The Cultural Animal

Roy F. Baumeister

The Cultural Animal

HUMAN NATURE,
MEANING,
AND SOCIAL LIFE

OXFORD
UNIVERSITY PRESS

2005

OXFORD
UNIVERSITY PRESS

Oxford   New York
Auckland   Bangkok   Buenos Aires   Cape Town   Chennai
Dar es Salaam   Delhi   Hong Kong   Istanbul   Karachi   Kolkata
Kuala Lumpur   Madrid   Melbourne   Mexico City   Mumbai   Nairobi
São Paulo   Shanghai   Taipei   Tokyo   Toronto

Copyright © 2005 by Oxford University Press, Inc.

Published by Oxford University Press, Inc.
198 Madison Avenue, New York, New York 10016

www.oup.com

Oxford is a registered trademark of Oxford University Press

Library of Congress Cataloging-in-Publication Data
Baumeister, Roy F.
The cultural animal : human nature, meaning, and social life / Roy F. Baumeister.
  p. cm.
Includes bibliographical references and index.
ISBN-13 978-0-19-516703-0
ISBN 0-19-516703-1
1. Psychology. 2. Social psychology. 3. Culture—Psychological aspects. I. Title.
BF57.B35 2005
302—dc22   2004002990

9 8 7 6 5 4 3 2 1

Printed in the United States of America
on acid-free paper

For my girls

Preface

Sometimes, I hear, one can set out to write a book according to a certain plan and actually keep to the plan, so that the final book closely resembles the original conception. More often, the project changes and evolves during the writing. This particular book changed in sweeping, fundamental ways.

My initial project was to provide a summary and overview of human nature, based on current lab findings in social psychology. There were, I thought, good reasons for trying to produce such a book. Psychology has amassed an impressive stock of research findings—but they are assembled piecemeal, in thousands of journal articles, each trying to make one or two small points. This mass of information is essentially beyond the reach of anyone except experts in the field. As a result, when scholars in other fields want some broad answers about what makes people tick, they often turn to Freud. I don't intend to indulge in the sort of Freud bashing that has been popular among psychologists in recent decades, and I would even list him as one of the greatest geniuses of all time. Still, he's obsolete at best. We should give him credit for his correct ideas, but we must also acknowledge that he was wrong about quite a few other things, and inevitably he simply overlooked quite a bit more.

It is therefore saddening and maddening to psychologists to see scholars in other fields continue to use Freud's model of human nature. I therefore decided to write a new model that would be based on all that we have learned in the decades since Freud died. All I would have to do would be to read a great many research findings and pull them together in some broad outline. The project was especially appealing because I was preparing for a sabbatical at the Center for Advanced Study in the Behavioral Sciences. The center is an interdisciplinary sabbatical hangout. I would be rubbing elbows on a daily basis with experts from the other social sciences. These contacts would help me get the perspectives needed for the task. After all, I am a lab researcher by training, and like all of my colleagues, I tend to get focused on a few narrow issues and questions. To write a summary of psychological knowledge, I wanted to be able to step back from my usual perspective and try to see what other fields would want to know from us. When I got to the Center and started working on the book, I began talking to the sociologists, economists, political scientists, anthropologists, historians, and others, always with an eye to learning what sort of knowledge or information they would wish psychology would give them.

The crucial thing about this approach to writing the book is that I started with few general ideas. I thought, well, psychology has a few major categories, so let me just summarize the main outlines of knowledge about each of them. The core chapters of the book still reflect this organizational scheme: motivation (what people want), cognition (how people think), emotion (how they feel), action (how they behave), and interaction (how they treat each other). I wanted to be as open-minded as possible, with no axes to grind or hidden agenda.

I worked on the book all year, usually for many hours every day. Each chapter took about a month. I still had no general ideas or overarching scheme; the book was written piece by piece, putting things in some sensible order but not imposing any grand ideas on them. In fact, I stayed with this plan so long that I actually generated a complete draft of the book on that plan. I mailed it off to several possible publishers.

But I wasn't happy with it. I had learned a great deal, and I thought the book would be a useful resource, but the lack of broad ideas made it seem like little more than a report on what I had read, or even a textbook. I cast around vaguely for some ways to integrate the mass of material, even including sections on "how everything fits together" in several of the chapters. But it was still a loose summary.

Then, one day, sitting by a rooftop pool while waiting to hear back from publishers, I began to think that the giant mass of information really did seem to be ready for integrative explanation. The human psyche is not just a randomly assembled collection of independent working parts. Perhaps it was designed for something very specific. Inner processes serve interpersonal functions. What goes on inside the person is there to facilitate the types of relationships we have.

Most big-picture explanations of human psychological functioning hark back to the two big causes: nature and culture. I had given the usual lip service to these, but I began to see that the standard way of talking about them was wrong in crucial ways. After some struggle, I came up with this book's main theme: Nature built us for culture. The human psyche is thus designed by natural selection to enable us to belong to a culture.

The conventional view is that nature instilled certain patterns in us, based on narrow contingencies of individual survival and reproduction; then came culture, building on what nature had instilled. The usual arguments revolve around how much latitude culture had to influence behavior, as opposed to attributing most behavior patterns to nature. Instead, I was proposing that culture had influenced nature.

Several criteria had to be satisfied to make that view even plausible. Fortunately, there have been a slew of recent advances that helped a great deal. The idea that culture influenced nature is more plausible if rudimentary forms of culture can be observed in other species, and recent evidence suggests that several dozen other species do have cultures. Another requirement was that culture had to offer benefits that could be measured in the cold biological criteria of survival and reproduction. There too, there is evidence that people survive and reproduce better as a result of belonging to a culture, even without needing to invoke modern technology and medicine.

Understanding the benefits of culture required me to have some knowledge about how systems work, including political and economic systems. Linking this back to biology pushed me to have some mastery over current thinking about evolutionary biology. I freely admit that I am not an expert in all of these fields. My Ph.D. is in social psychology, and that is still my primary expertise. Undoubtedly, I have glossed over important subtleties in those other fields. I am sorry for that, but I see no alternative. Only by traversing the long path from economics and sociology to biology could a suitable context for psychology's knowledge be provided.

Economists know that trade increases wealth, and division of labor increases productivity. Historians, sociologists, and scientists see how knowledge accumulates in a culture, thereby producing progress—something almost unheard of, even unimaginable, in noncultural animals. Hence being part of a system enables people to produce more and to live better than people who live alone. Those benefits can be measured in terms of survival and reproduction. And so, I propose, we evolved to be able to take advantage of these benefits of belonging to a cultural system.

Once I decided to recast the book by offering this explanation, I went through multiple stages. I wrote to the publishers reviewing the former draft and told them that I had some new ideas and wanted to rewrite the book. At first, I thought I could just give this overview in chapter 1, leaving the rest of the book as it was. Then I thought perhaps I would go through the chapters and point out links to the "cultural animal" theme here and there. Gradually, I realized that I would have to rewrite the entire book. This took another year, which involved a growing struggle with my own impatience. It is not easy for a time-conscious, schedule-driven person to spend a whole additional year on a project that was supposedly finished already and is now past its deadline. The excitement of the ideas sustained me through this, however. Each week, it seemed, some new insight or implication emerged. New ideas have always given me a thrill, and that was especially true during the rewriting of this book, though each new idea carried the burden of demanding further revisions. I had to keep telling myself that on this project, uncharacteristically, I should ignore the deadlines (both new and bygone) and put in as much time and effort as were needed.

I am grateful for the help and support that have made this work possible. The project benefited greatly from Kathleen Vohs, who read the entire manuscript (and some parts over and over!) and willingly discussed the ideas with me at great length. Those discussions led to some of the central reconceptualizations. Liqing Zhang read an early draft and gave me extensive and helpful comments. I also appreciate the input from the students in my graduate seminar at Case Western Reserve University in the fall of 2002, during which the book made the difficult transition from the first (human nature) draft to its current (cultural animal) focus.

Several other people made valuable contributions. I am grateful for the guidance of my editor, Joan Bossert, at Oxford University Press, whom I have long admired. It was great to work with her on this. Nathan DeWall and Matthew Gailliot provided valuable help in tracking down the far-flung reference citations, thereby making a hellish phase at least tolerable. Brad Bushman read the full manuscript and offered some suggestions, and Jonathan Haidt provided helpful guidance to several key literatures.

I must also express my appreciation to several institutions. I wish to thank Case Western Reserve University for giving me the sabbatical leave during which I researched and wrote the first draft. Though I have left that institution, I am forever indebted to it for the many years of support it gave me. The sabbatical itself was spent in the intellectually stimulating environment of the Center for Advanced Study in the Behavioral Sciences at Stanford University, and its staff and resources were particularly helpful. I am grateful to them also for the Fritz Redlich Fellowship, which supported me during my year at the center. More peripherally, I am grateful to Florida State University and the National Institute of Mental Health, whose financial support for my laboratory work freed up enough time for me to complete this project too.

Last, I wish to thank Dianne Tice, my wife, for her support and encouragement. While working hard to keep home and family together during a difficult and strenuous two years, she also read the evolving manuscript, offered helpful suggestions, and helped me shape and develop the ideas.

Contents

The Cultural Animal

I

Beasts for Culture

The mall was crowded that day because of the sale. Linda found some new jeans for the kids and then rushed to meet her husband, Jack, outside the department store. She waved when she saw him. He smiled and said he had just walked by a women's clothing store that had some lovely dresses at half price. They walked there together. She didn't like the items in the window, but inside she found a beautiful sweater that was perfect for her. Unfortunately, it wasn't on sale. Jack hugged her and said not to worry, and he pulled out his credit card and bought it for her despite the price.

As she came out of the store, Linda was delighted with the new sweater and overcome with love and gratitude toward her husband. She pulled him close and gave him a kiss, right there in the middle of the crowded shopping mall. He returned the kiss with pleasure, and he felt a surge of desire. They set down their purchases and began undoing each other's clothing. The floor of the shopping mall had a nice carpet which felt good against their bare skin as they embraced and made love. Some other shoppers paused to watch. One called out some joking words of encouragement, and two others engaged in a brief discussion about the movements of Jack's buttocks. But others hurried by, intent on their errands and their quest for bargains. After a few minutes of strenuous and satisfying intercourse, the couple finished, kissed each other once more, and started to put their clothes back on. "Anything else we need?" asked Jack, and Linda said she wanted to check whether the sports shoe store had the right brand of soccer shoes for their daughter.

As you may have surmised, this story is fictional. Human beings do not generally have sexual intercourse in shopping malls, or indeed in any public places. But why not?

After all, nearly all other animals are willing to have sex in the presence of others. True, there are a few circumstantial exceptions when they seek secrecy, such as when someone mates with another's regular partner. Human beings have their forbidden sex acts too. But human cultures *approve* of sex between married spouses, and so there is nothing forbidden about it. Adulterers and perverts might want to avoid being caught in the act, but why should married couples be reluctant to have other people watch their legitimate marital activities? If anything, they ought to be extra eager to have sex in public, where they can bask in society's approval.

Is it because people look foolish while having sex? This isn't a satisfactory answer. If you have seen rabbits, dogs, or other animals have sex, they look pretty silly too, but that doesn't stop them. The male rabbit's eyes bulge wildly, and he clings absurdly to the back of his furry sweetheart while his pelvis pumps away. Somehow, though, he is not deterred by the prospect that the other rabbits that witness his fornicating will laugh at him. In fact, they don't seem to laugh at him: they may stare at him, but it is hard to see anything resembling derisive mirth in their expressions. It almost seems that they lack the capacity to laugh at each other, failing perhaps in one of the prerequisites. They don't see themselves as belonging to a community of like-minded individuals with shared understandings—so they have no concept of identity threat, of jeopardizing one's dignity, and hence no basis for laughing at one of their fellows.

The reluctance to have sex in public is only one of many differences between humans and other animals. Sex is a biologically natural activity practiced by most (though not all) species, especially large mammals. Biologists and evolutionary psychologists observe human mating patterns and correctly note many similarities to what is seen in other species, but there are profound differences too.[1] No other species has latex fetishes, golden showers, professional flagellants, phone sex, mediated sharing of sexual fantasies (e.g., in the letters to *Penthouse*), and many more realms of idiosyncratic titillation. In recent years the similarities across species have garnered considerable attention, but the differences require explaining too. After all, if plain old animal sex works well enough for so many different species, why should it suddenly be transformed when human beings do it?

One standard way of answering these questions is to say that humans are shaped by culture as well as nature, and so due to historical circumstances Jack and Linda's culture has taught them not to have sex in public. That answer is not satisfactory either, however. Why should culture teach such things? As already noted, most cultures approve of sex between spouses, and most socially desirable actions are admired when performed in public. Moreover, why are so many cultures similar in this regard? It's not as if American tourists who travel to Spain, India, or Peru find themselves stumbling onto married couples who are absorbed in sexual intercourse in public thoroughfares or shopping areas. Nearly all nations have restaurants, but is it normal in any country for people to copulate while waiting for their food to be served (which, after all, would be an efficient way to pass the time)?

Au contraire, most humans in most societies seek privacy for most of their sex acts. Admittedly, sometimes (such as among the poor who cannot afford privacy) people have to compromise and settle for mere darkness. In human history, there have been long periods when many people lived in one-room huts, with family, and so people slept in the same room, sometimes in what is not unlike a dog pile. Spouses clearly had sex then, as proven by the fact that the typical marriage continued to produce pregnancies and children. Probably they did it late at night, when they presumed the kids and in-laws were asleep, and they probably tried to keep quiet so as not to wake up the gaggle of roommates.

That's how children were produced—with the maximum amount of privacy available and almost never by marital intercourse playing to a supportive audience who enjoyed the show and clapped after the good parts.

Again, though, why not? A penchant for sexual privacy seems to be part of human nature rather than a peculiar cultural prescription, but why? Societies approve of married couples having sex, and since through most of history most societies have wanted to increase the population, legitimate copulations were serving society's best interests. Why wouldn't people be spurred on to greater sexual feats by the encouraging presence of witnesses? Most likely, it's a design quirk of human nature, a side effect of some vital human quality.

In order to belong to a culture, people had to be able to see themselves as others would see them, and they also had to be concerned about how others would evaluate them. This awareness is detrimental to sexual response in both genders, and in the male its wilting effect is often sufficient to prevent intercourse. Even professional porn stars have difficulty getting and sustaining erections for their work (although in recent years, Viagra has helped many of these men overcome this occupational hazard). In order to make us capable of living in culture, nature had to bestow the capacity for self-awareness, and cultures everywhere have exploited this. Self-awareness, especially imagining how onlookers are evaluating you right now, is detrimental to sex.[2]

The theme of this book is that nature has designed the human psyche for participation in cultural society. This design has entailed two kinds of changes. One kind of change directly affected the biological makeup of the human being. The other was indirect: Our biology made us able to learn and change throughout life, so that cultural and social influences can continue to shape us. Together, these changes are responsible for many of the special, unusual features of human psychology.

The widespread hankering for sexual privacy is probably one side effect of these extensive changes. For example, human beings have a much greater capacity than any other known species to anticipate the thought processes and emotional processes of others. This pattern, called *mind reading* or *theory of mind*, makes us more sensitive to what others might be thinking about us. That ability to infer what others are thinking is vital to enable us to participate in complex social interactions, but it also probably makes it harder for us to engage in sex while others are watching. Rabbits look silly when they have sex, but they don't laugh at each other, and they probably don't have the mental capacity to be aware of how other rabbits that watch them might evaluate them. To you or me, a copulating male rabbit looks utterly ridiculous, but apparently he doesn't strike the other rabbits as ridiculous, and even if they did perceive him that way, he might not be capable of anticipating this. Therefore, when he gets a chance to score with some cute young bunny, he won't be bothered by the presence of gawkers. So rabbits don't mind having sex while their fellows watch, whereas humans balk. We are different, and this awareness of being evaluated might well interfere with sexual arousal. The ability to see ourselves as others see us, and to care about what they think, is a crucial part of what makes us human—and it is also utterly unavoidable, indispensable, if you are going to live in culture.

For want of a better term, let us say that human sex has become *culturalized.* This is not to deny that human sexuality has much in common with the sexual patterns of other mammals, nor that biology and nature remain important forces that shape human sexuality. On top of these, however, human sex is affected by the fact that human beings live in a cultural world. Cultural human beings are aware of themselves; they recognize that they are part of a network of similar beings; and they are well aware that their social group holds an assortment of beliefs and values—some of which may be applied by other people to evaluate each individual's sexual activities. These facts change sex in both the subjective experience and the objective behavior. We simply can't go back to the heedless frenzy to which the male bunny succumbs during sex. We don't even want others to watch us when the sex is legally, morally, spiritually, and socially legitimate. Legitimacy isn't enough.

I am not referring to cultural differences when I say that sex has been culturalized. The basic phenomena of self-awareness—anticipating how others perceive you, evaluating yourself and your actions according to collective beliefs and values, and caring about how others evaluate you—are an inherent part of belonging to any and every cultural society. I shall argue later in this chapter that focusing on cultural differences has caused many top-flight, rigorously disciplined social scientists to underestimate the power and importance of culture. Cultures and societies are broadly similar in many respects, and these similarities indicate crucial aspects of human nature. Indeed, these similarities may be what human nature was designed for.

To be sure, there are some cultural differences in human sexuality, especially along the lines of what kinds of activities are valued versus condemned. And there are also genuine continuities and similarities between human and other mammalian sex. But human sexuality has already changed from its animal heritage simply by virtue of the fact that human beings are shaped—first by their genes and then by their social environment—to live in culture.

Living in Three Worlds

Human beings are in many ways similar to other animals, and in many other ways we are different, as the example of public sex suggests. The usual way of explaining the mix of similarities and differences is to say that similarities between humans and other animals reflect the input of nature, while the differences reflect the teachings of culture. My account will accord considerable power to both nature and culture, but I will not weave them together in the standard way.

Nearly every expert who has tackled the nature-versus-culture question has assumed that nature comes first and culture comes along later. The dispute is therefore focused on the question of how far nature has laid down the outlines of human nature and hence how much leeway culture has had to alter the final shape of human psychology. My view will shift culture to an earlier and more prominent place in the causal chain. Culture has guided nature, and human nature was designed in part to be capable of culture.

This book seeks to give a comprehensive overview of human psychological functioning— desire, thought, emotion, action, and interactions— as well as how these facets affect each other. In order to understand how the human psyche is put together, we need to understand its functions, which is to say what it was designed to do. From that perspective, both the similarities and the differences make sense. Human beings have the same basic wants and needs as most other animals, but humans have taken a rather different strategy for satisfying them.

What is found inside any creature is there in large part because it helps the creature deal with what is outside. All organisms are the way they are so that they can deal effectively with their environment. Referring simply to "the environment" is too simple, however, because it mixes together several different things. It is useful to distinguish three different worlds in which we live. The human psyche has to have the inner structures that are suited to all three.

The first world is the physical environment. All living things must get certain things from their physical environment in order to survive. Almost all of them need some form of food, water, and air. And because (so far at least) nature has failed utterly to make any living thing immortal, every living thing has to find some way to reproduce in order that the species will continue to exist. Survival and reproduction are the universal hallmarks of biological success, and every living thing needs to achieve them. Human beings need these things too.

Every living thing therefore has some inner structures to help it get what it needs from the physical world. Most plants get what they need via roots and leaves. Most animals eat their food, and to do that they must have a mouth and some kind of digestive system. Finding food is also a common problem, and so animals must have some senses (e.g., vision, smell) to take in information about their physical surroundings, as well as something in the brain that can distinguish what is edible from what is not.

For some animals, that is enough. As long as each animal lives mostly alone and interacts directly with the physical environment to get what it needs, then the psyche does not have to be all that complicated. All it requires are sufficient inner structures to enable it to find and acquire what it needs to survive and reproduce.

Other animals, however, live in a second world, which is superimposed on the physical world. This is the social world. The social world came into being because it offered evolving animals a better way of dealing with the physical environment. A pack of wolves hunting together can corner and kill large animals that no one of them alone could kill. By working together in that and many other ways, social animals are able to survive and reproduce better than they could if they operated as loners. Social interaction is thus a biological strategy, whose success can be measured by the biological criteria of survival and reproduction.

Social life does not come cheap, however. In order to be social, animals must have additional inner structures beyond what they need to obtain their food and water. Social interaction requires some capacity for cooperating with others. It requires the animals to have some understanding of what others are going to do and how to respond, and it requires the ability to influence others and to be influenced by them. The animals must have the capacity to organize their groups and make decisions together. Wolves or bees can only operate as a pack or a swarm if they all work together toward the same goal, and somehow this goal has to be chosen for all of them together. At the least, they have to have some inner psychological mechanism that makes them join in and do whatever the others are doing.

Culture is the third environment. Few animals use this strategy, and only the human species has begun to take advantage of the potential power of culture to make life better. Culture is a better way of being social. That is, culture emerged as a strategy for dealing with the social and the physical environments. Ultimately, culture developed because it served the biological goals of survival and reproduction. To be sure, cultures have developed additional ideas, goals, and purposes, but the reason that natural selection created the capacities needed for culture is because some animals found they could survive and reproduce better by making use of culture.

Why do so few species use culture, if it is so great? Almost certainly, it is because culture is difficult for nature to provide. Living in culture requires considerably more inner structures than living in the social or physical worlds. It took natural selection a very long time to build those inner structures into a species so it could become capable of culture. As we shall see, the requirements of culture go far beyond what most social animals could manage.

The example of food illustrates the progression through the three worlds. All living things need to get some kind of food from their environment. Those who live only in the physical world require only the inner structures that will enable them to find their food and eat it. Those who live also in the social world require a psyche that can deal with other members of the species, and once those are in place the social animals can get more and better food than they could by operating alone. Last, we lucky few who live in culture need considerably more inner structures, but by making use of culture we can get more and better food than even the merely social species.

And we do eat better than they do. Even amid the bitter chill of a midwestern winter, when all is covered in snow and ice, people can eat fresh fruit, fish, and fancy meats. Modern humans in developed countries can say, with pride, that they don't kill their own food nor grow their own food—they buy their food in restaurants and supermarkets. In a pinch, they call room service. No other species has restaurants or room service. In the middle of a dry spell or a long winter, a wolf would probably love to be able to go to a supermarket and load up on prepackaged meats, but wolves do not have culture, and so they cannot create supermarkets.

The Essence of Culture

The term *culture* is used in different ways and by different fields, and so it will not be easy to forge a single definition that will make everyone happy. It is, however, necessary to spend a little time reflecting on what culture entails, if only to make the rest of my discussion intelligible. For years, anthropology claimed the concept of culture as its own, and other disciplines largely deferred to anthropology's understanding of it. More recently, some anthropologists have rebelled against how culture was understood in their own field, and this rebellion has left the concept of culture without its previous home.

The gist of the debate has been well summarized and criticized by anthropologist William H. Sewell.[3] Culture is in part a category or aspect of social life. Anthropologists have understood this in several different ways. First, culture is understood as learned behavior. It is the set of beliefs, practices, institutions, customs, myths, and the like that has been built up by a group of human beings and passed along from one generation to the next. Second, and related to the first, culture refers to a system of meanings and symbols. The famous anthropologist Clifford Geertz helped to elevate this understanding, which has been the dominant view in anthropology since the 1960s. When we say that a culture values a certain kind of activity or embraces a certain belief, we are using this approach.

The third view, which has rebelled against the second, has used the term *practice* to capture its vision of culture.[4] As the term implies, it emphasizes culture as a sphere of practical activity in which people grapple with the problems of living. Advocates of this view reject the implication that culture is a logical, coherent system of shared, uniform beliefs, pointing instead to conflict and disagreement. What makes Canada a culture are not the common beliefs, values, and symbols that all Canadians hold, but rather the common framework they use to conduct their daily activities. They drive their cars, do their jobs, pay the rent, purchase and eat their food, make love, fight illness, and educate their children within the Canadian cultural framework of laws, money, language, health care systems, highways, and the rest.

Yet these views of culture are not as incompatible as the academic debates would imply. Sewell himself exposes the false dichotomy.[5] System and practice go together well, as he points out. Perhaps previous generations of anthropologists erred by overestimating the homogeneity of culture, but that error can be corrected without throwing out the entire notion that cultures involve common understandings. In the United States, Republicans and Democrats may disagree as to what the best political policies would be, but their disagreements conceal common understandings and agreements, and they have enough in common to be properly regarded as part of the same culture. They live and act in the same *world of meaning*, even if they disagree about certain specifics. All that is needed is to recognize that culture is a world of meanings—one that isn't necessarily a perfectly coherent, uniform set of beliefs. Rather, culture is a set of loosely integrated assumptions, open to dispute, debate, and change.

Strictly speaking, without shared understandings, even debate would not be possible, and so the existence of debate hardly demolishes the belief in shared understandings. Americans can disagree honestly about issues such as whether abortion should be legal, but they carry on their debates by invoking assumptions and values that they do share even with their opponents, such as the value of human life, respect for the individual, the power of law, and the freedom to make one's own choices.

Practice likewise invokes shared understandings. Billions of people around the world know what a dollar is, and even though their attitudes toward dollars (or money generally) may vary widely, people agree on enough that they can use dollars effectively in buying and selling things, even when interacting with total strangers.

Moreover, even as anthropologists rejected the simpler views of culture as a static system, they lost contact with some of their subjects. Marshall Sahlins quoted one of his colleagues on this: "Whether anthropologists like it or not, it appears that people—and not only those with power—*want* culture, and they often want it precisely in the bound, reified, essentialized, and timeless fashion that most of us now reject."[6]

Culture extends the degree of social participation and interdependence. Much of what people do in a culture is linked to other people and indeed to the culture generally. Even a seemingly private activity such as brushing your teeth is a form of cultural participation. The brand of toothpaste you choose reflects what the market has produced to offer you, and if there are several brands your choice is probably shaped by cultural messages such as advertising slogans. In turn, your choices combine with those of many other toothpaste purchasers to determine which brands remain on the market and which ones fail and disappear. When a firm goes bankrupt, many individuals lose their jobs, and their families may face troubles. Moreover, brushing teeth is not instilled in our genes via some evolutionary process that weeded out non–tooth brushers and left us all with an innate urge to brush. On the contrary, you probably brush because you were taught to do so by your parents, and probably you sustain the practice because you believe other people will like you better if your breath smells fresh and your teeth look white (and you believe that brushing will promote those outcomes). You probably also accept on faith the cultural teaching that brushing your teeth will increase your dental health. If you fail to do it, your teeth will go bad, and either you or someone else will have to pay for treatment, such as filling cavities; the services of dentists are likewise provided as part of the economy.

In short, culture must be understood as encompassing both ideas and activities. It can be understood as a system of meanings that presides over a complex and possibly large set of actions and interactions. The meanings (symbols, beliefs, laws, and more) provide structure and guidance, thereby helping to organize behavior. To put it more precisely: Culture is an information-based system that allows people to live together and satisfy their needs. This definition will be sufficient for my discussion.

Differences among cultures have sometimes created the impression that the forms and impact of culture are almost arbitrary and can be almost anything. But that impression (though eagerly embraced by some) is misleading. The similarities among different cultures are not as eye-catching as the most peculiar and spectacular differences, but they are probably more revealing as to the essence and purpose of culture. Most societies have to solve the same basic set of problems in order to enable people to live together. These problems include obtaining and distributing food, providing for offspring, defending the group against enemies, managing conflict between individuals, accumulating wealth, and making collective decisions. The beliefs and values that make up the culture have important functions in helping to solve these problems.

The culture has to induce at least some of the people to perform particular social roles. Throughout most of history, most people were involved in obtaining food. In modern industrial societies, only a minority of people create the food, leaving others to do other things. But somebody has to obtain the food; somebody has to get it to those who will eat it; and somebody has to cook it or otherwise prepare it. Likewise, most societies need warriors who are available to fight enemies in case of attack. A certain number of them are needed, but there is no need for everyone to stand ready to use weapons to kill the enemy. Some people are usually needed to create and maintain shelters in which people can live, but it isn't necessary that every person be able to build a home (thank goodness, say people like me). And so on. My point is that the main beliefs in a culture supervise the process of getting people to perform their roles so that the members of the culture can survive, get along, and maybe enjoy life a bit.

In describing these processes, I am moved to speak as if nature and culture "want" people to do certain things. Clearly, this is just a style of speech rather than an objective reality. Neither nature nor culture is capable of wanting in a literal sense. I do not mean to reify these abstractions. If members of a species fail to reproduce, the species will die out, and so in that sense nature "wants" them to reproduce. Likewise, if a culture fails to induce any members to provide food, then people will starve or move away and the culture will cease to exist, and so in that sense a culture "wants" someone to provide food. It would be more cumbersome but more accurate to refrain from attributing wants to culture and to say instead that a culture will only survive and flourish if it can manage to organize people's behavior in particular ways so as to solve the basic problems that most societies face. But that's what I mean when I say that culture "wants" people to do something.

Speaking as if culture were a unity is also an oversimplification for the sake of a handy way of discussing phenomena, rather than a reality. Many cultures are open-ended, diverse, internally inconsistent, and so on.[7] A culture is not an elegant philosophical system but some degree of order imposed on what might otherwise be chaos. The success at imposing order may be only partial, but partial success is often sufficient for the sake of allowing the culture to survive and flourish.

My definition of culture includes the term *information-based*. This reflects the central importance of knowledge and meanings in culture. Cultures use information to organize people's activities and to improve efforts toward survival and reproduction. Indeed, the ability to use language to process meaning was a crucial step in human evolution, and it has helped set us far apart from our biological ancestors. No other animals have newspapers or books. We use information (meaning) to help us deal more effectively with the physical world, and we also use information to help us deal more effectively with each other in the social world. All cultures do this.

Evolution and Culture

One path of evolutionary development pushed toward more and more social life. Presumably this occurred because some creatures became more successful at survival and reproduction as they worked together. As nature was selecting for increasingly social beings, it reached the point where the first bits of culture became possible. Culture proved to be such a big advantage above and beyond social life that nature designed its next invention—our own species—specifically to be capable of both society and culture. And that's why we are the way we are.

Is this view plausible? The answer depends on several things. First, culture must exist in other species. Second, it has to have some value for survival and reproduction in those species. Third, biology had to be capable of increasing or exaggerating the traits that made culture possible. Let us consider each of these in turn.

Evolution does not normally produce something major out of nothing. If culture is one of the defining traits of our species, it had to exist in our biological ancestors, at least in rudimentary form. It is not plausible that nature would suddenly leap from, say, a fungus or a mouse to produce human beings whose culture has now accumulated to the point that they can program computers and travel to the moon. But if culture showed up in some other species, human beings might simply be a step or two farther down the same evolutionary path.

Culture is not uniquely human, for animal societies have been shown to exemplify patterns that qualify as cultural, in the sense that learned patterns of behavior are shared by other members of the group and then passed along to the next generation. The most famous of these is the potato-washing pattern among Japanese monkeys on the island of Koshima. According to the story, the monkeys were endlessly vexed by the problem that chewing sweet potatoes (their main food) was hard on their teeth because the dirt had an abrasive effect. Reportedly, one creative monkey, named Imo,[8] hit upon a solution to the problem. Imo washed off the potato in the water, thereby removing most of the dirt. This pattern was gradually picked up by other monkeys in her group. Eventually all of them, except the oldest males (who had the least contact with the younger ones and who perhaps had the least plasticity), adopted this practice, and moreover it spread to subsequent generations. When researchers fed the monkeys sweet potatoes from the human market, the animals washed them in the ocean, even though these potatoes came with hardly any dirt on them. The theory is that the practice was sustained because the salt water made the potatoes taste good. Some researchers began speaking of potato "seasoning" rather than washing.

Thus a behavioral innovation spread through the society and was transmitted to future generations, even though it had never been seen before. That seems sufficient to qualify the monkey society under most definitions of culture.[9] Crucially, there were genetically identical tribes of monkeys living nearby that did not wash their potatoes. Thus, the potato washing was an acquired pattern found within one group and sustained across generations, even while other groups did not do it.

There are other examples, such as devising specific forms of tool use. Some chimpanzees learn to crack open nuts using specific flat stones, and these stones appear to be kept in the same place and to be used by different chimps over long periods of time. Such cultural innovations have been documented by the eminent primatologist Frans de Waal.[10] Moreover, chimpanzees and monkeys are not the only animals to qualify as members of the culture club: De Waal proposes that other great apes, whales, dolphins, and elephants should also be included.

On the other hand, de Waal readily acknowledges that nothing animals do remotely approximates the full range or complexity of human culture. Washing potatoes in the ocean is not on a par with the Internet, transatlantic jet travel, Shakespeare's plays, or the *Encyclopaedia Britannica*. Hence even de Waal says that it is relatively easy to devise definitions of culture that rule out any species other than our own, although he prefers a broader, more inclusive definition. Our culture is so far beyond what other species have that we can point to plenty of qualitative, meaningful differences. Still, for present purposes, the point is that the beginnings of culture can be found in some other species. It is therefore plausible that culture appeared on the planet before humankind did. In a sense, nature recognized the benefits of culture and designed us to capitalize on them.

A similar view has recently been put forward by Merlin Donald.[11] Instead of focusing on culture per se, he has recognized social realities as large networks existing among people, and he thinks the brain (and consciousness) evolved to take advantage of this possibility. Language and culture offer immense advantages, but a creature has to have a sufficiently complex brain in order to appreciate and use them, just as a computer has to have certain processing capabilities before it can log on to the Internet. Crucially, and in my view correctly, Donald rejects the standard cognitive science opinion that thought is entirely contained in the single brain, because thought has to make use of language, concepts, and other realities that exist only in the shared assumptions that make up the culture. It takes at least two brains to have language—a solitary brain will not produce language. Once there is a network of brains, they can share information, compare notes, build up more knowledge, and the like. New members (such as children) can learn to join the same network and derive its benefits. This ability is what makes human beings so vastly more successful than other species, at least by some measures, such as taking control of the physical environment and engineering social relations.

The view that the brain evolved to take advantage of society and culture offers a profound mixture of nature and culture. Biology had to contribute its part, because without a sufficiently powerful brain, a person could not acquire language or participate fully in the network. But culture was not just a by-product or aftereffect of brain evolution—rather, in Donald's view at least, brain and culture developed together, because human beings who could master language and all of the rest of culture would collectively (and individually) have a huge advantage over those who couldn't.

In short, culture does exist in other species and probably existed before homo sapiens evolved. This is crucial for the approach to understanding the human psyche that this book will take. For decades, theorists have had to refrain from suggesting that culture influenced evolution, because biological change takes a long time whereas most cultures are of recent origin. For example, the Americans and the French are different, but no one says that those differences reflect different genetic endowments between the American and French populations. The thought police might want to haul me off to wrongheads' prison merely for suggesting that culture could influence biology, because such views are taboo—but they are taboo on the basis of the unfortunate assumption that culture equals cultural differences. The argument that specific cultures are too recent to have influenced biology may be entirely correct, but it misses the point. It makes the same error that I have already criticized, namely, of confusing cultural differences with culture.

Yes, the differences between modern American and modern French cultures are too recent and unstable to have shaped the genetic heredity of Americans and French people. But culture itself certainly has been around long enough to influence evolution. Biologists claim that culture can be found in various nonhuman species, including some that existed prior to homo sapiens. By definition, this means that culture was already present when the human species was evolving, and so it is plausible that the direction in which we evolved could have been to prepare us for participating in culture.

Most social scientists equate culture with cultural differences. Cultural differences do exist and are of considerable interest, but the biggest difference may be between culture and no culture. Cultural differences are mostly not rooted in biological differences, but culture per se could well be rooted in biology—it could in fact be what human biology and psychology are designed for.

Language illustrates the point and may help persuade skeptics. Language is a good example because it expresses meaning, and meaning is the building block of culture. It is widely recognized that some other species communicate spontaneously, and others are capable of learning the rudiments of language. Humans are not the only communicators and perhaps not even the only language users. But we use language far more extensively than other species, and as far as we can tell no other species has anything approaching human language, which includes written forms, an extensive vocabulary running to tens of thousands of words in each language, highly abstract concepts, and a complex grammar and syntax that frequently allow us to express novel ideas or statements by combining multiple concepts. Other species hardly use sentences at all and certainly not long or complex ones, let alone large-scale combinations of concepts such as one finds in a typical book. And it is the combining of symbols and ideas, rather than just having a vocabulary, that makes human language such a powerful tool. If you could only use one-word sentences, language would still be much better than nothing, but it would be severely limited. Try using nothing beyond two-word sentences for a day, and you will see how limited the thought processes of other animals must remain.

Is it too much to suggest that evolution shaped us to use language? No. Other animals developed rudimentary ways of communicating. These conferred sufficient advantages so that natural selection would favor language users over nonspeaking hominids.

Consider the vocal cords, for example, if you doubt that we were specifically selected by evolution to be language users. Human beings are better able to use language than other apes, as indicated by our vocal cords, which are capable of much finer control and a much greater variety of sounds than what other species can accomplish. Indeed, when researchers first wanted to see whether other apes could learn language, they initially tried to teach them to speak vocally. But the chimps could not manage to make enough distinct sounds to communicate effectively, and so the researchers could only make progress by using sign language. Chimps are not mute, but they cannot make enough different sounds reliably enough to support a spoken language. Humans can control the sounds they make across a remarkably broad assortment, far beyond what just about any other creature can do. A person who speaks two or three languages can probably produce more than a million distinct words, reliably and consistently, along with remembering their distinct meanings. Is this just a coincidence? Or did this extraordinary vocal capacity evolve so that we could communicate better than the other animals, whose communication is limited to grunts and gestures?

The same argument goes for the other aspects of human physiology that support speech. We have a large brain that has both an enormous memory capacity—capable of learning a vocabulary of many thousands of words—and, by most accounts, an innate readiness to learn grammar and syntax. Researchers who study chimpanzee sign language dispute how severely limited they are (the chimps, not the researchers) at becoming capable of grammar and syntax, as in combining words to make meaningful sentences, but hardly any experts think their potential capability is a match for the human speaker. So, again, the sequence in evolution appears to be that first there were some beginnings of language in other species, and then our own species evolved to be capable of far more extensive use of language. Mother Nature recognized the value of speaking before we appeared on the scene, and we were designed to capitalize on this. Natural selection probably registered that communication worked best by making sounds with the mouth. No other species has a written language, and so writing could not have contributed to our evolution. Vocalizing did exist and succeeded, however, and so natural selection favored new beings who could vocalize a large and controllable assortment of sounds.

This is not to say that all of culture's effects are filtered through biology. Reading provides an instructive example. No other species can read, and so it is not plausible that evolution designed us to read. But reading is vital for participation in modern society. No matter where you live in the world today, if you cannot read, your prospects are those of a second-class citizen. You can't use the technology very well without reading the instructions, and the top new technology (such as the Internet) is almost all based on reading. You can't drive a car properly if you can't read street signs. You can hold a few low-skill and therefore low-paying jobs, but you can't really verify that you are getting paid properly, although you can probably learn to cash your paycheck. Reading is vital to being a member of the culture, but it is all learned. (To be sure, we need vision to read and the brain power to handle a full human language.) In short, we were not designed by evolution to read, and reading is entirely a human cultural invention.

But nature designed us to be able to talk. To talk is to participate in the collective and its stock of knowledge. My argument simply extends this view: Nature selected us to participate in culture, because culture offered several benefits, of which language is one. We evolved not just to speak but also to share, to acquire and perform distinct roles, and in other ways to participate in culture.

The Individual and Society

What is the relationship between the individual human being and culture? This is one of the oldest and most debated questions in social inquiry. There are several possible views, each of which has had its adherents. At issue is how the inner processes and mechanisms that make up the human psyche fit together with the external social world of meaning and interpersonal relationships. Put more simply, how do the inner and outer worlds fit together for today's human being?

To complicate the question, no one (including Mother Nature) could have foreseen the kind of social and cultural world we live in today. Our basic human nature evolved under radically different circumstances. How do our evolved selves mesh with the society we now confront, and can our culture help us shape those into cultural selves that can bring us happiness in the unforeseen and rapidly changing social world in which we now find ourselves?

Let us consider the main approaches to how the individual is related to society. The first two can be dismissed rather rapidly, but the third and fourth require longer consideration. The theory of the cultural animal is the fifth. There is much at stake: Each points toward a different view of human nature, requiring a different set of traits, preferences, tendencies, vulnerabilities, and strengths.

Conflict and Struggle

One classic view of how the individual and society fit together is that of a square peg in a round hole. In this view, the human being is essentially a beast with a big brain, an otherwise typical animal that somehow got abnormally smart. Our intelligence led us to build a society haphazardly, but this grew into something that was ill suited to the rest of the beast. As a result, modern civilized life is a nasty problem for which we are not really prepared. People can be rendered capable of living in a cultural society, but this requires some rather extensive retrofitting of the psyche. Human nature has to accept some violent adjustments and accommodations in order to live in the modern world.

This approach can be traced back at least to Rousseau, who regarded society as a wicked influence that twists and distorts human nature. He thought people were born good but become corrupted by society, and his writings encouraged many people to seek to return to the simplicity and virtue that they expected to find outside of society. In America, Henry David Thoreau was one famous convert to this view. Thoreau went to live in a small cottage in the woods, where supposedly he could think, write, and cultivate his inner gifts safe from the corrupting influence of society. To be sure, his mother and sister visited him every week to update him on the gossip from back home and to wash his laundry, and his cottage was only a short walk from the town, so it is debatable how much he really managed to extricate himself from society. But his effort reflected the prevailing view that people are better off away from the destructive influence of society, and in the American imagination he has symbolized that sentiment ever since.

In social science thinking, the conflict view is probably best exemplified by Sigmund Freud,[12] who proposed that a substantial amount of suffering and difficulty are involved in making the human psyche capable of civilized life. He did say that cultural life offers benefits that to some extent make up for the sacrifices, but he was clear that the sacrifices are considerable. In his view, people are by nature not well suited to living together in civilized society, and in order to tame the inner beast it is necessary to direct the aggressive instinct inward, so that people torment and harm themselves. In his terms, the superego was formed (taking energy from the aggressive instinct) to enable people to live together, and the superego has a high cost. In particular, the sense of guilt that accompanies having a superego is one cost that is not offset by corresponding gains. Thus, living in civilization is a net loss.

There is something to be said for the view that humans are ill suited to culture. Clearly, the rise of culture has not resulted in universal peace and happiness. In the twentieth century, despite all of the improvements in everyday life that cultural advances produced, human beings used the tools and technologies of culture to slaughter each other on an unprecedented scale. If we are designing an optimal, utopian social environment in which to live, we clearly still have plenty of fine-tuning to do.

On the other hand, the view that culture is inherently inimical to human nature is hard to square with the facts of history. Movements to reject culture and return to nature arise periodically, but they are small and short-lived, as compared with the massive and widespread movement in the direction of more culture. People clearly want and like something about culture in general, even though they have not yet found the perfect formula for utopian life. Another crucial fact is that humans are always better off in most respects (including physical health, mental health, and longevity) when they live within a cultural society than when they live isolated or alone. This fact is hard to reconcile with the view that culture is bad for people, because culture is demonstrably good for them.

The view that people would continue to erect culture even though it is bad for them requires one to accept the premise that people will seek out ways of life that are bad for them. To Freud's credit for intellectual boldness and honesty, he did accept and even embrace that view, saying that people have an innate death drive that impels them to seek their own eradication. But the core idea runs contrary to the evolutionary view, according to which people (like all creatures) adapt in ways that make life better for them. The cultural animal theory is in a sense the opposite of the Freudian theory, because it proposes that culture is precisely what we are suited for, rather than being something that runs contrary to our nature and that has to be imposed on us with force and difficulty.

Culture as Defense Mechanism

A second view is that, being more intelligent than other beasts, we face special problems that others don't, and culture is a defense against them. This view is best represented by Ernest Becker[13] and his modern disciples.[14] In their view, human beings are individual beasts like most other species, except that our greater intelligence and consciousness have had one disagreeable side effect: We know that we are going to die. The recognition of our own mortality is profoundly upsetting and produces a gusher of existential terror. In response to this terror, human beings have supposedly created culture to defend themselves against it psychologically. By identifying with our culture, which supposedly will live beyond our own individual bodies, we can achieve a semblance of immortality, which serves as an anti-dote to existential terror. In short, culture is a defense mechanism to help us cope with the fear of our own individual deaths.

There are several important arguments against this view. In the first place, people mainly know they are going to die by virtue of cultural learning, so some amount of culture had to be there in the first place before the knowledge of death. That much culture, at least, was the cause rather than the consequence of the recognition of mortality.

More important, the fear of death is probably not pervasive enough to carry the weight of explaining all of culture. Yes, when people stop to think about death (or are reminded of it, as in the ingenious experiments conducted by researchers in this line of work), most of them are afraid of it, and they may seek in small ways to calm their fears or otherwise distract themselves. But the view that all human striving and all other cultural activities are driven by fear of death is far beyond what the evidence can support.

Becker's view may be correct in recognizing that some aspects of modern culture are designed to help shield people from the painful recognition of mortality, but culture is not primarily a defense mechanism. Culture does not shield us from death. More to the point, it does many other things much more effectively and successfully than shielding us from our own mortality—so, most likely, those are its functions, not defending against death. In everyday life, most people are much more worried about being humiliated publicly, or dumped by a loved one, or rejected by some major social group, or being a failure in their work, than about the fact that they will die some day. Culture doesn't prevent death, but it does help us to live together.

I am willing to accept fear of death as an occasional factor that contributes to various cultural activities. But it seems too far-fetched to elevate it to the primary, sole underlying cause of culture, as Becker and his disciples sought to do. Culture offers many more genuine and palpable benefits than helping one forget one's mortality.

Culture Constructs the Individual

A third perspective on the individual and society is the conventional wisdom in anthropology and related fields, which is that people are largely a product of culture and socialization. Culture can shape us in a wide variety of ways, and there is very little that is innate or inevitable. In this view, it is almost silly to try to write an overview of human nature, because the human psyche is a mostly blank slate that culture can shape in a vast variety of ways.

This view has much to recommend it, which is probably why it has been popular for decades. It recognizes the power and importance of culture, and it helps to explain variations in how people from different cultures think and act. But culture does not have a free hand in how it can shape individuals, and the evidence in recent years has begun to suggest that people are in many ways more similar than different, even across cultural boundaries.

My own sympathies lie more on the side of culture than nature, and so this view of all-powerful culture shaping the individual has held great appeal for me. Yet I can no longer defend it. Indeed, one impetus for writing this book is to offer an alternative justification for the importance of culture than can be found in the data on cultural differences. To be sure, there are many cultural differences on the surface. Underneath, however, the similarities are often more powerful. When you go to live in a different culture, you are at first overwhelmed by all of the differences. They use a different kind of money, and the bills are a different color from those in your native culture. They speak a different language. They may drive on the other side of the road. They have different holidays. They may practice a different religion, with different ceremonies and doctrines.

After a while, however, you begin to recognize that these large differences conceal underlying similarities. The color or name of the money does not matter so much as the fact of having a common money, which enables the people of the culture to trade with each other. The same goes for language: What matters is having a common language so that people can communicate. (Language, like money, serves essentially the same function in every culture.) Which side of the road you drive on is far less important than the agreement that everyone drives on the same side, so that people do not crash into each other's cars. Holidays serve the same functions and are celebrated in similar ways, even if they commemorate somewhat different events. Religion too serves largely the same functions, or tries to, in most different cultures, leading ultimately to the same battles over how far daily life and political government should be guided by religion.

In the next chapter, we shall examine at more length the implications of cultural relativity for human nature. For now, it is sufficient to point out that culture has often failed to mold people according to its goals and blueprints. If culture could shape people in almost unlimited ways, then communism would not have been such a colossal failure. After all, Soviet communism seemingly had all the tools it might need to mold people into ideal communists. It controlled education, enabling it to socialize children as it wanted. It controlled information, such as through the mass media, thereby enabling it to direct how people would think and speak. It held the power of life and death (and used that power liberally) over its citizens, thereby putting severe pressure on them to think and act as the culture prescribed. It permitted no dissent and infused every major institution in the society. It melded with patriotism, so that people's love of their country could be mobilized into support for communism. It should have worked. But it didn't.

In our own American culture, the limits of culture's power can also be seen. The shifts in thinking about gender socialization have reflected this increasing recognition of limits. Gender identity is one of the basic and seemingly universal facts of human life. Probably every functioning human being knows itself as male or female. Advocates of culture and socialization have emphasized how young children are taught to conform to socially sanctioned gender roles: Boys don't cry; girls don't play with guns; adult men hold doors for women; and so forth. Moreover, it is beyond dispute that the roles of males and females vary somewhat across societies. All this suggests that gender identity is a product of culture.

Indeed, the women's movement of the 1960s resulted in a great upsurge of influence of feminist thinking. One central feminist doctrine was that the differences between males and females were chiefly due to the way society taught boys and girls to think, act, and feel. Throughout most of history, men and women had lived in separate spheres, following different life paths and opportunities. When women began to ask why they could not pursue the opportunities that men had, at first they heard some answers suggesting that the innate differences between the sexes rendered women unsuitable for masculine occupations. Feminists bitterly attacked these claims and began to assert that innate gender differences were minimal. Instead, society—along with its prejudices and false lessons—created gender differences even where none existed by nature.

One of the most dramatic test cases began when a Canadian baby boy was to be circumcised by an overworked physician late one night.[15] The procedure went awry, and the boy's penis was badly, irreparably damaged. Rather than raise the child as a genitally damaged boy, the physician and parents decided to take the radical step of finishing the job of demolishing the penis and then raising the child as a girl. In this, they relied on the feminist-influenced theory of gender, which held that socialization is the main cause of whether someone grows up to identify self as male or female. Name the kid Brenda, put him in a dress, tell him and everyone else that he is a girl, and the child will grow up into a woman. (To be sure, they did anticipate having to give him some hormone treatments at puberty, to help his body become more thoroughly feminine in a biological sense.) They enlisted the aid of John Money, an internationally respected sex researcher who was well acquainted with the latest theories and methods. Money thought the project should go well, and he wondered only whether the child would grow up to have sexual desires toward men or toward women. If the latter, Brenda would be a lesbian.

The plan should have succeeded, if culture can shape the individual. All the major powers of socialization cooperated to raise the child as a girl. The parents both tried hard. The schools understood the issue and cooperated in treating the child as a girl. Psychotherapists were ready to lend help and support. The child had no inkling of what had happened to his/her penis and was thus brought up to know herself only as a girl. And the great expert Dr. Money was giving advice.

But it didn't work. Brenda didn't know what was wrong with her, but she was not like other girls. She didn't care for dolls or pretty clothes, and she preferred rough-and-tumble play more akin to what boys did. Her parents had her grow her hair long, but she couldn't be bothered to keep it combed or styled. Her dresses got torn and dirty from her antics. Once her mother found the child trying on the mother's soft leather gloves in the closet, and she was moved to tears to think that her daughter Brenda was finally appreciating feminine things. In reality, the child had been imagining that these were the kind of gloves that race car drivers might wear to get a better grip on the steering wheel while speeding through dangerous turns.

The problems were concealed for a long time. The parents really wanted the project to succeed. They furnished optimistic reports to Money, who passed them along. Textbooks on gender differences, which are heavily laden with feminist theory, reported that the girl was sailing along smoothly through her upbringing, experiencing a normal girlhood and headed for womanhood. To them, Brenda was further proof that the differences between the sexes were constructed by culture rather than dictated by nature and that socialization was the supreme determinant of male and female identity.

As puberty approached, the child began to be invited to some boy-girl parties where kids began to pair off or to play kissing games. Brenda wanted no part of these. Money was reluctant to concede defeat, especially since he had gained international fame by claiming victory already, but he did begin to tell the parents that their daughter might be a lesbian. The parents knew that the problems had been substantial, and they thought their child's sexual orientation was the least of their worries. Meanwhile, when researchers began to question whether it was really so easy to transform a baby boy into a girl, Money complained that he was the victim of antifeminist backlash.[16] He still tried to tell the world that the experiment was a success.

The time arrived for the hormone injections that were supposed to facilitate the transition to biological womanhood. Brenda rebelled. She threw violent fits and refused to accept any injections. Finally, the parents caved in and told Brenda the true story: She had been born a boy but because of the accident they had raised her as a girl. For the first time, Brenda had a sense that she understood herself and why she could not fit in with the other girls. Immediately she rejected her female identity. She cut her hair, changed her wardrobe, took a male name, and began moving toward manhood. When the person married, it was not to become a wife and mother, but to become a husband and father. The former Brenda was of course unable to father children biologically, but the young man married a woman who already had two children, and he became their father.

This case has had a profound impact. It showed that culture and socialization had serious limits, where previously their power had been widely assumed to be far reaching. Culture and socialization had some impact, but these were largely superficial, and Brenda was more a boy dressed in girls' clothing (and conforming reluctantly to norms for female behavior) than a genuine, self-accepting girl. Although Colapinto's recent book on the case made John Money out to be a charlatan and scoundrel who deliberately distorted the facts so as to advance his own career,[17] it seems more likely that Money sincerely embraced the reigning ideas of his time, which said that gender identity is mainly a product of socialization. In any case, he was far from alone in thinking that socialization—especially with the aid of hormone injections—could transform a baby boy into a normal young woman. But it couldn't.

In my view, the most telling set of evidence about the limits of culture's power is found in the debate about the "end of history," a phrase for which the influential political scientist Francis Fukuyama has taken considerable and unfair abuse.[18] The debate has been conducted outside of psychology, and few psychologists are even aware of it, but it has important implications for our craft.

In the Middle Ages, Europeans generally believed that history was a downward slide. There were powerful reasons for this. The Romans had built roads and aqueducts, but these were falling apart and not being replaced, so society's infrastructure was getting progressively worse. New diseases spread, and lawlessness arose as criminal bands victimized defenseless villages. Most people were farmers, and for them too life was steadily growing worse. They had not discovered crop rotation, and so most of them continued to grow the same crops in the same fields generation after generation, with steadily declining yields. Religion helped to cement the view that the high point of history had been when Jesus walked the earth, and the present was part of a downward spiral toward the end of time.

During the Renaissance or thereabouts, people began to see positive progress toward improvement in some respects. For a time, there was uncertainty about the long-term prospects. Gradually a new view emerged, which was stated in an influential manner by the German philosopher Hegel. According to Hegel, all events in the world had an interlinked inner logic that showed a gradual movement toward an "end of history" (his phrase). Hegel was rather vague about the details of this inner logic and about what the final state would look like, but he saw history as a process of making progress toward a final end state with a perfected, ideal society.

A half century later, Karl Marx leaped forward to fill in the details. He said he could tell how history was developing and where it was headed. Class conflict would increase; ethnic conflict would diminish; and capitalists would exploit the workers ever more grievously until eventually in the most advanced nations the workers would rise up and overthrow their masters. Then all property would be owned in common rather than privately. Money would be abolished. Central government would become unnecessary, after an effective interlude of central planning. Peace and harmony would reign in a socialist utopia.

Obviously, Marx was wrong in just about every major prediction. His utter wrongness discredited the view that history was moving toward a communist utopia. But Fukuyama revived the notion that history has a destination. As Fukuyama pointed out, the past couple of centuries have seen worldwide movements toward the same government and economic systems. First, the monarchies were overthrown, so that today hardly any country has a king or queen with any real power. Then, in the 1970s, the military dictatorships of South America began to be replaced by democracies. In 1989, the communist nations of Europe converted to capitalism and democracy. Asia has had a wide mixture of governments and economies, but these too have mostly moved toward democracy and capitalism.

At the beginning of the twenty-first century, there remain only a few places that have not accepted democracy and capitalism, including China, North Korea, the Arab Middle East, and parts of Africa. These places also tend to be lagging behind their neighbors in progress and quality of life, and more people want to leave them than want to move there. (You'd have to be seriously nuts to consider emigrating to North Korea!) Fukuyama's prediction, with which I agree, is that these are simply lagging behind the others and will eventually convert to democracy and capitalism too. Thus, Fukuyama says, there is an end of history after all: democracy and capitalism. More precisely, it is representative democracy and free-market capitalism with government regulation.

If one social system works best for everyone, then there is a human nature, and culture must serve it rather than the reverse. Many different systems have been tried, but some work better than others, and one works best of all. Culture cannot mold human beings to suit any arrangement it happens to favor. Rather, cultures ultimately succeed or fail according to how well they accommodate the innate, ineluctable tendencies built into human nature.

Culture as Evolutionary By-Product

A fourth view of how the individual relates to society is the conventional wisdom in biology. Essentially, it holds that culture is an accidental by-product of the evolution of intelligence. In this view, our brains evolved primarily to help us deal with the physical environment. A side effect of this increase in brain power was that we became smart enough to create culture, such as by copying each other's innovations.

High intelligence is undoubtedly one of the crucial, distinctively human characteristics. Most discussions of specifically human nature emphasize our large brains, and indeed we have named our species *homo sapiens* in honor of our putative intelligence. But for what exactly is the big brain designed?

According to the standard view of evolution and biology that most of us heard in high school science classes, problem solving is the crucial purpose. Our species emerged as more intelligent than its ancestors because intelligence enabled us to deal more effectively with the environment. We could spot patterns in the weather, figure out how to make better homes and other shelters, outsmart the animals we wanted to eat so as to catch them better, and not incidentally outsmart the animals that wanted to eat us. This explanation is pretty reasonable on the surface, but mounting evidence suggests that it is not the main explanation.

The biological anthropologist Robin Dunbar sought to test various versions of this theory by comparing brain sizes across different species and looking at what differences accompanied larger brains.[19] If the brain evolved for solving certain kinds of problems, then animals with larger brains should deal better with those problems. But this approach repeatedly failed. Larger brains did not show any consistent relationship with indicators of how the animals dealt with the physical world.

For example, the conventional view has held that larger brains might be useful for extracting more elusive or complex foods (such as fruit, which is distributed more erratically and goes bad faster, thereby making more demands on the fruit-seeking brain), or for constructing more thorough and wider mental maps (such as of larger territories). The fruit-seeking brain theory found no support. The mental map theory found at best a shred of evidence: The hippocampus, which is the part of the brain involved in spatial memory, is indeed larger among animals that roam across larger territories, but this small effect is irrelevant to the main variation in brain size.

The main differences in brain size were found in the part of the brain that is used for reasoning and conscious processes, the neocortex. Across different species, the size of this part of the brain was mainly linked to social structure.[20] These social indicators included the size of the typical group and the complexity of social relations. Big brains go with deception and the ability to detect deception in others, with forming coalitions and alliances (and remembering who else in the group has such a relationship), and with complicated mating patterns. Big brains seem to produce elaborate social skills.[21]

These findings are powerful. If the brain evolved to solve problems in the physical world, then bigger brains should go with better ways of dealing with the physical world. They don't. Instead, bigger brains go with more complex social worlds. This indicates that the brain evolved mainly for enabling animals to deal with other members of their own species. Dunbar calls this the *social brain hypothesis*. The brain evolved to support social interactions and social relationships.

Another of Dunbar's observations is telling. The size of the reasoning area in the brain (the neocortex) is linked to having a longer "juvenile" period, which is defined as the period of life between infancy and adulthood. Size of neocortex is not however related to having a longer period of brain growth prior to birth. As Dunbar puts it, this means that the crucial thing about the big brain is "software programming"[22] in the sense of social learning, rather than having a longer time to grow more brain tissue. The juvenile period in life is mainly used for mastering the complexities of social relationships, both in terms of individual relationships and in terms of the social system as a whole. The longer the animal spends on social learning, the larger the brain is. This does not of course mean that learning itself causes the brain to become larger. Rather, it suggests that the purpose of the large brain is to allow for maximal social learning. The more learning there is to do, the longer the juvenile period is, and the larger the brain is. Again, the brain is for social, interpersonal, and, ultimately, cultural purposes.

A different kind of argument for the same conclusion was put forward by Robert Boyd and Peter Richerson in their ground-breaking work, which applied evolutionary thinking to culture.[23] They emphasized that people's ability to learn through direct experience is fraught with risks of error, as well as extremely time-consuming and difficult. Instead, people rely much more on learning from others. Crucially, people often rely more on what they learn from others (from their culture) than from their own individual experiences. And they are often better off because of that.

Together, these findings point toward the conclusion that nature made big brains for the sake of social participation (although technically they do not prove that conclusion). Across different species, the brain's primary purpose is to promote social interactions and social relationships. The human brain is designed for learning from other people more than for learning through direct and difficult struggles with the physical environment.

Conclusion: Made for Culture

Thus far, I have considered and rejected four classic, influential views about the relationship between the individual and society. Their inadequacy paves the way for a new view, which is that evolution made us for culture. Yes, human cultures and societies have problems. But problems are part of life. The real question is whether people are better suited to any other form of life than in a cultural society, and the answer to that is no. The entire history of the human race can be seen as a series of clumsy efforts to create a workable system by which people can live together and satisfy their biological needs—in other words, to create an effective culture.

This fifth view is the radical position that our psyches are innately programmed by nature specifically to enable us to participate in culture and society. Or, more precisely, the human psyche emerged because natural selection redesigned the primate psyche to make it more suitable for living in a cultural society.

But why? The next section will consider the advantages of culture. Are they strong enough and basic enough that our fundamental human nature could have been shaped by biology and evolution expressly to take advantage of them?

The Biological Advantages of Culture

The argument thus far is that nature shaped us for culture. Natural selection shaped the human psyche in large part for the purpose of enabling it to participate in a society that has culture. In order for this argument to be plausible, culture must offer substantial advantages, indeed substantial enough to offset the difficulty and cost of overhauling and upgrading the ape mind. Thus, by one calculation, the human brain accounts for only 2% of the body's mass but consumes 20% of the calories that the average person takes in,[24] which makes it an extremely expensive organ to have and maintain. No wonder most creatures aren't any smarter than they are. Nature will mostly give a creature features that will pay for themselves, and so the human brain—consuming so many more calories than its weight—would only evolve if it led to a big enough increase in the total calorie intake to offset the brain's increased consumption. Put more bluntly, much 'of the body's food goes to feed the brain, and so the brain has to bring in more food to make itself worthwhile.

Moreover, the advantages of culture must ultimately be measured in biological terms. That means survival and reproduction. One might attribute all sorts of so-called advantages to culture, such as enabling us to have high self-esteem and to feel good about ourselves. But nature doesn't care a fig about how we feel about ourselves. Evolution would design people for culture only if culture improved people's success at survival and reproduction.

Certainly it seems to be working. We are surviving and reproducing quite swimmingly. Human life expectancy has improved remarkably, especially in industrialized nations. With reproduction, the picture is a bit more complex, because in the most modern and industrialized nations the birth rate has been dropping, sometimes below replacement levels, but these trends reflect the deliberate choices of individuals to have smaller families so as to increase the quality of life in other respects (fewer expenses, less stress, more leisure). Across the species as a whole, there is no question but that people have been extraordinarily successful at reproducing. From the first humans, estimated to have appeared around 200,000 years ago, humankind has exploded to a population of between 6 and 7 billion. Most habitable parts of the planet are full of people and the most desirable locales are crowded to overflowing. Human beings are not on the endangered species list—on the contrary, the danger of overpopulation is greater than that of extinction.

What are the advantages of culture that can possibly account for the success of humankind?

Progress: The Ratchet

One huge advantage of culture is progress. Cultural animals part ways with the merely social ones at the point of whether progress can be accumulated across generations. A pack of wolves (quite social animals) in the Arctic lives pretty much the same today as it would have lived 10,000 or 100,000 years ago. (The main differences would be those caused by the encroachments of humanity into their territory.) The strongest male is still the top wolf: Wolves have not invented new forms of government or social organization, let alone redefined gender roles in their society. Nor have they developed technology to improve their hunting practices, prolong food storage, or make more comfortable shelter. They don't have medical care to help injured wolves recover better and live to ripe old ages.

In contrast, human life has changed almost beyond recognition. Even much shorter intervals reveal extraordinary progress in the conditions of human life. At the turn of the twentieth century, most Americans didn't have indoor plumbing, electricity, or a car. Romance had not yet been revolutionized by cars and movies, and a "date" still meant only an assignation with a prostitute. Factory jobs at U.S. Steel still ran on a 12-hour day, 7 days a week. Newspapers were the main mass medium; moving pictures had barely been invented; and no television or radio was available. Sea travel was risky and air travel unknown. Minor infections would often prove fatal, because there were no antibiotics—indeed, it is sometimes asserted that the average visit to a physician failed to do more good than harm until around 1910.[25] All these features of daily American life are radically different, just a century later.

The contribution of culture to progress has been called the *ratchet effect*, based on an analogy with the tool that permits forward movement but prevents backward movement. Michael Tomasello,[26] an expert who has written extensively about both primate and human thought capabilities, summarizes the effect this way. Two things are needed for progress. The first is innovation: Someone has to come up with a better solution to a common problem. The other is preservation: The solution has to be transmitted to others and remembered, so everyone can continue using it even after the inventor or discoverer has died. Tomasello says that nonhuman apes actually are pretty good at coming up with novel, creative solutions to problems. For them (our biological relatives), the problem is with preservation. Even if the solver remembers the solution for a while, and even if a couple of his or her mates copy the solution and use it for a while, it is eventually forgotten, and the next generation has to start over.

With culture, knowledge is stored in the collective, not in individual minds. Each discovery can be shared with everyone and then transmitted to the next generation. Without progress, the children born today would have to figure out for themselves how to make fire, how to hunt or grow food, and what to do with their own babies, whose very arrival would be a surprise. But the collective pooling of knowledge enables each generation to start where the last one left off. On a planet of more than 6 billion people, it is enough for one single person to invent the videocassette recorder, and then this knowledge is available to everyone. The next generation can figure out how to make a better VCR, or a cheaper one. The pace is remarkable. Even though we now have accumulated many centuries of knowledge, one recent study estimated that the world's total stock of information doubled between 2000 and 2002. That is, the amount of new information in the past couple of years was equivalent to the entire stock of knowledge in the history of the world.[27]

Pooled knowledge is also more resistant to setbacks. The Black Death killed a third of the population of Europe, but the culture's stock of knowledge survived, because some people were left. (Putting knowledge into written form is itself an additional, powerful innovation that helps preserve and share knowledge.) In contrast, the knowledge of noncultural animals dies with them. If one of them has figured out a clever new way to get some tasty bugs, even if it shares those methods with others, the death of that animal means that the others won't get any more of those treats.

It is fundamentally misleading to say that human intelligence, based on our large brains, has been the cause of the great success of our species. We have reproduced ourselves in immense numbers and in the process taken over and utterly transformed the planet on which we live. To be sure, there are other hallmarks of biological success, and by some counts beetles or cockroaches may be following an even more effective strategy and may in the end dominate the planet more thoroughly than we do. Still, our species has been extraordinarily successful, and although intelligence is the standard explanation for this success, it is not, I think, the full or even the main answer.

Human society and culture should get the credit for our success. It is by working together with each other, sharing information and knowledge, and building upon each other's contributions that our species has done so well. Intelligence has had its effects by virtue of the accumulating power of society and culture.

Consider a different view. Suppose we were a species of brilliant but socially isolated problem solvers. How far would we have gotten? Even if every individual were smart enough to figure out how to start a fire and keep it going, it would have been a big effort that took years to achieve. Each new person would have to eat raw meat and sleep in the cold for many years. But with culture, whatever one person discovers or invents can be shared with the others, starting pretty quickly and continuing pretty much forever. It becomes part of the group's knowledge. New members simply learn it rather than needing to discover it for themselves. That head start frees up the new members to make different inventions or improve on what they were taught. In turn, the next generation benefits from this further progress.

The view that people share innovations fits well with what is known about even the earliest humans. Crops such as wheat were indigenous to the fertile crescent, and when people learned to farm them, the practice spread from there. At other places, where wheat was not indigenous, people began to farm wheat instead of the plants that were indigenous to their region—a clear sign that they learned methods from other humans (even those living relatively far away) rather than making discoveries locally. Likewise, archaeologists have found artifacts that seem to have traveled far from their point of origin, which is another sign that people were exchanging and sharing their cultural progress.

Division of Labor and Role Differentiation

As a schoolboy, Adam Smith once visited an ironworks factory in Glasgow, Scotland. The factory made such an impression on him that many years later, when he was a famous professor of philosophy, he described the factory at the beginning of his great book *The Wealth of Nations*, which helped to create an entirely new field of study (economics). The remarkable thing about the factory, according to Smith, was that ten people could in a day make nearly 50,000 pins. The key to this was not technology, though technology has also expanded human productive powers. The key was division of labor. The job of making a pin was divided into parts, and each task was performed by a different person. Ten people working alone could not produce anywhere near as many pins as they could by working together, cooperatively.

The division of labor is thus another huge and powerful advantage of culture. Nonsocial animals, almost by definition, cannot profit from division of labor. Animals that are social but not cultural can divide up labor in some ways. Cultural animals can, however, divide up labor extensively. Eventually, this culminates in the miracle of modern industrialized society, in which the vast majority of the population never kills or grows any food nor builds any shelter, but nearly everyone has ample food and shelter.

There are actually two forms of division of labor. One is based on doing separate tasks, and this one is not uniquely human. For example, social creatures such as birds and ants assign different jobs (building a home, laying eggs, caring for young) to different individuals. Human culture has many more different tasks and assigns them much more flexibly, but in this respect human uniqueness is a matter of degree, not of kind.

The second form of division of labor takes each task and divides it into parts. The assembly line is a vivid and extreme form of this: No one person has the job of building a car. Instead, the job is divided into dozens or even hundreds of little steps, each performed by a different person. This second way appears to be a relatively modern innovation, but it capitalizes on the same basic principle as the first.

Does division of labor make any difference? Yes. As people specialize, they can learn to perform their own roles better. In a sense, every job is performed by an expert, and so the quality of every task performance increases dramatically. Try to imagine yourself growing and processing your own food or building your own house: It would take years to master the skills necessary to do a merely adequate job of it, and even then your food and shelter might be quite poor in quality. With division of labor, your food and shelter are produced by experts, who perform their tasks on the basis of long-accumulated knowledge.

The bottom line is that there are powerful and undeniable benefits that come from both kinds of division of labor. Cultural beings can therefore accomplish a great deal more than noncultural beings, even if their capabilities are identical. Ten human beings who each live alone in the woods, doing everything for themselves, will not live as long or as well as ten human beings who work together, each specializing in different tasks.

Hence it is no accident that every human culture divides its tasks. (The fact that *every* culture uses division of labor makes this a feature of culture per se, rather than a matter of cultural differences.) Indeed, try to imagine a modern corporation that refused to use division of labor: It would quickly go out of business, if only because it could not possibly compete with other corporations that rely on division of labor. When factories were first invented, many of them were simply places where master craftspeople built entire products themselves, working side by side but not interacting. These factories had the first kind of division of labor but not the second. In the 1700s and 1800s, however, they were all replaced by factories that divided the manufacturing process into many parts and assigned them to different people. The advantages could be measured in money. A master craftsperson who builds the entire dining room set is expensive to hire, because the skill requires long and thorough training. And the craftsperson has to be paid at this expensive rate even when the required task is just tightening screws or sweeping up afterward. In contrast, if the task of building the table and chairs can be divided into parts, nobody needs to have as many skills as the one master craftsperson did, and some parts of the task, like sweeping the floor, can be performed by a cheap laborer who has almost no skills at all. The total work is cheaper, because fewer skills are required at every part. It is also probably better, because each part can be done by a specialist/expert, whereas the master craftsperson probably had a few weak points. Thus, role differentiation and specialization improve task performance overall, and so over time everything gets done better. The group's collective performance and output are increased.

To illustrate this advantage, consider football teams. If everyone on the team has the same skills, the team does not function as effectively as it does when each person develops a unique set of skills. Specialists outperform generalists. Sure enough, football has evolved over the decades toward increased specialization. In the early years and even into the 1950s, most players played both offense and defense, but that would be unthinkable today. Modern teams have specialists for specific situations, such as being a short-yardage receiver or a blocking back. To function effectively in such a system, you need to acquire specialized abilities.

Role differentiation also gradually produces another huge advantage of culture. This is the vastly widening circle of cooperation and reciprocal benefit. Social animals sometimes cooperate and help each other, but this mainly occurs between blood relatives and in narrowly circumscribed contexts. In contrast, culture allows people to interact with distant strangers in ways that benefit both. For example, consider any economic transaction. You arrive in a distant city and want food, so you pay a restaurant to serve you a meal. Both you and the restaurant are better off: You want food more than the money, and the restaurant's owners want your money more than their food. As with trade everywhere, both parties benefit. Even though you did not know them, had never heard of them before, and may never see them again, you and they manage to interact in a way that results in a good outcome for both parties.

At the heart of this is the network of economic exchange. A culture can produce a system in which many different parties perform different roles and exchange their outputs, so as to improve the lot of everyone. In this way, cultural animals can cooperate and reciprocate far beyond the intimate circle that limits social animals.

A culture is a system. To the extent that nature designed us for culture, it prepared us to be part of a system. Systems connect up multiple individual points (called *nodes*) so that the total can be more than the sum of its parts. For this, different roles are vital. A system in which every node was identical, doing exactly the same thing, would not be much of a system. In contrast, systems that link together different nodes that accomplish different things can be extremely powerful and can produce huge gains in productivity.

Language and Meaning

Language and culture are intimately linked, and it is not necessary to grapple with the chicken-and-egg question of whether language is a prerequisite for culture or vice versa. The important fact is that language is not an activity inside an individual brain but rather is part of the collectively shared and transmitted knowledge. Children learn the language that is spoken in their community, and once they have mastered this, they are able to communicate with many different individuals and gain access to the collective stock of information. People do not have languages by themselves or even language per se. (Indeed, it probably took early humans many centuries to create languages powerful and diverse enough to communicate the broad range of possible human thoughts.) Hence the only way for a person to be able to use language is to belong to a culture. And just as language is only had via culture, culture always includes language: There are no cultures that dispense with language. Culture relies on meaning, and language is the principal tool for accessing and using meaning.

Language may not be indispensable to thought,[28] but it greatly increases the power and range of thought, as well as enabling people to share their thoughts with others, thereby further improving the quality and quantity of possible thoughts. Let me quickly list some of the ways that language improves the cultural animal's ability to deal with the social and physical worlds.

First, of course, information can be coded in language and thereby transmitted much more efficiently. If a nonlinguistic creature solves a problem, it can only share it with others by demonstrating it. In contrast, cultural beings can explain their innovations to each other. Americans can read about new inventions in China and adopt them, and vice versa.

Second, disputes can be resolved by talking instead of by fighting. Disputes are probably inevitable in social life, given competition for limited resources, as well as other sources of aggravation. With language, two animals can explain their sides of the dispute and try to convince each other to yield, such as by appealing to commonly shared values. To illustrate, an episode of the television show "The Sopranos" depicted a meeting among professional criminals. One group reproached the other's boss for refusing to share the profits from a shady real estate deal, noting that the deal had been facilitated by insider knowledge from a source who was supposed to be "owned" in common by both families. The boss had belligerently refused to compromise on several other issues, which he could get away with because his organization was currently powerful and successful, but at this appeal to shared rules he paused, smiled guiltily, and said he would share the profits. Thus, might did not inevitably dictate right, even among professional criminals, who instead resolved their dispute on the basis of reasoning from common understandings about agreements and rules.

A third advantage that cultural animals enjoy, partly or largely on the basis of language, is a vastly expanded understanding of time. Most other animals are "stuck in time,"[29] meaning that they live in the present and have minimal ability to decide or alter what they do in the present on the basis of the past or future. Even such seemingly future-oriented behaviors as hoarding food are not based on a genuine understanding of future needs, because if circumstances are set up so that hoarding is futile, they continue to hoard. They hoard food (e.g., by burying acorns) "with no awareness of why they do it," in the words of one expert review of the research findings.[30] In an experimental study, monkeys were fed once a day, and by that time each day they were ravenously hungry. The researchers gave the monkeys all of the food they wanted at that point. The monkeys would eat their fill and then disregard the rest, sometimes even having food fights in which perfectly good food was hurled at other monkeys. They would have been better off had they conserved some of the leftover food for the hungry hours before the next feeding, but they never learned to do this.

By the same token, animals do not import the past into the present very well. They do learn, of course, but they mainly just learn when outcomes come immediately after the behavior, so that the connection between reward and punishment is obvious. In a famous study, rats had to choose between black and white cues and were rewarded for the proper response. If the reward came immediately, they learned the task quite easily and quickly. If the reward was delayed by only 5 seconds after the choice, it took them hundreds of trials to learn. If it came after 10 seconds, they failed to learn even after a thousand trials. Apparently rats can only connect the past with the present for a few seconds.[31]

In contrast, human beings can think and talk about the distant past and future. They can inform their current choices and change their actions based on events at other times. The human being can even draw meaning from events that occurred before the person was born (such as when people celebrate holidays) or that may occur long after the person is dead (such as when people make wills or enact laws to curb global warming).

Perhaps the single most important benefit to arise from the broad time perspective concerns tradeoffs in which the short-term benefits are opposed to the long-term ones. Cultural animals can vastly improve their lives, including surviving and reproducing better, by attending to long-term benefits and accepting short-term costs. As just one example, agriculture would be impossible without a long-term perspective, because people who are stuck in the present would eat (or even discard) their seeds rather than save them to plant for next year's crop. Many other choices, from using condoms to attending a university, are based on accepting costs and losses in the short run in order to come out better in the long run.

A fourth advantage, which again is probably based on language, is the ability to think of alternate possibilities. People can think beyond the present reality, not only into the past and future, but into other possible arrangements and circumstances. They can imagine how life could be made better by changing certain features.

A fifth and extremely powerful advantage is that people can learn to take advantage of the inherent structure of meaning so as to solve problems in the abstract. Logical reasoning and mathematical calculations are important examples of this kind of thinking. Only cultural animals can use linguistic, rule-based reasoning to solve mathematical problems—and these kinds of thinking greatly increase humans' ability to deal with the physical world (as in architecture) and the social world (as in the economy). Use of these advanced styles of thought depends on culture, because it has taken many generations of experts to develop them, and so most people who do use them have learned them in school.

A final advantage of culture's use of meaning via language is that rationality can be imposed on systems. The earlier example of division of labor illustrates this point too. Someone had to figure out that factories could be more profitable—that is, could make more and better goods more cheaply, thus benefiting the companies and their customers—by dividing the tasks into parts and assigning them to appropriate specialists, instead of having generalists (the master craftspeople) do the entire job.

Military logistics constitutes another example. Medieval armies just lived off the land, which is a polite way of saying that they stole food from the towns in their path or else they went hungry. Modern armies have elaborate staffs that calculate how much food and other provisions will be needed each day and where, as well as how to get it there. Some of these innovations were pioneered by Prussia, a small country in northern Europe that was surrounded by bigger, more powerful neighbors. Prussia needed to find some advantages to make it competitive. The traditionalists in other armies scoffed when Prussian officers began spending their days doing paperwork, but after the Prussians defeated them a few times they began to recognize the advantages of planning (as in having the right quantities of men, weapons, and food in the same place at the same time), and eventually they all began to copy the Prussian methods.

As with many things, there are better and worse ways to organize the behavior of groups of people, and sometimes even a person working alone can figure out a more efficient way of getting the same task done. The ability to use meaningful thought to solve these problems, and then the ability to change behavior so as to implement the improved system, has been a vital and powerful benefit of culture.

Postscript: Solving Problems

In describing the different views about how the individual relates to society, I criticized the high school biology class view that the brain evolved primarily for the purpose of solving problems in the physical environment. (Physical problem solving may have been a small gain from the larger brain, but the main purpose of the brain was for social life.) Yet, in a sense, the problem-solving view has reappeared, for in this section I have pointed out again and again how belonging to a culture has made people better able to deal with their physical world. Is there a contradiction?

The crucial point is that culture is, ultimately, a strategy for dealing with the social and the physical environment. It helps us deal better with the physical world, such as enabling us to obtain an abundant variety of food from stores and restaurants. And it helps us deal with the social world, such as by imposing laws, norms, and rules to guide how we treat each other—but, again, ultimately social life is itself a strategy for dealing with the physical world. The biological tests are survival and reproduction, and what evolution has given us has been given on the basis of improving those two outcomes.

It is not entirely wrong to say that the brain evolved to enable us to deal with the physical environment better, but the link between brain evolution and physical problem solving is indirect. Humans developed culture because, ultimately, culture has enabled us to survive and reproduce better. The brain and other features of the human psyche are there to help us deal with each other. That may have been the direct purpose, even though indirectly these features of the human psyche have indeed contributed to an enhanced ability to deal with the physical world.

Building a Cultural Ape

If Mother Nature set out to design a cultural animal, what features would go into the design? More literally, what were the principal changes from our apish forebears that rendered human nature capable of participating in a cultural society?

The two questions are not quite the same. If we could design the human being in any way we wanted, presumably we would all have the powers of Spiderman if not Superman, as well as twice the wisdom of Socrates, the sexual prowess of Casanova, the unlimited virtue of the Virgin Mary, and the resilient tenacity of cockroaches. But not everything is possible. Let us briefly consider what nature can and cannot accomplish, and then we can briefly speculate about just how nature might have made us into cultural animals.

Limits of Nature

I have already hinted at some of the limits to the power of culture (and will return to that theme in the next chapter), but nature has its limits too. I am proposing that nature designed us for culture. Clearly the job was less than perfect: We continue to have problems living in our culture, both individually and collectively. Probably everyone can think of ways that human beings might have been designed so as to be much better suited to modern cultural life. (For example, if I didn't need and like to sleep for 7 or 8 hours every day, I could get much more work done.) But perhaps these were not all possible.

Nature judges success and failure in terms of whether a species survives. A species that dies out is a failure, by definition. By this criterion, the most logical path to biological success would be for evolution to abolish death. If our species (or any other, for that matter) consisted of people who would live forever, it would be a huge success. Nature seems to have settled for an inferior substitute, namely, reproduction. When you think of all of the complex systems, mechanisms, problems, and dangers involved in having sex so as to make babies, it seems obvious that immortality would have been a much more efficient and reliable solution.[32] But living forever is not an option, apparently. It is precisely because aging and death are inevitable that nature has had to fall back on sexual reproduction to keep our species going.

Likewise, it seems to me that the human species would be better off if we could fly. Nature has created some flying animals, but it hasn't seen fit to bestow this blessing on us. One can't blame natural selection for our earthbound status. Certainly, if some humans emerged with the ability to fly, they would likely be successful. In ancestral times, they could have escaped from predators, scouted terrain from above, and prevailed in fights against other humans. In modern times, an athlete who could fly would probably earn millions playing professional basketball or football, and along with celebrity status one would likely attract a great deal of attention from the opposite sex.

The biologist Stephen Jay Gould has written persuasively about the limits of nature. Evolution can change existing structures much more easily than it can add new ones. For example, if there were some big advantage to being able to scratch your feet without bending your knees, humans might have developed longer arms. This would have been more likely than, say, growing additional arms out of the hips (so they could reach the knees). Lengthening the arm works with existing structures, whereas growing new arms would be far more difficult for evolution to accomplish.

Behavioral plasticity is a good and more relevant example. Many animals go through a juvenile/adolescent phase, during which their behavior is receptive to social learning. When that ends, they become set in their ways, and adults in most species do not easily adopt new behavior patterns. As Gould has argued,[33] this phase of plasticity is regulated by genes: One gene (or one combination) commences it, and another terminates the phase.

Evolution could alter the operation of one of those genes, provided it had a good reason, such as improvements in survival or reproduction. Humans retain behavioral plasticity throughout life to a much greater extent than most other species, and this may have been accomplished by simply altering the workings of the gene that was responsible for ending the phase of plasticity.

Why not make plasticity unlimited for humans as well as other species? And why not intelligence too? Certainly, if some is good, more is better. Here again, we encounter the limits of what biology can accomplish. Intelligence and plasticity may be adaptive, but they are costly too, and so natural selection can only increase them up to a point—and will only increase them as long as the rise in benefits outweighs the rise in costs.

Let us put this another way. If you were part of a committee designing a cultural animal, and you had carte blanche, you'd build in almost unlimited intelligence. But, as we have seen, brains consume far more than their proportional weight of the total energy intake. The rest of the body needs calories too, and so it may not be practical to increase the brain that much more. Indeed, many of our ancestors lived on a limited food supply, and so getting enough food to keep the body going was difficult. To increase a brain and as a result to require more food might end up causing the organism to starve. Being too smart could literally kill you.

The crucial implication of this for my argument has to do with the degree of resemblance and continuity between humans and other animals. Most theorists who write about human nature either seek to emphasize the continuities and similarities, indicating that we are much like other animals, or the differences, to argue that we are special and unique. The cultural animal argument requires a mixture of continuity and change. It is best supported by evidence indicating that the special features of the human psyche can be found in limited, rudimentary forms in other animals. Evolution thus took what was already there and increased it. Neither full continuities (in which humans are entirely the same as other hominids) nor radical differences (by which humans are unique) are really amenable to the cultural animal view. Human culture is unique in our planet's animal kingdom, but the biological structures that made culture possible were created by gradual alterations in the same traits and capabilities that other animals have.

Retrofitting the Ape Mind

Imagine that you have been appointed by some divine Mother Nature to be the chair of the committee that is responsible for designing new species. Imagine that homo sapiens had not evolved but is next in line to be developed. The approval has come through from the Big Boss, so your committee can start working. Mother Nature is giving you considerable latitude to make sweeping changes, but you should learn from past mistakes as well as past successes. Moreover—and this is the exciting part of the assignment—the recent experiments with rudimentary culture among other apes are proving successful, and so your committee is supposed to take them considerably further. In a sense, you are supposed to redesign the chimpanzee or ape to create a more thoroughly cultural being. What traits and attributes do you build into your cultural ape?

First, you would certainly want to make sure your new creation had strong urges to form social connections with others. Being cultural is an extension of being social, so at least you would want to retain the social inclinations of other animals, and possibly you would want to intensify them. A cultural animal should have a strong "need to belong," which keeps attention, effort, and behavior all oriented toward the goal of social connection. Both dyadic (one-to-one) and group relationships would be sought. The creature should form social bonds easily and be reluctant to break them. This might not be a big change from the chimpanzee, but the trait is certainly a prerequisite for culture.

Moreover, ideally, the need to belong could extend beyond connecting with individuals so as to make cultural animals identify with larger groups, possibly even up to the level of identifying with a nationality, university, corporation, or some other unit that might include thousands of people. Thus, the person should want to belong both in regard to specific individuals and to the broader cultural unit, such as a tribe or nation. Shifting the focus of the need to belong from connecting to an individual to (also) connecting with a collectivity would be helpful.

The cultural animal would presumably have some additional features built on top of the need to belong. A cultural animal has to do more than want to hang around with the other guys. It must also have what is called a *theory of mind*. It has to recognize that its fellows have inner states resembling its own, which make possible communication, empathy, social exchange, mutual understanding, deception, and other advanced features of cultural relatedness. It belongs to a community of others who have inner states and processes that resemble its own. Without this, cultural animals cannot share knowledge and work together.

To help them work together, moreover, cultural animals should ideally have some inclination and ability to make themselves act appropriately. They may require self-awareness, including the ability to anticipate how others perceive them, as well as the motivation to care about sustaining the good opinion of others.

Culture is potentially going to confront the new creature with a large stock of information. Dealing with information requires multiple things. First, the brain has to be intelligent enough to process this information. It will need a good reasoning capacity to work out the meanings and implications of events and of its own actions. A cultural brain will clearly need an extremely large storage capacity: It will need to remember an extensive vocabulary of words, people, events, social relations, and the accumulated knowledge of the culture. It will need to have good mechanisms for locating the most useful, important points in a chaotic mass of information, so it will have to be good at screening, sorting, labeling, and classifying. It will have to store information in a systematic manner, so it can retrieve what it needs at later points.

Cultural creatures will require a lengthy socialization process. They need to learn the culture's knowledge, and they will also need to learn the rules for behavior in their society. For socialization to be successful, the cultural animal will need several traits. For one, the creature will need to be willing to learn for many years. An old dog who can't learn new tricks won't do well in a cultural society. Actual dogs, as they get old, may lose their flexibility for learning and adapting, but senior citizens in our species need to learn to operate a VCR, log on to the Internet, and negotiate with new post-bereavement dating partners about condom use, and some of them do. We have already seen that Stephen Jay Gould proposed that nature's solution to this problem has been to make humans retain a childlike plasticity for a much longer period of time than what most other animals show. "Many animals display flexibility and play in childhood but follow rigidly programmed patterns as adults," he wrote. Unlike them, human beings retain juvenile patterns throughout life, even in terms of the shape of the human face. Gould was clear about the value of this: "[O]ur extended childhood permits the transference of culture by education."[34]

Thus, there has to be behavioral plasticity throughout life, and in particular the child and adolescent phases will need to be very long, because these especially promote socialization (curiosity, willingness to learn, and so on). Youngsters should be eager and quick to learn new things from other members of the species, whether older ones (as teachers) or peers.

Socialization also requires continued effort on the part of some of the grownups. A cultural being would benefit from having lifelong urges to nurture the young, to teach them, and to help them to become ready to take their places in the society. Given that cultural animals may need to continue learning and adapting as adults, it would be helpful to have older adults find some satisfaction in teaching (mentoring) young adults. Teaching the very young is not enough. Some experts on primate behavior have remarked on how the great apes fail to show any sign of intentional teaching, even though they may be smart and sociable in other ways.[35] Culture will succeed better if those who have mastered it are willing and inclined to teach.

Another need in a cultural animal would be for a sophisticated decision-making apparatus. Knowing how to act in a complex cultural society is going to be difficult. As the culture becomes more complex, each possible act may be transformed with multiple meanings and values. Novel and unforeseen circumstances will arise rather frequently, presenting new dilemmas of choice, and the person will have to decide what to do. So any simple mechanism for behavior control is likely to prove inadequate. Instead of building in rigid systems of responding, a cultural being will need multiple and highly flexible systems. At the least, the thinking system would have to be able to take over behavior and steer it, so to speak. The thinking system would have to understand various cultural meanings and then use them to dictate the courses of action. Essentially, the creature has to be able to perform rational calculations as to what is sensible, appropriate, and likely to produce a good result. Beyond that, a cultural animal requires some kind of mechanism that allows it to deal effectively with complex, unfamiliar situations.

The importance of inner controls on behavior is easily overlooked. Human beings can use meaning to analyze a situation and figure out what would be the best thing to do, in terms of producing the best long-range consequences. But this ability is useless unless they also have the ability to act on the basis of those thoughts. There has to be some mechanism that can override short-term natural impulses and instead implement actions that are based on the outcome of meaningful thought. Making choices will be a big part of cultural behavior. Simple decision rules that could be programmed into the brain at birth are not likely to be sufficient or flexible enough to deal with cultural social life. Instead, the creature should have some kind of "self" that can exert control and think through multiple possible courses of action and then choose one of them to pursue.

Rather than pussyfooting around with fancy jargon and carefully worded qualifiers, let me state the point with an overly blunt term: free will. That is, to make us suitable for living in culture, nature had to give us free will. As I will explain in chapter 6, there are many meanings of the term *free will*, and I do not claim the most extravagant of them. What is necessary for living in culture, however, is that the person can recognize several possible courses of action, can hold on to mental representations of their meanings and implications (including possible consequences) simultaneously, can analyze and compare them, and can choose among them in a way that is not fully and explicitly programmed in advance. The person must be able to make behavioral decisions that are not entirely determined by current circumstances, by innate proclivities, nor even perhaps by reinforcement history. (If the term *free will* is too grandiose for you, please substitute *controlled processes, self-regulation,* and *lifelong behavioral plasticity*.)

Put another way, a cultural animal will face both internal and external forces on its behavior, and it should not be entirely at the mercy of either of these. It should be able to override its own impulses, at least to the extent that it can eat, fornicate, urinate, and perform other actions in culturally approved ways and places. And it should not respond to the first signal or cue that comes from outside, because often the culture will send complex and conflicting messages about what to do. If you bought everything a salesperson recommended, you would soon be poor and overloaded with junk. A cultural being should be able to resist such pressures sometimes.

To use the terminology of the philosopher John Searle,[36] nature had to create a *gap* between cause and effect. There are inner and external reasons for acting, often multiple reasons for conflicting courses of action. The culturalized human self lives within this gap and is the agent responsible for linking reasons to action. This doesn't require free will in the extreme sense that a totally arbitrary choice can be made that is utterly free of internal or external causes. It does entail that nature has reduced the lawful determinacy of behavior, so that the self can sometimes use rational thought (or perhaps other guidelines) to choose among competing reasons and let action be guided by the best reason.

As I suggested above, a good way to conceptualize the change is by phrasing it in terms of *controlled processes*.[37] Controlled processes are not exactly the same as free will, but the discrepancy is more a matter of haggling than of radical dispute. The self has to do more than make choices. As already stated, culture is a system that thrives by division of labor and differentiated roles. In principle, people could be biologically slated for different roles, but this system would not function effectively, partly because of inflexibility. For example, if someone were biologically slated to be a blacksmith and performed well, he might prosper and hence reproduce, and the result could be a dozen children, all of whom were biologically slated to be blacksmiths. But if the village only needs one blacksmith, the rest would starve. Instead, the remarkable biological adaptation is to produce a flexible self that secures acceptance within the group and then seeks out or creates a more or less unique role for itself. The human self has to seek both common ground with others (to gain acceptance) and distinctive capabilities (to perform a unique role within the system).

For noncultural animals, automatic processing may be sufficient to guide behavior: Stimulus leads directly to response, and if there is any inner processing along the way, it follows standard and fairly rigid lines. As is well established, automatic processes are efficient and highly predictable, whereas controlled processes are costly (inefficient) but extremely flexible.[38] Culture will require the flexibility of controlled processes that can take over from the automatic, well-learned, or innate patterns of responding. Undoubtedly, it is a big and costly step for biology to give us the capacity for controlled processing, and as a result our capacity is probably limited, but what we do have is nonetheless extremely important and powerful.

Last, our cultural ape would benefit from having a strong inner mechanism that can override some of its responses and regulate itself. In a word, it should be capable of self-control. As the social world becomes more and more complex, it will be less and less helpful to do the first thing you think of or feel like, and a human being who always acted on first impulse would probably soon become an outcast if not a criminal. Complex and changing social circumstances will give a big advantage to creatures with the ability to alter their own inner states, as well as their action tendencies, to suit what will get the best results.

If your committee had come up with that list, it would have done its job well! Undoubtedly, there are other traits and abilities that would be helpful for a cultural being, but this list is sufficient to make the point and get us started. To be sure, any social scientist (myself included) is generally skeptical of this sort of armchair theorizing, and all the more so when most of the facts are already known. Still, this list of traits would almost certainly produce a better cultural being than their opposites. A lone-wolf, not-very-smart, rigid, and inflexible being with minimal self-control, a reluctance to learn new things, and a loathing to accept social influence would be a poor candidate for culture.

Lest anyone be misled, let us be clear that my little story about a committee redesigning the chimpanzee to make a human being is not of course the way humans evolved. The story is misleading in at least one important aspect. Evolution builds onto what is already there, making minor modifications. The committee story suggests that any and all changes would have been possible. But in reality only certain changes were possible. That is also presumably why communism and other utopian visions have failed: Human nature is still strongly linked to the traits of the animals from which we evolved. A committee might have designed human beings to be capable of living in a communist or socialist utopia, or in any number of other social arrangements. The reality is that the vestiges of our animal forebears are still there, and they constrain our social possibilities.

Plan of the Book

The rest of this book will build on these ideas. My purpose is to offer an explanation of human nature as revealed in psychology studies. Psychologists have accumulated a vast collection of facts about how people act and react, think, and feel, but there is little in the way of general or integrative understanding of how all of these fit together.

I am a social psychologist, not an evolutionary biologist or comparative psychologist. The cultural animal theory is a framework that in my view works well to integrate and explain what psychology has uncovered about human behavior. That is my goal. Proving that evolution selected us for these traits is a different task, one that requires a different expertise. Put another way, the goal of this book is not to prove that people evolved for cultural participation, but rather to use that assumption as a powerful explanatory framework for providing an integrated overview of social psychology and actual human functioning.

The next chapter will elaborate on these basic ideas about nature and culture. It will explain what is special about culture, of what culture is made, and what are some of the psychological requirements for participating in culture. The role of language and meaning will receive special attention, in view of its central importance to cultural life. The organization of the psyche into two parts (conscious and automatic) will be emphasized as a crucial theme that every other chapter needs in order to explain human functioning within culture.

After that, the book will proceed by examining the basic questions that people have for psychologists: How do we explain wanting, thinking, feeling, acting, and interacting? Chapter 3 starts with motivation, because that drives the truck. It is vital to understand what people want, or else their behaviors can make no sense.

Thinking comes next, in chapter 4. Thinking is a tool that serves wanting: People get what they want by means of figuring things out. Chapter 5 then examines emotions, whose role in psychological functioning has been elusive and enigmatic. Chapter 6 will focus on action control. It is easy but wrong to assume that people's behavior follows simply from their motivations, cognitions, and emotions. In my view, behavior is a separate system, and the welter of wants, thoughts, and feelings does not invariably or automatically result in clear sets of actions. People may want or think or feel without acting accordingly. Hence it is necessary to consider the action control system(s) separately.

Chapter 7 will then focus on interactions. Though psychology has generally focused its grand theories on the individual human self, thinking, feeling, wanting, and acting, interaction follows another set of rules.

Moreover, if we accept the premise that people are designed by nature for culture, then human interactions are worthy of separate treatment. To be sure, social life is already interactive, and so this chapter will focus on the differences between cultural and social interactions. Social interactions are mostly one-on-one, whereas cultural interactions involve a context that refers to the group or other collective. Hence this chapter will look at social behavior, such as family life, aggression, sex, and power, but it will emphasize how these interactions are transformed by being part of a culture.

2

The Human Psyche at Work

How many people have touched your dinner?

Taking a walk in the park is something people do mainly for relaxation and fun, but the animals they see are often hard at work doing what they do every day. Mostly, animals look for food and eat it. Some animals, like fish, hardly do anything else, whereas a few others have alternate activities, such as building a nest, but finding food is nearly always a major occupation. Moreover, when they find food, they usually eat it right then and there. Eating among animals is opportunistic. Waiting to meet up with relatives for a family dinner is relatively unknown, apart from a few practices such as when adult birds bring bugs and worms back to the nest to feed their babies. And even in those cases, hardly anyone else is involved. Animals may eat in the presence of each other, but the consumption is mostly a solitary activity, in which each animal obtains and consumes its own food.

Now, consider the family dinner in modern, suburban America. Unless they have tomatoes from their backyard garden, the family members probably did not obtain any of the food themselves directly from nature. It is sobering to try to calculate how many different people probably had a role in enabling the dinner to happen. The vegetables were grown on different farms, and the meat came from somewhere else, so all of those farmers and their workers are involved. Some of the food was processed before it was sold, at bakeries and slaughterhouses, so more people worked on it. Nearly all of it was packaged in some way. Truckers transported it from the plants to the grocery store, where the family bought it. Thus, there may be several dozen people who touched the food (or its packaging) before it reached the family's dinner table. Imagine if dogs devised a system by which 50 dogs would handle your food before it got to you. You would go hungry! The food would be lucky to make it past the second dog.

That's not all the people who were involved in the dinner, either. Plenty of others, who never actually touched the food, were less directly though no less vitally involved. The grocery store would not have been there without its management, possibly including corporate headquarters for the chain of stores. The trucking company also has its management. Banks probably financed the farm, the store, and several other businesses along the way, and so all the employees at each of those banks could be counted. The father purchased the food at the grocery store using money he obtained by virtue of his work, and so one can count all the people involved in making it possible for him to earn his salary, including the management of his company, the people who work with him to enable him to fulfill his duties, and his company's customers. He drove a car to the grocery store, so the car manufacturer and dealer could be counted as contributing to the dinner. The manufacturer of the stove on which the food was cooked could be counted, not to mention the companies that made and sold the refrigerator. In fact, the family members only can use that kitchen because they borrowed money from yet another bank to buy their house.

One could spin this example out further, but it is already apparent that a human family dinner in an industrialized society is much more dependent on other members of the species than is a dinner eaten by any other animal. At least 50 people handled the food en route to the table, and perhaps another 1,000 were indirectly involved. More than half of them never heard of this particular family and will never meet them. Nonetheless, their efforts were coordinated to make this dinner possible.

For such a system to work, culture has to organize the behavior of a large number of individuals. Most people who contributed to that dinner have specific, defined, individual roles. (Ants may work together in large numbers, but they have only a few differentiated roles.) When it works, it is great, and the immense advantages in efficiency produced by such large-scale coordination are responsible for the diverse successes in human activity. Without the system, those 50 people (or the 1,000) would not be producing that family's meal effectively. Such are the advantages of culture: It can organize and coordinate the actions of many individuals, so that the system is much more than the sum of its parts.

But if culture is so great, why have not most other species adopted it? The downside of culture is that it demands a great deal of the individuals. It is not as if you could hear about this terrific system and merely show up hungry in that family's dining room so as to reap the benefits. On the contrary, you have to find and sustain your own niche within the system. And the requirements for that are considerable.

Consider the birds again. Suppose that, for some reason, a bird lost its home, perhaps because a forest fire eliminated the tree where its nest was located. What would be required in moving to a new place? Essentially, the homeless bird has to find an unoccupied tree and build a nest. It can obtain food in the familiar fashion, by searching the area. For companionship, probably all it needs to do is find some birds like itself and hang around them for a while.

In contrast, a person who wants to live in a new place has a long series of tasks. Finding an apartment requires some mastery of cultural systems, such as knowing how to locate and decipher advertisements. The person needs a source of money, usually from a job, and so one has to know how to get a job. (And knowing how to find a job is hardly enough—often, years of education or other credentials are required to perform that job.) Acquiring a social life requires more skills, such as knowing how to make yourself attractive to others, what to wear and say, where to find them, and which people might be receptive to becoming friends with you. Romance requires further specialized knowledge.

Those two points, in a nutshell, hold the key to understanding how the human psyche is put together. The advantages of culture are so compelling that we cannot afford to spurn them. But animals can only take advantage of culture if they have elaborate inner structures that enable them to travel the long road to social acceptance. Even if some genius cat or bird were to design a cultural system for the species, the others would not be able to make it work, because they lack the inner capacities: the proper drives, cognitive abilities, and so forth.

The level of collective organization is one important difference between social and cultural animals. Human beings are not just connected to each other, as individuals. They are also connected to the system. (Again, we define *culture* as an information-based and organized social system.) Some animals may have an attachment to their herd, but these attachments are rudimentary compared to the complex attachments that people have to their systems of work, friendship, nation, and others.

Meaning as Resource

Culture is made from meaning. It is only by using meaning that one can store and communicate information beyond the simplest here-and-now facts. Meaning is also valuable for imposing organization on large systems. Meaning has other uses, too. People use language to access meaning, and language probably counts as the greatest invention of human culture, because without it none of the other achievements of culture would have been possible. Therefore, we begin by considering what meaning is and how people came to be able to use it.

Language and Thought

Among the most forceful and influential arguments for cultural relativity was the idea that language determines thought. It was made famous by Benjamin Lee Whorf and his student Edward Sapir, and it came to be called the Sapir-Whorf hypothesis. The central point was that different cultures use different languages, which express different concepts, and so people from different cultures will think in fundamentally different ways and will have potentially radical differences in how they experience themselves and their worlds. To illustrate the point, Sapir and Whorf furnished several classic examples. The Eskimos were reported to have 17 different words for different kinds of snow (or 3, or 50, or even 400),[1] thus indicating that they made conceptual distinctions that were important to them but invisible to us. In many ways, that was the most dramatic and exciting point of all: Their language allowed them to think thoughts that were incomprehensible to speakers of other languages.

Distinguishing among colors was another example used by supporters of Whorf and Sapir. According to physicists, the color spectrum is actually a continuum, and so dividing it into specific colors is somewhat arbitrary from the point of view of the physics of light—and so different cultures divide it differently. Thus our impression that red, blue, yellow, and green are naturally distinct colors, whereas light blue and dark blue are variations on the same color, is merely the arbitrary result of our cultural conditioning.

Most extraordinarily, Sapir and Whorf said that the Hopi (a Native American tribe) do not have a concept of time or of past and future, which their language supposedly reveals. Because of their language, the Hopi do not think of the past, the future, or other aspects of time in the same way that modern Americans do. If this is correct, then our very sense of time is culturally constructed and relative. We think time is out there in the world and we are at its mercy, but we are wrong: Time is constructed by us, using the ways that our culture has taught us to experience the world.

Moreover, these were presumed to be merely a few of the countless ways that languages differed from each other. If the Sapir-Whorf hypothesis is fully correct, then a great many thoughts—perhaps the majority—are the product of cultural conditioning and could scarcely be thought in another culture or another language. And if thinking is so utterly relative, then one can hardly speak of a universal human nature. Instead, one must assume that people from other cultures differ from us in innumerable and scarcely comprehensible ways.

The Sapir-Whorf theory was thus a major triumph for believers in cultural relativism. It seemed to prove that human experience is shaped so powerfully by language that the happenstance of growing up in some particular culture made some thoughts obvious to you while others were opaque and unattainable. Modern Americans could not hope to understand what life is like for people in Surinam or Nigeria or Myanmar, even if Americans tried to inform themselves about these lands. A good meal or an orgasm would be so utterly different that one could not imagine how someone from another culture would experience it.

The Sapir-Whorf hypothesis is more wrong than right, however. Subsequent work has discredited it point by point.[2] The Eskimos have many words for snow, but so do Americans (e.g., slush, sleet, flurries). More important, when Americans need to make finer distinctions—such as when they take up skiing and want to talk about the different snow conditions—they quickly develop the words they need (e.g., powder, corn). This fact is actually the crucial rebuttal of Sapir and Whorf, because it shows that thought is not constrained by language. Americans' language does not prevent them from recognizing the differences among various kinds of snow or from thinking about them. When the thought is needed, the language changes to accommodate it.

The Hopi seem to understand time pretty much the same way we do, and like everyone else they are able to talk about the past and the future. As for the color wheel, although it may be a continuum in terms of the physics of light, the human eye has the same color receptors everywhere, and so all cultures that distinguish colors end up with the same list. Some languages apparently do not distinguish all of the different shades that we do, but new colors are added in about the same sequence. That is, cultures that have only two color words almost always have them for light (white) and dark (black). If the culture has a third color, it is always red; the fourth is generally yellow or green; and the fifth is the other of those two; the sixth is always blue; and so forth.[3] Most cultures recognize the 11 basic colors and do so in precisely the same way. Maybe the color spectrum is a continuum in terms of light waves, but the receptors in the human eyes are not, and they attune us to certain colors. Anyone whose eyes work properly (that is, anyone not color blind) can tell the difference between red and green, regardless of culture and language.

Lately, there has been a trend to try to find a few bits of difference, such as that certain ideas can be expressed more easily in some languages than in others, making them easier to remember. These should, however, be regarded as finding scraps of linguistic relativity rather than reviving the idea that people from one culture cannot understand thoughts or concepts from another.[4]

Languages are far more similar than had previously been thought, and that universality suggests that the human brain is designed to understand the world in certain ways, which may also correspond to the structure of reality. Thus, all languages have nouns and verbs, modifiers (adverbs and adjectives), and names and pronouns.[5] Languages may differ as to the sequence of words in a sentence (e.g., verb in the middle or at the end), but sentences are always used. Even the sequence of words does not vary as widely as it could: Steven Pinker says that there are 128 possible orderings of the main parts of a sentence, but most languages use one of only two of those possibilities.[6] Crucially, most languages seem to have an almost identical list of concepts, and as a result nearly all words and sentences can be translated effectively from one language into another.

The acid test, in my view, is translation. If thoughts were dependent on languages, and languages were fundamentally different, then many ideas could be thought in one language but not in others. Translation would therefore be almost impossible. Yet translation is extremely accurate, probably losing only about 1% of the meaning (usually because of linguistic quirks like multiple meanings and connotations). People who read *Harry Potter* or for that matter *Wuthering Heights* in Spanish or Japanese probably don't miss out on much, as compared to reading the original in English.[7]

The important thing to appreciate about the Sapir-Whorf hypothesis is not merely that it is wrong, but how wildly and outrageously misleading the whole idea was. The important point, the one that offers the truly profound insight, is contained in the exact opposite view. It is the sameness, not the difference, that is the extraordinary thing about different languages and their resulting thoughts. Almost any thought can be expressed in almost any major language. That is what is remarkable.

The implication is that all languages use essentially the same concepts. It might deserve to be called the Anti-Whorf hypothesis: There is one basic universe of concepts, and all languages use it. They simply assign different sounds to the same concept, so that *dog, Hund,* and *chien* all refer to the same entity (in English, German, and French, respectively). This basic universe of concepts is an important common foundation for human thought, and it is pretty much the same everywhere, with only a few subtle differences here and there.

The common universe of concepts is an important resource. It indicates that there is a particular set of ideas—perhaps a very large set, but nonetheless one set—that most cultures and languages use. Without physical brains that can think these concepts, they would not have any impact on physical reality, but when brains begin using them, ideas can exert influence over physical reality. Until then, they existed only as possible thoughts that weren't yet being thought, but they were still part of the universe of concepts.

Thus, there is a universe of possible ideas, of possible meanings, that existed apart from human beings and essentially waited to be discovered. We can therefore distinguish three different processes. The brain evolved; language was invented; meaning was discovered. That is, the brain was created as a physical item, following the laws of physics, chemistry, and biology. Language was invented as a tool to enable the brain (or a community of like-minded brains) to make use of meaning. The universe of possible ideas was out there waiting for brains to come along and make use of it—as the human species has finally done, with enormous effect.

Consider an unusual number, perhaps something like 342,945,518,204, 337.41297436831. It is fair to assume that prior to the appearance of human beings, this number was never used on our planet. Plus the earliest humans probably did not make use of it. Suppose the first time anyone ever said or thought this exact number was in 1755. At that time, it determined some quantity of what was being sold, and so as a result of that number, one person paid another person a sum of money. In that sense, molecules were moved on the basis of that number in 1755, whereas up to that point that number (that idea) had never had a direct effect on physical reality. Still, the number existed as a possible thought prior to that. The number had to be there, waiting to be used. The number was not invented or discovered: All the numbers are there, waiting, for one to understand the concept of numbers (in this case, numbers with decimal places). All cultures that use numbers and mathematics will understand that number as signifying the same quantity (though they may write it differently and certainly will pronounce it differently). The value of that number is not subject to bias, distortion, or alteration by culture.

As a simpler example, consider the equation that 4 times 7 equals 28. This too is true everywhere. No peculiar cultural influence can dictate that 4 times 7 should equal 804, or indeed any other number than 28. If the importance of culture were to be found in cultural differences, then 4 times 7 might equal 25 in Greece, 26 in Spain and Mexico, 28 in China and Nigeria, 30 in Brazil and New Zealand, 32 in Israel and Canada. But it doesn't: The correct answer is 28 everywhere. At least, every culture that uses multiplication gets the same answer.

The idea has always been true that 4 times 7 equals 28, but it hasn't always necessarily mattered. It had no impact until we came along. It could only influence physical events by means of brains smart enough to understand numbers and multiplication, and so it was probably irrelevant to anything that happened in the world prior to the appearance of our species, and again even the earliest humans may not have figured out that 4 times 7 equals 28 or made any use of that fact. The equality between 4 times 7 and 28 is, however, built into the nature of meaning, and once human brains became able to think it and use it, that fact could begin influencing events.

Some theorists use the sameness of language to conclude that language is a result of the structure of the human brain. By that reasoning, the way we all use language derives from how evolution actually put the brain together. There may be some truth in that, but I do not think the evolution of brain structure was an accident. The universe of possible ideas was out there with its own concepts and relationships. The brain didn't create the structures of meaning; rather, it evolved so as to be able to recognize them and use them. It is not an accident of evolved brain structure that 4 times 7 equals 28; it is truth. The brain evolved to be able to appreciate that truth. If someday we travel across the universe to find other intelligent beings who evolved independently of our own species, and if they have mathematics, then for them too 4 times 7 will equal 28.

Language is our servant, not our master. It's a tool that people everywhere use to deal with the world, which presents mostly the same issues and problems everywhere. Hence, most languages mostly use the same concepts. Motherhood, a fight, good song, boy and girl, something good to eat, unfairness, bad weather, and countless other ideas generally are the same phenomena in all languages.

Human thought is much more similar than different across cultures. To be sure, there are a few important cultural differences in styles of thinking, as I shall cover in chapter 4. But by and large, people have the same thoughts everywhere. Even anthropologists who are committed believers in cultural differences have occasionally remarked that everyday conversations are fairly similar in topic and content the world over.[8] The same basic thoughts and ideas get expressed in every language: I'm hungry; the rain is here; I hereby marry you; it's too cold; you lost the contest; my child is sick; this is not fair; help me; I want to have sex with you; her father died; he told a lie; sit in the honor seat; please stop fighting; and so on. These are prominent ideas, much needed by people in every culture, and so every language has found the words for them.

There are immense advantages to being able to use meaning, many of which were surveyed in the previous chapter, and indeed the advantages of culture are mostly dependent on being able to process meaning. It is no accident that every known culture in the world has a language. My argument is that the brain evolved, via natural selection, so as to be capable of language, because language offered the essential tool to allow people to gain access to the universe of possible ideas and so to use meaning to think and communicate. The human brain took shape following the rules of physical causality, but the world of meaning is something quite different. Meaning is not made of atoms and molecules, though molecules can be made able to represent meaning and therefore to use it.

The distinction between meaning and physical processes underlies the important difference between social causality and physical causality. This distinction makes many modern thinkers uncomfortable, and so typically they deny that it exists but then go on using it in practice anyhow. But some clarification of causality is in order.

Cause and Effect

Before we start delving into the odd corners of the human psyche, we must gain some appreciation for how one thing affects another. Instead of going into intense technical detail about all the subtleties of the debates, I think it is sufficient to give a simple overview that everyone can follow relatively easily. I recognize, however, that specialists may accuse me of having glossed over the complexities. This is not a book about causality, however, and all that is necessary is that you grasp how things fit together well enough to read the rest of the book.

Although hardly anyone plays billiards any more, billiard balls are still one of the standard metaphors for causality. Billiards is something like pool, using pool balls but without the holes in the corners of the table. The image of causality involves one ball sitting quietly on the green felt table while the player knocks another ball toward it with a cue stick. The rolling ball smacks into the one sitting still and makes it roll. That's the image of cause and effect: The physical impact of the rolling ball caused the second ball to start rolling too.

This kind of causality can be quite effective in Newtonian physics, but things are rarely so simple and clear-cut in psychology. We might ask why Sam refused to help Jacob, and the answer could involve Sam's current mood, his childhood experiences, the temperature in the room, what Sam was recently thinking about, how Jacob phrased the request for help, the type of relationship Sam and Jacob have, and what happened a week ago when Sam asked Jacob for help. And all of those answers could be correct. In fact, they could be simultaneously correct, insofar as the issue of whether Sam helps on this occasion is affected by all of those things.

When one billiard ball hits another, the second one is sure to move, unless it is glued to the spot or something like that. This brings up another crucial difference. The temperature in the room and Sam's current mood may have a genuine effect on whether he helps Jacob, but neither determines it with anywhere near the 100% certainty that we have with the billiard balls.

The crucial point is that most causes in psychology take the form of changing the odds that some response will occur, not of guaranteeing it. Causes are probabilistic, not deterministic. Scientific journals that publish carefully controlled studies of human behavior are filled with evidence for one causal effect after another, but most of them show only a 5% to 10% change in behavior even under carefully arranged laboratory conditions. Outside the laboratory, where all sorts of factors may interfere with or supersede each other, many real causes may have barely a 1% impact. Yet that does not mean that all of that information should be discarded as trivial. (Indeed, an advertising campaign that increases sales by 1% might translate into millions or even billions of dollars for the advertiser, resulting in lavish bonuses and promotions in the shop, while competitors might have to fire staff.) Whether Sam actually does help Jacob or not may depend on how all those small causes add up. His mood, for example, might make only a 3% difference as to whether he helps Jacob—but that 3% is still a real cause. Sometimes, it might just be the crucial factor that determines the outcome.

Physical versus Social

Social causality is real. Many social scientists say this but do not really mean it, whereas I mean it. In this work, I will assume that physical and social causality are both genuine influences on behavior and are not the same thing.

Technically, the term *cultural reality* would be more precise than *social reality*. Meaning exists in culture, and it is possible to be thoroughly social beings without using meaning to understand the world. But the term *social reality* has already gained usage, and we are to some extent stuck with it. In parallel fashion, immigrants become American citizens by means of a process that is officially called *naturalization*, though nature has little to do with it, and *culturalization* would be a more appropriate term.

Physical causality involves the activities of atoms and molecules, chemicals and cells, and other aspects of physical reality. The laws of physics, chemistry, and biology are sufficient to explain these. Many social scientists profess to believe in social causality, but when pressed, they say they believe that all of psychology can be reduced to the laws of physics.[9] For example, they believe that thinking is ultimately nothing more than biochemical activity occurring within the brain. The brain is a physical entity, composed of nerve cells that operate through clear physical and chemical processes. If thinking is nothing more than brain cells firing, then perhaps the social level of analysis can eventually be discarded and everything can be explained according to the laws of natural science.

This idea is at best quaint, at worst absurd. Imagine a book trying to describe the American Civil War in terms of brain cell activity. It would be a long and boring book that would utterly miss the point of what the Civil War was about and even what happened. The causes and events of the Civil War cannot be adequately expressed in terms of brain cell activity, or even if you throw in muscle activity. The events of the Civil War meant something and were connected by meanings, and if you fail to appreciate those meanings, you cannot possibly understand the Civil War, nor even furnish an explanation of it. This is a radical point that contradicts the reduction of psychology to physics and chemistry. An account of the events of the Civil War in purely physical terms cannot possibly explain it.

It is perhaps radical to suggest that thought cannot be reduced to brain activity and (more generally) that psychology will not be able to be reduced to physics and neuroscience. If we want to attribute any genuine reality to social and cultural processes, however, it is essential to appreciate that they are not mere quirks of biochemical or molecular processes. That is where culture comes in. Culture is not a physical reality. It is grounded in a network or system of people. It is not contained inside a single brain, but rather sustained by the network of brains. In fact, the individual brains are replaceable: Culture continues to exist even though particular brains are eliminated from the network (such as by death) and new ones join it. Culture consists of meanings. The meaning of a sentence, an act, or an event is not something that has a chemical or molecular structure.

Meaning can be represented in physical structures. Brain activity is necessary to represent meaning, but the meaning is not contained in the brain activity. Rather, the meaning exists in the social and cultural network. This is why the meaning continues to exist even when some brains cease to function and are replaced by others. If the meaning were contained in the nerve cell firings of your brain, then when your brain died the meaning would cease to exist.

Meaning can thus only begin to influence the physical world when it is used and understood by a physical being. The biblical allusion to the Word becoming flesh can be understood best as referring to the origins of cultural life rather than to the creation of the physical world. Words become flesh in the sense that human beings can process meanings in their brains and then change the way they act on the basis of these meanings.

On the surface, languages differ widely. Those differences, plus the fact that language has to be learned, have encouraged many experts to regard language as the essence of culture and a crucial source of variation. More recent scholarship, however, has found strong similarities among languages.

The words are different, but the ideas and meanings are much the same. The order of words varies from one language to another, but the basic grammatical units are the same—nouns, verbs, subject and object, adjectives modifying nouns, and so forth. These characteristics have been found in cultures so vastly separated by geography and experience that one can assume that the languages developed independently of each other.

The view that the basic elements of grammar and syntax are built into the human brain is increasingly accepted. Of course, that does not necessarily settle the issue of whether brain structures cause language to take particular forms. The brain itself may have developed in a certain way because that is the best, or only, way to think. For example, maybe the reason that all languages have verbs is that the human brain has some peculiar structure that naturally formulates sentences containing verbs. But that very brain structure may be no coincidence. The brain may have learned to think with verbs because there is no other way, or at least no other way that works anywhere nearly as well for representing the realities of life. Verbs express action, change, movement, and being, and there is simply no way to describe reality without accounting for action, movement, and being. All languages have to express action in some way, because action is an ineluctable fact of life. This is essentially a broader version of the same point made in the previous section about multiplication. All cultures that do multiplication agree that 4 times 7 equals 28, and that is not an accidental result of brain structure. Rather, the brain evolved to be able to appreciate and make use of the external truth that 4 times 7 equals 28. In the same way, it evolved to be able to link different kinds of concepts, such as nouns and verbs, so as to express the external reality of action, movement, and being. The universal features of grammar may be inherent to the structure of meaning, and the brain simply evolved to be able to use them.

Can Ideas Move Molecules?

Probably the test case for whether someone genuinely believes in social reality is this: Do you believe that ideas can move molecules? In other words, is the distribution of physical matter in the universe ever altered, even slightly, by meanings or other nonphysical realities?

I think the answer is clearly yes, although only under limited conditions. Ideas can move molecules but only if there are people who can understand the ideas (in the sense of processing them in their brains) and change their actions on the basis of what they understand. Still, the ideas do have a reality that is independent of any particular brain. The ideas are rooted in the culture, which is held in common by a group of people. If one of those people dies or moves away, the ideas continue to exist, held by the people who remain.

As we have seen, there is essentially one universe of concepts upon which all languages and all cultures draw. This universe remained an irrelevant, abstract possibility until brains came along that were capable of processing it. The previous example of 4 times 7 equals 28 illustrates this point: That calculation was beyond what dinosaurs could do, and so it had no impact on the world in the dinosaur era, but now that human beings are capable of it and similar thoughts, that truth can affect how a skyscraper gets built or how much one person pays another.

For some obscure reason, many people have passionate beliefs about whether social reality can be explained in purely physical terms, and so I will not belabor the point. Let me, however, indicate what I mean by social reality and causality. To begin with, I hasten to add that I do not think that human behavior violates the laws of physics, chemistry, or biology. On the contrary, everything that people do has to be consistent with those laws. My point is only that there are additional, nonphysical factors that can affect human behavior. Physics is not enough; social causes must be appreciated too. Human behavior responds to meaning, which is not a physical reality but depends on the shared understandings of a cultural group.

To return to the brain, I agree that thinking is closely linked to brain cell activity and cannot violate the neurological and biochemical principles that govern the brain. In an extreme case, you can stop someone from thinking by smashing his brain with a golf club. But, crucially, the content of an individual's thoughts depends partly on nonphysical realities that are not part of his brain.

Sharedness is the essence of the social: Two or more (usually, far more) people have some understanding in common. Both their brains may represent the same idea by firing a special combination of brain cells—perhaps different cells in their respective brains—but the sharedness is the nonphysical aspect. Having something in common, and especially understanding it in common, is what is missing in physical causality.

Money is a good example. Money is not a physical reality. To be sure, some money takes the form of physical objects, such as bills and coins, but the value of those bills and coins depends almost entirely on shared understandings. As I write this, some European countries have abandoned their own money and begun to use a new, common currency (the euro). Dutch guilders and German marks are no longer worth anything. While packing to move recently, I found a 25-guilder banknote left over from a past trip to the Netherlands. It is the same physical item it has been for years, but I can no longer use it to buy beer or toothpaste, even if I go back to Holland. It has the same atoms and molecules, and our brains can recognize it just as well as ever, but its social reality has changed.

The nonphysical aspects of money can be appreciated in other ways too. Ten dimes equal a dollar, but this equivalence can never be found in the molecular structure of the metal coins and the paper bill. Furthermore, most people use money frequently without actually handling coins or bills—they purchase with credit cards, have their wages deposited directly into their bank accounts, write checks to the electric company, and so forth. If all of the coins and bills were retrieved and added up, they would amount to only about a third of the total money that officially exists—because the majority of the money exists only as abstract quantities in bank accounts and the like, without ever for a minute existing in the form of physical bills and coins.

The argument for social reality can thus be illustrated with the example of money. Money is real and can certainly influence people's behavior. People can think about money (sometimes at great length). The thoughts about money cannot be reduced entirely to electrical activity within single brains, because the thoughts depend on the collectively shared understanding of what money is. And money is not essentially a kind of physical matter. Money exists as shared understandings, and indeed money is possible only if a large number of people share the same implicit agreement and understanding of what money is. After all, why can you trade a dollar bill for a banana? That transaction cannot be explained by the molecular structure of the dollar bill, nor even by the neurological activity within your brain. Both of those are relevant—if your brain is not working, or if the ostensible dollar bill is made of the wrong molecules (such as aluminum or peat moss), then the transaction will fail—but the transaction can take place only if you and the banana vendor share the same recognition of the value of money. It's because of the system, the culture, that you can trade a dollar bill for a banana. The dollar bill has meaning, which depends on collectively shared assumptions and symbolic thought, and that's why it can garner a banana.

Law is another good example of a social reality. The law is not contained in individual brains, but rather it exists in the social system. It is not inevitable: There are countries that do not have the full rule of law, and generally these are terrible places to live. But people count on laws that they do not even know: For example, when you buy stocks, you count on all sorts of laws (for example, that the money you invest in the stock market won't be stolen from you by means of insider trading, whatever that is) to protect you. Otherwise you wouldn't buy. Your behavior is shaped by laws you may not even know. More generally, the large network of people manages to create, sustain, and obey laws. The individual brain enables the person to make use of laws and observe them competently, but it does not contain them.

As another example, consider the Boston Tea Party. In England, one man's brain cells instructed his lungs and vocal cords to make movements that created certain sound waves that came out of his mouth. As a result, thousands of miles away, molecules of tea ended up mixed with salt water instead of the fresh water that is the normal fate of tea. If physical causality were enough to explain that chain of causes, then something about the air molecules coming out of the king's mouth had to be able to produce physical and chemical effects that redirected the tea into Boston Harbor. But those molecules of air did not have any special physical properties. Had those tea leaves been intercepted by a modern chemist, he or she would have found nothing about them that would have revealed they would end up in salt water rather than fresh water.

In fact, identical molecules of air could have been created in the same room in England with no discernible effect on anything. If those words had been spoken by a floor sweeper when the room was empty, they would not have set in motion the chain of events that resulted in the Boston Tea Party. The shared understandings were crucial. Those sound waves had important meanings in the English language; those meanings were processed and implemented by the king's subordinates; and these had practical and symbolic implications for the colonists in Boston. Because of their shared values, they found the policy unjust; they decided to express their protest symbolically by dumping the tea into the harbor; and so forth. To be sure, none of the events contradicted the laws of physics, but they required an elaborate social system that cannot be reduced to physics. The molecules of air in the sound wave coming out of the king's mouth did not by themselves carry the causes of what was to happen much later and far away. Social causes were crucial.

Physical and social causations of behavior can operate more or less separately. Although they may often be intertwined in practice, still they can be distinguished. Behavior can be affected not just by brain activity but also by hormones, muscle fatigue, bodily pain and pleasure, and the like. The human body will recoil from pain as a natural response, and one does not need to invoke language or conceptual meanings to explain why people recoil from pain. Thus some behavior can be explained in terms of purely physical causes.

Social causes, however, are based on language and meaning. Norms and values guide how people act. Responses to certain problem situations may depend on how the person interprets them, such as who is to blame, or whether a given option is better regarded as an opportunity or a danger. Social causality does not operate alone, because it requires physical processes too—at minimum, the brains must process the information in order for behavior to be influenced by these meanings.

The intertwining of physical and social causality can be seen in a ball game. Kicking a ball certainly involves physical processes. The eyes transmit light to the brain, which determines where the ball is, and so forth. The brain cells fire in a certain pattern so as to regulate the movements of the leg so that the tip of the foot is brought into contact with the ball, sending it off on a certain trajectory. Without these physical processes, nothing would happen. Yet the physical processes are not a full explanation of what is happening. The reason that the kicker and the ball are there is understandable only in reference to the game, which exists as a shared understanding—shared by a couple of dozen players, coaches, referees, and perhaps some spectators. The rules of the game are understood even more widely, so that if perchance the game were to be televised and someone on the other side of the world were to turn it on, that spectator could quickly understand what was happening and why the player was kicking the ball (assuming, crucially, that the viewer understood the rules of the game). By the same token, the trajectory of the ball is a result of physical processes such as momentum, direction (vector), wind resistance, and the like, and these determine where it falls—but shared understandings can lead to big differences in everyone's behavior based on some differences in where the ball comes down (such as on one side of the goal post or the other, or across the out-of-bounds line) whereas other differences are trivial (e.g., half a meter out of bounds, or ten meters out of bounds). The rules of football cannot be reduced to molecules or chemicals. Therefore natural science and physical causality absolutely cannot provide a complete explanation of a football game.

None of this is meant to deny the reality of physical laws, nor even the influence of physical causality on human behavior. Genes and hormones do exert influence on human behavior that is largely independent of meaning. But a full appreciation of human action and psychology requires one to appreciate both physical and social causes. People respond to meaning as much as they respond to hormones, if not more. And there is overlap: The molecular and electrical processes in the brain allow individual human beings to understand and process meanings, so that their behavior can then be affected by social causes.

Beyond Here and Now

The visible world is all around us and undoubtedly has a strong impact on what people do. Indeed, the animals from which we evolved lived mainly in the world that confronted their senses, as do nearly all noncultural animals today. Human beings, however, can also respond to invisible phenomena, and this fact radically transforms human functioning.

We have already discussed the universe of possible ideas as an invisible reality. The world of meaning, such as mathematical principles and logical rules, does not exist as a physical fact but is available to physical beings who are smart enough to represent it mentally and make use of it. Human beings use meaning far more extensively than any other animal, and so already on that basis we are different.

Meaning allows people to represent possibilities and circumstances beyond their immediate surroundings, and this is also crucial. They can work toward goals that are off in the distant future, and they can coordinate their actions with those of people who are out of sight and even far away. For example, in 2003, the United States conducted an invasion of Iraq. In this operation, the actions of thousands of men and women scattered around the country of Iraq were coordinated by military commanders and politicians, some of whom were on the other side of the world (back in Washington, D.C.). Not only were invisible meanings crucial to executing the operation, but other invisible realities shaped it. The invasion was carried out amid international debates as to whether it was moral and legal. The United Nations—which is a collection of people living in the United States who are symbolically (invisibly) tied to all the different countries (defined by invisible borders and other symbolic determinations)—debated whether it should run the invasion, oppose and prevent it, or keep out of the way. And the biggest impetus for the invasion was that UN inspectors were unable to find certain kinds of weapons in Iraq. These invisible weapons were forbidden by invisible laws (some of which were, admittedly, printed on paper) but were nonetheless presumed to be somewhere in Iraq by those who urged the invasion.

Invisible phenomena may even be essential to the operation of consciousness. The philosopher Jean-Paul Sartre linked consciousness to non-being, noting that humans can be aware of a lack or absence.[10] A computer, for example, can "see" what is there but cannot really be directly aware of what is missing. At best, it can compare two representations, one with something and one without, and establish that they are different. In contrast, a person can look at a table and see immediately that his keys are not on it. If he is looking for his keys, he may not even recognize what actually is on the table, only that the sought-for keys are not there.

Even when a person sees what is there, consciousness may be informed by invisible realities. For example, people hear high-pitched tones as high, but of course *high* is a relative term that only makes sense in contrast to low tones. To hear a tone as high, consciousness must in some way be informed by the low tones that it doesn't hear. In the same way, people can look at a tool and imagine how it might be used, can look at an employee and wish that she might be better suited for the job, and can see a trashy neighbor or a roof leak as a threat to their property values. Probably relatively little conscious experience is a simple perception of some physical fact. Instead, perceptions are saturated with meanings, including implications, possibilities, and alternatives.

Furthermore, people are able to understand their worlds on the basis of invisible forces and facts. Even the most intelligent of other animals do not seem able to accomplish this. They can understand causality when cause and effect are both visible, but understanding the world as shaped by invisible forces appears to be utterly beyond them.[11] Humans understand some events in the physical world as influenced by things they cannot see: gravity, electricity, germs, acceleration, and the like, not to mention ghosts, gods, spells, and karma. They also apply this capability to the social world, interpreting the overt and visible behaviors of other human beings as based on invisible forces, including personality traits, intentions, norms, laws, and more.

Time is another invisible reality that informs and structures human life much more than that of other animals. Most evidence suggests that animals live in the immediate present, with little ability to recall the past (other than in the sense of having current response tendencies that were shaped by prior experiences of reward and punishment) or to plan for the future.[12] Hardly any animals can think more than about 20 minutes ahead. Some animal activities (such as squirrels burying nuts) seem like planning for the future, but careful research suggests that those are illusions. Squirrels bury nuts out of some current inner prompting. They do not, for example, change their behavior if many nuts are suddenly removed, so that their plans have been disrupted and they will need to store more if they are to find the same level when they go searching months from now.

Human beings are, however, genuinely able to incorporate the past and future into how they act in the present. These influencing events may be far off, even beyond the boundaries of their own lives. For example, each December, millions of Christians celebrate the birth of Jesus, which occurred more than 2,000 years ago. Many Christians also adjust their current behavior based on doctrines that predict what will happen after their deaths and even at the end of time.

Another way that animals are stuck in the present is that they can only learn if the interval is very short between their action and its outcome. Thus, rats learn pretty quickly and effectively if they are punished immediately after making a certain response. If there is a delay of only 5 seconds, however, it takes them much longer to learn, and if the delay is 10 seconds they do not learn at all.[13] In contrast, the human is able to learn with much greater delays. For example, a person may learn to avoid buying technology stocks even though it took 5 years between making the first investment and realizing how much money he lost. This ability to connect experiences across time greatly increases the human ability to learn, especially in a culture that is based in part on an understanding of time.

Indeed, culture itself is an invisible reality. You cannot ask for a box of culture, as if it were a physical thing that can be handled and measured. Culture exists in the sharedness of meaningful understandings. The actions and results it produces may be visible, but culture itself cannot be seen. Yet its influence is powerful. People pay taxes, vote in elections, and go off to war as a result of events that are outside their perceptual field and of structures that are by nature invisible. The organization that culture creates is also invisible. The economy and the legal system, for example, do not exist as physical items in some place where they can be seen. They are powerful forces that shape the actions of millions of people, but they are invisible realities.

Social animals do have social organization, but it is probably not maintained on the basis of explicit understandings of invisible realities. The alpha male can make the others do his bidding because he is bigger and stronger than they are. Humans, however, will do the bidding of someone much smaller and weaker than they are, simply because that person is wearing a police uniform, or because the little old lady giving orders happens to be your boss. Humans can see beyond the visible to respond to invisible systems of legitimate authority.

In short, the human psyche cannot be understood without appreciating how much it deals with invisible realities. We are not like any other creatures on the planet, because as far as we can tell they live in their physical surroundings and that is all. This use of invisible realities has greatly contributed to our ability to exercise control over the physical world and over the social world, and it has only been made possible by virtue of the use of language and meaning.

The Power of Culture—And Its Limits

The theme of this book is that culture is deeply embedded in human nature, but not in the way that such a statement is usually meant. Indeed, most advocates of the power of culture are deeply suspicious of any assertions about human nature. They believe that different cultures shape human beings in such widely different ways that hardly any generalizations about people will be valid across cultural boundaries. Thus, the advocates of the importance of culture have generally put their stock in cultural differences as the most promising source of support for their side. I think this has been a losing strategy. In my view, the data have not supported the radical view that culture can shape human beings in an almost unlimited and unpredictable range of variations. As these data have emerged, many social scientists have begun to doubt that culture is anywhere near as important as we once thought. But my view is that we have been looking in the wrong place. Focusing on cultural differences underestimates the power and importance of culture.

I don't mean this to detract in any way from the value of research on cultural differences. When solid, reliable methods prove that important cultural differences exist (as they do), these are often of profound interest. All I am saying is that there is more to culture than cultural differences, and when cultural differences are occasionally found to be minimal or superficial, we should not take that as a knock against culture per se.

The social and behavioral sciences (psychology, sociology, economics, anthropology, and others) are disciplines that try to apply the scientific method to understanding human beings. They are often compared somewhat unfavorably to the natural sciences (physics, chemistry, biology, and the like), and to be sure they have not been as successful, in the sense that our understanding of people lags behind our immense mastery of the physical world. Yet there are good reasons for the slower progress in the social sciences. Their task is more difficult, and scientists have not been working on it for nearly as long. (The respected science writer Jared Diamond recently proposed replacing the traditional classification of "hard" and "soft" sciences, which usually defined *hard* as physics and chemistry while psychology and economics are *soft*. Instead, he suggested, we should classify sciences as "hard" and "easy," with physics and chemistry in the easy category because their task is fairly straightforward compared to the enormous challenges faced in the "harder" fields of psychology, economics, and the other social sciences.) In any case, we should not be surprised that prevailing views have shifted dramatically in relatively short periods of time.

Throughout the middle of the twentieth century, the social sciences favored views that emphasized the power of socialization and culture. I recall my own first course in psychology in 1972, in which the professor asserted that human traits were mostly the product of experiences during childhood and that biologically inborn tendencies probably accounted for little actual behavior. Those assertions were in no way controversial at the time. They were mainstream. That was what most experts believed then.

Although that belief has changed substantially, we should not make the mistake of leaping to the opposite extreme, assuming that all human differences and tendencies are genetically determined and that society and culture are trivial or powerless. On the contrary, the current challenge is to find ways of answering the deep question: How much influence do culture and society have? In chapter 1, we touched on this issue in the discussion of Brenda, the boy who was raised as a girl. Socialization was not able to transform Brenda into a normal girl, but it has undoubtedly wrought some changes in gender roles. Many fathers participate in child-rearing activities to a much greater extent than their own fathers or grandfathers did. Meanwhile, whereas women who cared for the sick were once mainly nurses, women now become physicians in ever-increasing numbers, and recently women have begun to outnumber men in medical schools. Many other changes could be cited. Gender roles are not rigidly fixed by nature, any more than they are fully malleable by culture.

This new sense of balance has come as something of a shock to much of the social sciences community, especially insofar as we had previously embraced the view that cultures display almost unlimited variation. But let us consider some of the most dramatic clashes between nature and culture.

The nuclear family is a basic social unit everywhere that human beings live, but some cultures have tried to do away with it. In particular, communal living is threatened by individual family ties, and so cultures that promote communist or socialist ideals have sometimes come into conflict with traditional notions about family life. The Israeli kibbutzim initially made a serious effort to have all children raised collectively by all parents, so as to prevent individual parent-child bonds from becoming too influential. On a larger scale, the Soviet Union adopted the policy of doing away with the nuclear family, which it saw as a holdover from capitalist middle-class life and as oppressive to women.[14] It was also inefficient: Greater efficiency and thus widespread benefits could be obtained by serving everyone from one kitchen, even a "great public cauldron,"[15] instead of requiring every wife to have her own kitchen and cook meals for only a few people. Washing would be done by public laundries, sewing by public workshops, and so forth, until there was no economic force to keep husband and wife chained together (and women forced into the servant role).

Another way of getting rid of the nuclear family was to promote collective education and socialization of the young. Socialized child rearing was seen as an ideal system that would promote equality by giving all children the same start in life, would ensure that proper values and attitudes were instilled in all young people (thereby potentially improving the collective strength of the nation), and would reduce inefficiency so that women could assume equal places in the working world instead of having to stay home with their young.

The Soviet sociologist Vladimir Vol'fson asserted in 1929 that the family "will be sent to a museum of antiquities so that it can rest next to the spinning wheel and the bronze axe, by the horsedrawn carriage, the steam engine, and the wired telephone."[16] The Soviet Union's 1918 Code on Marriage, the Family, and Guardianship anticipated that the family would wither away (just like central government), and it sought to prepare the way.

Despite the government's efforts to implement these idealistic plans, they failed. People may be flexible in many respects, but so far no culture has been able to persuade them to give up their family ties. The Soviet leaders soon had to backtrack and change policies to restore the nuclear family to its central place in society. The Israeli kibbutzim likewise now allow members to live as families.

The sexual revolution of the 1960s and 1970s, in contrast, showed that cultural change can produce radical effects on the feelings and actions of many individuals, even if it is not a total victory of culture over nature. The causes of the sexual revolution are still debated, although some cultural changes seem almost certain to have contributed. First, the birth control pill enabled women to engage in intercourse with vastly reduced risk of pregnancy. Second, the women's movement and especially the sharp rise in female paid employment changed the basic social contract between men and women, which for many had meant that a woman gave her virginity to her husband in exchange for a lifetime of financial support. Third, the media began to display and even promote new lifestyles, and indeed Hugh Hefner has proposed that his magazine, *Playboy*, was an important cause of the sexual revolution. In any case, the sexual revolution produced sweeping changes in a short time. For example, premarital intercourse with several partners went from being stigmatized and statistically unusual to a normative expectation in fewer than 20 years.[17]

To be sure, the sexual revolution did not deliver all that was promised. Some gender differences in sexuality remained, or at least they reappeared after a period of experimentation.[18] Women were "set free" to be as shallow and promiscuous as men in their sexual choices, but after a while it emerged that they did not really desire to live that way. Moreover, as is generally true with sex, attitudes changed more than actual behavior. Still, behavior changed too, and far too quickly to attribute to any biological evolution of the species.

The wide variations observed in sexual practices and values indicate that culture can influence them substantially. Again, though, culture has sometimes overreached itself and failed. Many cultures, including that of the United States, have sought to eradicate homosexuality with laws, social stigma, education, and informal pressures that extend to violent oppression of homosexuals, but homosexuality is still very much with us. As another example, the Catholic church has upheld the ideal of lifetime celibacy for all of its priests and nuns, and it is reasonable to assume that most of these men and women are sincere about their sacred vows to renounce all sexual pleasure for life. Yet both survey data and the 1990s' series of clerical sex scandals prove that many men and women (perhaps especially the men) are unable to live up to their ideals. After many years of studying priests, one expert on the topic estimated that only 2% of them really achieve the goal of complete celibacy (including no masturbation) and another 8% are close.[19] That leaves 90% who aren't close to fulfilling their vows. These are cases in which culture should really have everything going for it: The ideals have the highest possible moral authority; a strong organizational and institutional structure supports them; public opinion is also supportive; and the individuals themselves embrace the ideals. But the sexual aspect of human nature is not conducive to celibacy. The failure to maintain celibacy reveals that culture's power is limited.

Alcohol and drug use also vary across cultures, but cultures have not been able to achieve the full extent of influence they seek. The United States outlawed all manufacture, sale, and transportation of alcoholic beverages during Prohibition, and some people did give up drinking—but many others did not. Even though the ban on alcohol was written into the Constitution, which is the supreme basis for legal authority in the country, the project failed so badly that the 18th Amendment had to be repealed. In a similar vein, recent data indicate that more young people use marijuana in countries like England, where it is illegal, than in the Netherlands, where its use is officially tolerated. Thus, the degree to which culture can prescribe patterns of alcohol and drug use is limited.

Then again, some might suggest that alcohol's effects should be entirely reducible to physiological processes, so we should be surprised if culture has any influence. Alcohol is a chemical, and when people drink it, it becomes absorbed into the bloodstream, with undeniable effects on the brain and other parts of the body. It is tempting to think that the effects of alcohol can all be explained in biochemical terms, without needing to invoke cultural and social norms. Even the psychological effects could be described in those terms, such as the old wisecrack that the superego is soluble in alcohol. And if cultural and social causes can really be reduced to physical and physiological processes (as many social scientists believe), then in view of our great knowledge of the physiological effects of alcohol, there should be little need to appeal to cultural explanations.

A careful study of drunkenness in different cultures yields a somewhat different picture, however. MacAndrew and Edgerton's classic cross-cultural study, *Drunken Comportment*,[20] revealed both similarities and differences, and so we cannot simply say that intoxication does or does not depend on culture. On the one hand, they pointed out, in all known societies and cultures, alcohol intoxication makes people physically less competent. Drunken people are less coordinated than sober people, less articulate, and less able to perform skillful tasks. Culture does not matter in this regard. Another common effect is that alcohol intoxication makes people become talkative and sociable.

On the other hand, alcohol does produce different patterns of some behaviors in different cultures. Many inhibitions remain in effect when people are drunk, at least in many societies, so the simple claim that alcohol reduces inhibitions across the board is wrong. In some societies, drunken men become more aggressive and are prone to getting into fights, but in others they do not. In some, they become more amorous and prone to make advances to nearby women, but in others they do not. In some cultures, there have even been historical changes in the effects of alcohol. MacAndrew and Edgerton said that when alcohol was first introduced in Tahiti, the natives disliked it, and those who tried it reported such negative, aversive experiences that they avoided it subsequently. After some years, however, there was a new phase in which Tahitians became deeply fond of alcohol, drinking heavily and often becoming violent under its influence. Then came a third era, in which Tahitians continued to drink alcohol heavily, but the fighting was mostly absent, and they became essentially happy and peaceful when drunk.

The role of culture is evident in another set of examples. The Bantu people of South Africa had long traditions of drinking alcohol, and these generally involved positive behavior patterns, such as singing and dancing. Fighting and other problems were not in their stock of inebriated behaviors. But as modernization disrupted tribal living patterns, people moved to the cities, where suddenly alcohol intoxication became associated with violence and bloodshed. Cultural context affects the Tecospans, a group of native people in Mexico, in a somewhat similar way: When they drink among themselves, they feel content and at peace, even to the point of regarding drunkenness as a pathway to spiritual feelings of community and brotherhood, but when they drink in the company of outsiders, they become hostile and insulting and often end up fighting.

How should we reconcile these different strands of evidence? MacAndrew and Edgerton pointed out that nowhere in the world is it true that "anything goes" when you are drunk.[21] Drunkenness seems to operate as a kind of time out, an interruption in the normal set of rules, but which rules remain in force versus which ones are suspended varies considerably. Even in lawsuit-happy America, drunks do not escape all responsibility. In a recent news story, a man sued six bars and liquor stores, as well as the electric company, over injuries he sustained when he got drunk, climbed over a fence with a locked gate, and then clambered up an electrical tower,[22] but he didn't win his case.

Only a mixture of nature and culture can begin to explain the impact of alcohol. Alcohol is a physical agent whose effects follow biochemical laws, and some of the behavioral effects (such as the sensorimotor impairments, which essentially make drunk people clumsy) seem universal. Moreover, the relaxation of some rules seems common, but different cultures suspend different rules.

A last set of examples worth considering comes from the advertising industry. Advertising is one form of cultural influence, and the immense amounts of money at stake give impetus to a continuing search for the strongest and most effective methods of swaying people's behavior. Advertising works, but only to a limited extent. Some ad campaigns have been extraordinary failures, such as the infamous effort by the Coca-Cola Company in the 1980s to switch its main product to "New Coke" and induce the world's masses to buy it. It flopped, and the company had to bring back the old Coke (called "classic" rather than "old"), and it eventually dropped the new taste entirely. In general, professional advertisers are content with small percentage shifts in behavior, because a slight increase in market share can translate into millions or even billions of dollars. Again, the record is one of genuine but limited success.

The opposing sides in the ongoing debate about the influence of nature versus culture can look at these examples and conclude, respectively, that the glass is half full or half empty. My point is to emphasize the halfness of the glass. Culture can influence behavior, but only to a moderate extent. In particular, some tendencies are deeply rooted in human nature and therefore highly resistant to social pressures. Others have much greater plasticity, and culture can have a big influence.

What, then, can we conclude about the relationship between the individual person and the broader society and culture? We can reject the simple model that society shapes people into any form it wants, with human beings no more than passive recipients of external influence. We can also reject the opposite model, that people are born a certain way and are bound to live and act along preset lines regardless of culture.

Most likely, culture has to work with the basic facts of human nature, in the sense that it can exaggerate them or stifle them. Gender differences are a useful example: Men and women are born with somewhat different tendencies, and society can either amplify them or minimize them. Society is, however, much less likely to succeed in creating them out of nothing or in utterly reversing them. Boys are more physically aggressive than girls, and society can encourage or stifle this difference, as is shown by cultural variations in the degree of physical aggressiveness. But culture does not seem able to reverse them, to make women generally more physically aggressive than men. Even despite a prolonged media campaign—on American television since the 1990s, women hit men fairly frequently and with approving laughter from the sound track, whereas men hitting women is rare and only presented with severe disapproval—men and women in real life hit each other with approximately equal frequency,[23] and men do more damage to women than vice versa.

Meanwhile, an individual is born with various natural tendencies and then confronts the immensely complex social structure that constitutes modern society. The individual's scope for changing the broader society is limited. Instead, people find their places in it and more or less take it as it comes. Each person has to develop some understanding of how society works and adapt the self well enough to fulfill some roles. The person's nature will influence how well she plays those social roles.

The Duplex Mind

A crucial fact about the human mind is that it operates on at least two levels. It has two large systems, where most other animals seem to have only one. The emergence of the second system is widely recognized as an important key to understanding the human psyche, although its origins and implications are widely disputed. Almost certainly, though, the emergence of this duplex organization of mind was an important, even crucial step in the evolution of the cultural animal.

This duality has been recognized over and over, although the names and dimensions of the two aspects have been revised. For Freud, there was the *conscious* and the *unconscious* (although he also sometimes spoke of a *preconscious*, referring to things that could be conscious but weren't being thought about right at that moment). Cognitive psychologists in the 1970s and early 1980s distinguished between *automatic* and *controlled* processes.[24] As those categories became more complicated, recent writers have distinguished between *reflexive* and *reflective* systems,[25] *experiential* and *rational* modes of thinking,[26] or *associative* and *rule-based* thinking.[27] Daniel Kahneman, one of the most highly respected thinkers in psychology today, flirted with *intuition* and *reasoning* but finally settled on *System 1* and *System 2* as the least problematic terms.[28]

"System 1 and System 2" may have the advantage of not invoking any misleading ideas, but they are cumbersome and hard to track. The point is that no terms are quite suitable, because any meaningful term—and by meaningful, I mean something that goes beyond labeling them as 1 and 2 or, indeed, as Fritz and Betty—brings along some baggage that can raise problems. Recognizing the problem, and freely admitting that the terms might bring a spluttering chorus of yes-buts and boos, let me use the approximate terms *conscious* and *automatic*. If you don't like them, please substitute any other terms you prefer.

What matters is not the specific names but rather the fact of duality. The human mind has two major processing systems at work, and they have different properties. Both get the same input from the senses: Both "see" what happens around you, but what they do with the incoming information is somewhat different.

The *automatic* system, also known as the intuitive or reflexive system, generally has many things happening at once. It processes things in many small ways, noting features, recognizing, and making crucial links via associations to what is already known. During a major race, when a car pulls into a pit stop, a half dozen mechanics leap into action at once: pumping gasoline, replacing tires, checking the oil, making various minor adjustments, and sometimes wiping the driver's brow or giving the driver a drink. This is a useful image for the automatic system. Many small things happen at once, simultaneously, and somewhat independently of each other. A single large task, such as figuring out what a written message means, may involve dozens of these small operations, from recognizing the individual letters to summoning up relevant contexts from memory.

In contrast, the *conscious* system does one thing at a time, yet it can process in depth and follow multiple steps. Its most powerful capacity may be symbolic logic: It can use abstract, rule-based reasoning to link together sequences of ideas in an impressive fashion, including figuring out whether they are true or false, consistent or inconsistent. Consistency at the automatic level is limited to whether things match each other or not in an obvious manner. Consistency at the conscious level can note that the logical implications of two ideas will lead to contradiction, even if there is no obvious clash between the original ideas.

Thus, both systems use meaning, but only the conscious system seems fully able to make use of the power of meaning and language. Its powers of reasoning enable it to take consistency beyond mere matching. In one series of experiments,[29] people were confronted with various words to ascertain their good or bad reactions. Words like sick, hurt, ugly, lost, enemy, and angry *automatically* evoked negative reactions, whereas words like friendly, bread, love, win, surgeon, green, and casual produced at least mildly positive ones. But what happens when the words are combined? The automatic system simply adds up the values of the individual words, but the conscious system will recognize that some combinations of good things produce bad things. Green and bread may both have positive values, and so when the automatic system sees "green bread" it gives a double positive vote. Yum! Only the conscious system recognizes that green bread is probably a bad thing. (To be sure, the automatic system can learn, and after one or two bad experiences eating green bread, it may know that it's bad. But this essentially forms a new category, "green bread," rather than integrating them separately as the conscious system may do.) A "casual surgeon" seems all good to the automatic system, whereas the conscious system doesn't want surgeons to be too casual. Conversely, it again takes consciousness to recognize that two bad things can combine into something good, as in "enemy loses."[30]

The conscious system can follow explicit, external, abstract rules, and so it can do many things the automatic system can't. The automatic system may be able to note small quantity differences and perhaps add or subtract a little, but it can't solve algebra problems or engage in any of the really useful mathematical reasoning. A recent study provides one example.[31] The experimenters approached someone with the following problem: Eddy bought a bat and a ball for $1.10. The bat cost a dollar more than the ball. How much did the ball cost? Most people, at least at Princeton where they ran the study, could soon come up with the right answer of 5 cents. But, crucially, most of them first thought of the answer "10 cents" and had to override and suppress that answer in order to get the right one. That shows the automatic system getting there first with an answer, but the slower, conscious system following along, correcting it, and getting the *right* answer. Crucially, when the experimenters stopped people who were busy and distracted, such as those hurrying across campus—times when the conscious mind is already preoccupied, and so the automatic system is left in charge of things like dealing with researchers and their math questions—people were more likely to say that the ball cost 10 cents.

In fairness to the automatic system, it may have had a hand in getting the right answer too. It was probably the automatic system that sent out the "alarm" signal that 10 cents couldn't be right or, at least, that the answer should be double-checked, perhaps because psychologists are tricky and so the obvious answer may be wrong. So the automatic system might have sent out an alarm signal, and the conscious mind would then turn its attention that way. Even so, it required the powers of the conscious system to follow the rules and calculate the correct answer.

That kind of decision process will be important again in this book, when we discuss action. That sort of delayed execution will turn out to be one key to "free will," in the sense of conscious control of action.

The conscious system is limited in its capacity, and so in many ways it can accomplish far less than the automatic system. You can only think one thing at a time in your conscious mind,[32] whereas your automatic system can do quite a few things simultaneously. Riding a bicycle, for example, may involve ongoing processing for keeping balance, moving the two separate legs in opposite directions to maintain motion, regulating speed with the brakes, watching for obstacles, and steering. All of this can occur while the conscious mind is replaying an argument with your roommate from two days ago. If consciousness is needed to guide action, such as if the way is blocked and the rider needs to plan an alternate route, the rumination about the argument has to be interrupted while the conscious mind devotes its limited capacity to planning an alternate route. Once the plan is made, the automatic system can handle the mechanics of propelling the bike, and the conscious mind can get back to what one should have said to the roommate the other day.

It is no accident that the conscious mind, in the biker example, had to intervene when the route was blocked. The conscious mind responds especially to problems. When things go smoothly, the automatic system can take care of almost everything. It has a great capacity and is highly efficient, but it is not very flexible. The conscious part of the mind is the opposite: highly flexible but not very efficient. For dealing with familiar, routine, or habitual matters, such as having breakfast and going to work, the automatic system works great. For unfamiliar or challenging situations, the conscious system turns out to be much more useful, because it can plan, reason, and in other ways figure out sensible ways of dealing with the unknown. The automatic system sends out a distress signal, it rings an alarm,[33] to get the attention of the conscious system. Emotions make good alarms: They react to current and changing circumstances, and they are felt immediately as good or bad. The conscious system takes over when things are difficult or complex.

There are other noteworthy differences between the two systems.[34] The automatic system operates rather effortlessly, and indeed it is hard to stop its relentless churning. In contrast, the conscious system often requires effort and exertion to make it continue. The automatic system is fast, while the conscious system is slow. The processes by which answers are obtained are largely invisible in the automatic system, whereas the conscious system is self-aware and can retrace its steps effectively. Undoubtedly, further research will identify additional differences. For understanding human nature, however, it is crucial to recognize that the human mind uses both levels.

The origins of the duplex mind are not known, but one may speculate. Let us assume that all mental processing requires some degree of attention, defined broadly as being able to take in information from the environment. The mind has a certain total stock of attention, which involves how much information (sights, sounds, words, feelings, and the rest) it can take in at any one time. Normally, that total stock of attention is dispersed throughout the automatic system, thereby allowing many different operations to occur at once, in parallel. A person walking through a train station is processing a cacophony of sounds and sights, and also processing information coming in from the feet about the slant of the floor in order to walk, and more.

Somehow, crucially, nature enabled the human mind to fuse together a large amount of attention (by no means all; perhaps a third or fourth of the total amount of attention) to make one giant processing space. This is the conscious system. Like any large system, it is slow and cumbersome, and it is rather heavily dependent on the quick operations of the automatic system to feed it information. It does, however, have the power to perform highly complex operations, such as those that involve following rules built into the structure of meaning (and also learned rules) to move from one idea to another. Hence logical reasoning and mathematical calculation, as well as the narrative construction of stories, fall into the province of the conscious mind.

These views are admittedly controversial. As we shall see in chapter 4, there are many experts who think human consciousness has hardly any function at all. They think it is a largely irrelevant by-product of how the mind works, that it is unable to exert any measurable influence on behavior, and that its ostensible activity is actually conducted in the automatic system. They are reacting against a traditional, commonsense view which holds that conscious choice and intention are essential to all human activity. In my view, they have erred by going from one extreme (consciousness is everything) to the other (consciousness is nothing). Consciousness is not a useless, trivial side effect of the human psyche, but one of its important achievements. It was probably quite difficult and expensive for nature to fuse that attentional capacity together so as to make people capable of being conscious. Nature would only do that if there were some significant advantages. Consciousness may do far less than the average person in the street naively assumes, but it probably accomplishes something extremely important. The functions I have already suggested, including reasoning, mathematics, and narrative, would alone confer great advantages.

The two systems are not limited to styles of thinking. They also reflect processes of action. Automatic behavior is governed by laws, prior experiences and their painful or pleasant outcomes, innate programs, habits, and external stimuli. The automatic processes are simple and inflexible and therefore require fairly little cognitive processing. This feature is often decisive, because the automatic system can dictate how to act or react at a moment's notice. In contrast, the controlled processes are highly inefficient, requiring a great deal of processing. They make up for their costly, cumbersome demands by being highly flexible. Controlled processes may require the person to stop and think, but as a result of this pondering the person can act in a novel, creative manner or in one that is consistent with broad, abstract principles—as opposed to acting by habit, routine, or simple straightforward response.[35]

The highly influential social psychologist John A. Bargh has identified four main hallmarks of automatic responding.[36] These do not invariably go together, and so certain responses may qualify as automatic in different ways. One is a lack of awareness: People may respond automatically without even realizing how they have been affected. Subliminal influences are an example of this kind of process. The second hallmark of automatic response is an absence of intention. Controlled behavior is generally intentional: You decide to do something and then do it. In contrast, automatic behavior may occur without the person intending to do it. The third hallmark is efficiency: As already mentioned, automatic behavior requires fairly little mental activity to perform, and indeed, the efficiency is an important advantage of automatic processing. Lack of control is the fourth and final hallmark. Automatic responses are not directed toward a particular outcome; in contrast, they just go on by themselves, without the person's having to do anything (or even being able to do anything) about them.

The relationship between the controlled and automatic processes is more than a simple master-servant relationship, in which the automatic processes carry out all the work (including doing the bidding of the conscious mind) unless the conscious, controlled ones override them. Many processes start out as controlled and become automatic. This is an important form of learning, called *automatization*. It may be most familiar in skill domains. Thus, when learning a new skill, the person usually has to pay considerable conscious attention to what she is doing. Through many repetitions, however, the process becomes more automatic, and eventually much of it becomes "second nature." In learning to ski or to play tennis, for example, a beginner must often think carefully about how to move feet, body, and hands, but an expert performs those same motions without needing to be aware of them. The expert can then do more, because of the benefits of automaticity (especially efficiency). Those mental resources that the beginner had to devote to gripping the tennis racket properly can instead, in the expert, be devoted to planning strategy or simply to enjoying the game.

There is a widely accepted, simple, plausible—but wrong—explanation for how this kind of learning proceeds. By this explanation, the brain learns how to perform a new task, like riding a bicycle. At first the connections between brain cells are uncertain and tentative, but as the person continues to practice, the same muscle commands follow the same neural pathways over and over. The brain cells adapt to this repeated exercise, until the brain cells that control riding a bicycle can function quite easily and readily. This theory seemed so obvious that hardly anyone questioned it until recently. Studies on brain processes have shown it to be wrong, however. Automatic, overlearned responses are executed in one part of the brain, while new learning through conscious supervision occurs elsewhere.[37]

The implication is that the conscious system is important in helping the person learn or acquire a new skill, but once the conscious system figures it out, it hands it over to the automatic system. The expert's brain is not really doing the same thing as the novice's brain, only better. The novice's brain is using the conscious system, whereas the expert's brain uses the automatic system to get the job done.

Almost certainly consciousness opens up new ways of learning, too. People do not just have to learn by trial and error. They can figure things out. They can learn systems. For example, some people never take a typing class, and if they work with computers or other keyboards they eventually develop a fairly smooth and automatic way of typing, but probably they will never type as effectively as someone who takes a typing class and learns the system for how to type most efficiently and effectively. Consciousness is far superior to other means of learning when one is trying to learn a system, as opposed to making single responses.

Consciousness brings indeterminacy by overriding the lawful running of the automatic processes.[38] If your tennis serve starts to go wrong, you may need to attend again to the details of the process. Thus the expert may occasionally have to focus consciously on how he holds his racket or how he tosses the ball. The problem with the serve is that the automatic processes have changed somewhat so that they now "automatically" do the wrong thing. Conscious, deliberate practice can correct the flaw and relearn how to serve properly, and once this has been accomplished, the automatic system can take over again.

Once a skill has been acquired, consciousness may even interfere with smooth execution. Essentially, this is what happens when people "choke under pressure."[39] A high-pressure situation means that it is extra important to do well. The conscious mind responds to the heightened pressure by paying extra attention to what the person is doing, so as to monitor everything and make sure it is done right. Unfortunately, the conscious mind no longer knows how to do everything just right—the automatic processes are the ones that perform best. When the conscious mind takes over, consciousness again brings indeterminacy. This time, however, indeterminacy is not good, for it makes the outcome unreliable. When serving for the Wimbledon tennis championship, you suddenly feel acutely conscious that the world is watching you, and you start attending consciously to how you hold and swing your racket. Instead of doing it the way your automatic processes have learned to do repeatedly and successfully, your conscious mind makes the outcome unreliable, and your serve hits the net or bounces wide.

A particular value of the conscious, controlled processes is that they can consult abstract principles and moral arguments. The automatic response interprets the situation in a certain way and initiates the standard response. The conscious mind can consider the situation from different angles. Consulting multiple interpretations can introduce novel approaches or solutions. In this way, consciously controlled behavior is likely to be far less predictable than automatic behavior, at least sometimes.

The wonderful thing about the human mind is that it possesses both kinds of processes. Conscious, controlled processes offer great flexibility, enabling people to deal in thoughtful, creative ways with a remarkably broad range of events and circumstances. But they are expensive, in the sense that they require energy and effort.[40] Automatic processes enable us to deal effectively with the immense volume of tasks that everyday life presents. Without automatic processes, the conscious mind would be hopelessly swamped. Without the conscious and controlled ones, people would be slaves of habit and of the impulses that their surroundings initiate. As William James wrote, "[T]he more of the details of our daily life we can hand over to the effortless custody of automatism, the more our higher powers of mind will be set free for their own proper work."[41] The physicist Albert Einstein, whose name has become a kind of synonym for genius, was known around Princeton in his later years for wearing gray sweatsuits every day. But as with so many things, he had a good explanation. Those simple garments freed his mind from having to deal with the mundane issue of choosing what to wear. A wardrobe of all gray sweatsuits may not enable you to shine at a discotheque, but it offers multiple advantages to a great mind trying to conserve its mental resources. Everything matches; it is easy to clean; and no choices are required.

Having sketched the main foundations for how the psyche operates, we turn now to examine its major functions. First, we will look at motivation, which is to say, human strivings and desires. To provide a psychology of human nature, it is necessary to explore what people want and how they want it.

3

What People Want

One cloudy afternoon, Henry walked into the post office to mail a Christmas gift to his mother. It was a small office, and no one was there except Jeff, a postal clerk who was sitting at his desk, looking out the window and eating a sandwich. Henry set the package down on Jeff's desk and asked for stamps. Jeff looked up at him and shook his head. He was eating and didn't want to be bothered. Henry asked again, but Jeff ignored him. Finally, Henry grabbed Jeff's sandwich and threw it out the window. He struck Jeff a few times on the side of his head. As Jeff pushed his chair back, Henry landed a punch in his stomach. "Okay, okay, I'll get the stamps," said Jeff hoarsely, out of breath. He stood up, moving more quickly now, and turned toward the file cabinet where the stamps were stored. To keep him moving, Henry landed a nasty kick on the seat of Jeff's pants. Jeff scurried back and retrieved the stamps, then brought them back to his desk. Henry counted out the cost of the stamps and gave Jeff the money. Then he licked the stamps and pasted them on the package. "Please put it in the mailbox," he said, and when Jeff hesitated, Henry raised his hand as if to strike him again, whereupon Jeff quickly deposited the package in the box with outgoing mail. His errand complete, Henry left the office and went back to his place of work.

Of course, this story is fictional: People do not generally have to hit and kick service workers in order to get them to do their bidding. But why not? Most social animals sometimes rely on some degree of aggression, or at least the threat of aggression, to influence a reluctant fellow creature to do what they want. Indeed, aggression probably evolved as a social influence strategy that enabled strong creatures to get their way in dealings with weaker fellow creatures of their own species. Human beings are social animals too, but in the process of becoming cultural, we have greatly tried to curb the use of aggression.

Aggression has hardly vanished from human life. In some ways, culture has increased the power of violence, especially by furnishing ever more powerful and advanced tools for inflicting harm. Other social animals hardly ever kill members of their own species, but that is partly because they do not have guns or bombs. If human beings could use no weapons except their own fists and feet, there would be far fewer murders and fewer battlefield casualties too.

What is remarkable is not that humans are sometimes violent but that we are so often not violent. Indeed, I began researching my earlier book on violence with the question: Why is there evil? But halfway through I had to shift to address the question: Why isn't there more evil than there is? The causes, incitements, and provocations for violence are seemingly endless, and the surprising thing is how rarely people actually do hurt and kill each other.

The rarity of violence in modern cultural life is especially shocking if one accepts some popular theories about the human aggressive instinct. According to them, people have a powerful inner need that bubbles up from within. Just as hunger arises on a regular basis because the body needs food, aggressive tendencies arise because people have an innate need to inflict harm and damage, or so the story goes. In Freud's theory, civilization depended on humans developing some inner structures (the superego, in his term) to restrain and redirect these aggressive impulses, so that people could live side by side without killing each other.

In this chapter, we will look at the question of what basic wants and needs are built into the human psyche. Some come from nature, insofar as our animal forebears acquired them because they promoted survival and reproduction. With these, the crucial question is: How have they been altered by evolution so as to make human beings suitable for living in culture? Other motives have roots in culture, though typically they build on what nature has already installed. The desire for money, for example, was not directly produced by natural selection, because money didn't appear on the planet until after humans had already evolved—but the desire for money probably has its roots in natural desires for food, shelter, comfort, and social acceptance, all of which are easier to acquire within a culture if you have money than if you haven't.

Human desires will be covered in three main groups, corresponding to the three environments (physical, social, and cultural). Yet these are not entirely separate, because the main thrust of this book is that the human psyche is an animal one that has been retooled for culture. Hence, we will explore the motivations that enable animals to survive in the physical world, such as the desire for food, the wish to avoid pain, and the self-preservation impulse—but it will be necessary to recognize how these drives have changed in cultural beings. Likewise, the motives pertinent to social animals may also have changed somewhat in human beings in order to make us suitable for culture. The third set of motives arises from culture, usually by capitalizing on some of the natural motives. For example, self-esteem is a widespread concern for most people in most cultures, but it is doubtful that evolution has instilled a "self-esteem instinct" into human nature. More likely, the concern with self-esteem arises because self-esteem is based on two deeply rooted natural motives, namely, the urge for control and the need to belong.

Desires Inherited from the Animal World

All living beings must get certain things from their physical surroundings, in order that they may survive and reproduce. Animals mostly have to perform various actions (like foraging) in order to get what they need, and so nature has instilled motivations in them to make them do things that will result in getting what they want. These do not necessarily match exactly; for example, nature requires reproduction, and it accomplishes this by motivating animals to desire the pleasure of sex, but to the animal itself (including many humans) the quest for sexual pleasure has no direct relationship with any wish to make babies, and in some cases pregnancy can be an unwanted side effect of sex.

The emphasis here is on how these basic, natural desires may have changed in order to make us capable of culture—and on how culture may have repaid those changes by making it easier to achieve the benefits. As was emphasized in the first chapter, evolution rarely makes something out of nothing, but it can tweak or retool existing structures for new purposes.

The human need for food is not a controversial drive, nor one that has powerful relevance to the cultural psyche. I begin with it because it provides a good illustration of several main themes, including evolutionary continuity and change, the benefits of culture, and the transforming influence of the duplex mind.

Food

All animals require food and water. Human beings do too, but the basic need for sustenance has become elaborated in industrialized societies into the quest for fine cuisine, tasty treats, and delicious hot and cold beverages. In modern America, culture has improved on nature to the extreme that, probably for the first time in the entire biological past on our planet, the rich and powerful are on average thinner than the poor and weak.

Crucially, culture enables people to eat more and better food than what would otherwise be available. Chapter 2 began by trying to reckon how many different people contributed to a single family dinner. Such a dinner depends on a vast web of interdependent relationships among hundreds if not thousands of people. Culture alone can produce and repeatedly modify such systems.

Culture has allowed people to develop ever more refined and sophisticated tastes. Anthropologists report that in some cultures people cannot afford to have food preferences, because in order to survive amid scarcity, people must eat whatever is available. In developed cultures, groups of friends will go to restaurants where every person orders something different, often asking for further alterations from the menu ("Can I have a baked potato instead of rice? And with butter rather than margarine, or else sour cream if there is no butter?"). Even when a family dinner is based on hamburgers for everyone, each person may want a different version: with ketchup, no mustard, with onions, pickles, one tomato slice, and many more variations.

What sustains this endless variety of taste preferences? The duplex mind has led to an emphasis on the conscious experience of food. Ingesting nutrition is not enough. Europeans sometimes hold stereotypes of Americans as willing to just take a few pills to provide all the nutrients they need, thereby dispensing with the need to eat, but the derogatory nature of this very stereotype points to the importance that people place on the conscious experience of enjoying a good meal.

Eating also takes on social and cultural meanings. Most people prefer not to eat alone, and so eating is a social occasion. Sharing food often has symbolic meanings, ranging from an affirmation of a social bond, to a hopeful prelude to a sexual relationship, to a religious celebration.

Pain and Pleasure

Like other animals, human beings are wired to feel pain when their bodies are being damaged and to feel pleasure when beneficial things happen. But these outcomes do more than alert the person to what has recently happened. People and animals are motivated to avoid pain and attain pleasure, and they organize their actions around those twin pursuits. Consistent with the principle that bad is stronger than good,[1] avoiding pain takes precedence over finding pleasure, but both are genuine motives.

Pain and pleasure reactions enhance survival and probably reproduction too. You might think that it would be wonderful to live without pain, but in reality people who lose their sensitivity to pain end up in bad shape. Many people know that lepers often end up losing fingers and toes, but they mistakenly think that the disease causes those disfigurements directly. It doesn't. Instead, leprosy causes the body to stop registering pain. Without pain, people do not realize it when a stone smashes a foot or when a hand grasps a dangerously hot cooking pot.

In the daily life of a cultural animal, pain and pleasure as physical sensations play a relatively small part. Emotions have largely replaced them. Daily life is guided by the quest to avoid emotional distress and to find positive emotional experiences. Chapter 5 will develop this theme more fully.

To be sure, cultural animals can still feel pain and pleasure when necessary. But one effect of culture is to reduce the amount of pain. Modern medicine, housing, dentistry, and other advances have greatly reduced the amount of pain we feel in our everyday lives.

The duplex mind has recast pleasure as happiness and other positive experiences. Undoubtedly, the simplest and most global answer to the question "What do people want?" is happiness. Sometimes people use happiness to refer to feeling good at the present moment, but for many people happiness is less a transitory feeling than a level of overall satisfaction with life. The term *subjective well-being* is used to describe this form of happiness. It essentially involves an appraisal of one's current life circumstances—and a comparison of that appraisal against some standard or ideal. The higher one's expectations, the harder they are to surpass and hence the less likely one is to be happy, at least in principle.

Subjective well-being and life satisfaction are probably peculiar to the cultural animal—unlike pleasure and the absence of pain, which can be registered by almost all animals. To be satisfied with one's life on the whole requires a meaningful assessment of many different aspects of one's life, including the past, present, and future, and comparing them with various standards, such as what you might have expected. Without meaning and culture, happiness cannot consist of much beyond feeling good right now. A cultural animal can, however, integrate many different experiences into a single outcome and compare it to standards. Culture can also manipulate the standards and expectations, along with the opportunities for achieving them.

In practice, people's standards and expectations rise and fall with current outcomes. One important set of insights into human (and animal) psychology is encompassed in *adaptation level theory*,[2] which emphasizes that people mainly respond to changes and then grow accustomed to the new circumstances. A raise in salary will make most people happy for a while, but then they grow accustomed to those new, bigger paychecks and cease to have much feeling about them either way. Some experts have likened the pursuit of happiness to a "hedonic treadmill,"[3] because one quickly adjusts to each step forward and therefore ends up in the same place in terms of how happy one is. In a famous demonstration of this principle, researchers showed that people who had won hundreds of thousands of dollars in the Illinois state lottery were no happier a year later than people who had not won anything.[4] Of course, at first, they were delighted to get all that money and probably they felt in a state of sublime euphoria for a while. But all too soon it wore off, sooner than anticipated.

The principle that bad is stronger than good applies to the adaptation level theory as well. The study of lottery winners also surveyed a sample of people who had had something terrible happen to them, namely, becoming paralyzed in an accident. These people did show some differences in happiness from the control group, reflecting lower happiness on some measures. The difference was not as large as one might assume, however, and there was evidence that the adaptation processes were at work. Still, it appears that positive events wear off faster than negative ones. This is probably the sort of thing Woody Allen had in mind when he said in *Love and Death,* "If God does exist, he's an underachiever." The world would be a more pleasant place if the human psyche could get over bad things rapidly while good feelings lingered for a long time. But in reality, it's the other way around.

Thus, happiness depends on changes from one's current situation. Happiness is therefore best maximized by having a series of gradual improvements and escalating successes, rather than making one big jump to a vastly better life. The big jump will undoubtedly produce good feelings, but these will wear off, whereas the series of upward steps affords more enjoyment.

If we put this in motivational terms, the quest for happiness will cause people to continue to seek improvements in life. This may well help account for much of progress in human life, because it offers an incentive for continued innovation and striving. What brought you happiness last year—whether it was finding a cave that was reasonably dry to sleep in, or getting your salary to the six-figure mark—will have worn off by this year, and so to find more happiness you will have to achieve something even better. This is perhaps the answer to Woody Allen's complaint about God. The fact that enjoyment of good things wears off is probably a major cause of human progress.

The present is not the only standard people use for assessing their lives and determining how happy they are. Social comparison is another one: People compare themselves against the average or against specific other people. The eminent British psychologist Michael Argyle noted the paradoxical contradictions in the relationship between money and happiness.[5] Although most people now (on average) have much more money than people did several decades ago, overall happiness has not improved. People do become happy when they get more money, but the good feeling wears off fast. Relative wealth seems to produce happiness, but an increase in everyone's wealth does not. Argyle concluded, "What people really want is to have more [money] than other people!"[6] Even among very poor people, those who have more than their neighbors will probably feel quite pleased, and by the same token the least affluent members of a rich community will tend to feel somewhat bad about their relative status.

The power of social comparison is also an important factor in human motivation. Cultural animals set their goals by what others in their community want. If nature had programmed us merely to find food, shelter, and someone with whom to sleep, people would have had little urge to find ways to make life better once those basic natural goals were satisfied. But the cultural animal tunes in to his society, and as society's standards change from year to year or century to century, each individual learns to want whatever currently signifies the good life. What is a luxury for one generation, such as cable television or a second car, is considered a necessity in the next generation. The shifting standards of happiness depend on human motivational plasticity, which is rooted in keeping up with one's neighbors. The constant factor is that cultural animals want to keep up with their peers.

Most animals want to feel pleasure and avoid pain. In human beings, as cultural animals, that same motivation is present, but it has been transformed into the search for happiness. Happiness depends on meaning, insofar as it requires an assessment of current versus expected circumstances (unlike the sensation of pain, which is a response of the nervous system and requires no meaningful thought). It is also found in conscious experience rather than momentary sensation.

Self-Preservation: Avoiding Injury and Death

Self-preservation encompasses a family of motives. The status and importance of the self-preservation motives can be debated, especially in modern Western societies where the average person rarely encounters famines or other life-threatening circumstances. At minimum, however, it is quite safe to assume that the instincts for self-preservation do shape behavior palpably whenever one's life is actually in danger. You may be listening to something on the radio that speaks to one of your main motivations, such as sex and relationships, but if another car veers into your lane and threatens to crash lethally into your car, self-preservation will take precedence over those other goals, and your mind will quickly cut away from the radio program to work on avoiding a deadly collision.

Motives for self-preservation do not necessarily have anything to do with culture. Noncultural animals have them, and even nonsocial ones do. They probably appeared early in evolution because they contribute directly to survival. A being that was indifferent to injury or death would not pass on as many genes as one who was careful to maximize life. But culture does help satisfy the self-preservation motives. In fact, one purpose of culture is to help individual humans survive, by helping them get the means for sustaining life. Culture organizes society so that tasks are divided up, and I have already sung the praises of division of labor. More can be created and accomplished, more effectively and more efficiently, if people specialize than if everyone does everything. The acid test is life expectancy, and across the centuries the average human lifespan has more than doubled, thanks in large part to culture, which affords us better food, better shelter, protection against disasters, better health care, and other advantages.

At what, specifically, do the self-preservation motives aim? Thus far we have emphasized that the threat of imminent death is typically (though not invariably) met with determined efforts to preserve life at all costs. The drowning woman struggles to stay afloat and reach land or ship; under attack by wild beasts the man looks to fight or flee; starving people will steal food; and so forth. Again, these may not be relevant to the everyday lives of middle-class citizens in industrial democracies, but when desperate circumstances arise, people will generally try to survive.

Some theorists have argued that there is a more profound link between self-preservation and human culture. The most ambitious theory of that kind was put forward by the anthropologist Ernest Becker in his 1973 book, *The Denial of Death*. Becker proposed that knowledge of one's own mortality is a uniquely human trait and gives rise to an existential terror of impending nonexistence, with the result that a great deal of human social behavior is designed to conceal the fact of death from oneself (hence his book's title). The thrust of his thinking was later taken up by a group of social psychologists who have likewise asserted that self-preservation is the "master motive" underlying all other human motivations.[7] In particular, Becker and his followers have asserted that culture itself is a defense against death, insofar as people seek to become valued participants in a collective enterprise that will go on after them, which reduces the threat of mortality. They may seek a symbolic immortality through their work, which will live on after them. (Woody Allen had a comment on this too, partly because he has spent much of his adult life in agonized terror over death. He pooh-poohed symbolic immortality: "It would be nice to live on in the hearts and minds of my audience, but I'd rather live on in my apartment.")[8] Likewise, these researchers propose that the quest for self-esteem is also a reaction against death. Anxiety, too, is seen as primarily if not exclusively a result of awareness of one's own mortality.

Stimulated by Becker's ideas about death, researchers have conducted a long series of laboratory studies that examine how thoughts, feelings, and behaviors change when people are prompted to think about death, such as by imagining the decay of their physical bodies shortly after their own deaths. These studies have failed to find much in the way of anxiety, but a variety of behavioral changes have been found, and there is much of value in that work. These findings chiefly show that death is a powerful existential cue that can alter priorities and perspectives. In particular, thoughts of death cause people to identify more strongly with their culture and its world views. After ruminating about death, people recommend more severe prison sentences for traitors and for criminals who violate society's values.[9]

Almost inevitably, however, these fall short of the project of proving that Becker was right to regard the fear of death and the self-preservation motive as the foundation of all human motivation and social activity. The studies show that fear of death makes people cling more strongly to their culture, but they hardly prove that people are always worrying about death or that culture is only (or even primarily) a defense mechanism against death anxiety.

In my view, the facts cannot support the conclusion that any motive, and certainly not avoidance of death, is the master motive that underlies all others. Although people perform plenty of actions that will sustain life, such as eating and drinking, they also risk or sacrifice their lives when sufficiently in the grip of other motives. Plenty of people have risked or sacrificed their lives for religious and political reasons, and many others have risked their lives pursuing money, power, and sex. The need to belong, in particular, has been shown to take precedence over self-preservation in many circumstances.[10] People will sunbathe despite the risk of skin cancer (even after a bout of skin cancer, some people soon resume sunbathing) because they believe the tan will make them more attractive to others. They take serious risks (such as riding a motorcycle without a helmet) in order to make a favorable impression on others. To avoid temporary embarrassment or the possibility of making a bad impression, they are often willing to have sex without using condoms, and recent findings suggest that making people think of death paradoxically increases their willingness to engage in sexual activities that carry a high risk of HIV infection.[11] They smoke cigarettes to curry favor with peers, seek out cosmetic surgery despite its risks and complications, and in some cases starve themselves to life-threatening degrees in the pursuit of fashionable thinness. And, of course, people do sometimes commit suicide, which is exceedingly difficult to reconcile with any assertion that self-preservation is the ultimate, all-encompassing motive. Self-preservation is one motive that competes with others, and sometimes the other motives win out.

None of this is intended to dispute the assertion that people prefer life over death and will strive to prolong life in most cases. Rather, the point is simply that self-preservation should be regarded as one human motive and must sometimes compete against the others. Plus, Becker's view about the link between culture and death has reversed them. People learn that they will die from their culture. Without culture, it is doubtful that people would know that they will die. Culture had to be there first.

Nonetheless, the findings do show that thinking about one's death and mortality can change one's perspective and alter one's priorities. The fact that people embrace their cultural world view more strongly after thinking about death may be an important sign that biology has created us to rely on the culture to help us survive. Likewise, as people approach death, they cease to desire new friendships and may even lose interest in casual acquaintances, but they reach out all the more strongly to their small circle of intimate partners, especially their families.[12] A brush with death as a result of a major illness causes people to reappraise their priorities and recognize that their time on earth is limited, so that petty concerns are downplayed, and they try to devote themselves to the things that matter most.[13]

From Curiosity to Understanding

Many animals exhibit a curiosity about their world, especially when they are young. Curiosity is a kind of eagerness for information, and it may contribute to survival because it helps the young creature learn about opportunities and dangers. Curiosity is an information-seeking instinct: It motivates the creature to want to discover some piece of information.

Information is the basis of culture, though, and so an information-seeking drive would be much more centrally important and adaptive to a cultural animal than to a solitary one. Maybe kittens can get on a little better because curiosity motivates them to learn a few facts about their worlds, but a cultural world has vastly more information. Most likely, human evolution included a great increase in the power of the curiosity drive. One result is what, in social psychology circles, has become something of a truism: People are lifelong, inveterate information seekers.

A big boost to the information-seeking drive in humans (as compared with other species) would be consistent with my account of how the human psyche developed. For one thing, we have seen that it is much easier for natural selection to increase or extend an existing structure than to make a wholly new one. It is undeniable that people are often open to new information, and many people spend part of almost every day acquiring new information. (No other species has anything resembling newspapers, science classes, oral histories, or "whodunit" entertainments, for example.) Moreover, the link of curiosity with youth in animals is enlightening, because one thrust of human evolution has been to prolong the youthful or adolescent traits throughout life. Kittens may lose some of their curiosity as they grow into old cats, but human beings remain curious right up into old age. More to the point, old dogs may not learn new tricks, but old people learn to surf the Internet.

In human beings, understanding is greatly facilitated by language, and we will return to the question of a "language instinct" later in this chapter. Language is purely cultural and has relatively little parallel in the animal world. The human fascination with language is most likely not a newly minted, independent instinct but rather a combination of the drive to understand and the social drive to belong (because communicating helps you to belong and to understand). For the present, the key point is that the human psyche is marked by a lifelong tendency to seek and acquire information. People strive to understand their world, in grand and small ways. Curiosity is not uniquely human, but the power of the drive, its persistence throughout life, and the formulation of understanding in abstract principles are all distinctive features of our species.

Human understanding does go far beyond what animals have been found to achieve, especially in terms of formulating knowledge in abstract principles. The desire to achieve a profound understanding of abstract principles has no apparent parallel in the animal world. Indeed, the understanding of events based on hidden causes that can be inferred may be beyond what animals are capable of and hence may be one of the distinctively human traits.[14] Probably this does not reflect a unique motivation but rather the same motivation (perhaps pumped up in power) combined with a powerful thinking tool, the human intellect. Curious kittens might like to understand their worlds in terms of abstract principles and hidden causes if they could, but they do not have the brain power to achieve this. And even if they had the brain power, they might not be able to infer abstract principles (e.g., force equals mass times acceleration) without language.

I have proposed that the drive to understand probably originated because it helped simple organisms deal more effectively with the physical world, and that evolution probably greatly increased the power and scope of this drive in order to make the cultural animal. There was quite possibly a big intervening step, however, insofar as the drive to understand may have been increased among social animals. Social interaction depends on some degree of mutual understanding, and so social animals should be curious about each other, at least. It is therefore plausible that the impulse to understand increased steadily, from an initial and simple curiosity about the physical environment, to a deeper and more enduring curiosity about one's fellows and their complex traits and habits, and finally to the cultural animal's full-fledged drive to understand.

Control

The quest for control is very deeply rooted in the human psyche, and it deserves a prominent place in any account of human motivation. People want to have control; they like to gain it; they resist losing it; and they are better off when they have it. Quite possibly, this desire will eventually be shown to be a family of innate tendencies, rather than a single drive. That is, the different motivations for control may be fairly independent of each other, and satisfying one will not satisfy the others. Power, mastery, money, skill, possessiveness, territoriality, self-efficacy, liberty—all these common human motives are fundamentally about control.

The drive for understanding may well be linked to the desire for control. Understanding does improve one's ability to control things. Even curiosity may be interpreted as one form of the drive for control, because curiosity leads to gaining information, which in turn facilitates mastery of the world.

The desire for control is not limited to cultural animals. Indeed, the quest for control would probably be beneficial even to very solitary species. Gaining control over events in one's physical surroundings contributes to both survival and reproduction, whereas a corresponding lack of control over the world leaves one vulnerable to failure on both counts. The beginnings of the drive for control may perhaps be seen in how bugs or other creatures struggle to right themselves if they are turned over onto their backs, or in making nests, or indeed in how creatures may change themselves to suit their environments better.

Undoubtedly, however, becoming social increases the payoff for control, because individuals can seek to control each other and thereby make use of others (or of the social system generally) to improve their own lot. Much of the human desire for control is focused in the social sphere: People seek interpersonal power, exert influence over other people, try to predict each other, strive to maintain some relationships and alter others, and in many other ways exert themselves toward regulating their social environment. All this is consistent with the view that social interaction is, at bottom, a strategy for dealing with the physical environment.

Thus, most animals need food to survive. One way to improve the food supply is to develop more control over the physical world, which can lead directly to more food becoming available. Another way to improve the food supply is to gain control over other creatures, especially members of one's own group, so that they provide you with more food.

Culture offers immense opportunities for gaining further control over both the physical and social environments, and culture can also make use of the human quest for control, even though the urge for control is probably not something the human race developed specifically to make it cultural. If anything, one could suggest that the drive to gain control was an important force that propelled us to develop culture, because culture vastly improved our ability to control our physical and social worlds. It is possible, however, that the human drive for control was extended or elaborated in some way during human evolution, so as to make people better able to exercise control by cultural means.

As we saw in chapter 1, a crucial difference between a cultural and a merely social animal is that culture permits progress. One animal can solve a problem or invent a better way of achieving something, and when that advance is appropriated by the culture, other members and even future generations can all enjoy the benefits of that innovation. Thus, culture greatly enhances the ability to gain control over the physical environment. But if the animals do not seek or enjoy control, they cannot make use of this advantage. It is plausible, therefore, that the evolution of the cultural animal depended to some extent on the drive for control.

The most basic form of the desire for control involves wanting to have an impact on one's surroundings. The person wants to do something that can reliably produce a reaction from the environment. Researchers on control believe that this kind of motivation is apparent in the acts of human infants as well as in nonhuman animals. Even if the effect is not beneficial in any apparent way, it is somehow pleasant and rewarding to be able to produce an effect. For me, personally, the idea that pleasure comes from having an impact on the environment is linked to a habit that my dog Warren developed some years ago. (I realize that stories by pet owners, like those of parents, are inherently suspect, so I offer this as mere illustration and not as proof of anything.) He was a sweet and gentle dog who loved to run but certainly not to fight. When I was at the University of Virginia, we lived out in the country, and I used to take Warren jogging in the late afternoon. We followed the dirt road past several farms and empty spaces. About a mile from our house, there was a small ramshackle trailer park, and between it and the road was a cluster of eight or ten doghouses—presumably for the pets of the trailer park residents. All the dogs were kept on long chains that permitted them to be in the house or near it, and of course the doghouses had to be far enough apart so that the dogs didn't get tangled in each other's lines. Mostly, in the late afternoon Virginia heat, they all retreated into the shade of their doghouses for a snooze.

Because we were deep in the country, I let Warren run off his leash, and he discovered the doghouse village, although in the standard territorial manner of dogs they did not like any intruders (and possibly resented Warren's freedom). Instead of making friends, as was his usual preference, he developed a new habit. When he and I rounded the bend heading toward the trailer park, he would take off at a rapid pace. Silently and swiftly, he would make his way directly to the center of the doghouse village. Upon arriving there, he would suddenly let out a couple of loud barks (uncharacteristically for him). Immediately, all the resident dogs would wake up and rush out of their doghouses in a mad frenzy of nonstop barking, as if they thought they were under attack by all the forces of evil. Warren would be long gone by then, making his way back to rejoin me on the road while the chaotic hubbub of barking slowly faded behind us. Any pleasure he got from this—and he must have gotten some satisfaction, because he continued to do this regularly—could only have been due to causing the hubbub, because he certainly did not achieve any other apparent benefit (no food, no fighting, no territory claimed, no sex). Producing that outburst was a form of control, in the basic sense of having a discernible impact on the environment, and that alone was enough to satisfy him.

Opinions differ as to whether the desire for control is innate or learned. The suggestion that it is innate, as favored by natural selection, has always seemed to me plausible and indeed very likely. Seeking control would be extremely adaptive, in the sense that it would be useful to the organism to help it achieve its goals of survival and reproduction. Biologists are well aware that the various forms of control represent life and death, including reproductive success, to many organisms: "The fundamental motivation of human beings, and all other complex organisms, is to achieve some level of control over the social (e.g., other people), biological (e.g., food), and physical (e.g., territory) resources that support life and allow one to reproduce."[15]

In contrast, others argue that it is learned as a general means of pursuing other things one wants. To obtain food, safety, warmth, sex, and belongingness, it is helpful to have control. People (and other animals) found that gaining control and using it was endlessly rewarding, because it brought them what they wanted. Meanwhile, lack of control was often marked by frustration and disappointment. A further argument is that parents and teachers reward children for small steps toward mastery, such as learning to tie one's own shoes or eat with a spoon. Hence many think that socialization and experience may be sufficient to explain the widespread desire for control, without postulating any innate inclination.[16]

Ultimately, though, it does not matter enormously whether the desire for control is learned or innate. The opposing view, that a desire for control is acquired through experience, points to so many experiences that are so common that everyone will end up with a desire for control even if humans are not born with it. (Thus, if control is part and parcel of getting most of the things one wants in life, a person could only evade wanting control by not wanting anything.) In practice, therefore, the urge for control will operate like an innate, universal need, even if it is not innate.

Control would seem to be learned if there is substantial cultural variation. Some experts assured me that other cultures and even other subgroups in our society do not desire control. They pointed out a recent study that showed differences between Western and Asian children: The Western ones worked hardest on tasks they had chosen for themselves, whereas the Asian children worked hardest on tasks their mother had chosen for them.[17] They also noted that some Eastern Europeans reported difficulty adjusting to the new freedoms they had when the repressive communist regimes were toppled.

But are those examples convincing indications that some people do not want control over their lives? The Asian children may simply have a broader conception of agency that includes close relatives and authority figures. They do not actively dislike having choice to the extent that they would prefer anyone other than themselves to make their decisions for them. As for the Eastern Europeans, some adjustments to freedom are to be expected, but those societies still unambiguously shifted toward greater freedom for individuals. A true counterexample would be a societal revolution in which people actively demanded a reduction in personal freedom for themselves, and history does not provide any clear examples of that sort. (Indeed, the satirical filmmaker Luis Bunuel highlighted the absurdity of that notion in his film *Phantom of Liberty*, in which a mob demonstrates and riots while chanting, "Down with freedom!") If we understand control in the broad sense defined above—encompassing power, money, ownership, knowledge, curiosity, and liberty—the weight of human history suggests a general, widespread desire for all of these things, and people only seek to relinquish them if they are confident that some other, greater good (such as religious salvation in heaven) will be theirs if they renounce these forms of control.

Deeply rooted motives can often be inferred from people's leisure activities, on the grounds that people's wants can effectively be determined by looking at what they choose to do when they have the freedom and leisure to let their own inner preferences dictate their choices (in contrast to behavior in work settings, for example, where behavior is constrained by external demands and forces). Plenty of movies have been devoted to sex, aggression, and relationships, indicating the seemingly bottomless fascination with those aspects of human life. Unlike those subjects, most video rental stores do not have specific shelves devoted to movies on the theme of control. (To be sure, if one broadens the understanding of control to include money, power, territory, and possessions, one can claim that control is a recurrent theme in many films and novels.) But perhaps watching a movie is not the optimal way to satisfy a deeply rooted desire for control, because in the final analysis the viewer cannot control the course of events.

Is control evident in other forms of recreation? Yes. There are many leisure activities that seem to revolve around control. The appeal of skill games in particular is based chiefly on the notion that gaining a sense of mastery is intrinsically satisfying. After all, the average video game bears no relation to real life and in that sense offers no useful information or abilities, and the solitary nature of such games shows that people do not play them for the sake of companionship. Moreover, my impression is that such games are satisfying as long as you are improving, whereas the game loses its appeal once you have fully mastered the game—indicating that the specific basis of enjoyment is the feeling of gaining control. Of course, video games are hardly unique in offering enjoyment based on developing a sense of control. Tennis, skiing, chess, billiards, and card games and tricks offer the rewards of skills that are gradually acquired over long practice. Thus, it seems fair to conclude that satisfying the desire for control is an important dimension of many leisure activities.

The fact that people seek out experiences of control even when there is no practical utility—such as by playing skill games—also suggests that the drive for control is somewhat independent of circumstances. The urge for control is more than just a response to practical circumstances in which control leads to material benefits.

The breadth of the concept of control was aptly captured in a classic 1982 paper by Rothbaum, Weisz, and Snyder,[18] who distinguished between *primary* and *secondary* forms of control. *Primary control* corresponded to the more familiar and traditional concept, namely, changing the environment to suit the self. *Secondary control* is the converse, namely, changing the self to fit the environment. Obviously, the common theme is creating harmony between self and world, so that the person can obtain safety and satisfaction from it. Rothbaum and his colleagues chose the names primary and secondary because they thought people (and other animals) would generally begin by attempting to change the environment and, when that failed, would go on to change themselves to fit in, so the names corresponded to an actual sequence of events. The researchers gradually changed their minds, however, as it became obvious that many people in many situations often go directly to secondary control, and sometimes changing the environment is even a second resort when efforts to adapt the self have failed. (For example, someone might seek a divorce only after she tried and tried, unsuccessfully, to accept her husband's faults.) Rothbaum and his colleagues also may have thought that the terms primary and secondary reflected a difference in adaptive value, in the sense that changing the environment is somehow preferable to changing the self, but on this also they later revised their opinions, because secondary control proved to be, if anything, more decisive in promoting happiness and adjustment.[19]

Secondary control can take multiple forms. Being able to predict an event, even if one cannot control it, allows one to brace oneself or be ready in other ways. The concept of *interpretive control* expresses the observation that people can tolerate things better if they feel they understand them, again regardless of whether this understanding enables them to avoid or prevent the problem. For example, research with sufferers of chronic pain has repeatedly confirmed that these patients can tolerate their suffering much better if the physicians can offer them some diagnostic label and explanation, even if there is no known cure or treatment. An unexplained, mysterious pain is far more distressing than one whose cause is known. A third form involves identifying oneself with an external power who has control, whether this is an authoritative spouse, a strong ruler, or a god or other supernatural power. Although one concedes that oneself cannot control the environment, one derives considerable comfort and satisfaction from linking oneself to someone who does have the requisite power. These secondary forms seem especially suited to a cultural animal, because they are based on meaningful understandings and interpersonal relationships. Thus, becoming a cultural animal was associated with gaining an expanded repertoire of ways to satisfy the desire for control.

Indeed, the initial idea behind the names primary and secondary may have derived from overestimating the centrality of dealing with the physical environment. In the social world, secondary control would probably have to be primary. To get along with others, it is more effective to change yourself to fit in than to expect everyone else to change to suit you. Simple arithmetic dictates this: If ten people live together, most of them are going to have to change to accommodate the group. There is no way that all ten can impose their will on all the others.

How important is control? One sign is whether people suffer negative consequences when they lack control. Interest in the health effects of control goes back at least to the classic "executive monkey" studies conducted by Brady and his colleagues in the 1950s.[20] Two monkeys are seated side by side at desks. Each has a button in front of him. If one of them, designated the executive monkey, fails to press his button over a 5-second span, both monkeys receive an unpleasant (but not harmful) electric shock. The other monkey, called the "yoked monkey," can press his button or not as he wishes, because it is not connected to anything and has no consequences. The two monkeys spend 6 hours "at work" at their desks, then have 6 hours off, and then back to work, day after day. Both get plenty to eat and maintain their weight. After about 3 weeks of this, the yoked monkey is rather bored but otherwise fine. The executive monkey is typically dead at this point; medical examination reveals that ulcers were the cause of death.

This research created a sensation when it was first published. In essence, the researchers had found that the simple act of having to press a button was sufficient to cause the death of a monkey. The electric shocks were not responsible for the death or ulcers, because the yoked monkey received exactly as many shocks as the executive monkey yet was fine. Actually, in most cases, neither monkey received very many shocks, because the executive monkey typically performed his duties very effectively. Americans were fascinated because the findings seemed to suggest that the pressures and responsibilities of executive life could be lethally stressful.

But wait. The executive monkey, after all, was the one who had control over the situation. Did Brady's findings indicate that having control might be bad for one's health? Follow-up studies cleared up the complex processes underlying the dramatic findings in the executive monkey studies.[21] Lack of positive feedback and a high demand for many responses were the main contributors to the stress of the executive monkey. Having control is itself a beneficial thing, and most subsequent studies confirmed that having bad things happen to you with no control is the most aversive and harmful situation. (The yoked monkey did not have control over the shocks he got, but then he hardly ever received any shocks, because the executive monkey performed well, and so the lack of his control did not matter in that study.)

The ill effects of lacking control have been documented in many studies. Getting ulcers from being exposed to bad events beyond one's control is only one form. Learned helplessness is another very destructive outcome of being subjected to uncontrollable events. This pattern was first demonstrated with nonhuman animals.[22] Thus, a dog would be put in a cage with a barrier between two parts, and shortly after a light flashed a mild electric current would be run through the metal flooring on one side. The dog would typically yelp with distress, run around, eventually stumbling across the barrier to safety. After a few trials, the dog would stand calmly by the barrier and step across as soon as the light flashed, thereby avoiding any pain. However, if the dog had previously been strapped down and subjected to electric shock that could not be escaped, it would fail to learn how to cross the barrier to safety, and instead it would simply lie down and cry when the shock commenced. Thus, intelligent animals seemed capable of learning that the situation was hopeless and that attempting to exert control was futile, and they would generalize that destructive lesson to new situations.

The eminent psychologist Martin Seligman proposed that learned helplessness was an important factor underlying many human failures,[23] including depression, voodoo deaths (self-fulfilling prophecies based on knowing that someone has cast a supposedly lethal spell on you), suicide, and school failure. Actually, the patterns of learned helplessness have not been found as consistently with human beings as with animals, although this may be due to the fact that college students (the most common research participants) have generally accumulated many years of experience in knowing that they can control their environment by the time they show up for a laboratory experiment. In other words, people have a strong expectation of being able to exert control. For example, when you put money into a vending machine and it refuses to give you a can of soda pop, you do not typically fall into learned helplessness. On the contrary, the typical response is to try that much harder to exert control, such as by pressing the buttons again, trying other buttons, or even banging on the machine. (In the United States alone, several deaths are caused every year when people are crushed by vending machines that they were attempting to manipulate by shaking and jostling—foolish and self-destructive, yes, but not helpless.)

One way to interpret these findings is to suggest that humans inherited the drive for control from other animals but the drive was somewhat changed in the process of human evolution. Perhaps evolution made humans more intent on seeking control by alternate routes when they failed at first. Alternatively, the human patterns may reflect the same desire for control as is found in other social species—but combined with the more complicated cognitive and action systems that human beings have. Just as people can substitute one response for another, they can quickly envision alternate routes to the same goal, and so when the first one is blocked they move along quickly to try another. In any case, the operation of the drive for control in humans does contain some features that seem to be distinctively human, especially the refusal to be discouraged or become helpless in response to initial failure.

The health benefits of control were demonstrated in a different way by Ellen Langer and Judith Rodin.[24] They noted a pattern that old people in the more expensive, seemingly more supportive nursing homes seemed to die more rapidly than the residents of the ostensibly less helpful homes, and they thought that the problem with the more expensive homes might be that everything was done for the person, thereby depriving the person of any direct control over the environment. In an experimental study, they gave a sample of nursing home residents the responsibility of taking control of their environment, while the rest were told that the staff of the nursing home would try to take care of them. In particular, people in the active responsibility group were each given responsibility for watering and caring for a potted plant, while those in the other group had plants put in their rooms but the nursing home staff took care of them. The people who were induced to take responsibility for themselves and for the potted plants did indeed become more active, and these gains were accompanied by greater feelings of happiness and alertness. More important, they fared better with regard to health, as indicated in physicians' ratings of the medical records at the nursing home. The most dramatic finding was that the people in the high responsibility group were less likely to die during the year and a half following the study. Thus, the results suggest that having control can lead to better health and longer life.

Even illusions of control can provide health benefits. Some women who suffer from breast cancer develop unsubstantiated theories about how they can gain control over relapse, and these women are rated by nurses and others as coping and recovering better than the women who do not cultivate such illusions of control.[25] Experimental demonstrations of the so-called panic button effect have confirmed that believing one has a possible escape route makes problems much more bearable. In these studies, people were first required to listen to stressful blasts of noise while they worked at some task. By random assignment, half the group was told that if the noise bothered them too much, they could press a button to turn it off, but the experimenter asked them to try not to press the button unless the noise got really bad. Nobody actually pressed the button. Still, these people showed fewer negative aftereffects of stress (including loss of frustration tolerance and inability to concentrate) than people who had endured exactly the same amount of noise without having the panic button.[26] Somehow, the false belief that they could potentially exert control reduced the stress that people suffered.

The panic button effect has profound implications. It suggests that what is harmful in stress is not the bad event itself so much as the threat that it could continue and get worse. The panic button did not objectively reduce the amount of noise, but it removed the threat. The person could say, "Well, if it gets worse, I can always press the button." Quite possibly, the same dynamic operates in many bad situations in life—fatigue, poverty, hunger, sexual frustration, dental surgery, and more. People can tolerate things much better if they believe they can exert control if it becomes necessary.

Control thus qualifies as a need rather than merely a want: People who lack control suffer seriously adverse consequences. There is, however, plenty of evidence that people want control too and feel upset or unhappy when they do not have it. In particular, a loss of control when one had previously enjoyed control often elicits sharp protests and distress, sometimes extending to aggression. Jack Brehm's *theory of reactance* proposed that people are widely and fundamentally motivated to maintain their freedom of action,[27] and many studies have shown that people resent having options taken away from them, even if these were not options that they had been intending to use. In one standard experimental paradigm, for example, the research subject looks at a series of posters and rates how much he would like to have each one. The experimenter has in fact promised that the subject can keep one of the posters. After the rating is done, however, the experimenter says that the subject's third-favorite poster is actually unavailable, and under some pretext the subject is asked to rate them again. Typically, the subject gives a higher rating to that poster after hearing that he cannot have it.[28]

Another response to lack of control is to cultivate false, almost superstitious beliefs of control.[29] That is, if real control is unavailable, people still prefer to imagine that they have control. Undoubtedly, a great deal of superstitious, magical, and even religious behavior is driven by the feeling that important outcomes can be controlled by ingratiating or manipulating these powerful, mysterious forces. For example, few theological experts believe that prayer can actually induce God to alter the trajectory of a ball, but many athletes and fans have been known to pray for divine assistance when the game is on the line.

There are many varieties and spheres of control. As already said, harmony with one's environment is one overriding goal, and changing either the self or the environment is a vital means of achieving that harmony. In particular, human life is marked by ongoing processes of change, both within the self (including both biological and psychological changes) and within the environment (both the physical and the social). Yet change is often stressful, in part because it can produce new problems, threats, and difficulties. Life is change that yearns for stability, and many human activities seem designed to make the environment more stable. And if the environment cannot be objectively changed to increase stability, then learning to predict the environment is a good substitute because the person can anticipate the changes and prepare for them.

The desire for a stable, predictable environment is well served if creatures provide for their future. Sure, there might be food and a dry place to sleep today, but what about next month? If one can do something now to prolong these benefits into the future, the goal of harmony with the environment would be much better realized. Most animals cannot do this effectively other than by fixed action sequences, such as nest building. Cultural animals who use meaning can, however, think about the future and make flexible, individually tailored plans to make it better, and this is hugely adaptive.

Let us briefly survey some of the major forms that the urge for control takes, especially among cultural animals.

MONEY

The desire for money is one common and familiar form of the urge for control. It is hardly necessary to amass statistics or research findings to prove that people like to get money and dislike losing it. Indeed, one entire social science (economics) is predicated on the view that people seek to maximize their financial outcomes, and economists often seem reluctant to concede that some humans will disregard the quest for profit or set it aside while they pursue other goals.

My own youth coincided with the youth rebellion and hippie movements of the 1960s and 1970s, and a particular target of hostility of that movement was the materialist, capitalist pursuit of money. My parents attempted to explain to me that they did not simply seek money for its own shallow sake. "Money gives you freedom," my mother recited to me on more than one occasion. It is a lesson that an idealistic, impecunious student may be reluctant to grasp or heed, but most adults sooner or later probably come to recognize the truth of it. In jobs, homes, health care, romantic partners, cars, leisure activities, and many other spheres, people with money have more options than people without money, and they are less likely to be stuck having to put up with something they do not really like.

Thus, ultimately, money is often sought as a form of control. When you do not have money, you are at the mercy of events and may have to do what you are told. When you have money, in contrast, you can get the things you want; you can refuse to do things you don't like to do; you can make other people do what you want; and you can cope with many misfortunes and problems. These things do not always happen, to be sure; the point is that there is a net gain. Popular wisdom has long sought to temper the human quest for money with trite claims that money cannot buy love or happiness, but in fact money does improve one's chances for both love and happiness. Many studies have found that people with more wealth or higher salaries are happier than poor people, although the size of the effect depends on other factors, and there are some suggestions that the effect is mainly found at the two extremes (in other words, in the middle class, differences in income are only weakly related to happiness, but the very rich and the very poor find that money has a substantial impact).[30] As for love, well, money can certainly purchase one facsimile (sex), and men with money find it easier than poor men to attract the love of women. For women, money is less directly related to romantic appeal, but it is well established that women are more willing to escape a loveless marriage via a divorce if they are able to support themselves financially than if they are dependent on their husbands for their money.

Money is quintessentially cultural, and so the pursuit of money is a form of control that is specific to cultural animals. I have already argued that money is a powerful and revealing form of social and cultural reality, because it depends on assumptions, beliefs, and implicit agreements that are shared by a large number of people. Money is one sign that culture exists, and it is a cultural medium of control.

POWER

Power is another common form of the urge for control. As with money, there is an entire social science, political science, devoted to studying power—and that is a persuasive sign that it is an important and fundamental aspect of human life. Power essentially involves control over other people. Researcher David G. Winter defined it as the ability to produce intended effects on another person's actions or emotions.[31] Some may seek power as a means to an end, such as on the assumption that once one is elected, one will be able to bring about certain much-wanted changes. But others probably seek power for its own sake and derive satisfaction directly from being able to make other people change the way they act. Actually, the specific goal of people with a high craving for power appears to be that they want to *have an impact* on other people's lives, which does not necessarily mean making people do things. Having an impact can be for good or ill, and a person with a high desire for power may enjoy giving money to a struggling family simply because it is satisfying to see how much she was able to change that family's life.

Power benefits the individual in at least two ways. First, as with money, power enables people to get what they want. Some human desires can be realized without power, but if other people make obstacles or difficulties, power can help resolve the problem in one's favor. Second, much of what people want involves other people, and power improves the chances that other people will treat us the way we want to be treated. Thus, we have seen that sex and belongingness are two innate human desires, and both depend on the cooperation of others. Powerful men can obtain sex more readily. (The American diplomat Henry Kissinger famously remarked that power is "the ultimate aphrodisiac," which presumably indicated some personal experience that despite being not very good-looking he was able to find willing sex partners when he held the most power.) Young men who score high on the motivation to seek power also report earlier commencement of sexual activity.[32]

In parallel fashion, power can increase one's opportunities for belong-ingness and reduce the risk of being abandoned. Powerful members of groups and organizations probably feel secure that they can retain their membership, in contrast to the relatively powerless, who often know they are dispensable. If nothing else, the powerful people are usually the ones who decide who must leave the group and who gets to remain.

Again, though, power is not always just a means to an end, but in many cases the pursuit of power becomes an end in its own right. In any case, it shapes many other activities. Young adults who score high in power motivation tend to join organizations that have more influence, such as newspapers. They take up official and powerful positions within organiza-tions. They are drawn toward sports in which two opposing parties vie for dominance (but not especially toward solitary sports, such as golf, swim-ming, or track), and they are more likely to suffer broken bones in sports (which is a sign of intense competition). They tend to show off so as to intimidate and impress others. They seek to build alliances and especially favor friends and allies who are not themselves power-seekers and hence are not threats or competitors.[33]

Power is inherently social and therefore not necessarily cultural. It would make no sense to talk about differences in power in a solitary being, but social animals usually have some form of power. Being social entails interdependence, and power is an imbalance in this interdependence: I have more power than you insofar as what I do affects your life more than what you do affects my life. The dominance hierarchies of many pack ani-mals are a form of distribution of power.

Indeed, one may argue that the pursuit and dynamics of power reach their peak in purely social species, and culture makes power problematic. Only a fool would deny that some human beings are driven to gain power, but this drive may be a holdover in our inheritance as social animals. Some aspects of culture increase the range and reach of power, but cultures also tend to place limits on power. The development of culture into its most advanced forms has been marked by a steady increase in the limits and constraints on the use of power, a theme that will be developed in more detail in chapter 7, on how culture transforms interactions.

POSSESSIONS AND TERRITORY

The quest for control can also be seen in possessive behavior. Animals and people show territorial patterns, in which they lay claim to some land (or other space) and aggressively maintain hegemony over it. Dogs mark their territory with urine and a few well-directed snarls, whereas human beings establish claims with legal documents, but the underlying theme is the same: Maintaining control over a specific area is deeply appealing and comforting.

Moreover, possessiveness extends beyond territory to include material possessions. Periodically, people are exhorted to try to live without material possessions, such as in some religious traditions, or under communism, but these idealistic systems fail to attract large numbers of people who want to live that way. In contrast, research studies have shown that even fairly trivial material objects gain abruptly in value when one owns them. Studies behind this so-called endowment effect will ask people to rate the value of some object such as a coffee cup with a certain design or logo, or to say how much they would pay for it, in order to obtain a baseline. Other people (or sometimes the same people, after they have made the initial ratings) are given the same object as a gift and asked to say for how much they would sell it or what its value is now. Almost invariably, they ascribe a higher value to the item when they own it.[34] If you have ever shopped for used furniture, you probably know how owners tend to overvalue what they have to sell.

Self and identity figure prominently in today's social psychology, because people are extensively motivated to find out who they are and to defend their good name against various threats and dangers. The origins of self are often traced to reflexive consciousness (that is, consciousness turned away from the world to look inward) and to having an identity in the matrix of interpersonal relationships. A less obvious but still important root is in possessiveness. Ownership presupposes an owner, and without a self or identity you could not really have anything nor care about whether others respect "your" possessions and rights. Among animals, possession is probably one of the earliest appearing steps toward selfhood.

Thus, the drives to own territory and to own items may be rooted in the motives for dealing with the physical environment, but they become more refined and developed in social beings, and cultural beings develop a much more elaborate sense of ownership. Having one's own territory or possessions is social in the sense that one usually makes a claim against possible claims of other members of one's species. If you were alone in the world, or even just on an island, you would not have much concern over claiming space or items. Ownership matters mainly within a group of animals or people, all of whom may want the same things. Culture produces far more things and far more elaborate systems of ownership—indeed, most cultures codify ownership into complex systems of rules. Buying a house or car is a process that depends heavily on legal documents. It also makes elaborate use of the economy, especially if one has to finance the purchase with loans, and we have already noted that the system of money is essentially cultural.

The Social Animal's Desires

All living things need basic nutrients from their environments. Some animals have adopted a particular strategy, social interaction, to get them. Human beings are descended from this social branch of the evolutionary tree. Hence human beings have inherited the psychological dispositions that have been designed by the trial and error of natural selection to make social interaction possible. In this section, we consider the principal motives that humans inherited from other social animals.

One qualification is needed. This section may read as if all of these motives appeared out of nowhere when animals evolved from solitary to social. That mode of presentation is more a heuristic simplification rather than a fair summary of the actual process, which was probably much more continuous. The aggression drive, for example, may have originated among solitary animals, which needed to use violence to kill their prey. I feature it here because aggression against one's own species is much more relevant to human activity and because such aggression presumes more complicated social relationships than predator-prey aggression.

Belongingness

The need to belong is one of the most basic and powerful human needs, as well as one of the most social. A drive to form relationships with other members of your species would be relatively trivial, even problematic, in nonsocial species that live by direct interaction with the environment. Of what use would a "need to belong" be in a tree, for example? At best, the tree would be upset to be away from other trees, whereas in reality it might do better to have some distance from the other trees, so they don't block its sunlight or preempt its water.

For creatures like us, however, evolution smiled upon those with a strong need to belong. Survival and reproduction are the criteria of success by natural selection, and forming relationships with other people can be useful for both survival and reproduction. Groups can share resources, care for sick members, scare off predators, fight together against enemies, divide tasks so as to improve efficiency, and contribute to survival in many other ways. In particular, if an individual and a group want the same resource, the group will generally prevail, so competition for resources would especially favor a need to belong. Belongingness will likewise promote reproduction, such as by bringing potential mates into contact with each other, and in particular by keeping parents together to care for their children, who are much more likely to survive if they have more than one caregiver.

One important difference between a want and a need is the scope of bad effects that attend not fulfilling it. By that definition, people want sex but they need belongingness. Sex is a want, and failure to get sexual satisfaction may make people feel bad, but it does not appear to do any actual harm. It is quite possible to live without sex, and many people (such as elderly widows) seem to forgo sex for many years without ill effect or complaint. In contrast, almost no one can live happily or healthily without some connections to other people. The evidence for this harm has been accumulating steadily. Already in the 1970s, Lynch's book *The Broken Heart* was able to summarize a sizable body of medical information indicating that "U.S. mortality rates for all causes of death . . . are consistently higher for divorced, single, and widowed individuals."[35] He found that unattached people have more fatal heart attacks than married people, and he noted that parallel effects had been clearly shown with several other major diseases, including cancer and tuberculosis, as well as for all diseases lumped together. These effects remain significant even after implementing statistical controls for other variables that might differ between married and single persons, such as cigarette smoking, speed of commencing treatment, and family income. Other work has begun to suggest that social isolation can have adverse effects on the immune system.[36] Lonely people are more vulnerable than others to stresses of all sorts, and their bodies are less successful at repairing the wear and tear caused by stress.[37] All of these findings confirm the power of belongingness for meeting one's biological needs, because a person's very survival is directly affected by having versus not having social bonds.

Belongingness is important for mental health as well as physical health, although many findings leave unclear whether the psychological problems are the cause or the consequence of being alone. Based on mental hospital admission patterns, one team of researchers concluded that mental illness is at least three times and perhaps as much as twenty times higher among divorced than among married people.[38] Their review observed that every single published study has found higher rates of mental illness in the unmarried group, and indeed the consistent pattern was that divorced and separated people had the highest rates of mental illness, never-married were intermediate, and currently married people had the lowest. In other findings, children who grow up either neglected by parents or rejected by peers have higher rates of psychopathology.[39] The greater rate of suicidal tendencies among socially unattached individuals was documented already in the 19th century by Durkheim,[40] one of the founding fathers of sociology, and that relationship was replicated through the 20th century.[41] The need to belong is literally a vital matter of life and death, health, welfare, and sanity.

Given the links between belongingness and both mental and physical health, it is hardly surprising that happiness is also correlated with belongingness. Socially connected people are happy, whereas lone or lonely people are generally not happy. The relationship is surprisingly strong. Whether someone has a network of good relationships or is alone in the world is a much stronger predictor of happiness than any other objective predictor, including money or income, health, place of residence, marital status, and other factors that people believe to be important.[42] No particular relationship seems essential, and so it does not matter a great deal whether people are connected to friends, relatives, children, spouse, teammates, colleagues, or others. But if you are alone in the world, your chances of being happy are statistically quite slim.

The fact that belongingness predicts happiness more strongly—far more strongly, in America—than any other external circumstance is another sign that the need to belong is exceptionally powerful. Satisfying the need to belong is more crucial and decisive than satisfying any other need.[43]

Experimental work has begun to confirm that belongingness plays a causal role, as opposed to simply being the result of mental and physical problems that might alienate potential friends and lovers. Laboratory studies have looked at what people do as a result of being socially rejected or made to feel alone or given the silent treatment. After something like that happens, people show a variety of destructive consequences. They are more likely to engage in short-sighted, self-defeating behavior, such as taking foolish risks; they show a reduced capacity for intelligent thought; they exhibit more aggressive and antisocial behavior and less prosocial behavior; and they seem less effective at regulating their own behavior constructively.[44]

Let us now consider the question of what, precisely, people desire in the way of belongingness.[45] As already mentioned, people vary significantly as to the strength and frequency of this motivation, just like the variations in the motivations for sex, aggression, and the rest. On average, it appears that most people want to have four to six close, important relationships with other people. People who are connected to fewer than four other people feel alone and may begin to suffer the symptoms of social deprivation. Above about six, there seems to be a pattern of diminishing returns such that few or no benefits are gained by adding additional relationships, although any new relationship may offer specific benefits that the others do not, such as if the seventh new person is the one who is willing to fix your car, have sex with you, or teach you to play tennis. It is possible that people simply do not have the time or energy to pursue emotional closeness with more than a half dozen people. Again, though, people do vary: Some people desire more social contact and connections than others.

Thus, there does seem to be a natural limit on the size of the desired social circle. One useful population to study in this regard is college students, because they come into contact with many other people of similar age and could potentially interact with someone new every day. Even in such people-rich environments, however, the vast majority of each person's social interactions are with the same four to six people.[46] In other words, people spontaneously restrict the size of their social circles even when they don't have to do so. American college students are hardly unique in this regard. All over the world, in all known societies, people organize their social lives around small groups, as opposed to living alone, orienting mainly toward very large groups, or having a constantly changing series of interaction partners.[47]

The goal of four to six relationships paints the need to belong as rooted in the social rather than the cultural animal. People are not programmed by nature simply to form more and more social bonds. Instead, they seem driven to live in small groups, with a handful of close relationships.

There is admittedly a gap between the limited size of the need to belong (i.e., seeking four to six close relationships) and the view of the cultural animal as someone who wants to connect with a broader culture. As it happens, psychologists have tended to focus on close relationships rather than any broader, vaguer desire to connect with large social entities, but there is some evidence. Some people—mostly men—can satisfy the need to belong by connecting with broad social and cultural entities, such as a corporation, a university, or a sports team.

Indeed, the tendency of researchers to focus on one-to-one relationships rather than larger units has led some experts to think that women are more social than men.[48] Those experts have probably been misled by a too-narrow understanding of belongingness, however. A more sophisticated and accurate understanding is that the need to belong is strong in both men and women, but the two genders tend to focus on and seek satisfaction in somewhat different spheres. Specifically, women seem more focused on the narrow sphere of intimate, one-to-one relationships, whereas men are often oriented toward larger social groups.[49]

There is ample evidence of the gender difference in social orientation, such that men are oriented toward broader groups but women are mainly oriented toward one-to-one close relationships. First, aggressive patterns show that male aggression is often aimed at other members of the larger social group, reflecting competition for dominance and other resources, whereas female aggression is mainly within the family or intimate group. (Domestic violence is the only sphere where women equal men; men are hugely more aggressive toward strangers or distant acquaintances.) Second, studies of helping show a similar pattern, with men being significantly more helpful toward strangers and other members of a larger social group, whereas women equal or surpass men in the amount of things they do within the family (e.g., child care, nursing the sick, housework). Third, males tend to identify with bigger groups (e.g., "my family" or "my company") whereas females describe themselves in terms of specific individual relationships. Fourth, observations of children on playgrounds repeatedly find that girls tend to pair off and play with the same partner for a long period of time, whereas boys spend just as much time in interpersonal play but they spend it with a revolving series of partners or, especially as they grow older, in coordinated group play.[50] Some experiments have let children form a dyad and then tried to introduce a third child to play along; boys are more receptive than girls to adding a new playmate, whereas girls prefer to continue the one-on-one play and therefore will tend to reject the new girl.[51] Fifth, the predictors of loneliness differ somewhat by gender. One team of researchers studied a large sample of Chicago residents, some of whom were lonely and others who were not. The absence of close, intimate relationships was a significant predictor of loneliness for both men and women. But the lack of a strong feeling of identification with a broader institution, such as one's corporation or university, was a strong predictor of loneliness for men but was essentially irrelevant for women.[52] Thus, again, males satisfy the need to belong partly by means of connecting with broad groups and institutions, whereas for females the one-to-one close relationships are seemingly all that matter.

The crucial part (regardless of one's opinion on gender differences) is that some humans go beyond one-to-one relationships in how they satisfy the need to belong. This may be an important step that helped move human beings from social to cultural animals. They connect not just individually with each other, but to larger collectives—teams, companies, ethnicities, nationalities. Possibly some other animals connect to groups rather than just to individuals, but this form of connection is vital to human culture, and it often involves abstract entities (again, e.g., nationalities). This shift in focus is just the sort of change that we have emphasized in understanding the human psyche: Nature took what was already there in our hominid ancestors and tweaked it a bit to make us more oriented for culture.

A need to belong sounds very positive, but there is one disturbing side to it. If people simply need to connect with somebody, are partners replaceable? Although certain relationships may offer special rewards, in general the need to belong does seem to accept substitutes quite freely, and the main human need is to be connected to others in whatever manner is convenient. This is illustrated by the adjustments people make when relationships change. For example, when two people develop a romantic relationship and start to become seriously close, they often withdraw from others, such as by spending less time with old friends.[53] In anticipation of breaking off such an intimate romantic relationship, people will often seek out new friends,[54] and most people rely heavily on social support from family and friends through the process of getting a divorce.[55] People are often quite distraught over romantic failures, particularly because they believe they will never find someone as good, but in most cases they soon find someone else—whereupon their distress over the previous failure recedes dramatically.[56] Friendships with peers are very important to the well-being of childless elderly people, and the more time they spend in such interactions, the happier they are—but elderly people whose children are in regular contact are less dependent on such friendships, and their happiness is unrelated to how many such interactions they have.[57] Thus, to be happy, old people can either have good relationships with their children or carry on some friendships with other adults.

It affronts our pride to realize how replaceable we are, especially in the lives of people we love, but the data are fairly merciless in this connection. As already shown, divorce increases people's risk for a large assortment of bad outcomes, including mental and physical illness, committing a crime, being a victim of crime (including murder), car crashes and other accidents, and suicide.[58] But remarriage drastically reduces or eliminates those risks. Undoubtedly, every spouse is unique and special in some ways, but when you look at the numbers with the cold eye of a statistician, it appears that in many respects, one spouse is as good as another, unless the marriage is unhappy or hostile.

When I was younger, the hit song "Somebody to Love" by the Jefferson Airplane struck many as odd, because it treated lovers as so interchangeable. "Don't you want somebody to love?" the song asked, as if anyone would do. The message was quite different from the thousands of other love songs one heard, because these nearly always emphasized a particular other person and often asserted that no one else could ever satisfy. The majority of love songs were closer to how love feels, because most people do regard their close relationship partners as special if not eternally irreplaceable. But the data suggest that those songs were wrong and the Jefferson Airplane may have had it right after all. The important thing is to find somebody, anybody (well, almost) to love. Hardly anyone is irreplaceable, and few people who are in love show any palpable sign of suffering from the loss of a previous lover.[59]

The need to belong can be subdivided into two more specific desires. These are, first, a desire for frequent interactions, and second, a context of ongoing mutual caring and concern. People who have either without the other often affirm the value of what they have but also will express dissatisfaction over what they miss. For example, people in so-called commuter marriages (defined by spouses living in different cities) often say how much they treasure the connection, but they also suffer over the lack of direct, face-to-face contact. Spouses of overseas (or underseas) military personnel or others in traveling occupations generally express similar sentiments, namely, valuing the connection but bemoaning the lack of interaction.[60] Thus, the social bond without regular interactions is experienced as only partially satisfactory.

Conversely, having many interactions without the overarching bond of mutual concern is equally unsatisfying. Most people consistently express a preference for having a few close friends as opposed to having many casual friends,[61] and many studies have found that people who complain of loneliness spend as much time as other people in interpersonal interactions.[62] Prostitutes are a relevant group, because they may have many seemingly intimate interactions but without any ongoing bond of mutual concern. Sure enough, prostitutes often say that meeting many interesting people is an appealing aspect of their jobs, but they also seem quite driven to form and maintain some lasting connections characterized by mutual concern. Indeed, the problematic and sometimes destructive attachments to pimps and others may be attributed in part to the prostitutes' craving for the ongoing framework of mutual caring, despite the frequent interactions.[63] Prostitutes also seem to prefer to cultivate long-term relationships with clients, which could have multiple explanations but again suggests that the interactions without the relationship are less satisfying. One researcher calculated that a prostitute could maximize her earnings by working in a brothel and servicing many customers quickly, but despite this financial inducement many of the women preferred to work outside brothels, in part because they could find better opportunities to cultivate relationships with repeat customers, including by spending more time with each one.[64]

To be sure, not all interactions are satisfactory. The need to belong is apparently not satisfied by hostile, conflictual interactions, and a bad marriage may make the person feel more alone than ever. Interactions do not, however, have to be positive or pleasant in order to be satisfying, for many people report comfort over seemingly neutral interactions such as doing chores or watching television together. The most precise formulation seems to be that the need to belong requires frequent but nonnegative interactions.

Sex

If belongingness is mainly for survival, sex is mainly for reproduction. This of course describes its ultimate biological function, not its immediate motivation. Many people engage in sex with no reproductive intent.

If anything, they are often trying their best to prevent reproduction. Sex is nature's way of making sure that people reproduce, whereas sex is often people's way of having fun and feeling good, expressing love, or even earning some much-needed cash.

To be sure, some people want children, and so they engage in sex for that purpose. But they may be in a minority at any given time. One of the intriguing mysteries of evolution is why so many human females do not know when they ovulate. Most of evolution, especially human evolution, has been marked by improved self-understanding and improved capacity for conscious control. Yet human women differ from most of our biological relatives in that there are hardly any outward signs of being ready to become pregnant. Among the leading candidates to explain this pattern is the idea that human women were too smart for their own good, or rather for the species' own good. If human women knew that they would become pregnant, they would refrain from intercourse, and the human race might dwindle toward extinction. It is abundantly clear from modern data that many women want to have sex without pregnancy, and early human women might well have recognized that abstaining from sex during the fertile days of the menstrual cycle would be an appealing way of avoiding pregnancy. But a woman who could not tell whether she was impregnable at the moment might well go ahead and take the chance, which could result (as it still often does) in an unplanned pregnancy. Evolution may well have found that women who knew when they could get pregnant managed to avoid doing so and thereby removed their genes from the human gene pool, ultimately leaving the field to their sisters who could not tell when they were most at risk for pregnancy.

In any case, the desire for sex is an easily understandable feature of human motivation. Perhaps it did not need to undergo much refinement as evolution moved from social to cultural animals. Then again, the remarkable wealth and diversity of human sexual expression suggests that the human sex drive is at least receptive to all sorts of cultural influences that are unknown in the sex lives of other species. No other species enriches its sexuality with pornography, phone sex, erotic spanking, striptease shows, cross-dressing, erotic tickling, shoe fetishes, vibrators, strap-on dildos, and many other variations that somehow appeal to assorted human beings.

Writers are fond of saying how natural sex is, and in one sense they are correct, but sex is also heavily culturalized. There are at least two steps in this cultural transformation of sex. The first is that among human beings, sex becomes saturated with meaning, and the meanings transform the experience as well as opening up new possibilities. People can have sex to symbolize their love for each other. They might engage in consensual sado-masochistic activity, in which they play elaborate roles and games involving submission to another person's ostensible power. Some people seek out sex as a symbolic conquest, so that they can have something to brag about to others. Fetishes show that inanimate objects can become invested with symbolic sexual power, and in some cases these meanings become indispensable to the individual's ability to feel sexual arousal.

The second aspect of the culturalization of sex involves attempts by culture and society to control people's sexuality. Many cultures have tried to restrain sexual desire and to prevent people from desiring or at least performing certain acts, such as homosexual activities. Many religions have preached that some forms of sexual activity are sinful. Many people have sexual inhibitions that are based on meaning. For example, one common thought experiment involves imagining that you are blindfolded and a member of the opposite sex is performing oral sex on you—and then imagining that the active person is a member of your own gender. Even though your sensations might be identical in the two scenarios, most people find one of them far more appealing and exciting than the other. The implications of this distinction go beyond thought experiments. In reality, some men like to dress up as women and perform fellatio on other men, but because of sexual taboos and fears, these cross-dressers risk being physically attacked if their partners discover that they are not the women they seem to be.

Thus, sexuality is subject to both physical and cultural causality. Sex is affected by physical factors, such as bodily health and hormones, and it is also shaped by meanings, such as when sex is enhanced by its symbolic messages of love and commitment. The influence of cultural causality on sex reflects the plasticity of the motivation.

Erotic plasticity is not equally distributed; there appears to be a sweeping gender difference. Women far exceed men in their erotic plasticity.[65] Most men find that their sexual desires adhere to the same patterns from puberty to old age, changing only as the aging process gradually diminishes their sex drive. Cultural influences also have relatively small effects on men's desires. In contrast, female sexuality changes shape more easily as a function of social and cultural influences. For example, the sexual patterns of highly educated men are not much different from those of men with less education, but the sexuality of highly educated women is vastly different from that of uneducated women. For example, the more educated ones are significantly more likely than less educated women to engage in oral sex, anal sex, same-gender activity, and a variety of other activities.[66] By the same token, highly religious women are far less permissive and adventurous in their sex lives than nonreligious women, but the differences between religious and nonreligious men are much smaller. The point is that cultural factors such as education and religion affect the sexuality of women far more than they do men. The female sex drive has some special receptivity to such influences.

The gender difference in erotic plasticity has important consequences. Female sexuality varies considerably across different cultures. It has also changed more across historical periods. The sexual revolution of the 1960s and 1970s brought much bigger changes to female than to male sexuality. Although individual men differ from each other, the general patterns of male sexual desire remain quite similar across time and culture. If a culture needs to bring about a change in sexual behavior, it can accomplish this better by changing women than by changing men. Meanwhile, within individuals, cultural factors and causes probably play a greater role in female than male sexuality. The greater erotic plasticity among women entails that questions such as "What does it mean?" will affect women's sexual responses more than men's.

What causes plasticity? The answer is not clear, but a promising guess is that it has to do with strength of motivation. A strong drive of any sort is less susceptible to the civilizing influence and transforming power of culture, as compared to a relatively mild drive. Is it plausible that women's sex drive is milder than men's? For some reason, this question became imbued with political significance, and as often happens, objective scientific inquiry took a back seat to politicized opinions. But eventually it became possible to set aside concerns about "equality" and "superiority," which are of doubtful relevance to the question anyhow, and to look at the evidence. And the evidence was overwhelming: In our 2001 survey of published studies, there was not a single finding on any measure in any investigation that indicated that women desired sex more than men. On the contrary, nearly every measure in every study depicted men as having the stronger sexual motivation. Men think about sex more often than women, are sexually aroused more often, desire sex more frequently at every stage in life and every stage in a relationship, want more sex partners, enjoy more different sex acts, have more positive attitudes about both their own and their partners' genitals, have more difficulty living without sex, expend more time, energy, money, and other resources to obtain sex, initiate sex more often and refuse it less often, have vastly lower standards for acceptable sex partners, masturbate more often, rate themselves as more sexually driven, and in every other way show themselves to have a stronger drive for sex.[67]

To be sure, *desire* for sex should not be confused with other concepts. Women are capable of having sex more than men, given the male refractory period and other limitations. Also, desire is not the same as enjoyment, and there is almost no usable information on the question of whether men or women enjoy sex more. Sex drive refers just to how often and how much someone wants sex.

Thus, men desire sex more than women, and the milder female desire may leave more opportunity for their desire to be shaped and influenced by sociocultural forces. As a parallel example, one might consider the desire to have and care for children. Most experts think that this desire is somewhat stronger among women than men, and so if lesser desire contributes to greater plasticity, fatherhood should be more susceptible than motherhood to the influence of culture. Sure enough, a variety of evidence suggests that the father-child relationship varies considerably across cultures, across history, and in response to other social influences, whereas the mother-child bond is much more constant and unchanging.[68] Thus, when men's desire is milder, their plasticity is greater.

In an important sense, then, sex responds to both physical and cultural causation, and men and women differ in the relative input. For men, sexual behavior seems more influenced by physical causes, including hormone levels and genetic heredity. For women, cultural causation is more prominent, including cultural influences and personal meanings. Female sexuality will therefore show much greater variation across history and cultures than will male sexuality. Sexual self-knowledge will also be more difficult for women than men, because for women one's own sexuality is a moving target, whereas for men it is a relatively fixed and obvious matter. Still, both men's and women's sex lives are based in nature but refined by culture.

All cultures have rules about sexual behavior, reflecting the fact that unrestricted sex produces a variety of social problems, including unwanted pregnancy and unplanned offspring, jealousy and violence, sexually transmitted diseases, and abusive sex. In view of women's greater erotic plasticity, societies may succeed at controlling sex better by directing their efforts at women. Then again, the greater sex drive among males entails that restraining the behavior of men is the more direct way of addressing some of the problematic forms of sex. In the United States, the vast majority of people arrested for sex crimes are men,[69] and probably this is true in most other societies as well. Even though the rules are enacted by predominantly male legislatures and enforced by predominantly male police, these rules seem to be directed mainly at restraining male sexuality. Probably because of the greater strength and inflexibility of male sexuality, it poses the main problem for society and hence is the target of more laws.

Cultural regulation is hardly the only influence of culture on sex. Remember, culture was supposed to be a benefit, not a problem. And culture does improve sex in many ways. Culture has provided human beings with many new opportunities to find sex partners: Dating services, classified advertisements in newspapers, and the Internet help people to find each other for sexual relationships. For those (mostly men) who want only sex, there is prostitution: Even a lonesome traveler who knows nobody in an entire city can usually find an "escort service" in the telephone book that will send over a woman to have sex with him for a fee. The Internet, pornographic books and magazines, cable television and sex videos, phone sex services, and other options provide sexual stimulation short of intercourse.

Meanwhile, culture has also offered technological innovations that reduce the risks of sex (such as condoms) or increase its pleasures (such as vibrators). The birth control pill has enabled millions of couples to enjoy sex without having to cope with unwanted pregnancies, and indeed one would be hard put to name any single technological innovation that has made a bigger contribution than the birth control pill to the well-being of the average healthy individual. Antibiotics enable people to recover from many sexually transmitted diseases, and on that basis modern lovers would be the envy of libertines throughout the ages.

Even the restrictions that culture has placed on sex are probably, in general, improvements to life, though sometimes at a high cost in short-term sexual pleasure. Cultures restrict sex so as to minimize the undesirable side effects, especially epidemics of sexually transmitted diseases and unwanted babies. Consistent with the emphasis on female erotic plasticity, cultures have aimed many of their efforts at suppressing female sexuality. This tendency has been decried by some feminists as a sign of antifemale prejudice and oppression of women. However, contrary to the female victimization view, the weight of evidence suggests that the suppression of female sexuality is largely enacted and maintained by women, who work together to restrain each other's sexuality because doing so brings significant economic benefits to women generally,[70] a pattern to which we shall return in chapter 7.

Let us turn now to consider the aims of sexual desire. No one will be surprised to hear that people want sex, but it is not easy to say more precisely what it is that people want. The intrinsic desire for sex is generally the desire for the pleasure of sexual acts. That pleasure can be found in genital stimulation. People desire the pleasure of that stimulation, and they also desire (although not exclusively) the peak of orgasm. There are, however, sexual desires that do not go all the way to orgasm or even genital stimulation, such as the desire to see someone naked. For example, many men like to watch films or shows with naked women even though they may do so in theaters where there is no opportunity for the men to receive genital stimulation (at least not without some risk of getting arrested). Some men even go out of their way to look under a woman's skirt to catch a glimpse of her panties. So the sex drive can motivate one to do and enjoy things that do not include genital stimulation. Orgasm is not even necessary for satisfaction, because some people (especially women) will sometimes report a high degree of satisfaction with sexual activity even when they do not have orgasms.

Some motivations (like hunger) seem to well up from inside, without needing any external stimulus to prompt them, whereas others (like aggression) seem to arise mainly in response to external circumstances. Sex shows both patterns. It would be absurd to dispute that sexual desire can be stimulated or diminished by what you see and hear. Every day, all over the world, people try to induce others to have sex with them, and to do this they often rely on sensory input, such as by wearing attractive clothing or makeup, saying certain things, and playing certain kinds of music. Even smells can play a major role: People use perfume and cologne to appeal to others, and they worry that various odors from their bodies will turn off potential lovers if not sufficiently concealed or disguised. The influence of odor on sexual response may be responsible for one widespread and puzzling pattern of sexual behavior, namely, that people mainly mate with members of their own race, even when they believe in racial equality and have ample opportunity to meet people from other races. Meanwhile, people who vow to maintain lifetime chastity generally try to surround themselves with nothing but homely, unadorned members of their own gender wearing shapeless clothes and bad haircuts, a pattern that again reflects a recognition that what you see around you can influence your level of sexual response.

The reality of external stimulation does not discredit the view of sex as an innate pattern, however. As we said, new theories of motivation treat it as a readiness to respond in a particular way if and when certain external circumstances arise. Much about sex fits this very well. When you encounter the right person in the right situation, your innately prepared response kicks into action, and you get turned-on sexually. You carry this readiness around with you, and so sexual arousal is a product of the meeting of inner and outer factors. On the other hand, external sources of stimulation are not always necessary either. Sexual desire can be stimulated from inside the person. Spontaneous sexual thoughts and sexual dreams, for example, can occur in the absence of external cues.

Sex is a want, not a need. People can live without sex. Some people go through their entire lives without any sexual activity, although such people are rare. Much more common, however, are people who will go for significant periods of time without sexual activity. Women in particular seem able to tolerate many months and even years of sexual abstinence, including no masturbation, without any visible signs of distress or harm.[71] It is rarer for men to forgo all sexual activity, although it can happen. More commonly, men maintain some level of sexual activity, generally falling back on masturbation when other outlets are unavailable. Thus, Kinsey[72] observed that some women may go through a period of several months between sexual relationships, and during that interval they will have no sexual activity of any kind—without regarding this to be a problem. When a man loses his sexual partner, he is likely to keep his orgasm count relatively steady by resorting to masturbation or other stopgaps (e.g., prostitutes). Men who really want to live without any sexual activity find the challenge daunting and, in the event, generally beyond their capabilities. For example, the Christian church, like many religions, has extolled the complete absence of sexual activity as the ideal way for a spiritual person to live. As this ideal came to be widely accepted, many Christian men despaired of ever reaching it and began to resort to desperate measures. Some eminent church leaders such as Origen (in the third century A.D.) took the extreme step of castrating themselves in the hope that the absence of sex organs would enable them to stop craving sex.[73] Eventually the church found it necessary to enact a law forbidding men to castrate themselves. Deprived of this admittedly extreme and dangerous option, Christian clergymen have always found complete celibacy an ideal that is mostly unattainable, and they have had to content themselves with varying degrees of sinful compromise.[74] The gender difference in success at celibacy is probably just one more illustration of the general pattern that men have a stronger sex drive than women.

Targets of sexual desire are typically well defined. The usual pattern is to desire a young adult of the opposite gender. Women are considerably more choosy than men. Studies asking things like "What is the minimum IQ someone would have to have in order to appeal to you as a possible one-night sex partner?" show that women have much higher standards than men.[75] Partly this reflects men's much greater difficulty of finding a partner, and men, as the beggars, cannot usually afford to be choosers. A couple of experiments were done in which various young men and women (on the research team) approached reasonably attractive strangers and invited them to have sex that night. The studies both found a huge gender asymmetry. Women who asked men for sex received positive answers about three quarters of the time. Men putting the exact same request to women got nowhere: Not a single "yes" answer was received by any man from any woman in two separate studies.[76]

Aggression

Social scientists have long debated whether aggression is an innate, instinctive tendency, as opposed to being entirely a learned pattern of behavior, and strong opinions have been expressed on both sides. Freud initially believed that aggression was caused by the thwarting of sexual desire, but after living through World War I he began to doubt that so much carnage and horrific violence could all be explained by sexual frustration. He therefore came to assert that sex and aggression were the two main drives in the human psyche. Similar conclusions have been reached via different methods by subsequent experts, such as Konrad Lorenz's observations on animals.[77] Meanwhile, other theorists have sharply disputed those conclusions, pointing to research such as the work of Albert Bandura, who showed how children learn aggression from observing and imitating others. From that perspective, aggression is a form of learned behavior rather than based on any innate tendency.

Considered more carefully, the two sides of the debate may both be missing the point, or at least missing each other's point. The fact that aggression can be learned does not rule out innate predispositions, because nature may prepare people to learn some things more readily than others. The apparent universality of the fact that young males are always the most aggressive members of every society suggests that some innate tendencies may underlie the learning. Boys play more roughly than girls, and young men commit more crimes, fight and kill more, and demolish more property than any other members of society. If anthropologists could identify some large cultures in which the bulk of violent crimes were committed by roving gangs of middle-aged women, for example, we might well have to scrap most of the assumptions about innate aggressive tendencies. But they don't.[78]

During my student days, I spent a year abroad, at the University of Heidelberg in Germany. Arriving late and not knowing the German system, I found myself without a dormitory room and unable to find anything I could afford near the university, and so I ended up living in one of the outer suburbs, which in Heidelberg meant far up one of the small mountains that surrounded the river valley where the city and university were located. I recall sitting at my desk one afternoon reading Freud's theories and looking out the window at the small neighborhood scene. In Germany at that time, the stores would deliver items to private homes. The family next door had apparently ordered a crate of soda pop, and the delivery people left it at the edge of the driveway. I didn't notice it at first, but I did see the 2-year-old son of those neighbors out by himself, exploring the world. He was all bundled up for winter, but no adult was in sight. Given our remote location, his parents probably just let him out to play, knowing he was safe. Well, he was safe, but the crate of soda pop wasn't safe from him. When he discovered it, he seemed fascinated by it, and he clearly had no idea what it was or why it was there.

After some experimentation, he learned that he could take one of the large glass bottles out of the crate, which was open on the top. He had to use both hands to carry it. He brought it over to the edge of the driveway, where there was about a 2-foot drop onto some stones. He carefully held it out and then dropped it. The glass shattered and the soda pop ran all around, fizzing and flowing, until it disappeared into the ground. I recall watching him stand there and stare at it. Then he toddled back to the crate, extracted another bottle, and repeated the experiment. Clearly, he enjoyed the spectacle of destruction, and more bottles met their demise in the same way before he lost interest and went calmly on to search for new wonders.

That image always came back to me in subsequent years whenever I had to lecture on Freud's theory of innate aggression. The theory holds that human beings are innately programmed to desire violent, aggressive activity. Smashing things or inflicting pain will bring pleasure and satisfaction to people. This theory was hotly debated on both sides for decades. Its opponents claimed that aggression was the result of sexual frustration or that all aggressive activity was learned from society. But I thought that the 2-year-old was clearly too young to have suffered so badly from sexual frustration, and although other frustrations were conceivable, he did not seem to have been frustrated or indeed upset in any way. Nor had society taught him to want to destroy his parents' newly purchased drinks. (If anything, the culture would try to teach him not to perform such costly stunts.) He simply seemed to get pleasure out of smashing the bottles.

To be sure, the child's seeming enjoyment is far from proof that people have an innate urge to smash things. Possibly he was just curious. Possibly the breaking glass reminded him of something he had seen on television, or perhaps he had seen a drunken uncle drop a glass and noticed that everyone laughed. Nonetheless, it has remained for me an illustration of one approach to aggression. The essence of this approach is that people have an inner craving for aggression and that they must satisfy this in one way or another. Smashing things is a direct source of pleasure.

Most theorizing about the aggressive instinct has followed more or less that same model, which was espoused by Freud in his later thinking. He thought that aggression is an innate desire or need and that it has to be satisfied in some way or another. People can satisfy this instinctual desire by wreaking destruction on material objects. Or they can satisfy it by inflicting harm on other people. Or they can satisfy it by turning it against themselves, in overt forms, such as suicide or masochism, or in milder ways, such as by developing a conscience that makes them feel guilty whenever they do something that violates their norms. But they have to satisfy it in some way. At least, that is the standard theory.

How does the aggressive drive work, according to that theory? It builds up from inside and needs to be discharged somehow. If the person fails to find some kind of aggressive outlet, the drive will become stronger and stronger, not unlike the way a hungry person will become hungrier hour after hour until she finds something to eat. The source of the drive is inside the psyche, and the outside world matters only for providing outlets.

But that kind of aggressive drive does not seem plausible any more. People do not seem to need to satisfy an endlessly refilled well of aggressive cravings. In particular, the emotional satisfaction called *catharsis* (more commonly known as "venting" your anger), which supposedly attends aggressive indulgences, does not seem to operate the way Freud thought. Freud said that people gain emotional satisfaction out of performing aggression (or even witnessing aggression), and as a result of this satisfaction they would be less likely to behave in an aggressive fashion afterward. Abundant evidence contradicts this. If anything, following an aggressive outburst, people tend to become more aggressive for a while. Two experts who reviewed the research on catharsis concluded that the whole idea is wrong and should be discarded.[79] More recent studies have found that even when people believe in catharsis, it fails to work for them.[80]

The crash and burn of the catharsis theory is important news. If people need to engage in aggression, then when that need is satisfied, they should be less aggressive than people for whom the need has not been satisfied. This is vital to the entire idea that a need is being satisfied. The analogy to hunger shows this: The body's need for food does steadily increase over time, but after people have had a good meal, their hunger is diminished, and they will be less likely to eat more food if it is offered to them, at least for a while. In the same way, satisfying the aggressive need should make the person less aggressive for a while. But it doesn't. More generally, people do not seem to suffer any ill effects from refraining from violent activity, and so it is hard to argue that people have an innate need to perform aggressive acts.

Thus, aggression may well be based in innate tendencies, but it does not seem to bubble up from inside the way hunger seems to do. Instead of thinking of a motivation as an inner need that builds up over time and demands some form of satisfaction, let us consider a different model. Suppose that some innate motivations are simply preprogrammed tendencies to respond in certain ways if certain kinds of situations arise. Until or unless those situations arise, there is no inclination to act in that way. Applied to aggression, this means that people are programmed to have the impulse to fight under certain conditions. The crucial difference is that, despite having innate aggressive tendencies, a person might in theory live his entire life without ever behaving aggressively—and yet might be fully satisfied. For example, if you always got everything you wanted, you might never feel the urge to behave aggressively. You could go your whole life without being aggressive, and this would be utterly fine. This is quite different from the standard "instinct" view of Freud and others, who believed that a person would have to let off aggression periodically, in order to remain sane.

This does not mean that aggression is a learned response to frustration. It may well be an innate, natural response. But it is a highly specific response nonetheless. The response only arises if it is triggered, and as long as nothing triggers it, there is no need for aggression. This is a radically different view of innate aggression from Freud's.

Put another way, aggression isn't a need. People don't have to have aggressive activity. Aggression may be an innate response tendency, so if a certain kind of provocation arises, people will react aggressively, but no aggression is required as long as those situations do not arise.

Remember my neighbor's little tyke letting the bottles drop and smash onto the rocks. Yes, the enjoyment of the aggression may have been quite natural. But if those bottles hadn't been delivered that day, he would have been just as happy doing something else, even something without any aggressive aspect. There was no built-up pressure from inner cravings that had to be satisfied by smashing those bottles—or, if the bottles had not been there, the craving would have had to come out in some other way, such as hitting his sister. The desire to smash the bottles only cropped up when he saw them and discovered what would be fun to do with them. Possibly his enjoyment was not based on aggression at all. Perhaps it was control: Smashing the bottles furnished the pleasant sensation of being able to produce an effect on his environment.

Hunger is a need, not a want, and that is why it provided such a poor model for motivation. Actually, it is probably both a need and a want, for people clearly want more food than they need to survive. The same may be said for some other needs, such as the need to belong and the urge for control. Yes, they are needs in the sense that people suffer pathological consequences if they are deprived for too long—but people also want more than they need. Aggression, however, is not a need in any sense, and people can live full, happy, healthy lives without ever engaging in aggression. Sex may be the same: a want, not a need. People can live full, healthy, happy lives without sex, and some of them do. If sex were a need, then people who did not have sex (or those who did not get enough sex) would show some kind of pathological outcome, such as illness. But research has not yet found any illnesses that are prevented by masturbation or intercourse.

If we understand aggression as an innate response tendency, how does it contribute to survival and reproduction, especially in a cultural animal? Aggression would seemingly have most value as a form of social influence. An aggressive creature can coerce others into doing what she wants. There are actually two forms of this. One is on a case-by-case basis: I want some of your dinner, so I attack you and make you let me have it. The other is a negotiation of the social hierarchy. Many social animals have a pack structure according to which higher-ranking animals, especially males, get better access to food, which helps survival, and sexual partners, which helps reproduction, than the lower-ranking animals. Aggression is a principal means of moving up in rank and thereby gaining the advantages that accrue.

As we move from social to cultural animals, however, a curious thing happens: The benefits of aggression diminish. They certainly do not disappear. Every day, all around the world, some individuals use force or the threat of force to get their way in some dispute with other people. And though culture prefers people to rise in the social hierarchy by nonaggressive means, such as by gaining education, inventing new products, or providing superior services, aggression has not passed out of the picture entirely. In fact, when most societies developed from warlike tribes into civilized systems, the fighters usually became the rulers. In some cases, the priests also took political power, but almost always the battlefield leaders became the political leaders too. The separation of military and political power is a relatively recent and still incomplete development: Many countries still suffer from actual or threatened military takeovers of civilian governments.

But the continued use of aggression in cultural societies may be just that: continued. Aggression is best suited to social but not cultural beings, and cultures strive to operate without aggression. In purely social beings, such as wolves, aggressiveness is an effective and even standard way of settling disputes and organizing the group's hierarchy. Aggression is far less effective and far less accepted in culture. In that sense, human aggression is a holdover from our evolutionary past as social beings.

Aggression is problematic (even inimical) to culture for multiple reasons. Probably the most important is the fact that culture typically organizes behaviors and interactions on a large, complex, integrated scale. Many different people are coordinated in order to accomplish tasks. This system greatly increases efficiency, so that the quality and quantity of what is produced are both improved. But violence disrupts the system and usually violates the basis for it. For example, most cultures negotiate the exchange of goods and services on the basis of money, but if people use force to take each other's money, then the incentive value of money is diminished. Why work hard to accumulate something if others will just take it away? And if people are killed by violence, then the system must replace them, which is costly and time-consuming, so the efficiency of the system is undermined.

Time perspectives reveal another reason that aggression is better suited to social than to cultural beings. When doing the research for my book on evil and violence, I was struck how scholars in one area after another had come to the same conclusion: Violent means of pursuing one's goals tend to bring short-term success but long-term failure. From terrorism and assassination to government repression to armed robbery and even spousal abuse, the resort to violence may bring a quick victory but in the long run, the perpetrators of violence fail. Terrorists may kill a leader whom they dislike, but in the long run they hardly ever get the government or system they want. Beating one's wife may win the current argument but in the long run the abuser does not get the kind of relationship he wants. Armed robbers may get their hands on a fair amount of cash quickly and sometimes easily, but few of them retire as wealthy, comfortable individuals—on the contrary, a career of crime is usually marked by longer and longer prison terms and an old age (if one lives that long) marked by few friends, little or no family, and little money.

The pattern of short-term gains and long-term costs is arguably one of the things that culture is specifically suited to thwart. Social beings, like zebras and apes, live in the immediate present,[81] whereas cultures and their citizens can organize the present based on improving the future. Culture improves life in part by providing for the future, so that crises are reduced.

Thus, perhaps, aggressive motivations reached their peak in the social stage of evolution, and they linger as problems in cultural animals. In practice, the process of cultural development involves putting more and more restraints on aggression. All known cultures have at least moral rules that prohibit members of the culture from killing each other.[82] As society evolves from the rule of morality to the rule of law, the prohibitions become more specific and complicated, sometimes delineating precise, exceptional circumstances in which killing is permitted, such as in self-defense, by police officers when there is a clear danger, or (sometimes, such as up until quite recently in Texas) when a man finds his wife having sex with another man. Sometimes, states reserve the right to execute criminals after a well-defined set of criteria and procedures has been satisfied.

Nor is killing the only target of cultural restraint. People are prohibited from hitting others, and increasingly even using corporal punishment to discipline children has become prohibited. Verbal aggression is less regulated, but sometimes people who believe that others have spoken or written derogatory things about them can sue their detractors and recover compensation in money. Willful damage to property is also restrained by law and public opinion, so the modern citizen cannot even act aggressively toward many inanimate objects.

With other motives, I have tried to indicate how culture improves the prospects for attaining satisfaction. Aggression is different, and probably most cultures would operate more smoothly and effectively if they could eliminate aggression entirely (setting aside the question of defending the community in war). It seems unlikely that the aggressive instinct was increased, extended, or retooled in the evolution of the cultural animal. It remains as a holdover from our evolutionary past as social beings, and when humans revert to acting more like social than cultural beings—such as when they are oriented toward the immediate present and having a conflict or dispute with someone else—they still sometimes turn to aggression to get their way. But the most important link between aggressive motives and cultural life is culture's attempts to restrain and minimize aggression.

Nature gave us aggressive impulses, but it also gave us the capacity to restrain ourselves and to learn (via socialization) cultural rules about when and how to aggress versus when to hold ourselves in check. People have plenty of angry and violent impulses, but most of these are stifled by inner, psychological restraints. The proximal cause of aggression is therefore usually some breakdown in these inner controls, which allows the impulse to erupt in violent action. Factors that undermine self-control—alcohol intoxication, strong emotion, disregard of the future, a reduced sense of personal responsibility, and the like—tend to make aggression more likely.

Self-control is one of the centrally important developments in cultural animals, as will be discussed in greater detail in chapter 6. For present purposes, the key point is that human evolution probably involved little or no improvement in the aggressive motivations but plenty of increase in the human individual's capacity to override and restrain those motivations.

The view that aggression is somehow a product of socialization—that cultures teach their boys and sometimes girls to be aggressive and that without such teachings there would be no aggression—was a lovely but implausible fantasy. Does anyone really think that American culture has something to gain by making its young people more violent?

Recent work by Richard Tremblay has suggested that the main impact of learning is to restrain aggression.[83] Tremblay's data have led to the somewhat startling conclusion that the age of maximum aggressive tendencies is actually in early childhood, perhaps at age two or three (different measures yield slightly different peaks), not adolescence as has usually been assumed. The only reason 2-year-olds get less press coverage for their violent activities than young adults is that, being small and weak and generally not permitted to roam the streets at night unchaperoned, they do less damage. As one sign of toddler disposition, Tremblay's observations of kids in daycare have found that a shocking 25% of social interactions between 2-year-olds contain some degree of physical aggression. Even the wildest groups of teenage boys or hardened criminals stop far short of that. The implication is that kids start off with an ample stock of aggressive impulses, and under the influence of socializing agents (parents, teachers, and the rest) they gradually learn to restrain them. Put another way, aggression is motivated by nature and restrained by culture.

Once I heard Tremblay at dinner after he had given a talk on his research, and he made what has been for me a persuasive and telling analogy. His point was to reject the old idea that society teaches aggression and to propose instead that children naturally seek to become aggressive while society tries to teach them restraint. He said this was not unique to aggression. Look at walking, he says. Children do not need their parents to teach them to walk, which would entail that if a parent were absent-minded, the children might remain on all fours for their entire lives. No, children eagerly acquire the capacity to walk, and the role of parents is mostly to teach restraint, such as not running toward the street, near obstacles, on the stairs, or with scissors. Nature says "go" and culture teaches "stop": Far from being a peculiar quirk of aggression, Tremblay thought this was the general pattern.

Thus, the process of growing up and being socialized is one of acquiring more and more capacity to restrain one's aggression. Culture finds only limited uses, and many problems, in the natural human inclinations toward violence. Culture makes much more use of nature's gift of the capacity to control and restrain ourselves. As we shall see in chapter 7, the strongest influence of culture on aggression has been to limit and restrain aggression.

Nurturance, Generativity, Helping

Another cluster of motivations makes people want to help others. Undoubtedly, many people do get some satisfaction from helping others and from providing care to young, vulnerable ones. One sign we have used to infer that people enjoy something is that they choose leisure activities based on it. Although relatively few games or films revolve around helping, pastimes such as gardening and pet ownership do show that people seem to enjoy exerting themselves to care for small living things and to help them grow.

I have chosen to treat nurturance, generativity, and helping as a separate set of motives, but they do seem to have much in common with the need to belong. Thinkers who want to keep the number of human motives to a minimum could probably get by with lumping these with belongingness. Whether we regard these as extensions of the need to belong or as distinct motives in their own right is not all that important. The important thing is to recognize their prominence in human nature.

The most common and widespread pattern of helping, especially across different species, involves caring for the young. Human babies are essentially helpless and incompetent, and without extensive care, none of them would survive to adulthood. Caring is, however, not elicited by such pragmatic, rational arguments but rather by a set of innately prepared mechanisms that make adults want to care for children, especially their own, and derive satisfaction or pleasure from doing so. There even seem to be some biological mechanisms, such as physiological responses to the sound of a baby crying, that prompt the adult to want to do something for the child (and not just to shut up that infernal racket).

True, some species seem largely indifferent to their young, and in some the adults (especially males) will even kill or eat their offspring. Most social species do, however, show some patterns of taking care of newborns. Probably this basic and widespread motivation underwent some expansion in the formation of the human psyche, so that human helpfulness is far more extensive and malleable than the helpfulness of other animals.

Indeed, even the impulse to care for infants has some distinctively human features. One is found in the willingness to raise someone else's children. Most biological and evolutionary thinkers have emphasized that the competition to pass along one's genes entails that animals are generally loath to care for young that are not biologically related to them. In a few species, an individual will help raise nieces and nephews, but there is still nothing like the eagerness in our own species to adopt children. Au contraire, the biological thinkers emphasize that most animals maintain a ruthless vigilance to avoid being duped into raising any offspring but their own. In particular, males are seen to employ extra care to prevent their females from becoming impregnated by other males, so that the male does not end up devoting his resources to providing for the other male's offspring. Sometimes males will actively seek to kill the offspring of others; for example, when a male lion finds a female mate, he will try to kill any cubs she has from previous fathers. And the reasoning is sound: If nature has programmed you to pass along your own genes, you want to put your resources and efforts only into taking care of youngsters who share those genes. All else is wasted.

In our own species, however, the situation is markedly different. Many modern citizens spend small fortunes simply to adopt a baby, even one from another race. Others try hard to do a good job as stepparents, and even if stepparents on average are not as loving and supportive as genetic parents, it is nonetheless true that many adults knowingly, even cheerfully, devote considerable time, effort, money, and other limited resources into taking care of children who are not theirs. And if one broadens the scope, such as by including a willingness among nonparents to vote for and pay taxes that support schools or daycare, or the willingness of people to donate money to international organizations that promise to help children on other continents, the human motivation to nurture children other than one's own is quite remarkably widespread. To be sure, sexual possessiveness and a preference for one's own offspring have hardly vanished from the human psyche, and there are ample signs that people do care more deeply and reliably for their own biological offspring than for those of others. But there is also undeniably a profound and widespread willingness to care for the children of others.

Why? A simple answer is that this reflects the greater plasticity of cultural beings. The motivation to nurture young animals is perhaps more flexible in homo sapiens than in other, less cultural species, and so it can be redirected toward children who are not one's own biological offspring.

There is probably a second important answer to the "Why?" question, however. The sense of self that a cultural animal wants to pass along is a cultural creation, and so in an important sense people can replicate themselves with someone else's genetic offspring. By adopting a child, you can pass along your values, teach someone what is important, expose the child to what you think is good and rewarding in life, and so forth. That is a crucial part of the appeal of adopting: Your cultural identity can live on into the next generation, even if your biological identity is not part of the formula. We identify ourselves with our cultural identity as much as with our genetic makeup, and perhaps more, and so passing that along to a new generation is appealing. Even becoming a "big brother" or "big sister," a kind of mentor to underprivileged kids, is a form of cultural reproduction: You want to show the youngster that if she adopts your values and approach to life, she can turn out like you.

The willingness and even desire to nurture people other than your own biological children reflects an important change in our species and probably contributed to enabling us to be cultural animals. It fosters ties that go beyond merely blood ties and helps the culture perpetuate itself. Indeed, a cultural animal almost by definition must accomplish much more learning, over a longer period of time, than a merely social animal, because of the complexity and change of culture. If your mother were the only one who cared for you and taught you anything, you would probably not be a competent member of society. Most likely, you have learned vital skills and information from dozens if not hundreds of people.

One important form of helpfulness outside of parenting involves helping younger people get started in your own line of work. The Freudian revisionist Erik Erikson proposed the concept of *generativity* to refer to the motivation to help the next generation come into its own,[84] and he thought this drive emerged after the adult has achieved some fulfillment of his own ambitions and strivings. In a professional career, for example, the young adult seeks to gain success and recognition for self. As the years go by and some amount of this has been accomplished, the middle-aged adult may begin mentoring younger people.

Generativity may be a refinement of the basic nurturing impulse. If so, it is one that seems especially well suited to a cultural creature. One of the hallmarks of culture is that socialization takes much longer, and so members of culture need help to learn their roles well into adulthood. An impulse among older, established adults to help young adults get started would be quite different from what most other species do, but getting help from older adults is certainly valuable for many young adult members of modern cultures. Older adults find it personally satisfying to mentor a young person in the same field, and there is not much sign that other, non-cultural species are capable of that satisfaction. Either nature changed us to add that form of satisfaction, or (more likely) it indicates that nurturance has become culturalized. In either case, it shows a special and adaptive side of the cultural animal.

Comparing ourselves with other species confirms the importance of teaching and mentoring for cultural animals. Although other primates sometimes mimic each other and learn about the world from each other, there is remarkably little intentional teaching. Michael Tomasello has noted the limitations in what other primates do.[85] For example, a mother might roll a log over and eat the bugs underneath, and later the baby chimp does the same. But it is not really learning the procedure from its mother: It is merely learning that bugs can be found under logs. Tomasello and his colleagues proved this in a series of clever experiments. In these studies, they demonstrated to human and chimpanzee children an inefficient way of getting something. The human children repeated the inefficient procedure, because they were truly copying what the model did, but the chimps quickly went over to the easier way of getting the same result.

Indeed, one of the major disappointments of research with chimpanzees has been that although people can teach sign language to individual chimps, the chimps do not seem to have any notion of teaching it to each other so they can communicate.[86] In contrast, when sign language first became available to human beings, deaf children picked it up rapidly and then improved on it and used it among themselves.[87] More broadly, however much chimps learn from humans, they do not seem to teach it to other chimps. The mentoring impulse seems to be lacking in noncultural species.

Helping is another pattern common in humans. In social psychology, two factions have bitterly debated the issue of whether helping is ultimately selfish. Robert Cialdini and his colleagues have shown that helping makes people feel better,[88] and in fact people are less helpful when helping will not make them feel better. For example, in one clever study, they showed that sad people will help if they think their mood can improve, but if they think that a side effect of a drug has made them unable to improve their current mood, they are less likely to help. On the other side, Daniel Batson and his group have showed that people will still sometimes help when there is no personal benefit involved, especially if they feel some bond of similarity with the person they are helping.[89]

The debate has gone on and on, with a steady stream of research findings on both sides. In my view, such a pattern of going in circles is often a sign that the basic question has been wrongly phrased. The debate has focused on whether people help in order to feel better. To me, the crucial fact is that helping does actually make people feel better. That is a positive aspect of human nature. We are psychologically constructed in a way that we find it satisfying and pleasant to lend help to others. The urge to help is deeply rooted in the psyche and may be a sign of these innately prepared motivational patterns. In other words, the human psyche is designed to make people want to help each other, in a way that seems to go beyond what is found in noncultural species.

Nearly all writers have assumed that nurturance toward children is stronger in females than in males. Indeed, nurturance toward loved ones generally is probably stronger in women, who not only care for babies but also for aging parents, sick family members, and the like. The consensus around this may have deterred researchers from bothering to test it, and indeed many studies of parental care or nurturance simply use mothers and fail to include fathers. There is some evidence that young boys and girls are about equally interested in caring for babies, but among older children the girls show more interest. For example, one careful study concluded that up until age 4, there is no gender difference in responsiveness to a baby, and children favor smaller children of their own gender.[90] From 4 to 6 years of age, there is still no gender difference in interest in babies, although both boys and girls respond better to girl babies than to boy babies. Starting at about age 7 and for the rest of life, females respond to babies more than males do. Although this could be interpreted as greater nurturance among females, these researchers cited findings that boys simply direct their nurturant impulses toward a broader range of targets, such as animals. Moreover, although girls and women provide direct care to babies, boys and men show concern by being protective, watchful, and helpful.[91]

Why do girls and women show more interest in caring for babies? There are several "obvious" answers, including that biology has programmed women to do this; men are pushed aside by women or socialized by society to refrain from what is seen as women's activity; or society oppresses women by forcing them to perform child care. Across many species (especially monogamous mammals), when females are able to rear infants without male help, they do so, and they only accept male help when the childcare tasks are beyond what females can do alone.[92] The latter is the case among human beings, and economic factors are important. In cultures where women work outside the home and earn money, fathers provide some direct care to the children, whereas in cultures where women mainly stay home and take care of children, fathers are much less involved.[93]

Some gender differences in child care fit the evolutionary theory about *paternity uncertainty.* A woman knows for certain that the children who come out of her body are hers, but a man can never be certain. The perennial issue of paternity uncertainty is reflected in the long tradition of jokes about it, such as the one in which a dying woman calls her husband to her bedside and tells him she has a terrible confession. "You know how we have ten children, and all of them have dark hair and dark eyes, except for Susie, who is blonde and blue-eyed," begins the woman. The man leaps to a worried conclusion: "Are you telling me that Susie is not my child?" "No, no," says the woman. "Susie is yours. But the other nine . . . "

Cross-culturally, variations in child care seem to fit that pattern. When promiscuity is culturally accepted and hence males have ample reason to doubt the paternity of their wives' children, the men often end up lavishing their efforts on their sisters' children (who are related to the men by blood, which is to say, genes) rather than on their wives' children. Among the Navaho, for example, a brother provides for his sisters' children and is their principal disciplinarian. In contrast, when adultery is relatively rare and so fathers can have higher confidence that their wives bear only their children, fathers direct their caring and providing efforts toward their own children.[94]

Other patterns of helping fit the view that people are biologically programmed to help in certain ways but that culture can work with those impulses and redirect them to some extent. Natural selection would favor those who help their relatives, especially younger ones, and across all species the majority of helping is directed toward relatives. Among human beings, helping is sometimes directed more widely, even to the extreme of propelling Americans to donate money to aid malaria victims in Africa or other far-off recipients whom the helper does not know, to whom she has no relation, and whom she will never meet. Some helping toward strangers in a group may be biologically mediated insofar as people have been selected to operate on a norm of reciprocity: If you help someone, eventually that person may repay your kindness by helping you, which might improve your chances for survival or reproduction. But human philanthropy is generally not directed toward anyone who will be in a likely position to return the favor, and so in such instances the natural impulse has apparently undergone significant transformation by culture.

The pattern of helping relatives suggests that helping is linked to belongingness. This seems confirmed by helping among nonkin, for people are most helpful toward those who are linked to them in some way. In experimental studies, people provide most help to those whom they perceive as similar to themselves[95] or who belong to the same group.[96] In fact, the very idea that belongingness is beneficial turns in part on the assumption of help. If members of a group did not help each other, there would be far fewer advantages to belonging, and the need to belong might not have evolved to be so strong and pervasive.

Helping and nurturance may be innately motivated, but they still appear to be response tendencies rather than needs. Plenty of studies have shown that an adult will offer help to someone who asks for it or seems to need it, but none of these findings indicates that the helpers had any drive or need to give help, which would have demanded finding another recipient if that one had not shown up. In the same way, adults and especially women may respond to an infant's crying with a hormonal surge and a feeling of wanting to care for the child, but again this is a response to a specific circumstance rather than an independent need.

As with aggression and belongingness, the crucial test is whether a person could in principle live a happy and fulfilled life without helping others, assuming that the person never encountered a situation in which somebody needed help. The evidence is clear that people do need to belong, and it looks like they do not need to aggress, but there is little clear evidence about helping. At present, there is no indication that people suffer harm or even distress as a result of not giving help, as long as they do not encounter anyone who needs help.

The evidence is somewhat murkier with regard to caring for children, however. One could make a case that people do have a drive to care for children, even before they have children. Indeed, many people try to have children, and it is quite plausible that one main reason is that they desire to care for them. Some people go to considerable expense, risk, and inconvenience to do so, such as by taking fertility drugs, undergoing surgery to increase fertility, or adopting children.

Against such arguments, one might point to the fact that nature has seemingly relied more on sexual desire than on reproductive wishes to ensure reproduction, for people want sex far more than they seem to want children. Certainly, most intercourse in the modern world is accompanied by precautions to make sure no children are conceived. Moreover, as birth control technology and changed attitudes have made it increasingly viable for people to refrain from having children, there has been a steady rise in voluntary childlessness. Even people who do have children have far fewer than their ancestors had, all of which suggests that any inner drive to have children is fairly weak. Conventional wisdom has long insisted that women could not be fulfilled without motherhood, but there is reason to suspect that this commonsense claim was more an ideological ploy foisted on women due to society's needs rather than a universal principle deriving from any true inner need that is innate to women.[97] Childless women are on the whole happier than those who become mothers,[98] which is a strong point against the view that women need to have children to be fulfilled.

In short, it seems safe to conclude that people want to care for children when they have them, but it is far less certain whether (and, if so, to what extent) people craved the experience of caring for children before the children were there to stimulate those cravings. Women exceed men in providing care directly to babies and children, whereas men surpass women in providing help to other members of the community. Both men and women show a preference for helping relatives over helping strangers, though, and in a similar fashion they help those similar to themselves more than those who are different. Generativity is perhaps the most specifically cultural form of helping, and it entails that middle-aged or older adults serve as mentors to young adults who may follow in their footsteps or have other things in common with them. These patterns suggest that the helping motivations are linked to the need to belong.

Culturally Created Motives

Nature may have programmed human beings to want certain things, but it is safe to assume that human wanting has generally been culturalized. To some extent, this consists of having culture channel and shape the basic wants; for example, every known society seeks to exert some control over sexual behavior and often this is accomplished by attempting to channel people's sexual desires. But in addition to this shaping and channeling, culture probably has to create some new motivational patterns. All cultures and societies offer certain kinds of rewards, especially ones that are invested with meaning by the culture.

The central issue involves the clash over self-interest. Nature makes each creature selfish, but culture functions best if people will sometimes set aside their selfish wishes and impulses in order to do what is best for everyone, that is, for the collective. To accomplish this, culture finds it an effective strategy to alter the shape of people's motivations, so that they want what will benefit the cultural system. To the extent that culture can make people want to do things that will be best for the culture, the culture will flourish.

Most likely, culture cannot create motivations out of nothing, and so culture has to work with the raw material of human nature. Cultural motivations are therefore generally rooted in natural and social motivations. By combining and refining these, the culture can get people to desire the rewards that the culture offers, and in this way the culture can organize people's behavior.

Money is a good example of this process. It is highly unlikely that natural selection instilled a burning desire for flat, round bits of metal or rectangular strips of colored paper. Yet people do want money, and they spend quite a big chunk of their lives and energies in trying to get money. The desire for money did not appear out of thin air, however. Culture made money a vital means to satisfy the basic desires for food, shelter, and other amenities. Money could make a person more appealing to potential mates, since it constituted status and resources for a man seeking to attract women, and in the form of a dowry it made a woman more marriageable. Money offered ways to control one's world.

In such ways, the cultural motives seem based on the natural, innate, and social ones. That does not mean there is no difference, however, and it is still possible to tell the natural and cultural motives apart, based roughly on what it is that the person ultimately wants. Language and meaning are important hallmarks of cultural activity, and so they can be used as rough criteria for spotting the influence of culture. Wanting things that take the form of meanings is a reasonable definition of cultural motivations. Animals, at least, do not base their wants on meanings and language, and so those wants are more distinctively human. A determined reductionist can perhaps see some animal behavior patterns as reflecting guilt, virtue, and self-esteem, for example, but such interpretations are debatable, and the discrepancy between guilt in humans and guilt in animals is much more substantial than is the case with sex, aggression, belongingness, and control—in all of which the ultimate satisfaction pursued by humans may be essentially similar to what other animals pursue.

How Culture Shapes What People Want

Cultural control of motivation has been a thorny and controversial issue. Undoubtedly, social influences can shape people's wants to some degree—after all, the multibillion-dollar advertising industry is based on the premise that human desires can be stimulated and altered by well-crafted messages. And certainly people learn to want things, such as good books and pantyhose and laptop computers, that are not found in nature and indeed have only been sought under circumscribed historical conditions.

Then again, cultures and socialization programs have often failed in attempts to control human motivation. Many governments, especially authoritarian ones, would find their tasks considerably easier if they could direct their populations to want certain things and not to want others. The persistence of homosexuality despite severe and often brutal societal condemnation is just one illustration of the limits to what culture can accomplish.

There is a good reason that cultural motivations typically build on natural motivations. It is much easier to extend and elaborate the basic, innate human wants than to go against them. Even the desire for laptop computers, those seemingly ultracultural creations, can be linked to natural motives: After all, they improve the person's ability to organize and store information and communicate with other people, and many owners use them to access online pornography, and so the desire for them may well have roots in the basic drives for control, belongingness, and sex. Promoting goals that go against natural motivations is more difficult. Most of the world governments now accept that widespread condom use will reduce the spread of HIV/AIDS, but condoms are perceived to reduce sexual pleasure and are therefore a difficult sell. In 2002, the president of Kenya, Daniel arap Moi, called on all the citizens of his country to abstain from sex for two years, in order to check the spread of AIDS. Although his plan would certainly help his society get this disease under control, its chances of success were slim insofar as it ran contrary to sexual motivations. Arap Moi was soon out of office, and his national celibacy plan was forgotten.

Nature has perhaps prepared the human being for culture by instilling a high degree of plasticity, including motivational plasticity. People are able to acquire new motivations, in the sense of having their original set of desires shaped and transformed into radically new forms. Human beings are good at acquiring extrinsic motivations and these can even seem to turn into intrinsic ones. Thus money is the quintessential extrinsic motivator, insofar as people want money for the sake of what it can buy them—but people can come to want money for its own sake. A miser loses sight of what money can do, preferring to accumulate it for its own sake without ever spending it.

In essence, culture capitalizes on the plasticity of human wanting in order to get people to do what the culture needs. Culture uses meanings to do this. By defining certain activities as valued—using prestige, money, and other rewards to lend substance to those values—it can make people aspire to do what is good for the culture. A culture that values education, invention, and philanthropy will succeed better than a culture that values ignorance, idleness, and profligacy.

Language and Talk

Because culture is constructed out of meaning and therefore relies on language, a language instinct would be a powerful aid to a cultural animal. Language is the best medium for communication and the sharing of information, which are hallmarks of culture. Language enables people to engage in systematic logical reasoning and calculation, without which consciousness would lose much of its value. Language enables people to form mental representations of the past and future as well as of other places, thereby freeing people's minds from what they can see around them at that minute. Indeed, language is a crucial requirement in the design of a cultural animal. A member of a culture has to be capable of using language, which requires a complex vocal apparatus that can make precisely tailored sounds and a brain that can handle grammar and vocabulary, and should also desire to learn and use language.

Certainly, people seem highly motivated to learn and use language. Language use is a universal feature found in all human cultures and all minimally competent members of them. Even cultures that never had contact with the wider world or modern culture have all had languages. Children learn language without needing to be required to do so. Parents rarely have the sense of having to force the child to learn to speak the way they might, for example, have to teach etiquette (waiting in line, taking turns, table manners) in the face of severe resistance. Children's active participation in learning language is reflected in the overregularization of patterns, which clearly goes against what other speakers do and what their parents and teachers teach. Thus, a child may initially learn to say *threw* as the past tense of *throw*, but after grasping the rule that the past tense is made by adding *-ed* to a word, the child will go through a phase of saying *throwed* as the past tense form. What impresses researchers about this is that the child initially did it correctly and then changed to do it the wrong way, which was almost certainly not learned from others (because other people do not say "throwed") and hence represents the child using a rule to override what it learned by imitation. When my own daughter went through this stage, we gently tried to correct her and prodded her to use the irregular verb forms, but she firmly rejected those suggestions: "My way sounds more beautiful," she declared.

Although language is clearly learned, the impetus to learn it could be innate, as its universality suggests.[99] Some writers have even spoken of a *language instinct*, implying that there is an innate drive to speak and communicate.[100]

But is a language instinct plausible? When discussing the limits of what nature could accomplish, we saw the importance of continuity: Evolution can alter structures readily, such as by increasing or diminishing them or refocusing them, but it cannot easily create wholly new structures. Some other species communicate, but none of them seem to have created language in the full-fledged sense in which humans use it. Most likely, therefore, the so-called language instinct is actually an elaboration of several more basic drives. These include curiosity, which is the desire for information, because language greatly increases one's ability to obtain information and to understand one's world. They also include belongingness, because language greatly improves a human being's ability to form and maintain interpersonal relationships.

The relevance of language to belongingness was highlighted by Robin Dunbar,[101] who proposed that people developed language precisely for the purpose of expanding their social circle. Apes maintain close relationships by grooming each other, which is a polite way of saying they regularly spend an hour or two picking the bugs off each other. That's their main way of showing affection and spending time together. As Dunbar notes, however, it's not very efficient: If you spend an hour picking bugs off one fellow, you may feel close, but there are only so many hours in the day, and you have to eat and sleep and do a few other things too, so the number of close partners you can have will be severely limited. In contrast, human beings can achieve and maintain intimacy by talking about themselves and their experiences, which is considerably faster. Moreover, one person can talk to several others at a time, whereas grooming is inevitably one-to-one, and so you can update your bonds to several partners at once. Even if we do not accept that this is the main or primary function of language, it is probably an important one, and in that sense the evolution of our species as language users may have been a good way to connect with others.

Indeed, Dunbar has phrased his thesis in the wonderfully startling form of saying that gossip was the purpose of language evolution. He notes that much of human speech is devoted to gossip, in the sense of telling stories about oneself and each other. To him, this indicates the goal of social connection. It seems to me, however, that gossip has value for a cultural animal that goes beyond maintaining social connections.[102] Gossip often consists of stories about how other people's actions have violated social norms, brought them trouble or woe, or perhaps brought about unexpected positive outcomes. Gossip thus may serve an extremely valuable function for learning. The cultural animal lives in a world full of events and circumstances for which her biological programming is inadequate, and so one might always encounter a difficult choice and not know how to act. Gossip tells the cultural animal how others have acted in unusual and important situations—what choices they made and how these turned out. I think Dunbar could be right that gossip is one of the driving forces behind language evolution, but biology may have impelled us to gossip as a way of gaining useful information about the consequences of possible actions.

Control is another innate motivation that may have contributed to the so-called language instinct. Language contributes greatly to control, in multiple ways. For one thing, language enables people to codify and share their knowledge. Obviously, all the scientific mastery of the world would have been extremely difficult to accumulate without language. For another thing, people use language to communicate what they want. My daughter seemed most eager to learn to speak because that way she could communicate what she wanted (speaking is far more effective than grunting or crying), and she seemed rather shocked to discover that even when she was able to tell Mama what she wanted, she would not always get it. It seemed that she had somehow believed that if only she could make her needs clear, Mama would satisfy them all, and language seemed the perfect solution so that she would never be disappointed or frustrated again. Children's eager, aggressive use of language to gain control can be seen in how children who are learning to speak spontaneously recite the names of items in their surroundings, how they narrate their own actions (which helps to bring one's behavior under conscious, linguistic control), and later in the months-long stream of "why?" questions.[103]

Did human evolution include a heightening of impulses toward communication and understanding? This question is difficult to answer, because there is a confound. That is, human beings certainly do communicate and understand far better than any other known species—but this does not absolutely indicate that we have a stronger motivation to do those things. Nature did give us a vastly increased capacity for both language and understanding, and so possibly our great successes in those spheres are due to the rise in ability, not motivation. But it seems a reasonable guess that nature created us as cultural animals by making us want to speak and learn, not just making us able to do so.

Comparisons between chimpanzees and deaf human beings are revealing. Both chimps and humans are capable of learning sign language, and both chimps and deaf humans find it difficult to master vocal speech. But there is a remarkable difference in the eagerness to master it. Deaf human beings are clearly driven to master sign language. They pick it up quickly and share it with each other. For the chimps, it seems to remain a peculiarity. They can learn to use it when human beings pressure them to do so, but they do not seem interested in teaching it to other chimps, and even when they meet another chimp who knows it, they don't use it much.[104] This discrepancy suggests that human beings are far more motivated than other animals to master and use language.

Thus, language is classified as a culturally created motivation because language only exists with culture, and so the existence of culture is a prerequisite for the desire to learn language. Language is an essential ticket to participation in culture, and as such it is almost indispensable for human survival and reproduction. A person who cannot speak or understand language is doomed to remain on the fringes of human existence, with severely restricted opportunities to find a mate for reproduction or even to obtain the necessities for survival. If culture is the main strategy our species has developed for survival and reproduction, language is essential to take part.

Self-Esteem

Some degree of selfhood can be found in animals, especially social animals, but life in a cultural society demands a great deal more of the self. Each person has an identity that marks a place in the social matrix of relationships. A cultural society also presents the individual with meaningful choices to make, and the self has to make them, which means that the self must have an elaborate structure of values and priorities, as well as knowledge about itself and its capabilities.[105]

A failure, for example, presents the individual with the dilemma of whether to give up or try again, and self-esteem turns out to be an important guide to making such decisions.[106] The expansion of self, and the correspondingly greater importance of self-esteem, are thus key steps in the construction of the cultural animal.

Self-esteem is an evaluation of the self, consisting of thoughts and feelings about how good the self is. It can be distinguished from public esteem, which refers to how other people feel about you, but in reality self-evaluation and evaluation by others are so deeply intertwined that the distinction does not carry much weight, and for present purposes I shall use them as interchangeable. As a motivation, the crucial point is that people seek and desire a positive evaluation of themselves, both in their own minds and in the minds of others.

Self-esteem is a promising vehicle by which culture can influence people's behavior. For this to succeed, culture must be able to set some of the criteria on which self-esteem is based. If people want to think well of themselves, they must do things that the culture values.

The desire for a favorable opinion of self is one of the most consistent and broadest assumptions in social psychology. People engage in a remarkably wide range of activities to sustain these favorable views. They selectively remember their successes while forgetting and downplaying their failures; they blame their failures on others while taking full (or even excessive) credit for their successes; they seek opportunities to shine while avoiding situations that risk loss of esteem.[107] They are highly sensitive to whether other people are watching them, and they carefully manage their public behavior so as to make a good impression and win the esteem of others.[108] When criticized or insulted, they often lash out at whoever has impugned their good name.[109]

In the 1980s, America "discovered" self-esteem as a promising key to success in life. A state commission in California led the way by exploring ways to solve California's social problems through enhancing self-esteem. Everywhere, schools developed programs to boost self-esteem among children. Trophies and awards proliferated, in many cases going to all participants out of fear that not getting a trophy would reduce somebody's self-esteem. Some sports programs stopped keeping scores in games, so that there would not be any official losers.

The vast amount of research information about self-esteem can be summarized with two succinct conclusions, one favorable to self-esteem, the other less so. The more disparaging conclusion is that high self-esteem does not confer a great many benefits. The California experts who were convened to summarize research findings linking self-esteem to various personal and social problems such as addiction, crime, school failure, and teen pregnancy came up with a very discouraging outlook: Self-esteem was at best weakly correlated with most of these problems, and in many cases self-esteem was the result rather than the cause. Thus, if you are a drug-addicted, pregnant teenage school dropout with no job, your low self-esteem may be a result of seeing what a mess your life is, rather than having been a cause of your problems. The school programs designed to boost kids' self-esteem succeeded in boosting self-esteem, but those boosts did not lead to improvements in school performance or good behavior. Newer, more extensive reviews of published findings point to the same dismal conclusion: Boosting self-esteem does not really produce many palpable benefits.[110]

The other conclusion, however, is that the desire to think well of oneself—the self-esteem *motivation*—is widespread and powerful. Much of what people do is concerned with maintaining a favorable opinion of themselves and making a good impression on others, which is closely linked with impressions of self. People have many strategies for boosting and maintaining self-esteem, and they use these often. Thus, they take credit for success but refuse the blame for failure. They compare themselves against goals or competitors that are chosen so as to afford a favorable outcome. They present themselves to others in ways that cast the facts in the most favorable light possible, and they sometimes ignore the facts if they think they can get away with doing so. They place higher value on attributes they have than on ones they lack. And so forth. Even Freud's defense mechanisms—one of his most popular set of ideas—appear to be aimed more at sustaining a favorable image of self than in regulating sex and aggression.[111]

These two conclusions raise a seeming paradox, however. Why would people care so much about something that confers so few benefits? After all, the psyche's various functions are aimed at helping the person to survive and prosper, and neither natural nor cultural evolution would presumably foster a strong drive to attain something that was inherently useless. If self-esteem has any benefits, it is a small improvement in initiative (such as being willing to criticize the group or to try again after failure) and a somewhat larger contribution to feeling good (people with high self-esteem are generally happier than those with low). Neither of these outcomes is likely to produce much in the way of palpable improvements in survival or reproduction, so why would nature or culture make people so motivated to preserve and increase their self-esteem?

One might try to answer this question by pointing to emotions. Gains in self-esteem nearly always bring pleasant emotions, whereas losses in self-esteem are generally associated with distress and dejection. But that answer is hardly satisfactory, because it immediately raises the question of why the emotional system should be so responsive to self-esteem if self-esteem is unimportant.

The most satisfactory answer, provided by Mark Leary and his colleagues,[112] is that self-esteem may be largely useless itself but serves as a valuable internal measure of something that is quite important—in their analysis, belongingness. As we have already seen, belongingness offers powerful advantages to the individual person in terms of health, happiness, and improved chances of succeeding at the most basic biological tasks of survival and reproduction. Leary et al. compare self-esteem to the gas gauge on a car, which contributes almost nothing to the successful functioning of the car, but which does provide the operator with helpful feedback about something that is absolutely vital, namely, how much fuel is in the tank. Drivers act as if the gas gauge is important, such as by seeking to keep the gauge away from the dreaded *E* (empty) point on the dial, just as people act as if self-esteem is really important.

The importance of belongingness dictates that the person has to keep track of interpersonal relations. Emotions provide day-to-day, even moment-to-moment feedback about changes in the status of important relationships. Self-esteem tracks a longer-term concern, namely, the challenge of being the sort of person with whom other people want to be affiliated. To be attractive to groups and potential relationship partners, it is vital to have some appealing trait, such as friendly charm or physical attractiveness, or some useful skill or knowledge, as well as to respect certain rules and obligations. Measures of self-esteem consist largely of questions about how the person appraises himself on those same dimensions: likability, attractiveness, competence, and morality.

The *sociometer theory* of self-esteem underscores the usefulness of the self-esteem motive for the cultural control of behavior. Again, cultures need to induce people to do things that will benefit the collective. Harnessing the desire for self-esteem to what is good for the collective (such as helping others, doing good work, and being a good citizen) will help motivate people to perform such acts. If the self-esteem motive is tied to the quest to be well regarded by others, then it is ready-made to make people behave in ways that will be beneficial to and valued by the collective. The inner meter will enable the person to know what aspects of self will and what aspects will not appeal to others. In principle, it should help the person manage social life effectively. In practice, people are often tempted to focus on the meter rather than on the underlying reality, which results in self-deception. For example, instead of being competent, you can simply find ways of persuading yourself that you are competent. Exaggerating your ability can be comforting, because you start to believe that your high ability will always help you find a job and maybe some friends too. Obviously, severe exaggerations and illusions about the self are vulnerable to being disproved by eventual facts. So people cannot just willy-nilly persuade themselves that they are great at everything. But that is not what they actually do. Instead of cultivating such extreme distortions, people seem to content themselves with pervasive but relatively small illusions. For example, many researchers have asked college students what their scores were on the Scholastic Aptitude Test (SAT), which is the main educational evaluation (similar to an intelligence test) that most students take when applying to college. These scores are often important to a student's self-evaluation of intelligence. Especially at selective schools, new students often nervously ask each other their scores, as a way of sizing up where they stand in the classroom competitions to come. There are three scores, each of which can range from 200 to 800. When researchers go to the trouble of checking the students' self-reported scores against their official records kept by the university registrar, the usual finding is that students inflate their scores a little (e.g., 50 points total). They are not precisely, scrupulously accurate, but neither do they overstate their scores wildly. More generally, it seems that many people go through life inflating their successes and attributes a little.[113]

The motive to think well of oneself can be subdivided into two parts, namely, the avoidance of losing self-esteem (*self-protection*) and the wish to gain esteem (*self-enhancement*). Occasionally these work against each other, such as when the person is deciding whether to accept a risky, public challenge that could potentially bring either glory or humiliation. The weight of evidence suggests that people whose self-esteem is already high tend to emphasize gaining even more esteem, whereas people with low or moderate self-esteem give first priority to not losing any of it.[114] This contributes to making people with low self-esteem more cautious, because risk to them represents the danger of loss, whereas the same risk might strike a person of high self-esteem as an opportunity.

In recent years, many researchers have turned their attention away from self-esteem per se to address a related construct called *narcissism*. The term *narcissism* is based on the Greek myth of the young man who fell in love with his reflection in the water, and narcissism therefore has a connotation of excessive or inappropriate self-love. Narcissism can be regarded as one subcategory of high self-esteem, and in particular it refers to people who hold favorable, probably inflated views of themselves and who are highly motivated to sustain them. Many people with high self-esteem are like that too, but high self-esteem also includes a category of people who are simply quite comfortable with themselves and not narcissistic. Thus, narcissism differs from the simpler concept of self-esteem in emphasizing two things, namely, the inflation of self-regard and the motivation to establish a highly positive image of self. Gender differences in narcissism are a bit larger than the differences in self-esteem, again suggesting that the main differences are that men are more concerned with social dominance than women and are more prone to inflate their self-appraisals.

Narcissism brings us back to the question of motivation: Exactly what do people want? The self-esteem motive is typically understood as the desire to think well of yourself, although it is closely intertwined with the desire to be regarded favorably by others. The two are linked because being liked and respected by others is often a prerequisite for liking and respecting yourself. Few people can sustain highly favorable views of themselves without getting some confirmation from others, whereas being widely admired is likely to prove to be a "cure" for low self-esteem.

To the extent that one can distinguish self-esteem from public esteem, the latter seems to be more important. The overriding motive of narcissists seems to be to obtain social approval from others.[115] That is, they spend much of their time and energy seeking ways to get others to admire them. In terms of being liked by others rather than admired, they are somewhat indifferent. That is, narcissists are no more nor less interested than anyone else in being liked. Being admired, however, is extremely important to them. In general, they do not seem overly concerned with proving something to themselves (possibly because they are already privately persuaded of their own good qualities), but they are quite interested in demonstrating their superiority to others. For example, if given a chance to tackle a difficult task and find out how good they are, narcissists put forth minimal effort if no one is looking, which is a sign that they do not really care about demonstrating their brilliance to themselves, whereas if others are watching, they put forth maximum effort in order to shine.[116]

The universality of the desire for esteem has been debated. One group of authors has recently argued that the Japanese do not show any desire to think well of themselves.[117] Others dispute this, arguing that the Japanese do want to think well of themselves, but for them the motive is expressed in a different way, which makes it harder for Westerners to see. In particular, Japanese people may base their self-esteem on being a good member of the group, such as a well-behaved child or a loyal employee.[118] Another perspective is that the Japanese may be modest and self-deprecating in what they say about themselves overtly, but secretly or even unconsciously they still strive to maintain positive views of themselves.[119]

From my perspective, self-esteem is based on the underlying motives of belongingness and control, which are probably found in every culture, but the specific concern with self-esteem and the forms that this concern takes may show great variation across cultures. And even if the Japanese are an exception, it is safe to assume that most people in most cultures want others to think well of them and prefer to avoid having a bad opinion of themselves.

The desire for esteem can be used effectively by society to influence how people act. Systems of prestige are found in all cultures, and in general prestige is used to recognize and reward people who do what is most useful to the culture.[120] People will labor for years, even decades, in the hope of securing the esteem of their fellows and the accompanying right to think well of themselves. By linking prestige and esteem to particular activities or accomplishments, a culture can direct many people to devote their energies in those directions. It is no accident that in small societies struggling for survival, prestige comes with bringing in large amounts of protein (hunting) or defeating the most dangerous enemies (fighting). By the same token, the prestige of motherhood probably rises and falls with the society's need to increase population, and the prestige of entertainers rises and falls with how much time and money the population can devote to leisure activities.

Guilt, Morality, and Virtue

Morality is an important category of human striving, and one that depends substantially on the cultural context. People want to avoid feeling guilty. They don't want their friends and neighbors to condemn them as immoral. The motivation to be a good person, or at least to avoid being a morally bad one, can direct actions in many ways. People may go to considerable expense and inconvenience to keep a promise. They may refrain from helping themselves to someone else's possessions. They may pass up a chance for a thrilling extramarital sexual encounter. They may hold their anger and refrain from attacking or hurting someone when they want to do so. Thus, even some of the most deeply rooted natural motivations may be thwarted by the desire to be good and to behave properly.

All cultures have morals, and although there are variations in moral imperatives, there are also many broad similarities. Moral rules that are sufficiently common as to qualify as universals or near-universals include prohibitions against murder, restrictions on sexuality (typically including prohibition of incest, however defined), and a reciprocity norm.[121] Few of the Ten Commandments would seem shockingly foreign to anybody, regardless of cultural background, although naturally the commandments to worship the Judeo-Christian god in particular and to respect the sabbath would not be observed in the same literal fashion in other cultures. But you will have to look long and far to find people who are surprised to hear that a society objects to stealing, murder, lying, and disrespecting one's parents.

Morality can be understood as a system of rules to allow people to live together. Hence moral rules are probably more strongly rooted in the requirements and challenges of group life than in the structure of the brain or the motivational system of the individual. People can live in close proximity best if they share some common understandings, such as respect for personal property, the importance of refraining from murder and violence except under very specific and consensually recognized circumstances, a standard of fairness and equity, appropriate partners and circumstances for sex and mating, and the special rights and obligations between family members.

Thus, in a sense, the innate motivation most closely linked to morality is the need to belong. People want to live together in groups, but group life requires that people follow some rules and restrain some of their impulses and inclinations. Still, morality is not directly derived from the need to belong—rather, it represents the compromises that must be made in order to satisfy that need on a long-term basis. Morality can, however, also be made effective by linking it to the desires to feel good and to avoid feeling bad, insofar as people can be taught to feel the aversive emotions of guilt or shame when they do something wrong.

Guilt has the reputation of being a solitary feeling, but it is a highly interpersonal emotion. It is rooted in the relationships people have, and its emotional basis includes empathy (i.e., understanding others) and separation anxiety (i.e., fear over losing the connection to others). Identical transgressions produce different degrees of guilt as a function of the person's relationship to the victim: You feel more guilt over lying to your mother than to a salesperson. In several studies about feeling guilty and being made to feel guilty, the most common cause of guilt is neglecting one's friends, family, or lovers. In short, guilt is an emotion that you feel when you hurt, neglect, or disappoint people about whom you care.[122]

Guilt can thus be understood as a vital part of the system that enables people to live together. It operates to strengthen and sustain good interpersonal relationships in a couple of crucial ways. First, it reduces interpersonal transgressions. In order to avoid feeling guilty, people will watch their behavior and refrain from actions that hurt other people. Second, and related, it drives people to repair damage to relationships caused by things they have done or failed to do. Guilt makes people confess, apologize, make amends, and promise not to repeat the transgression. If nothing else, the simple fact of feeling guilty (at least if the injured party sees that you feel guilty) can help to repair the relationship, because in many cases the damage caused by a transgression is less the material or practical consequences than it is the implication of not caring about the relationship. Thus, if you come home unexpectedly late and your partner cooked a meal for you that is now spoiled, the harm is not so much the cold potatoes but rather the apparent message that you did not care enough to call—a message that can be effectively counteracted if you feel guilty. Feeling guilty is a way of showing that you care about someone. Third, guilt helps to reduce power inequities in relationships. Powerful people do not need to induce guilt to get their way, because power allows them to influence others directly. Those who lack power can, however, get the powerful ones to do their bidding by expressing how hurt they will be otherwise. Because the powerful person would feel guilty over hurting the weaker one, the powerful person may do what the weaker person wants.

Thus, overall, guilt is an important cause of socially desirable, unselfish behavior. Guilt has a bad reputation in our society because people do not want to feel guilty, but a widespread reduction in guilt-proneness would be disastrous for social harmony. You would not want to have a lover, a boss, or a roommate who had no sense of guilt. Such individuals do exist—they are called psychopaths—but despite their initial charm they often wreak havoc on those around them, and by some estimates they are responsible for crimes, betrayals, and acts of violence far out of proportion to their numbers in the population.[123] The fact that people are motivated to avoid feeling guilty is an important foundation of society and culture.

The crux of the problem for group life is that individual self-interest may often clash with group harmony. One person might covet another's jewels, food, house, or sex partner. To act out of self-interest would entail attempting to take what you want, but who would like to live in a group in which one's cherished possessions were constantly stolen by others? Allowing one person to take another's goods is not a simple, even exchange, in the sense that one person's gain offsets the other's loss, so that for the group as a whole it is neutral. It undermines the possibility of harmonious group life and therefore undermines the group itself—in which case, everyone loses.

As I have already argued, nature makes each individual innately selfish, whereas culture must sometimes ask people to sacrifice their short-term self-interest for the benefit of group harmony. To live with others, you must be willing to refrain from taking their possessions or stealing their sex partners, except perhaps if this is done according to standard, agreed-upon rules. Likewise, society may expect you to pay taxes or send your children off to risk their lives in battle. At the least, you will have to wait your turn for many things.

Morality is therefore an important tool by which culture induces individuals to override their natural selfish or self-interested impulses. Morality therefore takes shape as a force that restrains individual self-interest in favor of the group, at least in the sense that it enforces patterns of mutual respect, nonviolence, and sharing, which allow the group to remain intact. The view of morality as mainly a set of restraints on self-interest explains its negative character: Moral systems have far more rules about what not to do than what to do. The majority of the Ten Commandments, for example, specify what "thou shalt not" do, such as killing, stealing, lying, and committing adultery. Even some of the commandments not phrased in "not" terms, such as the injunctions to honor one's parents and to keep the sabbath holy, implicitly specify things that should not be done (e.g., not abandoning your parents when they get old and not working on the sabbath).

Culture makes rules as to what is right and wrong. But rules are useless unless people have some motive to heed them. Culture must find a way to make people want to respect those rules and do what is right. There are two main solutions, which reflect different stages in social development. The first stage relies on the need to belong and related motives of the concern people have for one another in stable, long-term relationships. These are mediated by shame and guilt: People mainly feel guilty when they do something that could harm, offend, alienate, or otherwise disappoint the people about whom they care.

The main limitation on guilt as a motivator is that its power rests on the strength of the social bond. Guilt makes people do what will strengthen or preserve their relationships, and so the weaker the relationship, the less guilt there is.[124] If you get a phone message asking you to call back, and you neglect to do so, how guilty do you feel? Most people feel more guilty if the call is from a loved one, such as their mother or child, than if it is from a casual acquaintance, and they feel even less guilt over failing to return a stranger's call.

As cultures grow more elaborate and complex, social life consists of an increasing proportion of interactions with strangers. Guilt loses some of its power and so people are less motivated to treat each other properly when they do not expect ever to see each other again. That is why, as societies mature, the rule of law gradually replaces guilt and morality as the main impetus to make people behave well. Law is thus the second stage in how culture makes people do the right things: Abstract rules are enacted and enforced by a system that includes legislatures, police, courts, and prisons. Sealing a financial deal with one's word and a handshake may be effective in small towns with stable populations, because the person who broke his word would be known for many years thereafter as untrustworthy, and he would also probably feel quite guilty for betraying a member of his community, with whom he may have to deal for much of his life. In a more modern society, however, financial deals are generally between strangers who will possibly never interact again, and so to make people honor it the deal will usually be confirmed in some way that can be proven to be legally binding, such as a signed contract.[125]

The transition from morality to law is never fully complete, because people continue to live some of their lives in small, stable social groups where guilt and morality still can operate with great power. Most modern families have rules, but they do not hire a police officer to enforce them (e.g., by arresting kids for coming home after curfew). Families typically consist of stable, lasting relationships marked by mutual concern, and that context is sufficient to make guilt an effective motivator in most cases.[126]

Restraining selfish impulses requires self-control, which is defined as the capacity to alter and override one's inner responses and other psychological states or processes. Self-control therefore underlies most of the virtues, and most of the vices can be understood as failures or breakdowns of self-control. The Seven Deadly Sins of Christian theology, for example, refer mainly to indulging selfish impulses rather than restraining them in ways that might be better for others: gluttony, greed, lust, envy, sloth, pride or vainglory, and anger.[127] Thus, moral behavior requires the capacity for self-control and the motivation to use it for the sake of doing what is right. Chapter 6 will elaborate on self-control.

Success: Wealth and Fame

Success is also a cultural construction, and it normally consists of access to the rewards, both material and symbolic, that the culture values. Normally it is contingent on performing one's roles within the society effectively. A culture that cannot motivate people to want success according to its terms is not likely to survive, because without effective performance of social roles, the society will fall apart. But by defining success in a way that includes effective performance of social roles, and linking this idea of success to the underlying innate motives (such as social acceptance and control), a culture can encourage people to perform their roles effectively.

It is quite possible that people actually devote more energy to pursuing success than happiness. (We already covered the motivation to seek happiness as a culturally elaborated form of the basic desire to feel good.) Of course, the two are intertwined, and people imagine that achieving success will bring happiness. One of the causes of the so-called midlife crisis for many men is that they long entertained a somewhat mythical faith that if they could achieve their career goals, they would live happily ever after.[128] This faith sustains many a man in industrialized societies through a decade or more of overwork (typically his 30s). Many men of course do not reach their goals, but the fortunate few who do fulfill their aspirations encounter the cruel irony that all the other problems and aggravations are still there. Even though a man may be quite happy over finally getting the big promotion or award he coveted, this will soon wear off. So he ends up feeling about as happy as he always felt, instead of much happier, as he had hoped and expected. Still, for the purpose of understanding human motivation, the relevant point is that his efforts throughout that decade of overwork were guided more directly by the goal of success than the goal of happiness per se.

Success in modern, industrialized life is mainly understood in two forms, namely, money and social recognition. These correspond rather obviously to the motives for control and belongingness, and almost certainly they are culturally elaborated forms of those basic desires. To be rich and famous is the epitome of success today, and the pursuit of wealth and acclaim is hardly unique to the modern Western world. In past eras, perhaps, true fame was available only to a small privileged elite, whereas the modern world has promoted the view that at least in principle anyone can become famous.[129] There has also been a shift in the focus, from fame to celebrity,[130] in the sense that the modern individual wants to be celebrated for the entire person that she is rather than just, as in the past, for particular achievements.

These changes simply dramatize how the pursuit of fame is based on the need to belong, insofar as each person wants to be accepted, admired, and loved in totality, rather than given credit for a particular deed. Leo Braudy's survey of the history and mythology of fame concluded that fame is primarily appealing because it holds the promise (often a false one) of widespread and permanent social acceptance.[131] To be famous means to be loved forever. In reality, he noted, fame is painfully fleeting, so much so that by the time Braudy had finished his book, he had to go back and revise the examples he had used in the parts he wrote first, because many of the famous people in those examples (such as Farrah Fawcett, an actress) had faded to the point of scarcely being recognizable.

Researcher Jonathan Freedman conducted a series of large surveys of U.S. and Canadian samples, and he drew this conclusion: "It is not power that most people want, nor influence, but fame, and especially the kind of fame associated with glamour."[132] The emphasis on glamorous fame suggests that some sort of idealized version of the self is also envisioned. The implication is that fame boosts one's self-esteem, such as by validating the self as a worthy individual. As already noted, however, the self-esteem motive is itself strongly linked to the need to belong. In any case, this cluster of motivations seems ideal for a cultural animal: You want to be admired by other members of the society, both for who you are (your social identity) and for your achievements according to the culture's values. Such a pattern will tie the individual strongly to the culture.

The pursuit of fame is ironic in some ways because actual fame brings costs as well as benefits. It has become something of a cliché to hear newly famous people bemoan their unexpected problems. George Harrison, a shy young musician who became internationally famous as a member of the Beatles, complained about the adulation of screaming fans and sought to avoid it for most of his life: "I would never want that again," he said. He complained also that fame was constraining and said he disliked "going round and round the world singing the same ten dopey tunes."[133] Famous people find they cannot simply go shopping at the mall or dine at a neighborhood restaurant as they did in their days of anonymity, because people recognize them and make them the center of attention (such as asking them for autographs or simply wanting to chat), which soon becomes excessive and unwelcome. Then again, when their star fades, it seems unlikely that most of these people feel joy and relief at returning to anonymity. Either way, there appears to be an optimal margin of stimulation in the sphere of social approval: Either too much or too little is aversive.

Money is probably an even more widespread motivator than fame, for several reasons. First, money is more directly useful, insofar as it can be exchanged for a broad variety of goods and services (unlike fame, which has only a limited practical utility). Second, many occupations and careers offer little or no opportunity for achieving fame (for example, there are no national awards for being a good assistant manager of a convenience store), but they all offer money. Third, money can be measured objectively better than fame, and so people can keep track of their progress and compare themselves precisely against various standards or rivals.

In modern culture, money comes primarily from work. Attitudes toward work were sorted by Robert Bellah and his colleagues into three main categories: job, calling, and career.[134] In their definition, only the *job* was motivated primarily by money. In contrast, the *calling* is motivated by a sense of personal destiny and self-expression, and the *career* is oriented toward a (hoped-for) rising trajectory of achievement and recognition. But money tends to intrude on the callings and careers as well. Athletes, artists, and physicians may feel that their work is a means of expressing themselves, fulfilling their potentialities, and doing something they love (not to mention a path toward fame and recognition), but they also tend to be quite sensitive to how well they are paid. Likewise, a career-oriented person may successfully secure a series of promotions or awards, but unless these are accompanied by salary raises, the person is probably going to be discontented.

To be sure, there are differences, and some people are much more greedy for money or fame than others. Among other differences, there is a gender difference, such that men seem generally more oriented toward pursuing money and fame than women. Studies of materialism, for example, confirm that men are more oriented toward money than women, and in selecting jobs women tend to emphasize intrinsic satisfactions and social relations, whereas men place more emphasis on getting the highest salary.[135] Most likely this discrepancy contributes to the much-bemoaned salary gap between men and women. For the foreseeable future, men are likely to continue earning more money than women on average, because men pursue money more single-mindedly. To illustrate this, ask your friends the question: Would you take a job that involved a lot of aggravation and stress, including interpersonal conflict, and relatively little in the way of pleasure or satisfaction, but that paid a really high salary? More men than women would take such a job.

The pursuit of success by men, at least, may also owe something to the sex drive, because many men believe, with considerable justification, that fame and wealth will make them more attractive to women. Michael J. Fox, a short young man who rose rapidly to be a major television and movie star, commented that girls who never used to give him the time of day were now taking him home to bed. He said some people would occasionally ask him whether it bothered him that women only wanted to have sex with him because he was a celebrity. "My answer to that one was, 'Ah . . . nope!'"[136]

Although the pursuit of material resources may have an evolutionary basis, money is itself a creation of culture. Money may appeal to innate, natural motivations, but it goes some steps beyond them. As we saw in chapter 1, money is one of the clearest examples of social reality. The fact that people can come to want it so much is therefore a strong sign of the culturalization of motivation.

The failure of communism also shows the importance of money for human motivation. Communism reacted against capitalism and concluded (wrongly, it seems) that the quest for material gain was the root of most social evils. Hence it followed that abolishing private property would produce a better society, because the quest for material gain would become impossible. Soon after the Russian Revolution, the Soviet Union took the additional step of trying to get rid of money altogether. To accomplish this, the government started to print more and more money, so as to render it worthless. Lenin instructed the Russian treasury to print as much money as possible, and it pursued this policy for several years, only turning off the presses when the machines broke down from overuse. The result was a combined inflation across the First World War and early communist years of 650,000 to 1.[137] To put this in perspective, you have to imagine that at the start of the First World War you had saved up the equivalent of a half million dollars in Russian currency, and you never spent any of it; then 6 years later, the value of your savings was reduced to the equivalent of $1. Or, alternatively, if at the start of this period you tipped the porter $2 to carry your suitcases, at the end of it an equivalent tip would be well over $1 million. Despite these extreme measures, the leaders of the Soviet Union were unable to rid their society of money, and they ended up going back to a money-based economy.

The sweeping failure of communism was not based simply on the ineptness of central planning or even a quixotic monetary policy of hyperinflation, but rather it failed because it denied the usefulness of extrinsic (monetary) motivation. If people cannot profit by their work, they lose much of the desire to work, and so less work gets done. By all accounts, the productivity of communist workers was far below that in capitalist countries. When Germany was reunited and West German firms acquired control of formerly state-run factories in eastern Germany, almost invariably they started by reducing the workforce by more than half—and they started insisting that the remaining employees show up and work productively on a regular basis.

The so-called commons dilemma is another powerful consequence of money motivation (and another cause of the failure of communism). The motive to gain and maintain their wealth encourages people to take care of their property. Upkeep requires certain sacrifices, such as doing the unpleasant chores of waxing your car or trimming your hedges. Publicly owned property is felt to be owned by no one, and so individuals do not feel inclined to make such sacrifices. The term *commons dilemma* is derived from common grazing areas back in the days when many people had herds of animals. Grass will grow back after it has been grazed by animal herds, provided that they leave enough to replenish. Individual farmers and herders manage their grazing lands effectively, ensuring that they do not overgraze, but when grazing lands are commonly owned and shared by all, the problem of overgrazing is much more frequent and acute. Plenty of experimental studies have supported the same conclusion: Individuals can manage renewable resources very effectively, but groups consistently ruin them by depleting them.[138]

A Meaningful Life

Last but not least, people want to have a meaningful life. Meaningfulness is not the same as happiness, although there is some overlap. Specifically, lives can be meaningful without being happy, but people who regard their lives as meaningless are not usually happy. Put another way, meaningfulness is necessary but not sufficient for happiness. Terrorists and revolutionaries may have highly meaningful lives, for example, but they are not typically happy people. In contrast, people like the housewife in one research study who surveyed her life and summed up the lack of meaning by saying, "I was shocked when I finally realized that 'this is it,' that this would be my mode of living,"[139] are also not happy people. This is it, and it's not enough: such an outlook is not conducive to a joyful life.

Meaningfulness is another social reality that can be used by the culture to influence how people act. Though a culture cannot easily go completely against the subjective experiences of individuals, it can encourage them to find their lives more or less meaningful as a function of whether their actions contribute to things that are valued in the culture.

In a previous book, I surveyed the evidence about how people seek meaning in life, and I concluded that four distinct *needs for meaning* can be identified.[140] These can serve as a profile of what people specifically want in terms of achieving a meaningful understanding of their lives, which includes organizing their lives so as to furnish a satisfactory sense of meaning.

First, nearly all meanings of life include *purposes*, in the sense that past and current activities derive meaning from possible future circumstances.

The present is rarely understood as complete in and of itself, but rather it is understood in the context of some desired future state. People who lack goals or a general sense of purpose tend to be disoriented and discontented, and in most cases they try to fill in the future with something for which to hope and toward which to work. A concept of fulfillment, such as spiritual enlightenment or salvation, or simply love or happiness, can also serve as a purpose. This requires sophisticated meaningful thought, of which most noncultural animals would not be capable, because the present has to be interpreted with reference to the future.

Second, people require a sense of *efficacy*. Clearly, this invokes the desire for control, but it refers to the subjective perception. Illusions of control and other forms of secondary control will suffice. But people seem driven to understand their lives in a way that affords them some sense of being able to make a difference. After all, to have goals and purposes but no efficacy would hardly make for a meaningful life, because one would simply feel helpless about being unable to make progress toward those goals.

Third, some basis for *value* and *justification* is needed. All cultures have concepts of right and wrong, and the concepts of good and bad are among the first ones that children learn.[141] Some cultures, including modern Western ones, have problems in the sphere of values. These problems are not generally traceable to a lack of values, as is sometimes claimed, but rather they stem from having a multiplicity of competing values. The multiplicity removes the consensual basis[142] for regarding the values as firm, objective facts of life, leaving the individual with the need to find a way to choose among values. In any case, the need for value has two parts. One is some reliable basis for making judgments about what is good and what is bad. The other is some way, usually within that framework, of being able to see oneself and one's actions as good. That is, your life is not satisfactorily meaningful simply because you have a firm set of values, if all of those values condemn you and everything you do as evil and wrong. Even killers, slave owners, professional torturers, and other harm-doers strive to find some way to regard themselves as basically good people.

Last, people seem driven to find some way to understand their lives that affords them a sense of *self-worth*. In practice, this generally entails believing oneself to be superior to others. Although the quest for self-worth may be a property of the search for meaning in life, it is also part of the broader issue of self-esteem motivations (see above).

Levels of meaning are roughly correlated with time span, such that higher (also called "deeper") meanings are linked to longer time frames. The human lifespan has gradually risen from around three to around eight decades. Therefore, to draw higher meaning from a context, it must invoke something that spans at least a century and preferably a couple of centuries.

Also, given the centrality of the quest for purpose in life, the future may be more important than the past. A nation, a political movement, scientific progress, art, and similarly grand contexts are effective sources of meaning in life, because they are all larger and longer-lasting than the individual's life, and all of them offer the hope that the products of one's life and activities will continue after the end of one's own life. Many people draw meaning from their families, especially their children (who may be expected to outlive them), and in some cases by emphasizing their links to previous generations, such as in ancestor worship.

The invocation of these broad time spans, even longer than the anticipated duration of one's own life, is almost certainly unique to cultural animals. Ernest Becker may have been overreaching when he proposed that culture is itself designed to protect us psychologically from the anxiety over our own deaths, but there was a germ of a valid insight in his view. When people want to console themselves that their lives have meaning, they look for a context that goes beyond themselves, and this typically requires something that extends into the past and future (before their births and after their deaths). Culture has a monopoly on such broad contexts, because it enables people to think beyond the horizons of their own lives. And culture provides most of the meaningful entities—nationality, political movement, religion, science, art, multigenerational family lineage—that can achieve such time spans.

Religion has long been an especially powerful and popular source of meaning in life. Certainly, it has the broadest time frame—eternity—and by that measure at least can claim the highest possible level of meaning. Modern religions have typically been rich bases for values and have offered well-articulated concepts of human fulfillment (salvation), and in that sense they can satisfy two of the four needs for meaning.

Undoubtedly, part of the appeal of religion has long been rooted in control. Before the scientific view of the world came to predominate, many events in the natural world were attributed to the operation of supernatural powers, and so religion offered a way of understanding them (which is one kind of control). Some scholars have emphasized how religious groups are constantly tempted to offer more direct opportunities for control over life. Rituals, prayers, and other interventions are often presented as able to influence the gods (or other supernatural powers) to shape events in congenial, desired ways.[143] These promises cannot be reliably fulfilled, and the priests and shamans who claim to be able to cure the sick or end the drought risk being discredited—but if they refuse to make such promises, the desperate members of their congregations may follow a rival sect or holy man.

Although religions may not be able to bring about specific, desired outcomes by obtaining divine intervention in everyday affairs, they can help to satisfy the urge for control at least through secondary control. Identification with a higher power is one major form of secondary control, and there is no higher power than a supreme god. Understanding events is an important form of secondary control, and religion typically offers a fairly extensive means of understanding all sorts of events. The believer who is able to accept otherwise inexplicable events as being "God's will" may be satisfied with this form of interpretive control. The illusion of control may also be a powerful factor. Sick children do get better often enough to satisfy their parents that their prayers have been answered.

Indeed, the possibility of gaining meaning and understanding may be the single most important part of religion's appeal. Religion appeals most strongly to people who are confronted with misfortunes that are beyond their direct control. Sickness, accident, war, danger, and other events bring people to religion, and religion comforts them with ways of understanding and sometimes ostensibly dealing with these problems. My own review of research on religion led to the tentative conclusion that the modern decline in religious participation in industrialized societies is chiefly a result of the high quality of life in modern society.[144] In simple terms, we are too well off to crave the comforts of religious explanation. When modern individuals confront severe misfortune, however, such as a life-threatening illness in the family, they often find themselves reaching for their faith again.

Control is not the only basic need that religion satisfies. Belongingness is a major part of the appeal of religion. Studies on church membership indicate that people join and leave churches based more on social groups than on doctrines. For example, in the community where I grew up, people were acutely conscious of what kind of people went to which church, but they were considerably fuzzier about the doctrinal differences among the rival denominations. By the same token, studies on religious cults show that they are joined chiefly by people who are socially unattached and looking for friends and that the people who make friends in the cult tend to remain, whereas those who don't form ties quickly drift out of the cult.[145] Indeed, in recruiting new members, cults typically emphasize the chance to meet people or to join a warm, friendly community, rather than emphasizing their doctrines and beliefs.

Last, religion can appeal to the self-preservation instinct. Mircea Eliade's authoritative history of religious ideas asserted that the belief in life after death is one of the oldest religious ideas, dating back far into prehistory.[146] Conceptions of the afterlife have evolved over the centuries, and the idea of the afterlife as potentially a pleasant, blissful life (as opposed to a life as an unhappy ghost) rose sharply after religions began to espouse concepts of salvation. Christianity has long advocated two (sometimes three) afterlife locales, a very happy one and another miserable one, but even within those two there has been a gradual shift in favor of the more positive: Belief in hell has dwindled sharply over the last couple of centuries,[147] to the point where relatively few people now seriously believe that they are going to go to hell when they die. Thus, religions have helped people to escape the recognition of their own mortality, by asserting that death is not what it seems and that life will continue—preferably in a pleasant form. And modern religions also tend to promise that not only life, but also belongingness, will continue after death, for most people believe that life in heaven will include spending eternity with their families and other people they loved here on earth. The preacher Billy Graham said that one of the most common and difficult questions he is asked is whether people will be reunited with their house pets in heaven.[148] Presumably, what motivates this question is not the abstract theological issue of whether dogs have immortal souls, but rather the bond of belongingness between owner and pet, which makes it hard to conceive of spending eternity happily without one's beloved pooch.

The Laws of Wanting

Having considered specific motives in some detail, we move now to reflect more generally on how people want. All animals want some things, but there are some distinctive features of human motivation that probably reflect our evolution as cultural animals. Even when we want the same things as other animals, we may want them somewhat differently.

Motivation and the Duplex Mind

One of the biggest differences between human beings and other animals is the duplex mind and, in particular, the conscious system. Automatic responses are found in both humans and other animals. In contrast, the distinctively conscious processes, such as logical reasoning, narrative, and mathematical calculation, are more uniquely human. But what does consciousness have to do with motivation?

In humans, motivation takes on a quality that may differ from what is seen in other animals. The automatic system in humans and animals dictates how to respond to specific circumstances or stimuli, but the conscious system provides a salient, powerful subjective experience. Hence, in humans, motivation becomes centered around creating or avoiding various conscious states.

Consider sex. Animals can be prompted by hormones and stimuli to engage in sex when conditions are right. But consciousness enables human beings to savor the experience while it happens, to think back happily on what it felt like, and to long for it when it is not available. They can seek ways to intensify the pleasure, which is why human sexuality has been enriched through experimentation with different positions and various devices. The biological goal of sex is to make babies, and so that could be accomplished by a reflex occurring with little or no conscious involvement, but to a human being that would be a shame and a waste, because the conscious experience of sex has become the essence of what is desired. People tell jokes about one person being asleep during sexual intercourse, but animals would not get the point of such jokes even if they could understand language, because sex could still achieve its reproductive goal during sleep—whereas, for a human, to sleep through sex would mean missing out on a desirable conscious experience.

Likewise, the need to belong is found in many other species, but for human beings conscious experience is usually necessary for it to be satisfied. Love, in particular, is a conscious state, and most modern individuals believe that anyone who does not experience love has missed out on a vital element of fulfillment, even if everything else in life went perfectly fine.

Even food and drink reveal how conscious experiences have refocused human motivation. On the surface, humans resemble other species in the regular need for sustenance. But a closer look shows that people care not only about getting enough food to keep their bodies alive—they also want a conscious experience of eating and drinking something delicious. If you drank a $500 bottle of wine but failed to notice it, perhaps because you were engrossed in watching a game on television and paid no attention to what you were consuming, you would probably be disappointed to have missed out on the experience of savoring a presumably precious experience. Biologically, there would be no reason to complain: You ingested the same quality of drink and got the same physical effect.

Entertainments provide one sign of motivations, because they show what people do when there is no practical or external need to act in a certain way. I have used entertainments to indicate what some of the basic motives are. Entertainments also highlight the central importance of conscious experience. The information contained in a movie could probably be summarized in a paragraph that you could read in 3 minutes, but most people would prefer to watch the movie rather than read the summary. The desire for control is useful because it prompts people to master their environments in ways that can help them pragmatically. There is no pragmatic utility in playing billiards or tennis, but people enjoy those activities because they offer a conscious experience of mastery, even though if there were any utility to moving little balls around, the balls could be moved faster and more effectively via other means than cues or racquets.

Getting Begets Wanting

Motivation theory tends to focus on a simple cycle of satiation. You want something, you get it, and so you stop wanting for a while, until the cycle begins again. This is sometimes described as a *hydraulic model* in which pressure builds up and then is released when satisfaction is attained, resulting in a reduction of the inner drive for a while, until it builds up again. Although there is certainly some truth to this view, it does not provide an adequate fit to how people actually behave. On the one hand, it is true that many desires diminish as soon as the person finds some way to satisfy them. This is the simple model of hunger: As your body is deprived of food, it gets ever more hungry, but when you are able to eat a meal, the hunger goes away. On the other hand, there are some seemingly paradoxical patterns that work in the opposite direction. The more satisfaction you get, the more you want. Conversely, if you don't satisfy the desire, it gets weaker to some extent. Some experts think that even eating has elements of this pattern. For example, the influential diet mogul Dr. Robert Atkins asserts that the body has a physiological response to carbohydrates, by which its appetite for them increases when the person consumes more of them.[149] He contends that people who follow a low-carbohydrate diet gradually come to have less desire for carbohydrates. Informally, some vegetarians say the same about meat: They stop craving meat after abstaining for a while, whereas people who eat meat regularly start to want it more and more. Further converging evidence comes from the general difficulty of treating anorexia: People who starve themselves relentlessly gradually develop a loathing for eating, and so it is difficult to induce them to eat.[150] If hunger operated on a simple hydraulic model, the desire for food should grow ever stronger among people who are deprived of food.

These paradoxical patterns have not been studied extensively and are not well understood. One likely guess is that they are linked to the human ability to connect things across time better than other animals. As we saw earlier, animals can only have a response reinforced if the reward follows the behavior within a few seconds, but people can link things for a longer period. Hence, it is plausible that the subjective state of wanting something can be effectively reinforced if the person eventually gets what she wants. If you spend an hour craving a donut, and then you get one, the pleasure of eating it may operate like a reinforcer for wanting it, so that you soon feel that wanting again. Conversely, if you crave donuts every day but never get them, the cravings may dwindle and disappear. In technical terms, this would be an *extinction* of the wanting response.

In any case, there are many patterns that do seem to fit the paradoxical principle that more satisfaction leads to more wanting. Some people report that their sexual desires grow more frequent and intense during periods when they are having a lot of sex, whereas during periods of sexual abstinence, sex seems to recede into unimportance. Aggression also seems to become habit-forming for some, whereas people who do not engage in aggressive activity do not miss it. Video games are artificial and culturally created, and some players have similar patterns of becoming preoccupied with them when they play them frequently—whereas people can go for long periods without playing video games and never give them a second thought. Even belongingness shows some paradoxical patterns, at least with regard to specific attachments. People who spend enormous amounts of time together can develop strong attachments and become reluctant to be apart at all, whereas once someone is out of your life, you tend to miss that person less and less.

Addiction may be the most obvious form of a paradoxical satisfaction effect. One of the hallmarks of addiction is that the addict comes to want more and more, so it seems that satisfying the craving simply leads to ever-greater cravings. Conversely, strict abstention is supposed to reduce the cravings. The sixth month of staying clean and sober is generally easier than the first or second. Although addiction is usually understood in connection with drugs and alcohol, some social scientists have noted similarities to other behaviors and have suggested that a great many human motivations show similar patterns. Stanton Peele and Archie Brodsky first made this argument in their book *Love and Addiction*,[151] noting how people in love behave like addicts—yearning for the person they love, showing "withdrawal symptoms" when apart, seeking the "high" of new intimacies, and the like.

Religious asceticism might therefore have a valid psychological basis. Religions around the world have encouraged people to abstain from worldly pleasures in order to facilitate their salvation. Indulging desires may lead to stronger desires rather than to peace and satisfaction, and so refraining from indulgence may be the most reliable pathway to the abatement of desire. The ideals of celibacy among Christian clergy members (especially male clergy) have not generally been achieved, and most evidence suggests that the majority of priests eventually engage in masturbation and even some interpersonal sex.[152] Then again, priests may well be less troubled by sexual cravings than the average man, who enjoys a fuller sex life. Hence the example of priests does not necessarily contradict the paradoxical satiation pattern; it merely indicates that success is at best partial. The desires do not vanish entirely, but perhaps they do diminish. And sex may be harder to extinguish than many other cravings.

If getting does lead to more wanting, many issues need to be rethought. Is pornography a harmless outlet, even a valuable form of safer sex, which can substitute for other activities? Or does it simply promote all manner of other sexual desires? The policy and moral issues surrounding this question are formidable. For example, many people (including myself) now find an easy route to the moral high ground in opposing child pornography, because of the risk that children might be harmed in the making of it. But soon it will be possible to create virtual (that is, fully computer-generated) pornography without using any real people, and so child pornography can be made without the participation of children. Should this be allowed? Certainly some advocates of free speech are likely to say it should, on the grounds that no one is harmed. But if child pornography stimulates the desire for sexual contact with children, then the indirect harm of virtual pornography could be substantial.

Intrinsic and Extrinsic Desires

Human desires can be sorted into two broad categories, intrinsic and extrinsic. An *intrinsic motivation* means wanting something for its own sake. In contrast, an *extrinsic motivation* means wanting it as a means to some other end. This distinction, which was introduced by Ed Deci in 1971, has stimulated a flood of research.[153] Deci cautiously proposed the distinction as a way of making sense of contrary findings from his laboratory. In his studies, he had college students perform several tasks, gave them some rewards for doing so, and then surreptitiously watched whether they continued to perform these tasks when he left them alone. (The tasks were puzzle games that were popular at the time.) The students who had been paid money for performing the tasks seemed to lose interest in doing them in their free time. In contrast, the students who were rewarded by verbal praise did not show any decline in interest. Deci suggested that the verbal praise supported the students' intrinsic interest in the tasks, whereas the cash payments undermined it.

Plasticity is one of the hallmarks of the cultural animal, and motivational plasticity takes several forms. One of these is the susceptibility to extrinsic motivation. People can learn to desire something, not for its own sake, but for what it will lead to or bring. Animals can show a limited version of this, through classical conditioning. Pavlov's dog would drool at the sound of the bell, after the bell had been associated with food often enough. But that does not yet indicate that the dog came to desire the sound of the bell. The human capacity for forming complex chains of associations and for foreseeing distant outcomes makes it quite possible for us to be highly motivated about many things that have no intrinsic payoff, simply because we can anticipate that they will—or even that they *might*—lead to something that we do desire.

Extrinsic motivation is important in human beings, but it is not prominent in other species, and one could argue that in its full-fledged form it is unique to human beings. Extrinsic motivation typically relies on meaning, and so a complex thinking system is needed. You have to recognize that one activity leads to something else, and so you repeatedly engage in that activity for the sake of the reward that it promises to bring. Only human beings are fully capable of mentally representing chains of causes and consequences.

Culture relies heavily on extrinsic motivations, because culture requires a broad variety of actions that do not directly satisfy biological needs and probably do not feel good every step of the way. Think of working at a dull job, voting in an election, trimming your hedges, obeying the speed limit, and recycling your trash—all these cultural activities require extrinsic motivations. Human beings are extensively receptive to extrinsic motivations, probably more than other species, and this receptivity is probably important in making us cultural animals. A cultural being has to be able to be motivated extrinsically. Our complex society would not function well if people only did things that brought them immediate, intrinsic pleasure.

In that sense, the capacity for extrinsic motivation is an important and distinctive feature of human nature. Possibly this reflects a particular adaptation for which evolution selected us, in order to make us as we are. More likely, extrinsic motivations rely on other adaptations (intelligence and meaning) and constitute a crucial aspect of the culturalization of motivations. Culture teaches us to do things and even to want things based not on what they are but on their extrinsic consequences.

Moreover, when both intrinsic and extrinsic motivators are present, people are so susceptible to extrinsic motivation that extrinsic motives take precedence over intrinsic ones. If you pay people to do something they enjoy doing, they lose their intrinsic enjoyment and start to do it only for the sake of the money. That is what the monetary rewards in Deci's experiments accomplished. Deci suggested that the extrinsic reward of money made the task seem like a job, thereby undermining the sense that the research subjects were doing the task for enjoyment, whereas praise somehow reinforced the people's sense that doing the task was fun and satisfying.

Actually, a crucial factor in extrinsic motivation is that rewards must be presented in advance. If rewards come as a surprise, as praise usually does, they do not detract from the intrinsic enjoyment.[154] Anticipating a reward seems to transform the experience of performing the activity: "turning play into work," in the standard phrase. Getting the same reward as a surprise, after the task is done, has no effect on intrinsic motivation. These findings show the influence of meaning, and they suggest why extrinsic effects may be specific to our species. The person has to be able to interpret what he is doing now in the context of working toward some future, extrinsic goal.

Professional athletes constitute one group for whom large extrinsic rewards intrude on an activity that most athletes initially performed for love and enjoyment. Star basketball player Isiah Thomas once lamented that despite his million-dollar salary and numerous awards, he missed playing basketball for fun. He confessed that in his free time he would drive around Detroit to local parks and then sit in his car and watch enviously as kids played basketball informally. "I wish I was there again," he said in a nostalgic reminiscence about when "basketball was totally free" and he could play for hours simply for the enjoyment of the game.[155] A less poignant version of the same sentiment was articulated by Reggie Jackson, a baseball player whose salary at the time (in the 1970s) was $975,000 per year. When asked why he played the game, he admitted that he liked the money, but love of the game figured prominently too. He indicated he would be playing even if he made only $150,000. Although $150,000 a year may have seemed like small potatoes to him, to most people, that would have been a luxurious salary, and so his willingness to work for that amount did not go far in attesting to his intrinsic love of the game.

Thus, to understand why people might engage in some activity, two very different types of factors that make them want to do it must be understood. The intrinsic motivators involve desiring to do the task for the sheer pleasure or satisfaction of the activity. Extrinsic motivators involve receiving rewards as a result of performing the activity. Society cannot easily alter people's intrinsic motivations, which suggests that such desires are often deeply rooted in human nature. In contrast, society can give or withhold a great variety of extrinsic motivators, such as money, prestige, fame, imprisonment, and social approval or censure.

There is one important borderline case, which involves rewards that carry some message of competence. When rewards signify that you are good at something, they seem to foster satisfaction and sustain the intrinsic motivation to keep doing it.[156] As the section on control motivation noted, people like to be good at things and tend to enjoy and pursue things at which they are especially competent, so when extrinsic rewards carry this message, they support intrinsic motivation. The difference is roughly between being paid to perform (as in a guaranteed salary or wage) versus being paid if one performs well (as in prize money). Clearly, this is convenient for culture too: A cultural animal will enjoy doing things for the sake of symbolic rewards, especially when they indicate that the person is good at something the culture values.

In any case, the human susceptibility to extrinsic motivation is far greater than what is seen in other species, and this is probably a useful adaptation for living in culture. Human beings can come to desire a great many different things, including many things that are not directly pleasant or satisfying. This plasticity affords culture much greater power to shape the actions of the individual.

Conclusion: How They All Fit Together

Freud's vision indicated two basic roots of motivation, which opposed each other and which, through their conflicts and subsequent transformations, provided the basis for all of the specific desires and goals that guide human action. Contrary to that vision, however, recent findings have not given much reason to think that the various human motivations work or fit together in any kind of grand system. The opposite of Freud's vision—an anarchy of desire, in which various needs and wants lurk side by side in the psyche, operating more or less independently of each other—is, if anything, more plausible than the view that human wants are all interlinked.

Yet, these wants cannot operate completely independently. A person has only one brain, only one set of arms and legs, and so forth, and if these are engaged in pursuing food they cannot also be seeking to satisfy a need to belong. Sometimes the desire for sexual pleasure will conflict with the desire for self-preservation. Sometimes people must choose between continuing to pursue a love and preserving their self-respect.

In short, people must have some way of prioritizing their motivations so they can choose which to pursue when different ones clamor simultaneously for satisfaction. The most influential solution to this problem was the *hierarchy of needs* proposed by Abraham Maslow.[157] Maslow grouped the human wants and needs into five categories, and he proposed that people do not move on to satisfying the higher needs until the lower ones are satisfied.

According to Maslow, the most basic needs, which have top priority in his hierarchy theory, involve what the body requires for physical survival, such as food and water. One step above these comes safety, including the desire to feel secure from danger. Therefore, people will risk their safety for food, if both needs are sufficiently pressing. When those two types of needs are satisfied, belongingness and love needs are the next ones to take precedence. The need for esteem comes next, and the desire for self-actualization is the highest (and therefore least often satisfied) desire. Self-actualization involves fulfilling one's potential as a human being, such as through creative work.

The general consensus by now is that Maslow's hierarchy is too simple, although it has some limited validity.[158] Counterexamples, such as the "starving artist," indicate that people sometimes pursue higher needs even when the lower needs are not fully satisfied. Likewise, ample evidence indicates that in the Nazi concentration camps, inmates often helped and cared for each other despite being chronically undernourished and living under imminent danger of death, and these patterns suggest that social motives may be just as basic and powerful as physiological needs, contrary to Maslow's thesis that the social needs only emerge after the others are satisfied. Even the simpler view that the person's needs (defined as what is necessary for survival) take precedence over wants (all other desires) is not defensible as a general principle. People risk their lives for money, and they risk their marriages for sexual adventure, even though belongingness and survival certainly have greater claim to being needs than do money or sex.

Some researchers have attempted grand tests of Maslow's theory, mostly through using questionnaires. These have repeatedly failed to support the hierarchy of needs.[159] Longitudinal studies, which should show people satisfying one need and then moving up the list, have not been successful. At most, it can be said that there is some kind of hierarchy of motives, even if they are not quite the same list or in the same sequence as Maslow proposed.

Are we back to the anarchy of desire? Almost. Maslow's error may have been to propose that one hierarchy applied to everyone. He might have been on safer ground to suggest that each person has her own motivational hierarchy, and the various motivations might rank differently in different people. In one man, the craving for sexual novelty might be enough to cause him to risk his job, his reputation, his marriage, or even his life, whereas other people—for whom sex is less pressing a need—might well balk at the same risks. An artist might be willing to sacrifice material comforts, such as money, food, and a nice apartment, in order to pursue a creative vision, while others probably "sell out" after a spell of hardship and decide that they can do their artwork on future weekends after they have earned enough money to live comfortably. Some people will sacrifice their fast-track career prospects to spend time raising children, whereas others forgo having children in order to devote themselves to their work. In all of these decisions, one motivation is given priority over another, just as Maslow said—only not everyone makes the same decision.

After Maslow, a different approach to personality began to classify people based on how strong their various motivations were. Some people are desperate to gain and use power, whereas others are largely indifferent to power. Likewise, some seek achievement, esteem, affiliation, intimacy, and so forth, while these motives are weaker in others. This book is not going to devote much space to individual differences in personality, but these differences must be recognized as important. For now, they provide the seemingly best answer to the question of how the different motivations coexist in the same psyche. Some motives do take precedence over others, but the precise pattern varies from one person to another based on how strongly each person feels each different need.

There are probably variations within a person too. That is, the same person may desire achievement, sex, or security more at some points than at others. A given desire may subside temporarily after it is satisfied, but frequent satisfaction of some other desire may cause it to be felt all the more frequently, so that addictive patterns come and go across long periods of time. Thus, each person's hierarchy of motives should probably be recognized as dynamic rather than static.

4

How People Think

Thinking and communicating are vital to culture. Culture is based on shared understandings, and shared understandings require both thinking (for the understanding) and communication (for the sharing). Culture is made out of language, partly because language is such a powerful medium for both thinking and communicating. In the previous chapter, we considered motivation, in the sense of what people want and need, and we saw that human wanting is not all that radically different from what is found elsewhere in nature. Human thinking is much more profoundly different.

Still, thoughts and emotions are the servants of motivation. The desires have to be present in the first place. Human beings will survive only if people want some particular things that contribute to their survival and reproduction. But wanting is hardly enough: People have to be able to take action to satisfy their desires and reach their goals. The human brain is a terrific tool for pursuing our motivations. Thinking and feeling are extremely useful to help people accomplish whatever their inner promptings make them want.

The view of thought as the servant of desire has been nicely articulated by Steven Pinker.[1] He commented on the dying genre of movies in which computers become smarter than human beings and take over the world. In the real world, he said, plenty of computers can already think much faster and more accurately than people in many respects, but they have shown no inclination to take over the world. And why should they? he asks. What would they want? More floppy disks? Computers lack the capacity to want anything. No matter how well a computer can think, without motivation, it is only a tool. Agency—that is, acting as an independent, autonomous, self-starting actor—begins with motivation. It relies heavily on thinking and feeling in order to get the job done effectively, however. Without their own desires, computers are just tools waiting around for someone to come along and use them.

The world (and especially a cultural world) is a complex place full of information, but only a small part of that information can be used, and using it requires some degree of understanding and interpretation. Only a small part of the information can be processed. Essentially, the mind has to distill a few crucial facts out of a large chaotic brew of sensory impressions. The mind's jobs therefore include sorting through information and screening out irrelevant or useless material, simplifying it (such as by seeing regular patterns and general principles), storing useful information and vital lessons, and then retrieving them when needed.

Once upon a time, young men studied logic and philosophy to learn how to think. Those disciplines have devoted considerable effort to honing critical thinking and establishing what kinds of arguments permit what kinds of conclusions. But that is not our focus here. This chapter is concerned with how people actually do think, not with how they should or could ideally think. Actual thinking does bear some resemblance to the careful, disciplined reasoning of logicians, but only some. Actual thinking is full of shortcuts, not-so-educated guesses, predetermined conclusions, blind spots, rules of thumb, and other distortions. Initially, psychologists were eager to demonstrate errors, biases, and fallacies in the ways people think. These researchers were so successful that some have begun to wonder how people manage to get through life as well as they do, given their flawed patterns of thought.[2]

The range of possible topics for people to think about and understand is almost unlimited, but most human thought focuses on only a small corner of these possibilities. Specifically, people think about people much more than any other topic. Forming impressions of each other, trying to figure out why someone did or said something, analyzing relationship problems, telling stories about people, criticizing or praising, gossiping, consuming novels and movies about people, and many more activities reflect the way that the human mind is used primarily as a tool for navigating and negotiating relations with other people. It does sometimes get put to work on technical or physical problems, such as when your toilet is broken and you think you'll try to fix it yourself instead of calling a plumber, or you try to program a new VCR, or you navigate through an unfamiliar city. But well over half of the everyday thoughts of the average person involve other people. In chapter 1, we considered Robin Dunbar's evidence on the so-called social brain hypothesis.³ By that theory, the most powerful reason that brains evolved into ever more intelligent versions was for participation in social groups and relationships. Modern research with human cognition has confirmed that conclusion with very different kinds of data: Most human thought is about social and cultural life.

Thus, people use their intelligent brains mainly to think about other people, including the broader meaningful context of their interactions. This fits the view that the human mind is mainly used for the purpose of participating in culture and society.

Why Think?

As I already said, the mind and its activities are handmaidens and butlers for motivation: They help people get what they want. But how exactly does thought accomplish that? What are the specific goals and purposes of thought? The answer "to understand the world" is too broad and simplistic. Yes, an accurate understanding of patterns and principles that dictate what happens in the world is a desirable, useful goal. But the truth—full, accurate understanding—is not always pursued with unswerving zeal. Finding the truth is only one reason people think, and not always the main one. One compelling sign is that books of fiction outsell books of nonfiction, despite the latter's offering more true information. If people wanted only the truth, they wouldn't buy so many novels.

Instead of simply saying that the purpose of thought is to seek the truth, let us propose four competing goals. The truth is certainly one of them. People do exert themselves, at least sometimes, to attain a correct understanding of the world and to ensure that it is correct. At other times, however, people prefer a particular conclusion rather than just finding the correct one. The difference corresponds roughly to seeing the average person as a kind of amateur scientist as opposed to an amateur lawyer. A scientist tries to find the correct conclusion, whatever it may be. At least that's the general idea. Lawyers, in contrast, are paid to make the best possible case for a particular conclusion. If they don't do this, they won't be able to serve their clients. A lawyer whose court appearance consisted of saying "After reviewing all the facts, I have come to the conclusion that my client is guilty and so by law deserves to be sent to prison for a long time" would soon be out of business. Although people are not usually as obvious as lawyers in acknowledging that they are simply looking to make a good case for a predetermined conclusion, they will often try to support a favored conclusion. For example, evidence that supports what they want to believe will be accepted immediately and uncritically, whereas evidence that goes against their preferred conclusions will be subjected to careful scrutiny and critique.[4]

A third goal of thought is speed.[5] Sometimes the main goal is to make a decision, any decision, before a deadline expires. When you go to the video store to rent a movie, for example, you could probably make the best selection by carefully considering every movie in the store, reading reviews of them, asking people with tastes similar to yours what they thought of each, and the like—but you would not be able to finish in time to see the movie that night (or probably even that same week). Instead of finding absolutely the best movie, your goal becomes making a reasonably good choice within 10 or 15 minutes.

A fourth goal is not to work too hard or think too much.[6] Thinking requires energy and effort. To put it nicely, people naturally seek to conserve their resources. (A less charitable formulation is that people are mentally lazy.) In any case, we shall see ample evidence that people take shortcuts and skimp on mental effort in other ways.

Those four goals shape the course of most thinking. Clearly, they are incompatible with each other, so they compete against each other to take precedence. Circumstances give the edge to one or another. For example, when much is at stake and people are going to be held accountable for their decisions, they may go to extra lengths to think things through carefully and thoroughly.[7] In contrast, when people make decisions under time pressure, they cut short their consideration of multiple options and alternatives, stick more closely with their initial hunches, rely more on stereotypes and other entrenched attitudes, and search less thoroughly for helpful information.[8]

Although these four goals describe the everyday conduct of thinking, they do not fully answer the question about the purpose of thought—except for the goal of understanding the world, and as we noted, that goal fails to explain much actual thinking. Scientists assume that people think in order to understand the world, but scientists are professionally engaged in trying to understand the world, so they may be out of touch with everyday purposes of thinking. As we have seen, Dunbar has proposed that the evolutionary purpose of thinking is to enable us to interact with other people.[9] He thinks that gossip may be one of the major purposes of speech: Gossip enables us to share information about other people, including their faults, misdeeds, and peculiarities. That might help explain the seeming paradox that was noted earlier, which is that people prefer to read novels rather than nonfictional books. Novels are almost exclusively stories about people, and so they constitute a sophisticated form of pseudogossip. When people do read nonfiction, they again prefer stories about people, such as biographies, history, and psychology. These patterns fit the view that we mainly use our brains to process information about people.

Nature made us able to learn how to negotiate our way through a complicated social and cultural environment. To do that, we try to learn where the pitfalls, disasters, and opportunities lie. We also have to form and maintain social attachments, such as alliances and families. To succeed, we must learn what is the best way to act in each situation, which nature could not have foreseen, so we have no innately programmed response. We have to learn what to do. At worst, we learn from our own trials and errors. The sometimes glorious but often bitter experience of encountering our own fate is one way to learn valuable lessons. But how much gentler and more pleasant it is and also, crucially, how vastly more efficient and effective it is to learn from the mistakes (and occasional triumphs) of others. Gossip, defined as people's conversations about people, tends to focus on how someone else has done something out of the ordinary, especially perhaps something that has had humiliating consequences. It is much more wonderful and satisfying to learn useful lessons from the humiliating disasters of other people than from your own. This makes gossip into precious information, indeed almost biologically precious.[10]

Cultural Differences in Thinking

Psychology's recent love affair with studying the brain has encouraged the view that thought processes reflect the innate structure of the brain, which implies that human thought has common, universal patterns. Brains in all cultures are put together pretty much the same way, after all. In contrast, cultural relativists have long asserted that different cultures will have utterly different forms of thought. On their side, they have clear evidence that the majority of thought uses language and meaning, and therefore different cultures may have different languages and different systems of meaning. Language is undoubtedly learned, so there should be considerable scope for cultures to shape thought in different ways. Then again, the learning of language is itself so universal that many have proposed an innate basis for it.[11] And, as we have seen, beneath the surface, languages are far more similar than different, mostly using the same grammatical structures and the same set of concepts. Even if the brain is hard-wired for certain patterns of thought, it has to rewire itself to accommodate all it learns while participating in culture. Reading (literacy) provides a powerful example.[12] Natural selection could not possibly have prepared our brains specifically for reading, because reading did not exist in other species, and human beings have not been reading for long enough for natural selection to have changed the brain for the sake of reading. The brain is capable of reading, but this is a lucky accident. When people learn to read, however, their brains adapt in extensive ways so as to incorporate the processes and procedures needed to look at printed text, understand it, and store information gleaned in that way. Reading is participation in culture, and the brain has to be flexible enough to change so as to be able to perform it.

Most everyday thoughts are essentially the same in every culture. Still, some possible room remains for cultural variation. Recent work has proceeded cautiously to try to establish some limited, specific differences in thought patterns. In a sense, the ambitious skyscraper of cultural relativity has been demolished, and current researchers are trying to construct solid, well-built little bungalows in its place. The project is far less ambitious but much more likely to succeed.

Remember, though, that cultural variation is only a small part of the importance of culture. Indeed, it is in how cultures are the same that their main adaptive importance can be found. The broad similarity of thought in all cultures comes from the fact that all languages operate on the same universe of ideas, and most cultures have to solve the same basic set of problems. Sometimes, however, there is no single best solution upon which everyone converges, and instead different cultures choose somewhat different solutions. Sexual morality is a good example of the latter: There is no one perfect system for managing the sex lives of a large group of people, so different societies find different points on the continuum from liberal, anything-goes tolerance to prudish virtue. Still, even these cases don't usually entail that each culture is unique and special. Rather, there are a couple of different approaches (e.g., general sexual looseness or sexual restraint), and different cultures settle at different points along the continuum.

Thus, it is not how each culture is unique that matters, even when there are cultural differences. Rather, even when cultures differ, these differences signify that many different cultures fall at different points along one continuum or even within a dichotomy. It is not the uniqueness of a culture, but how it resembles others (even if the group differs from other groups) that is most relevant to understanding human nature.

So far, the evidence for cultural differences in thinking mainly concerns Eastern (Asian) versus Western (European and North American) thinking. The central idea is that Asians think more holistically, seeing how everything fits together, whereas Westerners think more analytically, focusing on particular entities in isolation.[13] This is a difference in emphasis, not a matter of utterly incompatible styles separated by a wide gap of mutual incomprehensibility. The difference begins with how people pay attention and then proceeds to how they understand and interpret.

According to Richard Nisbett and his colleagues,[14] the different thinking styles may originate in different social organizations. Western civilization was deeply influenced by the ancient Greeks, who developed early notions of democracy, freedom, and individuality. In contrast, Asian societies were influenced by ancient Chinese civilization, which emphasized *network* beliefs—for instance, that all people and all social roles exist in a structure of interdependent, reciprocal social duties and that actions and decisions flow from collective effort rather than individual agency. These different social organizations foster different styles of thought. It would be excessive to say that modern Chinese and Europeans think in radically or fundamentally different ways, but they emphasize different things and excel in different ways, and they will be prone to different kinds of errors and biases. Neither style is clearly better overall; each has its advantages and disadvantages, as the general tradeoff pattern would have us expect. Let us list some of these differences.

Cognition starts with attention, defined as what the person notices. With attention, "Easterners . . . see wholes where Westerners see parts."[15] Easterners have more difficulty understanding something or someone out of context, whereas Westerners are more prone to illusions of individual autonomy and control. Easterners are quicker to notice covariation, in the sense that they spot when two things go together.

In perceiving people and understanding behavior, Easterners are less vulnerable to the common Western error of underestimating situational factors. That is, Westerners tend to explain a person's behavior on the basis of what is inside the person—traits, goals, intentions, feelings. The person is treated as a self-contained unit, and the influence of the context is discounted. Easterners downplay these internal causes of behavior and focus instead on the situation. The Asian approach sees causality as highly complex and does not readily rule out possible causes. Nisbett and his colleagues describe studies in which Americans and Koreans were given a detective story with a lengthy list of facts. The researchers asked the subjects to indicate which facts were irrelevant to solving the mystery. The Koreans ruled out far fewer facts as irrelevant. In other studies, Asians expressed less surprise at new information that clashed with what they had already been led to believe, possibly because they were slower to draw definite conclusions. Even outright contradictions were less disturbing or surprising to the Asians than to the Westerners. Westerners exhibit a *hindsight bias*, which is to say, they think they knew something all along, but Asians show an exceptionally strong version of this tendency.

As we shall see, imposing organization on the welter of information is one of the crucial tasks of thought. There are, however, different possible ways to organize things. Asians tend to rely more on relationships and similarities (resemblances) in organizing things, whereas Westerners are more likely to formulate rules and principles and hence to form abstract categories. For example, would you group "notebook" with "pencil" or with "magazine"? Asians choose pencil because of the relationship (writing in the notebook), whereas Americans choose magazine because they both fit the category of written materials.

The two orientations also produce different approaches to resolving conflicts and disputes. The Western, individualistic approach understands conflict as a clash of two opposing entities and seeks to determine which one is right, often on the basis of abstract principles of justice and value. In contrast, the Eastern approach sees apparently opposing entities as part of a whole and tries to find a "middle way" that can avoid conflict by finding merit in both sides. It is hardly surprising that there are many more lawyers per capita in America than in Asia. Nisbett et al. report that Asians prefer to resolve each conflict by negotiation, on the basis of the particulars of the case itself, whereas Americans tend to look to general principles and precedents set by other decisions. Moreover, an ongoing source of conflict when East meets West is that Westerners regard a contract as firm and unalterable once it has been agreed, whereas Easterners assume that it can be continually modified as circumstances change. For example, if we have a contract that you will build me a house for a certain price, but then your labor and materials costs are increased, I (as an American) expect my price to remain the same, and the extra costs are your problem—but you (if you are an Asian) may have assumed that the price would be adjusted.

It is commonly suggested that the Japanese manufacture high-quality products efficiently but lack creativity. Even this difference may be misleading, however, for there is some evidence that the very concept of creativity differs by culture. Westerners understand creativity as developing something entirely new, and so radical innovation is the essence of creative work. In contrast, Asians think of creativity as making small improvements on something that already exists.[16] Hence it is not surprising that radical, ground-breaking innovations tend to originate in the West but often are improved and perfected in the East.

Thus, this line of research has established a set of cultural differences in thinking. They show a consistent theme (holistic versus analytical). Although they are differences along a continuum rather than vastly different or opposite forms of thought, the differences are large enough and consistent enough that they must be taken seriously. Still, let us not overstate them. For example, in the study about whether to group "notebook" with "pencil" or "magazine," both Westerners and Easterners understand both kinds of relationships, and it is simply a matter of favoring one or the other.

Today, the vast majority of cultural psychologists focus on comparing Eastern and Western cultures, because these are the most reliably different. Other differences are likely to be much smaller, with the possible exception of a few small and remote groups. Chinese and Americans may think differently, but one should not expect comparable differences in thinking to be found between Germans and Austrians, or even between Canadians and Spaniards. Moreover, many of the differences highlighted in this section were along single continuums between dichotomies, so there is no readily discernible way for yet a third set of cultures (e.g., African or native Australian) to be meaningfully different from both the Western and the Eastern. It may be safer to say that the two main styles of thought emphasize different things, as opposed to saying that all thinking is relative to its cultural background and that dozens (let alone hundreds) of profoundly different ways of thinking can be found around the globe.

Overview of Thinking

A great mass of information is available to people. Somehow, selected parts of it must get processed, and some of that gets stored away for future reference. Conscious thought is important, but a great deal of processing also occurs outside of awareness. The mind seems to operate on both levels (one conscious, the other automatic), having two systems that follow different operating principles and have different strengths. People vary in their degree of intelligence, and intelligence seems best described as the overall efficacy of the system. That is, smart people can perform the full set of mental operations faster and more accurately than not-so-smart people. The differences are also relative: The least intelligent human beings are still quite intelligent compared to most other species.

The mind's first task is to sort through the mass of available information by picking what to focus on. Multiple factors influence this focus, including expectancies and motivations within the person and patterns within the environment. Then this information is classified into categories and often simplified. To classify and simplify effectively often requires drawing on preexisting knowledge, so memory is accessed in order to deal with new material. Prior knowledge enriches current processing. The more you already know about something, the more fully (and yet also the more efficiently) you can process each new bit of information. Value judgments, causal inferences, and other interpretations may help classify new information. The interpreted material can then be stored in memory.

Reasoning can be done on material either entirely from memory or from a combination of new and remembered information. Reasoning tends to consist of conscious processes (such as following rules for deduction) supported by a great deal of nonconscious processing. For example, evaluating the moral appropriateness of an action may be a conscious process, but much of the categorizing and memory searching may be done by nonconscious processes, and even the moral judgment may be biased by factors operating outside of awareness.

Information is subject to biases and distortions arising from multiple sources. People want to know the truth, but they have strong preferences about what that truth will be, and they will consciously or unconsciously distort new information to fit their biases, expectancies, and preferences. Biases are especially strong with respect to self-knowledge and other issues that are highly relevant to the individual's wants and needs. Inaccuracies may also arise because the mind tends to take shortcuts to simplify its task, and these shortcuts (although generally accurate much of the time) increase the risk of error.

Most complex thinking relies on language and meaning. Thoughts are not entirely created inside the human brain—instead, they invoke systems of concepts that are shared throughout the cultural community, and the same basic set of concepts can be found with only minor variations in every language and every culture. Reasoning is constrained by rules of logic, which are not invented by individual brains but discovered and learned as if they are objective facts. When learning to think, each brain develops a competence in using the systems that other people in the community have developed.

Intelligence

Human beings seem weak and vulnerable in comparison with other species. We do not have sharp teeth or claws with which to tear enemies to shreds. We have no fur or leathery exterior, only a fairly delicate skin, to protect our vital innards from cuts and thrusts. We cannot outrun tigers or alligators. We cannot climb trees as well as monkeys and bears. Despite these handicaps, human beings have taken over the planet. Creatures that serve our needs, like cows and dogs, are allowed into our world in ways we decide. Those who threaten us, such as tigers and bears, are herded off into zoos or remote areas far from our suburbs. Only insects manage to keep pace with us, and we even win some battles against them. In terms of transforming the physical environment, no species has done anywhere near what human beings have achieved.

The human conquest of the planet was achieved not by physical bulk or sharp claws, but it did make use of the most powerful biological weapon of all: culture. By sharing information and knowledge, communicating with each other, building upon the advances of previous generations, and working together, human beings have relatively rapidly outclassed all other species.

Culture required intelligence, among other things. Intelligence underlies these big human advantages, namely, problem solving and social communication. Although it is fashionable nowadays to say that each species is well suited to its niche and therefore cross-species comparisons of intelligence are meaningless, there are still some thinkers who are willing to state the obvious: Human beings are capable of much more complex, abstract, and otherwise intelligent thought than any other known species.[17]

But what exactly is intelligence? Although experts have not agreed on a definition, they have identified some common themes. Intelligence refers to mental abilities. It enables people to process information rapidly and accurately. Hence, it enables people to learn and retain information. It also improves our ability to solve problems. It helps to recognize patterns and also contingencies (what depends on what) in the world. It produces abstract thought, so that people, unlike most animals, are freed from their immediate surroundings and can plan, imagine, analyze, and in other ways deal with information in other places and times. It enables people to build a large stock of knowledge and to retrieve and use it whenever they need it.

The value of intelligence goes far beyond competing with other species. Intelligence leads to success within human social and cultural life, especially in the competition among human beings. Intelligent people do better in many obvious ways, such as succeeding in school, but also in less obvious ones, such as avoiding criminality and remaining healthy. Intelligent people are more successful than their dimmer peers in every career that has been studied, including janitors and waitresses. (To be sure, its relevance to football was openly questioned by Joe Theisman, who was one of the smarter people in football, as shown by his success as a quarterback and later as a television commentator. Theisman said, "Nobody in football should be called a genius. A genius is a guy like Norman Einstein.") These patterns confirm the view of intelligence as the best all-purpose psychological tool (rivaled only, perhaps, by self-control): People with more of it end up better off than people with less of it.

Intelligence can be measured more accurately, precisely, and reliably than any other major psychological trait. Intelligence tests were launched early in the twentieth century and steadily improved throughout the century. Although they are sometimes criticized as tools that oppress some groups (by not accurately measuring their intelligence) and that rationalize the status quo,[18] IQ tests originally were developed to foster opportunities for disadvantaged people and to reduce the advantages of the upper class. The two institutions that took the lead in this movement were schools and the military. Both of these had traditionally given their best positions to rich, upper-class people. Indeed, in Europe for many centuries, the army and navy drew all of their officers from the aristocracy, in some cases by selling commissions for a fee (which therefore excluded poor people). In a similar fashion, the best colleges and universities had been accessible only to students from rich families who could afford their tuition fees. Intelligence (IQ) tests were designed to identify students from middle- and lower-class backgrounds who might benefit from more schooling and to help the army identify which recruits might be smart enough to be useful in ways other than becoming cannon fodder.

Is there a single entity called intelligence, or is it merely the sum of many separate abilities unrelated to each other? Common sense suggests the latter. We all know people who may be brilliant at higher mathematics but can't find their way around a grocery store, or someone who can formulate insightful theories about some obscure issue but can't remember people's names, or someone who has a tremendous vocabulary but can't balance a checkbook. The Scholastic Aptitude Test, which is given to assess whether someone is smart enough to succeed in college, gives three different scores, for verbal, quantitative, and analytical reasoning tests, and the existence of separate scores seems to invoke the principle that these are separate abilities.

Yet the data have consistently clobbered the commonsense theory that different abilities are unrelated. The British psychologist Charles Spearman, born in 1863, is generally credited with this discovery. He noticed that all of the various tests of mental abilities tended to be interrelated—in other words, the same people tended to score high on all of them, or low on all of them. He proposed that a single common factor is present in all different mental abilities and tests. This has become known as *general intelligence*, or *g*. True, there are also some variations in specific abilities that are independent of *g*, but *g* consistently emerges. It is impressive that Spearman noticed the correlation, because the statistical methods of his day were quite primitive in comparison with what is available now. In fact, his theory about *g* spurred the development of new statistical methods for discovering single factors that lurk inside many different measures.

In any case, the grand conclusion is that intelligence is mainly a single, overarching factor.[19] All mental abilities are interrelated to some extent. This connection does not erase the impression that some people are especially smart about certain things or in certain domains. But these are small variations within an overall quality. If the mathematical genius in the earlier example put his mind to it, he could figure out the grocery store—probably much better than the average shopper.

Some experts have attempted to extend the concept of intelligence by adding abilities. Raymond Cattell's distinction between *fluid* and *crystallized* intelligence[20] helps to explain why some scientists may do their best work in their 40s and 50s even though by that age their raw brain power has been in decline for years, having peaked in young adulthood. *Fluid intelligence* refers to the ability to understand new material and to solve unfamiliar problems (and hence corresponds most closely to *g*). *Crystallized intelligence*, in contrast, consists of what one has already learned, including skills for dealing with certain kinds of problems as well as knowledge. Fluid intelligence does reach a peak during young adulthood, whereas crystallized intelligence can continue to build for decades thereafter.

Creativity is not measured by IQ tests, which leads some authorities, such as Robert Sternberg,[21] to propose that a *creative intelligence* can come up with new ideas and deal with novel, unfamiliar situations. Sternberg also says that there is a *practical intelligence*, which consists of being able to deal effectively with everyday problems and the social world. To illustrate the latter ability, he offers the example of a man who loved his job but hated his boss. These conflicting sentiments came to a crisis when a corporate headhunter called to ask whether the man might be willing to change jobs. The man agonized over the question and then came up with a novel solution: He gave the headhunter his boss's name, and soon thereafter the boss was hired away to a different company. That way, the man could keep his job and be free of the despised boss.

Teachers and new parents like to think that they can boost a child's intelligence, but so far there is precious little proof that any specific method will reliably accomplish any improvement. When my own daughter was born, I was eager to learn what I could do to make her as intelligent as possible. Did she need to hear Mozart sonatas, to listen to tapes of foreign languages, to watch "Sesame Street" television shows, to have certain educational bath toys? I asked several of my colleagues who were experts in the study of intelligence what were the main steps for maximizing my baby's intelligence. They all responded in pretty much the same way, which was to give me a sympathetic look, hesitate, smile or grimace, and say something like "try not to drop her on her head." This advice was not very helpful, especially because my parental plans had already included trying to keep head injuries and brain damage to a minimum.

But my colleagues were simply following what the research has shown. No one has found clear support for any long-term improvement in intelligence that can be traced to any particular feature about how a child was raised. To be sure, there are plenty of ambiguous findings. For example, the more books there are in the parents' house, the smarter the kids grow up to be. Maybe the books caused an increase in the children's intelligence. More likely, though, parents who were smarter in the first place bought more books than other parents, because less intelligent people do not read as many (or any) books. And then, smart parents passed along the genes that made their children smart too. The books were a symptom, not a cause, of the intelligence that ran in the family.[22]

Some programs, such as Head Start, have been shown to produce significant increases in intelligence, even as much as 15 points (a full standard deviation, for the statistically inclined) on an IQ test. Unfortunately, these benefits last only as long as the child is still in the program. Put another way, kids in Head Start do score higher in IQ than other kids their age, but a year or two after the program ends, there is no difference. This has become known as the *fade-out effect*. In general, treating a child a certain way can boost intelligence in the short run but not in the long run. In the same way, adopted children do show a small tendency to become more similar to their adopted parents in intelligence, but this small tendency shrinks or disappears when they eventually move out of the adoptive home.[23]

The influence of genetic heredity on intelligence is unanimously supported by a large mass of data, much as some of us might wish otherwise. Current estimates say that from 40% to 80% of the variation in IQ scores is hereditary.[24] Adopted children are always more similar in IQ to their biological parents than to their adopted parents. Identical twins raised apart are more similar in IQ than nonidentical twins or siblings raised in the same family. (But identical twins raised together are even more similar.)[25] A researcher could get fame, prestige, and probably wealth too by proving that parents could do some particular thing for their kids that would produce a lasting improvement in their intelligence, but so far no one has been able to do so.

Though there is not much a parent can do to increase a child's intelligence, parental influence can apparently reduce it.[26] If you abuse your kids, molest them sexually, or starve them, you might end up lowering their IQs. The environment seems to have a bigger effect in the negative direction than in the positive, which illustrates the standard psychological principle that bad is stronger than good.[27] But fortunately such destructive practices are confined to a small minority of extremely bad parents. The effect of average or good parenting is simply to let the child reach the level of intelligence that the genes made possible.

What makes intelligence a useful tool? Obviously, intelligence helps people to solve problems and get the right answers to important questions. It helps them to recognize patterns in their surroundings, so they can spot important trends and developments and discover general principles. Smart people are faster than others even at fairly simple mental tasks.[28] It also appears that the entire mind works together better as an integrated system, so that smart people can coordinate various mental tasks and operations better than others.[29]

An All-Purpose Tool?

As the preceding section showed, intelligence is remarkably effective at improving performance at all sorts of tasks and jobs. Intelligent people do better than their less intelligent colleagues in every career that has been studied. Intelligence can be put to work on a remarkably wide array of problems and challenges. All of this suggests that intelligence is a wonderful all-purpose tool. However, there is some evidence that it did not evolve for that purpose, and indeed evolution does not generally promote multipurpose devices so much as design specific solutions to specific problems. Intelligence may therefore have evolved to solve a certain class of problems, ones that are of special importance to cultural animals.[30]

Evolutionary psychologists Leda Cosmides and John Tooby have provided some of the most dramatic evidence.[31] They proposed that the brain's thinking structures evolved specifically to deal with problems of social exchange, which is a centrally important requirement of cultural participation. A system of exchange between strangers requires people to play their parts and make their contributions, but the natural selfishness of organisms may tempt some to try to take the benefits of group life without contributing their fair share. Hence, according to Cosmides and Tooby, the advanced social brain (the cultural brain) was likely to keep a special lookout for such cheaters.

Their program of research used a classic reasoning problem, called the *Wason selection task*.[32] This task asks subjects to verify whether a logical rule of the form "if P, then Q" has been violated, by investigating cases known to correspond to P, not P, Q, and not Q. In a vivid example, the rule is "If someone is drinking beer, then he or she must be at least 18 years old," and the subject is asked which cases need to be checked: someone who is drinking beer; someone else, who is drinking soda pop; someone else, who is 25 years old; or someone who is 16 years old. (Thus, P refers to drinking beer, and Q refers to being at least 18 years old.) A more abstract version of the same problem runs, "If there is a D on any side of any card, then there is a 3 on the other side," with the added stipulation that every card has a letter on one side and a number on the other. The subject is then presented with cards showing D, R, 3, and 7.

The logically correct answers are D and 7, either of which could be turned over to reveal a D-7 pairing that would violate the rule, just as the correct answers in the underage drinking problem are to check the beer drinker and the 16-year-old. Many researchers have used the Wason task, and in general most people get it wrong, especially when it is presented in abstract form. When Cosmides and Tooby added the underage drinking version, however, suddenly many students got it right. Perhaps this was because they were familiar with that version of the problem, or perhaps it was because the brain is less effectively tailored for abstract reasoning than it is for detecting people who violate the group's rules and seek to obtain illicit benefits. To tease these explanations apart, Cosmides and Tooby tried a variety of other versions of their procedure, such as problems involving food and beverages, which presumably are familiar to students, who eat and drink every day of their lives.

These studies favored the conclusion that thinking is especially geared toward detecting cheaters. Perhaps the most dramatic study compared two similar but reversed versions of P and Q. In one, the rule was "If you take the benefit, then you pay the cost," and in the other, "If you pay the cost, then you take the benefit." The subject's job was to see if anyone was breaking this rule, by investigating any of these four: one accepting the benefit, one not accepting it, one paying the cost, and a fourth not paying it. The logically correct answers are different for the two rules, but subjects responded to both of them by searching for someone who might take the benefit without paying the cost.

The results of these and similar studies point to the important conclusion that the brain does not reason equally well about all problems, even ones that have similar logical structures.[33] Instead, human reasoning seems geared toward specific kinds of problems, specifically ones that violate the basic rules of social exchange. Put another way, the human mind seems naturally inclined not to search for logical fallacies but rather to search for cheaters. This is important confirmation of the view that the mind evolved for participation in cultural systems that rely on social exchange.

Meaning and Language

The previous sections explained the benefits of intelligence, but intelligence could not do much were it not for meaning and language. Meaning and language greatly improve the power of the human mind to understand events, control the world, and pursue human goals. Of course, meaning and language are essential to the fabric of culture, and all human cultures are based on language and meaning. Thus, again, the value of an inner process (intelligence, in this case) is closely tied to living within a cultural society.

Earlier, we discussed how most languages generally draw on the same universe of concepts and ideas. The same ideas get expressed in every language, for the most part. In a sense, this universe of meanings is out there waiting for creatures who are intelligent enough to make use of it. The big advantage of human intelligence is that it's powerful enough to offer access to this common set of ideas. Meanwhile, the human capacity for speech, which is rooted in having a voice box that can reliably produce a vast assortment of sounds, suggests that human beings were designed to be capable of meaningful communication.

Meaning and language embody the power of culture and show what it adds to nature. They also reveal the fallacy of the currently popular view that all human thought can be reduced to brain activity. Popular boosters of neuroscience, such as Steven Pinker, are fond of promoting the idea that human thinking is nothing more than the firing of brain cells. It is true that brain cells do indeed fire during thought, but the "nothing more" part of the assertion is where these reductionists go wrong. Thought is more than brain cell activity. Human thought generally uses language and meaning, which are social realities that are not contained in the brain.

The difference can be appreciated by invoking cognitive psychology's favorite metaphor for the human mind, namely, the computer. Starting in the 1970s, if not earlier, it became popular to think of the mind as a kind of computer that processed information—storing some of it, discarding the rest, recognizing things, analyzing, comparing, combining, and so forth. The electrical activity inside the computer is akin to the firing (also electrical) of brain cells, though they are not set up in quite the same ways.

Culture, with its meaning and language, is like the Internet. To say that human thought is contained in the brain, or is nothing more than brain cell activity, is like saying that the Internet is contained inside your computer, or that the Internet is nothing more than electrical activity inside your computer. But it's not. There is a world of difference between a computer that is linked to the Internet and one that is not, even though the two computers might be of exactly the same make and model. Two identical computers have the potential to perform all of the same operations, but the one that is hooked into the Internet will be of vastly more use and can end up actually accomplishing a great deal more. What happens inside that computer—corresponding to the thoughts that occur in a brain—will be much richer and more complex than what can happen in the computer that is not connected. In the same way, a brain connected to culture can think immensely more and better thoughts than a brain that is not connected.

The cells inside a brain, like the circuits inside a computer, are ultimately useful because they can *represent* meanings. That is, they can take on a special pattern that will stand for those meanings. The meanings themselves are not physical things, nor are they contained inside the brain or computer. The brain allows its owner to participate in culture, but without culture it can only accomplish a limited amount. Human thought consists of the brain making use of meanings—nonphysical realities—obtained from the shared space of culture. That's what the brain is designed to do.

Meaning and language have at least three crucial advantages for thought. As a result of these advantages, most people think in words (as opposed to pictures or some other medium), and language even lurks behind most of the small amount of thinking that takes place via mental pictures.[34]

The first advantage of thinking verbally is that language liberates you from the here and now. By virtue of language and meaning, you can think about possible future events, about people who are far away, about promises made in the distant past. A rat or insect essentially lives in the immediate present and can respond only on the basis of what it can see, hear, and taste. Language allows people to see the present through the lens of those other, invisible facts and even to imagine possible events that have never occurred. This facility is powerfully helpful and liberating. As just one example, animals that have no language cannot possibly understand that some of this year's harvest has to be saved for planting next year, and they might eat their seed corn when they got hungry. They would feel better in the short run, but next year they would have nothing to plant and hence no crop at all. It is hardly an accident that our species is the only one to engage in farming, even though a great many species eat plants.

The ability to transcend the immediate situation vastly expands our ability to control the world. Instead of being stuck with the world as it is, the way a dog or squirrel lives, the human being can see the present arrangement as only one possibility. The present can be compared to ideals and standards. Other systems can be considered as alternatives to the present.

A second advantage of thinking with language is that information can be processed according to the innate structure of meaning. Abstract reasoning, logic, numerical calculations, statistical modeling, and other forms of processing enable people to reach conclusions that would be impossible for someone who thought only in pictures. By using algebra and trigonometry, we can build a much better, more trustworthy, and more durable bridge or dam. If we could not use those mental tools, our building would be comparable to what beavers do, and their efforts are often washed away in the next heavy storm. Even in personal decisions, people can use rational analysis, moral principles, and other forms of thinking that go beyond the simple dialectic of what confronts them and what they feel like doing.

A third advantage is social communication, as noted in chapter 2. Information can be discussed with other people. As a result, knowledge can be shared, pooled, checked, and accumulated. Even if no single person understood how a modern airplane works, human beings could build airplanes that work very well—because different people understand different parts of the plane, and they can work together to build one. Mistakes can be corrected as people discuss them and contribute different insights. New knowledge can be learned by many people, written down, and passed along to the next generation, so that each new generation does not have to start over to solve all of the same problems. Instead, each new generation can take up where the previous one left off and add even more to the general stock of knowledge. This accumulation of knowledge has proven to be a crushing advantage of our species over all others. No matter how smart you are and how hard you work, if you have to start from scratch, you won't get far.

Human intelligence clearly works together with meaning and language. Indeed, skill at using language (even by the simple measure of a large vocabulary) is one factor that distinguishes the more intelligent human beings from their less intelligent peers. A fairly complex, intelligent brain is necessary in order to make use of language. In that sense, the brain was a prerequisite for language. On the other hand, once the brain reached the required level, language greatly increased what it could do. In that sense, language was a prerequisite for enabling the brain to begin fulfilling its potential.

Language is not uniquely human. Certain other species exhibit some degree of communication, and some nonhuman animals even learn limited amounts of human language. These indicate that the linguistic capacity of the brain is not all or nothing. Still, we should not be overly impressed by the vocabulary of dogs or by the handful of chimpanzees that learn sign language. Dogs can learn a fair number of one-word commands, but they cannot generally combine thoughts, so their thinking remains crude and concrete. Chimps can learn more complex language and by some accounts (and even these are disputed) even the rudiments of syntax, but they do not use this language to communicate with each other nor to solve abstract problems. The remarkable capacity of human thought depends not just on having words and symbols but on being able to make different kinds of combinations of them to construct an infinite variety of possible thoughts.

The essence of meaning is connection. Meaning connects things. The concept "flower" connects a wide assortment of plants together. More complex units of meaning, such as sentences and paragraphs, connect different concepts and ideas together. The natural metaphor for meaning is a web, because it involves connecting things that are in turn connected to others.

Distinction is another aspect of meaning. The concept of "flower" not only links all flowers together—it also distinguishes them from other things in the world, such as mountains, trees, bears, vegetables, and softball games.

The simplest thoughts therefore involve making a basic distinction or connection. Even animals with very small brains and limited intelligence can learn some associations, which are essentially a connection and a distinction. The famous early experiments of Pavlov showed that dogs (who are not among the stupidest of animals, although they are far less intelligent than humans) can learn by forming a simple association. A dog that hears a bell at feeding time will soon start to drool when the bell rings even if no food is in sight, because it has learned to connect the sound of the bell and eating food. Canine thought has not progressed far beyond such simple associations, but human thought has reached amazing levels of complexity.

The learning of language by human beings would be a source of astonishment if we were not so accustomed to taking it for granted. A well-known article by Miller and Gildea sought to show what a remarkable achievement it is for an infant to learn to speak—certainly much more impressive than acquiring a second or third language when one already has a language in which the new words can be translated or explained.[35] The vocabulary alone is remarkable. Even if we count each family of words (e.g., write, writes, wrote, writ, written, writing, writer) as consisting of one single word, then the average American high school student has a reading vocabulary of around 40,000 words. Adding in names of people and places, as well as idioms, would approximately double this tally, to 80,000. Learning 80,000 words in 16 years means that a growing child learns about 5,000 every year, or an average of 13 new words per day every single day, year in and year out. And that's not even the most remarkable part: Miller and Gildea pointed out that most experts on linguistics agree that the rapid acquisition of grammar is even more impressive than the vocabulary.

The basis of language is using sounds or other inherently meaningless expressions to symbolize things. Thus it begins with connection: A sound is connected to some entity. A flat piece of wood propped up by thin pillars is called a *table* in English, a *Tisch* in German, a *mesa* in Spanish. The sound is an arbitrary symbol, but the table is real, and the symbolic connection is the foundation of language.

What really enables human thought to reach its potential is not just having symbols but rather the combining of symbols. Instead of simply saying the word *table* when you want one, you can purchase a custom-made, L-shaped, oak butcher block trestle table to fit into a particular nook in your house for a particular intended use.

Here and there, some other animals can combine a symbol or two. But the real power of combining symbols depends on language, which can only exist in a community of minds. No matter how smart you are, you will only have language if you grow up in a community that has language collectively. It is existing within a culture that enables intelligence to use meaning and language to begin realizing the potential power of human thought. For that to happen, people must be able to recognize that they are similar enough to each other that they can share mental acts and meanings. This brings up the next crucial point.

Being One of Us

To describe humans as cultural animals is to say that they are designed by nature to participate in a community. This is only possible if people recognize that they belong to a group of people who have minds like their own and whose ideas they can therefore share. This is a crucial and possibly unique aspect of human functioning.

People generally, and psychologists in particular, are frequently fascinated by stories about children who were raised by wolves or in some other way survived long periods without human contact.[36] When these individuals finally do come into contact with human beings, they generally fail to turn into normal citizens. Some researchers conclude from this that experiences during childhood are vital for socializing a human being who can function in society and that once these critical periods of development are past, learning becomes almost impossible. Others are inspired to learn that a human being can grow up and survive without contact with other humans. Unfortunately, these isolated cases are difficult to interpret, not least because of the possibility that the wild children were autistic to begin with—which is perhaps why they were abandoned by their families, why they could survive without human contact, and why they cannot learn to fit in when human society "rescues" them from the wild. Most normal human children cannot stand to be deprived of human contact for even a couple of hours at a time, let alone years.

A famous passage in Jean-Paul Sartre's *Being and Nothingness* alluded to "the look" as a decisive cause of human consciousness and self-consciousness.[37] Sartre was referring to the experience of looking at someone and knowing that that person was looking back at you. When two people's eyes meet, each person is immediately, intimately aware that there has been some connection between minds. How could you not be self-aware once you recognize that another person is looking right at you and being aware of you?

Fascinating studies by Michael Tomasello and his colleagues have confirmed the importance of shared attention.[38] Indeed, Tomasello contends that humans share many mental processes with other primates, and so many of the principles we describe later in this chapter—sorting and classifying, finding patterns, simplifying, and the like—are not uniquely human. But knowing oneself to be part of a group of individuals who all have similar minds is uniquely human, he has concluded.

Consider the interactions between mother and baby. In many species, mothers and babies attend to each other and manage to communicate about what the baby needs and how the mother can provide it. In this, human beings are nothing special. But Tomasello has concluded that we are the only species in which mothers and babies signal to each other the presence of something else in the environment simply for the sake of enabling them to perceive it together. "Look!" is universally one of the earliest words that human mothers speak to babies and one of the first that babies use to communicate with mothers. Calling someone's attention to a bright light, pretty color, or peculiar flower does not seem all that remarkable, unless you realize that it is beyond what almost any other species can accomplish. (I have tried to get my various dogs to look at something, but typically no amount of pointing, gesturing, or shouting can get a dog to look where you want. They just stare at me stupidly, while outside the window the rabbits scamper by with impunity.) In fact, Tomasello emphasizes, human babies past the age of about 9 months often will spontaneously turn to see what Mama is looking at, without being instructed or exhorted to do so. To do this, they must apparently understand that Mama has a mind that is perceiving something and that they can perceive that same thing by looking in the same direction.[39]

What the human baby shares with other humans is not just the capability of joint attention, although that is hugely important. A related ability is the recognition of *intention*. Because you know that other humans have minds and inner mental states like you have, you quickly learn to attribute intentions to them, just as your own behavior is organized by intention. You choose a goal and then perform actions that are designed to bring about that goal—and, once you realize that other human beings are similar to you, you can interpret their actions as intentional.

Recent findings from neuroscience suggest that the human brain has an innate capability and tendency to read intention into the behavior of others.[40] A Swedish researcher developed a procedure by which he attached lightbulbs to a person's joints and then filmed the person moving around in a dark room.[41] All that showed up on the film was a bunch of moving points of light. When other people watched this film, they quickly and effortlessly recognized the light movements as indicating intentional movement by a human being. Even human babies as young as 3 months could tell the difference between these "human" light movements and a pattern of random movements with the same number of points of light. Other studies show that the brain seems to use its own experiences with movement to be able to infer intention from the movements of other people. Taken together, these studies indicate that the human brain is designed to perceive human movement in a way that leads to inferring intentions.[42]

Other work has confirmed that the human brain seems hard-wired to perceive intention.[43] In these, 18-month-old human babies watched either a human model or a mechanical device trying but failing to perform various actions, such as pulling something apart. The infants who watched a person fail would imitate the action themselves and succeed. Those who watched a mechanical device attempt the same act were not moved to copy or improve on it. Thus, even very young human beings interpret identical acts differently depending on whether they are performed by a fellow human being or by something else. In Tomasello's terms, we "identify with our species" much more than any other creatures do.[44]

Identifying with our species is not absolutely crucial to communication, but communication cannot get nearly as far without it as with it. An animal might bark or chirp out a warning to alert family members to the presence of food or the presence of a predator, and these patterns can be sustained simply because they improve the chances that one's partners will continue to be around. Identifying with the species entails recognizing that others have inner mental states similar to one's own. Chimps and other smart animals generally fail these tests.[45] For example, they do not distinguish between fellows who are ignorant versus those who are knowledgeable about some crucial fact. In some studies, a chimp has to choose another chimp to get a reward for it, and the chooser has observed that one fellow chimp saw where the food was hidden while another chimp didn't see it. Obviously, only the first fellow will be of any help, and so that's the one to choose. But the choosing chimp seems to choose at random upon which of the other fellows to rely, disregarding the crucial fact that only one of the others has the requisite knowledge.

Even more important, chimps do not seem to share knowledge deliberately. They seem to lack the capacity to recognize that communicative behaviors are intended to share some useful information. Chimps who learn how to cooperate with a human being to perform a difficult task (such as pulling two ropes to move a heavy box) do not seem to understand that newly arrived chimps don't know how to do that, and so they fail to teach or show the newcomer how to get the job done.[46] Intentional teaching is hugely helpful for transmitting culture, and the lack of it may help explain why human beings have been able to develop culture and benefit from it so much more than any other animals.

In short, human beings recognize other human beings as intentional agents like themselves. These capabilities enable humans to understand themselves as part of a community, indeed a community that is based on shared understandings—which are the essence of meaning and culture. Once people recognize that others are like themselves, they can communicate with them, learn from them, try to please and impress them, discuss each other with third parties, share information, initiate cooperation, and do many other actions that constitute culture.

Pattern and Consistency

An important function of intelligence is to recognize patterns in the world. The process of finding patterns can be described as a way of shifting from chaos to order. In an important sense, the mind imposes organization on a welter of sensory information. The essence of a pattern is connecting things, so the mind is predisposed to make connections. This would obviously be a useful and adaptive way for the mind to work. Finding patterns in the world increases our ability to predict what will happen, which is quite helpful in itself and can be even more valuable as an aid to exerting control. If we couldn't see the patterns, everything would surprise us all the time. Finding patterns is useful for dealing with the natural environment, and it is perhaps even more useful and important for dealing with the immensely complex social and cultural environment. Hence the cultural animal is a talented pattern finder (though some other animals are good at that too).

If the mind is in essence a pattern-finding tool, it should be liable to excesses along that line. More precisely, the mind should have a tendency to discern patterns that are not really there and to overestimate how stable and reliable these patterns are. A number of such tendencies have been well established.

A bias toward seeing patterns that aren't there would lead people to think they see orderly patterns in events that are actually random. People do tend to impose order on random events. People have certain (false)

preconceptions about what random sequences should look like. For example, if you are flipping a coin, the sequence "heads, tails, heads, tails, tails,
heads" will come up just as often as the sequence "heads, heads, heads, tails,
tails, tails," but people think the latter outcome is not as random. They will
be tempted to construe it as having some kind of meaning.[47]

The widespread belief in "hot streaks" and "slumps" among athletes
may be an example of misunderstanding random sequences. The definition of a hot streak is that an athlete's consecutive efforts are related to
each other, so that during the streak he will be more likely to make a
successful shot or play than at other times. Athletes, spectators, coaches,
and sportscasters all believe in hot streaks. Careful statistical analysis suggests that these beliefs are unfounded.[48] People continue to believe them
because they are imposing patterns that aren't there onto what are really
just random fluctuations around a person's average level of performance.
If you flip a coin several hundred times, sooner or later you are likely to
get five heads in a row. This will occur by chance, but at the time it will
seem like a hot streak.

Another instance of seeing patterns that aren't there is what is called
illusory correlation. People are quick to form an impression that two things
go together, even if there is no factual basis for their belief. These illusory patterns may arise because people have a reason to think that the two
belong together, or even because things stand out and grab attention. For
example, clinical psychologists have long used a test called Draw a Person to assess mental illness, and one of the standard ideas was that people
suffering from paranoia will draw characters with big eyes. Large studies
have disconfirmed this stereotype, but many clinicians continue to believe
it anyway. Researchers then turned their attention to the persistence of
this belief in the face of evidence. They would bring in drawings made by
mental patients, some of which had big eyes and some of which did not,
and they would label each one with the patient's psychiatric diagnosis. This
way, the researchers could set up the stack so that there was or was not a
link—in other words, they could control whether big eyes were more likely
to go with a diagnosis of paranoia or were not. The clinicians kept concluding that the stack had confirmed that people with paranoia drew big eyes,
even when in reality there was no relationship. In fact, in one study the
researchers set up a reverse relationship, so that if you tallied everything
carefully you would find that people with paranoia were less likely than
others to draw big eyes—but the clinicians who went through the stack still
concluded that people with paranoia were more likely to draw big eyes.[49]
In short, expectancies can make people think they see relationships and
patterns that are not there in reality.

The human tendency to find connections and patterns where none exist is an important basis for superstition and magical thinking. Many people long believed that witches cast their spells by means of magical connections. To cast a spell on someone, a witch would need one of two kinds of objects. One kind consisted of things that looked like the person, such as a picture or voodoo doll that supposedly resembled the person in some way. The other kind of magical object was something that had been in contact with the target's physical self, such as hair clippings or clothing. The principles seem to be that connections remain imbued with power: Things that look alike or things that have been in contact seem to retain a connection. These scientifically unfounded beliefs have persisted for centuries and provide the basis for countless superstitions.

Lest this kind of thinking seem obsolete and quaint, Paul Rozin and his colleagues have shown that these forms of magical thinking are still alive and well and strong enough to change the behavior of educated, modern adults.[50] To demonstrate the "contagion" pattern, they had people drink from a glass of apple juice. Next the experimenter put a sterilized, dead cockroach into the juice. Then the experimenter removed it, leaving the juice in the same condition it had been in a moment earlier—but nobody wanted to take a sip. In fact, most of the participants would not drink any apple juice, even if the experimenter poured them a new drink in a fresh, clean glass. The entire idea of apple juice had become contaminated by the temporary connection with the cockroach. In other studies, people refused to wear a sweater that had supposedly been worn by Adolf Hitler, even though the sweater was clean and could not produce any genuine negative effect on the new wearer.

The researchers also demonstrated the similarity principle in several clever ways. One was to ask research participants to bring a disposable photograph of a loved one. The researcher took the photo and put it in the center of a target and instructed the participant to throw darts at it. It does not do any actual harm to your mother or boyfriend to throw a dart at a photograph, but people were inhibited anyway: They were less able to hit the target with their darts than were control-group subjects who aimed at a clean target with no photo. In other words, people acted as if damaging the picture had magical powers to hurt their loved ones.

So far I have spoken about seeing patterns that are not there. A related tendency capitalizes on real patterns but exaggerates them. Roughly, "sometimes true" gets converted to "usually true" or even "always true"; more precisely, people mistake weak relationships for strong ones. In judging other people's behavior, for example, people will tend to overestimate the consistency of their personality traits. People tend to understand their own behavior as a response to the immediate situation, but they see others as acting the way they do because of their inner traits and intentions.[51] Thus, people tend to overestimate patterns in the actions of other people around them.

Stereotypes provide an important instance of finding patterns in the social environment. Although it has become fashionable to deplore stereotyping as immoral, there is probably no way to stop people from forming and using stereotypes. Forming general impressions of groups of people is one way to simplify the social world and to make the volume of information manageable, and people will probably have to continue doing it even though it does produce errors—and even though it goes against the American ideal of treating and judging each individual on the person's own merits.

Stereotypes can arise even in the complete absence of objective evidence, simply by virtue of salience. David Hamilton and his colleagues have repeatedly shown that research subjects will form stereotypes about fictitious, made-up groups if they stand out.[52] Suppose, for example, that a minority group commits crimes (or, in their studies, causes automobile accidents) at exactly the same rate as the majority. Because the rates are the same, there is no basis for regarding the minority group as more violent or criminal. But crimes are rare, so they stand out, and because minority group members are rare, they also stand out. As a result, crimes by the minority group members are hard to overlook. Hence people will form a stereotype even in the absence of any valid basis.

More commonly, stereotypes do have some genuine factual basis, but people may exaggerate its extent and overgeneralize. The stereotype that "women can't do math" has persisted for decades. The objective evidence confirms that girls and women are slightly less competent than boys and men at solving mathematical problems, but the difference is small. Jacqueline Eccles Parsons described how the national media reported the results of a large survey of mathematical aptitude scores among high school students.[53] The boys did better, but gender accounted for only 3% of the variance—yet the media ignored the smallness of the effect and depicted the results as if they suggested that girls should forget about trying to work with numbers. In the same way, a story in the *Chronicle of Higher Education* addressed the so-called publication gap between male and female professors. The cover illustration showed a man standing behind a stack of publications that was 16 times higher than the stack of publications in front of his female colleague, thereby implying that men produce 16 times as much work. In reality, female professors typically produce between 60% and 80% as much as their male colleagues.[54] The difference is thus much smaller than the impression people form. These examples illustrate the general pattern: Stereotypes take a small though real tendency and somehow transform it into the impression of a large, basic difference.

Expectancies

The psychologist Curtis Hardin told of traveling from his home in Los Angeles to Spokane, Washington, for a conference.[55] Arriving at night, he took a cab to the hotel, and along the way he asked the cab driver to recommend some good restaurants. The driver gave him some information and then added that the area was very safe; Hardin did not have to worry about walking around at night. Hardin assured him that, being from Los Angeles, he could take care of himself in any case. After checking in, Hardin went for a walk in the park near the hotel. He was quite surprised when a large man emerged from the darkness and said, "Give me all your money, or I'll knock you out." Hardin was so flustered that he asked the man to repeat what he had said, and the man obliged by reiterating the demand and threat. Hardin then objected, "But the cab driver said that it was safe to walk around here." The mugger was silent for a moment, and then said, "Well, that's probably right. OK, I won't knock you out, but can you still give me something?" Hardin gave him $3, and they parted amicably.

Thus, even novel interactions are shaped by expectancies. Hardin had been led to expect that walking was safe, and when he encountered a threatening stranger, the violation of his expectancy was so stunning that he didn't know how to behave, despite his earlier claims of big-city sophistication, to the extent that he tried to reason with the mugger because the cab driver had promised him safety. The absurdity of this objection was also presumably not what the mugger expected, and his own surprise left him at a loss for how to proceed, to the extent that he retracted his threat and simply asked for a small donation.

Expectancies are one of the most basic units of thought. Many animal researchers believe that nonhuman animals form expectancies. A rat that receives food every time a light goes on seems to learn to expect food when the light comes on, and the rat will show signs of dismay if the light comes on but no food comes. If this view of animal mentality is correct, then expectancies are one of the few forms of thought that do not depend on language.

Expectancies accomplish some of the main purposes of thought. They involve finding patterns in the environment and thus imposing order on chaos. An expectancy is typically based on extrapolating from a recognized pattern. In children's magazines, for example, the exercises in pattern recognition boil down to what the child expects to see next—grapes, grapes, apple, apple, grapes, grapes, apple, blank—and the child is supposed to fill the blank with another apple. To succeed, the child has to see the pattern, extrapolate, and hence expect that the next item will be an apple.

Another purpose of thought is to simplify the world to make it more manageable and comprehensible. Expectancies help here too. People's expectancies operate like a round hole, and actual experience is a peg that might or might not fit. If the peg is round or nearly round, you can plug it right into the hole without giving it further thought. On the other hand, if the experience is a square peg, the lack of fit stands out.

These two possibilities correspond to the responses called *assimilation* and *contrast*. Just as the almost-round peg can be treated as if it were perfectly round, expectancies cause people to exaggerate how closely reality fits their preconceptions. If you expect another person to be hostile, you will interpret her behavior as more hostile than it might actually be. This is assimilation. But assimilation works only if the reality is fairly close to what you expected. If you expect hostility and the person is unmistakably friendly and generous, then a contrast effect ensues, and you may even exaggerate the difference between what you expected and what you found. Put another way, expectancies can polarize reactions to events, driving them to either extreme: exaggerating similarity or contrast.

Seeing your expectancies confirmed is hardly on an equal footing with seeing them contradicted. When events conform to your expectancies, you can move along without giving the matter a second thought. But when events contradict what you expected, you have reason to think that you had the wrong pattern or wrong principle. Disconfirmed expectancies therefore prompt more thought. This tendency is well established in research: People spend a lot more time and effort analyzing events that violate their expectancies than events that confirm them.[56] Most likely, a violation of expectancies operates as one important alarm that calls the conscious system into action. When events go pretty much as expected, the automatic system can run things smoothly.

Emotions are also affected by expectancies. People react with much stronger emotion if an event is unexpected. Emotion too is often a spur to conscious processing, and so this is another sign that expectancy violations activate the conscious system. A dramatic illustration of this response occurred in connection with the terrorist bombings of the World Trade Center in New York in 2001. A hijacked airplane crashed into one tower and then, a quarter of an hour later, another hijacked plane crashed into the second tower. The news media focused on the towers after the first incident, allowing millions of people to witness the second crash live. Living in California at the time, we were asleep and heard about the events only after they had happened. We saw the crash replayed over and over on television, but by then we knew what was going to be shown and hence the emotional impact was muted. In contrast, our colleagues who were awake in time to see the second crash live—without expecting it—said that the emotional impact was unimaginably stronger. They reported being struck by an overwhelming wave of distress, which caused some to vomit and others to sob uncontrollably.

A less dramatic indication of the same phenomenon is evident among sports spectators. For years, the Super Bowl games have been among the most heavily watched shows in the history of network television, yet they were never replayed—even though the networks do replay a great many shows of limited and dubious appeal. But people do not like to watch bygone sports events when they already know the outcome. A social scientist might even have predicted the opposite pattern, namely, that people would prefer to watch reruns so they can avoid being disappointed by having their favorite team lose. Yet they don't. The suspense of the unexpected is apparently a vital factor in producing the emotional enjoyment of sports.[57]

Expectancies shape how people learn and remember. As you hear someone speak, your mind automatically projects what the person is likely to say next, and your projection makes it easier to understand what the person says. People know what kinds of things go with what context, and once they grasp the context, they know what to expect. When the further information fits the context, people learn it better than they learn the same information out of context. But when the information directly violates expectancies by being inconsistent with the context, people tend to learn it more poorly than they learn the same information without context.[58] Thus, expectancies can interfere with learning and memory, even though expectancies facilitate them too.

Actually, the effect of breaking expectancies has been somewhat controversial. Some experts claim that learning is impaired, and others say that it is facilitated. This contradiction can be resolved by noting that expectancies can be violated in two different ways, with different consequences. First, something may simply lie outside the realm of expectancy and seem to be irrelevant to it. This kind of violation tends to be forgotten, possibly because the mind doesn't readily know what to do with that information. Second, something may be the direct opposite of what is expected. This circumstance tends to get careful attention and be remembered, although some of the thinking is devoted to reconciling the contradiction.[59] Suppose, for example, that your stereotype of Asian Americans is that they are poor drivers but talented at mathematics. If you meet an Asian American who is a terrific driver and incompetent at mathematics, you may spend time wondering about the contradiction and dealing with the challenge to your stereotype. As a result, you may remember these characteristics of the person quite well, even though you may also come up with particular reasons that your stereotype is still valid. In contrast, finding out that this Asian American is good at knowing the names of birds and poor at mixing drinks will make less of an impression. These facts do not contradict the stereotype; they are simply irrelevant to it. Hence, they will tend to be forgotten.

The term *self-fulfilling prophecy* is undoubtedly the most famous and popular expression for expectancy effects. Some of these events involve interactions between people, such as when one person's expectancy leads to an actual change in the actions of the other, but others occur entirely inside the perceiver's mind.[60] The gist is that expecting to see something causes you to see it. To some extent, these are simply assimilation effects.

Yet other processes serve these expectancy effects too. The way we search for information is shaped by our expectancies, and it is always tempting to overlook things that don't fit. The great biologist Charles Darwin had a personal habit that illustrates this pattern. Whenever he found something that did not fit his theory, he insisted on writing it down in his notes immediately. He knew all too well that scientists tend to focus on facts that confirm their theories and hence might neglect or forget ones that don't fit, and he was trying to avoid that pitfall.

The tendency to search selectively for evidence that fits one's expectancy has been labeled the *confirmation bias*. A well-known study by John Darley and Paget Gross showed that this bias can sustain stereotypes.[61] Students watched a tape of a young girl and were told to form an impression of her scholastic ability. Half were told the girl came from an affluent background, attended good, modern schools, and had educated parents. The other half were led to think the girl came from a disadvantaged background, attended a poor school, and had relatively uneducated parents. Normally, one would expect the student from the better background to have higher ability, based on the advantages she has enjoyed. But the students who watched the tape did not predict any difference in the girl's ability or performance based on the background alone. In some cases, however, the students went on to watch the girl take an oral test. She did well in parts of the test and not so well in other parts. Everyone saw the same tape, so in a sense everyone should have been able to form the same impression of her ability. Ironically, the differences in impressions emerged only among people who watched the tape—even though they all watched the same tape. The students were able to "test" their expectancies by watching the tape, and the confirmation bias enabled them to see their (opposite) predictions confirmed. The students who knew that the girl came from an affluent, privileged background focused on the parts of the tape in which she performed well and concluded that she was quite smart after all. Meanwhile, the students who thought she was from a disadvantaged background focused on the parts of the tape in which she performed poorly, and these viewers saw their low expectancies confirmed.

The confirmation bias is another instance of how expectancies help to simplify the world. Although the confirmation bias can produce wrong conclusions, mostly it works well. In either case, expectancies help us sort through the chaos of possible information to focus on a few crucial and relevant things.

Screening and Sorting

Much of human thought is designed to screen out information and to sort the rest into a manageable condition. The inflow of data from our senses could create an overwhelming chaos, especially given the immense amount of information available in culture and society. Out of all the sensory impressions and possible information, it is vital to find a small amount that is most relevant to our individual needs and to organize that into a usable stock of knowledge. Expectancies accomplish some of this work, helping to screen out information that is irrelevant to what is expected, and zeroing attention in on clear contradictions. The processes of learning and memory are marked by a steady elimination of information. People notice only a part of the world around them. Then, only a fraction of what they notice gets processed and stored into memory. And only part of what gets committed to memory can be retrieved.

The elimination of information is far from random. To be sure, some information gets lost that you later wish you had. Remember taking a history test and wishing you remembered the names and dates that you did study but that somehow you can't summon up to answer the questions? In general, though, the mind has an elaborate sorting mechanism (again, relying heavily on expectancies), which is designed to help it find the important information and discard the rest. Likewise, people have general beliefs, assumptions, and ideas based on their experiences and knowledge. They know how a specific role is supposed to be enacted, what is appropriate in many situations, and the like. Stereotypes and prejudices also qualify as beliefs about the world. These forms of knowledge enable you to spot problems quickly or search for relevant, helpful information.

The view that cognition is the servant of motivation entails that people's wants and needs will influence their mental activity, and this assumption is widely accepted. On a long car trip, for example, many people notice that the highway signs and billboards for upcoming restaurants seem to stand out more as the passengers get hungry: The inner desire for food subtly directs their attention to the opportunities for eating. Relevance to the self is an important guide. Things relevant to the self get noticed more, thought about more, and remembered better.[62] The finding that people wake up to the sound of their own name more readily (even when spoken more softly) than to other words or sounds is an indication that the mind is extra watchful for information relevant to the self, even when it is sleeping.

One seemingly innate basis for sorting information is the principle that bad is stronger than good. People notice bad things more than good things. For example, one angry face in a crowd is spotted faster than one smiling face in a crowd.[63] We spend more time thinking about blocked goals, about people who express negative emotions, about lost bets, and about failed performances than about reached goals, people who express positive emotions, bets that were won, and successful performances.[64] We remember other people's bad behaviors better than their good behaviors.[65] The only exception seems to be that because people want to hold favorable views of themselves, they have inner defense processes that help them to dismiss and forget their own failures and misdeeds, especially after a fair amount of time has passed.

There is more to sorting information than simply deciding what is irrelevant and what should therefore be discarded. The information you keep has to be organized so it can be used now or stored in a way that allows it to be located and used in the future. To accomplish this, things and events are sorted into categories. There is a logical way to sort them, and if we programmed a computer to sort information, we would follow the logical method: Choose the criteria that define the category. Each new thing that comes along can be checked against the criteria. If it fits them, it goes in the category. If it doesn't fit any of them, it is excluded.

But that's not apparently how people actually sort. Instead, they rely on whether the new case resembles their mental image of the category. The mental image may be an ideal version, called a *prototype*, or it may simply be a highly familiar example.[66] But that's why people can classify some instances faster and with greater certainty than others, whereas a computer can decide all instances at about the same speed and with the same assuredness. Is a certain large plant actually a tree? Is a bat a bird? There are ways to make such judgments based on clear definitions, but most people approach them by trying to decide whether they are sufficiently similar to their mental images of a tree or bird. Compared to a robin, a penguin may seem less like a bird.

Sorting information into categories is a constant, ongoing process. It is one of the first things that happen with new information. Almost as soon as your eyes and ears (or nose or taste buds) get any little bit of incoming data, they categorize it. And almost all mental processes start off by working with categories.[67] People do much categorization without conscious thought or effort—rather, the mind automatically fits new information into categories as soon as the information arrives, and by the time anything shows up in consciousness, it has already been identified as belonging to some category with a definite place in a system of other categories. You recognize a friend's face, a telephone, or a flower without having to ask yourself what it is. Even when you do have some conscious uncertainty, some categorization has been done. For example, if someone smiles at you with obvious friendly recognition and you can't immediately recall his name, you have still succeeded at some categorizing: You know it is a face, male, adult, and so forth. Your uncertainty is limited to figuring out which of the people you have met is the owner of this face; you aren't likely to be wondering whether this is a face at all, as opposed to being a lobster, a melody, a shoe, or the battle of Gettysburg.

Some categories are already built into the mind at birth, although these are a minority. It has been shown, for example, that certain rodents are born knowing how to recognize the shadows of the birds that eat them.[68] The vision system is hard-wired to recognize certain visual properties, with certain brain cells allocated to recognizing horizontal lines, others vertical lines, and so forth.[69] Human infants may have an innate readiness to recognize certain facial expressions, such as a loving smile or an angry frown.[70] Still, most categories have to be learned, and one of the main jobs of growing up is to develop an effective system for categorizing information. People learn new categories throughout life. Undoubtedly, each new role they acquire brings with it new ways of sorting and classifying information, so part of mastering a role is learning a new way of thinking—starting with the basic categories that are needed. A new father, for example, may find himself mentally resorting all of his possessions on the basis of whether they represent a choking hazard for his baby.

People categorize other people too. It is no accident that the most prevalent stereotypes the world over are based on highly visible markers. You can usually tell a person's race and gender at first sight, even from a distance, and so it is natural—even if morally or politically undesirable—to categorize people on that basis. Likewise, visible characteristics such as disfigurations, handicaps, or obesity are readily used to categorize people.

Obesity is especially interesting, because it has come to mean something negative in most societies, whereas in some times and places, it has been a signal of wealth and prosperity. One of my friends returned from years of working in Asia to his home in New York, and after a couple of months he encountered another person who had just come back. "Hey, Ed, you're looking fat," said his friend with a big smile. When he saw the shocked look on Ed's face, he explained, "I meant that in an Asian sense!" In the Far East, where they had worked, the historical memory of chronic famine and undernourishment, which meant that only the rich would ever be able to gain weight, was still strong. But in opulent America, gaining weight is no sign of socioeconomic prestige, and indeed some people have suggested that ours is the first society in world history in which body weight and socioeconomic status are negatively correlated. Either way, though, weight is still obvious enough that it takes a deliberate effort not to use it to categorize people. The stigma of obesity in modern America is strong enough that it spreads to companions. In one study, normal-weight male job applicants were judged more negatively if they were in the company of an obese woman, as compared to being in the company of a normal-weight woman.[71]

Skimping on Thought

The human mind has only limited resources for dealing with the vast amount of information in the world. Again, if we were only dealing with the physical environment, we might be able to handle everything important, but the social and cultural environments multiply the amount of information so vastly that there is no way that even a great genius could process it all. The activities of screening out irrelevant information, as described in the previous section, are at least partly due to the necessity of culling the information down to a manageable quantity. The mind has developed a couple of ways to deal with information overload.

One of these is a general orientation to skimp where possible. The term *cognitive miser* was proposed by Susan Fiske and Shelley Taylor to describe this orientation.[72] Just as a miser seeks to avoid spending his gold, the social thinker tries to avoid expending mental effort and attention. Many patterns (though not all) fit this view. In particular, people adopt shortcuts and simplifying strategies to enable them to reach answers quickly and easily. And once they have formed an impression or belief, it is resistant to change. In a famous early demonstration of the latter phenomenon, Craig Anderson and his colleagues had people read stories about either risk-taking or cautious firefighters and then think of reasons that either risky or cautious people would make better firefighters.[73] After the participants finished their task, the researchers told them that the stories were fictitious and then asked them whether risky or cautious people made better firefighters. The research subjects had at this point learned that the evidence on which they based their theories was false, and they should therefore have been back to square one, but they weren't. The people who had thought up reasons that risk takers make better firefighters continued to believe that same conclusion, even after the evidence was demolished. Conversely, the people who had thought up reasons that cautious people make better firefighters continued to assert that their view was true. Other research has replicated these results and confirmed that, in general, people are reluctant to change their beliefs.

On the other hand, the view that people avoid thinking whenever possible has been contradicted by other findings. People try to skimp on thinking about many things, but on a few topics they are willing to devote a great deal of thought. At the extreme, some people dwell obsessively on certain topics or ruminate about particular events or problems. (Edgar Wallace once defined an intellectual man as one who had found something more interesting than women.) They may replay an embarrassing or unfortunate incident repeatedly or analyze yesterday's big game endlessly. The popularity of crossword puzzles shows that people are not simply averse to unnecessary thinking.

Perhaps triage is a better metaphor than miserliness.[74] The term *triage* comes from military medicine: Given the battlefield's constraints on time, medical staff, and medicines, not all of the wounded could receive care, so the military physicians developed a practice of quickly sorting the incoming patients into groups: who should receive immediate care (because they might otherwise die), who should wait (because their wounds were less severe), and who should not be treated (because they were too badly wounded to save). In the same way, people's motivations and circumstances dictate what topics are worth thinking about, even at great length, versus which ones should get minimal treatment.

Simplifying

Human thought also leans generally toward simple, even simplistic forms of understanding. The physical environment is somewhat complex,[75] and the social and cultural environments are extremely complex, and so a full understanding of our surroundings would stretch the capacities of even the most intelligent and energetic mind. It is therefore no wonder that people often favor simpler forms of thought.

The simplest, most basic form of thought is a distinction between two things, as in yes or no. The preference for simplicity entails that such dichotomous thinking is common. That is, the way people think about many aspects of the world is to invoke such simple categories: good and bad, us against them, my fault or not my fault. Often the underlying reality exists on a continuum, but people think of dichotomies anyway. For example, someone can be very angry, somewhat angry, slightly angry, or not at all angry. Indeed, degrees of anger could be graded along a 100-point scale. Yet people still treat anger as a dichotomy: "Are you angry or not?" The example of being at fault, which is to say, responsible for some event, is almost always a matter of degree, for all events have multiple causes, but people still speak as if fault were a dichotomy. Either you are to blame, or you're not.

Good versus bad is an especially strong and widespread dichotomy. It can be applied to entire persons or to individual actions. It can even be applied to seemingly neutral, inert aspects of the environment. Dieters, for example, tend to sort all foods into good and bad ones, sometimes irrationally.[76] To a dieter, salads are good, and cheeseburgers are bad, even though a salad with dressing may contain more fat and more calories than the cheeseburger.

Part of the simplifying process is demanded by the requirements for decision making. Decisions are often dichotomous. Should we buy this item or not? Should I accept that job offer or not? Should I marry this person or not? Can we trust them or not? Does she need surgery or not? Often these decisions require integrating several strands of information, all of which may come in the form of points on a continuum. The decision whether to marry someone, for example, may rest on how attractive the person is, how trustworthy, how rich, how easy to get along with—all of which can be compared against many other potential spouses. And there is one's own appeal to consider too: The most desirable potential spouse in the world probably would be highly sought after by many people and therefore would be unlikely to choose you. The other person's desirability and your chances also involve continuums. As the desirability of the potential spouse goes up, the chances of that person accepting your offer go down, and it might be foolish to pass up a pretty good opportunity in exchange for pie in the sky, although if you could attract your ideal person you might be happier than you would be with the one standing in front of you. Ultimately, all of this information has to be channeled into the simple yes-or-no decision.

Simplistic thinking is also reasonably effective, and so the effort to be more complex may not always seem worthwhile. Fiske and Taylor illustrated this principle by asking you to suppose that you thought a certain kind of dog, such as a terrier, was dangerous and prone to bite.[77] Perhaps a terrier bit you once and created this bad impression. It would be possible to evaluate whether this belief is correct. You could assemble a large sample of terriers and observe how often they bite people. Of course, that test alone doesn't prove whether they are more dangerous than other dogs, so you would need a comparison sample. Get an assortment of nonterrier dogs and observe them too, and record how frequently they bite. Then you can compare the biting rates of terriers and nonterriers. This procedure would get you a pretty reliable answer to the question of whether terriers are more dangerous than other dogs, especially if you collected your observations carefully and systematically, and you used statistical analysis to evaluate the difference. But it would take a lot of time and effort. Simply avoiding terriers would be much simpler and safer. Even if your belief is objectively wrong—that is, if terriers are no more prone to bite than any other dogs—you haven't lost much.

And, to be sure, simple conclusions are sometimes apt. In recent years, Great Britain has debated whether to ban fox hunting. A fox hunt is a traditional activity in which a fox is pursued through the countryside by an armed party of aristocrats, who are mounted on horses and accompanied by a pack of dogs. Jack Straw, the British home secretary, commissioned a study of the phenomenon by Lord Burns. The distinguished man reviewed the evidence about fox hunts, including the usual outcome, which is that the fox is either shot to death by the hunters or torn to shreds by the pack of dogs. In a memorable example of British understatement, Burns's report issued the judgment that this procedure "seriously compromises the welfare of the fox."[78]

Probabilities constitute a major human blind spot and hence a major focus for simplistic thought. Reality (especially social reality) is essentially probabilistic, but human thought prefers to treat it in simple, black-and-white categories. Many of the principal errors and fallacies in human thought can be understood as a matter of failing to appreciate how probability works. The simplest and most familiar of these is the gambler's fallacy. Everyone knows that heads and tails are equally likely outcomes of a fair coin flip, and in the long run heads and tails should come up equally often. Some people mistakenly extend this principle, however. They think that if the coin came up heads the last time, it is more likely to come up tails this time. This conclusion is false: Heads and tails are equally likely this time, regardless of what the outcome was last time, and even if the coin came up heads the last four times in a row, the likelihood of tails this time is still only 50%. (If anything, one should conclude that coming up heads four times in a row is a sign that there is something wrong with the coin or something shady about the person flipping it, and so the next outcome may be more likely to be heads again.) Likewise, if a baseball player's batting average is .250, which means he normally gets a hit one out of four tries, and he has struck out the last three or four times at bat, many spectators will think he is extra likely to get a hit the next time he is up. "He's *due* for a hit," they will say. But this prediction is unfounded and reflects a failure to understand how probabilities actually operate in the real world.

The base rate fallacy is a similar failure, although it is based not so much on lack of understanding as on failing to use information.[79] The standard classroom demonstration goes something like this: Michael is a slender man who wears glasses and likes to listen to Mozart. Is he more likely to be a truck driver or an Ivy League classics professor? Nearly everyone guesses that he is a professor, because he resembles the stereotype of a professor (slender, glasses, classical music). What they have overlooked, however, is the huge discrepancy in base rates between the two occupations. There are hundreds of thousands, perhaps millions of truck drivers in the world, but only a handful of male Ivy League classics professors. After all, there are only eight universities in the Ivy League; their classics departments are small or nonexistent; and some of the faculty are female. The odds are heavily stacked in favor of Michael being a truck driver, whether he likes Mozart or not. But people generally do not rely on base-rate information unless they have nothing else to go on, or unless they have been trained. As an example of the benefits of training, medical students gradually learn to apply base rates in diagnosing symptoms. A headache might indicate either a virus or a brain tumor, but viruses are much more common than brain tumors, and a physician generally knows to start with the tentative assumption that the source of any given headache is probably not a brain tumor.

The so-called regression fallacy is another indication of people's poor understanding of probabilities. A general statistical principle says that extreme cases are generally followed by less extreme ones. An athlete or team that plays exceptionally well in one game is unlikely to perform as well the next time. This is probably what lay behind the long-standing belief that athletes could be jinxed by having their picture on the cover of *Sports Illustrated*: The cover photo came after a great performance, and the subsequent games were statistically doomed to be less impressive. If the magazine had instead made it a policy to use its cover to recognize the worst performance of the week, it would have been known as having a beneficial effect rather than a jinx, because a disastrous outing would statistically be likely to be followed by something not quite so bad.

The children of genius parents are probably going to be less intelligent than their moms and dads. A week of record-breaking heat or cold is likely to be followed by milder weather. These facts follow directly from the nature of numbers, but people do not appreciate the statistical basis and instead tend to formulate special causal explanations. During a dry spell, if you do a rain dance every day, sooner or later the rain will come—and you may be tempted to think that your rain dance did the trick. (The illusion works especially well if you change your rain dance a bit each day, when it didn't work, so that when it finally rains, you think, *At last, I got it right!*) Medicine and psychotherapy thrive on regression to the mean. Whenever you feel bad, the odds are that you will feel better in a few days, and if you visit a physician in the interim, you will probably give her credit for your improvement. (And the doctor probably will be willing to accept your gratitude!)

The regression fallacy can trick people (and teachers and governments) into concluding that severe punishment is the most effective way to rule. The goal of both reward and punishment is to improve behavior. But even if reward and punishment are equally effective in reality, they won't be perceived as equal. The standard practice is to reward the child when she does well and to punish her when she behaves badly. The largest rewards will tend to be given after the best behaviors and the heaviest punishments after the worst. Regression to the mean will pull in different directions, however. The child's very best behaviors are likely to be followed by less praiseworthy behavior, whereas the child's worst behaviors will be followed by behaving better. This pattern will make reward seem ineffective—after all, from the parents' point of view, the child was good; they rewarded the child; and then instead of improving, the child's behavior took a turn for the worse. The parents end up thinking that reward doesn't accomplish much. In contrast, punishment will seem all the more effective because of regression to the mean: The kid acted up; the parents punished the child; and afterward the child's behavior got better. The parents will conclude that punishment caused the improvement, even though regression to the mean may have been entirely responsible. Laboratory studies with carefully controlled, random sequences of performance have shown that teachers and others will mistakenly come to the conclusion that punishments work better than rewards.[80]

Understanding Causes

Why did he say that? Why can't I solve this problem? Why did she die? A great deal of thought is devoted to inferring causes. In reality, events are the outcome of a tangled web of many different causes and processes. Events are affected by environmental conditions, even seemingly marginal ones like the weather (for example, if the temperature zoomed to 200 degrees, all human behavior would cease). Biological factors, such as hormones and genes, may contribute to outcomes. Social factors are at work, and indeed the potential meanings and social implications of a particular action can constitute an incredibly complex set of causes. Personality interacts with situational factors, so one person might act one way while a different person would respond to the same situation differently.

Understanding causality is helpful for dealing with the physical environment, but the simple processes of association and conditioning may be sufficient. Thus, if you eat the purple leaves of the plant and get sick afterward, you can just avoid those leaves henceforth, without really needing to understand the biochemical processes that intervened. Likewise, if a big hairy brown animal snarls and chases you back to your cave, you don't need extensive causal investigation to learn the lesson.

Social reality greatly complicates the understanding of causes, however. In order to live in a cultural society, the individual has to be able to understand not just physical causality but social causes, and this includes analyses of intentions and meanings. Hence human beings have become far more sophisticated (which is not to say more accurate) than other species in understanding the causes of each other's actions. A human action might, for example, be motivated by concern with taking advantage of a tax loophole, or maintaining plausible deniability in the event of a lawsuit, or an effort to respect the religious beliefs of others even though oneself does not share those beliefs. Such motives really do influence behavior, but they only arise within the context of a complex cultural society, and there is no evidence that any other species needs to recognize and infer such motives.

Recent studies suggest that human beings are uniquely able to think and understand reality in terms of hidden causal forces.[81] Chimpanzees are surprisingly good (and similar to humans) in understanding and learning about the visible properties of the world around them. But they do not seem to have the foggiest idea that patterns in the visible world can be understood on the basis of causal forces that cannot be observed. Human children by the age of 3 seem to have a working understanding of gravity, force, mass, and so forth, but chimps never attain this.[82] As a result, chimps may be able to make and use tools—an important step toward mastering the world as a cultural animal does—but they do not really understand how the tools work in terms of the properties of the tools and their functions.

If you are going to be competent to participate in human culture, you have to be able to think in terms of social causes. Evidence indicates that children start learning to understand social causes early in life.. Before the age of 5, most children go through a phase of asking "why?" relentlessly in response to almost everything they are told. To be sure, the "why?" questions may be driven in part by the child's enjoyment of control over an adult: The child has discovered that saying that little word can prompt a novel and interesting response from the adult. (If saying "jump" caused the adults to jump every time, some kids would probably favor "jump" over "why.") But the "why?" questions also elicit information about causality, which the child recognizes early in life as an important kind of knowledge. At the other extreme of sophistication, Kant's *Critique of Pure Reason* featured causality as one of the most important, basic, and pervasive categories of human thought.[83]

Needless to say, human thinking does not retain the full level of complexity. People think about causes in much simpler terms. Working under the clunky rubric of *attribution theory*, psychologists have been able to document the main outlines of how people draw conclusions about the causes of social behavior. Three dimensions cover most of the conclusions that people draw about the causes of human action. The first is whether the cause is *internal* or *external* to the person involved. In explaining the actions of others, people tend to focus on the traits of the person, but in explaining their own behavior, they emphasize the situation.[84] An observer of a violent act is likely to see the perpetrator as a wicked person, but the perpetrator is more likely to say "I was only following orders" or "I was only reacting to what someone else did."

Another dimension is whether the cause is *stable* or *unstable*.[85] Success can be attributed to high ability, which is stable, or to high effort, which is unstable, both of which are internal to the performer but which have different implications for how the person will do the next time around. External factors can also be stable (the task is easy) or unstable (it was sheer luck).

The third dimension involves whether the cause is *specific* or *global*. George may treat Sofie in a contemptuous manner because he despises her, or because he despises Bulgarians, or because he despises women in general, or even because he despises pretty much everybody. These reasons clearly make a big difference to how other people can expect George to treat them, depending on whether they are Bulgarian, or female, or merely human.

Any given explanation can usually be identified along all three dimensions. Columnist George Will once proposed naming a trophy for politeness after Alexander Blackwell, an adventurer who was beheaded in 1747.[86] According to the story, at his execution, Blackwell knelt in the wrong place on the platform and therefore put his head on the wrong side of the chopping block. The executioner pointed out the problem to him, and Blackwell apologized, adding by way of explanation that this was his first time being executed. Blackwell's explanation thus qualified as internal (he blamed himself, hence the apology), specific (an error that pertained only to this manner of execution), and unstable (this was his first—and, presumably, his last—execution).

People are reasonably logical and rational in much of their thinking about causes. They follow sensible rules: A cause must precede its effect; big effects tend to come from big causes; the cause must have some contact with its effect; and the like. Covariation is a factor: If the same effect occurs regardless of whether that ostensible cause is present, then something else must be at work. If someone acts the way everyone else does, there is no need to see that person's personality as playing a causal role. But if the person does the opposite of what everyone else does, then we see the person as responsible. Likewise, succeeding if you have huge advantages does not reveal much, but succeeding despite large obstacles attests to high ability and strong determination. People are held more responsible for the foreseeable consequences of their actions than for relatively unforeseeable ones.[87]

There are some less rational influences on how people infer causes, however. One of these is *salience*, which is defined as how obvious or noticeable something is. People tend to attribute causal responsibility to the most salient (obvious) factor.[88] For example, media attention and national sensitivities draw attention to drugs, so any form of wild, dangerous, or irrational behavior by someone who has taken drugs is typically attributed to the drug. Suppose, for example, that marijuana did not affect how well people can drive cars. Some marijuana users would still have accidents, because a certain number of accidents occur just in the normal course of events, and some drivers have used marijuana. These accidents will tend to be blamed on the drug use, because that is a salient factor, even though (as we assumed) marijuana did not actually play any role at all in causing them.

When it comes to drawing conclusions about their own lives, people have more sources of bias. The self tends to distort people's thinking in several ways. The self is highly salient and important, but people are also invested in maintaining a favorable view of self and not getting blamed for problems and failures. One well-established pattern is that people take credit for success but deny blame for failure.[89] This is called the *self-serving bias*. Ironically, this somewhat unfair and distorted manner of drawing conclusions is mainly found among healthy, well-adjusted people with high self-esteem. Depressed people and those with low self-esteem (two categories that overlap substantially) are much more evenhanded in taking both credit and blame.[90]

The self-serving bias can have historic and even fatal consequences. As just one example, consider the race to be the first men to reach the South Pole between a British team led by Robert Falcon Scott and a Norwegian team led by Roald Amundsen.[91] At the time (1911), relatively little was known about the best techniques for polar travel, and one question was whether to rely on dogs or horses. Scott was skeptical of dogs, and his skepticism was confirmed in his eyes when they performed poorly in a preliminary trial excursion. Yet in reality the dogs were better suited to the expedition, provided that one treated them properly. (The chronicler Roland Huntford explains, "[T]he relation between dog and driver had to be that between equals: a dog was not a horse, he was a partner, not a beast of burden.")[92] The British drivers on the trial excursion simply did not understand how to handle dogs properly, and they had trouble with them. Instead of admitting that he didn't know how to handle dogs—which would have entailed attributing the failure to self—Scott blamed the dogs.

From then on, he insisted that dogs were useless beasts, and he refused to rely on them for his ultimate trip to reach the South Pole. Even when other seasoned polar explorers such as Robert Peary tried to persuade Scott to use dogs, Scott refused to listen. In his eyes, his previous misadventures could not be his own fault, so the fault must lie with the dogs. Dogs were no good, regardless of what anyone else claimed.

In contrast, Amundsen exerted himself to learn all about dogs. He experimented with different breeds. He spent considerable time with Eskimos, who knew their breed of dogs well, and he learned how best to handle them. He learned how to coordinate using skis with using dogs and how to teach Europeans to handle dogs as well as the Eskimos did. When he set out for the South Pole, he had 52 dogs. He knew the British were coming also, and considerable prestige would go to whichever party got there first. His dogs and skiers were determined to make a good run.

Scott's British party relied mainly on ponies instead. They also had a few dogs along at first. Typically, Scott refused to acknowledge that the dogs were getting along better, scampering merrily through the snow while the ponies plodded miserably and sank up to their bellies in snowdrifts. Some of the ponies died, and the rest had to be shot. Scott still insisted the dogs were useless and sent them back.

The British paid dearly for Scott's self-serving biases, especially his refusal to attribute the early problems with dogs to his own incompetence. The Norwegians reached the South Pole first (at that moment, the British team was still nearly 400 miles away). In fact, after the first two men, a dog was the third creature to stand on the South Pole. They all then sped back to their ship, still pulled along by their energetic dog teams. The Norwegian team stayed on schedule, which meant that their rations held out and they had enough to eat. Although near the pole itself they had had some hungry days, they reached their food stores on the way home, and Amundsen even found that by the time he was back on the ship—10 days ahead of schedule, thanks to the dogs—he weighed a few pounds more than he had at departure.

The British reached the pole 34 days later than the Norwegians, thereby losing the big race. They had long been reduced to hauling their supplies themselves, and although their diets were roughly similar to the Norwegians', these were inadequate for the far greater expenditure of calories that man-hauling requires. Scott was disgusted to see the Norwegian flags and markers in his path on the final stretch, proving repeatedly that he had lost the race. On the way back, the British slowly ran out of food and fuel and began to die off. One man committed indirect suicide by deliberately going outside of the tent during a blizzard, bidding his mates good-bye (according to Scott) with the words, "I am just going outside and may be some time."[93] The last three men, including Scott himself, died of cold and starvation 130 miles from safety. Ironically, toward the end, the doomed men desperately hoped that the dogs they had sent back would come out with supplies and rescue them, and some of Scott's final notes blamed the dogs for this failure too. In his tent at the end, waiting for death, he wrote long letters, which he correctly expected others to find, in which he exonerated himself and attributed the catastrophe to bad weather, bad luck, and other external factors, while depicting himself as a heroic martyr who had done the best he could. Although historians have drawn varying conclusions about his attributions and claims, there is no disputing the fact that the Norwegians and their dogs had performed the feat faster and far more successfully than Scott's team.

In short, people are motivated to draw conclusions in a way that boosts or protects their self-esteem. The salience (obviousness) of the self is another way that the self influences thought. People are aware of themselves and especially of their actions, and as a result they may overestimate their own roles. A friend of mine lived downstairs from five people who shared a suite. She asked them individually how often each of them took out the garbage for the suite. One said he hardly ever did it, maybe 10% of the time. Another said he did it half the time. The other three each claimed to perform this chore 90% of the time. Although the answers should have added up to 100%, corresponding to all of the occasions that the trash got put out, these added up to 330%!

More systematic support for these same biases has been provided in laboratory and field research.[94] For example, husbands and wives both overestimate their contributions to family and domestic tasks, relative to each other, and members of research teams overestimate their contributions to laboratory tasks relative to each other. Several possible factors may contribute to this pattern, but the clearest is that people can remember their own actions better than they remember what their partners have done, so their estimates of their own contributions tend to be inflated by the salient memory of what they did.

There are also some signs that people prefer single-cause explanations, and they may choose ones that they favor. In reality, social causation is a tangled web of multiple factors, but people tend to pick one. The blaming of all manner of social problems on drugs (described earlier) is a good example; drugs serve as a simple explanation, so if drugs are involved, they are assumed to be the cause. A more transparent version of this kind of fallacy is evident in the explanation of a young couple struggling with a gambling problem that they refused to recognize. "Gambling is not our problem," the couple explained. "We enjoy gambling—both of us do. Our problem is this $100,000 debt."[95]

Self-Knowledge and Self-Deception

Most animals get by remarkably well without an elaborate self-concept and without apparently resorting to much in the way of self-deception. The cultural animal needs a vastly more complex and capable self, however. A cultural self is loaded with symbolic information about how one fits into the social matrix and how one measures up to cultural standards. The self also needs to make choices that are heavily laden with complicated meanings, value judgments, and down-the-road possible consequences. The cultural self is therefore itself a focus of extensive thought, belief, and bias, to the extent that people sometimes distort their information about themselves to fit what they want to believe.

Thus, a great deal of thinking (and a substantial part of the biases and distortions in thinking) is linked to the self. Not surprisingly, most people hold a prominent, privileged place in their own thought processes. They find it difficult to be fair and evenhanded in thinking about themselves.

The term *self-concept* became popular in the 1970s to refer to how people thought of themselves, but most experts now regard the term as misleading. A self-concept implies a unified, integrated understanding. Instead, it is more appropriate to think of *self-knowledge* as a collection of beliefs, specific memories, hopes, and other information. An apt image may be that of a large library without enough staff or shelves, so that some books are stored in a systematic, organized fashion while others are stacked haphazardly on the floor or shelved in the wrong place. Not only are some parts of self-knowledge quite unrelated to others, but a fair amount of contradictory information is stored in different places. At any time, only a small amount of the information is in use, and this part tends to be more consistent and coherent. For example, most people can think of times when they acted friendly and outgoing, and they can think of other times when they were shy and introverted, but these contradictory memories are not usually entertained at the same time.

As we have seen, the desire to think well of oneself and the overlapping desire to be well regarded by others constitute important parts of human motivation. It is hardly surprising that people's thought processes are biased so as to fulfill those desires. Indeed, the idea of self-deception can be traced back to Freud in psychological theory and considerably further in cultural history. Many historians consider the Calvinist and Puritan movements in Christian history to have led to an increased recognition of self-deception.[96] The doctrine of predestination meant (at least in the popular understanding) that your eternal fate was sealed from the moment you were born, and Calvin added that it was possible to tell by observing someone whether that person was destined for eternity in heaven or hell. Hence, many Puritans spent a great deal of time observing their thoughts, feelings, and actions for telltale signs of spiritual nobility or depravity. As they did so, they started to realize that they wanted to believe themselves to be among the elect (i.e., those destined for heaven), and therefore, they were trying to give themselves reason to believe good things about themselves. Self-knowledge never regained the confident certainty it had previously enjoyed.[97]

The notion of *self-deception* was elaborated by Sigmund Freud and again by his daughter, Anna, who proposed that people rely on an assortment of defense mechanisms to shield themselves from unwanted truths about themselves. In particular, the two Freuds thought people used these defense mechanisms to conceal sexual and aggressive impulses from themselves. More recent evidence suggests that people actually use these and other mechanisms to defend their self-esteem. Those two views (defending against sex and aggression versus defending self-esteem) are not really as different as they may appear at first blush. In the Victorian period in which Freud began his career and developed many of his main insights, sex and aggression were taboo, and so concealing such thoughts was probably an essential part of maintaining self-esteem (and public esteem). Nowadays, people are less afraid of their sexual and aggressive feelings—if anything, the lack of sexual desires is more likely to be a threat to self-esteem than their presence—but the need to maintain a favorable image of self is as strong as ever. So people continue to engage in self-deception.[98]

Methods of Self-Deception

The self-serving pattern of taking credit for success while refusing blame for failure is one of many ways that people boost their egos by processing information in a systematically biased way. Another is that people are selectively critical of feedback that makes them look bad, but are uncritical of anything that makes them look good. For example, when research subjects take a personality test and then are randomly assigned to receive good or bad feedback about their personalities, they rate the test as more valid if they received flattering feedback than if they were told bad news.[99] Another is that they spend minimal time attending to criticism, whereas they may linger over praise and explore all of its implications, with the result that the good news gets stored in memory much more thoroughly and effectively than the bad.[100] Sure enough, people do show better memory for their successes than for their failures overall.[101]

The behavior of others can also be interpreted in ways that bolster one's ego. People disregard their own responsibility for conflict, tending to blame conflict on the actions of others.[102] When a war begins, it is common for both sides to claim that the other started things by acting badly and

that their own behavior is merely an understandable response to provocation. Fights and arguments between small children show the same pattern.
Self-serving biases can also come into play with positive, desirable behavior.
Frans de Waal tells the story of a woman who claimed that the squirrels in
her back yard loved her deeply.[103] They visited her every day and accepted
food directly from her hands. Ostensibly moved by this love, she responded
by being generous, indeed spending well over $1,000 every year on food
for the squirrels. When the interviewer asked her cautiously whether her
liberal feeding practices might be causing their frequent visits, she said no.
They visited her because they loved her, in her view, which implicitly was a
testimony to what a wonderful and lovable person she was.

Memory can also be distorted by searching it in a biased fashion. As
already noted, people's memory for their own behavior often contains a
stock of loosely connected and sometimes even contradictory information,
and so it can be searched in a way that will lead to preferred conclusions.
One team of researchers told a series of ambitious Princeton students that
success in life was predicted by personality. The researchers secretly flipped
a coin to determine whether to tell each student that introversion or extraversion held the key to success. Later, when the students were asked to
reflect on their own past behavior, they each came up with the right kind
of memories that promised success. In other words, if they had been told
that introversion led to success, they recalled their own past behavior as
generally introverted, but the ones who heard that extraversion led to success remembered themselves as having been extraverts.[104]

Many traits are not objective qualities but depend on comparison
against other people. Being able to swim a mile in half an hour or perform
mental arithmetic with 90% accuracy is good or bad only in comparison
to how well other people can do. Moreover, not everyone else counts the
same as a target of comparison. After all, if you want to know how good
that half-hour mile swim is, you won't want to compare yourself with the
Olympic swim team, especially if you are a middle-aged woman with a job
and family and you never learned how to do flip turns. Evaluating yourself
therefore may depend on the targets against which you choose to compare
yourself. People often choose targets carefully so that they can outperform
them and hence think well of themselves.[105] Even people in low-perform-
ing groups can end up with high self-esteem this way. For example, women
and minority group members frequently earn less than white men, but they
maintain high self-esteem by comparing themselves only against members
of their own category.[106]

There is another important variation on the pattern of comparing
yourself against inferiors so as to bolster your feeling of superiority. People
shift their impressions of how similar other people are to them. They do

this in opposite ways, depending on the implications for self-esteem. It is better to have correct opinions, and one sign of correctness is agreement with other people. Hence, people tend to overestimate how much others agree with them. (This tendency is partly due to associating with like-minded friends, but some of it is pure distorted perception.) On the other hand, it is better to have unique abilities, because it is prestigious to be able to do important things that few or no others can. Hence, people tend to exaggerate the uniqueness of their capabilities. Furthermore, both tendencies—exaggerating the similarity of your opinions and the uniqueness of your abilities—are stronger among people with high self-esteem, suggesting that those tendencies are egotistically motivated.[107]

These and other esteem-boosting patterns do not fit the most stringent definitions of self-deception, which require that the person both know and not know the same fact (resembling interpersonal deception).[108] But they do achieve the same goal of allowing people to think more favorably about themselves than the cold, hard, objective facts would warrant. Ultimately, the average person ends up regarding himself or herself as above average.[109] Some researchers have called this tendency the *Lake Wobegon effect*, after the fictional town described by Garrison Keillor, in which "all the children are above average."

The dimensions of these patterns were assessed in an influential article by Shelley Taylor and Jonathon Brown.[110] The authors concluded that people show three broad patterns of pleasant, self-flattering distortions, which they termed *positive illusions*. First, people overestimate their abilities and other good qualities. Second, they overestimate their degree of control over events. Third, they overestimate the odds that good things will happen to them and bad things will not. Together, these make for a broad feeling of self-confidence and optimism that may be very appealing.

One sign of the benefits of these positive illusions is that they are most pronounced in happy, healthy, well-adjusted people. Depressed people see the world in a more accurate, balanced way. Psychology had long assumed that seeing reality accurately was the most beneficial and adaptive state of mind, and some authors devoted considerable effort to trying to understand just how depressed people managed to arrive at their negative, pessimistically distorted view of events. But many findings have suggested that depressed people are not distorting their view of the world, and instead they see it fairly accurately (indeed, that may be part of what makes them depressed). Rather, it is the happy, healthy people who distort, albeit in the opposite (optimistic and self-flattering) direction.[111]

What are the potential dangers of overestimating yourself? After all, overconfidence and overreaching have brought the downfall of many great figures of history. Napoleon's and Hitler's invasions of Russia are classic examples of the perils of overconfidence. In both cases, the leaders had produced a remarkable string of successes and had begun to think they could accomplish almost anything, and both invasions ended in utter disaster for the leaders, their armies, and their countries.

People avoid these problems in several ways. One is that optimistic, self-flattering illusions are kept within limited bounds, so they do not become too extreme.[112] Another is that people seem to be able to turn off their distorted views when they have to make a decision, so that for a brief time they become sober and realistic. After the decision is made, they can go back to their inflated self-confidence, which can even be helpful in carrying out a decision once it has been made.[113]

Maximizing self-esteem is not the only principle that guides self-knowledge. There are three distinct approaches to self-knowledge, and people favor different ones under different circumstances. One is to get accurate information about the self, such as by performing tasks that will furnish the most informative feedback.[114] Another is to get confirmation for what you already believe about yourself, regardless of whether it is good or bad.[115] This strategy helps people maintain consistent views about themselves, which serves the general goal of understanding the world as a stable, lawful, predictable place. The third is the desire to think well of oneself. There is some evidence that in general the desire for favorable feedback is the strongest, followed by the desire to maintain consistency, while the desire for accurate, informative feedback is back in third place.[116] There are variations among people and across situations in the relative strength of these three motives; for example, some people desire to learn the truth about themselves no matter how painful it may be, whereas others prefer to cling to their illusions as long as possible. Preferences are not the only consideration: People may prefer to hear favorable, flattering things, but they are more likely to believe things that confirm what they already believe.[117]

Many of the biases and distortions that perturb self-knowledge also operate on relationships. People try to persuade themselves that their relationships are strong and good. Indeed, in one study,[118] the researchers asked students to predict the future of their current dating relationships, and they also obtained predictions from the students' parents and roommates. Months later, the researchers checked back to see which predictions had come true. The roommates' predictions turned out to be the most accurate. The parents simply didn't have enough information to judge, and apparently individuals themselves were too biased by their own feelings to predict their own relationships accurately. People tended to overestimate the quality, strength, and durability of their own current relationships. The roommates, who were not affected by these biases, were able to size up the situation more effectively.

Sources of Self-Knowledge

Where does self-knowledge come from? Symbolic interactionism proposed that people learn about themselves mainly by means of feedback from others. The reality is not so simple. People's opinions of themselves do not actually match up closely with what their friends and family think of them.[119] On the other hand, self-concepts do conform rather closely to what people *believe* other people think of them. The gap is between how you think others see you and how they actually see you. This discrepancy is widely attributed to two sources. First, people do not always tell you the truth, especially with regard to what they see as your faults and shortcomings. Second, when clear feedback is provided, you (if you are like most people) are often reluctant to listen. Incoming information is distorted, especially when it is unpleasant or contradicts what you already believe.[120]

Introspection could also be a source of self-knowledge. Psychology's views on introspection have veered all over the map, ranging from a nearly exclusive reliance on introspection as the main source of psychological data in the early years, to the Freudian skepticism of introspection as reflecting only the tip of the iceberg, to sweeping contempt for it, and back to a sense that it is good for some things if not for others. If you want to know why somebody did something or what someone is thinking, is it reasonable just to ask? Most researchers today consider asking to be one good way of getting information about many topics, but it is vital to keep in mind that people may not know the answer and may not tell the full truth even if they do.

Introspection came under renewed attack in the 1970s. Richard Nisbett and Timothy Wilson proposed that people do not always know what goes on in their own minds—and moreover they often do not know that they do not know.[121] Hence, you may ask a person why he said something and he may give you a sincere answer that will nonetheless be wrong. A series of experiments confirmed that people do not always realize how their minds work. In one, for example, shoppers were asked to choose among four styles of nylon stockings. In reality, the stockings were all quite similar, and most shoppers ended up choosing whichever one came last in the sequence. (The experimenters shifted the different styles around so different ones came last, so they could verify that being fourth out of the four was what made a stocking be chosen.) But the subjects did not realize that they were simply picking the last one. Instead, they explained their choice as influenced by the color or texture or apparent quality of the stocking. The experimenter tried asking people if they chose that one because it was fourth, which was after all the actual cause of their choice, but they looked at him as if he were nuts.[122]

Another experiment made the point even more dramatically.[123] Researchers showed young men a series of car advertisements and asked them which car they would buy. The cars were different along many dimensions—style, safety, gas mileage, and so forth—and this information was described in the ads. One of the ads also featured a picture of an attractive woman dressed only in a black sweater and black lace panties, standing by the car with a big smile and holding a large spear. (The researchers thought the spear might appeal on some unconscious level as a kind of Freudian penis symbol.) They made up different versions of the ads so that each car was sometimes paired with the woman.

The young men generally favored the advertisement depicting the woman with panties and spear, and whatever car was paired with her was the one they tended to select as the car they would buy. But when the researchers asked them why they chose that car, they never explained their decision on the basis of the half-nude female warrior. Instead, they said they chose on the basis of whatever was good about that car. If they saw the woman in the ad with the car that was also recommended as having excellent gas mileage, the men said that gas mileage was important to them. If they saw her standing by the car with the top safety record, they said safety was their topmost concern.

The implication is that people do not know why they form the conclusions and preferences that they do. Introspection is an activity of the conscious part of the mind, and it does not realize how much of the work is done by the automatic system, which is mostly outside of awareness. When asked, they give answers that make sense logically, based on their beliefs about why people ought to form preferences, rather than actually looking inside their minds and describing what they see. People are supposed to choose which nylon stockings to purchase on the basis of color, style, or quality, not just whatever one they saw last. They don't realize that their actual decision process might be biased by serial position. When asked to explain their choice, they fall back on their general theory about how someone makes such a choice.

Introspection is not fully inept. People do know the contents of their minds. That is, they do know what they think, what their attitudes are, what their emotions are. Introspection works fine as a way of knowing what the current contents of one's mind are. But people do not know how they arrived at those contents. A sincere answer to "What are you feeling right now?" is likely to be accurate, whereas a sincere answer to "Why do you feel that way?" is much less reliable.

Conclusion: Self-Knowledge and the Cultural Animal

As we have seen, human beings typically maintain elaborate concepts and theories about themselves, and these are somewhat rooted in reality but also systematically distorted. The accurate parts of self-knowledge are not hard to explain. It is, after all, useful for a member of a culture to have accurate self-knowledge. You should know what you are capable of doing, so you can have an accurate idea of which roles in the society you can maintain. There is little point in trying to be a brain surgeon, an electrician, or even a parent if you lack the skills or other qualities that will be needed. Even finding friends and lovers will presumably be easier if you know what your good and bad points are, so that you can infer accurately which other people will be interested in you.

The distortions are harder to explain. The patterns of systematically overestimating your good qualities would seem to carry risks of getting you involved over your head, thereby setting you up for failure. But perhaps these risks are offset by certain possible benefits of distortion. First, confidence may actually help you perform better in many cases.[124] At the least, it supports the initiative to try new things and take more chances. Second, it feels good. Thinking that they are competent, attractive, likable, and so forth makes people feel good, and those good feelings appear not to depend on how well founded the favorable judgments about themselves are. In other words, being conceited is just as pleasant as having an accurate but equally favorable opinion of yourself (except, again, for the occasional risk of disconfirmation). More generally, self-esteem is strongly linked to happiness across many different walks of life and even across multiple cultures.

But why does it feel good? Probably the answer lies in the fact that people are motivated to gain social acceptance, and so nature has designed us to feel good when we are accepted by others. Presumably, nature's purpose in instilling that pattern of emotional reaction was to make us continue to strive for that acceptance. But human beings have found a shortcut to feeling good: Instead of actually becoming a good person so as to get others to accept you, you merely convince yourself that you are a good person, so you can comfortably assume that others generally will accept you. This is not unlike drinking coffee in lieu of actually having enough energy to do your work, or tampering with the mileage indicator on your car so as to make it seem newer and therefore more valuable. Because people's day-to-day behavior is organized by the pursuit of good emotions and the avoidance of bad emotions, people will often take shortcuts when they can get these positive feelings on the cheap. Self-deception and inflated self-esteem fall in that category of shortcuts. We saw that the duplex mind has oriented cultural animals toward the pursuit of conscious experiences, and self-deception may be one side effect of this.

What About the Unconscious?

The previous section indicated that people do not know their own minds. Not knowing your own mind was a central theme of Freudian thought as well. Freud and his followers blamed the failure on the *unconscious*, which they understood as a large area of the mind filled with powerful, influential things that the conscious mind is not willing to acknowledge.

If you ask a research psychologist today about the unconscious, you are likely to get an evasive, vague response accompanied by signs of discomfort. It is not much different from the response you might get if you asked a modern liberal Christian theologian about the virgin birth or the afterlife. It's not that these ideas have been proven wrong so much as that they represent obsolete ways of thinking, and to be required to use them is embarrassing for any expert who is up to date. Some of the phenomena Freud attributed to the unconscious were valid. And certainly a great deal of mental activity goes on outside of consciousness. But the notion of a gigantic unconscious that serves as a dungeon for wicked thoughts (thoughts that moreover may be plotting to escape in order to wreak mischief) is no longer tenable. The philosopher Jean-Paul Sartre was an early exponent of this position, although he is not given much credit for it any more.[125]

Self-deception, in this view, is one ostensible purpose for the unconscious. If you have traits or thoughts that are not acceptable to you, you supposedly consign them to your unconscious. As we have already seen, self-deception does not operate by simply thrusting ideas into a hidden back room of the mind. Instead, self-deception is accomplished by biased interpretations, selective searching for evidence, and other tricks. Consider the person who grabs all the credit for success but denies blame for failure by pointing the finger at others. No self-blaming thought has been shoved out of the conscious mind into another part of the mind where it lurks in full-blown form, waiting for a chance to burst back into consciousness and let loose a flood of anxiety or guilt. Rather, the idea of blaming the self may have been considered as a possible explanation but then rejected as wrong (as a result of a biased interpretation of the evidence). It exists in roughly the same place that "10" exists as an answer for "how much is 3 plus 5?"—that is, it might have been considered, but it was found to be wrong and discarded. The idea of "10" is not waiting in the unconscious ready to leap back into the conscious mind and wreak arithmetical mayhem. It is just gone. In the same way, the possibility of blaming the self for a particular misdeed has probably been discarded and deleted, once the person has managed to satisfy herself that the misfortune was someone else's fault.

Here is another thought-provoking illustration. Students were instructed to solve a series of word puzzles. For each, they were given five words, and the instruction was to make a sentence out of four of them (thus discarding the fifth). For example, the item "he it hides finds instantly" would be solved by crossing out "hides" and making the sentence "he finds it instantly." For half the subjects, some of the puzzles contained words relevant to stereotypes about elderly people, such as Florida, gray, careful, wise, forgetful, old, wrinkle, and bingo. The word *slow* was not included. The other half of the people in the experiment solved puzzles with words that were neutral with regard to stereotypes and aging.[126] After each person completed the puzzle, the experimenter said the study was finished and the person could leave. Then each departing person was covertly observed and timed while walking down the hallway to the elevator. The result? People who had done the puzzles containing the words relevant to the stereotypes about the elderly walked more slowly than the other people. When this was first observed, the professor in charge refused to believe the results and insisted that the entire experiment be repeated with a new sample of participants. It came out almost exactly the same the second time. Nor is this an isolated finding: There have been other, similar findings from other studies using other ideas and behaviors.[127]

There, in a nutshell, is the unconscious—or, in current terms, the automatic processing system that works outside of consciousness. Some words were slipped into a puzzle task. When people worked on the task, these words automatically but subtly activated other ideas, and these in turn led to a measurable change in the subjects' behavior (in this case, speed of walking). No one in the study recognized that the words in the puzzle had any bearing on the stereotypes of the elderly—rather, the stereotype got activated without people realizing it. No one believed that the words had any impact on behavior, although clearly they did. The findings are especially impressive given that none of the words referred explicitly to being slow or walking slowly. (The closest words were *careful* and *cautious*, but walking slowly to an elevator is hardly a standard form of caution.) Everything crucial happened outside of awareness. The automatic system of the mind picked up enough cues to activate the stereotype, then went to another part of the stereotype (walking slowly) that had not been mentioned, and then altered the person's own walking speed, all without conscious recognition.

We shall return in chapter 6 to the issue of conscious and unconscious processes in guiding behavior. For now, the crucial point is that plenty of mental activity occurs outside of awareness, and sometimes it can be so extensive and effective that a cue in the outside world can be processed and elaborated, leading to change in behavior, without the person realizing what is happening. This is not the unconscious in the sense that Freudian psychology made famous, but it is real and important. The social psychologist Timothy Wilson has proposed a new term for it: *adaptive unconscious.*[128]

Moreover, conscious thought and conscious control are not the same thing. People may think that their conscious minds and thoughts are under their control, but they can easily learn otherwise if they try earnestly to exert that control. This difference is most obviously encountered in meditation. Meditation exercises generally involve focusing the mind and concentrating on a specific stimulus, such as a word (a mantra), a problem, an image, or one's breathing. Focusing your mind on your breathing would seem to be the easiest thing in the world, especially if your thoughts were under your conscious control. Yet nearly every beginning meditator finds the task fiendishly difficult, if not impossible. Even when meditators use tricks such as counting their breaths (usually up to 10, then starting over), they soon find their minds are overwhelmed with other thoughts and often they lose count of the breaths. The internal monologue of the human mind is not typically a consciously directed process of thinking, even though we often mistake it for that.

Memory

The memory is a powerful aspect of human nature and crucial to many successes and accomplishments. Without memory, there would be no such thing as knowledge. Information would be essentially useless. There would be no learning. The intelligence of the human brain would be crippled, and culture would be impossible.

The capacity of the human memory is immense, and many experts believe that it is practically unlimited. Thomas Landauer tried to estimate how many bits of information the average person actually remembers.[129] Using several quite different methods, he came up with several answers that all clustered around a billion. More precisely, an average 35-year-old man may have acquired about a billion and a half bits of information in his life, and if we allow for memory loss of about a half billion bits,[130] about a billion would be left. He may actually use a bit less (perhaps a half billion) in the performance of his daily activities. To be sure, the maximum capacity of human memory is almost certainly significantly higher than that, because Landauer was only estimating how much people actually have in their memories.

The immense size of human memory capacity is another indication that we are cultural animals. If we were designed to solve problems in the physical world, we would never need so much memory storage. The physical world is not all that complex and variable, especially if you live in the same place your whole life, as most human beings always have. But the social world and the culture provide a great deal more information. Even just knowing the people in your group, including their relationships, reputations, goals, and personalities, already requires tremendous storage space. When we add the possibility of acquiring cultural knowledge, the demands on memory escalate even further. After all, if you only had to remember the problems you yourself had solved in life, you would not need all that much memory—but a member of a culture can learn the solutions to all of the problems that were solved by other members of the culture, even in previous generations. Thus, the surplus human brain power is probably another sign that the psyche evolved for culture.

If so much storage space is available, why is memory often so bad? There are several obstacles. In order for information to be available on demand from memory, it has to be stored in a way that permits it to be found. Information pours into the brain all day, but only some of it can be stored, and storing it effectively is even more difficult. Memory researchers distinguish between *long-term memory*, which encompasses information that is saved over long periods of time, and *working memory*, which includes one's immediate memory for what was just said as well as material that has been pulled up from long-term storage. The mind works on the information in working memory, interpreting it, linking it to other ideas and to material already in memory. The processed version, not the raw material that comes into the mind, gets put into long-term memory. This distinction explains why memory may be flawed and why people will remember the same event differently: People remember their interpretation of events rather than the events themselves. No wonder married couples sometimes disagree, even argue, about what exactly was said on a previous occasion: Both remember how they understood the conversation, including what they themselves meant to say and what they inferred the other person meant, rather than what was factually, literally, said and done.

The word *elaboration* is used to describe what happens as information is processed, interpreted, and made ready for storage in long-term memory. People elaborate what they see or hear by linking it to other information, by inferring what causes it, by judging it as good or bad, and so forth. The more thoroughly something is elaborated, the better it will be stored in memory, and hence the more effectively it can be retrieved in the future.

Memory thus operates as a large network. It is popular to think of memory as a library or file system, with lots of pieces of information lined up, but these images miss out on the crucial fact of interconnection. The contents of memory are linked together by chains of associations, and as people get older they can ramble along trains of reminiscences that are often only loosely related as far as anyone else can see. The chains of association help people find memories as well.

The web of memory can work in many ways, including helping a person to be happy or unhappy. At one extreme are people called *repressors*,[131] who seem happy and carefree even when bad things happen. These people can remember bad things, but their unhappy memories are largely isolated, and so it is rare for anything to remind the person of them.[132] In contrast, the memories of depressed people appear to be set up like a chain of doom. Many of the bad thoughts and experiences are linked together, so that any negative thought brings along another one.[133] Even when they stop trying to think about one bad thing, the next thought that comes to mind tends to be another unpleasant one (even if seemingly unrelated), and their overall mood remains dismal.

Most people cannot remember much from their early childhood. Freud famously proposed that this large gap is the result of repression: The Oedipal complex around age 5 is so traumatic, Freud thought, that the child is driven to hurl all of its thoughts and memories into the unconscious. As we have seen, expelling conscious thoughts into a kind of mental dungeon is no longer regarded as a valid metaphor. Most experts now believe that the amnesia for early childhood experiences has less to do with repression than with the primitive state of elaboration and encoding among young children. Because children have not yet built up much of a store of knowledge, they cannot easily interpret experiences on the basis of old ones, so they do not store information with plenty of links and tags that enable it to be found later on.

An important implication of elaboration is that the more you remember, the more you can learn, so that in the long run you will remember even more. This conclusion may seem paradoxical, especially if you subscribe to the image of a library, where once all the shelves are full, you cannot learn anything new until you forget something. As we have seen, however, the brain has a potentially almost unlimited capacity to store information, and the main limitation is on how to store it effectively so it can be found and retrieved later. Once you know a great deal, anything further that you learn can be connected to many parts of this knowledge store, so it will be remembered even better.

As I wrote this passage in 2001, the television in the next room registered the 69th home run this year by Barry Bonds. Will you remember that event years from now? The answer probably depends on how much context you can provide. If you have never played or watched baseball, the sentence may mean nothing to you, or at most it will be a vague statistic. In contrast, if you know a great deal about baseball, that particular event may be remembered in multiple contexts, including Bonds's quest for the home-run record (which stood at 70 and would be broken by Bonds in subsequent games), the fact that it won the game, the Giants' quest to make the playoffs, how the media treated Bonds and how he treated them, the other great home-run hitters of bygone seasons, and so forth. In this way, having more knowledge in your memory expands your capacity to learn and remember even more.

Memory often works by reconstructing the past on the basis of bits of information. Memory is the realm of what-must-have-been rather than what was. Reconstructing the past is, however, subject to influences, biases, and distortions. Simple errors can crop up easily, and when motivation is at work—that is, when people desire to remember something in particular or in a particular way—memory must be treated with suspicion.

Crucially, people's confidence in the accuracy of their memories is no reliable guide. "Are you sure this is the man you saw on the bridge that night?" the attorney asks the witness, and the jury listens intently to how sure the witness claims to be. But studies have repeatedly found zero correlation between how sure the witness is and how accurate the memory is in reality. The witness who says "I can't be sure, but I kind of think maybe he was the one" is no more likely to be correct than the one who says "I am absolutely sure."

Memory is certainly fallible. Daniel Schacter chronicled the ways that memory can go wrong in his list of the "seven sins of memory."[134] They provide a useful taxonomy of memory's shortcomings. First, memory fades. People forget things that they once knew. Second, people sometimes fail to pay attention at crucial moments, so information never gets properly stored (encoded) into memory in the first place. A variation on the second point is that information is put into memory properly, but the person fails to recall it and use it at the crucial moment. People may know what they need to know but still fail to summon up the information. You just didn't think of it then. Third, information may be in memory and the person may search for it but still be unable to retrieve it, because something blocks it. The "tip of the tongue" experience, such as the feeling that you know someone's name and can almost but not quite remember it, is an example of this phenomenon.

The fourth problem, called misattribution, can lead to dangerous and pernicious problems. The person remembers something, but the memory has become connected to the wrong person, place, or event. Schacter illustrated this failing with a famous incident in which the psychologist David Thomson, himself a memory expert who had spoken in public about the fallibility of memory, was suddenly accused of rape by a woman he did not know. The victim identified him with high confidence. Thomson eventually managed to gain acquittal because he had a good alibi: He was being interviewed at the time the rape occurred. Yet the victim really did recognize him, and there was a connection. Thomson's interview was being carried live on television, and the rape victim was watching that show when she was attacked. Her memory confused Thomson's face with that of the rapist. Thus her memory was correct in many respects, including recognizing Thomson and knowing that she had been raped, but it made the terrible mistake of misattributing the rape to him.

Fifth, memory can be highly vulnerable to suggestion, and therefore people may remember something that never happened. Leading or misleading questions about a previous event can change the way people remember the event, especially later on. Eyewitness accounts can be seriously distorted, especially by the time the witness has spoken about the incident on several occasions. Spurious information can get introduced into the memory and settle in there, and the next time the event is recalled, the spurious information comes right along with it. People are especially suggestible under hypnosis, and when hypnosis is used people may end up with vivid, compelling memories of events that never occurred—extending in some cases to ostensible memories of previous lifetimes via reincarnation, or childhood experiences that may include satanic ritual abuse, or abduction into flying saucers. So-called recovered memories are often fabricated (often unwittingly) rather than actually recovered.

The sixth sin is actually a composite, for it refers to distortion of memory by biasing factors. Schacter listed a variety of sources of bias that can shape and alter memory. Beliefs in consistency and change can alter memory so we see the past as more or less similar to the present. Self-serving biases can distort the past to support a preferred view of self, such as by forgetting stupid or malicious things one did or recasting them as reasonable, well-intentioned acts. Current knowledge can also alter the past in hindsight: "I knew it all along," someone says, even though moments earlier she was saying something quite different and obviously didn't know "it" at all. In a dramatic example, one research study followed a sample of married couples for 5 years.[135] Each year, the couples who remained together consistently reported that their love, commitment to each other, and satisfaction with the relationship had increased since the previous year. Yet a comparison of actual ratings from the preceding year showed no change. The couples wanted to believe that their love was growing stronger year by year, and their memories cooperated in supporting that belief, even though there was no factual basis for it.

The final sin is the opposite of the first two. Sometimes memories refuse to go away when they are no longer wanted. People are often unable to shut out the memory of something unpleasant or traumatic. Schacter illustrates this problem with the story of Donnie Moore, a relief pitcher who threw one of the most regretted pitches in history and could not seem to forget it. The pitch was the final one in a playoff game that would decide which team would go on to the celebrated World Series. Moore pitched for the California Angels, which had never made it to the World Series but which were leading in the final, decisive game at the very end. The opposing Red Sox were down to their last chance (two out, two strikes, and one man on base), but the pitch that should have ended the game with an Angels victory was instead hit for a home run, producing a Red Sox victory and sending them, instead of the Angels, to the series. Moore was unable to forget that catastrophic moment. His career went downhill, and fewer than 3 years later he shot his wife and himself to death.

Memory errors are not equal. In fact, there is a severe imbalance. Remembering something that never happened is an extremely unusual kind of error. Forgetting something that did happen is far more common. When biases and motivations distort memory, the most common path is to forget selectively. Thus accounts furnished by victims of misdeeds tend to leave out factors that are central to the perpetrators and that would reduce guilt, such as the fact that the perpetrator was upset or distracted, or especially that the victim had initially done something to provoke the perpetrator. Meanwhile, perpetrators tend to leave out some of the bad consequences of their actions, such as lasting damage done to the victim.[136]

Apart from deleting information, memory can be slanted by presenting things in an especially good or bad light. Suppose Sally refuses Joseph's love and breaks his heart, and suppose (as is common) that he doesn't immediately give up. His account of the episode is likely to say that he kept trying a few more times to win her affections, without making a big deal of his refusal to give up. Sally's account, in contrast, may elevate Joseph's persistence to the level of pathological stalking. Even though they agree that he kept trying, their memories differ in the extremity, irrationality, and duration of his perseverance.[137]

One general source of bias is that people distort their memories so as to flatter themselves. In this way, memory operates in service of self-esteem. The distortions we have seen so far—minimizing transgressions, emphasizing past successes, and the like—fit this view. Further evidence of the influence of self-esteem comes from studies on narcissists, who have the strongest motivation to glorify themselves. A study recruited young men to converse with an attractive woman, ostensibly as part of a study of dating.[138] In reality, there was no woman, and the men simply interacted with a tape-recorded voice that said the same thing each time. The researchers asked the young men to report on their dating history, including the number of girlfriends and sex partners they had had. Two weeks later, each young man was invited back to listen to a recording of the woman's appraisal of all the men with whom she had spoken. This judgment was a fake; everyone heard the same tape. By random assignment, half the men were told that she liked them very much, and the other half were told that she had formed a strongly negative impression and would not want to meet them. After this, the researchers told each participant that they had lost his dating question-naire and asked him to fill it out again. In reality, the former questionnaire was not lost—the researchers simply wanted to see how people's memory had changed after a blow to their self-esteem.

The revisions to memory depended on the young men's level of narcis-sism. Men who scored low in narcissism and who heard that the woman had disliked and rejected them responded with humility. They made only slight and negative changes in their assessment of how popular they had been with previous dating partners. In other words, after being rejected, they now recalled having been less popular with other women, as compared to what they had said on the first questionnaire. In contrast, the narcis-sists responded by boosting their retroactive reports. When they heard that the woman in the study had disliked and rejected them, they increased their tallies of previous romantic and sexual conquests. "Maybe this woman didn't like me," they seemed to say, "but plenty of others have, and so if there's any problem, it's with her, not with me."

Memory can also be distorted to fit people's a priori theories about themselves and their lives. If they believe they are consistent, then they distort memory to make themselves look consistent. People tend to deny that they have changed, even when they have. They accomplish this appar-ent sleight of hand by retroactively distorting what they had previously believed, to bring it into line with what they believe now. For instance, if you start out believing that alcohol should be banned from public beaches, and then someone persuades you in the name of civil liberty (or whatever) that it should be permitted, you are likely to think that you never were really opposed to it.[139]

People usually like to believe they are consistent, but sometimes change is preferable—and if so, they will revise memory to support the impression of change. A well-known study examined how people experience univer-sity classes in study skills.[140] Most universities offer them as a way to help students learn to study better. Most objective evidence indicates that these courses accomplish very little. Yet the people who complete them rate them quite positively and convince themselves that they learned a great deal. Obviously, this belief is difficult to sustain when you are still not studying effectively or getting better grades. How do they sustain it? By changing their impression of how bad they were beforehand. Although the person may have been about average before the study skills course and may still be about average afterward, he will think, *I was really bad before, so becoming average is a big improvement.*

Distortion in both directions was found in research on women's menstrual periods.[141] The researchers first asked women how bad their periods typically were. Then they had women keep a diary recording cramps and other discomfort over the course of one menstrual period. Later, the women were asked to say (without consulting their diaries) how bad that period had been. The women who said their periods were generally bad remembered the period as worse than they had actually described it at the time. Conversely, the women who said their periods were no big deal recalled them as less aversive than they had rated them at the time. In short, people have a priori theories about themselves and their lives, and memory is often distorted to fit these theories.[142]

Reasoning

When he was 9 years old, Billy spent a week visiting his aunt and uncle, who let him run more or less free in their semi-wild neighborhood. One day he got permission to construct a bonfire for burning on the beach that evening. He collected a great deal of driftwood. Some of the pieces were too long, so he hunted through the tool shed to find an old ax and began chopping them. Before long the ax got stuck in an old piece of wood, and when he yanked extra hard on it, it stuck briefly and then came loose with such unexpected speed that the back of it smacked into his forehead, drawing a little blood. As his aunt bandaged his forehead, he earnestly told her he had learned his lesson: "I think from now on, I should only use power tools." As you may have guessed, his aunt had not come to the same conclusion from the episode, and no power-driven chainsaws were put into 9-year-old hands. This story illustrates the hazardous nature of inductive reasoning: Different people can come to quite different conclusions from precisely the same evidence.

Reasoning has been studied in bits and pieces. The overarching question—whether people are rational—will be deferred until chapter 6. Irrationality emerges in action as much as, or even more than, in thought. People can decide logically what they ought to do, but then they may not actually do it.

The two main forms of logical reasoning are *induction* and *deduction*. Induction is the more hazardous and less reliable form. Deduction can be quite rigorous and will always lead to correct conclusions if done properly, although people sometimes do make standard mistakes. Induction involves making a generalization from a few cases or even from a single case. *Reasoning by analogy* is an important form of induction. It can also consist of *generalizing* from a few known cases to new cases. For example, most people have some ideas about how men and women differ, even though they have hardly made a systematic survey of all men and all women. Induction usually contains a higher risk of error than deduction, and people's generalizations about the differences between men and women are hardly infallible. But people observe a few differences between their male and female acquaintances and leap to broad conclusions about what women are like and how men are different.

Induction is common despite its logical weakness and the risks of error. It probably reflects the basic human tendency to seek patterns and order, which is one of the main functions of human intelligence. Let us pursue the example of gender differences. Some might wish that people would not make generalizations about men and women, because these amount to stereotypes, and they can result in unfair pressures on individuals to fit preconceived notions. But it is highly doubtful that people will ever stop generalizing about men and women. Mating is one of the central activities of life (indeed, it is essential to creating new generations so the species can survive), and mating depends on a man and woman negotiating some kind of mutual understanding. As men and women seek each other out, they need to know how to treat each other and what to expect from each other. When a dating relationship fails, people want to learn from their mistakes so their next relationship may be more successful. Generalizing about the opposite sex is an appealing strategy for achieving this goal. Instead of wishing that people would stop generalizing, it is probably more practical to hope that people can learn to make more accurate generalizations and perhaps to appreciate the diversity of people within each category.

Indeed, inductions are widely based on categories. This pattern starts early in life, suggesting that it is a natural tendency of the human mind. In one study, 2-year-old children were presented with categories and information, such as that black cats could see in the dark. Then the experimenter showed them two pictures, a black skunk and a white cat, and asked them which one could see in the dark. The children tended to pick the skunk, because it looked like the black cat. In another condition, the experimenter referred to both the black and white cats as cats while naming the skunk as a skunk. This had the effect of putting the two cats in the same category and the skunk in a different category. When these children were asked whether the skunk or the white cat could see in the dark, they chose the white cat.[143] Even these toddlers made their inductive generalizations on the basis of categories, and their answers depended on whether they were led to make categories based on color or on the name of the kind of animal.

The perennial problem with induction is how far to generalize. Suppose your boyfriend dumps you in favor of another woman. In principle, you might conclude that this was a once-in-a-lifetime event, but that seems unlikely, given how people are prone to generalize. But how far should you generalize? Perhaps this man is fickle in general. If he were from Indiana, you might conclude that men from Indiana are fickle, or men from the Midwest, or athletes (if he played basketball). Perhaps all white men or all nonreligious men are fickle. Perhaps all men are fickle. Perhaps all people are fickle, regardless of gender or basketball playing or Hoosier birth. The problem is, there is no simple way to determine how widely you should generalize from one incident.

To deal with this problem, people use several strategies.[144] One is to generalize cautiously and update their inductions as new evidence comes in. (For example, you can check whether your roommate's boyfriend, who is a midwesterner but not an athlete, also proves to be fickle.) People also decide how typical the individual case is for several categories. Suppose your boyfriend seemed unlike other midwesterners in his food preferences and speech patterns, but he seemed typical of other athletes you know in these respects. You would probably use his fickleness to conclude that athletes are fickle instead of concluding that midwesterners are fickle. The resemblance to the category is often an important guiding principle.

Deduction involves the strict rules of logic, and if deduction is done properly the conclusion is unassailably true (unlike induction, which always carries some degree of uncertainty and doubt). As Socrates taught his students thousands of years ago, if we know for certain that all Greeks are human beings, and we know that Socrates is a Greek, then we can infer beyond any doubt that Socrates is a human being. People are generally quite competent with this particular form of argument (called *modus ponens*). They use it and understand it seemingly naturally, which is to say without having to be taught. They are also quick to grasp transitive arguments: If George runs faster than Tom, and Tom runs faster than Bill, then George runs faster than Bill.[145] Indeed, there is some evidence that even pigeons can follow transitive logic in a simple, primitive manner.[146]

Other forms of deduction are more difficult for people to understand, however. Suppose we begin from the same premise that all Greeks are human beings, but we also stipulate that Socrates is not a human being (in this case, Socrates is the name of a dog). It follows that Socrates is also not a Greek. Although this argument is just as logically impeccable as *modus ponens*, people do not grasp or use it as readily.[147] This may again reflect the basic point that the mind is not an all-purpose reasoning machine but rather evolved to figure out certain particular and important problems (as we saw earlier with the cheating-detector and social exchange problems).

Last year, some friends and I were discussing New Year's resolutions. Several of us had made some, but one friend had not given the matter much thought. When pressed to articulate a resolution, he said that this year he planned to believe everything he read. This elicited general laughter: After all, professors such as my friend are supposed to be adept at critical thinking and skeptical analysis of all assertions. The idea that he would try to believe everything he reads was preposterous. Then again, some experts have concluded that you cannot refrain from believing everything you read—at first, at least. In this view, whenever new information arrives in the human mind, believing it is integral to understanding it. To reject it as untrue is a separate, later process. The important implication is that if people are distracted or interrupted or under stress, they may become more gullible.

The debate can be traced back several centuries at least. The French philosopher René Descartes proposed that the mind does two things when it encounters some claim or assertion: first it understands it, and then it evaluates it as true or false. Against that view, the Dutch philosopher Benedict Spinoza proposed that understanding it and regarding it as true are essentially the same act. A second act—rejecting the statement as untrue— may or may not occur. Subsequent generations of philosophers have sided with one or the other, without a clear winner.

The issue was taken up as a psychological question by Daniel Gilbert.[148] By the 1990s, the computer had become a powerful, dominating metaphor for how a human mind deals with information. Computers clearly follow the Cartesian two-step: They can accept information and hold it in their memories without making the slightest attempt to verify whether its statements are true or false. Gilbert, however, concluded that the human mind does not resemble a computer in this respect. Human beings believe first and may, or may not, doubt later.

A variety of evidence supports the conclusion that to understand is to believe, with doubt and rejection being a separate, possible state. Young children are presumably still learning to think, and if Descartes were right and true-false judgments were made in a single step, they should learn to make them at about the same time in development. But they don't: Children are notoriously gullible. They are inclined to believe whatever they hear. Skeptical doubt develops later and more gradually. In other words, child development shows that believing and disbelieving are not symmetrical—instead, believing emerges right alongside understanding, and disbelieving comes along later.

In laboratory studies, people who are distracted likewise become more gullible. They can process information and use it later, even if they are assigned to perform another task (like watching a screen for a number 5 or repeating a phone number mentally) at the same time. But they fail to reject false information. By the same token, many studies have shown that people are more easily persuaded (especially if the arguments are illogical or otherwise lame) if they are distracted or under stress, because they believe whatever they hear and fail to evaluate it critically.[149]

At the extreme, brainwashing succeeds better if people are rendered incapable of critical thought, for instance, by distraction, lack of sleep, or physical suffering.[150] Again, if understanding occurred first and true-false judgments were made later, brainwashing might not succeed under those circumstances: Exhausted and distracted people would perhaps be able to understand something, but they would judge it as neither true nor false, and so they would not be persuaded (or brainwashed). That's not what happens, however. Exhausted and distracted people believe something they are told as quickly as they understand it. They don't make it to the second step, which is purely a matter of rejecting it. Hence they end up believing it uncritically.

A particular challenge for reasoning arises when people's values conflict. This is a perennial problem for individuals and for entire societies. After all, who would be opposed to a measure that would save both lives and money? But in reality those two goals may be opposed, and at some point complex and expensive safety regulations may cost so much that the gain in safety is not worthwhile. Banning automobile travel altogether would certainly save lives, but it would demolish the auto industry, thereby having a costly effect on the economy. Plus, of course, requiring everyone to use public transportation exclusively would involve a substantial loss of time and efficiency. Hence, at some point, people favor keeping automobiles despite their high rate of casualties.

Philip Tetlock has devoted much of his career to studying how people deal with these complex tradeoffs among values. When a difficult choice arises, he found, people prefer to avoid it, but some cannot do so. Hence they respond with integratively complex reasoning—recognizing that there is a tradeoff and seeking a solution that balances both competing interests. Such reasoning is difficult and effortful, so people generally prefer to avoid it, but they will make the effort when the values in conflict are important to them.[151] Tetlock's conclusions fit the triage model of cognition: People will think a great deal about things that are important to them, while skimping on thought about less important topics.

Some people find ways of looking at life that emphasize a few simple values, and in that way they avoid painful tradeoffs and the need for complex thinking. Strict religious or political ideologies, for example, may be set up so that one or two values take priority over everything else. In that case, decisions are usually simple. But people who espouse complex sets of values often find it necessary to recognize that these may come into conflict. Both the right-wing and left-wing political extremes lean toward simple, black-and-white views of the world, whereas the moderate politicians tend to think and talk in more complex ways, recognizing the conflicts and tradeoffs that are required. In fact, politicians seem to change their own thinking as a function of whether they are running for office or having to make the hard choices that come with power. Simple value statements play well with the general public, and so they are prominent during election campaigns. A politician who is not in office can make strong promises and claims without acknowledging that there is any contradiction among them. Ronald Reagan famously claimed that he would be able to reduce inflation, lower taxes, increase employment, and offer other positive things that generally conflict with each other, and when pressed to explain how he would be able to afford all of these things, he said vaguely that eliminating all the waste in government spending would provide enough money to take care of everything. Once in office, however, politicians tend to recognize that pursuing one goal often requires sacrificing another, and their speech and thinking become more complex than they were during the campaign.[152]

Is this simply a matter of learning? Tetlock thought it plausible that politicians might not recognize the implicit contradictions in their policies until they were elected, or at best they might cling to pie-in-the-sky hopes like Reagan's idea of financing an economic surge simply by eliminating government waste. The data, however, did not support the view that a learning process is behind the shift from simplistic campaign rhetoric to complex thinking when in power. Instead, it seemed that politicians adopted a simple style in order to appeal to the voters and then quickly and thoroughly switched to a more complex style when dealing with the demands of governing. Tetlock found that politicians who were running for reelection were often quite simplistic in what they said during the campaign, even though their statements had been more complex while simply governing. Thus politicians seem to know that voters prefer a simple style of presenting the issues, and they cynically adopt this style while running for election and then go back to a more complex way of reasoning right after the election.

Moral Reasoning

Moral reasoning is a special category of reasoning, and one that is especially relevant to participation in a cultural society. It involves evaluating whether certain actions are right or wrong, according to standards and rules that are accepted in the culture. Most cultures rely to some degree on morals to induce people to restrain their selfish impulses and to do what is best for the group as a whole, such as following rules, and so cultural animals have to be able to apply abstract moral principles to specific behavioral dilemmas. For centuries, philosophers have debated the ultimate principles that determine rightness and wrongness. Psychologists have joined the fray in recent decades.

Undoubtedly, the most influential psychological work on moral reasoning was by Lawrence Kohlberg.[153] His theory emphasized that children acquire moral reasoning in a series of well-defined stages. Initially, children try to do what is right in order to avoid punishment. A slightly more advanced child sees rightness as fairness and will follow rules when doing so is in his self-interest (e.g., to avoid getting caught and punished). These *preconventional* stages are followed by *conventional* stages of moral reasoning. Here, what is right involves living up to the expectancies of others and doing what will maintain good relationships with others. A more advanced version of the conventional stage emphasizes fulfilling one's obligations and keeping one's word, as well as upholding the laws. Making a positive contribution to society or to the smaller social group is also seen as morally good. Eventually, then, the person may (but may not) reach the highest, *principled* level of moral reasoning. These stages involve, first, a respect for the different values and opinions that others may have, and then, finally, a recognition of universal ethical principles. Kohlberg describes this highest state as recognizing that laws and values are usually based on ultimate, universal principles, so one respects the underlying universal principle rather than the particular law.

An influential but possibly misguided critique of Kohlberg's views was put forward by Carol Gilligan,[154] who accused him of sexism and said that girls and women have a different style of moral reasoning. She said that Kohlberg's ideas emphasize abstract rules and fairness, whereas female morality features an "ethic of care," which tries to take care of everyone involved. Therefore, she says, if a disagreement arose during a children's game, the boys would appeal to abstract rules to resolve it and if the problem proved intractable they would eventually resort to doing the play over. In contrast, girls would treat the problem by trying to find a solution that would satisfy everyone and make everyone happy. Obviously, this style is better suited to one-on-one relationships than to larger groups, and sure enough most observers of playground activity say that large group games do not last long when they are made up of girls. In broader social contexts, the emphasis on caring for relationship partners rather than on respecting abstract rules of fairness might entail that female morality would be little more than opportunistic cronyism, if Gilligan were right. Regardless of how one interprets Gilligan's ethic of care, research has clobbered the idea soundly. A great many studies have repeatedly failed to find that boys and girls think differently. On the contrary, people seem to make very similar moral judgments regardless of gender.[155]

Most studies of moral reasoning have focused on how people deal with hypothetical dilemmas, such as the famous Heinz problem: whether it is morally acceptable for a poor man to steal some expensive medicine in order to save his wife's life. A recent work by Nicholas Emler noted that people don't seem to engage in a great deal of careful moral reasoning when facing a decision in their own lives.[156] Instead, they do whatever strikes them or feels right at the time. Emler said that this finding is a powerful challenge to the very idea of moral reasoning. Maybe people hardly ever bother.

Emler's response to this challenge was quite striking. He said that people do have to learn to master the rules of moral reasoning—but not for the sake of making their own choices. Instead, he says, people mainly use moral reasoning when they are arguing with other people. Moral reasoning is thus a tool for influencing others. If you can convince Jane that she is morally obligated to do what you want, then you can get your way. Moral reasoning is a way of exerting control in the social world.

Undoubtedly, people do use moral reasoning to argue with and influence others. There may, however, be a more subtle use of moral reasoning with one's own behavior, even if people rarely stop to engage in it when they face a difficult decision. True, they may make the decision based on what seems desirable and right at the time. Sometimes they will be wrong, however, and their actions will get them into trouble. Immoral actions engender interpersonal resentments and other costs. The person may feel guilty afterward. At this point, moral reasoning about one's own actions may become important. Feeling guilty is highly unpleasant, and moral reasoning can help in two different ways to help people avoid that awful feeling. First, of course, people may try to manipulate moral reasoning to justify what they did, so that they can convince themselves and others that they have no need to feel guilty. Second, moral reasoning can help people figure out precisely what they did wrong, so they can avoid making the same mistake again.

A more systematic attack on the traditional view of rational moral reasoning was presented by Jonathan Haidt.[157] He distinguished between *moral judgment* (determining if something is right or wrong) and *moral reasoning* (the process of thinking through implications of moral principles). Moral reasoning does not generally cause moral judgment, he concluded from much evidence. Instead, people typically have a gut reaction and base their moral judgment on that, and then they start using moral reasoning to defend their choice. In one of his studies, for example, he had people read a story about two adults, a brother and sister, who went on vacation together and then decided to have sex. The girl was on birth control pills and the boy used a condom; no one was hurt; they never repeated the act; and they concluded that it heightened their intimacy. Haidt found that when people read this, they almost universally condemned it as wrong, but they had trouble coming up with reasons. They brought up standard arguments against incest, such as the dangers of inbreeding and the possibility of hurting someone, but the story specifically made clear that there were no offspring and no one was hurt, so these arguments should be irrelevant. Still, the failure of moral reasoning had almost no effect on making people revise their moral condemnation. They would sometimes just shrug and say, "I can't explain why, I just know it's wrong."

The implication, as Haidt argued, is that people rely on their intuitions to make moral judgments, and they learn moral reasoning so as to defend their actions with others. Furthermore, moral reasoning can be used to teach or influence others, leading perhaps to changes in moral behavior in the future. Moral judgment should be studied as an interpersonal process, Haidt insisted.

Haidt's findings bring us back to the duplex mind. The automatic system operates by intuition and immediate feelings, and so it pronounces incest as wrong. The conscious mind has the capacity to reason, but often it merely follows along and provides a fancy rationalization to support the immediate judgment of the automatic system. And sometimes, to be sure, the conscious mind can actually reason things through and change the answer. After conscious reflection, the person might say, "I have a gut reaction that no brother and sister should be having sex, but apparently no harm was done, and they have the right to choose what they do, and so really there was nothing immoral about their actions."

Studies of psychopaths also show the limits of moral reasoning. Psychopaths lack moral emotions, but they are fully capable of moral reasoning. They know the right answers as to whether some action is morally acceptable or not, and they understand how to use general moral principles to reason about specific behaviors. But they don't care. Without moral emotion, they do not mind hurting others. They use their powers of moral reasoning to deal with and influence others.[158]

All of these lines of argument emphasize the social and cultural aspect of moral reasoning. People do not learn moral reasoning to help them make decisions at crucial choice points. Rather, they learn moral reasoning so they can participate in the cultural discourse: They can defend what they did; they can influence and even manipulate what others do; and they can improve their own relationships with others, at least by understanding why others might object to their actions and possibly by changing their future decision processes.

The importance of culture for moral judgment has several important aspects. One is that morality generally restrains self-interest, and self-interest is one of the most fascinating battlegrounds between nature and culture. Biologists have repeatedly rejected the idea that natural selection operates at the group level, and so biology only instills traits that benefit the individual. The "selfish gene" arguments of Richard Dawkins and others point irresistibly to the conclusion that people are inevitably designed to pursue self-interest.[159] Culture, in contrast, is by definition a matter of the group or collectivity, and in many cases it is necessary to encourage people to sacrifice their immediate self-interest for the sake of the group. At the extreme, people must sometimes be encouraged to sacrifice their lives for the sake of the nation, and the more common but lesser sacrifices (such as waiting one's turn or paying taxes) show the same shift. Moral principles and pressures are an important force that society uses to encourage people to do what is best for the group even if it is not clearly in their own individual self-interest.

Is morality unique to human beings? Not entirely. Other species seem to have some understanding of fairness, especially when one individual's rights or wishes have been thwarted. Only human beings seem to have morality based in the collectivity, however. As Haidt pointed out, only human beings show "widespread third party norm enforcement."[160] That is, people will expend their own or community resources to fight immorality even if they were not themselves the victims. They seem to recognize that maintaining morality is a generally good thing even when they are not directly affected. No other animal does this. If one dog steals a bone from another dog, the loser may protest and may even be said to have some moral sense that the stealing was wrong. But you will not see a third dog intervene to force the first dog to return the bone to the second. Only cultural animals use morality as a property of the larger society.

The dark side of moral reasoning is that it gives people a basis for condemning others. After all, morality establishes good and bad, right and wrong, and once a person has established what is right and good, he may feel perfectly justified in condemning others who deviate. This can extend to justifying violence.

Common Mistakes, Limitations, and Bad Decisions

We have already covered multiple sources of bias and distortion in human thought. These have not, however, exhausted the systematic tendencies toward error that researchers have uncovered. Let us consider several more factors that lead human thought down paths toward bad judgments and wrong conclusions. The effects of emotions on thinking will be covered later, in chapter 5.

One reasonably well-established pattern has to do with how people estimate along a numerical continuum, such as trying to guess how much money a house is worth. They follow the procedure that has been labeled *anchoring and adjustment*,[161] which is to find another example (the anchor) that is supposedly approximately the same and then to make adjustments for obvious differences. The anchor one chooses generally has a powerful effect on the final judgment, because the adjustments are nearly always too small. Hence, the final judgment is too close to the anchor.

We can use estimating the value of a house as an example. When you get ready to sell your house, you have to decide what price to ask. If you are trying to sell it yourself, you will probably consult the prices of recent houses sold in your neighborhood and then adjust up or down depending on how your house differs from them (e.g., your kitchen is nicer; your yard is smaller; your house has one fewer bathroom). Professional real estate appraisers do the same thing, only with more elaborate and systematic formulas, which likely include things about which you have not thought (such as rain gutters, easements, grounded outlets). Even so, they come up with quite different answers depending on the anchors with which they start. If they start with houses more expensive than yours, they are likely to come up with a higher estimate for the value of your house than they would have if they started with cheaper houses. The adjustments are generally too small.

Another kind of estimate that is generally too small crops up in planning. Planners tend to be optimistic, and many projects end up taking more time and costing more money than originally planned. When was the last time you heard of a building project, a highway construction, or a major movie that came in significantly under budget or way ahead of schedule? The Sydney Opera House, widely recognized as one of the most impressive and beautiful achievements of modern architecture, was undertaken in 1957. The planners estimated that it would cost $7 million and be completed early in 1963. In fact, it wasn't finished until a decade later, in 1973, even though the builders scaled back some of the original plans to save time and money. And as for money—the final cost was more than $100 million.[162] Although this was an extreme case, running late and over budget has been the norm with large projects everywhere.

Small projects are hardly immune. Students make comparable errors of optimistic overconfidence when planning their academic activities. For example, in one study, students were asked to predict how long it would take them to complete their theses.[163] They also were told to furnish their most optimistic ("assuming everything went as well as it possibly could") and pessimistic ("assuming everything went as poorly as it possibly could") estimates. Fewer than a third of them finished by the time they said was their most accurate prediction. Even more shocking was that fewer than half of them finished by their most pessimistic forecast. In other words, even when they tried to imagine everything possible going wrong and slowing their progress, they were still too optimistic.

The optimism bias appears to be limited to one's own efforts: People were able to predict quite accurately how long someone else would take to perform the task. Part of the reason is that people refuse to learn from their own experiences. Suppose, for example, that in the previous semester students had to write a 20-page term paper, which took them 2 weeks. Now, another course has assigned another 20-page paper. Do they budget 2 weeks? No. They might think, *But that took extra long because I had trouble getting the books from the library*, or *I didn't like that course very much, so it took longer*, or they'll rationalize that unexpected computer problems had delayed them. Somehow they assume that no delays will occur this time, so they expect to be able to finish the paper in 4 days. As a result, they are surprised when the new assignment also takes 2 weeks. Their roommates are less surprised, however: The distorted thinking applies mainly to one's own work.

Underestimating time can cause obvious problems for public policy-makers, military commanders, and many others. It can also be devastating in combination with tendencies toward procrastination. Procrastinators generally prefer to put things off until the last minute. In principle, procrastination might not cause any problem. If a project requires 30 hours to complete, it really doesn't matter whether you put in those 30 hours during the last 2 days before the deadline or 2 months ahead of time. But a project that looks like 30 hours may actually require 50 or 60 hours, and if the procrastinator has waited until the last 2 days to get started (because she thinks the project will require only 30 hours), there won't be enough time.

All of these patterns suggest a kind of overconfidence, and sure enough, overconfidence is a common kind of error. In particular, people are overconfident about the accuracy of their judgments, memories, and predictions. One of my classroom demonstrations asks students to make an estimate for which they are 98% but not 100% certain. Specifically, I ask them to give a range of numbers that they are 98% certain holds the correct answer to the question, which is the number of countries in the world. At present there are just under 200 countries in the world (depending on how one counts marginal cases). So if a student were to say that the number of countries in the world is between 10 and 1,000, she would be correct. The degree of accuracy can be measured from aggregating all of the responses in the class. If they were really estimating at 98% accuracy, then only 2 students out of 100 would have proposed an interval that did not contain the correct answer. In fact, however, about a third of the class gets it wrong. Thus, in trying to be 98% certain, they were only about 65% certain—a clear case of overconfidence.

Overconfidence is not surprising. What is surprising, even shocking, is that most estimates of confidence and certainty are unrelated to objective accuracy. We have already seen the irrelevance of subjective confidence with regard to memory and eyewitness accuracy, but the pattern is far broader. For example, one team of researchers combined the results of all studies dealing with how well people can tell when someone is lying.[164] In general, people are not very good at detecting liars, but the researchers went one step further to see how well confidence was related to accuracy. In other words, your guess that one person is lying might be based on a vague hunch, whereas you might express near-certainty that another person is lying. Would you be more likely to be correct in the latter case than in the former? The answer was no. Some studies did find a small positive relationship (high confidence went with high accuracy); some actually found the opposite (higher confidence went with lower accuracy); and many found no difference. When the results were all combined, the relationship was zero. Confidence in your judgment is unrelated to the accuracy of that judgment.

The consistent failure of subjective certainty may be yet another indication of the poverty of introspection. That is, people do not know how their minds work and cannot observe how they arrive at their conclusions. Hence they cannot form reliable impressions of the accuracy of their conclusions.

There is another way of looking at the inaccuracy of people's estimates of subjective certainty. Maybe people generally do not appreciate how much they do not know. This hypothesis would be plausible in connection with another form of bias, which is the tendency to be swayed by what is easiest to see and to overlook or downplay whatever is hidden, absent, or implicit.[165] People find it easier to list what someone is like than what the person is not like, even though logically the reverse should be true because there are more characteristics someone does not have than characteristics someone does have. Likewise, when people have to decide whether two things are the same or different, they make "same" judgments faster than "different" judgments (and speed is an indication of ease and efficiency)—even though logically the opposite should be true, because a single discrepancy can be enough to pronounce them different, whereas to say they are the same, it is necessary to compare the two on every dimension. When learning about something, we learn what it is faster than we learn what it is not.

Thus, people's thinking is not logically impeccable but rather is prone to various flaws and biases. Some of these reflect shortcuts. Other flaws may arise because of the influence of emotions, which at least in popular stereotype are widely assumed to subvert rational thought and to produce foolish, destructive outcomes. But is that stereotype valid? Why would evolution build the human psyche with an emotions system that routinely subverts one of its best abilities, namely, thinking? The next chapter will examine the effects and functions of emotions.

5

How and Why Emotions Happen

Life without emotions would be empty and boring, though some people might think they would like the peace and quiet that would entail. Emotions and other feelings (moods and affect) are woven into the tapestry of everyday life. But they are the most confusing and difficult piece to fit into the puzzle. Psychology has been far more successful at trying to understand thoughts, motivations, and behaviors than emotions.

Emotions are baffling in part because of their purpose. Conventional wisdom says that emotions make people do irrational things, but if that is all they did, natural selection would probably have weeded them out of our psyche ages ago. If emotions do have destructive or irrational effects, then they must also serve some extremely helpful function, because the positive benefits have to outweigh the negative—in order for our species to have retained them.

Full-blown emotions are conscious experiences and thus seem firmly planted in the conscious system (though, as usual, they have some roots in the automatic system). To talk about emotions without acknowledging the conscious dimension would miss one of their central attributes. Yet even the conscious feeling of emotions presents a further puzzle. Unlike thoughts and actions, emotions seem mostly immune to conscious control. A person can decide to think about dinner now and do so. Someone can decide to go for a walk and do so. But try deciding to feel jealous, guilty, angry, or joyful, or try to stop any of those feelings once it is in full bloom. Mostly, that doesn't work. You have to work hard to generate those states, such as by imagining previous experiences that involved those emotions. The problem is familiar to actors, who must produce displays of emotion on command (i.e., when the script calls for it). Some learn to fake it, but others try to generate the emotion itself. To succeed, however, they generally have to summon up vivid memories of past emotional experiences. Actors who use this method typically stock up on such emotional memories and, when they need to feel, use a series of mental tricks to take themselves back to those events. None of these tricks would be necessary if people could simply control their emotions by conscious will, the way they can control many other psychological processes.

Most likely, the reason we cannot control our emotions is so that they can control us. Emotions serve valuable functions in linking motivations to thoughts and actions. People will avoid actions that make them feel bad (aversive emotions). If they could simply turn off bad emotions by deciding not to feel that way, there would be no need to change our behaviors so as to prevent these bad emotions from arising. In chapter 3, we saw that people want to feel good and to avoid feeling bad. These drives are centered on pain and pleasure in most animals, but in human beings they extend to emotions. Hence people go through life pursuing positive emotional experiences and avoiding unpleasant ones.

For a cultural animal such as a human being, a crucial feature of the emotions system is its plasticity. Emotions can become attached to a wide range of circumstances and events. You can feel happy over a rise in the stock market, sad over a football team's loss, angry over injustice to others, ashamed over a bad tennis serve, embarrassed about the visibility of your underwear, envious of the discount someone got on a car, afraid of air travel, and in many other ways be susceptible to strong emotional reactions about culturally based experiences that did not occur during our evolutionary history and are not therefore fully natural. The emotions system is fairly malleable in its ability to connect with many different kinds of events, and this malleability is an important avenue by which the culture can shape people's behavior. To the extent that culture can connect emotions to different acts and outcomes, it can shape and influence people's behavior.

The rather primitive state of the psychology of emotions leads me to cover this topic in a manner different from the other chapters. I will start by presenting the main outlines of what we know about emotions. Then I will offer a tentative explanation as to how this knowledge fits the theory of the cultural animal. The purpose of this format is to enable readers to draw different conclusions from the facts if they are so moved, as well as to underscore the speculative nature of these ideas.

What Are Emotions?

Emotions are temporary states that differ from the normal, stable condition in several ways. There are bodily changes, ranging from an acceleration of the heartbeat to tears. There is the subjective feeling of emotional response, in which the impact of external events strikes the person much more intensely, as compared with non-emotional periods. Thought processes are also affected. Some experts distinguish emotion from mood on the basis of whether the person knows what has caused the state: Moods are felt without having a definite explanation, whereas an emotion is directed at a specific fact or event. In practice, however, many psychologists use the terms *emotion* and *mood* interchangeably.

Another distinction is made between emotion and affect, and this one is important. Full-blown emotions may consist of rich, complex, highly meaningful experiences. *Affect* refers simply to positive or negative feelings. At their simplest and most commonplace, affects are nothing more than small twinges of liking or disliking whatever you encounter. Although affects are simpler and seemingly more primitive than emotions, they may be far more important in influencing people's actions and responses. Affect is emotion reduced to one dimension, namely, positive or negative. Anger, sadness, anxiety, jealousy, and others are all lumped together as negative affect, and similarly, all of the various pleasant emotions are positive affect. Looking at affect instead of emotion therefore greatly simplifies the world, although it discards many of the rich variations and meanings that make up the full bloom of emotional experience. The greater simplicity entails that affect can have much broader psychological effects, as we shall see.

Affect and emotion also differ in degree, according to common usage. An emotion is a full-blown response, whereas affect can refer to a brief trace of positive or negative feeling. Attitudes, for example, include affect (such as liking a political candidate, a commercial product, or a suggestion), but it would be too much to say that attitudes consist partly of emotions. There is also a difference in speed: Affective reactions are extremely fast, arising within small fractions of a second, whereas emotions—especially when they include full-body arousal reactions—may take some time to develop.

The two patterns correspond well with the two systems in the mind. Affect seems perfect for the automatic system: quick, simple, reliable, and capable of arising in parallel. Full-blown emotion is more in keeping with the conscious system: slow, powerful, and all-encompassing. Emotion is normally understood as a conscious experience, whereas affect can occur at the margins of consciousness or even outside of it.

The broad usage of the term *emotion* is daunting. As two researchers wrote:

As psychologists use the term, [emotion] includes the euphoria of winning an Olympic gold medal, a brief startle at an unexpected noise, unrelenting profound grief, the fleeting pleasant sensations from a warm breeze, cardiovascular changes in response to viewing a film, the stalking and murder of an innocent victim, lifelong love of an offspring, feeling chipper for no known reason, and interest in a news bulletin. The experts do not agree on what is an emotion and what is not.[1]

A century ago, the James-Lange theory of emotion proposed that the physical response to external events comes first, and the mind's perception of these changes in bodily state constitutes the subjective feeling of emotion. This theory did not fare well in the laboratory, because the same bodily state seemed to accompany a broad range of emotions. This state is important to understand. It is what happens when the sympathetic nervous system kicks into action. The heart beats faster, breathing increases, and the bronchioles in the lungs dilate so that more oxygen gets into the blood. More blood gets pumped to the brain and the muscles. While these activities are stepped up, the body cuts back on its regular maintenance activities (homeostasis), such as digestion. The state can be mimicked by injecting the person with adrenaline.

A more familiar version may be the feeling of nervousness. When you are nervous, such as before an important performance, you may recognize your heart beating faster and your breathing increase; your hands will become cold as a symptom of the change in circulation; and you may feel that you want to go to the bathroom, which indicates that the body is trying to close down the digestive activities for a while. Nervousness can be regarded as a generic, all-purpose emotion.

The state of the body during these emotional moments is called *arousal*.[2] Arousal alone does not produce emotion, although it can intensify an emotional response. For example, injecting people with adrenaline does not produce a full-blown emotional response, although many people can recognize the similarity. If something happens to elicit emotion, however, the person who has had an injection of adrenaline may have an unusually strong reaction.[3] A cruder version of this response involves people who drink too much caffeine, possibly by accident (e.g., if they think they are drinking decaffeinated coffee or tea and unwittingly consume a big dose of caffeine). Some researchers find that people who jog in place or spend a couple of minutes on an exercise bicycle will have intensified emotional reactions later on—for instance, if someone insults them while their heart is still pumping harder from the pedaling, they may respond aggressively.[4]

Such observations led Stanley Schachter to propose that emotion has two components: the physical arousal and the mental label.[5] The physical arousal alone does not produce a full-fledged emotion, but it makes an emotion likely to be felt. The mental label is based on how the person interprets the situation, and so it determines which emotion will be felt. Schachter's theory of emotion can be crudely compared to a television set: The bodily arousal is the on-off switch and volume control, and the mental label resembles the channel selector.

If Schachter's theory were correct, then all emotions would have essentially the same physical state, and emotions might be readily converted into each other. Research has not found it easy to convert one emotion into another, because the arousal quickly becomes linked to the interpretive label. Unexplained arousal (such as if people unwittingly drink too much caffeine) can, however, be channeled into different emotions. Another limitation is that arousal states seem to come in at least two flavors, good and bad, and people cannot be made to confuse pleasant with unpleasant emotions, even if they can convert a pleasant arousal into a different pleasant emotion.[6] Apparently there is a barrier between the good and bad emotions, which may be rooted in the physiology of emotion, so that it is rare to confuse the two. Contrary to popular lore, hate is not easily mistaken for love, or vice versa.

Arousal in emotions has another implication that is important but easily overlooked. Emotions are inherently temporary. The body does not remain aroused for long—it has multiple inner mechanisms that are designed to return it to its normal, baseline state (homeostasis). The temporary nature of emotions entails that emotions are better suited to recognizing changes in one's circumstances than to recognizing circumstances themselves. Being poor is certainly unfortunate, for example, but if you have been poor all your life, you probably don't spend a great deal of time crying about it. In contrast, if you have been rich all your life and then abruptly become poor, you may cry hard for a while. Eventually, you will get used to your new economic circumstances, and the emotion will go away.

Key Facts About Emotion

In the absence of any generally accepted theory of emotion, it is helpful to review some of the main facts and conclusions about it. These contain valuable hints about how emotions help create the cultural animal. First, as already mentioned, emotions are inherently temporary. They depend on a bodily state of arousal, which soon wears off. Single emotional states do not last for months and normally not even for hours. Sigmund Freud asserted that repressed emotions remain intact in the unconscious, waiting to burst back into awareness, but this view is not accepted today. Emotions that are stifled tend to go away faster, although similar feelings can arise again if the underlying conflict or cause remains.

The temporary nature of emotions suggests that the purpose of emotions is to cope with current events. This could be useful for directing immediate action, although that will not be my conclusion. Another possibility is that emotions are mainly for evaluating changes.[7] And sure enough, when things remain the same for a long period of time, the stable facts do not generally evoke much emotion, whereas changes and departures from the status quo are more likely to yield emotions. Emotions draw the person's attention to something that has just changed, thereby guiding the person to think about the change and perhaps respond to the change in other ways.

Emotions are more temporary than people realize. Research by Dan Gilbert and Tim Wilson has confirmed that people's predictions about their emotional reactions show a standard kind of error: People predict stronger and longer emotions than they actually experience. If I asked you how bad you'd feel to find that your partner was having an affair, or how good you'd feel if you won $500,000 in the lottery, you'd probably predict that you would have a powerful emotional response that would last for a long time. If either of those events were to happen to you, your reaction might indeed be intense at first, but perhaps not as intense as you had predicted, and it would tend to pass much faster than you forecast.[8]

Affect is not so temporary. Affect seems able to remain in the system, at least in trace form, indefinitely, whereas emotions wear off. Emotions include physical arousal and other bodily changes that are inherently temporary. Affect boils down to a simple positive or negative feeling. When you encounter some person, situation, event, or even the possibility thereof, the association of a good or bad feeling will arise and color how you think and choose. You might run into someone you interacted with years ago. As soon as you recognize the person, you may have a good or bad feeling toward him, based on what happened between you years ago. The full details may not come back into memory for some time (if ever), and you may not have the time or energy to have a full-blown emotional reaction. Indeed, you may not reexperience a full-blown emotion from events that happened years ago, unless they were exceptionally strong. Even someone with whom you had a major conflict may not evoke a strong emotional response years later, but there is likely to be enough remembered affect to make you careful about how you deal with this person now.

Affect is one important component of attitudes, which is why attitudes toward most things can be assessed on a scale that simply asks for a one-dimensional rating of liking versus disliking. A complex range of emotional ratings is not needed to assess attitudes. And, as we shall see, attitudes are valuable guides to behavior. Often it is enough just to know whether you like or dislike something.

Another important fact about emotions is the finding that all of the positive, pleasant emotions tend to go together, and all of the negative, unpleasant ones go together, but the positive and negative ones are largely unrelated.[9] This view has had to fight off a series of statistical challenges,[10] but it has become increasingly influential. True, people cannot feel happy and sad at the same time, but people who frequently feel one bad emotion (such as anger or sadness) are prone to feel other bad emotions (such as jealousy or disappointment) more often too. This finding suggests that the human psyche has two separate emotions systems, one for positive and pleasant emotions, the other for unpleasant ones. Studies of the brain and nervous system have likewise supported the conclusion that there are two separate emotions systems, one for pleasant emotions and positive reactions, the other for the bad ones.[11]

The seeming independence of positive and negative emotions may actually reflect a mixture of two contradictory patterns. First, people cannot feel good and bad at the same time, so there is an inverse relationship. Second, some people are highly emotional and respond strongly in both directions, whereas others keep an even keel and do not generally have intense emotions of any sort, and this pattern produces a direct positive relationship (in other words, good and bad emotions go together). These two patterns offset each other statistically and produce the impression that there is no link between positive and negative feelings.[12]

Sorting emotions into two large categories is helpful, but a second dimension has also gained recognition as crucially important: arousal. As we have seen, some theories of emotion have emphasized arousal as a defining aspect.[13] But some emotions are marked by low arousal. Sadness, for example, does not usually involve a fast-beating heart and heavy breathing, and there is a kind of quiet, peaceful happiness that is also calm.

Using those two dimensions enables emotions to be sorted into four categories: high arousal pleasant, high arousal unpleasant, low arousal pleasant, and low arousal unpleasant. These groupings capture meaningful differences in how the emotions feel and how they affect people. To be sure, the four categories are only a rough condensation of what may actually be considered as a plane of space with two main dimensions. Some authorities think that it is best to think of emotions as arranged along a circle, so that some are very close to the two axes while others are farther from them.[14] For example, "tense" is a kind of aversive emotional state marked by high arousal, but it is not particularly negative and should therefore be considered closer to the positive emotions than, say, disgust or anxiety, which are intensely aversive. Even if you adopt that view, however, you still tend to recognize the dimensions of pleasantness and arousal as crucial.

The idea of mapping all emotions onto one or two dimensions is a handy way of making sense of the universe of emotional states, but some researchers question it and instead think that many basic emotions are innate and distinct. Lumping them together therefore loses some important categories. Yes, anger and fear may both be marked by high arousal and a negative (unpleasant) feeling, but those similarities do not change the fact that anger and fear are quite different emotions that serve different functions, produce different behaviors, and undoubtedly feel quite different to the person experiencing them. Some theorists have elaborated long lists of basic, discrete emotions.[15] Although the field as a whole has not gone along thus far, there is a growing recognition that a handful of basic emotions—joy, sadness, anger, fear, disgust, contempt—do deserve to be regarded as distinct.[16]

To complicate matters further, people do not usually have a single emotion in isolation. Several studies have found that when people report on their emotional and mood states, they usually list more than one at a time.[17] Even laboratory manipulations designed to induce a single emotional state tend to produce "blended" states of multiple emotions.[18] Although at first this observation raises obstacles to the study of emotions, it could actually hold one key to simplifying our understanding. James Averill,[19] a leading expert, compiled a list of 558 different names for emotions in the English language alone. Maybe we have so many words for emotional states because some of them have been coined to refer to common blends. Hence, it is possible that a dozen or so basic emotions could produce several hundred different emotion words to denote all of the blends. Perhaps the basic emotions exist in the automatic, affective system, but since unity of feeling characterizes conscious experience, the conscious mind needs many terms to label all of the blended emotions it feels.

One last and curious fact about emotions is their apparent immunity to conscious control. Most people cannot simply change their emotional state by an act of will based on deciding what they want to be feeling right now. In this respect, emotion is closer to motivation than to cognition, because people can often direct and control their thoughts, whereas (as we saw with the failure of priestly celibacy, for example) they cannot make themselves stop wanting something. Research on self-regulation reveals a stark contrast.[20] People can directly control their thoughts and their actions, including resisting temptation or regulating how hard they work at some task. (To be sure, some kinds of performance, notably skill-based ones, are partly outside of conscious control.) People regulate these actions mostly by sheer willpower. But willpower does not work with emotions, and so people tend to accumulate plenty of indirect strategies to regulate them. These indirect strategies include trying to create a different emotional state, such as buying oneself presents or seeking out the company of friends when one is depressed. They include controlling arousal, such as burning off energy through exercise when one is angry, or consuming energy-altering drugs like caffeine or alcohol. They include distracting oneself, such as by watching sports events to ward off one's worries, or even eating something tasty to get one's attention off personal problems.

Cultural Differences in Emotions?

The issue of cultural variation in emotions has been controversial. At first, it was widely believed that different cultures produced radically different emotional states, so that a person from one culture could not even begin to understand what someone from another culture was feeling. This research received a severe blow from evidence that people from very different cultures could translate emotion words effectively and even recognize facial expressions of emotion. A highly influential research program by Paul Ekman and his associates began with photographs of facial expressions that Americans would easily recognize as expressing different basic emotions: angry, sad, happy, and the like. Ekman and his group traveled all over the world showing the photographs to people in widely different cultures, including even some distant tribes that had had almost no contact with Western civilization. By and large, most people in every culture recognized the emotions expressed in those American faces. These results convinced most doubters that some aspects of emotions are innate and universal.[21]

Studies on infants have also favored the view of innate emotional tendencies rather than emotions being learned. Infants exhibit and express various emotions long before they have had much chance to learn facial expressions or to observe emotions in others. Indeed, babies who are born blind smile when they are happy; obviously, their smiling is not something they learned by observing others.[22]

The universality of facial expressions encouraged some experts to believe that the facial expression is a natural, innate part of emotion and may serve some function. Robert Zajonc revived a century-old theory that the face controls the blood flow to the brain and that different facial expressions channel blood to different parts of the brain, as appropriate to different emotions.[23] The brain controls the body, so it determines whether you will hug someone or hit him, and the emotions of joy or anger may help influence your choice by means of the facial expression, which channels blood toward the part of the brain that will direct hugging or hitting, respectively.

Although emotions may operate the same way in nearly all cultures, culture does have significant influence on how people deal with emotions. Some cultures believe it is appropriate to express emotions freely and dramatically. Others advocate keeping emotions under control and not letting them show. People can learn to indulge their emotions or to express them more freely.

There is an important caveat to the studies with Ekman's photographs of facial expressions. These studies only work when the photos are posed. That is, the models in the photos were instructed to do their best to express their feelings fully and clearly in their facial expressions. Another approach is to take photos of people in different emotional states as these occur naturally. When such photos are used, they do not elicit universal recognition.[24] In other words, when people look at someone from a different culture who is feeling an emotional state but not especially trying to show it, they cannot usually discern what the emotion is. Both findings are important, the successful and the unsuccessful. The successful studies show that there is some universal dimension of emotional expression. The unsuccessful ones show that there are also significant cultural variations.

My own reading of this literature points to the conclusion that emotions are natural and that the expression of them comes naturally, but culture can teach people to conceal their feelings. That's why people cannot recognize emotions as they actually occur: People don't make maximally expressive facial expressions when they have emotions in everyday life. The role of culture and society is not to create the emotions but to restrain and conceal them. And, as noted earlier, culture can use emotions to control behavior, insofar as culture can teach people to have various emotional reactions to particular events.

What Are Emotions' Purpose?

According to one standard view, emotions make people do crazy, irrational things. Emotions cause people to yield to impulses, and sometimes they do or say things they regret later. If people want to behave rationally and make sensible choices, they need to overcome or stifle their emotions. That view can't be the whole story, even if it were completely true. It depicts the impact of emotions as maladaptive—as an impairment of rational, sensible action. If that were all emotions did, natural selection would probably have phased emotions out of the human psyche thousands of years ago. Nature would only bestow or preserve emotions insofar as they confer benefits. And if there are costs to emotions, such as the occasional outburst of irrational behavior, that only means that the benefits have to be that much greater, in order to outweigh those costs.

One thing that emotions do seem to accomplish is to translate general motivations into specific feelings. After all, people mainly feel emotions regarding things about which they care, which is to say, when their motivations are engaged. When no motivation is involved, the person doesn't care one way or the other, and so no emotions are aroused. Emotions help evaluate events, but evaluation is not done in a vacuum—rather, evaluation has to compare current circumstances to some goal or standard. Emotions typically use the person's wants and needs as the basis for evaluating, and so emotions appraise events as good or bad insofar as they help or hinder the person's strivings.In that sense, the emotions serve to connect the motivation system with other activities. In particular, emotions communicate from motivation to both cognition and action. Emotions help to keep the cognitive system focused on things that matter (in the sense that they are relevant to the person's motivations). They also help to guide behavior so as to further the pursuit of what the person wants.

How exactly does this work? How do emotions guide cognition and behavior? There are several standard answers, not all of which can be credited. I will present them briefly here, and then we shall look more closely at how they fit the facts.

One obvious and traditional view is that emotions cause behavior. By this view, emotions consist of impulses to act. Possibly the emotion itself contains implicit muscle movements, as the noted aggression researcher Leonard Berkowitz has suggested about anger.[25] When an emotion arises, it sets the body in motion to carry out certain acts. Possibly it can bypass the entire thinking system and lead directly into action. The fact that many emotions include bodily arousal—the sort of energized feeling one gets from adrenaline—suggests that quick, efficient action is one purpose of emotions.

A second view is that emotions direct cognitive processing. Emotions grab attention and keep the mind from wandering. When you are upset about something, or when you are full of joy over something, your mind tends to stay focused on it rather than wandering off onto other topics. Consistent with this view, arousal narrows attention.[26]

A third view is that emotions serve some interpersonal functions. They may help people understand each other and even help them maintain good relationships. The fact that emotions tend naturally to reveal themselves, including by facial expressions and tears, suggests that emotions may serve some function of communication between people. An emotion may sometimes be a message rather than being simply a storm on the inner landscape.

These views are not necessarily contrary to each other, and in principle they could all be true. Let's take them one at a time, proceeding from the simplest (the interpersonal aspect) to the most complicated (action control).

Emotions and Interpersonal Relations

The cultural animal has to be a social animal first. This requires forming and maintaining relationships with others. We have already argued that human beings have a strong need to belong, in the sense of a motivation to make those important interpersonal connections. If emotions connect motivation to either cognition or action, then it should be easy to find that emotions operate to guide and support the efforts to belong. And it is easy. The evidence isn't hard to find, and it doesn't require careful scrutiny nor reinterpretation of obscure research findings. Au contraire, it is abundant and overwhelming. Essentially, all sorts of positive emotions are linked to forming or upgrading relationships, and all sorts of unpleasant emotions come from damaging or breaking off relationships.[27]

Forming new relationships is generally a cause of good feelings. Making new friends feels good, as does being accepted into a club or getting a new job. The strongest new attachments bring the strongest doses of euphoria, such as when two people form a romantic bond by falling in love. The irony is especially apparent when two people have a baby. Even though adding a child to one's family will in the long run cost a great deal of money, bring conflict and worry, and lower the parents' life satisfaction, the birth of a new child is treated everywhere as a joyous occasion.[28]

Forming a relationship is not the only source of joy. Anything that intensifies a relationship is also likely to bring happy feelings. When a couple converts their romance into marriage, the wedding ceremony is generally marked by an outpouring of joy. When professors get tenure—meaning that their temporary jobs become permanent—they too feel happy, and there are smiles all around. Confirmation into a church is also celebrated. Even hardened criminals, who tend to be a grumpy and suspicious lot, regard the cementing of relationships as a happy occasion for celebration, such as when a rising young tough is "made" a permanent member of the Mafia.

Meanwhile, a host of bad feelings are linked to all sorts of events that damage relationships. Nearly all experiences that separate people, set them against each other, or dissolve their bonds bring negative emotions. Sadness and depression are often associated with the loss of a relationship. Jealousy signifies a fear that your lover will leave you.[29] Grief typically involves mourning over the death or departure of a loved one. Guilt arises when you hurt or disappoint a loved one, especially in a way that might jeopardize the relationship.[30] Loneliness, described by Harry Stack Sullivan as possibly even worse than anxiety,[31] comes from a lack of interpersonal connection: Even though lonely people have as many contacts with other people as nonlonely people, they lack the feeling of mutual concern and ongoing connection. Chitchat with casual acquaintances or coworkers isn't enough to satisfy most people.

Anxiety is widely regarded as the most powerful form of emotional distress. Anxiety feels like fear or panic and is acutely unpleasant. Freud himself accorded anxiety an ever more prominent and central place in his theorizing as he continued to revise his ideas in light of new observations, and by the end of his career, anxiety—and the need to avoid it—figured as one of the prime movers in the psyche. Some people suffer from *anxiety neuroses*, which are characterized by recurrent feelings of panic and impending disaster.

What causes anxiety? Dianne Tice and I reviewed the published literature on the topic and found that all of the assorted studies and findings could be easily grouped into two main categories, corresponding to two main causes of anxiety.[32] For example, if we look at what the people who suffer from anxiety neurosis actually worry about during their panic attacks, these fall into two main categories, and there is hardly anything else. The less common and less powerful category was fear of injury or death. That is, some people have anxiety that they are going to get sick and die, that they will have a car crash, that they will sustain a major injury and be crippled, and the like.

The other, more prevalent and powerful source of anxiety was what we called *social exclusion*. It consisted of fears of ending up alone. These anxieties focus on being rejected by loved ones, abandoned by partners, or otherwise shut out of desired relationships. Even strangers can evoke anxiety if they represent the threat of rejection. Shyness and social anxiety often have the effect of making the person avoid meeting other people, going to parties, or entering other settings where there are people present, because the shy person fears being rejected by them.[33] When people report their emotional reactions to various kinds of memories and scenes, social rejection is the most consistent cause of anxiety.[34] Situations that involve interpersonal evaluation are highly prone to cause anxiety,[35] which is an indication that people fear that others will reject them if they evaluate them badly. Interacting with people from different social groups or different races tends to produce *intergroup anxiety*,[36] probably because the odds of being accepted and included by someone from a different group are markedly lower than the odds of acceptance from one's own group.

Anger is the one emotion that might seem not to fit. After all, anger may seem like a bad thing that would harm or jeopardize relationships rather than preserve them.[37] But anger is often a response to something that a partner does that might itself damage the relationship. People get angry when others treat them unfairly or hurtfully. If the anger is communicated, it can help people resolve their conflicts. Otherwise, the only choices are to walk away from the relationship or to engage in physical violence. A discussion and possible compromise, prompted by the display of anger, may therefore be better for the relationship in the long run.[38]

In sum, the roster of emotions seems well attuned to interpersonal belongingness. To the extent that people want to feel good emotions and avoid bad ones, they will seek to form and maintain good, stable relationships.

Another interpersonal aspect of emotions involves expressing them. The fact that emotions are naturally, easily expressed suggests that they serve some interpersonal function. Otherwise, they might easily just take place inside the person's head or body, like thoughts or actions. Most likely, members of groups gain some benefits by knowing each other's feelings. These benefits would have to extend to biological advantage, which normally means improved prospects for surviving and reproducing, and they would have to benefit the individuals involved rather than just the group as a whole. We may speculate about what these benefits might be. Fear, for example, would seemingly put the person at a disadvantage in some ways, at least vis-à-vis the predator, because showing fear may reveal one's weakness and vulnerability to the enemy. But a clear expression of fear (such as a scream) could benefit one's genes by alerting family members that danger is present. Sadness may elicit sympathy and support from others, thereby enabling the person to recover faster from misfortune or loss. Joy and other positive feelings make the person fun to be with and therefore help to attract others. Showing guilt over a misdeed can help a relationship recover, not least because it shows that the guilty person cares about the relationship—something that might be especially important to affirm after you have done something bad, which might imply you don't care about your partner. Indeed, one of the largest sources of guilt that people report is over failing to pay enough attention to relationship partners, and so simply expressing guilt may directly counteract that message of neglect.[39]

Thus, emotions may be useful for the social animal in at least two ways. Inside each person's psyche, emotions exert some influence to push the person to maintain strong relationships. Meanwhile, emotions also function between people, insofar as emotions help people to communicate a variety of helpful, valuable messages and therefore to understand each other better.

Emotions and Thought

Emotions help to link motivations and cognitions. That is, emotions push people to think about the things that matter (as defined by the person's wants and needs). You don't have emotional reactions to things you don't care about, by and large. So emotional reactions are strong indications that some motivation is highly relevant to what is going on. Emotions keep your attention focused on these important issues, and you go on to think about them.

The mental effects of emotional arousal are important. During emotions, you are highly alert and typically focused quite narrowly on the here and now. When you are beset with strong emotions, because your child is hurt or your lover has left you or you have just learned you are to receive a major award, your mind does not wander. Indeed, the effects of arousal on attention involve some of the oldest ideas in research psychology. One long-standing and well-replicated conclusion is that people (and even nonhuman animals such as rats) perform best at intermediate levels of arousal.[40] Low arousal produces indifferent, sluggish performance, and high arousal can be disruptive. The so-called Easterbrook hypothesis[41] held that this pattern is due to the progressive narrowing of attention as arousal increases. A person with low arousal will take in any information available, including material that is not relevant to the current task, and so the openness to all sorts of information produces distraction and relatively poor performance. As the person becomes more aroused, the mind manages to screen out irrelevant, extraneous information and concentrate on the task at hand. Performance improves. At some point, the person has it just right: All irrelevant information is ignored, and all relevant information is noticed and processed. Beyond that point, further increases in arousal continue to eliminate information, but because all of the irrelevant information has already been screened out, the mind now starts to eliminate or neglect information that is helpful and relevant to the task. This interference will therefore impair performance.

Suppose you were a divine power designing a human being. For it to survive, you would want it to take care of itself and its offspring. By this point, you have endowed it with a rich mind full of possible things about which to think. It can pursue long stretches of ruminations and interesting ideas, and it can also jump from one idea to another. But when its child falls in the river, it would be best for the human to focus specifically on that problem and not to drift off into other thoughts, such as how nice the clouds look. Emotions can help the mind focus. Emotions direct attention to the here and now and indeed to a narrow part of it. As we already noted, emotions also get the body ready for action. The child whose parent felt no emotions would be at greater risk of drowning than the child of a parent whose system has a strong emotional response to get the body and mind working together, without distraction or interruption, to accomplish a rescue.

Emotions often take some time to develop and therefore may sometimes be too slow to guide responses to a rapidly occurring crisis. But emotions could still be valuable for linking motivation and thinking even if they are delayed. When the crisis has passed, you may still feel lingering emotions. These keep attention on what happened, and so you may continue to think about it. By focusing thinking on the issue, you may be able to learn the right lesson and store it in memory for the next time a similar situation arises. Even if emotions are too slow to help you respond to the first crisis, the emotions from the first time may help create the memory trace that helps you know how to deal with a similar situation the next time.

The effects of emotions on thought are not uniformly helpful, though. The emotions system focuses on only half of the relevant information, and this can lead to bad decisions. A purely rational decision maker would appraise each possible outcome by looking at both its value and its likelihood. Should you spend your $3 buying milk for your children or buying lottery tickets? If you won the lottery, you could buy all the milk your kids would ever need, plus plenty of other things they might want. But the odds of actually winning the lottery are slim. In contrast, some milk will do them a little good, and there is hardly any uncertainty involved. Your accountant might tell you that the milk is the better buy, considering the long odds against winning the lottery. Your emotions, however, tend to disregard probabilities and merely look at the size of the outcome, and they might well sway you to buy the lottery tickets instead.

Actually, emotions seem to register only two levels of probability: definitely and maybe. The many shades of maybe don't register. In one classic study, participants were told that at a certain point in time, they might get an electric shock. The odds were either 50% or 100%. The researchers measured people's emotional arousal physiologically. As the fateful moment approached, arousal went up, not surprisingly. The stronger the shock was anticipated to be, the greater the arousal—thus, emotion was in proportion to the size of the outcome. But the level of arousal was essentially the same whether the chances were 50-50 or certain.[42]

Other studies have come to the same conclusion.[43] The implication is that emotions arise in connection with the image of the anticipated outcome, such as winning plenty of money or getting a shock, and they do not pay much attention to differences in the odds.[44] George Loewenstein and his colleagues convey this message by asking you to consider the difference between winning $10,000 versus $10 million in a lottery. These seem quite different—the $10 million will change your life in a way that $10,000 cannot begin to do. In contrast, consider two lotteries with identical prizes, but one offers a 1 in 10,000 chance of winning, whereas the other offers 1 in 10 million. That difference in probability is hard to translate into an emotional image, and so people will have about the same feeling toward both. The difference between 10,000 and 10 million is the same in both examples, but emotion will respect it in the one case and disregard it in the other.

The special emotional power of zero chance was shown in studies that asked people how much extra they would be willing to pay for product safety. Thus, one study asked people what they would pay for an improvement to an insect spray that would reduce the chances of inhalation poisoning or skin poisoning. In one condition, the risk reduction was described as going from 5 in 10,000 to zero. In the other, from 15 in 10,000 to 5 in 10,000. The second improvement is twice as good as the first in terms of the number of people saved, but consumers were willing to pay more for the first improvement than for the second.[45] The reason is presumably that the emotion system doesn't distinguish very well between different probabilities unless one of them is zero. Zero risk has a powerful emotional appeal.

When we do learn to notice odds and probabilities so that our emotions can register them, sometimes the effect is still irrational and counterproductive. Experiments by Paul Slovic and his colleagues show that people rely on affect to make choices and sometimes are led astray as a result.[46] For example, imagine an airport safety measure that is projected to save 150 lives. Sounds somewhat good, right? In contrast, imagine an airport safety measure that is projected to save 98% of the 150 lives that would otherwise be at risk. Strictly speaking, the second measure isn't as good as the first, because it only saves 147 lives (98% of 150), whereas the first saves 150. But the 98% probability sounds great. People who saw only the second measure gave it higher ratings than people who saw only the first. In fact, even a safety measure that would save 85% of 150 lives elicited more support than the guaranteed saving of 150 lives. These preferences make no rational sense, but they can be explained by the impact of emotions: Saving 98% or 85% of lives functions as a cue that the measure is good, thereby boosting the affective evaluation of the measure. The difference probably reflects the duplex mind pattern. The automatic system simply adds up the affective values: Saving lives is good; 85% is good; so it's a double good, whereas saving 150 lives is only a single good. Only the conscious system can calculate that saving 85% of 150 lives is not as good as saving 150 lives.

The impact of judging by anticipated emotional tones has been dubbed the *affect heuristic* by Slovic. The general idea is that people rely on these little good and bad feeling tones to make judgments and decisions. The automatic system uses affect in a simple-minded fashion that probably works well in many situations but is ill equipped for complicated decisions and probabilities, like the life-saving example above. In another demonstration, people were offered the chance to win a prize by drawing a red bean from an urn full of beans. In one case, there were 7 red beans out of 100; in another, 1 red bean out of 10. The latter case offers the better odds, but people often preferred the former, presumably because they were swayed by the higher absolute number of red beans.[47]

The subtle power of affect may help explain many peculiar things. Slovic and his group invoke it to explain why performers change their names: "John Denver" presumably sounded more pleasing than the musician's real name of Henry Deutschendorf, just as "Judy Garland" probably appealed more than Frances Gumm.[48] They even note some evidence that political candidates with more pleasing names are more likely to win elections. Likewise, the affect heuristic may explain the widespread use of background music in movies and television shows: Music guides the affective reactions of the automatic system and helps people understand what is happening. Smiles are another cue for positive affect, which is why models in commercials and catalogs are often depicted with big, happy smiles.

Affect can lead people astray. Full-blown emotions can have even more dramatic effects. Irrational and self-destructive behavior is most often found among people who are emotionally upset. Emotional distress tends to make people focus on outcomes and disregard risks, and so people in that state may take foolish risks that sometimes will bring disaster on their heads. In one study, people were offered a choice between two lotteries, one of which was a long shot for a big prize, while the other offered a good chance of winning a small prize. If you appraised the risk properly, the way a statistician would (by multiplying the odds times the payoff), it was clear that the play-it-safe lottery was the better choice. Sure enough, people in good or neutral moods tended to pick that one. People who had just been through either a frustrating or embarrassing experience chose the long shot, however.[49] They were drawn by the big prize and ignored the odds, even when the chance of losing carried some additional penalties such as having to undergo a noise stress experiment. Moreover, if people were instructed to list the pros and cons of all of the options before choosing, then even the emotionally upset people made the right choice. The implication is that emotional distress makes people respond quickly, ignoring risks and focusing just on an outcome that appeals most to them, without thinking through the downside of the risk.

Emotions thus influence cognitive processing and decision making, but they do not always produce the optimal result. Emotions may well deserve part of their reputation for irrationality, but then again people who lack emotions seem to have considerable trouble negotiating their way through human social life. The bottom line must be that emotions do more good than harm, even if the results are far from perfect. If emotions mainly disrupted thinking, then people who were relatively immune to emotions would be wiser and more rational. This view was popularized by the character Mr. Spock on the old "Star Trek" television shows. Spock was from a different planet and race, and although he was similar to human beings in most respects, he did not have emotions. He never tired of explaining to his earthling colleagues that decisions should be made on the basis of reason and logic rather than on emotions, and in the show he was one of the most rational and reliable characters.

Yet human reality is quite different. Researchers such as Antonio Damasio have studied people who have suffered brain injuries or other problems that prevent them from having emotions.[50] They are not superbly wise, calm, and rational beings like Mr. Spock. Instead, they show poor and erratic judgment and are prone to engage in highly impulsive behavior patterns that mess up their lives badly. Emotions remain important aids to rational thought and self-control. To live in human society today, it is important to have the entire system functioning properly. Having no emotions to help guide your behavior would be just (or almost) as disastrous as acting solely on the basis of emotions.

One of Damasio's observations is especially relevant. Some of his emotionless patients find it difficult to make up their minds. In one anecdote, he offered one of these patients a choice between two dates for their next appointment. The patient was able to think endlessly about the implications of these two choices but was not able to pick one. He spent the better part of an hour discussing all of the possible costs and benefits of the two dates, such as possible other things he might want to do on those dates and even what the weather might be like. Finally, Damasio just picked one, and the patient immediately said, "That's fine."[51]

This indecisiveness could well indicate what emotions are supposed to do, namely, link motivations to cognitions. Without emotions, the person was unable to decide what he wanted. The thinking system just rambled on endlessly, identifying plenty of relevant ideas but not able to sort them out effectively. The impulsiveness of other such patients may reflect the same problem, even though on the surface being impulsive is making too-hasty choices whereas being indecisive is being too slow to choose. In both cases, the person is not getting the helpful input from the emotions system that normally enables people to navigate their way through the complex choices that come with living in a cultural society.

In short, without emotions, the thinking system just spins its wheels. Emotions are vital for evaluation. Thinking without evaluating has limited practical utility. Evaluation is done by referring to what is important—again, the person's set of wants and needs. Emotions are a crucial link between motivation and cognition. Mr. Spock might have been useful for thinking up all sorts of possible consequences and implications of any decision dilemma, but he would not have been good at picking the best choice of action.

Imagine again that you are on the committee charged by Mother Nature to design a cultural animal. You have already decided to give it a large brain so that it can participate in culture and think through many issues. Ultimately, though, it is going to face choices that cannot be imagined (or programmed) in advance. These may be extremely complicated choices, involving multiple dimensions and possibly options that have little in common with each other. What kind of choosing system could you install that would be able to handle all sorts of complex, unforeseen dilemmas?

The matter would be simple if all choices involved only common features. For example, if you had to choose between a charming, sensitive, and rich husband versus an obnoxious, aloof, and poor one, the selection is easy. Likewise, the choice of whether to take the job that pays $50,000 or the one that pays $60,000, with all else being equal, is not hard. But life in a cultural society is not like that. The job that pays $50,000 may offer other benefits, such as better prospects for advancement, or the chance to live in an area with nicer weather, or a more stimulating set of colleagues. How do you integrate those aspects with the difference in salary?

Consider even the decision about how to spend a Sunday afternoon. You could clean the house, watch football, visit your mother, read up on the stock market, or write a poem for your beloved. There is only one afternoon, so you can't do them all. The crux of the dilemma is that they have so little in common. The various benefits—a clean house, some enjoyment, fulfilling family obligations, an improved chance of making money, or possibly attracting some reciprocation of your feelings—are so different that there is no obvious way to say which of them is better.

Emotions can rescue you from this dilemma. Each of the options can be associated with how it will make you feel. To be sure, even these may be complicated by mixed feelings. For example, watching football might make you feel good during the game, but then again you might end up being upset if your favorite team loses, and you also might feel guilty because you neither cleaned the house nor visited your mother. Still, even these can be added together.

Emotions thus serve a crucial, valuable function that has been overlooked by many theorists: It constitutes a kind of common currency for the decision process. Anticipated emotions enable people to compare and choose among various options that seemingly have nothing in common. All people have to do is translate each option into its anticipated result in terms of how they will feel emotionally. The option that promises the best emotional outcomes is probably a pretty good choice.

Economists like to analyze decisions in terms of *utility*—the anticipated value of outcomes. By and large, they express utility in terms of money. The rational investor, for example, will choose the form of investment that looks like it will yield the most money. In that sense, money works as a way for evaluating investments. But much of life involves decisions that are not easily translated into money. In the Sunday afternoon example, what is the dollar value of visiting your mother? Moreover, even when some possibilities can be converted into money, it is far from clear that people actually do so. Thus, we could calculate the dollar value of cleaning your house, such as by finding out what a professional maid service would charge for the same labor. But when debating whether to clean your house, do you ever try to put a dollar value on it and use that to compare with the appeal of watching a football game? Few people do.

Emotions are therefore probably the true internal measure of utility. Almost all options can be converted into emotions. A big advantage of emotions is that these calculations of affect are extremely rapid and ubiquitous. As soon as you consider doing something, you probably already have an affective reaction: cleaning house will be tedious, but it will feel good to have it done; watching football will be fun, but Mom will make me feel guilty; writing the poem might be frustrating or satisfying, depending on how it goes, and if it does help win over your beloved's heart, there will be bliss. And remember that emotions tend to discount the odds, focusing just on how appealing the outcome is, so bliss looks like a winner—write the poem.

None of this says that emotions will invariably lead to the best result. Rational analysis and especially moral reasoning can sometimes show that you should not pursue the course of action that might feel best. As we have already seen, emotions and affect do not properly appreciate complex probabilities and may occasionally push people toward choices that seem wrong by careful logical analysis. These occasional failures are beside the point, however. The emotions system will often yield the best answer, or one of the best answers. And in any case, it is an efficient and easy-to-use system for making complex decisions. Nature had to give us some way to choose among multiple, diverse options that differ in too many ways to make rational analysis a reliable guide. Otherwise the cultural animal would freeze up at all sorts of dilemmas, like a computer asked to do something for which it does not have the proper program or adequate data. Choosing by affect and emotions is a remarkable solution to this design problem. Certainly we don't have to follow our hearts, and nature has made us able to do something other than what the affect heuristic favors. But at least the affect heuristic can weigh in, and quickly, with a recommendation, so people are not stuck for hours trying to choose what to eat for lunch or which letter to open first.

Emotions and Action

One standard view is that emotions create impulses to behave in beneficial ways, even if these may be too simple for dealing with the complex modern social world. Nico Frijda used the term *action readiness* to describe this function of emotions: Emotions prepare the body for action.[52] The known features of emotional arousal do seem well suited for action: More blood (and therefore more oxygen) is sent to the brain and muscles, so you can notice more, think faster, and summon more physical strength.

On the other hand, emotions don't really cause behavior in any reliable or direct manner. We will return to this issue when we discuss how people act, but for now the relevant point is that emotions are rather slow for causing behavior and seem on the face of evidence to be unreliable as a factor. Many emotions fail to cause any discernible behavior: People can have emotional reactions while watching a film, for example, yet may sit quietly until the movie ends. When emotion does affect behavior, it does so indirectly, such as by affecting how people process information.

It is possible that emotions evolved as a way of guiding behavior but that they no longer serve that function in human beings. There are some data on brain patterns to fit that view. Emotions in animals are marked by activity in the limbic system. In human beings, however, emotions also set off considerable activity in the newer (frontal) parts of the brain. The human system for controlling action is considerably more complex than what other species have or need, especially since our behavior is based in part on appreciating meaningful aspects of situations and cultural values.

The question of how emotions actually operate in the psyche is far from settled, and the next decade or two will bring more data to bear. In the meanwhile, however, the theory of the cultural animal can propose some ideas about what emotions are for and how they link motivation to behavior.

My conclusion is that it is wrong to say that emotions are for initiating behavior, and it is even mostly wrong to say that emotions cause behavior. Instead, behavior pursues emotions. Emotions are an important consequence of behavior rather than a cause. There are two major implications of that view. First, as we have already begun to see, actions are sometimes decided on the basis of anticipated emotions, though action is helped along by affective signals. Second, emotions contribute to learning, and so future actions benefit from past experience to the extent that emotions resulted from the past experiences. Without emotions, people may fail to profit from experience.

The old view, that emotions caused behavior directly, typically used fear as its best example. Fear makes you run away, according to this analysis, and as a result you are less likely to be killed—hence better able to survive and reproduce. Yet in many cases people report that they did not experience fear during the emergency. Fear, like other emotions, may be slow to arise, sometimes too slow for dealing with the current emergency (wherein it might be counterproductive anyhow). When you realize that the other car is about to crash into yours, you do not have time to become afraid, nor would fear do you much good. The next time you go to make a left turn, however, fear may arise, as if to persuade you not to put yourself in danger.

The new, alternative view, that behavior pursues emotions, may perhaps be appreciated in the example of guilt. Guilt does not directly make people move their bodies in any obvious manner. Rather, guilt comes after one has done something wrong, such as hurting a relationship partner. Guilt makes people think about what they did wrong and about how to avoid repeating that mistake, so that they will not have to feel guilty again. One study of guilt experiences, for example, found that guilt led to a high rate of learning one's lesson and changing one's behavior subsequently.[53] And henceforth, guilt operates primarily via anticipation. When you face a decision on how to act, you realize that one action could lead to your feeling guilty, and so you tend to avoid that course of action. Guilt can therefore exert a great deal of influence over behavior without the person feeling guilty very often, because people simply avoid doing things that will make them feel guilty.

Emotions seem well suited to help people learn lessons from their behavior, even if the emotions contribute almost nothing to guiding the course of action at the time. As we saw, emotions focus attention on what happened to cause the emotion. Therefore a strong emotional reaction will keep your mind focused on what just happened, and this thinking may help you analyze what you did right (if the emotion is positive) or wrong (if it is negative).

Why didn't I do something different? How could I have avoided this? If only I hadn't said the wrong thing—there is some evidence that emotions stimulate *counterfactual thinking*, defined as imagining events or outcomes that differ from reality.[54] This seems ideal for learning: The conscious system can consider alternative possibilities, especially including things that you could have done differently, and hence you will learn from your mistakes.

The importance of emotions for learning is supported by observations on when emotions occur. Wendy Wood and her colleagues have shown that people mainly experience emotions when they are performing new, unfamiliar actions.[55] When they act out of routine or habit, emotions are much less common. Habitual and routine acts don't generally require learning, almost by definition. In contrast, learning is mainly associated with new acts, and that is where one finds emotions.

Emotions can thus facilitate learning by making people think and analyze their recent actions. This form of learning is highly suited to a cultural animal, for whom action is meaningful and must be understood within a system of values, expectations, communications, and other ideas. There is however an even more basic way that emotions can prompt learning, and that is by the basic processes of reward and punishment. As we will see in our exposition of action, the laws of learning operate effectively in many species, even those with fairly limited intelligence. An action that is punished (that is, followed by something bad) becomes less likely to be repeated, whereas one that is rewarded (that is, followed by something good) is more likely to be repeated. Emotions probably serve as salient, powerful regulators. Pleasant emotions reward actions, and aversive emotions punish them.

Most animals negotiate their way through life guided by pleasure and pain. In modern human life, pain is rather unusual and predictable, and pleasure has also become tamed and managed into predictable doses. Emotions, in contrast, are frequent and often unexpected. Emotions, rather than pleasure and pain, are probably what guide people through their daily lives. Emotions reward and punish actions, thereby changing the odds that the person will perform a similar action the next time around.

One sign of the importance of emotions is that people who lack emotional reactions often make bad decisions. This is shown by studies with people who have had brain damage that prevents them from having fear or other emotional reactions.[56] In one study, people played a game in which they could turn over cards. Each card signified either winning or losing some money. There were four decks of cards. Two of them included high payments, and two contained low payments. The catch was that the high-paying deck also contained some very large losses, and if you kept going to that deck, you would end up losing money. The low-paying deck was "safe" in the sense that you would never lose money by drawing cards from it. Both normal and brain-damaged patients would initially try out all of the decks and, as soon as they encountered a big loss, would avoid the risky deck for a while. The difference emerged in how fast they went back to the risky deck. The healthy people avoided it for a longer time and hence made out relatively well. The brain-damaged people, however, were prone to go back sooner to the risky deck, and many of them ended up going bankrupt in the game. (The researchers did not actually take their money away, of course.) The point is that without emotions, people were more prone to take dangerous, destructive risks.

Even so, this study indicates that the effect of emotions is to consolidate one lesson so as to influence future behavior. It doesn't show that current emotions help people to perform better. Drawing a costly card from the bad deck produced a negative emotional reaction (in normal people), which then left enough of an affective residue to steer them away from that deck the next time. The emotional reaction was essential for learning: Without emotions, people didn't learn from their mistakes. So they continued to take the same dangerous risks.

This function of emotions helps explain one of the key facts about emotions that we noted earlier, which is that emotions are relatively immune to conscious control. People cannot normally just change their emotional state by an act of will, the way they can change their thoughts or their actions. The reason for this immunity of emotions is that emotions are there to help us learn. When we do something wrong, it is important that we feel bad in order that we learn the lesson. If we could simply feel better by deciding to feel better, there would be much less incentive to learn from our mistakes.

In other words, emotions guide us and teach us. If we could control our emotions, they would lose their ability to guide and teach us. If you say something that upsets your mother or your boyfriend, you feel guilty, and so henceforth you avoid saying such hurtful things so that you won't feel guilty again. If you could just stop feeling guilty by simply deciding to feel happy, you wouldn't have to change your behavior. Guilt would not deter wrongful actions if guilt could be banished by fiat. Immunity to direct control is essential for the emotions to serve their function.

But isn't there plenty of evidence that emotions do directly cause behavior? Actually there is much less than one might think. And, crucially, even that evidence is open to reinterpretation. On closer inspection, many signs that emotions cause behavior actually indicate that behavior is pursuing emotions.

Research on helping, for example, has shown that people who are sad or upset are more helpful than people who don't feel bad.[57] This looks like emotions causing behavior: Sadness leads to helping. But it could also be that sad people help because they believe that helping will make them feel better—in which case, behavior pursues emotions. The conclusion that people help specifically in order to feel better was demonstrated with a clever procedure by a team of researchers at Arizona State University.[58] They gave half their subjects a placebo (sugar pill) and told them that it was a mood-affecting drug, not unlike marijuana and alcohol, except that its specific effect was to freeze and prolong whatever mood you felt when the pill took effect. This meant that there was no point in trying to change your mood or emotional state for the next hour or two. The subjects were also put into a bad or a good mood by artificial mood-induction procedures. Then everyone was asked for a favor. Without the mood-freezing pill, the bad moods led to greater helping, consistent with previous findings. But the people who had taken the (bogus) mood-freezing pill did not help more even if they were sad. Thus, sadness leads to helping only if you think that it will change your mood and make you feel better. The helping by sad people is a strategy for bringing about a change in their own emotional state.

Aggression is also done for the sake of improving a bad mood. Angry people tend to be more aggressive, and this tendency is especially pronounced among the many people who believe that acting out their anger will make them feel better. When these angry people take a mood-freezing pill, however, they do not become more aggressive.[59] In some way, people seem to believe that lashing out at someone will enable them to feel better and escape their angry, upset mood.

There is even more evidence that what looks like emotions causing behavior is actually behavior pursuing emotions.[60] Depressed people eat more cookies and junk food than happy people, but only because they expect the food will make them feel better. Upset, guilty people seek immediate gratification in the hope of feeling better right away. People procrastinate on difficult assignments in order to do fun things that promise short-term good feelings.

We saw earlier that emotions often don't last as long as people had anticipated they would. In a sense, this means that emotions are inflated in their anticipation. That too probably means that the anticipation is one of the important aspects of emotions, consistent with the view that people regulate their behavior based on what they expect to feel as a result. After all, if the opposite were true— future emotions were typically underestimated—this would undermine their usefulness in guiding behavior.

Conclusion

Thus, emotions operate as an internal system that rewards and punishes actions. Full-fledged emotions often come after the behavior is finished, whereas the twinges of positive and negative affect can help steer behavior automatically in certain ways. Emotions stimulate thoughtful learning, such as by making people think about what they just did to cause a good or bad outcome. Emotions narrow attention, thereby facilitating mental processing of some information rather than others. Anticipated emotions can be an important factor in dictating how people choose to act. Indeed, anticipated emotions are a compelling common currency, which allows cultural animals to translate different possible options, which differ in many unrelated dimensions, onto a single factor and therefore select among them. Emotions guide people to form and maintain good relationships, to behave in rational and prudent ways, and generally to function effectively within the complex world of culture.

We can now proceed to consider human action itself. Motivation, thought, and emotions all make some contribution to push people to act in various ways. None of those systems is an end in itself—instead, the value of each can be read in what it contributes to behavior. Sometimes motivation (wanting), cognition (thinking), and emotions all push in different directions, but the person has only one set of hands and feet, and so the crucial outcome is which push manages to win and dictate what the person does. The next chapter will focus on action.

6

How People Act and React

Though all cultures have rules, they vary in how strictly people comply with them. Stories about Peruvians arriving two hours late for a lunch appointment, or Englishmen standing in line waiting their turn to loot a store, reflect these different degrees of strictness. In Europe, the Germans are known to be exceptionally rule-bound, in contrast to the more easy-going Italians. The difference in rule orientation informs the following (possibly apocryphal) anecdote. A German was preparing to travel by train to Italy for his vacation. At the time, most European trains were designed with small compartments with three seats on each side. From past experience, this man knew that he was prone to motion sickness when he rode facing backwards, and so when he made his reservation he insisted repeatedly that he be assigned a forward-facing seat, and he was assured that he got one. When he boarded the train, however, he found to his dismay that his seat faced backward after all. The next day he got off the train in Italy in a very grumpy mood and went straight to the station master to complain. The Italian seemed unfazed by his complaint, especially since it was not his personal fault and in any case it was rather too late to do anything about the problem. Not getting any satisfaction, the German persisted and insisted how terrible the journey had been. Finally the Italian said "You should have just asked the person sitting across from you to change seats. I'm sure anyone would agree, considering how you were suffering." The German replied, "Well, I couldn't do that—no one was sitting in that seat."

Whether strictly or more casually enforced, rules are a major part of human life. Rules reveal how the control of action changes between cultural and merely social animals. Social animals have only the most rudimentary sense of rules, most of which involve direct enforcement of some privilege by the stronger animal at the expense of the weaker one. That is, a big animal may punish a smaller animal for displeasing it, and over time the smaller one may learn to avoid that behavior, at least in the presence of the larger animal. But this is a far cry from how human beings follow rules. They understand the rules as abstract prescriptions that exist independent of any particular person. Strangers meeting for the first time can follow rules (such as taking turns, shaking hands, or using money) in dealing with each other without even needing to discuss what those rules are. People can also debate the legitimacy of rules, dispute whether certain rules apply to the current situation, and argue for changes in rules. Only cultural animals can do such things.

The main differences between cultural and merely social groups is the cultural reliance on systems of meaning (which include rules). Ultimately none of that can accomplish anything unless people are able to alter and guide their behavior on the basis of meanings. Even rules mean nothing if behavior is dictated by hormones, genes, reinforcement history, or indeed any other factor that does not take current rules into account. The behavior of social animals can be driven by their impulses, together with some influence from the other animals who are present at that moment. In contrast, the actions of cultural animals reflect the influence of many factors not currently visible: not just laws, morals, and other rules, but also plans and goals that remain in the distant future, obligations and debts carried over from the distant past, and the expectations or wishes of people who may be thousands of miles away.

What these have in common is meaning, especially abstract meaning. The key difference between social and cultural animals is that only the latter act on the basis of abstract meanings, such as rules and plans. Animals who do not have language cannot make use of abstract meanings, because they cannot process them. The culture is a giant system that uses these invisible forces to shape the behavior of the various individuals, such as by laws, that enable the system to function so that it can work its magic (accumulation of knowledge, division of labor, and the like) and make the members generally better off.

Cultural animals therefore need a complex and flexible inner mechanism for action control—certainly much more complex and flexible than what other creatures need. It is possible for nature to program some creatures with precisely how to respond to every situation they will encounter. For other creatures, a simple learning mechanism may be sufficient to enable them to develop the repertoire of actions they need to get through their lives. But culture presents the individual with novel, complicated choices and multiple ways of construing various decisions and dilemmas. Acting purely on the basis of innate impulse or previously reinforced behavior is not a reliable guide to the best response, and so cultural animals must be able to override some impulses and inclinations in order to do something else instead.

Ultimately, the cultural animal needs to have free will, or at least what it would understand and describe as free will. The cultural world presents the individual with new, unforeseeable circumstances, and it would not be possible for genetic evolution to program strict response sequences for all these circumstances.[1] Instead, the person has to be able to modify his or her own behavior along the way and develop new programs to guide his or her own action. This vast expansion in plasticity (flexibility), subject to the person's own control, constitutes one important form of free will.

I realize of course that free will is a controversial concept that sets off all sorts of bitter debates and strong opinions, many of which are not relevant to my point. Let me therefore back off from saying simply that evolution gave us free will so we could benefit from culture. The idea of free will can be re-stated in a way that will be more palatable to all but the most rigid determinists. To enable human beings to participate in culture, evolution gave us the ability to override our initial responses, choose among different options, and let behavior be guided by meanings (including rational analysis, abstract rules, and long-term planning). In addition to programming some of our tendencies and reactions, evolution created us to be able to re-program ourselves. It gave us controlled processes, self-regulation, and lifelong behavioral plasticity. It enabled us to use the results of complex, logical reasoning (occasionally!) to alter our behavior.

As this chapter indicates, we should understand the human being as having a behavior system, which the cognitive and emotional and motivational systems may or may not influence. Probably that view reflects how the human psyche actually developed. Even cockroaches, rats, and worms can make behavior, so behavior obviously does not require much intelligence or cultural learning. In order for human beings to be cultural animals, however, nature had to change the behavior-producing system so as to make it receptive to meanings. Meaning is the vehicle by which culture influences behavior. People use meaning to allow their behavior to benefit from culture.

How Action Happens

How does behavior occur? Based on common sense, the answer should go something like this. The person surveys the situation to see what the various options are (i.e., various possible actions). Then he or she does a quick cost-benefit analysis of those options, in order to pick the best one. Then the mind tells the body to act in that way. Sometimes, to be sure, emotions break through and hijack the process, causing behaviors that the person wouldn't rationally select. Also there might be some kinds of behaviors that are swayed by unconscious or subliminal influences. Still, by and large the process goes from information processing (with appraisal) to mostly rational choice and then action. There is much to be said in favor of this standard view. It fits both common sense and some data. It should only be rejected with caution.

Nonetheless, let me propose an alternative. Behavior is not the end-product of cognitive processes, but rather behavior goes on all the time with or without rational thinking. A "self" can sometimes use rational thinking to intervene and hijack the behavior process, however, and when it does so the results are often adaptive and beneficial. So it learns to do this. Even so, rational thought is not always emphasized as a way of making here and-now choices in everyday life. In substantial part, people may just do whatever seems appropriate at the moment, following the obvious path. When things go bad and they feel a big dose of negative affect, then—and mainly then—do they engage in rational thought, to try to figure out what they did wrong. They come to some conclusion and possibly figure out an if-then rule for how to act if that situation comes up again in the future. The next time that situation does arise, relatively little rational analysis is needed in order that the behavior be better chosen. Some residue of the bad feelings from the previous disaster arises quickly, helping the person to steer behavior (perhaps invoking if-then rules) so as to produce a more desirable result.

How do people explain their own actions? In many cases they say they simply did what felt right at the time. This account should not be dismissed. Feeling right may be a matter of simple affective cues. Emotions can leave those affective traces that will guide behavior. Also, as we saw in the chapter on emotion, the role of emotion in this process is not so much to erupt into the process and wreak irrational, destructive havoc. Instead, emotion surfaces sometimes after the fact of good or bad behaviors, depending on their consequences, and the emotion helps stamp in the lesson of whether this was the right way to act in such a situation. Behavior is aimed at producing good emotions and avoiding bad ones. In this way, the point is not that emotion causes behavior, but rather that behavior pursues emotion. And, recognizing that behavior leads to emotion-relevant outcomes, behavior is then altered or directed in anticipation of these emotional outcomes.

The emotions themselves are linked to the motivations. You don't have strong feelings when you don't care about something. You feel good when things satisfy your emotions, and you feel bad when events thwart your wishes in all the various ways this can happen. Essentially, emotion carries messages from the motivation system to the cognitive system, and that in turn can pass preferences along to the behavior system. This applies to both the natural and the cultural motivations. Culture can exert much of its influence this way too. Culture can shape motivations in effect by linking various emotions to various actions or accomplishments. If the culture can teach people to feel good or bad (respectively) when performing various particular actions, it can shape their behavior. People will act so as to avoid bad emotions and if possible to attain pleasant ones.

There is probably some sense in which cognition contributes to ongoing behavior. In this it is probably just processing information so as first to understand the situation and second to see how to pursue one's goals. When driving down the highway you know where you are going and how to get there, yet you have to process information to make the trip successfully. You probably have to change lanes now and then so as to pass slow cars, and occasionally you heed road signs so as to connect onto other roads, and so on. And then if a passenger tells you that she needs to go to a bathroom, you make various other adjustments to get her there. So cognition participates in executing the behavior. But it's more like carrying out if-then rules: "When the sign says junction for route 80, exit route 91 and drive onto route 80 heading east." "When the next rest area comes along, exit and park there instead of continuing to drive down the road." The automatic system may be sufficient to carry these out, so conscious thought and its elaborate powers of reasoning are not required. But conscious thought may contribute by changing the programs, such as by creating the if-then rules in advance, and perhaps by modifying them when they are not working out.

Action and the Duplex Mind

A recent news story reported that the president of a local anti-violence group in Sarasota, Florida was arrested for punching a referee during a flag football game. The man was not even a player in the game—it was his 7-year-old son's game, and the man was the team coach. The man had been reprimanded several times during the game for yelling at the referee, and his behavior had even resulted in his son's team being penalized. Even these penalties didn't have the intended effect, however, and later in the game he charged out onto the field and clobbered the referee with a punch that made the poor fellow's ears ring. The 270-pound, 34-year-old man had to be pulled off the referee by other spectators. Police locked him up and later released him on bail.[2]

That people become angry with sports officials is hardly news. That they sometimes resort to violent protest is fortunately rare enough that it still qualifies as news. But what made this story remarkable was that the offender was the leader of a group devoted to reducing violence. The organization "Mad Dads" was founded in Nebraska and has 60 chapters in 15 states, all geared toward steering young people away from criminal and violent behavior. To become president of such an organization, the man must presumably have been sincere about promoting nonviolence. But then how could he attack a referee at a sporting event, in front of all the players and spectators and even in front of some members of his family? It's as if Gandhi were caught beating his wife. The irony was not lost on the man, who later apologized and resigned as coach (though apparently not as president of the anti-violence group!).

Action is in many ways the end product of all we have discussed so far. The impetus to act begins with either motivation (what the person wants) or some external demand. Thoughts and emotions come into play to elaborate on this impetus, scoping out specific possible acts, noting potential problems, getting the body ready to act. Of course, what the person actually does may or may not follow from these sensible calculations. No doubt the "Mad Dads" president could have explained in detail (and later did) how people are supposed to control and express their anger without punching anybody. There are undoubtedly links between thoughts and actions, but there are some gaps too. Perhaps the duplex mind is at work again: The conscious system embraces nonviolence, but the automatic system acts on the violent impulses that arise when the referee appears to be mistreating your son. To put this another way, you have two different mental systems, but only one set of hands and feet. You can only do one thing at a time, especially when the competing options are incompatible. Do the hands and feet do the bidding of the automatic system, when it has an impulse to tackle the referee, or do they obey the conscious system and its commitment to nonviolence?

The fact that cognitive processes and reasoning do not necessarily produce the wisest or most helpful action points to a broader truth that must be kept in mind. Behavior happens all the time. Even animals with very small brains and limited cognitive capabilities manage to produce a constant stream of behavior. Likewise, in our own species, there is no sign that stupid people produce any less behavior than smart people, even if one might sometimes wish they did. The implication is that all this thinking and other processing is not necessary for behavior. The conscious mind and its rational thinking function as a usurper or hijacker. Thinking can show you how to act differently than you otherwise would have acted, and sometimes the agent system responds to those calculations by altering the course of action.

Because behavior happens all the time, with or without much help from the conscious system, it is easy to conclude that the automatic system runs the show: Behavior is mainly guided by automatic processes. Then again, it seems likely that the conscious system must accomplish something relevant to behavior. Otherwise it is doubtful that nature would have created it in the first place. The bottom line is that human behavior will be influenced by both parts of the duplex mind.

One view that is gaining in popularity is that consciousness is like a high-level executive, deciding broad issues of policy but not in charge of moment-to-moment operations. When a break in the meeting is called, you may decide whether to go back to your hotel room to get a sweater. The conscious mind calculates whether there is enough time to get there and back before the meeting resumes, and also evaluates how desirable the added comfort would be. If the decision is favorable, then the automatic system takes over, controlling the legs and feet, pressing the elevator button, operating the room key, searching through your suitcase for the sweater, and then returning (perhaps in a hurry) to the meeting room. The conscious system did not decide which finger to use to press the elevator button, nor did it supervise each footstep. It only formulated the grand plan.

People like to think they are in conscious control of all their actions, but more and more findings are accumulating to show that nonconscious, automatic processes are often very involved. We saw some of these in our initial discussion of the duplex mind in chapter 2.

The influence of automatic processes on even major life choices— where careful, conscious deliberation really ought to be paramount—has been established in some remarkable work by Brett Pelham.[3] This work built on the name-letter effect, which indicates that people have a special affection for the letters in their names.[4] They prefer the letters in their names (slightly) above other letters. Pelham has found that people's choice of residence and occupation are sometimes affected by this seemingly trivial preference for the letters in their name and in parallel fashion for the numbers in their birthdays. People named Dennis are more likely than people with other names to become dentists, for example, and people named Laura are extra likely to become lawyers. People born on the 12th of the month are more than usually likely to live in places that have the number twelve (such as Twelve Oaks), and the same goes for other numbers. People named Virginia and Georgia are more likely to live in the states with that respective name (and to move there during their lives, which counters the possibility that they were simply named after their state of birth) than to the other state.

These effects are admittedly small, but they are statistically significant, and as such they challenge our view of human beings as rational decision makers. It seems highly unlikely that people would consciously choose their homes or occupations based on the letters in their name. The implication is therefore that people's preferences are swayed by their affection for those letters without realizing it. Even when making major life decisions, these biasing factors enter into the decision process, again presumably without full awareness. The idea of becoming a dentist just feels a little more right to Dennis than it would have felt if his name were Ronald or George. Given the small size of these effects, it would be wrong to assume that being a dentist becomes the sole, overriding goal of his life from early on, or that parents can guarantee his future financial security by naming him Dennis and thereby steering him inexorably into dentistry. But perhaps when he has narrowed the choice down to two or three similar occupations that seem quite similar in most respects, the name letter bias gives him a small push toward becoming a dentist.

Does that mean that the conscious mind is irrelevant? Not necessarily. As I said, the conscious mind can choose goals and set the process in motion. The idea that parts of the process of pursuing the goal are carried out outside of awareness is undeniable. For example, when you decide to walk to the bank, you may consciously attend to initial factors such as making sure you have your bankbook or bankcard, but once you set out you do not consciously move your leg and foot muscles every step. In fact, during the walk your conscious mind is more than likely somewhere entirely different, such as remembering a conversation you recently had or thinking about what you might do later on. Your body executes all the complex actions needed to bring it to the bank with hardly any guidance required from the conscious mind. (To be sure, if your normal route is blocked, you may pause to think consciously about an alternate route; but perhaps that also might be done outside of awareness.)

Again, the great advantage of controlled and conscious processes is their flexibility. Automatic responses work well for carrying out standard, well-learned courses of action in predictable, familiar situations. The conscious mind is however able to consider a broad range of possible actions and to override or interrupt other responses.

My best guess is that the conscious mind's capacity for taking control developed first as a way of overriding those automatic responses. The capacity to resist responding based on every impulse or a first reaction would be extremely helpful and adaptive. Julian Jaynes[5] suggested, for example, that when well-armed soldiers ride into your village and say they want to take your food and perhaps your wife, your first and natural impulse may be to resist aggressively, in which case you would probably be killed. The ability to override that impulse consciously and substitute another response (such as meekly giving them what they want, while perhaps storing up information in case the future brings you a chance to get even) would enable you to survive.

A second crucial advantage of the conscious system is its ability to use logical reasoning and rational analysis to guide behavior. This too is one of the hallmarks of being a cultural animal. We shall have considerably more to say about these advantages (overriding impulses and making rational choices) in the subsequent sections. But let us first understand how the automatic system behaves. Its systems for controlling behavior are largely inherited from our biological ancestors. The simple ways that animals react and learn have not been erased from the human psyche, and indeed the automatic system in the human psyche probably contains slightly improved versions of them.

Acting Like Animals

Before telemarketing, many companies relied on traveling salesmen who went from one home to another in the attempt to persuade people to buy their products. The salesman would start each encounter by walking up to the door and ringing the doorbell, which is such a simple, familiar, and commonplace act that few people give it a second thought. It is however possible for years of experience at ringing doorbells to be overridden by a single experience, and a salesman named George Foster[6] developed a serious phobia about doorbells. As he was doing his job one day, he came to a house that unbeknownst to him had been deserted for several months. The lack of anybody home was not a serious problem, but the slow gas leak in the kitchen was, for it had gradually filled the house with flammable natural gas. It was a house-sized bomb just waiting for any spark to ignite it. Unfortunately the doorbell had a short circuit, and so when George Foster pressed it there was a spark, and house blew up in his face. He was knocked off the porch and had to be hospitalized.[7]

When he returned to work, he found that it was extremely difficult to bring himself to ring any more doorbells (which was an indispensable part of his job). Consciously he knew that the house explosion was a highly improbable freak accident that would be unlikely to be repeated, and moreover he could reduce the very low risk even further by only approaching houses that showed signs of being occupied. But somehow his rational understanding was unable to calm himself down, for his body went into panic mode whenever he approached a doorbell. After a while, however, the fear went away and he was able to resume work effectively.

This episode illustrates one way that behavior is learned in human beings and other animals. Behavior is a function of its consequences. This was articulated by Thorndike as the *law of effect* and made famous by B. F. Skinner under the rubric of *operant conditioning*. Whenever a behavior is followed (soon after) by some pleasant event, the creature becomes more likely to perform that behavior again. In contrast, when something bad happens after any sort of behavior, the bad event makes the behavior less likely to be repeated. In this case, having a house explode in one's face was an extremely bad outcome, and so some deep level of the man's psyche learned to want to avoid pressing any more doorbells.

This kind of process is very simple: a good outcome increases the behavior, a bad outcome decreases it. Because it is so simple, it doesn't require a highly intelligent brain, and so even very simple creatures follow these principles. But these principles aren't just for rats, they work on people too. People have other ways of acting, and they can even sometimes analyze a problem rationally or debate the proper moral course of action, and then act based on these thoughts. Still, the basic animal patterns of learning remain at work in human beings.

Another important point about George Foster is that his reactions did not depend on conscious choice or self-regulation. If anything, he needed conscious self-control to make him start pressing doorbells again, because his automatic system was quite satisfied that doorbells were utterly too dangerous ever to touch again. He had to use conscious reasoning to convince himself to ignore his panic and press the new doorbell anyway. Thus, his automatic system was capable of learning and changing his behavior, without needing much help from the conscious system, and indeed the conscious system was opposed to this learning (and eventually helped overcome it).

The fact that people can learn behaviors without consciously trying to learn anything is important, because it shows how the automatic system can learn and change behavior without needing the conscious system. There are ample anecdotes of psychology classes whose students form a conspiracy to shape the behavior of the very professor who has lectured them on these principles, without the professor's awareness. Thus, one class made a pact to see if they could control where the professor stood. When he moved to the left part of the stage, they acted as if fascinated by his lecture: they looked at him closely, kept quiet, visibly took notes on what he was saying. When he moved to his right, they looked away from him, rustled papers, dropped things on the floor, coughed, whispered a bit, and generally conveyed the impression that they were not following him. Sure enough, as the lecture wore on, he spent more and more time on the left part of the stage. It is said that by the end of the hour they had nearly conditioned him right out the door!

The automatic system probably learns mainly by reward and punishment. During the long reign of behaviorist theories, psychologists insisted that human behavior followed the same principles observed in white rats, even if people were a little smarter and more complicated. Nowadays few psychologists would insist that the principles of animal learning are sufficient to explain all human behavior. But those principles still do apply. And in particular, they apply to the automatic system.

The conscious system may look down on this simple kind of learning. To the conscious mind, learning from reward and punishment is "trial and error," a slow, clumsy, and occasionally painful way to learn something. Figuring it out with conscious reasoning is altogether more satisfying and pleasant, if it can be done.

The ability to figure things out is one of the biggest advantages of the conscious system and thus of the duplex mind itself. It affords much better and faster improvements. Most of the great inventions of the world, such as automobiles and televisions and space rockets and birth control pills, were more based on coming up with ideas than with blind trial and error. The ability of animals to produce such insight-based solutions is very limited. Among the most famous was Kohler's ape, who couldn't reach the banana from his cage but after considerable time realized that if he fit together the several sticks on the cage floor (none of which could reach the banana by itself) he could fashion a long stick that could reach it. Such an insight is at the high point of animal intelligence, but humans are much more sophisticated in their ability to perform imaginary operations to solve problems. Undoubtedly language has greatly increased the human capacity to use reasoning, logic, and insight to solve problems.

Operant learning typically takes some time and multiple failures. The earlier example of the house explosion is somewhat unusual in that a single event had such a strong influence on the man. These so-called one-trial learning episodes are relatively rare. Most learning, as Skinner's research showed, occurs much more gradually, under the influence of a sequence of rewarding or punishing outcomes. The sequence generally starts with random behavior which happens to elicit a reward or punishment, resulting in a slight change in the probability of repeating that behavior. If every time the baby makes the sound "mama" the mothering one gives it an affectionate hug that is pleasant to the baby, the baby will gradually learn to say "mama" more frequently, sometimes running to several hundred times per day!

Furthermore, behavior patterns gradually disappear when the rewards and punishments stop. George Foster was able to resume his job and even go back to ringing doorbells without having a panic attack every time, because there were no more instances of exploding houses. Behavior responds to incentives such as rewards and punishments, and when these incentives are withdrawn, behavior gradually—not right away, but gradually—reverts to its baseline. After a while, it just wears off. It's not necessary to try to undo some pattern you have learned, although sometimes trying can help. As long as the rewards and punishments that sustained it are clearly absent, the pattern will disappear of its own accord, just as a road that is no longer used will gradually become covered by weeds.

There are several additional principles that emerged from the study of animal learning and that are relevant to human nature. Consistency of reward and punishment is an important factor. Some behaviors might be rewarded (or punished) every time, whereas others only bring consequences intermittently. Not surprisingly, consistent incentives produce faster learning. If you want your child or assistant to learn something, reward him (or her) every time he does something right. And punish him every time he does something wrong.

Less obvious, but still important, is the fact that intermittent incentives produce more durable behaviors, especially after the incentives are withdrawn. If you learned to do something based on intermittent rewards, and then the rewards stop coming, you will keep it up longer than if you had learned it on the basis of being rewarded every single time. (For one thing, it takes longer to notice that the rewards have stopped, because you are accustomed to going without reward for periods of time.)

For most animals, the reward or punishment must come immediately after the behavior in order for learning to occur. (Even a five second delay makes learning much slower and more unreliable, and with a ten seconds delay rats will fail to learn at all.[8]) The expanded time processing of people may stretch this out, so we can learn from delayed rewards and punishments. Still, quick and consistent ones work best. This is an issue with criminal behavior, for example, in which the effectiveness of the death penalty toward deterring crime is debated. But the death penalty is administered only rarely, and then after years of delay through many legal processes. Speed and certainty of punishment are far more powerful than severity of punishment. Far more crimes would be deterred by administering a relatively mild punishment every time and right away, than by the threat of a possibly severe penalty in the distant future.[9]

Learning in general depends on rewards and punishments. Which is better? Almost certainly the optimal situation for learning is to have both. That is, you should praise and reward the person for right answers and good behavior, but criticize and punish the person for wrong answers and bad behavior. Getting both kinds of feedback provides the greatest amount of information and therefore allows the fastest learning. This may seem obvious, but in recent decades many American parents and educators have gone from emphasizing mainly punishments (under the fear of spoiling children) to relying almost exclusively on praise (under the influence of the self-esteem movement).

Still, if there is some reason to choose between the two, then current evidence suggests that punishment promotes faster, more efficient learning than reward. This is probably yet another example of the general principle that bad is stronger than good. A variety of studies have pitted rewards against punishments, such as having a teacher say "correct!" in response to correct answers but nothing in response to wrong answers, as opposed to saying "wrong!" in response to wrong answers but nothing in response to correct answers. The general finding is that students learn more and better in the "wrong!"-only condition than in the "correct!"-only condition.[10] Other work has sought to equate rewards and punishments by giving children marbles and making marbles contingent on learning to perform various tasks. In the reward condition, the child would start out with an empty jar and receive a marble for doing something right. In the punishment condition, the child would start with a jar full of marbles and lose a marble each time she did something wrong. Children learned more effectively in the punishment than in the reward condition.[11] Nor is this effect limited to a particular age: Other studies have found that punishment promotes learning more effectively than reward across many different ages.[12]

This evidence may shock some parents and teachers, who often like to think that punishment is bad and they should strive to use mainly rewards. (Then again, as we saw in the earlier discussion of the regression fallacy, experience may tend to mislead teachers and parents into thinking that reward is less effective than it really is, so that they lean toward overreliance on punishment.) If learning were the only consideration, it is clear that punishment should be favored. But learning is not always the sole consideration. On the contrary, people usually want their child (or student or trainee) to do more than learn a particular behavior. They want the person to have a cooperative attitude toward the task and perhaps to sustain a good relationship with the teacher. Punishment probably has undesirable side effects. Spanking your children or students may get them to learn proper behavior rapidly, but it may also foster a sense of resentment and rebellion, so that in the long run you do not get the outcome you sought. These side effects could reduce the overall effectiveness of punishment. Nonetheless, in the short run punishment is superior to reward for promoting learning. If you want the best learning, however, it is obvious that the best technique is to use both reward and punishment in a judicious, consistent fashion.

The laws of learning do have their limits. People and other animals are innately predisposed to learn some things more easily than others. Animals cannot be trained to learn any arbitrary behavioral response, but rather they show certain preferred ones. A classic paper by Robert C. Bolles pointed out that animals in the wild would not have sufficient opportunities to learn to avoid predators via reinforcement and other operant principles, because they would have been devoured before the learning could take place.[13] Instead, they are predisposed to learn to flee or hide from large, dangerous looking animals. Even tame laboratory rats quickly learn to distrust human beings and treat us as threatening possible predators, indeed faster than they learn many other reactions, and the difference is indicative that they are predisposed to learn the one rather than the other. Thus, innate tendencies place limits on learning.

Social (Observational) Learning and Gossip

Learning by trial and error—operant conditioning, as used by rats and by the human automatic system—is effective. But it is also painfully slow and, well, sometimes it painfully painful! Many complex behaviors cannot be left to operant conditioning. How would you like to learn to drive a car that way? You'd have to smash up several dozen vehicles and break plenty of your own bones before you'd have it right. Or imagine what it would be like if dentists or surgeons had to learn by trial and error—tedious for them, hellish for their patients.

Fortunately there are other ways. One important one that piggy-backs onto the simpler animal learning patterns is *observational learning* (sometimes called *social learning*). People can learn a great deal by watching others. In fact, observational learning fails to get the respect it deserves. Most psychology textbooks spend one or two dozen pages describing operant conditioning and then tack on a page or two to mention observational learning, as if observational learning were only about one-tenth as important, but some of them at least acknowledge that in daily life the reverse is closer to the truth: Most learning involves observation by others, rather than direct experience.

Observational learning is well suited to a social or cultural animal, because it relies on at least some primitive form of identification of the watcher with the one being watched (called the *model*). In human beings, such bonds of identification are especially potent, and so observational learning may be especially effective. The importance of interpersonal connections is easily apparent: People learn best from watching models who are similar to themselves, are attractive, or are high status, all of which are prominent mediators of social relations.[14]

At least two different mechanisms contribute to learning by observation. One is simple *imitation*. The other is *vicarious conditioning*. Imitation appears to be hard-wired in the brain: People simply imitate movements that they see others doing. But if you see someone get into serious trouble by acting in a certain way, you don't necessarily imitate it, and indeed you may learn to avoid actions simply by seeing the misfortunes of someone else.

Human language allows us to learn from the mistakes of others without even having to see them. This is probably one important function of gossip. Robin Dunbar has emphasized that gossip is a way of making social connections and exchanging information about each other, but this analysis, however correct, overlooks the power of gossip for learning.[15] A great deal of gossip is not the exchange of personal information for the sake of learning to understand each other better. Rather, it focuses on the misdeeds and misfortunes of others. Moreover, these aren't usually physical mishaps such as putting too much salt on your food. Rather, they involve overstepping or violating some of the intricate rules that govern social life in a culture. Sexual mishaps, money problems, symbolic affronts, social mistakes—these are the preferred stuff of gossip.

Gossip is often regarded as malicious, because its content makes its targets look bad. And it is quite possible that malice plays a role, insofar as people might prefer to repeat stories that reflect badly on their rivals or enemies. But they also repeat stories about celebrities and public figures, and even about their own friends and relatives. Stories about people who break the culture's implicit rules and norms and come thereby to grief seem widely interesting regardless of one's relationship to them.

Gossip is a very powerful extension of observational learning, though of course it is limited to cultural animals because it relies on language. Its power makes use of meaning, and indeed both the medium of gossip (speech) and its content (often rule violations) highlight the centrality of meaning in the life and behavior of cultural animals. For example, a group of adolescents may be struggling to master the newly relevant norms for dating and sexual behavior, as well as the options and limitations within a new school. Each one can learn the rules by direct reward and punishment, which would be a long and painful process, or by directly seeing what happens to others who break the rules, which will be somewhat less painful but still slow. In contrast, if every major rule violation and its consequences are repeated throughout the group, everyone can learn from everyone else's mistakes. In this way, people can learn a long and complicated set of rules in a reasonable amount of time.

Teasing serves some of the same function, though it starts earlier in life. Much of teasing is based on norm violations. For example, one child asks another whether there is a flood, and when the other says "No, why?" in a mystified manner, the first one points out that the second one's pants are somewhat short at the bottom (a common problem in rapidly growing children!) and suggests that the second child wore those pants to keep them dry. The other kids laugh (a little). The humor in such teasing is often rather weak, especially to the target of teasing. Why bother teasing someone in this way? The teaser gains social status, however, by showing that she understands the norms: Pants should cover the ankles. By teasing, the teaser wins a victory over both the target and the audience, because the teaser was the first to spot that a norm was being violated.

Parents use a form of gossip to teach their children, also. No mother wants to wait for operant conditioning to teach her child not to play in the street. That would require letting the child be hit by several cars, until the accumulated injuries produced a stoppage of street play. Instead, she will tell her offspring about other children who played in the street and were hit by cars and suffered terrible injuries. Such repeating of others' misfortunes is neither designed to build relationships with the subjects of those stories nor to be malicious. Rather, the mother tells the story by way of helping her child learn the rules of the culture. Roads are used by dangerous, heavy, fast-moving cars and are therefore unsuitable for children's play. And even when gossip does take on a malicious aspect, it still often serves to illustrate the culture's rules and the penalties for breaking them, and so it still has value for learning.

Meaningful Action

To nearly all animals, eating is straightforward and uncomplicated. The main problem is finding enough to eat. If something good to eat is available, and the animal is hungry, there is no mystery about what is going to happen. In contrast, eating in human beings can be determined by a vast array of meanings that go far beyond the simple biological urge for sustenance. Eating may be guided by long-term considerations such as dieting to become slim or avoiding high-cholesterol foods in the hope of avoiding a heart attack. Eating can be a social occasion in which the people are not very hungry and scarcely notice the food because they are engrossed in conversation. Scarlett O'Hara in *Gone With the Wind* ate a private meal before attending a banquet because she believed that attractive women should not be seen to eat very much in public, and research studies have confirmed that many people (especially women) eat less on dates or in other situations where people can see them than when they are alone. The category of "comfort foods" consists of foods that people associate with happy childhood memories and mother's love, and as adults they may consume similar foods when upset or under stress. In some cultures, norms stipulate that men may not harm others with whom they have shared food, because eating together creates a meaningful social bond. Christians eat crackers and drink grape juice or wine during their sacred rituals in church, and their belief that these foods become the body and blood of Jesus has earned Christianity the label of "the cannibal religion" among some people who believe in other faiths and feel a bit queasy about the Christian practice of eating their savior's flesh and drinking his blood. Jews, meanwhile, will refuse to eat perfectly good pork because of traditions and religious guidelines. Women who suffer from anorexia may refuse to eat almost anything, as a way of gaining a sense of mastery and control. Many people eat even when they are not hungry, simply because it happens to be lunchtime.

In short, eating has become culturalized. What for most animals is a relatively simple activity has become saturated with meaning and therefore transformed. One point in favor of meaning and culture is that our species tends to eat better than many others: We have gained control over our food supply in a large-scale, coordinated fashion to an extent that is unheard of in other species. What other species can have a whim to eat a delicacy from another continent and be able that same day to obtain an imported ration of it?

With meaningful action, we shift focus from the animal to the (almost) uniquely human. That is, the conditioning and basic learning processes covered are common to human beings and other animals, but meaningful action is minimal if not completely absent in most other species. Symbolic gestures, the pursuit of far-off goals, religious rituals, idealism and virtue, and similar forms of action are essentially unknown outside the human species, but all figure prominently in any attempt to understand people. Only a cultural animal can act meaningfully, because meaning is obtained from the culture. Indeed, meaningful action is one hallmark of the cultural animal, and the ability to base action on meaning rather than just blindly following stimulus-response links is one of the major advantages that cultural animals have over others. We shall return to this point when we talk about rational action, because the advantage of culture is most obvious there: A rational person can use reasoning and logic (inherent to meaning) to ascertain the best way to act and then can alter his or her behavior on the basis of those thoughts.

We should not equate meaningfulness with consciousness, however. The human automatic system can process meaning. In that way, the human automatic system is more powerful than the automatic systems of other animals. The conscious system can perhaps use meaning more powerfully and effectively than the automatic system, such as logical reasoning, construction of narratives, and mathematical calculation. But both systems have and use meaning.

Meaning changes the nature of behavior. Instead of simply responding in preprogrammed ways to the immediate environment, people can act in a wide variety of alternative ways. Actions can be symbolic. They can be coordinated with the actions of people who are not even present. They can be guided and altered by events that lie in the indeterminate future or the ancient past. In particular, meaning allows a person to string together a long series of actions that might seem to have little in common, in order to achieve some long-term goal such as buying a house or getting an education.

Meaning is one aspect of the all-important liberation from the immediate surroundings. Most animals and plants can only react to their current situation. In contrast, a human being can act based on events in the distant past or future, or on the basis of concerns about people who are far away, or about possible events and abstract perspectives. Meanings are vital for this liberation because they bring those distal concerns into the present. The person can mentally represent possible future events, or perspectives of others who are not there, or symbolic links to the past. People observe holidays that commemorate long-ago events, worship unseen powers in religious ceremonies, preserve their virginity to give to an as yet unknown future partner, vote in national elections for candidates they haven't met or against issues that represent what they regard as unfair possible changes to society, and more.

None of these would be possible without meaning. Lab rats and chimps couldn't possibly comprehend commemorating or worshiping. Voting in a national election, for example, would seem incomprehensibly absurd to most laboratory rats or wild birds. Voting brings no tangible benefit to the voter and requires a fairly complex (and sometimes quite cumbersome) transaction with the environment. Why would someone do something that is inconvenient and brings no obvious payoff? But of course voting has value and meaning that go far beyond the act of standing in a voting booth and pulling a lever or marking some spots on paper. Indeed, the payoffs of voting are invisible in that situation, and only a creature who can represent far-off outcomes could possibly understand that value of voting. Thus, language and meaning enable the cultural animal to move far beyond the immediate situation—and for those distal concerns to guide current action.

The intrusion of meaning is the basis for social causality. That is, people's actions can be determined by something beyond the mere twitching of neurons, reflexes, and molecular transactions. (The neurons do still have to fire, of course.) They can instead be influenced by factors far beyond the immediate situation, such as historical, political, economic, religious, and other abstract meanings. Meaning thus takes us beyond physical causality.

The simple learning processes already covered can be explained entirely in terms of physical causality, although it may be a bit clunky to do so. The animal's body performs actions, consequences are directly registered by the animal's brain, and the likelihood of repeating those actions is adjusted accordingly. An account of the molecular and chemical processes in the brain and muscles of the animal may be entirely sufficient to account for these patterns. In contrast, meaningful action depends on the linguistic and cultural system of meanings, which is something shared in common by large numbers of people. To explain why someone might vote for a third-party candidate as a symbolic protest against the two dominant political parties in a nation election, for example, requires some reference to national politics, the record of the main parties and their candidates, the individual's values, the system of voting, and other processes that go beyond the single person's brain and muscles. To be sure, social causality does not violate the laws of physics and chemistry. But it is not easily reducible to them.

Most behaviors occur simultaneously at many different levels of meaning, and people may be aware of one level but also operate (albeit less consciously) on the others.[16] The action of voting, for example, refers to an intermediate level of meaning. At a lower level, the same action can be described as moving one's hand. At a higher level, it can be understood as helping to shape our nation's history or participating in democracy. High-level meanings tend to involve long time spans. Low-level ones are here and now. People tend to prefer to understand their actions at the high levels, but when there is a problem they shift back to lower levels. Thus, the voter might be thinking about how his vote may help steer the direction of national policy over the next few years if his candidate is elected. But if the voting machine doesn't work right, he will quickly shift out of those grand meanings and start attending to how his hand movements can be altered so as to get the machine to respond properly.

To change the meanings that guide someone's actions, it is often useful to shift temporarily to low levels of meaning.[17] Actions at low levels are stripped of meaning and hence new meanings can be superimposed on them. Therapy for test anxiety, for example, may involve getting the student to stop thinking of the test as a huge threat that will ruin her life. Eventually the therapist may want her to look upon the test as a step toward finishing her schooling and getting a rewarding job, or as a challenge that will allow her to display her knowledge. But you can't just switch her from the one to the other. Instead, it is useful first to get her to think of taking the test as a matter of putting marks on paper or of tackling the first question and trying to rule out one of the possible answers. Once she can proceed through a test at this low level of meaning—doing one question after another, moving her hand to mark her answer on the sheet—then the troublesome meaning ("ruining my life!") is gone, and then a new higher meaning can be introduced.

People who want to avoid recognizing the broad meanings of their actions also may prefer to remain at low levels of meaning. Criminals, for example, usually spend very little time dwelling on the grand moral principles they are violating. Instead, they focus on procedures and techniques. In the same way, the Germans who carried out the killings of Jews and other victims did not probably think long and hard about the historical enormity of their actions as genocide. When they did think in high level terms, they tended to construe their actions vaguely as doing their duty and helping to create a better world by eliminating evil influences. Mostly, however, they probably kept their awareness at low levels: checking lists, reciting instructions, counting, directing people where to stand, pressing buttons.

Much meaningful action is found in role performance, and many roles come with scripts. These are essentially bodies of information about how one is supposed to act, and as such they are embedded in the culture. People rely on these scripts to perform the role, although they may deviate from it or put their own twist on it. When James Carter was sworn in as President of the United States, he followed the script for the ceremony except that he asked to sworn in as "Jimmy" rather than by his formal name "James." Likewise, although most American weddings involve some exchange of vows, some couples prefer to compose their own vows so that they can personalize the ceremony to some extent rather than simply following a standard script. But the personal vows do not generally range far afield ("Grace, my bride, I promise that after we are married I will not make obscene sounds with my mouth when your mother comes to visit.") People start with the standard script and make small adaptations and refinements as they see fit.

Pursuing Goals

A goal is an idea of a possible future, one that the person wants to make come true. As ideas, goals are made of meaning, and in order to think of goals one has to be able to use the power of meaningful thought to envision circumstances different from the here and now. Goals thus make clear the advantages of transcending the immediate environment. The goals confer meaning on the present choices, linking one's actions to future possible outcomes. Organizing your behavior in that way allows people to achieve much more than they could otherwise, especially in terms of goals that may be years away. For example, humans are the only animals who effectively retire from work, but retirement usually depends on years of planning and saving. Truly goal-directed action, in the sense that the actor chooses the action based on the intention of pursuing that goal, is a powerful and important form of meaningful action.

It actually took psychology several decades to realize that human action is largely directed toward goals. The old school behaviorists studied rats, and rats do what they do because of what has happened to them previously (the reinforcement history), not because of what they intend to happen next (a goal). But by now most psychologists believe that people, at least, have goals and that most human actions are goal-directed.

Whether animal behavior is truly goal-directed is controversial. They can pursue outcomes that they can see in their immediate environment, but they do not have much capacity to think of (and act upon) possible future events in other surroundings. This means that animals can follow very short-term goals, such as when an animal chases another in the hope of catching and possibly eating it. Such goals do not really require the animal to form mental representations of future possible states, however, and so goals that do go substantially beyond the present may be more than animals can pursue. Without language, animals cannot easily think of goals, and so their actions cannot be organized toward distant goals in the same way human action can.

Complicating the question of animal goals is the fact that some behavior may appear goal-directed when it is not. One psychologist who lived with a chimpanzee for a year noticed that it began imitating her washing the dishes. But the chimp didn't really have the same goal as the psychologist, namely to get the dirt off the dishes and render them clean. The chimp just enjoyed rubbing the dishes in warm soapy water and perhaps enjoyed imitating what the psychologist did. It would wash clean dishes just as readily as dirty ones, and even with dirty ones it didn't really get them clean.[18] Thus, it could perform the same behavior as the humans in one sense, but the behavior was not goal-directed for the chimp as it was for the human. At most, the goals that deliberately pursue are likely to be linked to short-term changes in the immediate stimulus environment. As I have said all along, one crucial advantage of meaningful thought is that it liberates the thinker from the immediate stimulus environment. Humans can make here-and-now choices based on goals that are years and miles away, unlike any other animal. Such is the power of meaning.

This view of human action as goal-directed stands in contrast to the behaviorist tradition, which used rat behavior as the model and assumed that rats (and by extension people) acted in certain ways simply because they had been rewarded for similar behaviors in the past. In contrast to such past-oriented models, it seems beyond dispute that much of human behavior is aimed at producing future outcomes. A goal is a mental idea of some desired future state.[19] People are sometimes assigned to pursue particular goals, and other goals they choose for themselves, but in either case the present behavior is oriented toward reaching the goal.

Goal pursuit thus depends on being able to think about a future state. Humans can pursue goals that are decades or even centuries away, and indeed some religions exhort people to change their behavior now on the basis of what will supposedly happen at the end of time, thousands or even millions of years into the future. Thus, we have the familiar pattern in which evolution takes something that animals can do on a small scale and gives humans the ability to do it on a grand scale, aided by language and the other tools of culture.

Not all goals are the same. You can have a goal of getting an education and graduating from college, and you can also have the goal of getting tonight's assignment done in time for tomorrow's class. The time span is a crucial difference: Goals can be either short-term (*proximal*) or long-range (*distal*).[20] The proximal ones are on the order of getting today's assignment finished, in contrast to a distal goal of getting an education and graduating from college. If animals do pursue goals, they are proximal goals, where the outcome can be anticipated clearly and realized in a very short period of time. By virtue of meaningful thought, people can pursue goals that may take decades to realize, and in some cases they pursue goals that will not be realized until after they are dead.

People are most effective if they have both the distal goals and the supporting structure of proximal goals that lead up to them. (Not that they necessarily know which is which. Football running back George Rogers once told reporters that his goal for the upcoming season was to gain 1000 or 1500 yards rushing, "whichever comes first.") A high school student may aspire to be a U.S. senator, but without a clear idea of what first steps to take toward that goal, the goal itself is likely to be impossible to realize and this may be quite discouraging. In contrast, someone who has only proximal goals may go through life without really getting anywhere, because each day is spent just taking care of immediate needs and demands.

The combination of distal and proximal reveals the power of meaningful thought: A distal goal is realized by following an organized succession of proximal ones, but only if the mind can process and represent that organized series of steps. This ability to organize goals into hierarchies and chains is a powerful advantage of the human psyche and its ability to apply the advantages of meaningful thought.

Pursuing a goal involves a shift between two very different mental states.[21] During the first (*deliberative*) stage, the person reflects on whether to pursue a particular goal. This phase is marked by cost/benefit calculations, sober realism, and consideration of alternatives. The other phase comes after the goal has been chosen. As its name (*implemental*) implies, it is concerned with implementing the goal. It is characterized by narrowing of attention to the goal (thus non-consideration of alternatives), optimistic illusion and confidence, and focus on information about how to do the task. The person in an implemental mind-set may reject questions about whether the goal is worth pursuing and whether alternatives are better. To him or her, those questions are no longer relevant and may distract from getting the job done.

The transition from the deliberative mind-set to the implemental one is sometimes marked by forming particular kinds of specific intentions.[22] These have an if-then structure: "If I can get home before it gets dark, I'll go jogging." These help people get started working toward their goals, and they also help people keep working toward the goals once they have started. In effect, these if-then intentions turn over control of behavior to the environment and the automatic response system. As soon as a certain situation is encountered (the "if" part), the behavior is more or less automatically set in motion. (Again, the if-then format is a meaning structure that is almost impossible to use without language, and so using language to process meaning enables people to take advantage of if-then logic to control their behavior in ways that non-cultural animals cannot.)

These two states represent different relationships between the automatic and conscious systems. Both terms (deliberative and implemental) describe what the conscious system is doing. In the deliberative state, the conscious system is considering the alternatives and their costs and benefits (some of which, no doubt, the automatic system is busy calculating, perhaps even adding a few affective shadings to them). In the implemental state, the conscious system has turned over the operation to the automatic system, and it merely waits optimistically for the outcome.[23]

Once a person has chosen a goal and made some personal commitment to pursue it, there are some standard patterns. The person's desire to reach the goal may actually increase, almost like inner pressure building up, until the goal is reached. As shown in the so-called Zeigarnik effect, if people are interrupted in the middle of pursuing some goal, thoughts of the goal tend to intrude on them while they are doing other things, which suggests that the mind is trying to get the person back on track moving toward the goal. Goal pursuit continues despite obstacles. If one path is blocked, the person will often find alternative pathways. Most goals, especially distal ones and ones that arise in cultural life, can only be pursued a step at a time and with regular interruptions for dealing with other aspects of life. Hence resuming work after an interruption is an important feature of successful goal pursuit, especially for cultural animals.

Looming above the process of goal pursuit is some sort of supervisory attention that keeps the goal in mind and keeps track of progress toward it. This too is one of the distinctively human adaptations enabling it to make use of meaning so as to improve control of behavior. Cybernetic theory has long emphasized how mechanical systems—and human ones too—regulate progress.[24] All that is required is a periodic check of the present status against the goal, followed by initiating some action to bring the self closer to the goal. The imagined future state (the goal) is compared with the actual present state. Much of this is probably automatic, though it may result in conscious feelings of satisfaction or dismay.

Although people certainly feel happy when they reach their goals, as a general principle, happiness is not limited to reaching the goal. Simply having the sense that one is making good progress toward the goal may be enough to bring positive, pleasant emotions.[25] Conversely, people may feel distress when their progress toward the goal is even temporarily blocked. Emotions thus seem important parts of regulating one's day-to-day (even moment-to-moment) progress toward goals.

All in all, goal pursuit represents an important form of action control in the cultural animal. Current behavior can be guided meaningfully by future possible events, and indeed current successes, failures, and other events draw meaning from these goals. The mind also seems to have a goal pursuit mechanism (in the automatic system) that nudges you to get back to work on goals when progress has been interrupted. The historical achievements of human culture would have been difficult, perhaps impossible, without these forms of action control.

Consciousness is Optional

How do plans, goals, wishes, and intentions get translated into action? This is an elusive problem that most theories of human action go to great pains to conceal. Dan Wegner, a respected psychologist whose research on free will we will cover later, effectively disarms many skeptics by asserting readily that "thought can cause action."[26] By saying this, he acknowledges that mental processes exert a causal role, thereby evading the accusation that he is dismissing human mental life as irrelevant to behavior. This charge may sound foolish, but for decades psychologists in general insisted that behavior could be explained without assigning any role to mind or thought. The school of behaviorism championed by B.F. Skinner and many others noted that animals behave without being able to think about events in abstract, verbal terms, and these psychologists insisted that human behavior essentially followed the same principles. (These are the principles that were covered in the "acting like animals" section above.) Modern psychologists, like Wegner, are careful to distance themselves from the anti-mind faction of behaviorists.

But does thought cause behavior? The matter may not be as simple as it seems. One model is that a person thinks *I want to go to the store*, and this thought causes her feet to start moving. She may also think to take some money and presumably she will draw on her knowledge of where the store is and what is the best way to get there. Yet did that thought really cause her feet to move? When you read the preceding paragraph, your mind contained the thought *I want to go to the store*, but if you are still reading it is safe to say that your feet did not start carrying you in the direction of the store. Thus, that same thought failed to cause behavior in your case. Something else, above and beyond the thought, is needed to translate thought into action.

The person who starts moving toward the store must have had some brain activity that sent out signals to the leg muscles that got the feet moving. Still, those signals probably did not show up in conscious thought. Meanwhile, the thought *I want to go to the store* was conscious. Thus, there was a conscious thought that she entertained, but it was separate from what actually got her feet moving. Whether the conscious thought played any role in helping to get the feet started is not clear. On the one hand, people who think *I want to go to the store* are probably more likely to end up going than people who do not have that thought. Still again, perhaps the conscious thought is just a symptom of the non-conscious process that eventually leads to going to the store, and the thought itself plays no causal role.

Has Skinnerian behaviorism crept back into the picture? If we embrace the latter view—that the conscious thought is simply a symptom that has no causal power—then behavior is guided by processes that operate outside of consciousness, and these might well follow the principles of behavior and learning that Skinner emphasized. But why is the conscious mind there at all, if it doesn't do anything except to observe and occasionally to comment on what is happening? The Skinnerian view reduces the human mind (at best) to a helpless spectator of what the body is doing. Natural selection went through a great deal of trouble and expense to give us the capacity for conscious thought, and it would be surprising if it couldn't do anything useful. More likely, nature gave us that capacity because it would make our lives better in some way (as reflected, ultimately, in improved survival or reproduction).

Another point in favor of the Skinnerian behaviorist view is that conscious thought, especially in the complexity of human language, is clearly not a prerequisite for behavior.[27] Most animals in other species manage to emit behavior constantly without ever having a verbal thought in their entire lives. As far as we can tell, most of them are not conscious in the sense that human beings are. If consciousness has any effect on behavior, it is one that can be dispensed with entirely. Consciousness is optional as far as behavior is concerned. The key to the answer may lie in recognizing that consciousness is optional, however. The seemingly large gap between conscious thoughts and behavior may be easier to bridge if consciousness does not have to initiate all behavior but instead can merely intervene now and then to change the course. Behavior is happening all the time, with or without the thought processes in the conscious mind. The mind can jabber along with its thoughts while behavior occurs. Or occasionally, perhaps, conscious mental activity can take over and alter the flow of behavior.

In this view, there are two main circumstances that require consciousness to exert a causal influence on behavior. The first is when the body does not know what to do. This might come about because the person has conflicting impulses and does not know which one to follow, or even because a choice is required and the person does not have any basis for making the choice (such as if you are ordering dinner in a foreign country and cannot understand any words on the menu, or worse yet have only a few vague hunches about what some of the words might mean but not enough to form an idea of what you would be getting). The second is when some behavior is in progress but the person is able to realize by means of conscious thought that this not what he or she should be doing and therefore has to override the response. "Not a good idea," one says, and this expression literally captures the point: The meaningful representation (the idea) of the act, put in context, reveals it to be undesirable. Only a cultural animal can recognize ideas as bad, because only a language-using animal can put those ideas into contexts so as to evaluate them. Only a cultural animal can alter behavior based on ideas, because ideas consist of meaning, and only a cultural animal can process meaning, because you need language to process meaning, and language exists in the culture.

Another alternative is that behavior follows from pre-set programs, including meaningful maxims. Consciousness can however set and alter these. Maybe consciousness is too slow to guide behavior when split-second choices are required, but consciousness can work after the fact—even just seconds after the fact. Within an event or conversation that takes an hour or two,[28] consciousness can exert plenty of influence. In this view, conscious thought does not directly control behavior, which is under the control of the automatic system, but consciousness can guide behavior indirectly by prompting the automatic system.

What About Free Will?

A tree's roots will grow out in a more or less straight line, following the blueprint that nature instilled into the DNA of trees. What happens when a large stone is in the way? The tree cannot follow its program of continuing to grow the root forward. Nature has however programmed just what is to happen in this circumstance: The root changes direction, and its continued growth makes a detour based on the stone. Natural selection thus programmed what the tree should do, and it also programmed the alternative response when the first one is blocked. The tree cannot cope with an unlimited variety of changes, but within a small range the tree is rather rigidly programmed for how to respond.

It is fair to assume that nature programmed many creatures with how to respond to various problems, dilemmas, and choice points in their worlds. However, it is impossible to program a human being in advance with the precise response it should make to every problem, dilemma, or choice that it will ever encounter. Culture is complex and changes rapidly. Many of the dilemmas people face today were unheard of a couple generations ago: how to prevent hackers from borrowing credit card information through computer fraud, how to diagnose a transmission problem in an automobile, how much to rely on social security payments in planning for retirement. There is no way nature could have programmed us for how to respond to these specific threats. It didn't have time: Evolution is slow, while cultural change is fast. Several hundred thousand years, versus fifty years. Therefore, instead of programming us for how to respond to every situation, nature had to give us the freedom to program and re-program ourselves. Nature had to give us free will—in a sense.

The term *free will* has multiple meanings, and often it evokes bitter controversy or disdain. Dan Wegner, the Harvard psychologist who has conducted several ingenious experiments to show that sometimes people are mistaken about whether their own actions have caused various outcomes, has derided anyone who believes in human freedom as a "bad scientist."[29] His position is comfortably supported by a host of other established thinkers who reject free will as an impossible, inconceivable absurdity. The rejection of free will comes partly from cultivating an absurdly restrictive definition. Philosophers and psychologists have gradually defined free will as having to reside in actions that are utterly independent of any external cause or impetus. Such an action would reflect a random choice that was not guided by input from the world around us. But why would nature give us an ability to act in those ways? What benefits for survival or reproduction would make evolution select us to be capable of such acts? Random, irrelevant choices have little value for survival or reproduction.

Consider instead what nature could give us that would be beneficial and adaptive. What would free the animal from its slavery to stimulus and response would be a capacity to use meaningful thought and reasoning to determine how to act in a way that will pay off in the long run—and, crucially, to be able actually to act on the basis of those calculations. The philosopher John Searle has noted that rationality and freedom are linked, because rationality is useless if you cannot do what you have decided is best.[30] Rational thought without rational action is pretty worthless.

This, then, is the version of free will that is central to cultural animal theory: Nature designed the human psyche to be able to act on the basis of its meaningful thoughts (including logic and reasoning, moral rules, symbolism, relation to distal goals). In order for this to happen, some inner mechanism probably had to override the automatic responses built into the system we inherited from other animals. Indeed, the ability to override one's first response and do something else is hugely helpful for living in culture, as we shall cover in the next section. Free will thus starts with "free won't," in the sense of not acting on the first impulse that arises, and instead doing something that you voluntarily choose on the basis of your thinking processes. More generally, though, free will (such as it is) is likely an inner mechanism to allow human beings to act on the basis of meanings.

The Arguments

The question of free will versus determinism rears its ugly head in debates among psychological theorists from time to time. *Determinism* is the view that everything that happens is the inevitable result of a cause (or set of causes) that preceded it in time. Nothing other than what actually happened was even possible: or, put another way, the total set of possible events precisely equals the set of actual events, because everything was determined. You may have the subjective impression that there are different possibilities as to what movie you will watch tonight, or which person you will date or marry, or where you will go on vacation next year—but your sense of multiple possibilities is an illusion. Causal processes are already in motion that will make one and only one outcome inevitable. Your belief in multiple possibilities is a result of your ignorance of how these processes will turn out. At least, that is what determinists believe, and there are many of them. In contrast, the *doctrine of free will* believes that there are really multiple possibilities and you can autonomously decide which of them will come true.

Most psychologists are skeptical of free will, which they tend to interpret as meaning that the person's behavior is utterly immune to all previous events that might cause it. The majority of cognitive scientists generally believe that the laws of physical causality are sufficient to explain all behavior.[31] (This is actually an extreme position, because it says that even social causality is essentially an illusion. If physical causality explains everything, then meaning never causes behavior, unless you think that meaning can somehow be reduced to atoms and molecules.)

Psychology generally purports to show that behavior is caused, which seems to contradict the subjective impression people have of free will. In a sense, every new success by psychologists at demonstrating how human behavior is caused seems another defeat for the idea of free will. Indeed, the very scientific enterprise is based on the assumption that causal principles and causal patterns exist to be found. Furthermore, part of the liberal faith of most social scientists is that people are products of their environment and so changing the environment is an effective way to change behavior. The belief that people should be held personally responsible for their actions and misdeeds is a politically conservative view, and most social scientists distance themselves from that end of the spectrum.

On the other hand, a good scientist ought perhaps to be skeptical about determinism too. Yes, some things are caused, but everything? Inevitably? Strict determinism is an unproven and unprovable assumption, not an empirical finding. It also runs counter to our everyday experience (of having multiple possibilities and making choices), which is another reason to be skeptical. If you eat an apple every day, and then they tell you that apples don't exist, you have a right to be more skeptical and demand more proof, as opposed to their telling you that unicorns don't exist when your own experience has nothing to contradict that.

And on closer inspection psychology's vast stock of research findings do not really support determinism all that well. Strict determinism requires 100% certainty—but psychology's findings of causal relationships fall far short of that. In fact the overwhelming majority of psychology research findings merely signify slight changes in the odds of any particular response. Actual research findings in psychology are generally probabilistic, not deterministic. Thus, psychologists find that a certain factor increases or decreases the chances of some behavior, not that it guarantees it. Changing the probabilities by a few percentage points is more suited to a view of the world as not fully determined than to the deterministic vision.

In my view, this debate is missing a few crucial considerations. First, the concept of free will has changed and in some ways degenerated over recent centuries, making it less acceptable than it otherwise has to be. When Immanuel Kant grappled with the idea of freedom in his philosophical classic work, the *Critique of Practical Reason*,[32] he came up with solution that deserves more attention from psychologists. He said that there are two modes of behavior. One is simply to be driven by environmental stimuli, which is the sort of determined, not-free behavior that psychologists are fond of demonstrating. The other is to behave according to practical reason, especially morality. You can choose to do the morally right thing despite a situation that tempts you into sin and indulgence. To do so is free.

Try for a minute accepting Kant's definition of free action: behaving on the basis of practical reason, especially when the situation and environment pull in some other direction. Certainly this does happen. In that sense, determinism would be defeated. Of course, psychologists might respond that using reason is actually another form of causality, and so it is not truly free. But to define freedom as utterly independent of any identifiable influence is an absurd, impossible requirement. Moreover, morality exists socially, not physically, and so at the very least a decision based on moral reasoning cannot be reduced to purely physical causation. Yes, the brain has to process the moral principles and issue the instructions to the muscles, but the moral principles are not themselves composed of molecules or chemicals. At very least, Barsalou's faith in physical causality as a total explanation of all human behavior is untenable.

That brings up a second point. Another of Kant's memorable tomes— the *Critique of Pure Reason*[33]—contended that causality is one of the basic, innate categories of human understanding. If he was correct, then the proponents of free will can never win the argument, even if they are right. Human minds (including, of course, the minds of all psychologists) can only understand events as being caused. And so any explanation of human behavior will have to invoke causality. This is why theorists are so skeptical of the idea of a totally free will: They cannot explain how it works, because any explanation would consist of a causal mechanism—and once you postulate a causal mechanism, the very freedom disappears, by definition. Therefore, by definition, no psychological theory can explain free will in causal terms. Most of the serious arguments against free will boil down to this little semantic trick.

The fact that we can't construct a theory without invoking causality doesn't necessarily mean that freedom is nonexistent. Our explanations of the world don't necessarily match the world precisely. In physics, for example, there is the problem of whether light is a particle or a wave, and the idea that it is somehow mysteriously both is something that is supposed to be accepted on faith as necessary to fit the data. Likewise, indeterminacy in particle physics (where causality again looks probabilistic rather than deterministic) is another shortcoming of our way of thinking about the world. Perhaps the world just fails to conform to the way we are able to think about it. Freedom of action can be another example of this.

The concept of a totally free will is therefore one that will not be able to find much of a place in psychological theory (even if it would exist in objective reality). A *partially* free will is however more understandable and should be palatable to most psychologists. That is, behavior may be dictated by lawful patterns of habit, routine, and automatic responses much of the time, but it is possible that these may sometimes be overridden. The overriding process thus "frees" behavior from certain causes, indeed ones that might otherwise have determined how the person would act. What the person then does may be affected by a new, different set of causes, but still the act of overriding achieved partial freedom.

Freedom in the Real World

Free will finds more believers (at least in practice) outside of psychology. The legal system, in particular, is largely based on a belief in free will. After all, if people's actions are the direct and inevitable result of their innate tendencies and their past experiences, how can we hold them responsible and punish them for these actions? You could not possibly have acted any other way than you did, according to the determinist, so how can we blame you for not having acted otherwise? In fact, legal trials often depend heavily on whether the person acted freely or not. If a person was forced to do something, or otherwise was unable to avoid the action, then we do not convict and punish the person (or at least not nearly as severely). If your new car crashes into another car because the brakes fail, that is the manufacturer's fault, not yours, whereas if you were careless and caused the accident, you are at fault. (And if you deliberately crashed the car into the other, your fault is that much greater, and your punishment more severe.) Most legal systems even recognize psychological causation beyond the individual's control as a mitigating factor. Crimes committed in the so-called heat of passion are regarded as less blameworthy and are punished less severely than crimes committed in a calm, deliberate state of mind.[34] Somehow people can differentiate quite effectively between different degrees of freedom of action.

One of the big news events of the 1970s was the kidnapping of Patricia Hearst, a young woman of one of the richest and most powerful families in the country. According to reports, she spent many months in the power of her kidnappers but gradually came round to join them. The saga reached a climax when she participated in a bank robbery, herself holding a gun and helping her kidnappers to carry out the robbery. Eventually she went to prison for this crime. The trial hinged on whether she had freely participated in the robbery or had done so under pressure from her kidnappers. The jury knew the importance of free will, and the legal system institutionalized it. If she had been forced to take part in the robbery against her will, then she should not be punished, but if she had participated voluntarily, then she was guilty of a crime.

Some psychologists are especially familiar with free will: those who work with addicts.[35] Those psychologists know free will is important because their patients (the addicts) know it, and in fact it is a big part of what an addict's life is about, or at least that of an addict who is in therapy. The addict knows there is an important difference between being driven by external events in relation to your own unrestrained cravings—versus being able to do what you know is right and best in the long run. To an addict, *not free* is being at the mercy of events and cravings, whereas *being free* means doing what your topmost self thinks is right and best. In my view, the addicts and their therapists are right, and there is an important distinction between those two kinds of action. And they are right that one of them is more free than the other. That's enough to put free will on the table as a useful and empirically testable idea.

The idea that human action is sometimes free, in limited ways, and other times fully determined may be unsatisfactory to either extreme side of the debate, but it may be correct. Occasionally the conscious mind can override some responses and change the programming of the automatic system. Indeed, this partial freeing may be one of the crucial functions of consciousness. Overriding one set of causes to allow behavior to be guided by a different set would be highly adaptive and would greatly increase the range and flexibility of human behavior.

Freedom and Consciousness

One of philosophy's most strident advocates of free will was Jean-Paul Sartre. Sartre contended that people were inevitably free—"condemned to freedom," in his famous phrase.[36] People could always do something different from what they actually do, and in that sense every human action is free. Yet his illustrations of this argument suggest that deliberate conscious choice is necessary for the sake of freedom. In one of his passages, he gave the example of a hiker who grows exhausted and finally sits down, saying "I can't walk another step." Sartre disagrees: The man could have walked another step, even another fifty steps, if necessary. The man might also have stopped sooner had he come to an appealing spot for a rest. But to go on longer, the man would have had to make a conscious effort to go a little farther. His body reached the point at which it was tired enough to warrant stopping, and so it stopped. This was the result of lawful, causal processes in his body. He might have overridden them and gone on a bit farther—but only with the aid of a conscious override of the processes that said to stop and sit right here.

Thus, the point is that much of human behavior is causally determined. If there is freedom, even partial freedom, it may depend on the conscious mind overriding these chains of causal responses, so that the usual behavioral outcome does not happen. Turning off the one cause creates some indeterminacy as to what will happen. Perhaps the person consults moral rules or other meaningful ideas in order to let one of them dictate what he or she will do. Perhaps some other cause lurking deep in the psyche lurches forward deterministically and hijacks the behavior process. Still, behavior was freed from what it would have been.

This view of consciousness is also consistent with a remarkable book on the emergence of human consciousness by Julian Jaynes.[37] Translating his work into modern terms, he proposed that early human beings operated entirely on the basis of automatic processes. Rulers gave commands and the brain repeated them to keep the person carrying them out. When rulers died, their commands were still heard (generated by the brains of their surviving followers), which gave rise to the idea of gods. In many cultures, rulers were explicitly promoted to gods when they died. People reported hearing the voices of gods on a daily basis, indeed whenever a choice had to be made. Eventually, however, there got to be so many gods, some of whom disagreed with others, that the intrapsychic system collapsed, and people had to make up their own minds. In Jaynes's view, this was the cultural, historical origin of consciousness. Thus, consciousness had to be developed as a way of making choices when the inner babble of competing automatic responses pulled in contrary directions. After that, people ceased to hear the voices of the gods on a daily basis, instead having to resort to prayer, divination, trance, scripture, and the like.

The sense of free choice does not correspond precisely to actual volition. Experiments by Wegner indicate when people have the thought of doing something shortly before it happens, they think they have caused it to happen, even if this is not correct (e.g., even if something else—perhaps manipulated by the experimenter—is the actual cause).[38] For example, in some studies, people heard a tape recorded voice say "swan" and then a cursor on a computer screen selected a picture of a swan. The participant's hand was not the only hand on the mouse, and in reality a research confederate gently moved the cursor to the swan picture, so the participant was not responsible for that movement. But sometimes the participant thought he or she was responsible—specifically, when the word *swan* occurred in the participant's mind one to five seconds before the cursor moved. If the thought occurred 30 seconds before, the participant did not feel responsible for moving the cursor, nor did people feel responsible for it if the word came one second after the cursor moved. Having the thought right before the action was crucial.

Hence, in some cases people falsely believe that they have caused a certain outcome to occur, and in other cases they falsely believe that they did not cause something to occur. These may be interpreted as indicating that freedom and volition are illusions, and certainly they show that illusions are possible. They may however simply mean that the mind's method for recognizing its own acts of volition can be fooled.

If Wegner's results are broadly correct—that is, if they fit most behavior, well beyond the few situations that he has studied in the laboratory—they indicate only that there is no direct link from conscious will to behavior. The automatic system is generally the one to control behavior. But conscious will could still have an indirect effect. Thus, the direct and immediate control of behavior may always follow from automatic behavior (as Wegner suggests)—but the conscious system can direct the automatic system, at least sometimes. That would be a sufficiently important and powerful role to justify its existence. And why else would nature have given us the conscious system?

Conclusion

A cultural animal encounters many more difficult, complex, and unforeseeable decisions than non-cultural animals. One way or another, nature had to instill a vastly more flexible system for controlling action, if cultural life was to be possible. People had to be able to change how they would respond based on cultural meanings, to think about different possible courses of action at the same time so as to compare them and decide which might be best, and to confront and make decisions in circumstances that they had never previously encountered. In common terms, nature had to give people free will in order to make them capable of living in a cultural society. It is best to understand free will in a relative sense. As is clear to the addicts and lawyers, there is an important difference between acting in ways that are driven entirely by external circumstances and acting in ways that reflect one's own choices based on rational judgment.

Perhaps the most lofty and extreme definitions of free will cannot be fit into our preferred way of thinking about the world (especially the emphasis on causes). But nature clearly instilled mechanisms into the human psyche that increased its power to do several very useful, adaptive things. First, people can override their initial reaction or first impulse. Second, they can grow and change throughout life. Third, they can alter their behavior on the basis of reasoning and rational analysis.

We do know that some automatic reactions are based on previous activity by the conscious system. When a person learns a new skill such as skiing, for example, the initial efforts are made very consciously and deliberately, but once the conscious system begins to figure out how to perform the skill, the task is turned over to the automatic system. Likewise, conscious calculation and planning can figure out when you have to leave for the airport in order to catch your plane, and once that is determined the automatic system can take care of watching the time and ensuring that you get there. The conscious system may not generally control one's muscle movements, but if it can make policy for the automatic system, that would be a highly adaptive and useful form of free will.

Impulse and Restraint

In the early 1600s, the Scottish king James I ascended to the throne of England, thereby uniting the two kingdoms and supposedly bringing an end to the long period of bitter, bloody hostility between British and Scots. One evening soon after that event, a British gentleman gave a dinner party for a large number of distinguished guests. As was customary, there was a good deal of drinking, and as the liquor began to animate the men, one of the guests, an English general named Somerset, stood up to address the other guests. He politely said that he wished to inform the company that when he fell under the influence of alcohol, he often had the unfortunate habit of insulting the Scottish people. He concluded, "Knowing my weakness, I hope no gentlemen in the company will take it amiss." There was a moment's pause, and then a Scottish nobleman, Sir Robert Blackie, stood up to address the company also. He politely said that when he fell under the influence of alcohol, he too had an unfortunate habit, which was that if he heard anyone insult the Scottish people he would usually kick and throw the man out of the house, often breaking a few of the man's bones in the process. He concluded, "Knowing my weakness, I hope no gentlemen will take it amiss." Despite these announcements, neither man's habitual practice was enacted that evening!

This anecdote was used by Craig MacAndrew and Robert Edgerton[39] to conclude their survey *Drunken Comportment*, which examined the effects of alcohol in different times and cultures. They noted that alcohol is widely believed to cause or at least release various forms of behavior, and indeed Somerset's announcement to the dinner party invokes the principle that inebriation would cause him to perform a certain kind of behavior, as if that behavior were out of his control. Yet after Blackie's announcement, Somerset apparently discovered that he could control the behavior after all.

What exactly do we infer? Somerset had some animosity toward the Scots, and alcohol probably did make him more willing to denigrate them on many occasions. His announcement was therefore accurate up to a point. It seems fair to assume that on other occasions alcohol really did unleash an anti-Scot tirade from him. But his announcement sought to liberate him from responsibility for obnoxious behavior, invoking the assumption that when inebriated he could not stop himself from making insulting remarks. This assumption, crucially, was false, for when faced with the prospect of possibly having some of his bones broken by a burly, surly Scotsman, Somerset was quite able to refrain from making any such remarks after all. For present purposes, the crucial point is that behavior is often a result of the interplay of two types of forces. Something creates the positive impulse to act, but this may be opposed by restraining forces. Whether the behavior actually occurs depends on the strength of the impulse versus the strength of the restraint.

Neuropsychologist Jeffrey Gray[40] has proposed that the brain actually has two different systems for these different tasks. He has labeled them the BAS, or behavior activation system, and the BIS, or behavior inhibition system. (He also proposed that fight-or-flight responses are rooted in a third, separate system.) Evidence for his work is not limited to human beings and indeed emerged from studies on the brains of rats. Thus, nature appears to have separated activation from inhibition long before human beings evolved. Starting and stopping are not part of one system but depend on entirely separate systems. If impulse and restraint are indeed rooted in separate, independent systems, then factors can in principle affect one without affecting the other—but these effects might shift the balance between the two.

There are two separate faculties at work in controlling any given behavior. One is to perform it. The other is to stop it from happening. When only one is at work, such as when you are starting to kiss the person you love passionately, then the outcome is easy and predictable. But in many cases, there is a battle between positive and restraining forces. The example of alcohol is useful. The idea that alcohol produces all manner of wild and crazy behavior was tested in a careful meta-analysis (which combines results from many different studies) by Claude Steele and Lillian Southwick.[41] They rejected that view that alcohol causes such misbehavior. Instead, they concluded that alcohol produces wild or otherwise problematic behavior only in cases in which the person had an inner response conflict, which meant that the person both wanted to do it and wanted to not do it. As they put it, alcohol inhibits the inhibitors. In terms of the present discussion, alcohol impairs the restraints but does not affect the impulses or the activating system. Alcohol does not give rise to new desires or inclinations—it merely weakens the restraints, so that the desires already lurking in the psyche have a better chance of turning into action.

The split between impulse and restraint may also shed light on how culture can affect behavior. Although this is difficult to prove, my sense is that culture generally is more successful at shaping behavior by means of restraints than impulses. To make people want something, culture generally has to build on pre-existing natural motivations, and so its hands are somewhat tied. Nor can culture easily eliminate deeply rooted desires or impulses. But it can shape and strengthen people's inner restraints. For example, culture may be unable to cause husbands to stop feeling sexual desire toward women other than their wives, but it can give them the capacity to refrain from acting on those desires.

Even what is known about emotion fits the view that culture and socialization aim at the restraining systems. As we saw, the link from emotion to causing behavior is tenuous, but emotion does at least create a tendency to express the emotion. In that connection, it is oversimplified but still crudely accurate to say that the expression of emotion is natural whereas its restraint is cultural. Facial expressions that have been posed to express emotional states are recognized the world over, largely the same way in all cultures.[42] But the effect is only found for carefully posed faces. Candid photographs of people who are actually experiencing emotions show much more variation and are recognized far less reliably.[43] The implication is that the pure expression of the emotion is universally recognizable, but culture teaches people to conceal some of their emotional expressions, so the way emotions normally affect people is more variable. The same conclusion is also suggested by observing children, of course. Small children express all their emotions in highly vivid, easily recognizable manners, and indeed the intensity of their emotions contributes to why small children are often perceived as charming. As they grow up, they learn to hide their feelings and express them in more limited ways, according to the feeling rules that are accepted within their culture. Thus, again, culture socializes people to learn to inhibit and restrain themselves.

Undoubtedly some of culture's strongest means to influence behavior are contained in morality. One of the seeming paradoxes of moral theory is the asymmetry between prescriptions to act and prescriptions to refrain from acting. Specifically, most moral rules tell you what you should NOT do as opposed to telling you what you *should* do. In Western culture, for example, the most famous set of moral rules is the Ten Commandments, allegedly given to Moses directly by the universal god. Those commandments are mainly commandments about what not to do, as opposed to what to do. Eight of the Ten Commandments are clearly rules about what you should not do (e.g., stealing, lying, killing). The other two are ambiguous: Honoring your parents includes both doing and not doing, such as not insulting or disobeying them; and keeping the sabbath holy also encompasses a wide range of restrictions on behavior, namely all the things that you are essentially forbidden to do on the seventh day of each week. In short, morality aims most of its force at strengthening and directing the restraint system, to prevent various behaviors, rather than on initiating behaviors.

The distinction should not be overstated. Nature has certainly provided us with the capacity to restrain impulses, and culture can help shape behavioral impulses too. Thus both nature and culture are involved in both impulse and restraint. Still, they may not be equal partners in both. Nature favors "go," while culture promotes "stop."

This view of impulse and restraint as a form of nature versus culture is probably another manifestation of the clash over self-interest. Nature made us want things, including satisfaction of many drives and impulses. Culture needs people to restrain some of these impulses, in order that people can live together in reasonable peace and harmony. Culture can't stop us from having our selfish wants and feelings, but it can promote the structures that restrain them. Culture is not very successful at creating new wants. As we saw in the chapter on motivation, the culturally derived motives generally are based directly on the natural ones, sometimes combining several of them. (The desire for money, for example, cannot be innate because money does not exist in nature; but culture instills a desire for money by linking money to things people do want, such as food, shelter, comfort, respect, and love, all of which are more available to the person who has money than to the one who does not.) Most of the work of culture on the psyche has to do with the "stop" systems rather than the "start" systems. Impulses are rooted in nature, restraints are cultivated by culture.

Isn't this too simple? Culture does help tell us how to act, after we have restrained initial impulses. At a restaurant, you may see some delicious-looking food being served to a patron at another table, and if you are bigger and stronger than that person you might naturally feel like taking that tempting item away from the other patron so as to enjoy it yourself. But you don't do that, and instead you demurely take your seat, order something from the menu, wait until your food is brought, and then pay for it. Does that sequence show that culture does more than restrain animal impulses? In a sense. Then again, following the culturally prescribed "restaurant script" is merely a means to get food for yourself, thereby satisfying in innate and natural desire, while also not being thrown out of the restaurant and possibly arrested, both of which outcomes would be (naturally as well as culturally) aversive.

Restraining impulses is thus a crucial aspect of the free will that nature gave us to make us cultural. A savage (uncivilized) beast would not be able to live in culture, because it would act on almost every impulse, which would violate the rules and systems that make culture possible. We can only enjoy the benefits of culture if we participate in the system, which requires restraint. Yet complex inner mechanisms are required in order for the cultural animal to be able to refrain from acting on impulses.

Self-Control

The restraint of impulses is part of the larger project known as self-control or self-regulation. This capacity is crucial for the success of the cultural animal, and indeed most experts believe that humans can regulate themselves far more extensively than other animals. In particular, self-control allows human beings to stop what they are doing in the middle, which is quite difficult for most animals. Put another way, humans can override responses that are already in progress. Self-control enables us to alter our own inner states, responses, and behaviors. As a result, it produces a degree of flexibility and plasticity that is breathtaking. The immense diversity of human behavior, compared with the predictable and stereotyped behavior of most other animals, is attributable in substantial part to this capacity.

As we have seen, following rules is a vital part of cultural participation and a crucial difference between human and animal behavior. Self-control is a powerful help for following rules. Rules often exist to prohibit people from doing what they might feel like doing, and so obeying such rules (including morals and laws) often requires the person to override an impulse so as not to act it out. Self-control does precisely that.

Recall the basic principles of animal behavior we covered earlier. The animal is wandering around and discovers something that would be good to eat. The food elicits attention and interest, and the animal's innate wants and needs for food are activated. The brain tells the paws to take the food and put it in the mouth, and eating commences. The process is well established and straightforward. Among human beings, however, there is a mechanism that can override this and stop the sequence of responses in the middle, before the food is eaten. Even though the person may be just as hungry as the animal and just as knowledgeable about how to eat the food, other considerations may intrude (such as realizing one does not have enough money to pay for the food, or that the food violates one's religious prescriptions, or that if you try to take food from other restaurant patrons you will be thrown out and will remain hungry).

Self-control probably evolved in order to turn responses off. Obviously this would greatly increase the range and flexibility of human behavior. Once we are able to resist always acting on the first impulse that crops up in response to any situation, we can act in a vast range of different possible ways. The negative thrust of self-control parallels the negative thrust of morality: Culture wants us to override responses and not-do what we might feel inclined to do, and self-control is the vital inner mechanism that makes this possible.

One of the most important forms of self-control—and one that might have been sufficient by itself to ensure that the capacity evolved, because it was so adaptive and beneficial—is the ability to delay gratification. In a program of research pioneered by Walter Mischel,[44] researchers would bring children to his laboratory and offer them a choice between having one small candy bar right away or two or three large candy bars in half an hour. This dilemma corresponds to the kind of choice that many people have faced in many circumstances throughout history. When you are a peasant farmer whose family is desperately hungry because of famine, do you eat your last ox and your seed corn? When you get your wages, should you buy something you want right now or save the money in case you really need something later? Is it worth putting up with the sacrifices and efforts required for getting a college degree instead of moving out on your own and getting a job?

Thus, there are two key things to say at the outset about the ability to relinquish short-term gains in order to pursue long-term benefits. First, it is distinctively human. Most other species have very little capacity to do it. Even behaviors that seem to conform to that pattern often turn out on closer inspection to be driven by short-term presses. For example, birds seem to sit on eggs, thereby pursuing long-range goals of having offspring instead of the short-term attraction of flying about in search of food or other pleasures. But sitting on the eggs turns out to be driven by such mechanisms as an uncomfortable rise in body temperature that makes it pleasant to sit on the cool eggs. The birds are not making sacrifices for the sake of the future, as humans would. Even the burying of nuts by squirrels does not really indicate that they are planning their dinners for the coming months. If researchers disrupt the process, they carry on unfazed. Apparently one set of innate impulses tells them to bury nuts, and a separate and unrelated set of impulses later makes them search and dig for buried nuts.

Unlike squirrels and birds, people are mentally capable of thinking about the future and altering their current behavior on the basis of those ideas. Indeed, successful delay of gratification often depends on thinking about the delayed reward.[45] People use language and meaning to transcend the immediate present, and those broad thoughts and contexts enable them to resist the impulses that are aimed at the immediate present.

The second point follows from the first. In evolutionary perspective, the human ability to pursue delayed gratifications is relatively recent and hence somewhat fragile. We should not be surprised that people often fail. Put another way, people's errors will be asymmetrical. They will be far more prone to seize the immediate satisfactions (even when small) and thereby lose out on greater long-term advantages, as opposed to the opposite mistake of neglecting large immediate rewards in order to pursue lesser but delayed rewards. When people go astray, it will be in the direction of impulsive, short sighted actions rather than the opposite.

People regulate their own behavior in at least four main areas. First, they seek to *control their thoughts*, such as by making themselves concentrate on tasks or trying to avoid remembering unpleasant things. Second, they try to *control their emotions*, such as by seeking to escape from bad moods. Third, they engage in *impulse control*, which typically involves trying to resist various temptations such as to eat, consume alcohol or drugs, smoke, or hit someone. Fourth, they try to *regulate their performance*, such as by persisting in the face of failure or achieving up to the level of their abilities. All of these requires overriding some contrary responses and controlling or changing one's inner states.

Successful self-control is an important key to success in life generally. People who manage to regulate their own behavior effectively do better than other people. They perform better in school and work. They have better interpersonal relationships and are better liked and trusted by others. They have fewer personal problems and are better adjusted psychologically.[46] Self-control ranks alongside intelligence as one of the best all-purpose psychological capacities. Conversely, failure at self-control is centrally involved in many if not most personal and social problems, including addiction and substance abuse, unwanted pregnancy, sexually transmitted diseases, crime and violence, underachievement, debt and other money problems, eating disorders, emotional excesses, smoking, and lack of exercise. The link to crime has been especially well researched, and it is important because crime is by definition a breaking of the culture's explicit rules—and often the basis for committing crimes appears to be an impulsive lack of self-control.[47] Many failures at role performance (e.g., marital infidelity, spouse or child abuse, impulsive decision-making, embezzling and corruption) are basically failures of self-control.

There are three main ingredients to self-control, and a breakdown in any of them can cause self-control to fail. The three ingredients are standards, monitoring, and strength or willpower. Given the importance of self-control failure, each of these deserves a brief explanation.

The first ingredient consists of *standards*. These are the rules, goals, ideals, intentions, or other guidelines for proper action. When you try to change yourself, it is often because you have a clear idea of how you want to be, such as physically fit, calm and not angry, or reliable and trustworthy. Unclear, ambiguous, or conflicting standards make self-control more difficult and prone to failure. Probably the most common form of conflict involves a clash between the desire to feel better (based in emotion control) and the desire to achieve long-term goals. This is because emotional control is often in direct conflict with other themes and goals of self-regulation. The goal of feeling better is generally immediate: When you are upset, you want to feel better right now, not next year. Moreover, most of the things people want to regulate and control involve resisting some immediate pleasure or satisfaction—but these immediate pleasures can seem mighty appealing when you want to feel better. For example, a person who is upset may blow her diet by eating cake and cookies, because she thinks that the pleasure of eating those foods will cheer her up.[48] Even aggressive behavior may be performed in the hope that striking out at someone will make the angry, unhappy self feel better.[49] Thus, people who are upset often make trying to feel better their first priority, and their other patterns of self-control are often compromised.

The second ingredient of self-control is *monitoring*. This is essentially a matter of watching yourself and keeping track of how your behavior matches up with your goals or standards. A landmark book by Charles Carver and Michael Scheier[50] recognized that self-awareness—that bane of adolescence and boon to vanity—often serves a crucial function of helping people regulate themselves. Self-awareness is usually more than just noticing something about yourself. Rather, it involves comparing oneself to various standards: Does my hair look good? Am I thin enough? Have I done the morally right thing? Am I going to succeed at this? Will I be sorry later? Carver and Scheier borrowed the concept of a feedback loop from cybernetic theory and suggested that human self-regulation has much in common with a room thermostat. The feedback loop involves the four steps called test, operate, (re-)test, and exit. The first *test* is a self-check: Just as the thermostat discovers that the room is too cold, the person recognizes that he or she is not meeting expectations. The next phase, *operate*, involves making a change to resolve the problem. (For a thermostat, this involves turning on the heat.) The third phase is another self-check, which may signal continued efforts to make a change, but at some point the problem is resolved and so the feedback loop is *exited*.

Monitoring yourself is often the single best way to improve self-control. If you want to develop a program of regular exercise, mark your calendar or diary each day as to whether you exercised, so that by the end of the month you have a clear record of how often you worked out. If dieting is a goal, record your food intake and weight each day. If managing money is your problem, keep a written record of all your expenses. Self-control fails when monitoring breaks down. One of the main effects of drinking alcohol is that it reduces self-awareness.[51] As a result, nearly every form of self-regulation is impaired by alcohol intoxication. People who have had alcohol drink more, eat more, spend money more recklessly, engage in violent behavior, and so forth. In the same way, any other processes that reduce self-awareness or prevent people from monitoring their behavior will contribute to failures at self-control. When people start an eating binge, for example, they seem to turn off their inner monitor that keeps track of how much they ate (which among dieters is often very strict and scrupulous most of the time).

The third ingredient consists of the ability to make the changes. The conventional name for this capacity is "*willpower.*" After all, you may know what you want to do (i.e., have standards) and may monitor yourself plenty, but if you lack the willpower to make the necessary changes then your self-regulation will fail.

Willpower operates like a muscle. Its strength is a limited resource: After engaging in one act of self-control, your ability to control yourself in other ways is reduced.[52] The limited resource is one main reason that so many changes occur when people are under stress. They use their self-regulation strength to cope with the deadline or other problems, and they don't have enough left over to regulate their emotional outbursts (so they become crabby), or to keep up their good habits (so they stop washing their hair and flossing), or to resist temptations (so they go back to smoking cigarettes or drinking too much alcohol, or they break their diets).

The strength of the self-control muscle can be restored by rest, such as sleep. There are also some signs that it can be strengthened by repeated exercise.[53] The latter is more traditionally known as "*building character*," as in everyday acts of self-discipline. Maintaining good posture, waiting your turn, brushing your teeth, and resisting temptation have value far beyond their immediate practical results: They strengthen the self's capacity to control itself in other ways.

No doubt we would all be better off if we all had more willpower. Still, what is remarkable is how much we have rather than how little. Self-regulation is an important ability for living in culture, and to create the cultural animal nature endowed us with a much greater stock of this resource than other animals are known to have. Somehow, the human body is able to put some of its energy at the disposal of a "self" that can use it to alter and override its responses. The benefits are enormous in terms of being able to follow rules, pursue goals, build a better future, and get along with each other in the present.

Choice and Decision Making

How do people make choices and decisions? This question has occupied specialists for decades, but it remains elusive. Pieces of the answer are falling into place, but there is no consensus on a general model of human decision-making.

What Is Choice?

Perhaps surprisingly, the question of what constitutes a choice is still a stumbling block. The problem remains because very different answers follow depending on whether one looks at the question objectively or subjectively. Objectively, which is to say looked at from outside, people make choices all the time. Viewed from inside, however, people make far fewer choices. To illustrate, consider the question of what to eat for breakfast. Viewed from outside, there is a broad range of possibilities. A person might choose to eat anything in the refrigerator. There is also the possibility of going out to a restaurant (which is actually not just one but a great many possibilities, considering all the restaurants that are open at that time and all the items on all their menus). And of course another option is to skip breakfast entirely. The *ontological horizon*, which is the technical term for the range of options available to someone at any given point in time and space, is remarkably broad, and so each bite of each breakfast represents the result of an impressive series of choices among many possibilities.

But the actual inner processes of the person are likely to present a very different picture. Most people do not begin each day by debating among all the wealth of breakfast options in their world. Most people follow a very standard routine for breakfast, in which they eat almost exactly the same sort of thing they ate yesterday and every day last week. Thus, they do not go through any psychological process of choosing what to have for breakfast each morning. Put another way, the question of choice can be phrased in terms of whether the person could do something different (*implicit choice*) or in terms of whether the person actually engages in an inner psychological process of weighing, deliberating, and making a selection among options. By the first definition, life is filled with choices.

By the second, people go through their daily lives making only a handful of choices.

The Burden of Choice

Rather than choose between those two widely different definitions, let us instead try to appreciate the significance of the distinction. Life, and especially modern life, is filled with potential choices and a constant stream of multiple options, but most people ignore most of those options most of the time. Thus, one basic and pervasive principle of human functioning is that people avoid many possible choices. Consistent with the general thought patterns of screening and simplifying, people ignore many options that are objectively available to them, and they follow standard routines and habits instead of embracing the full diversity of selections. People may have free will, but they try not to use it very much.

Let us not overstate the case. People clearly do not like to be deprived of options, and they often resent being told what to do or being forced into certain lines of action. It appears that human nature prefers an intermediate level of choice, neither too much nor too little. The long-term trend in history is toward greater freedom and more options, and so people have long struggled to gain some latitude for themselves to choose and to change certain aspects of their lives. Then again, the modern world has gradually created an almost absurd, intimidating range of options and choices. One study of American supermarkets concluded that the average one in 1976 had approximately 9,000 different products, and so each time you entered the store you could in principle be faced with making nine thousand separate decisions about what to buy. As if that weren't bad enough, however, fifteen years later the average American supermarket had over 30,000 different choices![54] Even just the average "produce" (fruits and vegetables) section had gone from stocking 65 items to offering nearly 300. Nor are supermarkets alone in this trend: Look at the range of options available on television (in the 1960s, when I was a boy, everyone had the same three channels, and that was all), in investment opportunities, in religious denominations, and so forth. Barry Schwartz, a psychologist who has denounced this trend as "the tyranny of freedom,"[55] tells the story of walking into a store and asking to buy a pair of blue jeans and being met with an utterly bewildering series of questions about what manner of blue jeans: stone-washed, flare, boot cut, pre-stressed, designer, stovepipe . . . until finally he had to say, "I want the kind of blue jeans that you got when there was only one kind of blue jeans," whereupon the young salesperson had to go find an older employee who might know what this odd customer was talking about.

People who lack options generally want to gain some, but when many options are available they act so as to screen out most of them. Even the breakfast food example does not really mean that people wish there were no choices. People want there to be enough choices so they can have just what they want, but then they arrange to have the same thing every time. Many folks have the same food for breakfast every day, but that is not the same as if there were no choices and everyone were forced to eat oatmeal every day. Lots of us don't like oatmeal. The wealth of options enables you to have just what you want every day, without making a choice every day. By the same token, there are dozens of possible routes from your home to your office, and in theory you could choose a different one each day (or could review the options and consciously choose pretty much the same route every day), but that is not how people operate. Instead, what nearly everyone does is to figure out the best route and then automatically follow it every day. They don't wish they were forced to take some other route, so the multiplicity of options is good, and occasionally it is handy to have alternatives in case your preferred route is flooded or there is a traffic jam. Thus, people want to have options, but they seek to avoid the process of choosing, especially in the sense of making conscious choices over and over. One key reason for this is that choosing requires effort. Making an explicit choice is hard or unpleasant in some way, and so people try to minimize having to go through that.

The self's capacity to choose operates like a muscle with a limited amount of strength—just like self-regulation. Making a choice drains some of that strength. Because the strength is limited, people operate so as to conserve it. In a sense, you can only make so many conscious decisions in any given day, and so you want to save up this capacity in case something important comes up—as opposed to squandering it all on breakfast. Free will depends on a limited resource, and people conserve it.

Laboratory studies have confirmed the view that making choices and decisions depletes the same resources that are used in self-regulation. In one study, people were told to prepare a speech on a pre-assigned, controversial topic, and either they were told that the decision was ultimately up to them or that they were simply assigned to it and had no choice. Everything else was exactly the same except for the inner choice. Later they were given a difficult set of puzzles (supposedly unrelated to the speech) and the researchers measured how rapidly they gave up. The people who had made the choice gave up faster on the puzzles. Thus, making that conscious, deliberate decision took something out of them, which was then no longer available to enable them to keep working on the frustrating puzzles.[56] In another study, people were confronted with a long list of everyday products. Some were told to rate their use of them and familiarity with them; others were instructed to choose between them (in pairs). Both groups were told they would eventually receive one of the items, and those in the choice condition were told that their pattern of choices would dictate which one they received. Again, making the choices was found to be psychologically draining, as indicated by subsequent behavior in an ostensibly unrelated setting.[57]

Attitudes help make choices. Having clear, well-defined attitudes enables you to confront each decision point smoothly and pick the option that corresponds to what you know you prefer. In contrast, if you do not have an attitude, you must struggle to find a way to choose. The highly respected researcher Russell Fazio once described the difficulties he had faced in having a room built on to his house in terms of how stressful it was to have to form attitudes rapidly with regard to many issues about which he had never thought nor cared, such as light fixtures, doorknobs, and window panes. You can't avoid making a decision: The contractor shows you fifty or sixty different options, and you have to find a way to choose one.

Attitudes are thus vital benefits in helping the person avoid expending precious resources in making choices. If you have the simple attitude that one political party is always the best one, then voting is a simple matter. If you think different political parties have different strengths and weaknesses and no one is always right, then voting becomes much more draining because you have to think about the relative merits of all the candidates for each office. In light of these advantages, it is not surprising that people who have many clear and well-formed attitudes tend to find life easier and to experience lesser levels of physiological stress when faced with choices to make.[58]

How to Choose?

Processes of choice have been much debated. Rational approaches emphasize the calculation of costs and benefits. In this, as in much else, bad is stronger than good, and so people's decisions are biased toward minimizing loss, harm, and other costs, instead of increasing benefits. (People do want to maximize benefits too, of course; the point is merely that minimizing loss gets priority.) For example, researchers[59] asked people whether they would accept a bet on a coin flip: if they won they would gain ten dollars, and if they lost they would lose ten dollars. According to an objective cost-benefit analysis, the expected outcome of this bet is precisely neutral, because the 50% chance of gaining ten dollars is precisely offset by the 50% chance of losing ten dollars, and if these are added together the total *expected gain* (the statistical term from risk appraisal) is zero—the same as if you refused to bet and therefore neither won nor lost anything. In principle, then, betting or not betting is exactly the same, and one might expect people to be evenly divided as to whether they bet or not. Instead, however, most people refused to take the bet. Losing ten dollars is perceived as a more extreme outcome than gaining ten dollars. In a sense, you know you will be more unhappy about losing ten dollars than you would be happy about winning the same amount, and so you refuse, even though a statistician or accountant would approve of taking the bet.[60]

Departures from Rationality

A more systematic analysis of rational choice emphasizes two features: expectancy and value.[61] By this so-called *expectancy-value theory* (also known as *expected utility theory*, with subtle differences), people evaluate their decision options on the basis of two questions. First, if I choose this option, what will probably happen to me? And, second, how good or bad is that outcome? A slight chance of a very desirable, positive outcome may thus be roughly equivalent to a much larger chance of an outcome that is only slightly good. To invoke statistical risk appraisal again, a 5% chance of winning a hundred dollars is roughly equivalent to a 50% chance of winning ten dollars or even a sure thing of five dollars.

Of course, people's judgments and preferences do not map precisely onto those statistical principles. If they did, no one would ever buy a lottery ticket. Or at least no one would if he or she had any understanding of statistics—which is what prompted one wag to define a state lottery as "a tax on people who are bad at math." The state, or the casino, or whatever institution that runs the lottery wants to make some money from it. To do this, it has to take in more money than it pays out in prizes. Suppose, for example, that the state sells a million lottery tickets at a dollar each, saves $200,000 for the state budget, and gives out the remaining $800,000 as one big prize. Each person who buys a ticket is therefore irrational, because he or she pays a dollar but gets only a one-in-a-million chance at $800,000—which means that the expected value of each ticket is only eighty cents. (Divide the $800,000 by the million tickets.)

Paying a dollar to get an eighty-cent value is economically foolish in an objective sense. But that fails to take subjective values into account. If nothing else, the dollar purchases a day of engaging in a pleasant fantasies about what you could do if you won all that money, and the enjoyment of those fantasies may be worth substantially more than the missing twenty cents on your investment. Moreover, some people may regard the dollar as so small as to be trivial, whereas they think the $800,000 would enable them to live happily ever after, and so in a sense they have lost nothing but gained an opportunity for something wonderful to happen. In these ways, human decision processes diverge from strict statistical rationality.

One major difference between cultural and social animals is the ability to think in subtle, complex, nuanced terms. For social animals, the world exists here and now and in stark, yes-or-no terms. Conscious, rational thought can understand that there are continuums, probabilities, and other shades of meaning. But when rational thought fails, people will fall back into the simpler modes of thought.

Hence one important way that human decision-making departs from rational, expected-utility models is the so-called *certainty effect*.[62] Suppose, for example, you have to play Russian roulette. How much would you be willing to pay to remove one bullet from the gun, depending on whether (1) there are four bullets in the six chambers, and so removing one will reduce the bullets to three, or (2) there is only one bullet, and so removing it will reduce the danger to zero? Most people say they would pay more for the latter (from one to zero) than the former, but statistically the improvement is the same, and if anything one could make a case that you should be willing to pay more for the former (four to three), because money becomes irrelevant if you are dead, and the former case has the larger chance that you will die. But people pay extra for the certainty of moving from a slight chance to zero, so that they can be absolutely sure they are completely safe.

Likewise, participants in other studies were offered a choice between a guaranteed \$3,000 or an 80% chance of winning \$4,000 (but of course with a 20% risk of getting nothing). Most people preferred the sure thing, even though statistical rationality says taking the chance on the four thousand is the better bet (expected gain = .8 times \$4,000, thus \$3,200). Nor are people even entirely consistent on favoring all outcomes that are certain. If the problem is phrased in terms of losing money rather than gaining, then people prefer to take the risk (80% chance of losing \$4,000) rather than the guaranteed loss of \$3,000—which, again, is irrational statistically. In short, people prefer to take sure-thing gains and avoid sure-thing losses.

Thus, people assign extra importance to certainty. This is matched by assigning extra value to immediacy.[63] For example, would you rather have a thousand dollars today, or a thousand and two hundred dollars in two weeks? It is financially rational to take the delayed reward, because it is larger, and there is little likelihood of increasing your money by 20% in just two weeks if you take it now and invest it.. But people tend to prefer the immediate reward. Economists have tried to treat this as rational by proposing that there is some logical diminishment in value of anything in the future. For example, if you were to die a week from now, you might have been able to enjoy the immediate reward whereas you would never be able to collect on the delayed reward. Economists therefore try to calculate the degree to which subjective value declines with time delay.

Unfortunately, there is a further complication, as shown by the fact that people's preferences reverse if the question is posed this way: Suppose you could choose either $1,000 a year from today, or $1,200 in a year and two weeks? Logically, the discrepancy is the same: if you wait an extra two weeks, you get a reward that is larger by 20% (that is, 200 extra dollars). Yet people do not treat them as the same: They choose the sooner-smaller reward when it is today but take the later-larger one when deciding for next year.

Why do most people think the extra wait is worth it in the one problem and not in the other? The only apparent explanation is that there is something special about the present. If you are going to wait a year, you might as well wait the extra two weeks for the larger reward, but if you can have the money immediately, the wait of two weeks is less appealing. As we have seen, cultural animals use conscious thought to orient themselves toward the future and figure out what will be best in the long run, but sometimes these elaborate structures fail and they return to the present. We saw that the ability to delay gratification is very adaptive and rational, but sometimes it fails and people grab for immediate satisfaction.

The effect of immediacy resembles the certainty effect: People prefer the immediate gain just as they prefer the guaranteed gain. And both of these suggest that underneath the sophisticated thinking processes of the cultural animal, there still lurk the simpler needs and inclinations of the social animal. Sometimes these win out. People hardly ever depart from rationality by pursuing uncertainty or by taking smaller rewards that are further delayed into the future. Certainty and immediacy please the social animal, and those are what tempt the cultural animal away from enlightened, rational choices.

Egotism is another source of departure from rationality. People wish to think well of themselves and to have others regard them favorably, and when these favorable views of self are threatened, people react in ways that again depart from rationality, sometimes with costly results. For example, sometimes athletes sit out the season, thereby forfeiting millions of dollars of salary, because they think they deserve more money than their contract specifies. Another example would be when two sides go to court rather than settle a dispute, with the result that both sides pay immense amounts of lawyers' fees and court costs. This kind of pattern has been studied under the rubric of the "Ultimatum Game."[64] In the typical experiment, two people play the Ultimatum Game toward the end of an experiment in which they have worked together to earn some money. The experimenter gives one of them (the Divider) the opportunity to divide a $10 payment between the two of them. The other person has no say in the division but does have the option of refusing the deal—in which case both players get nothing. Now, rationally, something is better than nothing, and so if people were simply motivated by material self-interest, the Divider could well say "I'll take $9, and you get $1" (or even "I'll take $9.75, and you get a quarter)—and the other person should still take the deal. In practice, however, Dividers usually split the money around seven dollars to three dollars, and if they do try to take more than that for themselves, the other person tends to refuse the deal. Refusing may seem irrational, because that person gets nothing instead of at least the single dollar, but pride and indignation enter into the decision process and make the person refuse to accept such a seemingly unfair, inequitable decision.

Blows to pride also jeopardize people's ability to make rational decisions. In one series of studies, participants earned money by playing a video game, and then the experimenter offered to let them bet any part of their winnings for a triple-or-nothing payoff on one last game. Players could do well by refusing to bet and keeping their money, and they could do even better by betting heavily and then performing well. They would only lose out if they bet heavily and then failed. Hence they had to predict their own performance and bet accordingly. Most of the time, people with high self-esteem managed to do this quite effectively in general, either betting and winning or refraining from betting. However, in one condition of the experiment participants received a blow to their pride just before the game, such as being told that they had performed very poorly on an earlier test of creativity (which had no relation to the video game). Then, abruptly, people with high self-esteem bet quite foolishly, often losing all their money in one trial. Many people with high self-esteem hate to be criticized, and so they react with foolish risk-taking and bravado.

In yet other studies, egotism has been shown to make people reluctant to abandon a losing endeavor. Sometimes people's choices turn out not so well, and the person has to face the difficult decision of when to cut his or her losses. The more the person's pride has been linked to the initial choice—such as when the person made a public commitment to the decision, especially in the face of arguments by others who voted against that course of action—the longer they stick with the losing cause, often suffering vastly greater losses. It is harder to admit you were wrong when your pride and identity are tied up with the decision.[65]

Choice Is Lovely

Choice has a variety of positive psychological consequences. For one thing, people like what they choose more than they would like the same thing if assigned to them. This was shown most rigorously in studies of cognitive dissonance. In hundreds of such studies, people have been asked to make a speech favoring a certain position or advocating a certain belief. Before each session, the experimenter flips a coin to assign the person either high or low choice. In the low choice condition, the research subject is simply assigned to advocate a particular belief. In the high choice condition, the experimenter asks the person to advocate a particular belief but emphasizes that "the final decision is entirely up to you." Nearly everyone agrees to do it in both conditions. Afterward, however, when the experimenter surveys what the subject actually feels about that belief, the people who chose to advocate it have become significantly more favorable than the ones who were merely assigned.[66]

This has important implications for public policy and for handling people. Letting people think they have some choice in the matter is a powerful tool for securing compliance. One relevant examples comes from the school desegregation movement during the 1950s and 1960s. In many places states simply required everyone to attend racially integrated schools. Some of these laws led to riots, bomb threats, and other forms of violent protest. North Carolina, however, proved an interesting exception.

The prospects for smooth school integration were certainly not good. North Carolina had a long tradition of segregation and had of course briefly joined the rest of the South in seceding from the Union in response to the national election victories by the anti-slavery Republican party. In 1955 the North Carolina state legislature even passed a resolution stating that "the mixing of races in the public schools cannot be accomplished." In 1956, however, under pressure from the Eisenhower administration and the Supreme Court's landmark decision that segregated schools were unacceptable, they passed a plan that desegregated public schools. To appease the residents, however, the desegregation bill established a procedure that enabled families to obtain state funds in order to send their children to segregated private schools. Thus, people were given a choice: They could either go along with integration, or they could decide to attend segregated schools and get help from the state taxpayers. In reality, the procedure was quite cumbersome, requiring both the individual family and the prospective school to fill out many documents and clear other bureaucratic hurdles in order to qualify. Ultimately only one family ever actually received public funds to send their children to a segregated school. Still, the very existence of the procedure had great symbolic value in that it gave people a choice, so no one was actually forced to attend integrated schools. Unlike other states, North Carolina managed to achieve school integration with virtually no violence or other protest.[67]

The value of choice is not unlimited. People are more satisfied with their outcome if they had more choices, but only up to a point, and having more options beyond that point produces a negative reaction. Thus, in one study,[68] people were able to choose a chocolate treat from among either six options or from 24 options. Choosing from among six options produced a very positive response, but choosing from among 24 led to less satisfaction. (Possibly people feared they had not made the best choice among the 24.)

Despite these occasional negative reactions, people want to have choices and options. The clearest sign of this is that when options are removed, people become upset. Studies under the rubric of *reactance theory* have offered people a range of options, such as various posters, and then taken one of the options away.[69] These were covered in chapter 3. When a toy, a gift, or an activity is offered and then withdrawn, the person suddenly finds it more appealing. The underlying theme is that we resist having an option taken away.

Thus, people like to have choices, even though they may not always make use of them. The most dramatic evidence of this is the panic button effect, also discussed in chapter 3.[70] Exposure to stressful noise had various harmful effects—but not if the people believed, even falsely, that they could turn off the noise if they wanted to do so.

This panic button effect is remarkable. The false belief that one could escape from a stressful situation eliminated the bad effects of the stress—even though no one ever made use of the escape option. Put another way, people were profoundly affected by something that never happened. (Such effects depend on transcendence—that is, seeing beyond one's immediate physical surroundings—and are almost surely unique to cultural animals.) The panic button effect suggests that the worst aspect of many stressful situations is the feeling of being trapped. If you think you could potentially escape in the future if you wanted to do so, you can tolerate a great deal more.

The panic button effect may have a broad range of implications for human social life. For example, the possibility of divorce may make many marriages much more tolerable, even among people who never resort to it. (Indeed, the rise in unmarried cohabitation in recent decades may be one manifestation of the panic button effect: A partner seems more tolerable if you could in principle leave at any time, as compared with the much greater difficulty of divorcing that same person if you are married.) Conversely, the perception that there is no escape makes everything much worse. Aerial or artillery bombardments, health risks, pressures at work, and financial problems may all be much more upsetting to the person who thinks there is no escape, as compared to someone who believes that there is a way out that is available. One might even speculate that the reason women can tolerate living without sex more easily than men can is that women think they could obtain sex if they ever really wanted it, whereas men cannot. Even hunger and thirst or a need to urinate may be less oppressive to the person who believes that relief could be readily obtained than to the person who does not see any such opportunity available.

Conclusion: The Choosing Process

Thus, ultimately, how do people make choices? Sometimes they rely on habit or conformity to avoid choosing. When that does not work, they may be guided by their intuitive preferences, arising from the automatic system and its stock of affective tags: good and bad feelings that are quickly activated in connection with almost anything you think about. Alternatively, the conscious system may use logic and reasoning in order to make a rational decision. This may require overriding the immediate impulses and affective intuitions, but ultimately it allows people to use their powers of reasoning and the laws of meaning in order to do what will be best for them in the long run.

When reasoning is used, it first has to simplify the complexity, diversity, and multiplicity of options into a manageably simple choice. This fits what we saw in the chapter on thinking: Much human thought is devoted to simplifying things. In an influential theory, Daniel Kahneman and Amos Tversky[71] proposed a two-step theory of decision-making. The first phase (called "*editing*") whittles down the array of options into a few major ones and a simplified version of the decision. If multiple possible events are linked together, the person might combine them together or eliminate certain factors from consideration. The second step involves *assigning subjective values* to the various options. These may not correspond precisely to the objective values as a statistician or economist might see them. Factors such as the certainty effect come into play here. Emotions and anticipated emotions are also involved. But somehow this subjective weighting allows the person to pick one option and let the others go. People clearly do not always make the best choice, but on the whole people do pretty well.

Some people, and some of their choices, are undeniably more rational than others. We turn next to consider the outlines of rationality and irrationality.

Rationality

Rational action means that what you do is based on good reasons. You use logic and reasoning to figure out what is the best course of action, and as a result of this analysis, you choose that course of action. In that sense it is uniquely human, because no other animal has sufficient intelligence and language to engage in logical reasoning. Rational behavior is one of the crucial advantages of a cultural animal, and indeed it is probably essential. Life in cultural society offers many different possible paths and actions, and people have to find reasons for choosing one of the others. In a sense, rationality represents the supreme achievement of evolution: Cultural animals can use language to access the basic structures of meaning, use their conscious system to follow rational rules to figure out what is best to do, and then employ their self-control and other resources to make those calculations the basis for their action.

By relying on logic and reasoning, people are able to make choices rationally. The definition of rationality is generally understood along the lines of the enlightened pursuit of self-interest. Self-interest means doing what is best for the self, and in that respect rationality is not so far removed from the innate selfishness of any organism. The qualification "enlightened" is a vital addition to distinguish rationality from mere opportunistic hedonism (as in doing whatever feels good right now). Cultural animals enjoy the ability to respect extended time frames in their thoughts and decisions, and so they can make choices that will be best in the long run even if they do not offer the best immediate payoffs. Hardly any other animals can do this. The dilemma of delayed gratification, as covered in our earlier discussion of self-control, is one place where we can distinguish enlightened self-interested from the other (un-enlightened) kind. Often the delayed rewards are larger than the immediate ones and so in the long run the person will be better off pursuing them. Enlightened self-interest would therefore say to pursue the delayed rewards rather than the smaller, immediate ones.

For example, some people go to work after high school, while others go to college. In the short run, the young person who goes to work has it much better: money is coming in, so the teenager can purchase a car, get a decent apartment, and so on. The one who went to college is usually spending the parents' money and possibly going into debt, as opposed to earning anything. Despite spending more, the college student usually lives in near poverty, having to share a room in a dormitory with another student, eating low-cost cafeteria food much of the time, and putting up with various other deprivations. But in the long run, the college education pays off. Despite starting work later than the high school graduate, the college graduate earns more over a lifetime, by a six-figure margin.

In terms of money, rationality means doing what is best for the self in the long run. This includes attending to incentives and adjusting one's behavior accordingly. Without the enlightened capacity to pursue delayed gratification that is best in the long run, no one would ever save money for retirement, for example. People would spend their money as soon as they got it, because the short-term choice is between getting something for your money or not getting anything for it (such as when you simply put in the bank rather than spend it). Enlightened self-interest requires saving money for retirement and for other needs that arise beyond the narrow horizon of the here and now.

Undoubtedly the most rational procedure for making a decision is to calculate the costs and benefits of each option, suitably weighted for subjective importance and uncertainty, and compare them. In practice people sometimes take short cuts, such as stopping at the first option that seems acceptable, but the shortcuts must be recognized as designed to approximate the goal of full rational calculation (again, costs and benefits). Short cuts are necessary because of uncertainty (such as when the full costs and benefits cannot be known) or in the quest for efficiency (because calculating all the costs and benefits of all the options would take too long or be too tiring).

"Live each day as if it were your last." This is one approach to life that has periodically been extolled by some philosophers and religious leaders. But is that really viable? If this day were your last, you wouldn't bother with flossing your teeth, or doing your laundry, or eating vegetables, or resisting temptation. You certainly wouldn't spend your last day on earth cleaning your apartment or paying your bills. But if you actually lived every day that way, you'd soon be poor and sick and possibly arrested. The whole recommendation is absurd.

Economic incentives do generally have a significant impact on human behavior. Economists often take this as a sign that people are generally rational. It would be an overstatement to say that people are always rational, but it is hard to dispute that basic economic rationality does succeed as a general principle for explaining and predicting(and controlling) a great deal of human behavior. For example, when Congress wants people to save more for their retirement—presumably so that the burden of supporting them in their old age will not fall entirely on the taxpayers and the federal budget—it offers people some additional incentive for saving. They may say that the money you put away for retirement is exempt from income tax, which in effect means that you can save a great deal more out of your salary than you could otherwise and still have the same amount to spend each month. When such incentives are created, people do respond to them, although not everyone takes full advantage of them. Thus, people are somewhat rational in the sense that they take advantage of these opportunities, even though some people fail to do so and others do so only partly.

Many people regard violent crime as the essence of irrationality, but in fact organized crime (at least) is fairly rational. Diego Gambetta's[72] history of the Mafia explains the incentive structure that gave rise to the Mafia and sustains it in modern times. The Mafia originated in Sicily, which is an island off the southern tip of Italy. Sicily was very spread out. There was no central government or police force. Farmers supported themselves and many grew enough to sell, but this created a problem. To sell their produce, they had to make the journey of a day or two to reach one of the cities with a marketplace. Because of the lack of police, the island was infested with bandits, and any farmer who sold his produce faced a high likelihood of being robbed on the way home—which would thus nullify the value of taking the trip. Gradually farmers realized that they could hire an armed guard or two for the journey as a protection against the bandits. Crucially, selling the farm produce yielded enough money so that the farmer could pay his guards and still turn a profit. These guards were the forerunners of the Mafia: They sold protection. When the law and police couldn't protect people, the Mafia found a market for their services.

Even today, that is what the Mafia mainly sells: protection. Gambetti said that it is misleading to think of the Mafia (as many do) as the "industry of violence," because violence is not their main product, and indeed they prefer to operate without using violence. Like the farmer's guards, they hope that the threat of violence will be enough to deter others. In modern society, the police provide protection to most citizens and most businesses, but people whose products are outside the law are still quite vulnerable. Prostitutes and drug dealers cannot go to the police when they are cheated in business transactions. Hence they rely on illegal forms of protection, such as organized crime. Knowing that a prostitute or drug dealer is connected with organized crime is often enough to deter anyone from attempting to cheat her. That is also why many thinkers and pundits, across the political spectrum, recommend legalizing prostitution, drugs, and other so-called vices—having fewer illegal industries means fewer opportunities for organized crime.

Consistency is another hallmark of rationality. Rational people are expected to think and act consistently across time and to keep their actions consistent with their values, beliefs, attitudes, and other principles. A rational person would not make opposite choices on consecutive occasions, such as casually giving ten dollars to a panhandler but then going to considerable trouble to try to save fifty cents on a tank of gasoline. A recent news story provided an amusing example of irrational inconsistency.[73] The story is based on the standard practice of allowing a criminal facing execution to have anything he wants for his last meal (within a limited budget of something like twenty bucks). In June of 2001, Juan Raul Garza requested that his last meal include french fries, steak, onion rings—and a Diet Coke. The combining of a diet soda with so much fattening food is one form of irrationality. The other is of course the point that if the man is going to be executed the next day, why is he still worried about his weight? Why not enjoy the full flavor of a real Coke?[74]

Psychologists have studied consistency rather extensively, and the verdict is again intermediate: People are somewhat rational in general, but there are significant failures and shortfalls. That is, people do exhibit a general effort to be consistent, but they also show plenty of inconsistency at times. The intermediate outcome probably reflects the incomplete evolutionary success of bringing the impulsive inner animal under the enlightened control of reason.

Consistency and inconsistency were the basis of the theory of *cognitive dissonance*.[75] According to this theory, people are motivated to try to maintain consistency in a broad, loose sense. Inconsistencies among their thoughts, feelings, attitudes, and actions give rise to cognitive dissonance, which is an unpleasant feeling marked by arousal and discomfort.[76] Naturally the dissonance arises mainly when people become aware of inconsistencies. They might hold inconsistent beliefs or attitudes for years without any problem, as long as they were never forced to recognize or reconcile the contradictions. Many experiments have confirmed the basic idea of cognitive dissonance. When people are induced to speak or write something that contradicts their beliefs, they experience dissonance, and the typical response is to alter their belief or attitude so as to resolve the discrepancy.

In the first published study on the topic, Leon Festinger and J. Merrill Carlsmith[77] induced participants to tell someone (who was playing the role of the next participant) that the task was enjoyable and interesting. In reality, as the participant had just recently learned through personal experience, it was tedious and downright boring. Hence people found themselves in the position of having to tell a lie. Some participants were well paid for this deception, while others received only a token payment of a dollar. Later, the researchers asked each participant how interesting the task had actually seemed to them. The ones who had lied for a small amount of money reported that the task was more interesting than the ones who had been very well paid, and more than the ones who didn't lie. The implication is that the inconsistency between "I told someone the task was interesting," "The task was actually quite boring," "I do not tell falsehoods unless it's for a very good reason," and "The money was so small that it is not a good reason," gave people dissonance, and so they resolved the inconsistency by changing the second statement to "Well, the task was kind of interesting after all."

Thus, people do rationalize their behavior by changing their attitudes after the fact so as to bring them into line with their behavior. This shows a concern with consistency. Still, it must be noted that researchers have generally been quite successful at getting people to perform the inconsistent behavior in the first place, so the consistency motive is not strong enough in most cases to prevent people from inconsistent behaviors. The implication is that people try to maintain consistency but it is hardly their top priority. Act first, rationalize later: that seems to be the main plan for maintaining consistency!

The consistency issue brings up the broader question of how consistent people actually are. In particular, do people behave in ways consistent with their attitudes? The very concept of attitude has held a special, privileged place in social psychology for decades, because it was assumed that knowing attitudes was the key to understanding human behavior. If we knew what people liked and disliked, believed and rejected, favored and opposed, we could predict how they would act.

Unfortunately, when the merciless criteria of cold statistical analysis were applied to the question, attitudes suddenly began to look weak if not irrelevant. A classic paper by Wicker[78] surveyed many different studies on attitude-behavior consistency and found the correlations to be disappointingly low. Wicker even concluded by suggesting that psychology should abandon the concept of attitude! He cited study after study showing that people would say one thing but then do something quite different. In one of the earliest demonstrations, for example, a researcher[79] wrote to hotel owners in the American South to ask whether Chinese persons would be permitted to stay there as guests. Most wrote back to say no (this was before all the laws against racial discrimination were enacted). But when the Chinese couple actually showed up, most of the time they were accepted as guests with no problem.

Wicker's critique of attitudes provoked a crisis in the field. The defenders of attitudes have managed to counteract the damage to some extent. One response was to note that most of the studies Wicker reviewed surveyed general attitudes, whereas behavior is highly specific.[80] Thus, a researcher might measure a person's attitude toward helping others (an attitude) and then measure whether the person was willing to give blood that day (a behavior). Most such studies found very weak correlations, but perhaps that was because helping others is a broad, general value, whereas giving blood today is a highly specific, one-shot behavior. Better correlations could be obtained by making the attitude and behavior more commensurate. Thus, one could measure the person's attitude toward giving blood that day, and then see if the behavior was consistent. This brings higher correlations, but some people object that the point is trivial, because it renders general attitudes worthless, and that implies that people must form and maintain thousands of highly specific attitudes rather than a few general ones. To salvage the general attitudes, one might try aggregating a broad set of behaviors instead of a one-shot measure. That is, if you want to see whether people act consistently with their general attitude about helping others, you should measure whether they will give blood, donate money, volunteer time and effort for various causes, stop to help a stranger in an emergency, help friends with chores, and the like—and do so on multiple occasions.

A more elegant response to the attitude-behavior gap was based on recognizing that many people do not consult their general attitudes when a specific behavioral choice is met.[81] You might be in favor of helping others in general, but when someone asks you to give blood you do not see it as a test of your helpfulness in general. Rather, you may see it as an inconvenience, as a possibly painful procedure, or something that will make you too light-headed to do well on the chemistry test or tennis match you happen to have scheduled for later that day. General attitudes may or may not come into play during a particular situation. If they do, then they will shape and guide behavior so as to produce consistency. If they don't, then there is no reason for expecting consistency. These researchers showed that when people interpret the immediate situation as relevant to their general attitudes, then behavior becomes much more consistent.

Irrationality: Self-Defeating Behavior

The pursuit of enlightened self-interest is the hallmark of rationality. Conversely, doing the opposite of enlightened self-interest is the essence of irrationality. Thus, any action that proves self-defeating or self-destructive behavior is of particular interest, because it reveals the limits of human rationality. If rationality is one great advantage of the cultural animal, then irrationality shows that our adaptations are incomplete.

Self-defeating behavior is defined as intentional action that brings failure, suffering, or misfortune onto oneself. The tricky part of the definition involves whether the self destructive result was intended or foreseen. As we shall see, the topic is defined too narrowly if we include only deliberate attempts at self-destruction. But it is defined too broadly if we include pure accidents. After all, thousands of people die every year in traffic accidents, but it is hardly appropriate to define driving a car as self-destructive.

Self-defeating behavior has garnered fascination far beyond the intramural debates of psychologists. (The terms *self-defeating* and *self-destructive* are here used interchangeably.) When people do colossally stupid things, pundits and even ordinary people often speculate about their motives. For example, when Senator Gary Hart was campaigning for the presidential nomination of the Democratic party, there were rumors about his marital infidelities. He addressed them head-on, denied the truth of the rumors, and went so far as to challenge the media to prove otherwise. Reporters took up his challenge. Eventually they documented him engaging in sexual hijinks with his mistress on a yacht. His candidacy was ruined and his career ended ingloriously. In retrospect, many proposed that he must have been deliberately or at least unconsciously self-destructive to have challenged the media to catch him when he must have known all along that he was guilty.

The idea of unconscious impulses toward self-destruction was stated formally by Freud in the *concept* of the *death wish*. Late in his career he proposed that people have separate, innate impulses toward life and toward death. By extension, he proposed that people perform many self-destructive acts because of this deeply rooted, unconscious motive toward death and defeat. Freud's follower Karl Menninger elaborated Freud's ideas into a well-known book, *Man Against Himself*,[82] in which Menninger proposed that such ordinary actions as alcohol abuse and automobile accidents stem from an innate tendency toward self-destruction.

The idea of an innate death wish or self-destructive instinct would pose a serious challenge to the idea of the cultural animal—indeed to many theories. How on earth could natural selection instill self-destructive tendencies? They would not have value for survival, by definition, and their payoff for reproduction would be dubious at best. I have proposed that nature makes people (and other creatures) basically self-serving, but it would be hard to reconcile a self-serving orientation with the existence of self-destructive impulses. Fortunately for our theory, the idea of a death wish or innate self-destructive urge has largely been discredited. Indeed, our review of "what people want" earlier in this book did not include any mention of self-defeating or self-destructive motives. Modern research psychologists have searched long and hard for evidence of deliberate, intentional self defeating behavior, but without success. It is doubtful that the lack of success reflects some kind of bias on the part of researchers. Those who have tried to gain an understanding of self-defeating behavior—myself included—all know that any proof of deliberate self-destruction would be a great feather in any researcher's cap and a boost to his or her career. But despite decades of research efforts, no such proof has been forthcoming. At some point one has to accept the repeated failures and conclude that the sought-after pattern is simply not there to be found.

It is important to be precise. People do engage in self-defeating behaviors, indeed plenty of them. But they do not do so out of a death wish or self-destructive urge. In fact, there is no evidence that people seek failure, suffering, or misfortune for its own sake. Even the Freudian idea that people want to be punished when they feel guilty[83] does not appear correct. A man may be quite guilty and may feel guilty too, but even so he doesn't usually want to be punished. More likely, he hires a lawyer and does everything else he can to avoid punishment. Guilty people may admit to their crimes and misdeeds sometimes, but they are generally hoping for forgiveness or at least leniency, not for punishment.

How do people then defeat themselves, if not out of a deliberate intention to do so? There are two main answers.[84] The first and less interesting one involves going about things in ways that backfire. The person pursues some positive, desirable goal, but chooses a strategy that produces the opposite result. For example, some people try drinking alcohol when they are depressed, only to discover that drinking can make them even more depressed.[85] Likewise, the pattern of choking under pressure reflects a strategy that backfires. When it is especially important to do well, people focus more attention on what they are doing, but the extra attention disrupts the smooth, "automatic pilot" aspect of skilled performance, and they end up performing worse than usual.[86]

The second form of self-defeating behavior involves tradeoffs. In this case, they are usually pursuing some positive outcome that is connected to a bad outcome, and so they get the bad with the good. This pattern is well illustrated by smoking cigarettes. People do not smoke in order to kill themselves with lung cancer, regardless of what Dr. Menninger may have thought. Instead, they smoke for the sake of positive outcomes, such as pleasure and satisfaction, or perhaps to be regarded as fashionable and debonair. The lung cancer is an unwanted side effect that accompanies the pleasure. Smoking cigarettes is self-destructive (especially insofar as the costs, namely cancer and death, outweigh the benefits), but it is not done for the sake of self-destruction.

An interesting tradeoff of this kind was labeled *self-handicapping* by researchers.[87] In self-handicapping, people create obstacles to their own success. Making one's own work or performance more difficult is certainly a puzzling form of self-destructive behavior, but there turn out to be substantial benefits that people may pursue through such strategies. In particular, failure may be blamed on the obstacle rather than on the self. And, meanwhile, success despite the handicap is all the more impressive. Thus self-handicapping can serve to protect a favorable image of self against any possible disconfirmation and may even strengthen that image. For example, consider a writer or musician who achieves remarkable success with his first effort—and then is soon reported to be struggling with a drug or alcohol problem. This scenario is banally familiar to anyone who follows the lives of celebrities in the talent professions. Pundits periodically ask why such a brilliant young man (the pattern is found most often in men, but it is there among women too) would blight his own fabulous potential by loading himself down with drugs or alcohol. Yet there are hidden benefits to this seemingly destructive path. A huge initial success brings considerable pressure to live up to one's reputation as a genius. When it is time for an encore, the nervous young man may have doubts about his ability to live up to that reputation by producing another brilliant work. An alcohol or drug problem furnishes a perfect excuse in case the second album or second novel turns out to be second-rate. Without such an excuse, the second-rate second product would send everyone the message that the ostensible genius had actually been overrated. Without the excuse of a drug problem, people will look at the mediocre second effort and discount the first success, saying that maybe he just got lucky one time, but at heart he's nothing special. At best, a one-shot wonder. Not the genius we thought.

And that's the crunch. Once someone has the reputation for genius, it is a terrible fate to have that review revised downward. It is far, far more attractive to be recognized as a troubled genius whose struggles with the demons of drugs or alcohol have prevented him from reaching his true potential—than to be seen as a mediocrity after all, whose early success was a flash in the pan. Self-handicapping insulates his reputation for brilliance against any possible disproof. And, as an added bonus, if the second product does turn out to be terrific, the person gets extra credit: He (or she, though this form of self-handicapping also has been found more among men than women) managed to perform outstanding work despite the drinking problem and hence must be really superb. People will say, imagine what he could do without that handicap! Of course, alcohol and drug problems really do lower the quality of someone's work, and so the self-handicapper ends up trading away substance for the sake of illusion. That is, the self-handicapper produces a lower quality or quantity of work in order to sustain the image of being brilliant. This is a classic pattern of a self-defeating tradeoff.[88]

Even suicide fits this pattern. In some ways, suicide is the ultimate form of self-defeating behavior, because it literally destroys the self. And since people intentionally commit suicide, one might be tempted to conclude that they do seek harm for its own sake. However, research on suicide suggests that it is generally a tradeoff. People accept the prospect of being dead in exchange for other rewards. Most commonly, these rewards consist of an end to a long nightmare of trying to ward off bad feelings. Oblivion is preferable to anguish and emptiness. Other times, people choose suicide as an escape from disgrace or dishonor, or from a painful or humiliating illness that is incurable. But in some twisted way the choice seems rational: Death looms as more pleasant than continued life under unacceptable circumstances.[89]

What causes people to engage in self-defeating tradeoffs? One standard pattern is that the rewards are immediate but the costs are delayed. Another is that the rewards are guaranteed but the costs are merely probable or possible. Again, smoking illustrates both these patterns. The pleasure of smoking comes within seconds, whereas the lung cancer does not materialize for many years thereafter. Likewise, the pleasure is reliable and almost guaranteed, whereas the lung disease may never occur at all.

Procrastination is another self-defeating tradeoff that is important in its own right and also as a good example of self-defeating patterns. Procrastination allows immediate pleasure, because the person can enjoy pleasures of the moment rather than the tedium or anxiety of working on the project toward the far-off deadline. In fact, there is some evidence that student procrastinators are healthier than non-procrastinators early in the semester! The freedom to spend an afternoon or weekend engaged in reading poetry, conversing with friends, playing frisbee, watching television, and the like reduces stress, while those task-oriented individuals who get right to work on their assignments pay some penalty in terms of illness and reduced enjoyment.[90] But procrastinators pay a steep price down the road. At the end of the term, when the deadlines are imminent, procrastinators have a great deal more stress and are considerably more prone to illness than their colleagues who got to work earlier. In fact, if you add up the early and the late health data, the procrastinators end up being sicker overall.[91] They are so much sicker in the long run that this reverses the early benefits they gained. In that sense, procrastination is self defeating and fits the pattern of short-term gains and long-term costs. Moreover, their work suffers too. Although some procrastinators rationalize their dawdling by saying that "I do my best work under pressure," the evidence says otherwise. One longitudinal study of student procrastinators found that they did worse than other students by about two thirds of a grade (thus, the difference between a B and a C plus) on every examination and test. The short-term pleasures of enjoying the present moment are paid for not only in terms of stress and health but also in terms of poorer work and lower grades.

A last cause of self-defeating behavior is emotional distress. Over and over, research has found that people who were upset, angry, anxious, worried, embarrassed, or in some other bad mood were more prone to fall into some kind of self-defeating pattern.[92] On the surface, this resembled the old Freudian idea that guilt makes people want to suffer and be punished. But there was no sign of any intentional self-defeat. Instead, the unpleasant emotions made people more likely to fall prey to self-defeating tradeoffs or counterproductive, backfiring strategies. The link between emotions and self-defeating behavior revives long-standing ideas about emotions as irrational. Again, self-defeating behavior is fundamentally, essentially irrational, and if emotions cause it, then they too are linked to irrationality in some crucial way. The rational pursuit of enlightened self-interest is hampered and sometimes thwarted by emotions. But how exactly do emotions produce this effect?

It took years of laboratory work to find the answer, but after many promising theories were scrapped the result has begun to take shape. In essence, it appears that emotions that are both unpleasant and marked by high arousal interfere with careful thinking, leading to impulsive and risky action. When people are happy or calm, they think through the various options carefully and note the pros and cons of each. If there is some degree of risk involved, they appraise both the chances of good and bad outcomes and the size of these outcomes. In contrast, when they are upset, they cut short their consideration. They look for some desirable possible outcome and grab for it, disregarding both the odds and the alternatives. This pattern will favor high-risk, high-payoff lines of action that will often (by definition) lead to many failures and other bad outcomes.[93]

The implication is that self-defeating behavior comes from a failure of what makes the cultural animal special. People sabotage themselves by not using self-control. When the cultural animal reverts to impulsive, short-term, selfish patterns of action, the result is often failure and misfortune (even death) in the long run. Nature gave the cultural animal the ability to pursue enlightened self-interest in a complex, meaningful environment. This ability included the capacity to use reason, plan for the future, and use self-control to resist short-term temptations. But when people fail to make use of those capacities, they bring woe (sometimes) on their own heads.

Moral Action

Morality represents a set of abstract rules for behavior, and in that sense it is a distinctively human form of action. Other species cannot comprehend those abstract principles and therefore cannot base their actions on them. Morality is thus a clear instance of what is special about the control of behavior in culture animals.

The source of moral rules is a subject of debate. One major tradition has regarded morality as means by which people can pass from their natural, animalistic state into a higher form of being.[94] Religions in particular have emphasized moral action as one requirement for spiritual advancement. In Christian religion, behaving in a morally proper fashion is a main criterion for receiving salvation and being admitted to heaven after one's death. Beyond a certain number of immoral actions, a person would be doomed to hell. Lifelong virtue, in contrast, earned the person a place in heaven, alongside humanity's best. Then Christian faith receded from its medieval role as a shared set of assumptions underlying all social interactions. Morality was left as a set of rules without any clear reason for people to obey them, and in recent centuries moral philosophers have groped for ways to replace the religious imperative.[95] For example, Kant proposed that the moral laws were built into the very structure of the human mind, so moral duties and obligations followed directly from simply existing as a human being. Other philosophers have rejected Kant's conclusion, but then they are left with the empty view of morality as nothing more than a set of socially prescribed rules, with no inherent reason for anyone to follow those rules.

Perhaps a more useful way of understanding the function of morality is to look beyond the individual person. It is often hard to see how an individual benefits from doing what is morally right, especially when moral obligations require the person to make sacrifices or thwart his or her own self-interest. But groups clearly benefit from moral rules. Moral rules can thus be seen as a set of rules and guidelines that allow people to live together in some degree of peace and harmony.[96] In that way, morality reflects the influence of culture. Culture uses morality to shape the behavior of individual persons, so as to mold them to the organizing scheme that the culture seeks to impose on the group. For example, a society is clearly better off if everybody pays his taxes and nobody dumps her sewage into the river. Moral obligations benefit the society, sometimes at the expense of individuals.

Both the similarities and differences among different cultural moralities can be understood in this way. On some issues, such as prohibiting impulsive murder of fellow citizens, pretty much all cultures have to agree, because it would be very difficult for a society to survive in which people could kill each other whenever they felt like it. On other issues, such as sexual morality, there is much more variation, because the important thing is to have some set of common understandings and agreements about what sexual practices are appropriate, but there is no single code of sexual morality that will be best for all societies.

Moral rules typically require individuals to sacrifice their own wishes and self-interest for the sake of the greater good. It thus supports culture over nature in the battle over self-interest, and indeed morality is one of culture's principal weapons. Stealing might benefit the individual, for example, but morality enjoins people to refrain from stealing the possessions of others, and the group as a whole is better off if nobody steals. If the moral consensus is strong enough, people can trust each other not to steal from them, and they do not need to watch over their possessions or take expensive precautions. When my parents bought a house in such a safe suburb, the previous owners claimed they had never once locked their doors! In contrast, people who live in societies without such a moral consensus may have to employ multiple locks and expensive, electronic security systems whenever they go out, and still they worry that they will return to find their home ransacked and pillaged.

The emphasis on a moral consensus raises a broader issue for social groups. If everyone agrees, more or less, then the moral rules become woven into the fabric of social life. It is difficult to be different, and there will usually be pressure on those who think and act differently to conform. This is to some degree compensated by the secure feeling of trust and community that comes with those shared assumptions. Diversity brings with it greater freedom for individuals to be different, but the cost of diversity is that the moral consensus is undermined, because different people may be assumed to have different values.

There is an African proverb that "It takes a village to raise a child," which was appropriated by First Lady Hillary Clinton as the title of her book. But that proverb is actually an anti-diversity slogan. A village can only cooperate in raising each child if the village's inhabitants all share the same values. Would you want other adults to discipline your child, especially if the child was doing something you had taught him or her was acceptable? In contrast, in tightly knit communities that share common values, all the adults can use the moral consensus to regulate the behavior of each other's children. Probably you would want other adults to report or even punish your child for breaking your rules. The system works if you and the other adults agree on the same rules.

Sacrificing one's own self-interest for the greater good requires self-control, and hence it is reasonable to regard self-control as "the moral muscle."[97] In fact, most of the major virtues have some form of self-control as central to them, just as most immoral actions contain some substantial flavor of failed self-control. The Seven Deadly Sins of medieval Christian theology, for example, are mostly a litany of major failures of self-control. The sin of gluttony is a failure to control one's impulses and desires, especially for food. The sin of sloth (laziness) means lacking the self-discipline to do one's work. The sin of anger or wrath involves acting in a hostile manner and possibly failing to control one's feelings. Sins of lust involve giving in to sexual impulses and desires. Sins of envy involve wanting what other people have and possibly trying to take them for oneself. Greed is also a failure to control one's appetites, desires, and impulses. The last sin, pride, is less obviously a failure of self control, but in practice it too often means indulging one's impulses to feel superior to others and to claim special privileges or entitlements for oneself. Society works better if people restrain all these feelings and impulses.

Moral judgments are undoubtedly subject to bias. People do certainly rationalize some of their misdeeds and apply more lenient standards of moral judgment when examining their own actions, as opposed to how someone else acted.[98] Still, in principle moral rules allow for disputes to be resolved and enable people to find a solution that everyone can agree is right and good. Thus, again, it is a useful way for a group to handle conflicts and maintain harmony.

Thus far we have considered wanting, thinking, feeling, and acting. That would seem to cover the main functions in the human psyche. But before closing, it is helpful to consider interacting too, because behavior has special properties in interaction. The next chapter will examine the special properties of interactions, and especially how they are transformed among cultural animals.

7

How People Interact

Karen is miserable today. She feels all alone in the world. Last year, she and her husband got a divorce. Since then, he and his friends have essentially disappeared from her life. Her son has started college on the other side of the continent, and she hears from him barely once a month. She had several good friends in the neighborhood where she lived with her husband, but since she sold the big house and moved to an apartment building, those friends have drifted away, and she hasn't made new friends in the impersonal apartment building. Her best friend, Lynn, is still in contact, but Lynn recently changed jobs and is quite busy most of the time, plus they have less in common now that Lynn is so immersed in office politics. Karen wishes she lived in a society where people's relationships were firm and stable and you could count on people to always be there.

Jana is miserable today. Last night at dinner, her mother-in-law, who lives with Jana and her family, made a series of disparaging remarks about Jana's cooking and housekeeping and thus humiliated her in front of everyone. Two nights ago, Jana's husband kept coughing all night and she hardly got any sleep, and so yesterday afternoon she tried to take a brief nap to catch up on her rest after she got the laundry hung out to dry, but during her nap it rained, and she knows the neighbors are making snide, gossipy jokes about what she must have been doing while her laundry was hanging in the rain. She knows her next-door neighbor is likely to tell everyone, because the next-door neighbor has held an assortment of grudges against her dating back 11 years to when she painted the fence that borders their property and the paint accidentally killed some flower bushes on the neighbor's property. (If the neighbors had painted their side of the fence like they were supposed to do, that whole problem never would have arisen.) There is another couple down the street who have also been Jana's enemies for many years, but there seems to be no possibility of either getting away from them or making up. Last week, Jana noticed some new wrinkles on her face. She wishes she could wear more makeup and some jewelry, but every time she does this, people gossip about her. She is sick of the feeling that everyone else watches, knows, and talks about every little thing she does, so that her only solution is to try to be just exactly like everyone else and to do precisely what everyone expects, so that she doesn't attract attention to herself. This is especially hard because Jana had more education than the other women, and so she stands out. She wishes she had some friends who had more education and who would like to talk with her about current events and literature. Jana wishes she lived in a society where she could escape from people she didn't like and could have more choice about what sort of people with which to surround herself as friends and companions.

These two stories highlight one fundamental dilemma of human social life. Probably most people anywhere in the world would agree on the same ideal arrangement, which would involve being surrounded throughout life with a stable network of people who share many of their interests, values, and goals, who respect them and care for them, and who can be counted on to be there year after year. Unfortunately, that is mostly an impossible, unrealistic ideal. It is unrealistic because it combines two essential features that are largely incompatible, and so ultimately it is necessary to choose one or the other. The two features can be called *stability* and *matching*. *Stability* means that the interpersonal connections are more or less permanent: This person will be in your life for a long time. *Matching* means that the person is well suited to be a good companion to you. This is best accomplished by letting people choose each other freely. The unfortunate problem arises because allowing people the ongoing freedom to make choices undermines stability. The dilemma is thus the tradeoff between having a stable social network and having the freedom to choose the people in your social network.

The endless societal controversies about divorce capture the dilemma in a nutshell.[1] In some societies, divorce is impossible. This makes marriage highly stable: You can count on your spouse being there until you are parted by death. On the positive side, the commitment is totally firm and reliable, and each couple can accept the importance of trying to work out their differences rather than screaming for divorce at the first hint of conflict. It also ensures that most children will grow up with the advantages of having two parents. The drawback is that many individuals will spend most of their lives inextricably bound to someone they do not love and may not even like, unable to escape from a wretched coexistence with someone they may come to despise, even if they find someone else who would make a perfect, ideal partner for them. And even if they don't come to despise one another, they may simply feel stuck together without being particularly happy about it.

Meanwhile, in other societies, divorce is freely available. This has the advantage that people can escape from bad marriages and go looking for someone new who will be a better match. Even if the marriage was initially good, the couple may grow apart for many years and gradually reach the point at which they both want something different, and so they can split amicably and live with someone who suits them as they are now, as opposed to someone who seemed like a good match 20 or 30 years ago but is no longer satisfying. But this societal approach has its drawbacks too. Many children end up being raised by single parents or by stepparents, who often do not treat them with the same love and affection that a natural parent shows. Usually, the children's relationship to at least one of the divorced parents suffers considerably. Couples may rush to divorce instead of solving their problems, only to realize later that they would have been better off staying together. One person may not want the divorce but may end up dumped by a spouse who has simply become infatuated with a new potential partner. Divorce may bring loneliness and anxiety, especially if one had been overly optimistic about how easy it would be to find someone new.

Another crucial point is that the choice between stability and freedom is not made solely or even primarily at the individual level. To Karen and Jana in the examples above, the problem reflected their own narrow social worlds. But the society as a whole also takes a position and to some extent forces people to construct their lives in a certain way. Divorce laws exist at the level of society, and individuals have to accommodate themselves.

That is the theme for this chapter: Cultural beings do not relate to each other only as individuals. Rather, their relationships are shaped by the broader social network. That network is a crucial difference between social and cultural animals, because the merely social animals essentially interact one-to-one. Even if one dominates the group, such as an alpha male, whatever practices that animal introduces into the group will likely die with him. In culture, however, the innovations of individuals are retained by the group and so outlive them. More broadly, the backdrop of culture organizes behaviors and interactions in ways that transform them, and so cultural interaction is more—and more complicated—than merely social interaction.

Many biologists, evolutionary psychologists, and comparative psychologists have been quick and insightful at seeing parallels between human and animal interaction patterns. Like most social animals, people devote time and energy to relationships with kin, prefer them over unrelated fellows, and generally have a family life. Like most social animals, people engage in sex and aggression. Like most social animals, people will occasionally perform helpful acts even when some sacrifice or risk to themselves is involved. But the human versions of these have an added dimension that transforms them. Culture imposes its organization, rules, scripts, and expectations onto family life, sex, aggression, and helpfulness.

When two social animals interact, they are often essentially alone in the world, and no one else is relevant. When two cultural animals interact, however, there is often the implicit presence of a third party, namely, the culture as a whole. Laws, morals, rules, norms, and other manifestations of the collective are present to constrain the interaction. Even sexual intercourse between spouses is not entirely their own private affair, and one or both may go to prison because the culture says they did it incorrectly.

Another major advance is that culture uses meaning, and so the interactions of cultural animals are meaningful. This enables them to be controlled and informed in many ways. In chapter 6, we saw that the shift toward following rules was a major feature of the shift from social to cultural beings. Rules are most common for regulating interaction, not simple action. In short, cultural beings are connected to the collective in addition to being connected to each other with individual bonds. Knowledge, organization, and other information exists at the collective level. Cultural animals respond to this level as well as to individual others.

Living, Working, and Playing Together

Two creatures can interact in many ways: cooperating, competing, making love, fighting, playing together, and so on. Our focus here is on how those one-to-one interactions are transformed in human beings because of our belonging to a culture. The collective reaches into the dyad to shape and organize it. Or, looked at another way, the one-to-one relationships and interactions have to change in order to sustain the existence of the collective. Just as all societies must meet the basic material requirements of life, as in ensuring that people can obtain food, water, and shelter, they must also satisfy certain social requirements. The innate need to belong is not enough to enable people to coexist and cooperate for long periods of time.

What are these basic requirements? Some shared understanding of fairness has to be achieved. All known societies have some form of reciprocity norm, by which whatever A does for or to B is appropriately repaid by something B does for or to A.[2] The great Chinese philosopher Confucius was once asked if there were any single word that could serve as a guideline for all of one's life, and he answered, "Reciprocity."[3] Although that may be a tad overstated, there is little doubt that people have a keen sense of reciprocity as fair, in both help and harm.

Equity and *equality* represent two different conceptions of fairness, and these are different. That is, does everyone get an equal share in the reward money or the available food—regardless of individual need and contribution? That is equality. Equity, in contrast, entails that those who contribute the most effort or resources are entitled to greater rewards. Either system can work, though probably larger groups will lean toward equity, because equity has the advantage of rewarding those who contribute or achieve the most, and so it encourages achievement.

Cultures also gain advantages by assigning people to distinct, differentiated roles. This may start with division of labor. All known societies have some form of division of labor, because there is simply no way to deny the immense social benefits that stem from dividing up tasks and letting everyone master a few things, as opposed to having everyone do everything. This increases the interdependence of each individual and each couple on others.

All societies and most groups need ways of making decisions. Different systems exist, usually based on majority voting or on having a leader issue decrees. And there are highly complex systems such as the American democracy in which the people elect representatives to two legislative chambers, which have committees to recommend bills upon which everyone votes, whereupon the two chambers reconcile their differences. The president is permitted to veto, which can be overridden by additional legislative procedures, and if necessary the Supreme Court can declare the enacted laws to be unconstitutional, which cannot be overridden, except by changing the Constitution itself.

Some system is also necessary for dealing with the everyday concerns of individuals. These include material possessions. Groups must have rules as to what ownership rights entail and under what circumstances they can be set aside. Sexual relations usually require some kind of collective agreements, especially with regard to what are the limits of permissible behaviors. Disagreements need to be resolved with a minimum of harm and violence. All of these problems are faced by giant nations and by small families.

As a member of a group, the individual confronts two main projects or superordinate goals,[4] namely, getting along and getting ahead. *Getting along* involves developing positive, pleasant relationships with other people, so that interactions can be pursued in a friendly, cooperative manner. *Getting ahead* refers to rising in power, status, prestige, or some other indicator of place in the hierarchy. Getting ahead breeds competition and even antagonism.

There are may ways that people relate to each other and many ways that large groups deal with their ongoing problems and challenges, but many of them operate on similar assumptions. What is needed is therefore a summary of the major sets of assumptions, which will furnish an account of the different types of relationships people can have. The anthropologist Alan Page Fiske did this.[5] He concluded that there are four major types of human relations, which correspond to four basic structures of human social life.

Communal sharing is Fiske's first form, and as the name implies, it is based on the principle that the members of the group all own and use everything in common. People can take what they need and contribute what they like. Whatever benefits they get do not have any necessary relation to what they contribute. All that matters is belonging to the group. Fairness is based on equality rather than equity. Margaret Clark and Judd Mills have observed that in modern America, most close relationships operate on the basis of communal norms, in the sense that people are supposed to care about each other, share things, take care of each other, and not keep track of whether one person did more or received more than a fair share.[6] Indeed, the notion of "fair share" is foreign to communal sharing. "What's mine is yours" is the motto of communal sharing. Conformity tends to be high. Decisions are made by consensus, that is, the group looks for a solution with which everyone can agree. Usually, there is a strong sense of group unity and identity. Communal sharing works well in connection with intimate relationships, but it may become cumbersome and inefficient in large groups. It is impossible to imagine a large modern nation operating on that basis, partly because it would require people to share all of their goods and possessions with strangers. This was the communist ideal, but even communist societies never implemented anything close to it on a large scale.

The second form, *authority ranking*, is based on a hierarchy. Those higher in the ranking take precedence over those lower in it. Decisions can be made by the superiors, who then simply issue commands to the subordinates. The superiors enjoy more prestige and get better resources, as compared with those lower in the ranking. Sometimes, the superiors have an obligation to take care of their underlings, just as parents may take care of children and just as kings and presidents may feel responsible for the welfare of those beneath them. The ranking is transitive, which means that if Bob outranks James while James outranks George, then Bob also outranks George. Subordinates are expected to be loyal to their superiors and to obey them. Throughout world history, many large and small groups have used this system, and it seems especially effective under difficult or stressful times. It is no accident that military organizations almost always use it.

Fiske's third form is *equality matching*. In this form, everyone counts the same and expects to be treated the same. Everyone gets the same resource, regardless of need or desire. Reciprocity is a powerful norm and may take the unusual, narrower form of insisting on exchange of precisely the same services: You should do for me the same thing I do for you. (More commonly, reciprocity consists of doing things of roughly equal value, not identical things, such as when the vegetable farmers and the fishing villages give each other some of their food.)[7] Group effort is based on taking turns or by some other system that enables everyone to contribute the same amount. Decisions are typically based on pure democracy, in which every person has a vote that counts the same, and the majority rules. (Alternative modes of decision making would involve a lottery or rotating positions of authority such that everyone gets an equal turn.) Justice is based on eye-for-an-eye or tit-for-tat principles, and fairness begins with the principles of equality and reciprocity.

Market pricing is the fourth and final form of social relation. Individual interactions and even individual relationships are based on a broad network of relationships (the market) in which everything is assigned some degree of abstract value. People relate to each other as buyer and seller. The market value system allows things to be exchanged even if they do not resemble each other at all, unlike in equality matching. For example, you might trade a used car for a piano and some paintings. Resources are allocated in due proportion to what each person has contributed. Fairness is thus based on equity rather than equality: That is, those who contribute more get more in return. The market allows strangers to have significant interactions that are mutually beneficial and satisfactory. Market incentives, including costs and benefits, govern social influence in place of conformity or obedience. Decisions are left up to the market, which sets prices and values, and then individuals can depart from these (e.g., by demanding more than the going rate, if they can get it) if they want.

In terms of the evolution from social to cultural animals, the first two of Fiske's forms (communal sharing and authority ranking) can exist in purely social species, partly because they do not require much in the way of meaningful regulation of action. Equality matching already imposes significant meaning to constrain behavior, and market pricing depends heavily on a cultural network and meaningful understandings.

Apart from Fiske's typology, there is another structural variable that is helpful for understanding human interaction. It is usually described with reference to the clunky mathematical term *zero sum*. More precisely, most human relationships and even fleeting interactions can be characterized as either *zero sum* or *non–zero sum*, and those two categories bring with them a host of different rules, implications, and consequences. Zero sum actually refers to a simple concept from the theory of games. In most games, such as tennis, chess, or football, there is one winner and one loser. Mathematicians would score the outcome as plus one for the winner and minus one for the loser, and when you add these together across both players or teams, the outcome is zero. Even in games like poker, there may be one winner and four losers, but the amount of money that the winner gets is precisely equal to the amount lost by everyone else, so poker also is zero sum. In a nutshell, zero sum entails that one person's gain is linked to another person's loss, and so all of the gains and losses add up to zero.

Many social interactions other than games are zero sum. Fiske's discussion of market pricing invokes the principle that buying and selling are ultimately zero sum, even if the price departs from the true market value. The seller gets as much money as the buyer gives up. Even if the buyer pays twice the appropriate price, the outcome is still zero sum, because the buyer's excessive loss is equal to the seller's excessive gain. Power and influence likewise tend to be zero sum, because the more power one person has, the less the other has.

On the other hand, many human interactions and relationships are not zero sum. Both parties may benefit, or both may lose. A friendly conversation or romantic date may bring pleasure to both people, for example. Even exchanges based on market pricing may depart from zero sum if individuals have subjective values that depart from the general market value. You have an ugly old painting that reminds you of your unhappy childhood, so you just want to be rid of it and think that getting fifty bucks for it is an unexpected bonus, whereas to me the same painting is beautiful, inspiring, and perfect for my study, and since I had expected to have to pay much more, the purchase seems a tremendous bargain. Thus, we both believe we have gotten the better deal. Or, suppose I have excellent hearing but also have hay fever, so I cannot abide yard work but don't mind tuning your family's piano, whereas you are tone deaf but enjoy any outdoor activity, so you are happy to mow my lawn in exchange for getting the piano tuned. We can do each other favors and both gain in the process.

Indeed, the very principle of market pricing, and the associated division of labor, conceals a non–zero sum aspect even if every transaction is precisely fair and seemingly zero sum. The market itself, and the division of labor, allows everyone to gain: The net total wealth is increased. Everyone works at a job with a narrow set of duties, and as a result everyone manages to get food, shelter, and countless other comforts, by virtue of the network of exchanges. If we all had to build our own houses and grow and prepare all of our own food, we would all live much more poorly than we do.

The two goals mentioned earlier (getting along and getting ahead) differ in their zero sum nature. That is, getting along is non–zero sum, because it entails constructing mutually beneficial and satisfactory relationships. Getting ahead, in contrast, tends to be zero sum, because there is a relatively fixed amount of status and influence, and so one person's gain is another person's loss.[8]

The zero sum dichotomy is roughly comparable to cooperation versus competition. Competition tends to be zero sum, in that there are winners and losers, and the winner's gain equals the loser's loss. In contrast, cooperation tends to be non–zero sum, because both people may benefit. Cooperative interactions look and feel very different than competitive ones. The reasons people engage in them, how they carry them out, and how they come away from them are all quite different.

Selfish Impulse Versus Social Conscience

Self-interest is one perennial source of conflict between nature and culture. Evolution almost inevitably makes each organism do what is best for itself, with the main exceptions involving possible willingness to make some sacrifices for kin (the "selfish gene"). In contrast, culture requires individuals to restrain their self-interest and to act in ways that are best for the group. Selfish individuals will not want to pay taxes, wait their turn, risk their lives in war, respect others' ownership of things they want, and the like, but culture demands that they do so.

In chapter 6, we saw that self-control is the principal inner mechanism that culture uses to override selfish impulses. Here, our concern is with how the cultural system itself dictates the desired modes of unselfish behavior. Morality and law are the two main cultural mechanisms for this.

Morality and law may operate in different spheres. Lawrence Friedman's history of law in America makes the profound point that law is the logical replacement for morality as the latter gradually loses its power, and the change depends on how much people interact with kin as opposed to strangers.[9] Morality depends on social bonds. Morality can have sufficient force to restrain selfishness and to promote socially desirable behavior within stable, long-term relationships, especially among kin and friends. It is considerably weaker at regulating interactions among strangers, and so the rule of law has to step up and take its place.

The operation of morality depends on guilt, and guilt is strongly linked to close relationships. The emotional basis for guilt appears to be concern about maintaining close social bonds. The same transgression arouses different degrees of guilt depending on whom is victimized: You feel much worse about neglecting to return a phone call from your child, mother, or lover than you do about failing to return a call from a stranger, a casual acquaintance, or someone from the department store.[10] Guilt is one of the most interpersonal emotions, and most instances that people report of feeling very guilty involve misdeeds against those they love or those about whom they care strongly.

Guilt is thus valuable and helpful for making people behave properly toward family and friends. It is much weaker at making people treat distant acquaintances and strangers properly. Loss of love is a palpable threat that can motivate people to do right by their relationship partners, but the only threat that a stranger can enforce against you is to regard you as immoral. A moral or immoral reputation is also somewhat influential in small villages or towns where everyone knows everyone and where most people continue to live for many years, but in modern societies people move around a great deal more, and so even the threat of a bad reputation loses its force.

Hence as society becomes ever more modern, people must be governed more and more by the rule of law rather than by the implicit pressures of morality. Morality continues to operate, however, within the narrow spheres of intimate relationships. Friedman points out that most modern families have rules for how the members are expected to behave, but they do not hire a police officer or security guard to arrest a family member who comes home too late. The emotional bonds of the intimate relationships lend sufficient force to morality to make it work. But when people leave home and begin to deal with strangers, they need law to make them obey the rules.

Culture organizes behavior on a large scale, often coordinating the actions of distant acquaintances or even total strangers. Getting people to play their roles properly and to treat strangers fairly and decently is often essential to the smooth functioning of a cultural society. Therefore, societies will gradually need more and better laws, along with social systems (such as police and courts) to enforce the laws.

Breaking the Social Contract

People may obey laws because they fear the legal consequences of breaking them, but a broader understanding is needed for people's willingness to continue to make the sacrifices required by morality and law. Why don't people simply run off and live by themselves instead of making the sacrifices necessary for living in culture? Some individuals have done so. What keeps the rest in place?

The most obvious answer is that the rewards of living in a cultural society are immense. Despite the sacrifices required of culture—having to wait your turn, curb your impulses, respect the rights of others, pay taxes—these are compensated by the advantages that culture can bestow. Between income tax, property tax, sales tax, and other mechanisms, the government takes more than half the salary you earn, but you still live a much more lush, comfortable, well-fed, and generally agreeable life than you would by heading off into the wilderness to seek your fortune by yourself.

Life in modern society (and probably in most premodern societies too) thus depends on an implicit contract. The individual obeys the rules, which means curbing a great many selfish impulses and making herself behave in socially desirable ways. In exchange, the society provides the individual with all of the great rewards that come from belongingness, ranging from the direct satisfaction of the need to belong all the way to the advantages that derive from participating in the economy and enjoying the social safety net of welfare, military defense, health care, and the rest.

Either side can break this contract, which seems quickly to cause the other to renege also. Individuals who fail to exhibit the requisite self-control are often rejected by others. Criminals are put into prison; selfish, impulsive, aggressive people are shunned by others; dishonest employees are fired; dealers who cheat their customers gradually lose their business or are prosecuted; and those who betray trust are abandoned by their lovers. Thus, continued acceptance by the social network depends on a continued willingness to make the necessary sacrifices to do what is best for the collective as a whole.

Conversely, people who find themselves rejected by groups often revert to impulsive, selfish patterns of behavior. Even in laboratory studies that choose people at random to receive messages of social exclusion, being rejected makes people more willing to behave aggressively, to cheat, to refuse to cooperate or help others, to pursue short-term gains despite long-term costs or losses, and in other ways to show signs of diminished self-control and antisocial tendencies.[11] This is an important sign that people obey rules and control themselves precisely because they expect to reap the rewards of belonging.

The Family

It is safe to say that human nature contains a penchant for living in families. All over the world and throughout history, people have lived in families. To be sure, the definition and typical formula for a family has been somewhat flexible. But the family is here to stay. "Families is where our nation takes hope, where wings take dream," said a tired George W. Bush during a Wisconsin speech in his 2000 campaign for the presidency, and presumably he was trying to invoke the standard theme of support for families as a central task of government. Politicians and pundits periodically wring their hands and gnash their teeth over statistics about divorce rates, absentee fathers, socially isolated elderly widows, and the like, as if these portend the imminent demise of the family. But no demise of the family is imminent.

Divorce may be less of a threat to the ongoing survival of family ties than people think, because marriage is not as important to the family as is often assumed. One scholar surveyed both historical and cross-cultural findings and concluded that the core meaning of *family* in most societies is the parent-child bond, not the husband-wife bond.[12] The emphasis on the husband-wife bond as the core of the family is a modern and Western pattern that departs from what has generally prevailed. And the parent-child bond has proven extremely durable. Indeed, as noted earlier in this book, determined attempts to eradicate the parent-child bond have been complete failures. Both the Israeli kibbutzim and the Soviet Union tried to have children raised communally, without the usual parent-child bond, and both soon gave up on these efforts. Marriage can be altered and has in fact gone through multiple forms, including polygyny, occasionally polyandry, serial monogamy, and so forth, but the parent-child core of the family (perhaps especially the mother-child relationship) is much less amenable to radical restructuring.

My purpose in this and the subsequent sections is to explain how interaction patterns are shaped by the link to the collective. Families exist everywhere, in human life and in much of the animal kingdom. But how does culture affect families?

The family is normally a vital connection between the single individual and the broader culture. The family locates and identifies the individual. The family prepares the child to become a member of the culture in multiple ways. In some societies, the family connection is so vital that without it, people have little chance of securing their own place. In bygone centuries in our own society, the family fed and clothed you, educated you, arranged your marriage, and placed you in your occupation. If it couldn't do that for you, it steered you into the military or the clergy. If it failed at those, or if you didn't accept the place it found for you, you probably became an outlaw.

Modernization has in some respects diminished the importance of the family for connecting the individual to society. Probably the most important change in the history of the family was the loss of its socioeconomic function and its subsequent evolution into a haven of intimacy. The classic sociological work by Ernest Burgess and Harvey Locke articulated this change.[13] As they pointed out, throughout history most people were farmers, and on a family farm most members of the family usually worked together as an economically productive unit. The many farming tasks were divided among father, mother, sons, daughters, and other family members, so that the farm could grow food for the family and perhaps some surplus for trade. Exploring each other's feelings and cultivating a self-actualizing sort of psychological growth were not high priorities—indeed they were mostly irrelevant to the vital family project of running the farm. The family was first and foremost the unit by which you participated in the economy, if only by means of growing food to sell.

With the industrial revolution, some changes occurred, but the family continued to be primarily an economic partnership. The family was what connected the individual to the broader society and its economic system, and a person without a family was at best in a precarious position. Your family fed you, clothed you, got you a job, gave you crucial possessions, made it possible for you to marry, took care of you when you were sick, and supported you in your old age. This was before nations had systems like Medicare and Social Security or public school liberal arts educations that led directly to job opportunities. The family used to serve all of those functions as best it could.

Modern Western couples marry for love and decide at their leisure whether to have a child or not. This is radically different from the lives that most of our ancestors led. For them, marriage was impossible until an income was available, and the family helped you get this, such as by willing you the farm. Moreover, children were a vital economic asset, and once you got married you usually wanted to start having them as quickly as possible. Their contribution to farm work was vital. Later, they worked in factories and contributed their wages to the family income. In old age, people depended on their children for their subsistence. For a couple to remain childless was generally a disaster for them—again, not for emotional or fulfillment reasons, but for purely economic ones.

The modern form of the family took shape over several centuries. Young people began to marry for love rather than accept marriages that their parents arranged. With that shift, the husband-wife bond became an expression of emotional intimacy and romantic passion rather than an economic merger between families. The financial incentives for having children dwindled progressively and eventually disappeared. That is, in bygone days, money flowed from you to your children when they were small, but when you got old it flowed back to you from them (at least in the form of food, housing, and other vital aspects of life support). Children were therefore a sound economic investment. But no longer: Almost no American parents realize a profit on their children, and indeed money tends to flow from parents to children right up until the death of the parents. No doubt this reality has contributed substantially to the decline in family size. Why have lots of children when they are an unending drain on your financial resources? Instead, people have one or two children and then stop.

Obviously, few families in the modern world are engaged in joint economic production, whether on farms or in other milieux. Families are not even necessary to place a person in a job, in most cases. Instead, students go to school, and when they graduate they seek employment on their own. Even in families in which everyone is employed, the different jobs are likely to have no relationship to each other. Father works as an accountant; mother is a nurse; son has a job with a magazine; daughter works for a department store. This is a far cry from all of them working together to operate the family farm. The family continues to connect them to the broader society, but in more indirect ways. Thus, the family lives in a certain neighborhood, which dictates which schools the children can attend, and later the family's wealth and related circumstances help to dictate the quality of university education the offspring can obtain. The children's own lifetime incomes depend much more on the education they get than on their family connections. Thus, how the person fares in the society depends only indirectly on the family.

Instead of economic advantage, people seek emotional satisfaction in their families. Ideally, the members meet in the evening, share their problems and concerns, provide emotional support for each other, and seek satisfaction or fulfillment in their interactions and relationships with each other. (Or, at least, they watch television together.) If the relationships fail to provide them with the emotional fulfillment they seek, the individuals leave the family. The parents may divorce, or the children may move away and stay only vaguely in touch by means of the occasional phone call.

Society has a continuing interest in sustaining families, because they do form such useful units to take care of individuals and connect them to the broader cultural system. When families break apart, children may be left without anyone to care for them, and so society must find ways to provide care—daily food, clothing, and shelter require both the institutions to provide these and the funds to pay for them. Even if the children of a disintegrating family can remain under the care of one parent, which is the normal result of modern divorce, there are some costs to society. Single parents have less money, time, energy, and other resources, and as a result the children of single parents on average contribute less to society and demand more from it. They do less well in schools, commit more crimes, create less wealth, and often go on to have less stable families of their own.

Though most societies try in various ways to support families, other developments in the culture may weaken or undermine them. Systems of welfare that give more money to single mothers than to married parents effectively constitute incentive structures that discourage marriage. Liberal divorce laws make people more willing to abandon a marriage when it ceases to be fully satisfying, as opposed to working on the marriage to repair its problems.[14] Increasing the rights and economic opportunities for women and, more generally, making it more economically viable to live alone, have produced an increase in divorce and single life, because people are less willing to continue living in unhappy marriages. All of these processes and systems have advantages and may be desirable in some ways, but they have side effects of weakening families.

Cultures also make laws to regulate families, and so gradually family life has come under the control of the state. Although the Catholic church struggled for much of the Middle Ages to gain primary control of marriage, by now marriage is primarily a legal relationship and religion plays at best a supporting role. Current legal debates in America reflect the government's control of marriage, such as by dictating who may marry whom. A man may only marry a woman, for example, so homosexuals are generally prohibited from forming a true family that will be recognized by the state. In a recent case in Ohio, a man was undergoing a sex change operation and intended to live as a lesbian with his/her girlfriend. They applied for a marriage license. The judge insisted on a medical examination to establish that the groom-to-be still had a penis on his wedding day, or else the marriage would have been illegal because both parties would have been women. Likewise, the rule is one wife at a time, so if a man wants to marry another woman, he must first divorce his previous wife; the law does not allow her the option of remaining in his family. Stepfamilies are systematically regulated, such as by highly complex rules about which children will inherit what from whom. And of course the traditional purpose of the family—transmitting wealth from parent to child, especially when the parent dies—is something the government watches and manages carefully, sometimes giving tax breaks to parents so they will have more money to spend on their children, but also usually stepping in to claim a sizable share of the inheritance when the parent dies.

In short, the family is more than a network of people who are related to each other and may live together. In culture, families are regulated by the rules of the society at large and are treated as important links between the individual and the culture.

Sex

Sex may seem like a private act between two individuals, but most cultures influence and regulate sex in many ways. When two rabbits, two dogs, or two elephants have sex, the community of other animals is essentially absent and irrelevant, but when two people make love, their culture is often very much present and relevant. What two people do together in bed is often shaped extensively by many people who are not there with them.

The most obvious influence of culture is to provide meaning. Among humans, sex usually means something—a dimension that is generally lacking in the copulations of other species. A sex act may be a mortal sin, an act of rebellion, a rite of passage, an expression of love, a purposive attempt to create a child, or a symbol of one's desirability.

All known societies have rules governing sexual interactions. This universality probably signifies that unregulated sex is a potential threat to the social order. In fact, sex probably represents multiple threats. Most of these problems (especially unwanted pregnancy) center on intercourse, whereas masturbation, kissing, petting, and even oral sex are less dangerous. Still, societies may sometimes regulate these other behaviors too, perhaps on the assumption that they lead to intercourse. This is one of the most important and unresolved policy questions about sex: Could people be satisfied with halfway measures, or do the halfway measures increase the tendency to go all the way? For example, if society were to tolerate oral sex for all premarital and extramarital activity, would people be satisfied and stop there? If so, then people could enjoy those pleasures without problem. If not, however, then society might need to crack down on them too, and a more puritanical approach would be vital if sex is to be controlled.

The major problems of unregulated sex are as follows. First, sex causes pregnancies, and society ends up bearing many of the costs of children who lack an adequate family environment. Babies born outside of wedlock (either premarital or extramarital) may not receive either adequate material care or adequate socialization.

Second, sexually transmitted diseases (STDs) can cause significant problems. At present, AIDS is projected to decimate the populations of several African countries, with catastrophic impact on these nations' economic and cultural structures on top of the human toll of death and misery. And the rates of infection with HIV and other STDs worldwide continue to rise. Even nonfatal sexual diseases can cause problems. There are several African societies, for example, in which all manner of sexual expression is encouraged.[15] People have many premarital and extramarital partners throughout life. This may sound appealing to people who would like to enjoy a rich variety of sexual experiences, but the STDs end up rendering between a third and a half of women permanently infertile. This too has significant human cost as well as bringing about socioeconomic disruption.

Third, sex can lead to violence. Some degree of sexual possessiveness is found in all societies and cultures.[16] Hence people become upset when others copulate with their mates. Moreover, extramarital sex appears to represent a threat to the primary relationship,[17] even if the primary partners have agreed to permit each other to have sex with others. Thus a society that condones extramarital activity will likely have to contend with an elevated rate of divorce, along with all of the disruption that brings.

It is no surprise that cultures use morals and laws to regulate sex. Cultures influence sex in more subtle ways, too, however. Within a community, the sexual activities of many individuals are loosely connected in a kind of economy. The sexual economy rests on the assumption that sex is a female resource and so men give women other resources in order to get sex.[18] Women may desire sex, but men desire it more. The risks and costs of sex also tend to fall more heavily on women than on men. As a result, men often have to sweeten the deal by offering women other incentives to engage in sex: gifts, money, respect, commitment, love, and so on. Thus, men will buy dinner or spend money on other attractions, will offer jewelry, will make long-term promises and commitments, and will even give women cold hard cash in exchange for sex. It is rare for women to give men any such resources in exchange for sex.

The exchange of resources for sex (even if disguised) creates a sexual marketplace within a society. Each couple's sexual decisions draw meaning from what the norms are in their community, and these norms consist of an ostensible "going rate" in the sense of an accepted price. The price may vary substantially according to market forces.Consider supply and demand. In the sexual economy, men constitute the demand; women constitute the supply. Variations in the gender ratio will change the price of sex.[19] When there are more women than men, supply exceeds demand, and so the price of sex will go down. Such circumstances may arise after a major war that kills off large numbers of young men, or in low-income minority communities in which a substantial proportion of men are lost to violence and prison. The low price of sex means that the men who are there often can engage in premarital and extramarital sex rather easily, and women cannot demand much in terms of commitment, money, love, or other resources. If a woman withholds sex, a man can soon find another, more willing partner.

In contrast, the price of sex rises when there are more men than women, such as the situation that is produced by the selective abortion or infanticide of female offspring. Premarital and extramarital sex become rare. The community becomes rather prudish. A man must often sign on for a permanent commitment before he can get into bed with a woman. This commitment may include promising to provide food, housing, clothing, and other goods for her for the rest of her life, as well as forgoing any chance to have sex with anyone else. That may seem like quite a lot to give for a little intimacy, but when women are scarce, many men will pay that price. Indeed, recent studies have uncovered patterns that seem paradoxical without the supply-and-demand analysis of the sexual marketplace. For example, the rate of teen pregnancy goes up when there is a shortage of men.[20] Because women get pregnant by having sex with men, a shortage of men should seemingly reduce the risk. In the extreme case—no men at all—women would presumably not get pregnant at all. Therefore it seems quite surprising that as fewer men are available, a higher proportion of teenage girls become pregnant. Put another way, if you were trying to guess how many out of 100 teenage girls would get pregnant in a given year, you would probably assume that more of them would get pregnant if they lived in a community with 200 young men, as opposed to only 30 young men. But you'd be wrong: Somehow, the 30 men cause more pregnancies than the 200.

The social exchange analysis can resolve this apparent contradiction. When men are in short supply, women must compete all the more fiercely among themselves for the men, and female competition will take the form of reducing the price of sex (just as stores may offer sales and bargains when there are not enough customers). Making sex more freely available to men will result in an increase in the rate of unwed pregnancy. Consistent with this analysis, fashion trends reveal that women wear shorter skirts when there is a shortage of men, and this too suggests greater competition for male mates, because women wear short skirts to advertise their sexual charms.[21]

These findings on teen pregnancy bring up the broader issue of competition for mates. Part of the tendency for women to restrain each other's sexuality is probably due to concern over restraining competition. After all, a woman who offers more sexual activity than other women is likely to be popular with the men, and so she can potentially steal boyfriends from other women. (Research has confirmed that offering sex is a far more common and effective technique for women who want to steal another's mate than for men trying to steal another man's mate.)[22] If women restrain each other so that all offer roughly the same degree of sexual activity, then competition among them does not produce an escalating spiral in which each woman has to give sex more and more freely.

In a sexual economy, women will have conflicting impulses, and indeed the conflicting pressures on women seem likely to produce chronic ambivalence. On the one hand, the woman does desire and enjoy sex. In fact, the advantage she has over the man is there as long as he desires it more than she does, so she is free to desire and enjoy it up to a fairly substantial extent. On the other hand, women want the price of sex to be high, and as with any resource, high prices are best achieved when the demand outstrips the supply. Women therefore have an incentive to restrain each other's sexual behavior. Just as the men may want women to be economically dependent so that they will offer sex for relatively little money, women want men to remain somewhat sex starved so that men will be willing to offer a great deal in order to get sex.

The view that women try to restrain each other's sexuality is well supported. Indeed, the cultural suppression of female sexuality appears to be largely enacted by means of women influencing each other, as opposed to men suppressing women.[23] In modern Western cultures, the pressures on women and girls to restrain their sexual activity come from other women: mothers rather than fathers, female friends and peer groups rather than male ones. The so-called double standard that allows men to engage in sexual activities while condemning and punishing women for the same actions is supported mainly by women. In some non-Western societies, surgical techniques are used to curb female sexuality, such as sewing up the vagina (infibulation) or cutting off the clitoris (subincision). These practices are almost entirely maintained, initiated, carried out, and defended by women. Typically they occur in societies in which women lack financial, political, legal, educational, and other opportunities to create comfortable lives for themselves. For such women, sex is almost the only ticket to a good life, and so each woman needs to get the highest possible price for her sexual favors. It seems safe to predict that as these societies begin to offer women more rights and opportunities, there will be a sharp drop in the practices of genital surgery aimed at curtailing sexual desire.

Men also compete among each other to attract women. As we saw, male sex appeal depends on status, resources, and prestige, and so men compete for these. Indeed, the high and sometimes excessive levels of career ambition that are found among men more than among women may be attributable to the male belief that occupational success will produce sexual and romantic success, whereas women don't see career success as a strategy for attracting suitors. Most evolutionary biologists assume that the specifically male concern for reaching the top of the status hierarchy is linked to its promise of sexual and reproductive success, and human beings are no different. The only important difference is that human men must negotiate their place in the cultural system in order to achieve status and to attract women.

In sum, sex is often regarded as a private and animalistic activity, but for human beings, sex has become culturalized. Sex is shaped by a cultural context that includes norms, rules, morals, and laws, and it is also powerfully affected by the sexual economy based on men giving women resources in exchange for sex. An economy is a cultural system, and so the sexual economy reveals the importance of culture for transforming sex.

Violence and Aggression

If societies must control sex, they find it even more imperative to control violence. Letting people work out their disputes by violent means, even up to the point of killing each other as they see fit, has never proven a workable system over the long term. All societies prohibit murder in some form, and nearly all set other limits on violent conduct. In most cases, formal laws punish people for violent acts. Even more important, people are socialized to restrain their angry, aggressive impulses, and the inner, psychological restraints created by socialization are crucial to the success and harmony of human social life. And just as sex means something, aggression means something too. Aggression upholds a principle, or defends someone's honor, or solves a problem.

Aggression and sex are not on the same level, however. People desire sex for its own sake, but violence is usually done as a means to obtain some other goal. This does not deny that aggression may have an innate basis, but it does say that linking aggression to some genetic or biological tendency will fall short of explaining actual aggression. Much aggression and violence can be understood as a means of resolving conflicts and exerting influence over others.[24] When two people want different, incompatible things, there are many ways to decide which one will get his way—but aggression is certainly one of those ways and, moreover, one that is recognized and used throughout the world.

In chapter 3, I proposed that aggression is social more than cultural. That is, social animals use aggression as a social strategy to influence others, claim a place in the status hierarchy, increase their power, resolve conflicts in their favor, and defend their territory and pride against challenges. All of these goals remain important among cultural animals, but cultures generally find better and preferable ways of achieving them. A modern male is supposed to prove his manhood and rise in the status hierarchy by such means as getting an education, earning a high salary, and providing a privileged start in life for his children, not by beating up other men (or, worse, beating up women). His pursuit of education and occupational success will benefit society, whereas if he turns to violence society may be disrupted.

Cultures will be more successful to the extent that they motivate people to pursue their goals through these nonviolent means.

Nonetheless, evolution has certainly not had time to erase aggression from the human psyche just because the shift from social to cultural life has rendered violence somewhat obsolete as an optimal means of goal pursuit. In fact, in the short run, violence often seems to succeed at helping people reach their goals, which will make it all the more difficult for human evolution to outgrow aggressive tendencies. In particular, many individuals will find that peaceful, culturally approved means of reaching goals do not work for them. It is fine to say that if you want to be financially secure, you should obtain an advanced degree in law, medicine, or dentistry, but far more people apply for such training than can receive it, and many others do not even reach the point (of graduating from college) where they can apply. Some paths to wealth are long, difficult, and restricted to a chosen few. In contrast, almost anybody can buy a gun and demand money from passersby.

As a result, every culture is put in a position of having to control and restrain aggression. In this respect, at least, Freud was right when he argued in his classic *Civilization and Its Discontents* that people's innate aggressive tendencies pose a problem for culture (though he may have been wrong about the nature of aggression and the nature of the problem it poses).[25] Civilized life would be more efficient, smoother, and easier if people did not periodically resort to aggression to resolve their problems.

Moral objections aside, why really should cultures oppose violence? There are two main answers, both of which I think are correct, and together they frame the context for the cultural efforts to minimize and restrain human aggression. The first is that aggression will tend to interfere with the social system. Part of the essence of culture is imposing organization on people and their actions, typically by means of a set of interlocking roles and rules. Performing one's role often requires training for both skills and rules. If someone is murdered, however, she will be unable to fulfill that role, and so someone new must be trained. If aggression is widespread enough, rules become unsustainable and effectively meaningless. For example, most economies rely on personal ownership of property, including money, but if people use violence to take what they want from others, possession becomes meaningless and money essentially useless. After all, why spend money to buy something if it will be stolen right away? And why accumulate money if you can't use it, or if the money itself will be stolen? Another way of putting this point is that violence is often not zero sum. It is worse than zero sum, in the sense that the losses outweigh or outnumber the gains.

That brings up the second reason that culture opposes violence. The essential purpose of culture is to make life better by providing goods and services to satisfy people's needs. Such goods and services have value, and culture makes progress by increasing the total amount of value within the society. Violence, in contrast, decreases that total amount of value. When researching my book on evil,[26] I noticed a pattern that seemed to come up in one sphere after another, each time presented as if it were a novel finding by each different scholar: What the perpetrator gains by violence is almost always less than what the victim loses. I called this the *magnitude gap*, which refers to the size or quantity of the loss, but essentially it is a loss of value. The thief or burglar gets less value for what he steals than what the victim loses, because stolen goods are worth less than new ones, plus sentimental value is lost. The victor in war may gain new territory, but often it has been damaged during the war, so its value is less than what it was before the war. Any sexual pleasure that a rapist or child abuser gets is almost surely less than the trauma and suffering that the victim experiences, and the pleasure is usually gone in minutes whereas the suffering may last for years. Most obviously, there is hardly anything that a perpetrator can gain by murdering someone that will equal the victim's loss of life.

The point of this discussion of the magnitude gap is that acts of violence inherently reduce value. Scholars may treat violence and aggression as just other means of influence, in the sense that they help people get what they want, but although this is largely correct, it misses the point that violence and aggression are collectively costly. They do not just transfer goods from one person to another, but they typically reduce the value of those goods in the process. Hence it is not surprising that cultures universally seek to curb violence and to induce people to use other, more peaceful methods to get what they want.

Cultures use many different means to restrain aggression. Violent individuals are often shunned and ostracized by others. This starts even in childhood, insofar as aggressive children and bullies are often avoided by other children. Socialization processes teach children to restrain their aggression and to find peaceful ways of expressing their feelings or pursuing their wants. All cultures have moral restraints on at least some violent acts,[27] and most large modern cultures have extensive laws against them. Less obvious, but still important, is the fact that cultures promote alternative ways of resolving disputes, such as lawsuits.

Even when violence is accepted as inevitable, cultures may organize it so as to control and restrain it. The practice of dueling provides an excellent example. Dueling is, at its core, a violent individual battle over a point of honor or some other cultural construction, but dueling is generally surrounded with extensive rituals and rules that seek to keep it in bounds, to prevent vendettas from forming, and to provide clear stopping points.

Other restraints on aggression include rules of warfare. Although the rules are sometimes broken, the rule breakers usually know they are breaking the rules and moreover that breaking the rules risks stiff penalties should they be found out. In modern life, war is conducted in the context of clear rules specified in international treaties. These rules specify how combatants should be identified, how they should treat each other, how prisoners are to be treated, and the like. The rules continue to evolve, although throughout history efforts to make rules for war have been only partly successful. One of the most high-minded was the medieval Christian church's attempt to impose limits on warfare such that battles should only be held on Mondays, Tuesdays, and Wednesdays.[28] Thursdays through Sundays should be reserved for prayer and other sacred activities. These rules were not very successful. Another failure was the efforts by the Crusaders to outlaw ambushes. The armor-clad European knights could generally vanquish the Muslims in face-to-face combat, so the Arabs developed a more mobile form of warfare, which involved leaving the battlefield and then ambushing the pursuers at an advantageous spot. The Crusaders resented this and deemed it unfair, but they never managed to persuade the Arabs to abandon this highly effective tactic.

The example of war brings up a crucial point, however: Sometimes cultures do use violence rather than just restraining it. Societies can gain by violent means. One might have thought that the world would have learned the futility and cost of violence from World War II, but apparently this was hardly a thorough lesson: By one calculation, the 4 decades following the end of that world war contained only 11 days of world peace, and that was not even counting civil wars.[29] In other words, even in the modern world, there is almost always a war going on somewhere. Societies compete, just as individuals do, and sometimes one of them will think that resorting to violence will help it achieve its goals. The same constraints do apply, however, and in the long run the world economy would probably flourish best if war could be ended.

There is another case in which culture may promote violence, and this is particularly important because the violent perpetrators may sincerely believe that what they hope to gain is equal to or even greater than the victim's loss (although the victims probably will not agree). This case involves idealistic killing.[30] The most notorious bloodbaths of recent history were all perpetrated by groups that thought they were creating a better society, even a kind of utopia. They believed that killing certain people (sometimes by the millions) was a necessary precondition toward creating a society that would be so wonderful that it would justify the violence and bloodshed. More than 20 million people died in China's Maoist Cultural Revolution, and a similar number perished in Stalin's purges in the Soviet Union. Perhaps 11 million died in the multiple genocidal projects of Nazi Germany. Two million may have died during the brief Khmer Rouge regime in Cambodia—a smaller body count than the others, but a larger proportion of the country's population. In all of these cases, the killers were encouraged by their culture to believe that the violence was a necessary, justified step toward making a better society.

Idealistic killings are probably so bloody for precisely that reason: The perpetrators sincerely believe, or try their hardest to believe, that the violence achieves some greater good, which will outweigh the cost to the victims. The violence may be officially justified or rationalized by appealing to the culture's highest values. In the United States, the most common recent version of idealistic violence involves the protests at abortion clinics, which sometimes use bombs or guns to damage the facilities and injure or kill the people who work there. Although the use of such violence is illegal and morally offensive to most thoughtful people, the perpetrators often believe that they are acting in accord with sacred values by protecting the lives of unborn children.

The belief in the great positive value of the outcome does more than allow perpetrators to rationalize or justify their violent acts. Indeed, that belief makes it a positive duty to ignore one's qualms so as to carry out the bloody tasks. Idealistic violence is often especially cruel and thorough because perpetrators feel a moral obligation to inflict all of the harm that is assigned to them, and so—unlike most violent perpetrators—they may continue killing and harming far beyond the point at which they have any impulse or inclination to do so and even past the point at which they may deeply wish to stop.

Disputed resources, conflicting claims, and utopian dreams are not the only things over which people fight. A substantial portion of aggression revolves around self-esteem and interpersonal esteem.[31] In particular, people become aggressive toward someone who attacks their favorable images of themselves.[32] Criticism, disrespect, insult, dishonoring, and other blows to pride often elicit aggressive responses. This can work at both the individual and the group level, and indeed group violence, mob action, and even international wars have sometimes been motivated by the sense that collective pride had been besmirched. Violent people tend to hold positive, even inflated views of themselves, and the very favorability of these views may make them especially vulnerable to feeling that someone has not treated them with sufficient respect. It is possible to view such violence as simply a humanized form of status fighting among pack animals, such as when males fight to establish their place in the dominance hierarchy. However, culture has also greatly increased the importance of self and identity, and accordingly cultural beings feel a greatly increased need to maintain their honor, respect, and dignity. Hence such violence is in part traceable to cultural life, even in a culture that generally discourages violence.

All in all, then, human aggression is profoundly different from what is found among other species, even if there are significant and biologically based similarities too. The meanings constructed by the culture form part of the context of human aggression. Sometimes, aggression arises from these meanings. In other cases, culture seeks to constrain and reduce aggression. When two animals fight, their battle is essentially between the two of them. Human aggression is, however, often influenced by third parties and by the broader culture itself.

Helping and Cooperation

Helping encompasses a broad range of social behaviors. People donate money to charities and to individual panhandlers. Fathers carry their tired children to bed. A bystander jumps into freezing water to save a drowning person. A motorist witnesses an accident and telephones an ambulance.

Early theories were skeptical that people could naturally be helpful. Konrad Lorenz (1966) concluded that evolution would inevitably shape animals to be purely selfish. To give some of their food to another animal would reduce their own chances for survival, and so natural selection would eliminate any organisms that were inclined to act that way. In retrospect, these arguments overlooked two points. First, natural selection is for genes rather than for individuals, and so helping a relative (who shares some of your genes) may actually improve the prospects of that gene to survive and flourish. Thus, if mutation produced two families that were identical except that one group was inclined to help each other out whereas the other group did not help each other, it is plausible that the helpful family would end up surviving better and producing more offspring.

Second, the simple view of helping as inherently opposed to selfishness assumes that helping is purely a zero sum proposition. When it is a matter of one animal giving its food to another, this does look like a zero sum proposition: One animal's gain is equal to the other's loss. (Then again, even that may not be precisely zero sum, especially if the first animal has more than it needs or can eat but the other is starving.) In contrast, helping may sometimes benefit both parties and therefore qualify as a non–zero sum form of interaction. When helping produces better than a zero sum, it effectively enriches the social network by creating additional value. This is the opposite of evil and violence, which according to the magnitude gap often produces outcomes that are worse than zero sum, thus effectively reducing the amount of value that exists in the social system.

The benefits of helping are most evident in cases of reciprocity. That is, if two people help each other, both may benefit in the long run.[33] This is particularly true insofar as people have different abilities, talents, and resources. Hence each can help in ways where the benefits to the other outweigh the costs to the self. In the long run, both gain more than they give. This is one of the major benefits of culture, after all: Individuals specialize and can therefore do specific jobs better than average, so all jobs get done better, and the total wealth increases as a result of cultural exchange. It is hardly surprising that reciprocity norms are found in all known societies, as noted earlier. Moreover, individual people often seem acutely attuned to issues of reciprocity. They are less willing to accept help if they see no prospect for returning the favor,[34] and they certainly notice when others fail to reciprocate their favors.

Another clear benefit of helping is that it feels good. Many people derive satisfaction from helping others, and indeed helping increases when people feel bad, in part because people seem to give help based on their expectation that helping will make them feel better.[35] This too produces net outcomes that rise above the zero sum. For example, if you give someone $10, then your monetary loss and the recipient's gain do add up to zero—but if you both feel better as a result of the gift, then there is a net benefit. The custom of widespread gift giving undoubtedly contributes to the general sense of joy, love, and harmony that make people love the Christmas season. From a purely financial perspective, the givers and receivers have roughly equal sums, but the mutual pleasure and satisfaction create a collective outcome that is significantly positive rather than neutral.

Our concern here is not with the evolutionary roots but in how culture changes the interaction patterns. For this, it is useful to observe not just continuities but also differences between human helping and the helping of other animals. Many writers have emphasized that human helping shows some of the same biases found among animals, especially the preferential helping of kin. Thus, people help their immediate family most, followed by other relatives, followed by friends; and people are far less helpful toward total strangers.[36] On the other hand, many animals from which we evolved show an even sharper drop-off, such that they will give essentially no help to strangers. Perhaps the truly noteworthy fact is that people help strangers at all, rather than that they help strangers less than family members. Human beings do donate money, time, and effort to help people they do not know and whom they will never meet.

Likewise, stepparents and foster parents often make great efforts and sacrifices to care for children who are not biologically related to them. Researchers have correctly pointed out that stepparents on average do not treat their children as well as biologically related parents do, but this seems an unfair comparison. In the animal world, many creatures are indifferent if not murderously hostile toward youngsters to which they are not related. Compared to them, human stepparents are remarkably caring and nurturing.

Underlying these patterns is a sense of the collective or community. Americans donate money to feed hungry children in Africa or South America because they recognize them as belonging to a common community (which is facilitated by empathic identification with these children) and because their culture places a positive moral value on helping fellow human beings regardless of biological relationship. The connection to the collective therefore promotes a wider sphere of helping than nature alone creates.

Another uniquely human response is third-party intervention to promote fairness. Animals may have a sense that they are being treated unfairly and may even be said to have a simple understanding of justice, but these apply mainly to their own outcomes. If you have two dogs and give a biscuit to one of them, the other will watch reproachfully, seemingly quite aware that it did not get its fair share. If one dog eats the other's food, the other will know it has been cheated in some way and will feel something akin to resentment. However, you will not see a third dog intervene to tell the first dog to return the stolen food to the second. Among humans, in contrast, people often intervene to put things right between others. And many will recognize that unfairness or mistreatment violates the culture's rules. Indeed, human culture has developed large institutional structures to enable third parties to intervene on behalf of fairness and justice. At the individual level, police officers intervene to stop fights and disputes, and judges resolve disputes between others. At the collective level, the United Nations organizes troops from different countries to intervene so as to stop large-scale killings. In such cases, we have a dispute between two parties— just as can occur among any social animals. But we also have a third party intervening to act as an agent of the culture, representing and enforcing its rules. Only cultural animals have that.

These tendencies seem linked to culture insofar as they become more and more prominent as culture develops. Thus, any list of the most developed cultures in the world would have to include the modern Western nations of North America and Western Europe, and the mostly white men who ran these during the twentieth century gradually instituted remarkably extensive interventions and policies to promote the rights and welfare of other groups, even groups that despise them. The Supreme Court of the mid-twentieth century often consisted of white men only, but these judges passed a series of rulings that vastly expanded the rights of women, African Americans, and other groups. Indeed, the affirmative action laws enacted by mostly white males in the 1960s and 1970s dictated that members of other groups would be given preferential treatment over white males. There is no way to argue that any sort of evolutionary or genetic self-interest was served by making rules that put their own group at a disadvantage. But they did it anyway, because of their commitment to the moral values linked to a vision of a culture in which all individuals would participate as equal members regardless of external categories.

The penchant for third-party intervention has been suggested in recent studies in behavioral economics.[37] Even in the laboratory, people will engage in *altruistic punishment*, which is defined as a willingness to punish for the sake of the greater good, even if the punishment is costly to the individual punisher and produces no material gain for that person. Some studies have focused on the free rider problem, in which people work together collectively but not necessarily equally, and everyone benefits from the collective work. *Free riders* are those who enjoy the benefits of the group effort without making a contribution. The participants in these studies were willing to pay some of their own money in order to "fine" (remove money from) the free riders. There was a very high rate of administering such punishment: 84% of the people administered punishment at least once, and the punishments were often harsh. These responses were especially disturbing to economists, because the discipline of economics is wedded to a view of people as rational and profit-maximizing—and giving up one's money to punish someone else reduces one's profit, so it seems irrational. Yet most people did it anyway.

Moreover, altruistic punishment had important effects for promoting cooperation. The researchers compared how the game proceeded when people could versus could not punish the free riders. When free riders went unpunished, people became stingier with their contributions to the group, and more and more took free rides. In contrast, when free riders were punished, free riding diminished over time, and people contributed increasing amounts to the group. Because cooperative contributions produced the greatest return for the whole group, everyone was best off in the latter situation—that is, in which free riders were punished and so everyone cooperated. Thus, sharp and harsh punishment of free riders promotes collective cooperation and beneficial results for the entire group.

The patterns of altruistic punishment are not limited to one culture. An ambitious cross-cultural project showed that a concern for fairness tends to triumph over ruthlessly rational self-interest everywhere that was studied.[38] These researchers studied people in widely dispersed and different cultures, including nomads and hunter-gatherers. The research included the Ultimatum Game, in which one person can divide up the reward any way she wants and the other can either accept the division or veto it, in which case neither one gets anything. There were also common goods games and dictator games in which one person can divide up the reward and the other has no say in the matter. In all societies, the simple profit-maximizing style of decision making was disconfirmed in general, although occasional individuals acted that way. Much more common was a pattern of exhibiting some sense of fairness, such as equity or equality.

My point is that nature gave us the capacity to adopt a perspective on helping and cooperation that goes beyond any biologically rooted impulse to help kin, and this capacity has been important in enabling human beings to be cultural animals. As a result of it, people show cultural patterns of helping and cooperation that are based on a connection to the collective. In nature, perhaps, shared genes can lead to helping and cooperation, but humans will act on the basis of shared humanity. And human beings everywhere seem guided by the abstract idea of fairness.

That sense of common community also explains the rise of institutionalized helping in human cultures. Much human helping is not a simple matter of one person benefiting another, but rather creating cultural structures that dispense help where it is needed. Modern societies have firefighters who are supported by taxes (thus paid by most members of the society) and who will travel to any burning home or building to save it. They support coast guards who roam the waters to rescue boaters who are in danger. Churches and philanthropies have long dispensed a broad range of help, often running hospitals, poorhouses, schools, and orphanages.

Modern societies often engage in extensive redistribution of wealth, essentially taking money from the rich to give to the poor. The more you earn or have, the more you pay, and indeed progressive income taxes dictate that the more you earn, the greater proportion of your earnings you pay in taxes, some of which is then used to help the poorest people to afford food and housing. Many governments also encourage helping by allowing charitable contributions to be tax deducted, and this amounts to a cultural structure that helps people to help others. All of these forms of helping would be inconceivable without culture, and nothing resembling them has been found in any other species.

Mating and Relationships

Like many other creatures, human beings form partnerships based on sexual intercourse and raising children. In the animal kingdom, the duration of such partnerships varies widely, ranging from a few scant moments of sex to lifelong monogamous unions. Our own species all by itself encompasses just as broad a range. Sexual matings range from one-night hook-ups to lifelong faithful marriages.

Many writers have emphasized that human matings have much in common with those in the animal world, reflecting the common evolutionary heritage and the common problems of sexual reproduction. But there are important differences too, and many of these involve the link to the collective community and the meanings it confers on mating. If James and Lynn have sex on Monday and again on Friday, with a marriage ceremony on Wednesday, the meaning of those two acts is demonstrably different. The first is premarital sex, which has been illegal and morally stigmatized in many societies, whereas the second occurs with the blessing of the state and indeed is a standard, expected feature of marriage. There is no such distinction in the couplings of other animals.

The importance and power of collective meanings are even more obvious in the breaking up of sexual relationships. Such relationships have endings in many species, but these simply happen and are more or less a private matter between the two individuals who have lost the wish to be together. No other animal has to get a lawyer or appear in court in order to separate from a sexual partner who is no longer wanted.

The (even) greater involvement of the community in the dissolution of sexual partnerships, as compared with forming sexual partnerships, reflects a common policy. Most countries make it easier to marry than to divorce, because they want to encourage people to marry and to stay married. This is not just some accident of random religious doctrine. As we saw in the section on families, states and communities have a vested interest in keeping families together. Families connect individuals to the country and society at large, and they also encourage people to do things that help the culture work. Hence states want to promote strong families. At the extreme, some countries have absolutely forbidden anyone to get a divorce.

Are human beings naturally monogamous? Opinions differ.[39] Monogamy is now the dominant law and practice in most modern countries, and it seems unlikely that monogamy would become law if it went violently against the grain of human nature. Then again, polygamy has been practiced by a majority of cultures in the history of the world, so the ascendancy of monogamy is a fairly recent development. Moreover, even in the modern world, the practice of monogamy is admittedly imperfect. Many Americans in fact marry several times. The monogamy laws simply require that they divorce one spouse before marrying another. Most are probably quite willing to do this, though others might have preferred to keep one partner even when adding a new one. The effect of the laws is to require people to manage their matings in a certain way, specifically producing serial monogamy.

Likewise, many married people mate briefly with someone other than their spouse. Recent animal studies have confirmed that this is far more common than previously thought, such that even supposedly monogamous species engage in a substantial amount of extra-pair couplings.[40] Evolutionary theory has suggested that such motives may run deep and be quite natural. Natural selection has favored males who spread their genes to multiple partners. Sure enough, throughout history, rich and powerful men have generally had it both ways, typically having one wife, who produces the most favored offspring, but also having an assortment of mistresses, concubines, lesser wives, or other lovers.[41] Biology also favors females who combine their own genes with the fittest possible male, even if that male is not willing to stick around to raise the child. Hence, one common and adaptive pattern is for a female to form a partnership with one man who can be counted on to support her and her children, while secretly having sex with a higher-status or genetically superior male so as to get pregnant by him. All of this is natural, but human cultures seek to regulate if not prohibit it. Adultery was widely illegal in many places and periods in history, and though in modern America most such laws have been repealed, it is still grounds for divorce and can be problematic and expensive in various other ways.

Culture is also relevant to mating at the front end. Finding and attracting a potential partner may seem like a private matter for individuals, but there are norms, scripts, rules, expectations, and many other signs that the mating process is shaped by collective meanings. Even just the things people do to make themselves look appealing to the opposite gender are heavily informed by culture. In some places, people engage in seemingly bizarre (to Westerners) practices such as putting metal rings around their necks to elongate them, or stretching the skin of the penis. More commonly, people use jewelry, makeup, hairstyles, and clothes, the fashions of which change from one time to another. These changes suggest that there is no single ideal of human beauty (though to be sure there are common themes, such as symmetry and youthful appearance) and that success in the mating market requires a demonstration that one knows what is currently valued and admired in the collective society. Fashions or hairstyles that were attractive in the 1930s or 1950s will appear old-fashioned today, and so the person must present himself in accordance with the current ideals.

By the same token, acquiring a mate requires an elaborate series of steps that follow a script that may be fairly uniform within a culture even though it varies across cultures. In the late 1800s, courtship consisted largely of visits by the young man to the young woman at her home, where the couple might sit on the porch in the presence of her parents and carry on polite conversations. The automobile revolutionized the process by allowing the couple to travel elsewhere where they could conduct their conversations in private and possibly do some kissing. (Youngsters at the time dropped the term *courting* and instead adopted the term *date*, which up until then had referred exclusively to an assignation with a prostitute.) Trips to movies became a staple of dating through much of the twentieth century. The point is simply that in order to find a partner, one had to know the current practices that prevailed in the community and to follow them.

The unfolding of the relationship is also shaped by collective meanings. These include moralistic notions about how much sexual activity is appropriate, which may depend on things such as how many dates the couple has had. They also include explicit laws, such as the recent efforts to curtail date rape and sexual harassment. All in all, the community and its meanings continue to be a powerfully present force in the process of mating.

Power

Social animals face problems of power. Solitary creatures that satisfy their needs purely by interacting directly with the physical world do not need to worry about power. A grove of trees does not really have a power structure, in any meaningful sense. Power conflicts can also be avoided even among social creatures as long as they are programmed always to want and share the same things and to behave harmoniously so as to get them. But as soon as individual creatures want different outcomes—and especially if they both want something that only one of them can have—the social group has to have a system by which the wishes of one can prevail over the wishes of another. Power resides in that system.

Power is thus essentially an aspect of situation structure. Power entails that one person has control over another person's outcomes. Someone has power over you to the extent that she can alter how much money you get, how much pain or pleasure you experience, your access to food and other resources, and the like. You may well do what the powerful person wants simply because she could potentially change your life in some meaningful way. The use of power involves influencing another person's behavior. In an act of power, one person makes a second person behave in a way that the person would not otherwise behave and might not want to behave. Power thus operates on a zero sum basis, by and large. Either I do what I want to do, or you make me do something different. We cannot both have our way, and so there is a winner and a loser. To the extent that I do what you want, I give up doing what I want. If we want the same thing, power is irrelevant. Put another way, there is a fixed amount of control over what happens, and it has to be divided up among the people who are involved, and so one's gain is the other's loss.

In social animals, power is typically based on fighting, and success at fighting is based on size, strength, ruthless meanness, and perhaps mastery of tactics. Often power is accorded to the strongest male, who can boss the others around and keep the females for himself. Needless to say, most cultures today do not make their group decisions by letting the biggest, meanest man tell everyone else what to do. Thus, the dynamics of power change as we move from merely social to cultural animals. The effect of culture on power is chiefly found in two main trends, which may at first glance seem to be opposites. The first of these is an extension of power due to the tools of culture. The second is a far-reaching and progressive curbing of the power of individuals by changes in the cultural design.

To appreciate how culture initially extended power, it is useful to contrast how power works in nonhuman social groups. Among wild horses, for example, power is held by a strong and mature male and is usually gained by physical fighting and intimidation. One such alpha male will rule for a year or two. During that time he claims exclusive sexual access to all of the females, but maintaining that requires constant vigilance. He has to herd the females together and run off any other males. There is little time for sleep. He may father a group of young horses by copulating eagerly with every female. The accumulated strain of fighting, watching, chasing, and copulating takes a severe toll on the fellow, often leaving him physically exhausted or even broken for the rest of his life.[42] Thus, the alpha male horse maintains his power by constant physical exertion, and his power extends only as far as his physical prowess can prevail.

Human culture, in contrast, allows power to be sustained and exercised by many other means. Though some rulers have certainly been killed in their sleep, there was never a general pattern of trying to stay awake throughout one's entire reign. Underlings could be recruited and to varying degrees trusted to enforce the ruler's power. The network of supporters, combined with the transmission of information, has enabled human rulers to exercise power over people they never see and who may live vast distances away. During the height of the British empire, for example, it was hardly necessary for the king or queen to sustain direct physical intimidation over every individual subject. Instead, the sovereign could rule from home over millions of people, including many in India, Australia, and Africa.

Yet the king was not really like the alpha male horse only with better means of enforcing his rule. This brings up the second trend, which is that the evolution of culture has put more and more limits on individual power. The British empire may have seemed superficially to be an elaborate system to serve the will of a single person, but in reality the king's decisions and actions had to conform to a steadily tightening network of rules and restrictions. The king's powers were explicitly limited already in 1215 by the Magna Carta, which ceded some of his power to the aristocrats. In the so-called Glorious Revolution of 1688, Parliament removed the king and invited another fellow to come over from Holland and take the British throne, thereby establishing that Parliament was superior to the king. Over the centuries, the popularly elected House of Commons gained power at the expense of the hereditary House of Lords. Some kings who failed to conform to the will of the people (however defined) were thwarted and even beheaded. The alpha male horse at least got to enjoy sex with all of the females, but by the 1900s the British king was not even allowed to marry the one woman he desired (because she was an American divorcée), and so he had to abdicate his crown. Today's British monarch is a symbolic figurehead with almost no real power, and the government is run by a succession of elected officials.

Much the same process has occurred (or is still occurring) everywhere. Whereas once every land was ruled by some sort of king or queen, now only a few have them, and most of these have no real power. In the move to modernity, one state after another did away with kings and queens altogether, but only a tiny handful (such as the Netherlands) have changed in the opposite direction and added a royal monarch. For a time, strongman dictators held extensive power in lands that had dispensed with their hereditary monarchs, but the list of such dictators grows ever shorter and their hold on power ever more tenuous. At present, it is hard to predict just how long these few old men, such as Fidel Castro and Robert Mugabe, can maintain their iron grip, but it is a good bet that when they leave or die, they will be replaced by new rulers who will be more accountable to the people in their countries.

The United States was founded by men who had an acute belief that the concentration of power in one person's hands is detrimental to society. They therefore wrote a constitution that dispersed power widely through many different people and offices. Once, in some places, a king might decree a new tax or law, but in America no person or small group can accomplish that. The law must be passed by two houses of Congress, which are composed of officials who depend on the votes of many adults. The president can do no more than sign or veto the law, and even his and Congress's mutually agreed decisions can be overthrown by the appointed judges on the Supreme Court. The implementation of the law depends on the actions and interpretations of countless police officers and various others. The American president is the single most powerful person, but he cannot make laws (only sign them), and his power depends on having a majority of the voters elect him (and he only may serve up to a maximum of 8 years). In addition, the alpha male horse would probably sneer at the president's sexual opportunities, especially considering that one recent president nearly lost his job in connection with a few banal minutes of oral sex with a young woman who worked for him.

The cultural curbing of power is not limited to the men at the top but appears instead to be a pattern of cultural evolution throughout the society. The so-called robber barons who made fortunes in America in the 1800s could not repeat their exploits today. John D. Rockefeller, for example, assembled a remarkable business empire in the oil industry that controlled the market both vertically and horizontally, but the antitrust rules and monopoly-busting mechanisms of modern government ensure that no company can gain such power today. Even in the small sphere of the family, the power of the head of household has been radically diminished. Today's husbands and fathers cannot impose their will on the other family members, including not being able to beat or strike their family members as bygone patriarchs could. Husbands are no longer entitled to have sex with their wives without their consent, and instead the husband must persuade the wife to copulate, or else he will remain celibate.

Thus, cultural life has progressively extended power in some ways— and progressively restricted it in other ways. These are clearly opposing trends in terms of their impact on the power of individuals, but at another level they complement each other. Both involve transforming power from the property of single individuals to something that resides in the collective. The king served as a symbol for the collective. Unlike the wild horses, the decline or death of the king did not typically create instant anarchy that had to be resolved by open competition for power. Instead, typically, the king's death was followed by an orderly succession during which the designated heir would take over. Most of the rest of the power structure could remain in place, and the ministers, officers, and others continued to perform their duties, smoothly transferring their loyalty to the new ruler. The smoothness of this transition is an important sign that the power actually rested in the system rather than in the individual, because it was not dependent on the particular individual.

The collectively shared meanings do more than make specific rules to prevent abuses of power. Exercising power in a cultural context, as opposed to a merely social (might makes right) context, generally requires legitimacy. One does what the ruler says, not from direct fear that the ruler will beat or kill you (though those are still influences of last resort), but because you and everyone else acknowledge that the ruler has the legitimate right to tell you what to do.

The maintenance of power is thus often dependent on *legitimizing myths*.[43] These are ideas that purport to explain why those in power deserve to be in power. In an ostensible meritocracy, those in power have to contend that they have superior merit, such as by being smarter, more virtuous, more talented, or harder working than those who rank below them. After all, some degree of inequality is inevitable, and nearly all societies have power structures, so the crucial question is whether the inequality of power is fair and legitimate or not. The individuals or groups in power must typically find some reason—persuasive enough that everyone will accept it—for establishing that their power is indeed fair and legitimate.

The people who hold power are often chronically in quest for ways to justify and legitimize their power. As one group's hold on power loses its legitimacy, it can soon lose its power too. In South Africa, for example, the white minority retained a firm hold on political power until it gradually lost its legitimacy. The international outcry against apartheid gradually compelled the white ruling party to yield its privileged position and to share power with the black and colored (i.e., mixed race) majority. On a much smaller scale, in America, husbands were once automatically recognized as the natural heads of households with an innate right to make the decisions and give commands, and wives and children were expected to obey. Gradually, that view was questioned and lost its presumptive legitimacy, and most families shifted toward more egalitarian systems in which the wives had a greater say in decisions. Far fewer modern husbands expect to be able to issue unquestioned commands and make all of the major decisions themselves as compared with several generations ago.[44]

Throughout history, the frequent links between religion and politics have been driven partly by religion's ability to lend legitimacy to the power arrangement. As we have seen, ruling groups have the chronic problem of justifying their hold on power, and religion can claim some of the highest and most powerful values. If the religion says that the king rules by divine right, for example, then he can issue his commands and edicts with little need to worry about having them questioned.

Religions change when they become allied to the status quo and the ruling class. The history of Christianity provides a typical example.[45] Like many religious movements, Christianity started out by appealing to the downtrodden and powerless, and it offered a profound critique of the worldly system of power and society. Once the Roman emperors were Christians, however, Christianity became allied with the ruling class. At this point, Christianity was called upon to help shore up the government by legitimizing the status quo. Instead of offering a critique of the current political system, it began to explain that God had created the current system for divine reasons, and people should be content with their station in society rather than aspiring to change. In St. Augustine's famous analogy, the whole of society is like a human body, and a person should no more wish to change to a different position in society than a finger should wish to become an eye.[46] Such doctrines encourage the relatively powerless to accept their status and position and to accept that those who hold power deserve to hold it.

In short, the quest to bolster legitimacy is typically an ongoing problem for those in power. Even as they hold and exercise power, they must remain on the lookout for ideas or values that can justify their position of power and their influence over others. The need for such legitimizing myths is unique to the cultural context of power and thus unknown to the exercise of power in merely social animals. (The wild horse who rules the pack does not need one.) It also reveals how power depends on cultural meanings that reside in the collective.

The restrictions on the exercise of power and the need for legitimizing myths both can be seen as moves that reduce discrepancies in power and thus empower the people who start out with less power. By definition, subordinates lack the means to get their way or to force others to do what they want. There are, however, a variety of "weapons of the weak" by which people low in power can redress the imbalance and exert some influence, at least to some degree. The reciprocity norm puts some constraints on power and prevents powerful people from simply exploiting those underneath them.[47] Perhaps especially in close relationships marked by unequal power, the obligation to be kind and helpful to those who have benefited you can serve as an important force to make the more powerful person confer benefits on the less powerful partners.

Guilt is an important weapon of the weak. By making the powerholder feel guilty, the subordinate can influence the powerholder to do what the subordinate wants. Guilt is therefore a means of reducing power inequalities.[48] The use of guilt as a countermeasure to objective power depends on having the powerholder care about the subordinate. Boiled down to its simple core, guilt-based influence is a matter of saying, "What you are doing is hurting me," and the powerholder is supposed to respond by changing his actions so as not to inflict that hurt. If the powerholder's response is "So what?" then guilt cannot get any leverage toward bringing about the desired changes. Only to the extent that the powerholder desires not to hurt the subordinate will guilt be an effective force for changing the powerholder's behavior and allowing the subordinate to get his way. Likewise, guilt depends on empathic identification and hence on theory of mind. Animals that lack the sense of identification with other minds cannot spontaneously feel guilty, though perhaps they can be made by others to know that they have broken a rule and might be punished.

Guilt often depends on meaning too, and in that sense it invokes the collective prescriptions for how to feel. Guilt can be deflected and perhaps ended by appealing to moral rules that say the powerholder is doing the right thing. Some of these include abstract rules that apply to everyone.

Others may invoke the ruler's legitimizing myths, which supposedly make it acceptable for her to dominate others—sometimes even to send them to their deaths.

Relations Between Groups

Throughout this book, I have emphasized the advantages of belonging to a group. These are substantial and abundant. But there is a hidden dimension that probably intensified the evolutionary push toward group life. Life in nature involves competition, and groups can certainly compete better than individuals. The hidden dimension is that individuals cannot usually compete against groups. Therefore, once groups exist anywhere, everyone else has to join a group, if only for self-protection. Put another way, this book has emphasized what happens inside groups, but some features of human nature have been shaped by what happens between groups. The so-called intergroup dimension is an important factor in understanding human behavior. Nature probably prepared us to align ourselves with others and to square off against other groups.

Intergroup relations are often competitive, sometimes hostile, and occasionally brutal. Though individuals may occasionally be responsible for wars and other violence, in general, warfare is group against group. Wars (both international and civil), genocide, gang fights, oppression, and many more evils of human history are further manifestations of the natural tendency for groups to oppose other groups.

In today's America, there is a strong public sentiment to overcome and end certain forms of prejudice, especially those against various racial and ethnic groups. This is historically unusual and reflects the high moral aspirations of American society. But the task is a steep uphill battle, because prejudice is simply one more manifestation of the basic tendency for groups to regard each other as threatening rivals. Stereotypes and prejudices are a meaning-based version of the basic readiness to regard other groups as enemies. One well-established finding in social psychology is that people tend to identify with their own group against outsiders, even if the group has relatively little significance. If they have a chance to divide up some rewards or resources, they will give a bigger share to members of their own group than to others. Groups may be formed on the basis of seemingly minimal, even trivial criteria, but people still cleave together and square off against others.[49]

What gives rise to this pattern of *in-group favoritism*? Several researchers set out to test this theory with a seemingly foolproof plan.[50] They decided they would start off with groups that were so meaningless and trivial that there would not be any in-group favoritism, and then one by one they would add in other factors such as perceived similarity, common goals, shared values, extended opportunities to get to know each other, and the like. Then they could see at what point people started showing preferential treatment to their own group. The plan seemed good, but it failed for a surprising reason—the researchers could never get to the starting point. That is, they were unable to construct a group that was so trivial or random that people didn't show in-group favoritism. Even when people knew that everyone had been assigned to the groups utterly at random, that they did not necessarily have anything in common, and that the group was only temporary and had neither a purpose nor a future, people still directed more resources toward their group members than toward members of the other group.

Thus, people have a very strong and pervasive tendency to band together with others and to sort the world into "us" and "them." It is perhaps noteworthy that in these studies there were always two groups, and so it is not clear whether being a member of the in-group or the out-group was more salient. There is relatively little evidence to distinguish these two, but in cooperation versus competition studies, it has been found that individuals and groups behave differently, and when an individual is playing against a group, the individual already starts adopting the more aggressive, competitive style that is typical of groups.[51] This is one sign that membership in the out-group is more salient than membership in the in-group, but perhaps it just reflects the way that antagonistic styles prevail over cooperative ones. In any case, the readiness to form groups and to act as if strong, important bonds exist do seem quite plausible as tendencies that would have been selected in evolution. When a lone individual goes up against a group, he is at a serious disadvantage, and if the dispute is over some resource (such as access to food or water), the group is likely to win. People may have evolved to recognize the presence of an enemy group and to seek to form bonds and alliances for their own protection.

An unpleasant implication of this work is that prejudice against outgroups is likely to be the normal, natural tendency. For decades, it has been fashionable for social scientists to claim that prejudices are simply the result of socializing pressures and misinformation that people pick up from their misguided culture.[52] Such a view is appealing because it holds up the hope that if we can simply stop society from teaching children to dislike others, prejudice will vanish and society will be filled with tolerance and harmony. Reluctantly, I have come to see this view as naïve. I do not know of any society that has been shown to be free from prejudice—certainly not any society that consists of multiple groups or that has regular contact with other societies. Moreover, prejudices seem to form quite quickly and easily, and it takes considerable training and effort to overcome them.[53]

Problems of Groups

In this book, I have generally emphasized the advantages of working and living in groups. Nonetheless, social psychologists have found a variety of drawbacks, and these deserve brief mention before we close our discussion of interaction.

The major advantages of culture are best achieved when people work together in an organized fashion, which entails that people have distinct roles (permitting meaningful division of labor) that complement each other. Sometimes, however, working in groups simply means that people submerge themselves into the group, such that their relative efforts and contributions are indistinguishable. This result is far less effective and can produce destructive side effects. The crucial difference appears to be whether the situation is set up so that people will know who does what and therefore will hold each other responsible for their actions.

One important form of submerging the self in the group is called *diffusion of responsibility*. This term was coined by John Darley and Bibb Latane in their efforts to understand why bystanders may fail to come to the aid of a victim of a crime or other emergency.[54] This line of work began with the famous incident in 1963 in which a young woman was murdered outside her apartment in New York. A man attacked her, left, returned, attacked her again, and then left and returned a third time, over the course of 45 minutes. Nearly 40 people saw or heard at least one of the attacks, but no one took any action (not even making a phone call) to save her. The news media discussed the incident at length because there were so many people who could have saved her, but no one did anything. Darley and Latane showed that the presence of so many onlookers probably worked to her disadvantage, because everyone thought that someone else would do something. Their laboratory experiments staged emergencies with varying numbers of people present. If someone thought he was the only person who could help the victim, he was likely to do so. But if he thought that there were many other people who were also aware of the situation, he tended to leave it to them. Ironically, with everyone leaving the action up to everyone else, the victim was less likely to get help from a group than from an individual.

Diffusion of responsibility happens in many settings other than emergencies. Many couples find that chores do not get done unless someone is designated as responsible for them. If both members pay the bills, for example, you might think that the bills would be all the more likely to get paid, but instead it may occur that each one sometimes assumes the other will do it, and the bills end up overdue.

Social loafing is a particularly pernicious extension of diffusion of responsibility. Social loafing (also known as the free rider problem, as discussed above) is a tendency to let the other group members do the work while you coast along.[55] Lab studies have confirmed a broad tendency for people to put out less effort when they are merged into a group than when they work alone or when their inputs to the group are kept individually identified. It occurs most commonly when no one keeps track of how much each person contributes. It is no accident that most corporations, factories, and other profit-making institutions have shifted toward greater individual accountability over recent decades. Accountability essentially means keeping track of how much each individual accomplishes, and it is a powerful antidote to diffusion of responsibility and social loafing.

The basketball player Stacey King once made a joke that illustrates the principle behind social loafing. King was in his rookie season and, when he wasn't sitting on the bench, played alongside Michael Jordan, who was generally regarded as the greatest player ever. After one memorable game, King spoke to reporters after the game and, using standard sports phrasing, said, "I'll always remember this [game] as the night Michael Jordan and I combined for 70 points." Scoring 70 points would indeed be a remarkable feat for two players, and so cooperating with Jordan to reach that goal would reflect well on him. If one pursued individual accountability to examine the score more closely, however, one would have found that Jordan had scored 69 and King only 1.

The infamous *commons dilemma* is also related to the lack of individual responsibility. The term comes from animal husbandry and refers to grazing areas that were open to anyone who wanted to use them. Any farmer or shepherd might therefore bring his herd to feast on the grass that was owned and shared in common by all. Sharing resources in this way might seem like a potentially efficient and friendly way of managing them. Unfortunately, it leads to a pervasive problem of overgrazing, with the result that the grass is unable to grow back, and eventually the resource is depleted or even destroyed. The grass will replenish itself as long as it is not entirely exhausted, but because no individual takes responsibility for limiting the usage, it tends to be exhausted utterly.

Although the commons dilemma originally referred to feeding herds of sheep or other animals, the world is now suffering from the same problem with a different element, water, and the animals that live in it. Grasslands can be owned by individuals who can take responsibility to manage them effectively and make sure that they are not depleted past the point of replenishing themselves. This strategy doesn't work with water, of course, because fish can easily swim from one area to another. Indeed, even national governments often cannot maintain control, because fish swim across the imaginary lines in the ocean that define the boundaries between countries. Each fishing boat will take its own catch from the common stock of fish, and each boat has a financial incentive to catch as many as it can. No individual boat endangers the stock of fish, but collectively the boats do gradually catch so many fish that there are not enough left to reproduce the stock. (After all, the number of new fish hatched each season depends on how many adult fish are still alive to lay and fertilize eggs.) Overfishing has become a severe problem in many parts of the world.

Another failure of groups is responsible for the disappointing performance of so many committees. Gordon Stasser and his colleagues approached this problem by acknowledging the standard justification for forming committees in the first place, namely, that drawing multiple people together will help bring more information to bear on an issue and result in a more enlightened, rational decision than a single person could make.[56] Ideally, every member of a committee would contribute unique information to the discussion, and the committee as a whole would reach a higher level of wisdom than the sum of its parts would predict. It's a lovely principle. Unfortunately, the data suggest that committees often work in the opposite way.

Stasser's experiments asked groups to decide which job candidate to hire. Each member of the committee was given some information about two candidates. The experiments were carefully set up so that there were more reasons to hire candidate Anderson than candidate Baker, but the pro-Anderson reasons were scattered through the group, whereas everybody had the pro-Baker reasons. For example, each person might have one reason to hire Anderson and four reasons to hire Baker. Everybody had the same four reasons to hire Baker but a different reason to hire Anderson. Only if they pooled their information—which is the ostensible purpose of a committee—would they realize that Anderson was the better candidate. Instead of combining their reasons, however, the groups converged on Baker as the better candidate. They did not bring up their unique perspectives or special knowledge. Instead, they talked about what they all had in common, namely, the many reasons for hiring Baker.

Thus, sadly, committees appear to work by ignoring much information and focusing on what they have in common rather than by each member sharing her own unique perspective. The group ends up being less than the sum of its parts.

Part of the problem for groups is that members are often reluctant to disagree openly with each other. If a committee is really going to succeed at integrating diverse viewpoints, the members must be willing to bring up views or information that clash with what someone else has said. But people don't want to make waves. Irving Janis borrowed the term *groupthink* from George Orwell's novel *1984* to refer to this pattern.[57] Groups want consensus and feel best when everyone agrees. Hence they avoid possible disagreements and suppress any urge to question what the other members of the group (especially a leader) may have said. Janis concluded that these tendencies have led to many historical catastrophes. For example, President John Kennedy's advisors were committed to consensus and reluctant to disagree with each other, so they went along with the plans for an invasion of Cuba that turned into the costly Bay of Pigs disaster. Moreover, because people keep their doubts and objections to themselves, everyone gets a false impression that everyone else agrees enthusiastically. Some people will even act on this assumption and exert pressure on the occasional individual who will deviate from the group consensus or question what the group is thinking. The objections are then stifled, thereby contributing all the more to the illusion that everyone is in agreement.

Groupthink goes beyond the pressure for consensus and uniformity.[58] The group gradually develops a sense of being invulnerable. This tendency may be especially strong among privileged, powerful, elite groups (such as Kennedy's advisors in the example above). This sense of being highly powerful contributes to an exaggerated optimism, and as a result the group may take foolish risks. It also fosters a sense of moral superiority, so that groups may ignore ethically questionable implications or consequences of their decisions. The Committee of Public Safety that ran France after the French Revolution had this sense, as did the Russian communists after the Russian Revolution. These groups gradually began to sentence large numbers of people to death, buoyed by their sense of historic mission and moral superiority.

Along with the sense of omnipotence and moral superiority, groupthink tends to promote derogatory views of the external world. Warnings and danger signs are ignored once the group has its plan, and members may support each other in rationalizing that potential problems will not be taken seriously. Opposing forces and leaders are likewise dismissed either as weak and incompetent, hence not worth worrying about, or as evil and hence not worthy of compromise and negotiation. The attack on Pearl Harbor illustrates the latter point.[59] Both sides regarded the other as evil and incompetent. Racist prejudice probably contributed to both perceptions. Japan and the United States perceived each other as wicked warmongers bent on conquering other peoples for selfish reasons.[60] The Japanese believed that the weak and decadent Americans would give up after Pearl Harbor, being unwilling to bear the costs and sacrifices of war. The Americans refused to believe that the Japanese were capable of carrying out a strike against the American stronghold, and even after Pearl Harbor many top American military experts continued to think that the Germans must have planned the operation for their Japanese allies. The American commanders in Pearl Harbor had various warnings that an attack could take place, but they dismissed them. One of the admiral's staff of advisors was asked during testimony whether they had considered the reports of various junior officers that a dawn attack by the Japanese could achieve complete surprise and inflict serious damage on the American fleet. "Yes, we considered this point, but somehow or other, we always felt that 'it couldn't happen here.'"[61] Admiral Husband E. Kimmel himself, the commander of the entire Pacific fleet, responded to warnings from Washington, D.C., that negotiations with Japan had broken down utterly by saying, "[T]here was no chance of a surprise air attack on Hawaii at that particular time."[62]

The failures of groups bring us back to human nature and culture. Culture operates by linking together many different people who perform different roles. To benefit from culture, people must belong to a group, but they must also have distinct, individual identities. When they lose their individual identity and melt into the group, the results are often counterproductive or destructive.

Epilogue

Why do people think, feel, and act as they do? Psychology has created a great number of narrow, specific explanations for particular thoughts, feelings, and actions. Its ultimate explanations, in contrast, generally hark back to the two eternal themes of nature and culture.

In psychology, the nature side of the question has recently been dominated by evolutionary psychologists, and their research emphasizes the *similarities* between human beings and other animals. To be sure, the evolutionary psychologists also have some interest in differences, especially gender differences, but their influential accounts of these still go back to similarities. That is, they tend to point out that the roles played by human males and females are fundamentally similar to the male and female roles in other animal species. In contrast, the culture side has been the province of cultural psychologists, and their stock in trade is *differences*, specifically, differences between cultures. When one sees the word *culture* in the title of a research talk or article, one can almost always safely predict that the focus will be on cultural differences.

In this book, I have sought to switch those perspectives. Evolutionary similarities and cultural differences are not the only ways to think. A more positive and powerful view of human nature can be created by focusing on evolutionary differences and cultural similarities. That is, to understand what makes us distinctively human, psychologists should look hard for biologically based differences between humans and other species. And we should also survey what all cultures have in common.

Crucially, those are linked. If nature has indeed shaped the human psyche for participation in culture, then the keys to understanding human nature lie in the biological differences between us and other species—which are, I have proposed, largely aimed at facilitating the features that are common to culture in general. The similarities between cultures are vitally intertwined with the evolutionary differences that separate humans from other animals.

I have proposed that culture is a strategy, in the sense that culture appeared because it served the biological goals of survival and reproduction. Cultural animals survive and reproduce better than their biological relatives that are not cultural. Culture must offer advantages that produce those benefits.

How are those benefits created? In a good system—and there are many good systems, though many bad ones too—the whole is more than the sum of its parts. Everybody working together in a large system produces better results than everybody working separately, alone. All in all, there is more to go around when people work together in a system, and so nearly everybody is better off. That's why nature made us for culture: Because culture would multiply our individual powers, so that everyone together would create a better life for everyone (well, almost everyone).

The benefits do seem to be quite real. Human life expectancy in developed nations is moving steadily upward, and with a healthy lifestyle and a bit of luck the average person will soon be able to anticipate living for a century or more. This is close to triple the life expectancy that people had in the not-so-distant past. What other species has managed to triple its life expectancy by dint of its own efforts and interventions? Culture alone has made it possible for humans to achieve this astounding feat of extending individual life. Likewise, reproduction has succeeded remarkably. In the relatively short span of 200,000 years, the human population has gone from a single woman to more than 6 billion souls.[1] If the planet were larger, we would probably have more, and indeed most of the recent efforts by the culture have aimed more at curbing than furthering the increase in population. We have all the people we need, and overpopulation is now a much greater threat than extinction.

To be sure, culture has brought its share of new problems. The advance of technology has created some monsters, such as weapons of mass destruction, efficient genocide, pollution, and economic crises, not to mention alienation, moral decay, and bad haircuts. My ideas have been criticized (with some justification) for having a positive view of the impact of culture, neglecting all of the terrible things that it also brings. Yes, culture creates tools that can be used for evil purposes. Remember, though, that nature's criteria for success are survival and reproduction, and by both criteria the human population has done very well, despite its occasional ugliness and misbehavior.

What are the basic, universal features of culture that ultimately help people to live longer and raise more healthy children? I have suggested four main ones. First, culture (not individuals) can create and sustain language, which greatly increases the power of human thought. Language enables people to access the world of meaning and to apply it to their social and physical environments. Ideas can be communicated, analyzed logically, improved, and stored. Inherent structures of meaning, such as grammatical and mathematical relationships, as well as reasoning, can be used in ways that other animals cannot even imagine. Moreover, language enables the human mind to think beyond the present surroundings, extending into the past and future as well as to far-away places. Language is the brain's software, without which its power would be ineffective.

Second, culture permits the collective accumulation of knowledge. The new generation learns what the old generation knew, rather than having to figure everything out for itself. Over the centuries, this has proven to be a remarkably powerful engine of progress. And progress—in understanding, in technology, in altering the physical surroundings to suit us, and even in revising the systems of culture so that people treat each other better—sets humanity apart from what other creatures have been able to do.

Third, division of labor produces immense gains in the quality of work and task performance. Division of labor is simply, indisputably better than its alternative. If someone tried to start a corporation today that did not use division of labor and instead had everyone perform every task, it would not be even remotely competitive and indeed would almost certainly be out of business within a year. The advantages of division of labor are so ubiquitous and ineluctable that even nature has recognized them: Most species have some division of labor based on gender. But culture greatly increased the power of division of labor, starting perhaps with hunting groups that relied on differentiated roles instead of simply mass action. As different people perform different roles, they become specialists and experts, and so each task is performed by an expert rather than by a jack-of-all-trades. The result is better overall performance.

Last, culture can create a network of exchange relationships. Many animals cooperate and help, so that mutually beneficial interactions can and do occur, but mostly these are limited to blood relatives. In a human economic system, however, people can have mutually beneficial interactions with total strangers. Money (or some other medium) allows people to exchange goods and services in ways that benefit both parties, and this leads to the general increase in wealth that is (almost) everywhere produced by free trade.

That list is not necessarily exhaustive. Perhaps there are other ways that culture produces benefits that ultimately help people to survive and reproduce better. But those four benefits of culture are already quite substantial and could well be sufficient to explain why nature selected in favor of hominids who could participate more fully in culture.

The evolutionary process of creating a cultural animal was presumably one of modifying traits already found in our biological ancestors, rather than creating wholly new capacities, though by using those biological traits in a cultural context, some wholly new capacities, such as reading, space travel, and musical composition, emerged. Our biological forebears were somewhat intelligent; human intelligence is much higher. They had a fair-sized memory; human memory is dramatically larger. They had a motive to form social bonds; humans form bonds not just to each other but also to large communities. They had curiosity about their environments, especially when young; humans seek to understand and explain much of what happens around them all through their lives. Other animal minds could combine information only to a small extent; human beings can use the conscious processing space to integrate a much larger amount of information. Some animals could restrain impulses under direct threat; humans can alter their behavior much more extensively and in response to far more abstract, distal, or indirect reasons. They could recognize and respond specially to other members of their species; humans understand each other as having similar minds and similar inner processes, which can be inferred or anticipated with empathy, thereby creating a community of minds.

Unfinished Tasks

My goal in this book was to present an integrated, comprehensible, systematic account of human nature. To keep it to a reasonable size, it was necessary to skip some parts of the question, and I am the first to admit that the entire project would benefit from further inquiry. Let me note what seem to me to be the most obvious gaps.

The main source of information on which this work is based is the accumulated knowledge in my own field of social psychology. The book has had to draw on ideas from a much wider sphere, ranging from economic systems theory to evolutionary theory. Undoubtedly, I had to cut some corners and simplify some of the complexities of current thinking in those fields. In particular, my account of human evolution is fairly speculative. The core argument—that nature designed us for participation in culture—was derived from, and based on, a survey of what social psychologists have learned about how people think, act, and feel, and not from any original study of fossils or DNA records. I have proposed that natural selection favored human beings who could exploit the potential advantages of culture so as to better their chances of survival and reproduction, but this process occurred long before the first social psychology laboratory began functioning, and so my database cannot prove that conclusion. It is also plausible that ideas of coevolution could greatly enhance the account offered here, such as if people coevolved with language, division of labor, and the like. As evolution moved from our apelike ancestors through the hominids to our own species, there may have been some reciprocal steps such that creatures who could talk some fared better than those who could not, and those who could combine words fared better than those who could simply use single words, and so forth. Likewise, hominids who could sort themselves into separate roles, thereby specializing in different tasks, would generally outperform hominids who had all the same other abilities but did not divide labor according to individually differentiated roles.

My original plan and indeed my first draft contained a chapter on development, but that had to be removed to make way for the lengthening coverage of other topics, and I still regret its absence. Biologists know that the sequence of development is important for understanding the life course and functioning of an organism, and social scientists recognize correspondingly the central power of socialization for molding a little savage into a productive, responsible citizen. Developmental psychologists have amassed a great deal of information about the processes and steps by which children grow into functioning adults, and this could undoubtedly help inform a full understanding of cultural animals.

The focus on general patterns has led to an unfortunate neglect of the fact that people are different in many ways. Most human traits show variation, and this is certainly true of the centrally important cultural animal traits as well: Some people are more intelligent than others, have more self-control, more empathy, and so on. My neglect of individual differences is ironic, because the quest for a working model of human nature has been one of the central goals of personality theory for many decades, and I have embraced that goal while neglecting the extensive work that personality psychologists have done in mapping out and understanding all of the ways that people differ from each other.

Gender differences are a particularly important and perennially interesting set of differences among people. My initial plan for the book was to provide two models of human nature, one male and one female. Gradually, however, as the focus shifted to the cultural animal theory, the emphasis on recounting important gender differences receded, and the topic is mostly absent from this book. The theory of the cultural animal offers a potentially powerful new perspective on gender differences, though in the current climate of politically charged discussions, it is difficult to look at data on gender in an open-minded manner. Elsewhere, I have proposed that men and women specialize in different spheres of interpersonal relations, with women excelling and favoring the narrower sphere of close, intimate relationships, while men seem more suited to larger groups and less intimate interactions, such as with strangers or acquaintances.[2] To me, this offers the possibility of reinterpreting the history and current status of gender differences without the usual insistence that all must be explained in terms of sexist men banding together to oppress women. In any case, there may be value in trying to view gender differences through the lens of biological evolution as it was connected to cultural systems.

Social and Cultural Animals

Thinkers throughout the ages, from Aristotle to Aronson, have referred to the human being as "the social animal." That designation is correct as far as it goes—but I think it does not go nearly far enough. Humans are not the only social animals. Arguably, they are not even the most social of animals. For example, does an ant ever seek out some time for itself, to be away from everyone else? The emphasis on being social has helped illuminate many important aspects of human life, but it does not go to the heart of what makes human beings distinctively different.

Rather, culture is what is special about human beings. That explains my choice of title for this book. To be sure, the beginnings of culture have been observed in several dozen other species, so culture per se is not uniquely human. But no other animal uses culture to anywhere near the extent that humans do. It is fair to say that nearly all human beings rely on culture for their survival, and in this respect they are widely different from the other animals in which some forms of cultural activity (such as potato washing or tool use) have been recorded. Without their culture, those animals' lives would not be much different. Human life without culture is almost impossible to imagine, however, and to the extent it could be imagined, it would be vastly different (and vastly worse) than the life we know. Without culture and its language, we could scarcely even think, let alone get a cooked meal.

The differences between the merely social animals and the fully cultural animals are central to this understanding of human nature. Let me revisit a few. Social animals gain some advantage by means of mass action, in which they work together to achieve a difficult goal. Cultural animals, however, use division of labor to perform complementary roles and tasks, thereby realizing the startling gains in quality and quantity of performance that come from expert specialization within a working system.

Social animals solve problems and occasionally copy each other's solutions, thereby enabling them to benefit from each other. However, these advances are rarely sustained for long, and the next generation usually has to start over. In contrast, cultures store knowledge in the collective and transmit it to the next generation. In principle, once any member of a culture solves a problem, it is solved for everyone forever. Over the centuries, the progress of cultural animals is immense, while social animals essentially run in place.

Social animals sometimes cooperate with and help each other, so that both can benefit in the long run. Altruistic behavior may have benefits for survival and reproduction, but in social animals, it is mostly limited to close relatives. In contrast, cultures promote exchanges between people who are not related, thereby vastly increasing the sphere of mutually beneficial interactions. Today, an American may invest money in stock in a Japanese company, for example. The Japanese firm gains the benefit of having the money with which to work, and the American gains from the payoff from her investment. This interaction between total strangers living on opposite sides of the world is thus mutually advantageous. Such a thing would be essentially impossible in merely social animals. These interactions and transactions create wealth, so that there is more for everyone.

Some degree of conflict is inevitable wherever resources are limited and organisms must compete for them. Among social animals, there are not many options for resolving conflicts other than aggression or invoking the dominance hierarchy, which is itself based on and often sustained by aggression. Cultural animals have far more elaborate and sophisticated means of resolving disputes: They can appeal to morality, to laws, and to abstract ideals of fairness; they can hire a judge or arbitrator; and they can reconceptualize the situation in ways that may offer some benefit to everyone involved in the problem.

And, of course, language itself is a major difference, in multiple ways. Social animals often have some rudimentary form of communication, but human language far outclasses the communicative efforts of all other species. Language permits the storage and transmission of knowledge. It facilitates reasoning. It enables people to think about the past and future. Very possibly, language was important in the emergence of human consciousness, because the power of language for combining concepts made it possible to create a mental processing space that could integrate many ideas at once (as in a long sentence, like this one). Undoubtedly, it facilitates efforts to organize groups and to maintain an efficient system of exchange or of division of labor.

When nature produced social animals, it capitalized on the advantages of togetherness. Culture has brought the advantages of systems: organization, efficiency, specialization.

Ultimately, one of the biggest differences between social and cultural animals is in the power of meaning to cause behavior. Human behavior is often caused or influenced by meanings: honor, pride, justice, patriotism, ambitions, goals, religious promises and other obligations, allegiances, legal restrictions, inferences, and countless others. With language, cultural animals could begin to use meaning on a grand scale, and so human behavior is caused by what something means to the actor—a type of causality that is essentially absent in other animals. The reliance on meaning and hence on cultural causality underlies most of the other differences between social and cultural animals. Meaning combines information, and without that, culture would be impossible. All of the unique successes of the human race—science and technology, economic systems, morality and the rule of law, artistic creativity, democratic government, education systems, and the rest—depend on the use of meaning to combine information.

Culture, like any good system, is a whole that is more than the sum of its parts. A hundred people linked by culture will outperform a hundred people who live and work alone. That, perhaps, was the crucial factor by which natural selection produced the human race. By evolving people who could be part of a culture, nature enabled human beings to become greater, more powerful, and more successful beings, because they could share the systems of culture.

Any baby boy or girl born today, in the twenty-first century, especially in one of the more developed countries, can dream (at least) of great achievements and a beautiful, happy life. Had nature fated us to live and work alone, the child's prospects would be limited instead to the struggle with nature for mere survival and occasional pleasure or comfort. Even the most talented baby would face dangers, risks, and at best the prospect of being able to find a few ways to make a hard life slightly easier. Instead, today's baby inherits the priceless gift of thousands of years of accumulated knowledge and some highly sophisticated social systems that will shelter him or her from bad weather and predators, present an abundance of tasty and nourishing food that has been repeatedly screened for safety, bring miraculously powerful medical care as needed, offer a suitable assortment of companions and playmates, provide abundant pleasures of toys, music, and video images, and promise a place in an established school system to inculcate some of the knowledge the child needs to become a fully functioning member of the society. If that child, like most of the others, can take the thousand easy and the few harder steps along the path to adult citizenship, then one day that child will become a productive member of the culture too. Participating in culture will allow that person to become more than a person could ever become or achieve alone.

Half a century ago, the existentialists told us that we all are born alone and die alone. Strictly speaking, they were probably wrong: Most people in developed countries are born and die in hospitals, surrounded by the culture's latest technology, attended by its expert trained professionals, and supported by its financing. But even if there is a solitary aspect to birth and death, it's what is in between that counts most. During those steadily increasing decades of the human lifespan, people are not alone, even when they sit by themselves in a hotel room or walk along the public beach. A person's innermost thoughts, wants, and feelings drink from the common well of culture, using its language, revolving around its tasks and people, knowing its values and expectations. Even your most secret thought, the one that you never told anyone, is partly made from the culture. It almost certainly exists in your own culture's language and is concerned with some issue that the culture has created (and probably about which it has ample opinions). In a functioning human psyche, almost nothing is truly private. It is not in human nature to be alone.

Instead, human nature is designed to enable each individual person to belong to culture. Culture helps us to become something much more than the sum of our talents, efforts, and other individual blessings. In that sense, culture is the greatest blessing of all, because it multiplies all of the other advantages that nature gave us. Culture enables human beings to dominate our planet and reinvent our lives like no other animal can.

Alone, we would be but cunning brutes, at the mercy of our surroundings. Together, we can sustain a system that enables us to make life progressively better for ourselves, our children, and those who come after. Not only *can* cultural animals do this—we already have.

Notes

Chapter 1

1. Diamond, 1997.
2. Masters & Johnson, 1970, made this point central in their work. Normal bodily sexual responses, such as arousal and erection, are impaired by self-awareness, even just when people act as their own spectators and seek to evaluate how they are doing.
3. Sewell, 1999.
4. E.g., see Biernacki, 2000.
5. Sewell, 1999.
6. Sahlins, 1999, p. 403; also see Brumann, 1999, p. S11.
7. Sewell, 1999.
8. Obviously, the name was given by human researchers; as far as we know, monkeys and other animals do not spontaneously name each other.
9. De Waal, 2001.
10. De Waal, 2001.
11. Donald, 2002.
12. E.g., Freud, 1930.
13. Becker, 1973.
14. E.g., Greenberg, Pyszczynski, & Solomon, 1986.
15. See Colapinto, 2000.
16. Colapinto, 2000.
17. Colapinto, 2000.
18. Fukuyama, 1992. A decade later, Fukuyama revised his thesis somewhat to suggest that the unpredictable vagaries of ethnic identification will prevent any genuine end to history, but for the present purposes, his earlier argument is still valid and relevant.
19. Dunbar, 1998.

20. As is standard, these calculations are made proportional to body size and sometimes with other controls. Thus it is not raw brain size. Proportional brain size is a better guide to actual intelligence. This can be seen by looking at gender differences in human beings. IQ tests show that men and women are almost exactly equal in intelligence. This finding is hard to reconcile with the fact that men have larger brains than women and the assumption that raw brain size contributes to intelligence—unless one corrects for body size, because men's bodies are also larger than women's.

21. Dunbar, 1998.

22. Dunbar, 1998, p. 185.

23. Boyd & Richerson, 1985.

24. Dunbar, 1993.

25. Will, 2002b.

26. Tomasello, 1999.

27. Lyman & Varian, 2000.

28. See Carruthers, in press, for a thoughtful and detailed discussion of this point.

29. Roberts, 2002.

30. Roberts, 2002, p. 484.

31. Grice, 1948.

32. Actually, this argument is more complicated. A species of immortals who did not reproduce would not be all that flexible. And nature cannot rule out death by accidents and killing, so that a species that didn't age would still gradually die out. Arguably, reproduction is better than not aging, in terms of allowing the species to survive. Still, if nature could make some creatures not age and live for an unlimited time, it would be a big mark of biological success.

33. Gould, 1979.

34. Gould, 1979, p. 36.

35. Tomasello, 1999.

36. Searle, 2001.

37. See Schneider & Shiffrin, 1977; Bargh, 1994.

38. Bargh, 1982; Schneider & Shiffrin, 1977.

Chapter 2

1. See Pullum, 1991.

2. Brown, 1991; also Pullum, 1991.

3. Berlin & Kay, 1969.

4. For a fairly recent compilation, see the volume edited by Gumperz & Levinson, 1996, especially their introductory chapters and those by Lucy, Slobin, Kay, and Levinson.

5. Brown, 1991.

6. Pinker, 2002.

7. To be sure, poetry does not translate well, because it relies on both meaning and sound, and if the translator gets the meaning right, the words won't sound the same (e.g., they won't rhyme). All this proves is that languages sound different. The crucial point is still that different languages can express the same ideas.

8. This point was made by Brown, 1991.

9. See Barsalou, 1992.

10. Sartre, 1943/1974.

11. Povinelli & Bering, 2002.

12. Roberts, 2002.

13. Roberts, 2002.

14. See Gordon, 1993.

15. Gordon, 1993, p. 6.

16. Quoted in Gordon, 1993, p. 1.

17. E.g., Laumann, Gagnon, Michael, & Michaels, 1994.

18. E.g., Rubin, 1990; Smith, 1994.

19. Sipe, 1995.

20. MacAndrew & Edgerton, 1969.

21. MacAndrew & Edgerton, 1969, p. 82.

22. Will, 2002a.

23. Archer, 2000.

24. Bargh, 1982; Schneider & Shiffrin, 1977.

25. Lieberman, Gaunt, Gilbert, & Trope, 2002.

26. Epstein, 1994.

27. Sloman, 2002.

28. Kahneman & Frederick, 2002.

29. Reviewed in Barsalou, 1992.

30. T. D. Wilson, 2002, discusses this; see Greenwald, Klinger, & Liu, 1989, for data.

31. Kahneman & Frederick, 2002.

32. Lieberman, Gaunt, Gilbert, & Trope, 2002.

33. Lieberman, Gaunt, Gilbert, & Trope, 2002.

34. Kahneman & Frederick, 2002; Lieberman, Gaunt, Gilbert, & Trope, 2002.

35. Schneider & Shiffrin, 1977; Bargh, 1982.

36. Bargh, 1994.

37. Lieberman, Gaunt, Gilbert, & Trope, 2002.

38. Kimble & Perlmuter, 1970.

39. Baumeister, 1984.

40. They are also expensive in the sense that it was probably difficult for evolution to create the structures that made such processes possible.

41. James, 1890, p. 122, quoted in Bargh, Gollwitzer, Lee-Chai, Barndollar, & Trötschel, 2001.

Chapter 3

1. Baumeister, Bratslavsky, Finkenauer, & Vohs, 2001.

2. Helson, 1964.

3. Brickman & Campbell, 1971.

4. Brickman, Coates, & Janoff-Bulman, 1978.

5. Argyle, 1987; see also Diener & Biswas-Diener, 2002.

6. Argyle, 1987, p. 207.

7. Pyszczynski, Greenberg, & Solomon, 1997.

8. Quoted in Farndale, 2002.

9. See Pyszczynski, Greenberg, & Solomon, 1997.

10. Leary, Tchividjian, & Kraxberger, 1994.

11. Mikulincer, Florian, & Hirschberger, 2004.

12. Carstensen, 1992; Carstensen, Isaacowitz, & Charles, 1999; Fredrickson & Carstensen, 1990.

13. Taylor, 1983.

14. Povinelli & Bering, 2002.

15. Geary, 1998, p. 11.

16. See Geen, 1995.

17. Iyengar & Lepper, 2000.

18. Rothbaum, Weisz, & Snyder, 1982.

19. F. Snyder, letter, circa 1970.

20. Brady, 1958.

21. E.g., the series by Weiss, 1971a, 1971b, 1971c.

22. E.g., Overmier & Seligman, 1967.

23. Seligman, 1975.

24. Langer & Rodin, 1976; Rodin & Langer, 1977.

25. Taylor, 1983.

26. Glass, Singer, & Friedman, 1969.

27. Originally proposed in Brehm, 1966.

28. See Brehm, 1966; Brehm & Brehm, 1981.

29. Langer, 1975.

30. Diener & Biswas-Diener, 2002; Diener & Diener, 1995; Diener & Fujita, 1995; Diener & Oishi, 2000; for reviews, see Argyle, 1987; Baumeister, 1991; Myers, 1992.

31. Winter, 1973.

32. Winter, 1973.

33. Winter, 1973.

34. Beggan, 1992; also Kahneman, Knetsch, & Thaler, 1990.

35. Lynch, 1979, p. 38.

36. Kiecolt-Glaser, Garner, et al., 1984; Kiecolt-Glaser, Ricker, et al., 1984; Kiecolt-Glaser et al., 1987.

37. Cacioppo, Hawkley, & Berntson, 2003.

38. Bloom, White, & Asher, 1979.

39. E.g., Bhatti, Derezotes, Kim, & Specht, 1989; Bowlby, 1969, 1973; Hamachek, 1992; Rutter, 1979.

40. Durkheim, 1897/1963.

41. E.g., Trout, 1980.

42. E.g., Baumeister, 1991; Myers, 1992.

43. There are several statistical complications here that should be acknowledged. Degree of correlation can be affected by restricted range and degree of variation. For example, satisfying the sex drive might in principle be just as important as satisfying the need to belong, but belongingness would correlate more strongly with happiness if all Americans got equal degrees of sexual satisfaction whereas they varied in how much belongingness they enjoyed. Also, genes and temperament contribute substantially to happiness, indeed arguably more than external circumstances. I think the data support my conclusion, but one could argue that the final proof is not yet available.

44. Twenge, Baumeister, Tice, & Stucke, 2001; Twenge, Catanese, & Baumeister, 2002; Baumeister, Twenge, & Nuss, 2002; Williams, 2001.

45. From Baumeister & Leary, 1995.

46. E.g., Wheeler & Nezlek, 1977.

47. E.g., Brown, 1991.

48. For example, see the way Cross & Madson, 1997, explain gender differences in terms of women's greater concern with maintaining relationships.

49. Or, in some cases, a particular woman, such as a mother or daughter.

50. Belle, 1989; Benenson, 1993; Benenson, Apostoleris, & Parnass, 1997.

51. Feshbach, 1969; Feshbach & Sones, 1971.

52. Gardner et al., 2002.

53. Milardo, Johnson, & Huston, 1983.

54. Vaughan, 1986.

55. Spanier & Casto, 1979.

56. E.g., Baumeister & Wotman, 1992.

57. Beckman, 1981.

58. Bloom, White, & Asher, 1979.

59. To be sure, people who lose a child or a spouse of many years say they never entirely get over it. A new attachment can provide some joy, but one still occasionally misses the lost love.

60. Gerstel & Gross, 1984; Winfield, 1985; Bunker, Zubek, Vanderslice, & Rice, 1992; Beckman, Marsella, & Finney, 1979; Snyder, 1978; Harrison & Connors, 1984.

61. Reis, 1990; also Caldwell & Peplau, 1982.

62. E.g., Cacioppo, Hawkley, & Berntson, 2003; Wheeler, Reis, & Nezlek, 1983.

63. Adler, 1980; McLeod, 1982; Symanski, 1980.

64. Symanski, 1980.

65. Baumeister, 2000.

66. Laumann, Gagnon, Michael, & Michaels, 1994.

67. Baumeister, Catanese, & Vohs, 2001.

68. E.g., Fukuyama, 1999.

69. Federal Bureau of Investigation, 1998, reports that men are the accused perpetrators in 99% of arrests for rape, 40% for prostitution and commercial sex, and 92% of all other sex crimes.

70. Baumeister & Twenge, 2002.

71. Kinsey, Pomeroy, Martin, & Gebhard, 1953; Laumann, Gagnon, Michael, & Michaels, 1994.

72. Kinsey et al., 1953.

73. Tannahill, 1980.

74. Sipe, 1995.

75. Buss, 1994.

76. Clark & Hatfield, 1989.

77. Lorenz, 1966.

78. There is some basis for arguing that younger males—boys—are also quite aggressive. The reason that the young men have the "badder" reputation is that the children just can't do that much damage, not being allowed to be out at night, operate heavy machinery, or purchase guns. This does not change the conclusion much, though. The age profile for violent crime shows a steep drop as men move through their 20s, and the slowdown as they move out of middle age is significant. Almost no men take up violent crime past the age of 40 (Gottfredson & Hirschi, 1990; Sampson & Laub, 1990, 1993).

79. Geen & Quanty, 1977.

80. Bushman, Baumeister, & Stack, 1999.

81. Roberts, 2002.

82. Brown, 1991.

83. See Tremblay, 2000, 2003; also Nagin & Tremblay, 1999; Broidy et al., 2003; Tremblay et al., in press.

84. Erikson, 1950, 1968.

85. Tomasello, 1999.

86. Tomasello, 1999.

87. Pinker, 1994.

88. Cialdini, Darby, & Vincent, 1973; Manucia, Baumann, & Cialdini, 1984.

89. E.g., Batson et al., 1981.

90. Fogel, Melson, & Mistry, 1986.

91. Fogel, Melson, & Mistry, 1986.

92. Wong, 2000, p. 60.

93. Wong, 2000, p. 82.

94. Wong, 2000.

95. E.g., Batson et al., 1981.

96. Gottlieb & Carver, 1980; also note extensive findings on in-group favoritism, e.g., Turner, 1985; Brewer, 1979.

97. E.g., Margolis, 1984.

98. I reviewed many research findings that confirmed this point; see Baumeister, 1991.

99. Brown, 1991.

100. Pinker, 1994.

101. Dunbar, 1998.

102. See Baumeister, Zhang, & Vohs, in press.

103. E.g., Kagan, 1981.

104. See Pinker, 1994.

105. Baumeister, 1986.

106. E.g., Baumeister, Campbell, Krueger, & Vohs, 2003; McFarlin & Blascovich, 1981; Shrauger & Sorman, 1977.

107. E.g., Taylor & Brown, 1988.

108. Baumeister, 1982; Schlenker, 1980.

109. Baumeister, Smart, & Boden, 1996.

110. See Baumeister, Campbell, Krueger, & Vohs, 2003; Emler, 2001; Mecca, Smelser, & Vasconcellos, 1989.

111. For review, see Baumeister, Dale, & Sommer, 1998.

112. Leary, Tambor, Terdal, & Downs, 1995; Leary & Baumeister, 2000.

113. E.g., Taylor & Brown, 1988; see Baumeister, 1989, on the optimal margin of illusion.

114. Baumeister, Tice, & Hutton, 1989.

115. Morf & Rhodewalt, 2001.

116. Wallace & Baumeister, 2002.

117. Heine et al., 2000.

118. Sedikides, Gaertner, & Toguchi, 2003.

119. Kitayama & Uchida, in press.

120. Derber, 1979; see also Brown, 1991.

121. Brown, 1991.

122. For review, see Baumeister, Stillwell, & Heatherton, 1994.

123. See Hare, 1999.

124. Baumeister, Stillwell, & Heatherton, 1994.

125. Friedman, 2002.
126. Friedman, 2002.
127. Lyman, 1978; Schimmel, 1992.
128. E.g., Levinson, 1978.
129. Braudy, 1986.
130. Lasch, 1978.
131. Braudy, 1986.
132. Freedman, 1978, p. 208.
133. "George Harrison," p. 77.
134. Bellah, Madsen, Sullivan, Swidler, & Tipton, 1985.
135. Kasser & Ryan, 1993.
136. Fox, 2002, p. 28.
137. Conquest, 1986, 1990.
138. E.g., Platt, 1973; Knapp & Clark, 1991.
139. Lopata, 1971, p. 129.
140. See Baumeister, 1991.
141. E.g., Cassirer, 1925/1955.
142. See Berger, 1970, on "plausibility structures."
143. Stark & Bainbridge, 1985.
144. Baumeister, 1991.
145. Stark & Bainbridge, 1985; see also Robbins, 1988.
146. Eliade, 1978.
147. Aries, 1981.
148. Graham, 1987.
149. Atkins, 2001.
150. Bell, 1985.
151. Peele & Brodsky, 1991.
152. Sipe, 1995; Murphy, 1992.
153. Deci, 1971; also see Lepper & Greene, 1978.
154. Lepper, Greene, & Nisbett, 1973.
155. Graeff, 1990.
156. Rosenfeld, Folger, & Adelman, 1980.
157. E.g., Maslow, 1968.
158. See, e.g., Mook, 1987.
159. See Wahba & Bridwell, 1983.

Chapter 4

1. Pinker, 1997.
2. E.g., Funder, 1987.
3. Dunbar, 1993.
4. See Baumeister & Newman, 1994; Kunda, 1990; Lord, Ross, & Lepper, 1979.
5. Kruglanski, 1989; Kruglanski & Mayseless, 1988.
6. Fiske & Taylor, 1984.
7. Tetlock, 1983; Tetlock & Boettger, 1989; Tetlock & Kim, 1987.
8. Jamieson & Zanna, 1989; Keinan, 1987; Kruglanski, 1989; Kruglanski & Mayseless, 1988.
9. Dunbar, 1993, 1996.

10. Baumeister, Zhang, & Vohs, in press.

11. E.g., Pinker, 1994.

12. E.g., Donald, 2002; Ehrlich, 2000.

13. Nisbett, Peng, Choi, & Norenzayan, 2001.

14. Nisbett, Peng, Choi, & Norenzayan, 2001.

15. Nisbett, Peng, Choi, & Norenzayan, 2001, p. 296.

16. Kim & Markus, 1999.

17. E.g., Donald, 2002.

18. See Gould, 1996.

19. Jensen, 1998.

20. Cattell, 1963.

21. Sternberg, 1997.

22. Still, to be on the safe side, my publisher recommends that every parent buy many copies of this book and keep them all around the house.

23. Detterman, 2001.

24. Detterman, 2001; Jensen, 1998.

25. Jensen, 1998, gives IQ correlations of .86 for monozygotic twins raised together, .60 for dizygotic twins raised together, and .75 for monozygotic twins raised apart; see p. 177.

26. Rowe, 1998; Rowe, Jacobson, & Van den Oord, 1999.

27. Baumeister, Bratslavsky, Finkenauer, & Vohs, 2001.

28. Jensen, 1998.

29. Detterman, 2001.

30. Boyd & Richerson, 1985, develop this argument in other ways.

31. See Cosmides, 1989; for overview, see Cosmides & Tooby, 1992.

32. Wason, 1966; Wason & Johnson-Laird, 1972.

33. See Cosmides & Tooby, 1992, for review.

34. Vivid memories may seem to exist as images and pictures, but often they are not really stored images—instead, they are reconstructed from verbal information. For example, when asked to recall the last time they went swimming, many people summon up an image of a scene in which they are swimming in a particular pool or lake. When pressed, however, they concede that their "memory" is viewed from overhead, as if a camera perched on the high diving board had filmed them swimming down below in the water. Because you cannot actually see yourself from high above, it is obvious that these ostensible memories are not actual recordings of sensory impressions. Rather, they are reconstructed. You remember that your last swim took place at such-and-such a time and place, fill in the memory of that place, and put an image of yourself in the water. The verbal record of information about the last swim thus formed the actual memory, and the image was created in the present on the basis of that verbal information (Jaynes, 1976).

35. Miller & Gildea, 1987.

36. E.g., Itard, 1962.

37. Sartre, 1943/1974.

38. Tomasello, 1999.

39. There is some argument that our closest primate relatives may have the rudiments of shared attention. Even if that is correct, and it may not be, it amounts to relatively little, in contrast with its central importance in human psychology.

40. See Blakemore & Decety, 2001.

41. Cited in Blakemore & Decety, 2001.

42. Blakemore & Decety, 2001.

43. See Meltzoff, 1995.

44. Tomasello, 1999.

45. Povinelli & Bering, 2002; Tomasello, 1999.

46. Povinelli & Bering, 2002.

47. Gilovich, Vallone, & Tversky, 1985.

48. Gilovich, Vallone, & Tversky, 1985.

49. Chapman & Chapman, 1969.

50. Rozin, Millman, & Nemeroff, 1986.

51. Jones & Nisbett, 1971.

52. Hamilton & Gifford, 1976; Hamilton, Dugan, & Trolier, 1985.

53. Eccles Parsons, 1982.

54. Hardin used this story in his presentation at the Self Preconference for the Society of Experimental Social Psychology, Spokane, October 2001.

55. Janet Hyde presented these data at a colloquium at Case Western Reserve University in March 2001.

56. Abele, 1985; Pyszczynski & Greenberg, 1987; Holtzworth-Munroe & Jacobson, 1985.

57. Yes, ESPN has started a network that replays old games. Even so, the network has found that it cannot simply rebroadcast the same game, but must try to juice up the presentation as a documentary by having people in the present reminisce about the game or reflect on its historic meaning.

58. Palmer, 1975.

59. E.g., O'Sullivan & Durso, 1984.

60. Darley & Fazio, 1980.

61. Darley & Gross, 1983.

62. E.g., Rogers, Kuiper, & Kirker, 1977.

63. Oehman, Lundqvist, & Esteves, 2001.

64. Fiske, 1980; Gilovich, 1983; Klinger, Barta, & Maxeiner, 1980; Weiner, 1985.

65. Dreben, Fiske, & Hastie, 1979; Bless, Hamilton, & Mackie, 1992.

66. See Fiske & Taylor, 1991.

67. Barsalou, 1992.

68. Eibl-Eibesfeldt, 1972, 1975; see also Barsalou, 1992.

69. Hubel & Wiesel, 1959, 1962.

70. Ekman, 1973, 1989.

71. Hebl & Mannix, 2003.

72. Fiske & Taylor, 1991.

73. Anderson et al., 1981.

74. Pete Ditto, 2002, in conversations.

75. To be sure, a full understanding of the physical environment, as exemplified in modern physics and chemistry, is certainly complex, but dealing with the environment under the conditions of evolution did not require such an advanced scientific understanding. As just one example, sailboats operate by splitting the air flow unevenly and thereby creating a vacuum that sucks the boat forward. But humans sailed boats and ships for many centuries before they understood this. Indeed, a proper understanding of the physics of sailing only emerged in connection with modern airplanes, not sailboats.

76. Widely reported in news media at the time, especially in the *Economist.*

77. E.g., Herman & Polivy, 2003; Hoch & Loewenstein, 1991; Loewenstein, 1996.

78. Fiske & Taylor, 1991.

79. Tversky & Kahneman, 1973.

80. Schaffner, 1985, showed this when rewards and punishments worked equally well, as stipulated by experimental design. To be sure, there are some objective signs that punishments do often work better than rewards; see Baumeister, Bratslavsky, Finkenauer, & Vohs, 2001.

81. Povinelli & Bering, 2002.

82. Povinelli & Bering, 2002.

83. Kant, 1787/1956.

84. Jones & Nisbett, 1971.

85. Weiner et al., 1971.

86. Will, 1990.

87. For review, see Fiske & Taylor, 1991.

88. Pryor & Kriss, 1977.

89. E.g., Zuckerman, 1979.

90. E.g., Campbell, 1986; see Taylor & Brown, 1988.

91. Huntford, 1999.

92. Huntford, 1999, p. 78.

93. Huntford, 1999, p. 523; Huntford is, however, skeptical of Scott's account.

94. Ross & Sicoly, 1979.

95. "Look Out, Vegas," 2000.

96. E.g., Weintraub, 1978.

97. See also Baumeister, 1986.

98. Freud, 1936; for recent review, see Baumeister, Dale, & Sommer, 1998.

99. Pyszczynski, Greenberg, & Holt, 1985; Wyer & Frey, 1983; see also Kunda, 1990.

100. Baumeister & Cairns, 1992.

101. Crary, 1966; Kuiper & Derry, 1982; Mischel, Ebbesen, & Zeiss, 1976.

102. See Jones & Nisbett, 1971.

103. De Waal, 2001.

104. Kunda & Sanitioso, 1989; see also Kunda, 1990.

105. E.g., Wills, 1981.

106. Crocker & Major, 1989.

107. Campbell, 1986; Marks, 1984; Suls & Wan, 1987.

108. Gur & Sackeim, 1979; Sackeim & Gur, 1979; Sartre, 1953.

109. See also Baumeister, Tice, & Hutton, 1989, on self-esteem scores.

110. Taylor & Brown, 1988.

111. See Alloy & Abramson, 1979; Lewinsohn, Mischel, Chaplin, & Barton, 1980.

112. Baumeister, 1989.

113. See Gollwitzer & Kinney, 1989.

114. Trope, 1983, 1986.

115. Swann, 1987.

116. Sedikides, 1993.

117. Shrauger, 1975; Swann, Griffin, Predmore, & Gaines, 1987.

118. MacDonald & Ross, 1999.

119. See Shrauger & Schoeneman, 1979.

120. See Kenny & Albright, 1987.
121. Nisbett & Wilson, 1977.
122. Nisbett & Wilson, 1977.
123. Smith & Engel, 1968.
124. Then again, high self-esteem does not seem to produce a broad pattern of improved performance; for review, see Baumeister, Campbell, Krueger, & Vohs, 2003.
125. Sartre, 1953.
126. Bargh, Chen, & Burrows, 1996.
127. See Bargh, Chen, & Burrows, 1996; also Chartrand & Bargh, 1999.
128. Wilson, 2002.
129. Landauer, 1986.
130. Landauer notes that his estimates of the extent of memory loss are less reliable than his estimates of what is acquired.
131. Weinberger, Schwartz, & Davidson, 1979.
132. Hansen & Hansen, 1988.
133. Wenzlaff, Wegner, & Roper, 1988.
134. Schacter, 2001.
135. Sprecher, 1999.
136. Baumeister, Stillwell, & Wotman, 1990.
137. Baumeister, Wotman, & Stillwell, 1993.
138. Rhodewalt & Eddings, 2002.
139. Bem & McConnell, 1970.
140. Conway & Ross, 1984.
141. Ross, 1989.
142. Ross, 1989.
143. Barsalou, 1992, pp. 307–308,
144. Barsalou, 1992.
145. Barsalou, 1992.
146. Von Fersen, Wynne, & Delius, 1991; see also McGonigle & Chalmers, 1977.
147. Barsalou, 1992.
148. Gilbert, 1991, 1993.
149. E.g., Festinger & Maccoby, 1964; Petty & Cacioppo, 1986.
150. Gilbert, 1991.
151. Tetlock, 1986.
152. Tetlock, 1981, 1986.
153. E.g., Kohlberg, 1985.
154. Gilligan, 1982.
155. See Jaffee & Hyde, 2000.
156. Emler, 1998.
157. Haidt, 2001.
158. E.g., Hare, 1999.
159. Dawkins, 1976.
160. Haidt, 2001.
161. See Tversky & Kahneman, 1973.
162. Buehler, Griffin, & Ross, 1994.
163. Buehler, Griffin, & Ross, 1994.
164. DePaulo, Charlton, Cooper, Lindsay, & Muhlenbruck, 1998.
162. See McGuire & McGuire, 1992, for review.

Chapter 5

1. Russell & Feldman Barrett, 1999, p. 805.
2. Arousal is a complicated concept and resists simple definition. Also there are some nonaroused states associated with parasympathetic activity.
3. See Schachter & Singer, 1962; Maranon, 1924.
4. Zillman, 1993.
5. E.g., Schachter & Singer, 1962.
6. E.g., Zanna, Higgins, & Taves, 1976; also Maslach, 1979.
7. Frijda, 1986, among others, has argued that emotions are for evaluation.
8. Gilbert, Pinel, Wilson, Blumberg, & Wheatley, 1998; Gilbert, Brown, Pinel, & Wilson, 2000; Wilson, Meyers, & Gilbert, 2001; Wilson & Gilbert, 2003.
9. Diener & Emmons, 1984; Watson & Tellegen, 1985; Watson & Clark, 1992.
10. E.g., Green, Goldman, & Salovey, 1993; Green, Salovey, & Truax, 1999.
11. Cacioppo, Gardner, & Berntson, 1999.
12. Diener, Larsen, Levine, & Emmons, 1985.
13. E.g., Schachter & Singer, 1962.
14. E.g., Russell & Feldman Barrett, 1999.
15. E.g., Izard, 1977.
16. E.g., Niedenthal, Halberstadt, & Innes-Ker, 1999.
17. Diener, Larsen, Levine, & Emmons, 1985.
18. Polivy, 1981.
19. Averill, 1980.
20. See Baumeister, Heatherton, & Tice, 1994, for review.
21. Ekman, 1973; Ekman & Friesen, 1971; Ekman et al., 1987.
22. Freedman, 1964.
23. Zajonc, 1985.
24. Russell, 1994, though Ekman hotly disputed this point; see Ekman, 1994; Russell, 1995.
25. Berkowitz, 1989, 1990.
26. Easterbrook, 1959.
27. Reviewed in Baumeister & Leary, 1995.
28. For review, see Baumeister, 1991; Myers, 1992.
29. Pines & Aronson, 1983; Buss, 2000.
30. Baumeister, Stillwell, & Heatherton, 1994, 1995a, 1995b.
31. Sullivan, 1953.
32. Baumeister & Tice, 1990.
33. Schlenker & Leary, 1982.
34. Craighead, Kimball, & Rehak, 1979.
35. Kendall, 1978; Smith, Ingram, & Brehm, 1983.
36. Stephan & Stephan, 1985; see also Ickes, 1984.
37. Tavris, 1989.
38. Averill, 1982.
39. Baumeister, Stillwell, & Heatherton, 1994, 1995.
40. Yerkes & Dodson, 1908.
41. Easterbrook, 1959.
42. Monat, Averill, & Lazarus, 1972.
43. See Loewenstein, Weber, Hsee, & Welch, 2001, for review.
44. Loewenstein, Weber, Hsee, & Welch, 2001; see also Damasio, 1994.

45. Viscusi & Magat, 1987.
46. Slovic, Finucane, Peters, & MacGregor, 2002.
47. Denes-Raj & Epstein, 1994.
48. Slovic, Finucane, Peters, & MacGregor, 2002.
49. Leith & Baumeister, 1996.
50. Damasio, 1994.
51. Damasio, 1994.
52. Frijda, 1986.
53. Baumeister, Stillwell, & Heatherton, 1995a, 1995b.
54. See Johnson-Laird & Oatley, 2000, for a summary of the literature.
55. Wood, Quinn, & Kashy, 2002.
56. Bechara, Damasio, Tranel, & Damasio, 1997; Damasio, 1994.
57. E.g., Cialdini, Darby, & Vincent, 1973.
58. Manucia, Baumann, & Cialdini, 1984.
59. Bushman, Baumeister, & Phillips, 2001.
60. Tice, Bratslavsky, & Baumeister, 2001.

Chapter 6

1. Some of this has been anticipated by Dennett, 2003.
2. Associated Press, 2001.
3. Pelham, Mirenberg, & Jones, 2002.
4. Hoorens & Todorova, 1988; Prentice & Miller, 1992; Jones, Pelham, Mirenberg, & Hetts, 2002.
5. Jaynes, 1976.
6. Not his real name.
7. Bolt, 1987.
8. Roberts, 2002. To be sure, there are some exceptions, such as the "Garcia effect" in which animals will learn to dislike a taste when they become nauseous an hour or two after eating something with that taste.
9. Fox, 1993.
10. Spence & Segner, 1967.
11. Costantini & Hoving, 1973.
12. Tindall & Ratliff, 1974.
13. Bolles, 1970.
14. See Gazzaniga & Heatherton, 2002, p. 185.
15. Dunbar, 1993.
16. Vallacher & Wegner, 1985, 1987.
17. Vallacher & Wegner, 1985, 1987.
18. Pinker, 2002, p. 61.
19. Oettingen & Gollwitzer, 2001.
20. Bandura & Schunk, 1981.
21. Oettingen & Gollwitzer, 2001; also Gollwitzer, 1990.
22. Gollwitzer, 1999.
23. See Lengfelder & Gollwitzer, 2001.
24. See Powers, 1973; also Carver & Scheier, 1981.
25. Wegner uses this in his oral presentations, but see also Wegner, 2002.
26. Carver & Scheier, 1990.

27. Again, here we are using *conscious thought* to refer to full-blown consciousness as an integrated mental system. There is another, much looser form of consciousness, sometimes called simply *awareness*, which refers merely to receiving any information through the senses, and this of course is necessary for behavior.

28. See Donald, 2002.

29. Wegner, 2002.

30. Searle, 2001.

31. Barsalou, 1992, makes this assertion.

32. Kant, 1797/1967.

33. Kant, 1787/1956.

34. E.g., Averill, 1982.

35. Miller & Brown, 1991.

36. Sartre, 1943/1974.

37. Jaynes, 1976.

38. Wegner, 2002.

39. MacAndrew & Edgerton, 1969, p. 173.

40. Gray, 1989, 1990.

41. Steele & Southwick, 1985.

42. Ekman, 1973; Ekman & Friesen, 1971; Ekman et al., 1987.

43. Russell, 1994.

44. E.g., Mischel, 1974, 1996.

45. Mischel, 1974.

46. Tangney, Baumeister, & Boone, in press; see also Mischel, Shoda, & Peake, 1988; Shoda, Mischel, & Peake, 1990.

47. Gottfredson & Hirschi, 1990.

48. Tice, Bratslavsky, & Baumeister, 2001.

49. Bushman, Baumeister, & Phillips, 2001.

50. Carver & Scheier, 1981.

51. Hull, 1981.

52. E.g., Baumeister, Bratslavsky, Muraven, & Tice, 1998; Baumeister & Heatherton, 1996; Muraven & Baumeister, 2000.

53. Muraven, Baumeister, & Tice, 1999; Oaten & Cheng, 2002.

54. Waldman, 1992.

55. Schwartz, 2000.

56. Baumeister, Bratslavsky, Muraven, & Tice, 1998.

57. Vohs, Twenge, Baumeister, Schmeichel, & Tice, 2002.

58. Blascovich et al., 1993; Fazio, Blascovich, & Driscoll, 1992.

59. Kahneman & Tversky, 1979.

60. To be sure, many people do like to gamble. But perhaps the structure of gambling avoids the dilemma when winning and losing are equal. Mostly, people like to bet small sums on the chance of winning large ones. I don't know of any casino that works on the opposite principle, insisting on large bets with small payouts.

61. Gollwitzer, 1999; Gollwitzer & Brandstatter, 1997.

62. Kahneman & Tversky, 1979.

63. See Loewenstein & Elster, 1992; Loewenstein, Read, & Baumeister, 2003.

64. Elster, 1998; see also Loewenstein, Weber, Hsee, & Welch, 2001.

65. Brockner, Rubin, & Lang, 1981; Fox & Staw, 1979; Teger, 1980.

66. Linder, Cooper, & Jones, 1967.

67. Cooper, 2001.

68. Iyengar & Lepper, 2000.

69. Brehm, 1966.

70. Glass, Singer, & Friedman, 1969; Glass & Singer, 1972.

71. Kahneman & Tversky, 1979.

72. Gambetta, 1993.

73. Herman & Polivy, 2003.

74. "Drug kingpin executed in Indiana federal prison," *New York Times*, June 19, 2001.

75. Festinger, 1957.

76. Zanna, Higgins, & Taves, 1976.

77. Festinger & Carlsmith, 1959.

78. Wicker, 1969.

79. LaPiere, 1934.

80. Ajzen & Fishbein, 1980; Fishbein & Ajzen, 1975.

81. Fazio, Powell, & Herr, 1983.

82. Menninger, 1938.

83. See Piers & Singer, 1953/1971.

84. Baumeister & Scher, 1988; Baumeister, 1997; Berglas & Baumeister, 1993.

85. Billings & Moos, 1984.

86. Baumeister, 1984.

87. Jones & Berglas, 1978.

88. See also Berglas & Jones, 1978.

89. Baumeister, 1990.

90. Tice & Baumeister, 1997.

91. Tice & Baumeister, 1997.

92. See Baumeister & Scher, 1988, for review.

93. Leith & Baumeister, 1996.

94. MacIntyre, 1981.

95. See MacIntyre, 1981.

96. E.g., Baumeister & Exline, 2000.

97. Baumeister & Exline, 2000.

98. E.g., Baumeister, Stillwell, & Wotman, 1990.

Chapter 7

1. See J. Q. Wilson, 2002.

2. Gouldner, 1960.

3. Quoted in De Waal, 2001.

4. Hogan, 1983.

5. Fiske, 1991.

6. Clark & Mills, 1979.

7. See Gouldner, 1960.

8. In many large systems, the amount is not quite so fixed, and so there is some departure from the strict zero sum pattern. Military soldiers can get promoted to a higher rank without anyone else necessarily moving to a lower rank, and in the same way corporations promote people far more than they demote them. Still, much of this is made possible by people leaving the organization, through retirement, death, or taking a job elsewhere. The zero sum aspect may be muted, but it does not disappear.

Ultimately, for example, a corporation has only a fixed amount of money to spend during a given year, and so it is not possible to double everyone's salary. If it doubles the number of vice presidents, it will have to pay them all less.

9. Friedman, 2002.

10. For review, see Baumeister, Stillwell, & Heatherton, 1994.

11. Twenge, Baumeister, Tice, & Stucke, 2001; Twenge, Catanese, & Baumeister, 2002.

12. Macfarlane, 1986.

13. Burgess & Locke, 1945.

14. J. Q. Wilson, 2002.

15. Bailey & Aunger, 1995.

16. Reiss, 1986.

17. Blumstein & Schwartz, 1983.

18. Baumeister & Tice, 2000; Baumeister & Vohs, in press; Symons, 1979.

19. See Guttentag & Secord, 1983.

20. Barber, 2000.

21. Barber, 1999.

22. Schmitt & Buss, 2001.

23. For review, see Baumeister & Twenge, 2002.

24. See Tedeschi & Felson, 1994.

25. Freud, 1930.

26. Baumeister, 1997.

27. Brown, 1991.

28. Clebsch, 1979.

29. Keegan, 1993.

30. Baumeister, 1997.

31. See Tedeschi & Felson, 1994.

32. Baumeister, Smart, & Boden, 1996.

33. Gouldner, 1960.

34. Fisher, Nadler, & Whitcher-Alagner, 1982.

35. Cialdini, Darby, & Vincent, 1973; Manucia, Baumann, & Cialdini, 1984.

36. E.g., Burnstein, Crandall, & Kitayama, 1994; Cialdini, Brown, Lewis, & Luce, 1997; Essock-Vitale & McGuire, 1985; Kaniasty & Norris, 1995.

37. Fehr & Gächter, 2002.

38. Henrich et al., 2001.

39. Barash & Lipton, 2002.

40. Barash & Lipton, 2002.

41. Betzig, 1986.

42. Gould & Gould, 1997; see also Ridley, 1993.

43. Chen & Tyler, 2001.

44. See Burgess & Locke, 1945.

45. See Stark & Bainbridge, 1985.

46. Quoted in Weintraub, 1978.

47. Gouldner, 1960.

48. Baumeister, Stillwell, & Heatherton, 1994.

49. Tajfel, 1970; Tajfel & Billig, 1974; Tajfel, Flament, Billig, & Bundy, 1971; Brewer, 1979.

50. Tajfel, Flament, Billig, & Bundy, 1971; see also Turner, 1985.

51. Hoyle, Pinkley, & Insko, 1989.

52. See Sullivan, 1953.
53. E.g., Devine, 1989.
54. Darley & Latane, 1968.
55. Latane, Williams, & Harkins, 1979.
56. E.g., Stasser & Titus, 1985, 1987.
57. Janis, 1982.
58. Janis, 1982.
59. Janis, 1982.
60. See Dower, 1986.
61. Janis, 1982, p. 73.
62. Janis, 1982, p. 75.

Epilogue

1. This as accepting the *African Eve theory*, according to which all human beings are descended from a single woman (or possibly a group of sisters with very similar DNA), who lived in Africa back then.

2. Baumeister & Sommer, 1997.

References

Abele, A. (1985). Thinking about thinking: Causal, evaluative, and finalistic cognition about social solutions. *European Journal of Social Psychology, 15,* 315–332.

Adler, P. (1980). On becoming a prostitute. In E. Muga (Ed.), *Studies in prostitution* (pp. 22–26). Nairobi: Kenya Literature Bureau.

Ajzen, I., & Fishbein, M. (1980). *Understanding attitudes and predicting social behavior.* Englewood Cliffs, NJ: Prentice-Hall.

Alloy, L. B., & Abramson, L. Y. (1979). Judgment of contingency in depressed and nondepressed students: Sadder but wiser? *Journal of Experimental Psychology: General, 108*(4), 441–485.

Amato, P. R., & Gilbreth, P. R. (1999). Nonresident fathers and children's well-being: A meta-analysis. *Journal of Marriage and the Family, 61,* 557–574.

Anderson, C. A., Lepper, M. R., & Ross, L. (1980). The perseverance of social theories: The role of explanation in the persistence of discredited information. *Journal of Personality and Social Psychology, 39,* 1037–1049.

Archer, J. (2000). Sex differences in aggression between heterosexual partners: A meta-analytic review. *Psychological Bulletin, 126,* 697–702.

Argyle, M. (1987). *The psychology of happiness.* London: Methuen.

Aries, P. (1981). *The hour of our death.* (trans. H. Weaver). New York: Knopf.

Associated Press. (2001, November 7). "Mad Dad" head arrested for battery. Sarasota, FL.

Atkins, R. C. (2001). *Dr. Atkins' new diet revolution.* New York: Avon.

Averill, J. (1982). *Anger and aggression: An essay on emotion.* New York: Springer-Verlag.

Averill, J. R. (1980). On the paucity of positive emotions. In K. Blankstein, P. Pliner, & J. Polivy (Eds.), *Advances in the study of communication and affect* (Vol. 6, p. 745). New York: Plenum.

Bailey, J. M., & Pillard, R. C. (1995). Genetics of human sexual orientation. *Annual Review of Sex Research, 6,* 126–150.

Bailey, R. C., & Aunger, R. V. (1995). Sexuality, infertility and sexually transmitted disease among farmers and foragers in central Africa. In P. Abramson & S. Pinkerton (Eds.), *Sexual nature, sexual culture* (pp. 195–222). Chicago: University of Chicago Press.

Bandura, A., & Schunk, D. H. (1981). Cultivating competence, self-efficacy, and intrinsic interest through proximal self-motivation. *Journal of Personality and Social Psychology, 41,* 586–598.

Barash, D. P., & Lipton, J. E. (2002). *The myth of monogamy: Fidelity and infidelity in animals and people.* New York: Freeman.

Barber, N. (1999). Women's dress fashions as a function of reproductive strategy. *Sex Roles, 40,* 459–471.

Barber, N. (2000). On the relationship between country sex ratios and teen pregnancy rates: A replication. *Cross-Cultural Research, 34,* 26–37.

Bargh, J. (1982). Attention and automaticity in the processing of self-relevant information. *Journal of Personality and Social Psychology, 43,* 425–436.

Bargh, J. A. (1994). The four horsemen of automaticity: Awareness, intention, efficiency, and control in social cognition. In R. S. Wyer, Jr., & T. K. Srull (Eds.), *Handbook of social cognition* (pp. 1–40). Hillsdale, NJ: Erlbaum.

Bargh, J. A., Chen, M., & Burrows, L. (1996). Automaticity of social behavior: Direct effects of trait construct and stereotype activation on action. *Journal of Personality and Social Psychology, 71,* 230–244.

Bargh, J. A., Gollwitzer, P. M., Lee-Chai, A., Barndollar, K., & Trötschel, R. (2001). The automated will: Nonconscious activation and pursuit of behavioral goals. *Journal of Personality and Social Psychology, 81,* 1014–1027.

Barsalou, L. (1992). *Cognitive psychology: An overview for cognitive psychologists.* Hillsdale, NJ: Erlbaum.

Batson, C.D., Duncan, B.D., Ackerman, P., Buckley, T., & Birch, K. (1981). Is empathic emotion a source of altruistic motivation? *Journal of Personality and Social Psychology, 40,* 290–302.

Baumeister, R. F. (1982). A self-presentational view of social phenomena. *Psychological Bulletin, 91,* 3–26.

Baumeister, R. F. (1984). Choking under pressure: Self-consciousness and paradoxical effects of incentives on skillful performance. *Journal of Personality and Social Psychology, 46,* 610–620.

Baumeister, R. F. (1986). *Identity: Cultural change and the struggle for self.* New York: Oxford University Press.

Baumeister, R. F. (1988). Should we stop studying sex differences altogether? *American Psychologist, 43,* 1092–1095.

Baumeister, R. F. (1989). The optimal margin of illusion. *Journal of Social and Clinical Psychology, 8,* 176–189.

Baumeister, R. F. (1990). Suicide as escape from self. *Psychological Review, 97,* 90–113.

Baumeister, R. F. (1991). *Meanings of life.* New York: Guilford.

Baumeister, R. F. (1997). *Evil: Inside human violence and cruelty.* New York: Freeman.

Baumeister, R. F. (2000). Gender differences in erotic plasticity: The female sex drive as socially flexible and responsive. *Psychological Bulletin, 126,* 347–374.

Baumeister, R. F., Bratslavsky, E., Finkenauer, C., & Vohs, K. D. (2001). Bad is stronger than good. *Review of General Psychology, 5,* 323–370.

Baumeister, R. F., Bratslavsky, E., Muraven, M., & Tice, D. M. (1998). Ego depletion: Is the active self a limited resource? *Journal of Personality and Social Psychology, 74,* 1252–1265.

Baumeister, R. F., & Cairns, K. J. (1992). Repression and self-presentation: When audiences interfere with self-deceptive strategies. *Journal of Personality and Social Psychology, 62,* 851–862.

Baumeister, R. F., Campbell, J. D., Krueger, J. I., & Vohs, K. D. (2003). Does high self-esteem cause better performance, interpersonal success, happiness, or healthier lifestyles? *Psychological Science in the Public Interest, 4,* 1–44.

Baumeister, R. F., Catanese, K.R., & Vohs, K.D. (2001). Is there a gender difference in strength of sex drive? Theoretical views, conceptual distinctions, and a review of relevant evidence. *Personality and Social Psychology Review, 5,* 242–273.

Baumeister, R. F., Dale, K., & Sommer, K. L. (1998). Freudian defense mechanisms and empirical findings in modern social psychology: Reaction formation, projection, displacement, undoing, isolation, sublimation, and denial. *Journal of Personality, 66,* 1081–1124.

Baumeister, R. F., & Exline, J. J. (2000). Self-control, morality, and human strength. *Journal of Social and Clinical Psychology, 19,* 29–42.

Baumeister, R. F., & Heatherton, T. F. (1996). Self-regulation failure: An overview. *Psychological Inquiry, 7,* 1–15.

Baumeister, R. F., Heatherton, T. F., & Tice, D. M. (1994). *Losing control: How and why people fail at self-regulation.* San Diego, CA: Academic.

Baumeister, R.F., & Leary, M.R. (1995). The need to belong: Desire for interpersonal attachments as a fundamental human motivation. *Psychological Bulletin, 117,* 497–529.

Baumeister, R. F., & Newman, L. S. (1994). Self-regulation of cognitive inference and decision processes. *Personality and Social Psychology Bulletin, 20,* 3–19.

Baumeister, R. F., & Scher, S. J. (1988). Self-defeating behavior patterns among normal individuals: Review and analysis of common self-destructive tendencies. *Psychological Bulletin, 104,* 3–22.

Baumeister, R. F., Smart, L., & Boden, J. M. (1996). Relation of threatened egotism to violence and aggression: The dark side of high self-esteem. *Psychological Review, 103,* 5–33.

Baumeister, R. F., & Sommer, K. L. (1997). What do men want? Gender differences and two spheres of belongingness: Comment on Cross and Madson (1997). *Psychological Bulletin, 122,* 38–44.

Baumeister, R. F., Stillwell, A. M., & Heatherton, T. F. (1994). Guilt: An interpersonal approach. *Psychological Bulletin, 115,* 243–267.

Baumeister, R. F., Stillwell, A. M., & Heatherton, T. F. (1995a). Interpersonal aspects of guilt: Evidence from narrative studies. In J. P. Tangney & K. W. Fischer (Eds.), *Self-conscious emotions: The psychology of shame, guilt, embarrassment, and pride* (pp. 255–273). New York: Guilford.

Baumeister, R. F., Stillwell, A. M., & Heatherton, T. F. (1995b). Personal narratives about guilt: Role in action control and interpersonal relationships. *Basic and Applied Social Psychology, 17,* 173–198.

Baumeister, R. F., Stillwell, A., & Wotman, S. R. (1990). Victim and perpetrator accounts of interpersonal conflict: Autobiographical narratives about anger. *Journal of Personality and Social Psychology, 59,* 994–1005.

Baumeister, R. F., & Tice, D. M. (1990). Anxiety and social exclusion. *Journal of Social and Clinical Psychology, 9,* 165–195.

Baumeister, R. F., & Tice, D. M. (2000). *The social dimension of sex.* New York: Allyn & Bacon.

Baumeister, R. F., Tice, D. M., & Hutton, D. G. (1989). Self-presentational motivations and personality differences in self-esteem. *Journal of Personality, 57,* 547–579.

Baumeister, R. F., & Twenge, J. M. (2002). Cultural suppression of female sexuality. *Review of General Psychology, 6,* 166–203.

Baumeister, R. F., Twenge, J. M., & Nuss, C. (2002). Effects of social exclusion on cognitive processes: Anticipated aloneness reduces intelligent thought. *Journal of Personality and Social Psychology, 83,* 817–827.

Baumeister, R. F., & Vohs, K. D. (in press). Sexual economics: Sex as female resource for social exchange in heterosexual interactions. *Personality and Social Psychology Review.*

Baumeister, R. F., & Wotman, S.R. (1992). *Breaking hearts: The two sides of unrequited love.* New York: Guilford Press.

Baumeister, R. F., Wotman, S. R., & Stillwell, A. M. (1993). Unrequited love: On heartbreak, anger, guilt, scriptlessness, and humiliation. *Journal of Personality and Social Psychology, 64,* 377– 394.

Baumeister, R. F., Zhang, L., & Vohs, K. D. (in press). Gossip as cultural learning. *Review of General Psychology.*

Bechara, A., Damasio, H., Tranel, D., & Damasio, A. R. (1997). Deciding advantageously before knowing the advantageous strategy. *Science, 275,* 1293–1295.

Becker, E. (1973). *The denial of death.* New York: Free Press.

Beckman, K., Marsella, A. J., & Finney, R. (1979). Depression in the wives of nuclear submarine personnel. *American Journal of Psychiatry, 136,* 524–526.

Beckman, L. J. (1981). Effects of social interaction and children's relative inputs on older women's psychological well-being. *Journal of Personality and Social Psychology, 41,* 1075–1086.

Beggan, J. K. (1992). On the social nature of nonsocial perception: The mere ownership effect. *Journal of Personality and Social Psychology, 62,* 229–237.

Bell, R. M. (1985). *Holy anorexia.* Chicago: University of Chicago Press.

Bellah, R. N., Madsen, R., Sullivan, W. M., Swidler, A., & Tipton, S. M. (1985). *Habits of the heart: Individualism and commitment in American life.* Berkeley: University of California Press.

Belle, D. (1989). Gender differences in children's social networks and supports. In D. Belle (Ed.), *Children's social networks and social supports* (pp. 173–188). New York: Wiley.

Bem, D.J., & McConnell, H.K. (1970). Testing the self-perception of dissonance phenomena: On the salience of premanipulation attitudes. *Journal of Personality and Social Psychology, 14,* 23–31.

Bem, D., & McConnell, H. K. (1971). Testing the self-perception explanation of dissonance phenomena: On the salience of premanipulation attitudes. *Journal of Personality and Social Psychology, 16,* 23–31.

Bem, D. J. (1996). Exotic becomes erotic: A developmental theory of sexual orientation. *Psychological Review, 103,* 320–335.

Benenson, J. F. (1993). Greater preference among females than males for dyadic interaction in early childhood. *Child Development, 64,* 544–555.

Benenson, J. F., Apostoleris, N. H., & Parnass, J. (1997). Age and sex differences in dyadic and group interaction. *Developmental Psychology, 33,* 538–543.

Berger, P. L. (1970). *A rumor of angels: Modern society and the rediscovery of the supernatural.* Garden City, NY: Anchor.

Berglas, S. C., & Baumeister, R. F. (1993). *Your own worst enemy: Understanding the paradox of self-defeating behavior.* New York: Basic.

Berglas, S., & Jones, E.E. (1978). Drug choice as a self-handicapping strategy in response to non-contingent success. *Journal of Personality and Social Psychology, 36,* 405–417.

Berkowitz, L. (1989). Frustration-aggression hypothesis: Examination and reformulation. *Psychological Bulletin, 106,* 59–73.

Berkowitz, L. (1990). On the formation and regulation of anger and aggression: A cognitive-neoassociationistic analysis. *American Psychologist, 45,* 494–503.

Berlin, B., & Kay, P. (1969). *Basic color terms: Their universality and evolution.* Berkeley: University of California Press.

Betzig, L. (1986). *Despotism and differential reproduction: A Darwinian view of history.* New York: Aldine.

Bhatti, B., Derezotes, D., Kim, S., & Specht, H. (1989). The association between child maltreatment and self-esteem. In A. M. Mecca, N. J. Smelser, & J. Vasconcellos (Eds.), *The social importance of self-esteem* (pp. 24–71). Berkeley: University of California Press.

Biernacki, R. (2000). Language and the shift from signs to practices in cultural inquiry. *History and Theory, 39,* 289–310.

Billings, A. G., & Moos, R. F. (1984). Coping, stress, and social resources among adults with unipolar depression. *Journal of Personality and Social Psychology, 46,* 877–891.

Blakemore, S.-J., & Decety, J. (2001). From the perception of action to the understanding of intention. *Nature Reviews: Neuroscience, 2,* 561–567.

Blascovich, J., Ernst, J. M., Tomaka, J., Kelsey, R. M., Salomon, K. L., & Fazio, R. H. (1993). Attitude accessibility as a moderator of autonomic reactivity during decision making. *Journal of Personality and Social Psychology, 64,* 165–176.

Bless, H., Hamilton, D. L., & Mackie, D. M. (1992). Mood effects on the organization of person information. *European Journal of Social Psychology, 22,* 497–509.

Bloom, B. L., White, S. W., & Asher, S. J. (1979). Marital disruption as a stressful life event. In G. Levinger & O. C. Moles (Eds.), *Divorce and separation: Context, causes, and consequences* (pp. 184–200). New York: Basic.

Blumstein, P., & Schwartz, P. (1983). *American couples.* New York: Morrow.

Bolles, R. C. (1970). Species-specific defense reactions and avoidance learning. *Psychological Review, 77,* 32–48.

Bolt, M. (1987). *Instructor's resources to accompany David G. Myers' Psychology First Edition.* New York: Worth.

Bowlby, J. (1969). *Attachment and loss: Vol. 1. Attachment.* New York: Basic.

Bowlby, J. (1973). *Attachment and loss: Vol. 2. Separation: Anxiety and anger.* New York: Basic.

Boyd, R., & Richerson, P. J. (1985). *Culture and the evolutionary process.* Chicago: University of Chicago Press.

Brady, J. V. (1958). Ulcers in "executive" monkeys. *Scientific American, 199,* 95–100.

Braudy, L. (1986). *The frenzy of renown: Fame and its history.* New York: Oxford University Press.

Brehm, J. (1966). *A theory of psychological reactance.* New York: Academic.

Brehm, S. S., & Brehm, J. W. (1981). *Psychological reactance.* New York: Wiley.

Brewer, M. B. (1979). Ingroup bias in the minimal intergroup situation: A cognitive-motivational analysis. *Psychological Bulletin, 86,* 307–324.

Brickman, P., & Campbell, D. T. (1971). Hedonic relativism and planning the good society. In M. H. Appley (Ed.), *Adaptation level theory: A symposium* (pp. 287–302). New York: Academic.

Brickman, P., Coates, D., & Janoff-Bulman, R. (1978). Lottery winners and accident victims: Is happiness relative? *Journal of Personality and Social Psychology, 36,* 917–927.

Brockner, J., Rubin, J. Z., & Lang, E. (1981). Face-saving and entrapment. *Journal of Experimental Social Psychology, 17,* 68–79.

Brody, L. R. (1996). Gender, emotional expression, and parent-child boundaries. In S. Fein, R. Kavanaugh, & B. Zimmeberg (Eds.), *Emotion: Interdisciplinary perspectives* (pp. 139–170). Hillsdale, NJ: Erlbaum.

Broidy, L. M., Nagin, D. S., Tremblay, R. E., Bates, J. E., Brame, B., Dodge, K., Fergusson, D., Horwood, J., Loeber, R., Laird, R., Lynam, D., Moffitt, T., Pettit, G. S., & Vitaro, F. (2003). Developmental trajectories of childhood disruptive behaviors and adolescent delinquency: A six-site, cross-national study. *Developmental Psychology, 39,* 222–245.

Brown, D. E. (1991). *Human universals.* New York: McGraw-Hill.

Brumann, C. (1999). Writing for culture: Why a successful concept should not be discarded. *Current Anthropology, 40*(Suppl.), S1–S13.

Buehler, R., Griffin, D., & Ross, M. (1994). Exploring the "planning fallacy": Why people underestimate their task completion times. *Journal of Personality and Social Psychology, 67,* 366–381.

Bunker, B. B., Zubek, J. M., Vanderslice, V. J., & Rice, R. W. (1992). Quality of life in dual-career families: Commuting versus single-residence couples. *Journal of Marriage and the Family, 54,* 399–407.

Burger, J. M. (1992). *Desire for control: Personality, social and clinical perspectives.* New York: Plenum.

Burger, J. M., & Solano, C. H. (1994). Changes in desire for control over time: Gender differences in a ten-year longitudinal study. *Sex Roles, 31,* 465–472.

Burgess, E. W., & Locke, H. J. (1945). *The family: From institution to companionship.* New York: American.

Burnstein, E., Crandall, C., & Kitayama, S. (1994). Some neo-Darwinian decision rules for altruism: Weighing cues for inclusive fitness as a function of the biological importance of the decision. *Journal of Personality and Social Psychology, 67,* 773–789.

Bushman, B. J., Baumeister, R. F., & Phillips, C. M. (2001). Do people aggress to improve their mood? Catharsis beliefs, affect regulation opportunity, and aggressive responding. *Journal of Personality and Social Psychology, 81,* 17–32.

Bushman, B. J., Baumeister, R. F., & Stack, A. D. (1999). Catharsis, aggression, and persuasive influence: Self-fulfilling or self-defeating prophecies? *Journal of Personality and Social Psychology, 76,* 367–376.

Buss, A. (1989). Temperaments as personality traits. In J. Bates, G. Kohnstamm, & M. Rothbart (Eds.), *Temperament in childhood* (pp. 49–58). New York: Wiley.

Buss, D. M. (1994). *The evolution of desire.* New York: Basic.

Buss, D.M. (2000). *The dangerous passion: Why jealousy is as necessary as love and sex.* New York: Free Press.

Buss, D. M., & Schmitt, D. P. (1993). Sexual strategies theory: A contextual evolutionary analysis of human mating. *Psychological Review, 100,* 204–232.

Cacioppo, J. T., Gardner, W. L., & Berntson, G. G. (1999). The affect system has parallel and integrative processing components: Form follows function. *Journal of Personality and Social Psychology, 76,* 839–855.

Cacioppo, J. T., Hawkley, L. C., & Berntson, G. G. (2003). The anatomy of loneliness. *Current Directions in Psychological Science, 12,* 71–74.

Caldwell, M. A., & Peplau, L. A. (1982). Sex differences in same-sex friendship. *Sex Roles, 8,* 721–732.

Campbell, D. E. (1995). *Incentives: Motivation and the economics of information.* New York: Cambridge University Press.

Campbell, J. D. (1986). Similarity and uniqueness: The effects of attribute type, relevance, and individual differences in self-esteem and depression. *Journal of Personality and Social Psychology, 50,* 281–294.

Carruthers, P. (in press). The cognitive functions of language. *Behavioral and Brain Sciences.*

Carstensen, L. L. (1992). Social and emotional patterns in adulthood: Support for socioemotional selectivity theory. *Psychology & Aging, 7*(3), 331–338.

Carstensen, L. L., Isaacowitz, D. M., & Charles, S. T. (1999). Taking time seriously: A theory of socioemotional selectivity. *American Psychologist, 54*(3), 165–181.

Carver, C. S., & Scheier, M. F. (1981). *Attention and self-regulation: A control theory approach to human behavior.* New York: Springer-Verlag.

Carver, C. S., & Scheier, M. F. (1990). Origins and functions of positive and negative affect: A control-process view. *Psychological Review, 97,* 19–35.

Caspi, A., & Roberts, B. W. (2001). Personality development across the life course: The argument for change and continuity. *Psychological Inquiry, 12,* 49–66.

Cassirer, E. (1955). *The philosophy of symbolic forms: Vol. 1. Language* (R. Manheim, Trans.). New Haven, CT: Yale University Press. (Original work published 1925)

Cattell, R.B. (1963). Theory of fluid and crystallized intelligence: A critical experiment. *Journal of Educational Psychology, 54,* 1–22.

Chapman, L. J., & Chapman, J. P. (1969). Illusory correlation as an obstacle to the use of valid psychodiagnostic signs. *Journal of Abnormal Psychology, 74,* 271–280.

Chartrand, T. L., & Bargh, J. A. (1999). The chameleon effect: The perception-behavior link and social interaction. *Journal of Personality and Social Psychology, 76,* 893–910.

Chen, E. S., & Tyler, T. R. (2001). Cloaking power: Legitimizing myths and the psychology of the advantaged. In Y. Lee-Chai & J. Bargh (Eds.), *The use and abuse of power* (pp. 241–261). Philadelphia: Psychology Press/Taylor & Francis.

Cialdini, R. B., Brown, S. L., Lewis, B. P., & Luce, C. (1997). Reinterpreting the empathy-altruism relationship: When one into one equals oneness. *Journal of Personality and Social Psychology, 73,* 481–494.

Cialdini, R. B., Darby, B. L., & Vincent, J. E. (1973). Transgression and altruism: A case for hedonism. *Journal of Experimental Social Psychology, 9,* 502–516.

Cioffi, D., & Garner, R. (1996). On doing the decision: The effects of active vs. passive choice on commitment and self-perception. *Personality and Social Psychology Bulletin, 22,* 133–147.

Clark, M. S., & Mills, J. (1979). Interpersonal attraction in exchange and communal relationships. *Journal of Personality and Social Psychology, 37,* 12–24.

Clark, R. D., & Hatfield, E. (1989). Gender differences in receptivity to sexual offers. *Journal of Psychology and Human Sexuality, 2,* 39–55.

Clebsch, W. A. (1979). *Christianity in European history.* New York: Oxford University Press.

Colapinto, J. (2000). *As nature made him: The boy who was raised as a girl.* New York: HarperCollins.

Conquest, R. (1986). *The harvest of sorrow: Soviet collectivization and the terror-famine.* New York: Oxford University Press.

Conquest, R. (1990). *The Great Terror: A reassessment.* New York: Oxford University Press.

Conway, M., & Ross, M. (1984). Getting what you want by revising what you had. *Journal of Personality and Social Psychology, 47,* 738–748.

Cooper, J. (2001, December). Personal communication (letter) regarding choice and school desegregation in North Carolina.

Cosmides, L. (1989). The logic of social exchange: Has natural selection shaped how humans reason? Studies with the Wason selection task. *Cognition, 31,* 187–276.

Cosmides, L., & Tooby, J. (1992). Cognitive adaptations for social exchange. In J. Barkow, L. Cosmides, & J. Tooby (Eds.), *The adapted mind* (pp. 163–228). New York: Oxford University Press.

Costantini, A. F., & Hoving, K. L. (1973). The effectiveness of reward and punishment contingencies on response inhibition. *Journal of Experimental Child Psychology, 6,* 484–494.

Craighead, W. E., Kimball, W. H., & Rehak, P. J. (1979). Mood changes, physiological responses, and self-statements during social rejection imagery. *Journal of Consulting and Clinical Psychology, 47,* 385–396.

Crary, W. G. (1966). Reactions to incongruent self-experiences. *Journal of Consulting Psychology, 30,* 246–252.

Crick, N. R. (2000). Engagement in gender normative versus nonnormative forms of aggression: Links to social-psychological adjustment. In W. Craig (Ed.), *Childhood social development: The essential readings* (pp. 309–329). Oxford: Blackwell.

Crocker, J., & Major, B. (1989). Social stigma and self-esteem: The self-protective properties of stigma. *Psychological Review, 96,* 608–630.

Cross, S. E., & Madson, L. (1997). Models of the self: Self-construals and gender. *Psychological Bulletin, 122,* 5–37.

Cunningham, M. R., & Shamblen, S. R. (2001, July). *The erosion and revitalization of love: Social allergies and pleasantries in romantic relationships.* Paper presented at the Conference of the International Network on Personal Relationships, Prescott, AZ.

Damasio, A. (1994). *Descartes' error: Emotion, reason, and the human brain.* New York: Grosset/Putnam.

Darley, J. M., & Fazio, R. H. (1980). Expectancy confirmation processes arising in the social interaction sequence. *American Psychologist, 35,* 867–881.

Darley, J. M., & Gross, P. H. (1983). A hypothesis-confirming bias in labelling effects. *Journal of Personality and Social Psychology, 44,* 20–23.

Darley, J. M., & Latane, B. (1968). Bystander intervention in emergencies: Diffusion of responsibility. *Journal of Personality and Social Psychology, 8,* 377–383.

Dawkins, R. (1976). *The selfish gene.* New York: Oxford University Press.

Deci, E. L. (1971). Effects of externally mediated rewards on intrinsic motivation. *Journal of Personality and Social Psychology, 18,* 105–115.

Denes-Raj, V., & Epstein, S. (1994). Conflict between intuitive and rational processing: When people behave against their better judgment. *Journal of Personality and Social Psychology, 66,* 819–829.

Dennett, D. C. (2003). *Freedom evolves.* New York: Viking/Penguin.

DePaulo, B. M., Charlton, K., Cooper, H., Lindsay, J. J., & Muhlenbruck, L. (1998). The accuracy-confidence correlation in the detection of deception. *Personality and Social Psychology Review, 1,* 346–357.

Derber, C. (1979). *The pursuit of attention: Power and individualism in everyday life.* New York: Oxford University Press.

Detterman, D. K. (2001). Intelligence. *Microsoft Encarta Encyclopedia.* http://encarta .msn.com/find/Concise.asp?z=1&pg=2&ti=761570026.

Devine, P. G. (1989). Stereotypes and prejudice: Their automatic and controlled components. *Journal of Personality and Social Psychology, 56*(1), 5–18.

De Waal, F. (2001). *The ape and the sushi master: Cultural reflections of a primatologist.* New York: Basic.

Diamond, J. (1997). *Why is sex fun?* New York: Basic.

Diener, E., & Biswas-Diener, R. (2002). Will money increase subjective well-being? A literature review and guide to needed research. *Social Indicators Research, 57,* 119–169.

Diener, E., & Diener, C. (1995). The wealth of nations revisited: Income and quality of life. *Social Indicators Research, 36,* 275–286.

Diener, E., & Emmons, R. A. (1984). The independence of positive and negative affect. *Journal of Personality and Social Psychology, 47,* 1105–1117.

Diener, E., & Fujita, F. (1995). Resources, personal strivings, and subjective well-being: A nomothetic and idiographic approach. *Journal of Personality and Social Psychology, 68,* 926–935.

Diener, E., Larsen, R. J., & Emmons, R. A. (1984). Person X situation interactions: Choice of situations and congruence response models. *Journal of Personality and Social Psychology, 47,* 580–592.

Diener, E., Larsen, R. J., Levine, S., & Emmons, R. A. (1985). Intensity and frequency: Dimensions underlying positive and negative affect. *Journal of Personality and Social Psychology, 48,* 1253–1265.

Diener, E., & Oishi, S. (2000). Money and happiness: Income and subjective well-being across nations. In E. Diener & E. M. Suh (Eds.), *Culture and subjective well-being* (pp. 185–218). Cambridge, MA: MIT Press.

Diener, E., Suh, E. M., Lucas, R. E., & Smith, H. L. (1999). Subjective well-being: Three decades of progress. *Psychological Bulletin, 125,* 276–302.

Donald, M. (2002). *A mind so rare: The evolution of human consciousness.* New York: Norton.

Dower, J. W. (1986). *War without mercy: Race and power in the Pacific war.* New York: Pantheon.

Dreben, E. K., Fiske, S. T., & Hastie, R. (1979). The independence of evaluative and item information: Impression and recall order effects in behavior based impression formation. *Journal of Personality and Social Psychology, 37,* 1758–1768.

Duckworth, K. L., Bargh, J. A., Garcia, M., & Chaiken, S. (in press). The automatic evaluation of novel stimuli. *Psychological Science.*

Dunbar, R. I. M. (1993). Coevolution of neocortical size, group size, and language in humans. *Behavioral and Brain Sciences, 16,* 681–694.

Dunbar, R. I. M. (1996). *Grooming, gossip, and the evolution of language.* Cambridge, MA: Harvard University Press.

Dunbar, R. I. M. (1998). The social brain hypothesis. *Evolutionary Anthropology, 6,* 178–190.

Dunton, K. J. (1988). *Parental practices associated with their children's moral reasoning development.* Unpublished doctoral dissertation, Stanford University.

Durkheim, E. (1963). *Suicide.* New York: Free Press. (Original work published 1897)

Easterbrook, J. A. (1959). The effect of emotion on cue utilization and the organization of behavior. *Psychological Review, 66,* 183–201.

Eccles Parsons, J. (1982). *Sex differences in achievement patterns.* Unpublished invited address, American Psychological Association, Washington, DC.

Ehrlich, P. R. (2000). *Human natures: Genes, cultures, and the human prospect.* Washington, DC: Island Press/Shearwater.

Eibl-Eibesfeld, I. (1972). Human ethology: Concepts and implications for the sciences of man. *Behavioral and Brain Sciences, 2,* 1–57.

Eibl-Eibesfeldt, I. (1975). *Ethology: The biology of behavior* (2nd ed.). New York: Holt, Rinehart & Winston.

Eisenberg, N., & Lennon, R. (1983). Sex differences in empathy and related capacities. *Psychological Bulletin, 94,* 100–131.

Ekman, P. (1973). Cross-cultural studies of facial expression. In P. Ekman (Ed.), *Darwin and facial expression* (pp. 169–222). New York: Academic.

Ekman, P. (1989). The argument and evidence about universals in facial expression of emotion. In H. Wagner & A. Manstead (Eds.), *Handbook of social psychophysiology* (pp. 143–164). Chichester, England: Wiley.

Ekman, P. (1994). Strong evidence for universals in facial expressions: A reply to Russell's mistaken critique. *Psychological Bulletin, 115,* 268–287.

Ekman, P., & Friesen, W. V. (1971). Constants across cultures in the face and emotion. *Journal of Personality and Social Psychology, 17,* 124–129.

Ekman, P., & Friesen, W. V. (1975). *Unmasking the face: A guide to recognizing emotions from facial clues.* Englewood Cliffs, NJ: Prentice-Hall.

Ekman, P., Friesen, W. V., O'Sullivan, M., Chan, A., Diacoyanni-Tarlatzis, I., Heider, K., Krause, R., Lecompte, W. A., Pitcairn, T., Ricci-Bitti, P. E., Scherer, K., Tomita, M., & Tzavaras, A. (1987). Universals and cultural differences in the judgments of facial expressions of emotion. *Journal of Personality and Social Psychology, 53,* 712–717.

Eliade, M. (1978). *A history of religious ideas: Vol. 1. From the stone age to the Eleusinian mysteries* (W. Trask, Trans.). Chicago: University of Chicago Press.

Ellis, B. J., & Symons, D. (1990). Sex differences in sexual fantasy: An evolutionary psychological approach. *Journal of Sex Research, 27,* 527–555.

Elster, J. (1998). Emotions and economic theory. *Journal of Economic Literature, 36,* 47–74.

Emery, R. E. (1999). *Marriage, divorce, and children's adjustment* (2nd ed.). Thousand Oaks, CA: Sage.

Emler, N. (1998). Sociomoral understanding. In A. Campbell & S. Muncer (Eds.), *The social child* (pp. 293–323). Philadelphia, PA: Psychology Press.

Emler, N. (2001). *Self-esteem: The costs and consequences of low self-worth.* York, England: York Publishing.

Epstein, S. (1994). Integration of the cognitive and psychodynamic unconscious. *American Psychologist, 49,* 709–724.

Erber, R., & Fiske, S. T. (1984). Outcome dependency and attention to inconsistent information. *Journal of Personality and Social Psychology, 47,* 709–726.

Erikson, E. H. (1950). *Childhood and society.* New York: Norton.

Erikson, E. H. (1968). *Identity, youth, and crisis.* New York: Norton.

Essock-Vitale, S. M., & McGuire, M. T. (1985). Women's lives viewed from an evolutionary perspective: 2. Patterns of helping. *Ethology and Sociobiology, 6,* 155–173.

Farndale, N. (2002, March 17). Living on his nerves. *Sunday Telegraph Magazine,* pp. 12–19.

Farrington, D. P. (1998). Youth crime and antisocial behaviour. In A. Campbell & S. Muncer (Eds.), *The social child* (pp. 352–392). East Sussex, England: Psychology Press/Taylor & Francis.

Fazio, R. H., Blascovich, J., & Driscoll, D. M. (1992). On the functional value of attitudes: The influence of accessible attitudes on the ease and quality of decision making. *Personality and Social Psychology Bulletin, 18,* 388–401.

Fazio, R. H., Powell, M. C., & Herr, P. M. (1983). Toward a process model of the attitude-behavior relation: Accessing one's attitude upon mere observation of the attitude object. *Journal of Personality and Social Psychology, 44,* 723–735.

Federal Bureau of Investigation. (1998). *Crime in the United States.* Washington, DC: U.S. Government Printing Office.

Fehr, E., & Gächter, S. (2002). Altruistic punishment in humans. *Nature, 415,* 137–140.

Feshbach, N. D. (1969). Sex differences in children's modes of aggressive responses toward outsiders. *Merrill-Palmer Quarterly, 15,* 249–258.

Feshbach, N. D., & Sones, G. (1971). Sex differences in adolescent reactions toward newcomers. *Developmental Psychology, 4,* 381–386.

Festinger, L. (1957). *A theory of cognitive dissonance.* Stanford, CA: Stanford University Press.

Festinger, L., & Carlsmith, J. M. (1959). Cognitive consequences of forced compliance. *Journal of Abnormal and Social Psychology, 58,* 203–210.

Festinger, L., & Maccoby, N. (1964). On resistance to persuasive communications. *Journal of Abnormal and Social Psychology, 68,* 359–366.

Fishbein, M., & Ajzen, I. (1975). *Belief, attitude, intention, and behavior: An introduction to theory and research.* Reading, MA: Addison-Wesley.

Fisher, J. D., Nadler, A., & Whitcher-Alagner, S. (1982). Recipient reactions to aid. *Psychological Bulletin, 111,* 27–54.

Fiske, A. P. (1991). *Structures of social life: The four elementary forms of human relations.* New York: Macmillan/Free Press.

Fiske, S. T. (1980). Attention and weight in person perception: The impact of negative and extreme behavior. *Journal of Personality and Social Psychology, 38,* 889–906.

Fiske, S. T., & Taylor, S. E. (1984). *Social cognition.* New York: Random House.

Fiske, S. T., & Taylor, S. E. (1991). *Social cognition* (2nd ed.). New York: McGraw-Hill.

Fogel, A., Melson, G. F., & Mistry, J. (1986). Conceptualizing the determinants of nurturance: A reassessment of sex differences. In A. Fogel & G. Melson (Eds.), *Origins of nurturance* (pp. 53–67). Hillsdale, NJ: Erlbaum.

Fox, F. V., & Staw, B. M. (1979). The trapped administrator: Effects of insecurity and policy resistance upon commitment to a course of action. *Administrative Sciences Quarterly, 24,* 449–471.

Fox, J. A. (1993). The death penalty: Foolproof or foolish? *Boston Sunday Globe*, September 28.

Fox, Michael J. (2002, March 18). How Parkinson's saved my life. *Daily Mail* (England), pp. 28–30.

Fredrickson, B. L., & Carstensen, L. L. (1990). Choosing social partners: How old age and anticipated endings make people more selective. *Psychology & Aging* 5(3), 335–347.

Freedman, D. G. (1964). Smiling in blind infants and the issue of innate versus acquired. *Journal of Child Psychology and Psychiatry, 5,* 174–184.

Freedman, J. (1978). *Happy people: What happiness is, who has it, and why.* New York: Harcourt Brace Jovanovich.

Freud, A. (1936). *The ego and the mechanisms of defense.* New York: Hogarth.

Freud, S. (1930). *Civilization and its discontents* (J. Riviere, Trans.). London: Hogarth.

Friedman, L. M. (2002). *Law in America: A short history.* New York: Random House.

Frijda, N. H. (1986). *The emotions.* Cambridge: Cambridge University Press.

Fukuyama, F. (1992). *The end of history and the last man.* New York: Free Press.

Fukuyama, F. (1999). *The great disruption: Human nature and the reconstitution of social order.* New York: Free Press.

Funder, D. C. (1987). Errors and mistakes: Evaluating the accuracy of social judgment. *Psychological Bulletin, 101,* 75–90.

Gambetta, D. (1993). *The Sicilian mafia: The business of private protection.* Cambridge, MA: Harvard University Press.

Garcia, J., Ervin, F. T., & Koelling, R. A. (1966). Learning with prolonged delay of reinforcement. *Psychonomic Science, 5,* 121–122.

Gardner, W., Seeley, E., Gabriel, S., Pennington, G., Solomon, J., Ernst, J., & Skowronski, J. (2002). *The role of "his" and "her" forms of interdependence in everyday life: Gender, belonging, and social experience.* Unpublished manuscript, Northwestern University.

Gazzaniga, M., & Heatherton, T. F. (2002). *Psychological science.* New York: Norton.

Geary, D.C. (1998). *Male, female: The evolution of human sex differences.* Washington, DC: American Psychological Association.

Geen, R. G. (1995). *Human motivation: A social psychological approach.* Pacific Grove, CA: Brooks/Cole.

Geen, R. G., & Quanty, M. B. (1977). The catharsis of aggression: An evaluation of a hypothesis. In L. Berkowitz (Ed.), *Advances in experimental social psychology* (Vol. 10, pp. 1–37). New York: Academic.

Geertz, C. (1973). *The interpretation of cultures.* New York: Basic Books.

Geertz, C. (1974). *Myth, symbol, and culture.* New York: Norton.

George Harrison: Obituary. (2001, December 8). *Economist,* p. 77.

Gerstel, N., & Gross, H. (1984). *Commuter marriage: A study of work and family.* New York: Guilford.

Gilbert, D. T. (1991). How mental systems believe. *American Psychologist, 46,* 107–119.

Gilbert, D. T. (1993). The assent of man: Mental representation and the control of belief. In D. Wegner & J. Pennebaker (Eds.), *Handbook of mental control* (pp. 57–87). Englewood Cliffs, NJ: Prentice-Hall.

Gilbert, D. T., Brown, R. P., Pinel, E. C., & Wilson, T. D. (2000). The illusion of external agency. *Journal of Personality and Social Psychology, 79,* 690–700.

Gilbert, D. T., Pinel, E. C., Wilson, T. D., Blumberg, S. J., & Wheatley, T. (1998). Immune neglect: A source of durability bias in affective forecasting. *Journal of Personality and Social Psychology, 75,* 617–638.

Gilligan, C. (1982). *In a different voice: Psychological theory and women's development.* Cambridge, MA: Harvard University Press.

Gilovich, T. (1983). Biased evaluation and persistence in gambling. *Journal of Personality and Social Psychology, 44,* 1110–1126.

Gilovich, T., Vallone, R., & Tversky, A. (1985). The hot hand in basketball: On the misperception of random sequences. *Cognitive Psychology, 17,* 295–314.

Glass, C. C., & Singer, J. E. (1972). *Urban stress.* New York: Academic.

Glass, D. C., Singer, J. E., & Friedman, L. N. (1969). Psychic cost of adaptation to an environmental stressor. *Journal of Personality and Social Psychology, 12,* 200–210.

Gollwitzer, P. M. (1990). Action phases and mind-sets. In E. T. Higgins & R. Sorrentino (Eds.), *Handbook of motivation and cognition* (Vol. 2, pp. 53–92). New York: Guilford.

Gollwitzer, P. M. (1999). Implementation intentions: Strong effects of simple plans. *American Psychologist, 54,* 493–503.

Gollwitzer, P. M., & Brandstatter, V. (1997). Implementation intentions and effective goal pursuit. *Journal of Personality and Social Psychology, 73,* 186–199.

Gollwitzer, P. M., & Kinney, R. F. (1989). Effects of deliberative and implemental mind-sets on the illusion of control. *Journal of Personality and Social Psychology, 56,* 531–542.

Goodenough, F. L. (1931). *Anger in young children.* Minneapolis: University of Minnesota Press.

Gordon, W. Z. (1993). *Women, the state and revolution: Soviet family policy and social life, 1917–1936.* New York: Cambridge University Press.

Gottfredson, M. R., & Hirschi, T. (1990). *A general theory of crime.* Stanford, CA: Stanford University Press.

Gottlieb, J., & Carver, C. (1980). Anticipation of future interaction and the bystander effect. *Journal of Experimental Social Psychology, 16,* 253–260.

Gottman, J. M. (1994). *What predicts divorce?* Hillsdale, NJ: Erlbaum.

Gould, J. L., & Gould, C. G. (1997). *Sexual selection: Mate choice and courtship in nature.* New York: Freeman/Scientific American.

Gould, S. J. (1979, May). Mickey Mouse meets Konrad Lorenz. *Natural History,* pp. 30–36.

Gould, S. J. (1984). *Hen's teeth and horse's toes.* New York: Norton.

Gould, S. J. (1996). *The mismeasure of man.* New York: Norton.

Gouldner, A. (1960). The norm of reciprocity: A preliminary statement. *American Sociological Review, 25,* 161–178.

Graeff, B. (1990). On the NBA: Thomas is unhappy celebrity. *Cleveland Plain Dealer, Sports section,* p. 2.

Graham, B. (1987). *Facing death and the life after.* Waco, TX: Word Books.

Gray, J. A. (1989). Fundamental systems of emotion in the mammalian brain. In D. Palermo (Ed.), *Coping with uncertainty: Behavioral and developmental perspectives* (pp. 173–195). Hillsdale, NJ: Erlbaum.

Gray, J. A. (1990). Brain systems that mediate both emotion and cognition. *Cognition and Emotion, 4,* 269–288.

Green, D. P., Goldman, S. L., & Salovey, P. (1993). Measurement error masks bipolarity in affect ratings. *Journal of Personality and Social Psychology, 64,* 1029–1041.

Green, D. P., Salovey, P., & Truax, K. M. (1999). Static, dynamic, and causative bipolarity of affect. *Journal of Personality and Social Psychology, 76,* 856–867.

Greenberg, J., Pyszczynski, T., & Solomon, S. (1986). The causes and consequences of self-esteem: A terror management theory. In R. Baumeister (Ed.), *Public and private self.* New York: Springer-Verlag.

Greenblat, C. S. (1983). The salience of sexuality in the early years of marriage. *Journal of Marriage and the Family, 45,* 289–299.

Greenwald, A. G., Klinger, M. R., & Liu, T. J. (1989). Unconscious processing of dichoptically masked words. *Memory and Cognition, 17,* 35–47.

Grice, G. R. (1948). The relation of secondary reinforcement to delayed reward in visual discrimination learning. *Journal of Experimental Psychology, 38,* 1–16.

Griffitt, W. (1981). Sexual intimacy in aging marital partners. In J. Marsh & S. Kiesler (Eds.), *Aging: Stability and change in the family* (pp. 301–315). New York: Academic.

Griggs, R. A., & Cox, J. R. (1982). The elusive thematic-materials effect in Wason's selection task. *British Journal of Psychology, 73,* 407–420.

Gumperz, J. J., & Levinson, S. C. (Eds.). (1996). *Rethinking linguistic relativity.* Cambridge: Cambridge University Press.

Gur, R. C., & Sackeim, H. A. (1979). Self-deception: A concept in search of a phenomenon. *Journal of Personality and Social Psychology, 37,* 147–169.

Guttentag, M., & Secord, P. F. (1983). *Too many women: The sex ratio question.* Beverly Hills, CA: Sage.

Haidt, J. (2001). The emotional dog and its rational tail: A social intuitionist approach to moral judgment. *Psychological Review, 108,* 814–834.

Hamachek, D. (1992). *Encounters with the self* (4th ed.). San Diego, CA: Harcourt Brace Jovanovich.

Hamilton, D. L., Dugan, P. M., & Trolier, T. K. (1985). The formation of stereotypic beliefs: Further evidence for distinctiveness-based illusory correlations. *Journal of Personality and Social Psychology, 48,* 5–17.

Hamilton, D. L., and Gifford, R. K. (1976). Illusory correlation in interpersonal perception: A cognitive basis for stereotypic judgments. *Journal of Experimental Social Psychology, 12,* 392–407.

Hansen, R. D., & Hansen, C. H. (1988). Repression of emotionally tagged memories: The architecture of less complex emotions. *Journal of Personality and Social Psychology, 55,* 811–818.

Hare, R. D. (1999). *Without conscience: The disturbing world of the psychopaths among us.* New York: Guilford.

Harrison, A. A., & Connors, M. M. (1984). Groups in exotic environments. In L. Berkowitz (Ed.), *Advances in experimental social psychology* (Vol. 18, pp. 49–87). New York: Academic.

Haselton, M. G., & Buss, D. M. (2000). Error management theory: A new perspective on biases in cross-sex mind reading. *Journal of Personality and Social Psychology, 78,* 81–91.

Headey, B., Veenhoven, R., & Wearing, A. (1991). Top-down versus bottom-up theories of subjective well-being. *Social Indicators Research, 24,* 81–100.

Hebl, M. R., & Mannix, L. M. (2003). The weight of obesity in evaluating others: A mere proximity effect. *Personality and Social Psychology Bulletin, 29,* 28–38.

Heine, S. J., Lehman, D. R., Markus, H. R., & Kitayama, S. (1999). Is there a universal need for positive self-regard? *Psychological Review, 106,* 766–794.

Helson, H. (1964). *Adaptation-level theory: An experimental and systematic approach to behavior.* New York: Harper.

Henrich, J., Boyd, R., Bowles, S., Camerer, C., Fehr, E., Gintis, H., & McElreath, R. (2001). Cooperation, reciprocity and punishment in fifteen small-scale societies. *American Economics Review, 91,* 73–78.

Herman, C. P., & Polivy, J. (2003). Dieting as an exercise in behavioral economics. In G. Loewenstein, D. Read, & R. F. Baumeister (Eds.), *Time and decision: Economic and psychological perspectives on intertemporal choice* (pp. 459–490). New York: Sage.

Herrnstein, R. J., & Murray, C. (1994). *The bell curve: Intelligence and class structure in American life.* New York: Free Press.

Hoch, S. J., & Loewenstein, G. F. (1991). Time-inconsistent preferences and consumer self-control. *Journal of Consumer Research, 17,* 492–507.

Hogan, R. (1983). A socioanalytic theory of personality. In M. Page & R. Dienstbier (Eds.), *Nebraska symposium on motivation* (pp. 55–89). Lincoln: University of Nebraska Press.

Holtzworth-Munroe, A., & Jacobson, N. S. (1985). Causal attributions of married couples: When do they search for causes? What do they conclude when they do? *Journal of Personality and Social Psychology, 48,* 1398–1412.

Hoorens, V., & Todorova, E. (1988). The name letter effect: Attachment to self or primacy of own name writing? *European Journal of Social Psychology, 18,* 365–368.

Hoyle, R. H., Pinkley, R. L., & Insko, C. A. (1989). Perceptions of social behavior: Evidence of differing expectations for interpersonal and intergroup interaction. *Personality and Social Psychology Bulletin, 15,* 365–376.

Hubel, D. H., and Wiesel, T. N. (1959). Receptive fields of single neurons in the cat's striate cortex. *Journal of Physiology, 148,* 574–591.

Hubel, D. H., and Wiesel, T. N. (1962). Receptive fields, binocular interaction and functional architecture in the cat's visual cortex. *Journal of Physiology, 160,* 106–154.

Huesmann, L. R., Eron, L. D., Lefkowitz, M. M., & Walder, L. O. (1984). Stability of aggression over time and generations. *Developmental Psychology, 20,* 1120–1134.

Hull, J. G. (1981). A self-awareness model of the causes and effects of alcohol consumption. *Journal of Abnormal Psychology, 90,* 586–600.

Huntford, R. (1999). *The last place on earth.* New York: Modern Library.

Ickes, W. (1984). Compositions in black and white: Determinants of interaction in interracial dyads. *Journal of Personality and Social Psychology, 47,* 330–341.

Itard, J.-M.-G. (1962). *The wild boy of Aveyron* (G. Humphrey & M. Humphrey, Trans.). New York: Appleton-Century-Crofts.

Iyengar, S. S., & Lepper, M. R. (2000). When choice is demotivating: Can one desire too much of a good thing? *Journal of Personality and Social Psychology, 79,* 996–1006.

Izard, C. E. (1977). *Human emotions.* New York: Plenum.

Jaffee, S., & Hyde, J. S. (2000). Gender differences in moral orientation: A meta-analysis. *Psychological Bulletin, 126,* 703–726.

James, W. (1890). *Principles of psychology* (Vol. 2). New York: Holt.

James, W. H. (1981). The honeymoon effect on marital coitus. *Journal of Sex Research, 17,* 114–123.

Jamieson, D. W., & Zanna, M. P. (1989). Need for structure in attitude formation and expression. In A. Pratkanis, S. Breckler, & A. Greenwald (Eds.), *Attitude structure and function* (pp. 383–406). Hillsdale, NJ: Erlbaum.

Janis, I. L. (1982). *Groupthink*. Boston: Houghton Mifflin.

Jaynes, J. (1976). *The origin of consciousness in the breakdown of the bicameral mind*. Boston: Houghton Mifflin.

Jensen, A. R. (1998). *The g factor*. Westport, CT: Praeger.

Johansson, G. (1973). Visual perception of biological motion and a model for its analysis. *Perceptual Psychophysics, 14,* 201–211.

Johnson-Laird, P. N., & Oatley, K. (2000). Cognitive and social construction in emotions. In M. Lewis & J. M. Haviland-Jones (Eds.), *Handbook of emotions* (pp. 458–475). New York: Guilford.

Jonas Savimbi: Obituary. (2002, March 2). *Economist*, p. 82.

Jones, E. E., & Berglas, S. (1978). Control of attributions about the self through self-handicapping strategies: The appeal of alcohol and the role of underachievement. *Personality and Social Psychology Bulletin, 4*(2), 200–206.

Jones, E. E., & Nisbett, R. E. (1971). *The actor and the observer: Divergent perceptions of the causes of behavior*. New York: General Learning.

Jones, J. T., Pelham, B. W., Mirenberg, M. C., & Hetts, J. J. (2002). Name letter preferences are not merely mere exposure: Implicit egotism as self-regulation. *Journal of Experimental Social Psychology, 38,* 170–177.

Kagan, J. (1981). *The second year: The emergence of self-awareness*. Cambridge, MA: Harvard University Press.

Kahneman, D., & Frederick, S. (2002). Representativeness revisited: Attribute substitution in intuitive judgment. In T. Gilovich, D. Griffin, & D. Kahneman (Eds.), *Heuristics and biases* (pp. 49–81). New York: Cambridge University Press.

Kahneman, D., Knetsch, J. L., & Thaler, R. H. (1990). Experimental tests of the endowment effect and the Coase theorem. *Journal of Political Economy, 98*(6), 1325–1348.

Kahneman, D., & Tversky, A. (1979). Prospect theory: An analysis of decision under risk. *Econometrica, 47,* 263–291.

Kaniasty, K., & Norris, F. N. (1995). Mobilization and deterioration of social support following natural disasters. *Current Directions in Psychological Science, 4,* 94–98.

Kant, I. (1956). *Kritik der reinen Vernunft* [Critique of pure reason]. Frankfurt, Germany: Meiner. (Original work published 1787)

Kant, I. (1967). *Kritik der praktischen Vernunft* [Critique of practical reason]. Hamburg, Germany: Meiner. (Original work published 1797)

Kasser, T., & Ryan, R.M. (1993). A dark side of the American dream: Correlates of financial success as a central life aspiration. *Journal of Personality and Social Psychology, 65,* 410–422.

Kay, P. (1996). Intra-speaker relativity. In J. Gumperz & S. Levinson (Eds.), *Rethinking linguistic relativity* (pp. 97–114). Cambridge: Cambridge University Press.

Keegan, J. (1993). *A history of warfare*. New York: Knopf.

Keinan, G. (1987). Decision making under stress: Scanning of alternatives under controllable and uncontrollable threats. *Journal of Personality and Social Psychology, 52,* 639–644.

Kendall, P. C. (1978). Anxiety: States, traits—situations? *Journal of Consulting and Clinical Psychology, 46,* 280–287.

Kenny, D. A., & Albright, L. (1987). Accuracy in interpersonal perception: A social relations analysis. *Psychological Bulletin, 102,* 390–402.

Kenya: No swots, please, we're Masai. (2002, March 23). *Economist,* p. 45.

Kiecolt-Glaser, J. K., Fisher, L. D., Ogrocki, P., Stout, J. C., Speicher, C. E., & Glaser, R. (1987). Marital quality, marital disruption, and immune function. *Psychosomatic Medicine, 49,* 13–34.

Kiecolt-Glaser, J. K., Garner, W., Speicher, C., Penn, G. M., Holliday, J., & Glaser, R. (1984). Psychosocial modifiers of immunocompetence in medical students. *Psychosomatic Medicine, 46,* 7–14.

Kiecolt-Glaser, J. K., Ricker, D., George, J., Messick, G., Speicher, C. E., Garner, W., & Glaser, R. (1984). Urinary cortisol levels, cellular immunocompetency, and loneliness in psychiatric patients. *Psychosomatic Medicine, 46,* 15–23.

Kim, H., & Markus, H. R. (1999). Deviance or uniqueness, harmony or conformity? A cultural analysis. *Journal of Personality and Social Psychology, 77,* 785–800.

Kimble, G., & Perlmuter, L. (1970). The problem of volition. *Psychological Review, 77,* 361–384.

Kinsey, A. C., Pomeroy, W. B., Martin, C. E., & Gebhard, P. H. (1953). *Sexual behavior in the human female.* Philadelphia: Saunders.

Kipnis, D. (1972). Does power corrupt? *Journal of Personality and Social Psychology, 24,* 33–41.

Kipnis, D. (1976). *The powerholders.* Chicago: University of Chicago Press.

Kitayama, S., & Uchida, Y. (in press). Explicit self-criticism and implicit self-regard: Evaluating self and friend in two cultures. *Journal of Experimental Social Psychology.*

Klinger, E., Barta, S. G., & Maxeiner, M. E. (1980). Motivational correlates of thought content frequency and commitment. *Journal of Personality and Social Psychology, 39,* 1222–1237.

Knapp, A., & Clark, M. S. (1991). Some detrimental effects of negative mood on individuals' ability to solve resource dilemmas. *Personality and Social Psychology Bulletin, 17,* 678–688.

Kohlberg, L. (1985). Resolving moral conflicts within the just community. In C. Harding (Ed.), *Moral dilemmas* (pp. 71–97). Chicago: Precedent.

Kruglanski, A. W. (1989). *Lay epistemics and human knowledge.* New York: Plenum.

Kruglanski, A. W., & Mayseless, O. (1988). Contextual effects on hypothesis testing: The role of competing alternatives and epistemic motivations. *Social Cognition, 6,* 1–20.

Kuiper, N. A., & Derry, P. A. (1982). Depressed and nondepressed content self-reference in mild depression. *Journal of Personality, 50,* 67–79.

Kunda, Z. (1990). The case for motivated reasoning. *Psychological Bulletin, 108,* 480–498.

Kunda, Z., & Sanitioso, B. (1989). Motivated changes in the self-concept. *Journal of Experimental Social Psychology, 25,* 272–285.

LaFrance, J., & Banaji, M. (1992). Toward a reconsideration of the gender-emotion relationship. In M. Clark (Ed.), *Emotion and social behavior* (pp. 178–201). Newbury Park, CA: Sage.

Landauer, T. K. (1986). How much do people remember? Some estimates of the quantity of learned information in long-term memory. *Cognitive Science, 10,* 477–493.

Langer, E. (1975). The illusion of control. *Journal of Personality and Social Psychology, 32,* 311–328.

Langer, E. J., & Rodin, J. (1976). The effects of choice and enhanced personal responsibility for the aged: A field experiment in an institutionalized setting. *Journal of Personality and Social Psychology, 34,* 191–198.

LaPiere, R. T. (1934). Attitudes vs. actions. *Social Forces, 13,* 230–237.

Larson, R., & Pleck, J. (1999). Hidden feelings: Emotionality in boys and men. In R. Dienstbier & D. Bernstein (Eds.), *Nebraska symposium on motivation: Gender and motivation* (Vol. 45, pp. 25–74). Lincoln: University of Nebraska Press.

Larson, R., Richards, M. H., & Perry-Jenkins, M. (1994). Divergent worlds: The daily emotional experiences of mothers and fathers in the domestic and public spheres. *Journal of Personality and Social Psychology, 67,* 1034–1046.

Lasch, C. (1978). *The culture of narcissism: American life in an age of diminishing expectations.* New York: Norton.

Latane, B., Williams, K., & Harkins, S. (1979). Many hands make light the work: The causes and consequences of social loafing. *Journal of Personality and Social Psychology, 37,* 823–832.

Laumann, E. O., Gagnon, J. H., Michael, R. T., & Michaels, S. (1994). *The social organization of sexuality: Sexual practices in the United States.* Chicago: University of Chicago Press.

Leary, M. R., & Baumeister, R. F. (2000). The nature and function of self-esteem: Sociometer theory. In M. Zanna (Ed.), *Advances in experimental social psychology* (Vol. 32, pp. 1–62). San Diego, CA: Academic.

Leary, M. R., Tambor, E. S., Terdal, S. K., & Downs, D. L. (1995). Self-esteem as an interpersonal monitor: The sociometer hypothesis. *Journal of Personality and Social Psychology, 68,* 518–530.

Leary, M. R., Tchividjian, L. R., & Kraxberger, B. E. (1994). Self-presentation can be hazardous to your health: Impression management and health risk. *Health Psychology, 13,* 461–470.

Lee-Chai, A. Y., Chen, S., & Chartrand, T. (2001). From Moses to Marcos: Individual differences in the use and abuse of power. In A. Lee-Chai & J. Bargh (Eds.), *The use and abuse of power* (pp. 57–74). Philadelphia: Psychology Press/Taylor & Francis.

Leitenberg, H., & Henning, K. (1995). Sexual fantasy. *Psychological Bulletin, 117,* 469–496.

Leith, K. P., & Baumeister, R. F. (1996). Why do bad moods increase self-defeating behavior? Emotion, risk taking, and self-regulation. *Journal of Personality and Social Psychology, 71,* 1250–1267.

Lengfelder, A., & Gollwitzer, P. M. (2001). Reflective and reflexive action control in patients with frontal brain lesions. *Neuropsychology, 15,* 80–100.

Lepper, M., Greene, D., & Nisbett, R. (1973). Undermining children's intrinsic interest with intrinsic rewards. *Journal of Personality and Social Psychology, 28,* 129–137.

Lepper, M. R., & Greene, D. (Eds.). (1978). *The hidden costs of reward: New perspectives of the psychology of human motivation.* Hillsdale, NJ: Erlbaum.

Levinson, D. J. (with Darrow, C., Klein, E., Levinson, M., & McKee, B.). (1978). *The seasons of a man's life.* New York: Ballantine.

Levinson, S. C. (1996). Relativity in spatial conception and description. In J. Gumperz & S. Levinson (Eds.), *Rethinking linguistic relativity* (pp. 177–202). Cambridge: Cambridge University Press.

Lewinsohn, P. M., Mischel, W., Chaplin, W., & Barton, R. (1980). Social competence and depression: The role of illusory self-perceptions. *Journal of Abnormal Psychology, 89,* 203–212.

Lewis, M. (2001). Issues in the study of personality development. *Psychological Inquiry, 12,* 67–83.

Lieberman, M. D., Gaunt, R., Gilbert, D. T., & Trope, Y. (2002). Reflection and reflexion: A social cognitive neuroscience approach to attributional inference. In M. Zanna (Ed.), *Advances in experimental social psychology* (Vol. 34, pp. 199–249). New York: Elsevier.

Linder, D. E., Cooper, J., & Jones, E. E. (1967). Decision freedom as a determinant of the role of incentive magnitude in attitude change. *Journal of Personality and Social Psychology, 6,* 245–254.

Lifton, R. J. (1989). *Thought reform and the psychology of totalism: A study of "brainwashing" in China.* Chapel Hill: University of North Carolina Press.

Loewenstein, G. F. (1996). Out of control: Visceral influences on behavior. *Organizational Behavior and Human Decision Processes, 65,* 272–292.

Loewenstein, G. F., & Elster, J. (Eds.). (1992). *Choice over time.* New York: Sage.

Loewenstein, G. F., Read, D., & Baumeister, R. F. (Eds.). (2003). *Time and decision: Economic and psychological perspectives on intertemporal choice.* New York: Sage.

Loewenstein, G. F., Weber, E. U., Hsee, C. K., & Welch, N. (2001). Risk as feelings. *Psychological Bulletin, 127,* 267–286.

Look out, Vegas. (2000, July 15). *Economist,* pp. 30–31.

Lopata, H. Z. (1971). *Occupation: Housewife.* Westport, CT: Greenwood.

Lord, C., Ross, L., & Lepper, M. (1979). Biased assimilation and attitude polarization: The effects of prior theories on subsequently considered evidence. *Journal of Personality and Social Psychology, 37,* 2098–2109.

Lorenz, K. (1966). *On aggression.* London: Methuen.

Lucy, J. A. (1996). The scope of linguistic relativity: An analysis and review of empirical research. In J. Gumperz & S. Levinson (Eds.), *Rethinking linguistic relativity* (pp. 37–69). Cambridge: Cambridge University Press.

Lyman, P., & Varian, H. R. (2000). How much information? Retrieved from. http://www.sims.berkeley.edu/how-much-info on July 21, 2003.

Lyman, S. (1978). *The seven deadly sins: Society and evil.* New York: St. Martin's.

Lynch, J. J. (1979). *The broken heart: The medical consequences of loneliness.* New York: Basic.

MacAndrew, C., & Edgerton, R. B. (1969). *Drunken comportment: A social explanation.* Chicago: Aldine.

Maccoby, E. E. (1998). *The two sexes: Growing up apart, coming together.* Cambridge, MA: Harvard University Press.

MacDonald, T. K., & Ross, M. (1999). Assessing the accuracy of predictions about dating relationships: How and why do lovers' predictions differ from those made by observers? *Personality and Social Psychology Bulletin, 25,* 1417–1429.

Macfarlane, A. (1986). *Marriage and love in England: Modes of reproduction 1300–1840.* Oxford: Basil Blackwell.

MacIntyre, A. (1981). *After virtue.* Notre Dame, IN: Notre Dame University Press.

Malinosky-Rummell, R., & Hansen, D. J. (1993). Long-term consequences of childhood physical abuse. *Psychological Bulletin, 114,* 68–79.

Manucia, G. K., Baumann, D. J., & Cialdini, R. B. (1984). Mood influence on helping: Direct effects or side effects? *Journal of Personality and Social Psychology, 46,*
357–364.

Maranon, G. (1924). Contribution a l'étude de l'action emotive de l'adrénaline. *Revue
Française d'Endocrinologie, 2,* 301–325.

Margolis, M. L. (1984). *Mothers and such: Views of American women and why they
changed.* Berkeley: University of California Press.

Marks, G. (1984). Thinking one's abilities are unique and one's opinions are common.
Personality and Social Psychology Bulletin, 10(2), 203–208.

Maslach, C. (1979). Negative emotional biasing of unexplained arousal. *Journal of
Personality and Social Psychology, 37,* 953–969.

Maslow, A. H. (1968). *Toward a psychology of being.* New York: Van Nostrand.

Masters, W. H., & Johnson, V. E. (1970). *Human sexual inadequacy.* Boston: Little,
Brown.

Mayer, J. D. (1993). The emotional madness of the dangerous leader. *Journal of Psycho-
history, 20,* 331–348.

McCord, J. (1979). Some child-rearing antecedents of criminal behavior in adult men.
Journal of Personality and Social Psychology, 37, 1477–1486.

McCrae, R. R. (2001). Traits through time. *Psychological Inquiry, 12,* 85–87.

McFarlin, D. B., & Blascovich, J. (1981). Effects of self-esteem and performance
feedback on future affective preferences and cognitive expectations. *Journal of
Personality and Social Psychology, 40,* 521–531.

McGonigle, B. O., & Chalmers, M. (1977). Are monkeys logical? *Nature, 267,*
694–696.

McLahahan, S., & Sandefur, G. (1994). *Growing up with a single parent: What hurts,
what helps.* Cambridge, MA: Harvard University Press.

McLeod, E. (1982). *Women working: Prostitution today.* London: Croom Helm.

McGuire, W. J., & McGuire, C. V. (1992). Cognitive-versus-affective positivity asym-
metries in thought systems. *European Journal of Social Psychology, 22,* 571–591.

Mecca, A. M., Smelser, N. J., & Vasconcellos, J. (Eds.). (1989). *The social importance
of self-esteem.* Berkeley: University of California Press.

Meltzoff, A. N. (1995). Understanding the intentions of others: Reenactment of
intended acts by 18-month-old children. *Developmental Psychology, 31,*
838–850.

Menninger, K. (1938). *Man against himself.* New York: Harcourt.

Mikulincer, M., Florian, V., & Hirschberger, G. (2004). The terror of death and the
quest for love. In J. Greenberg, S. Koole, & T. Pyszczynski (Eds.), *Handbook of
experimental existential psychology* (pp. 287–304). New York: Guilford.

Milardo, R. M., Johnson, M. P., & Huston, T. L. (1983). Developing close relationships: Changing patterns of interaction between pair members and social networks. *Journal of Personality and Social Psychology, 44,* 964–976.

Miller, G. A., & Gildea, P. M. (1987). How children learn words. *Scientific American,
257,* 94–99.

Miller, L. C., & Fishkin, S. A. (1997). On the dynamics of human bonding and
reproductive success: Seeking windows on the adapted-for human-environmental
interface. In J. Simpson & D. Kenrick (Eds.), *Evolutionary social psychology* (pp.
197–235). Mahwah, NJ: Erlbaum.

Miller, W. R., & Brown, J. M. (1991). Self-regulation as a conceptual basis for the
prevention of addictive behaviours. In N. Heather, W. R. Miller, & J. Greeley

(Eds.), *Self-control and the addictive behaviours* (pp. 3–79). Sydney, Australia: Maxwell Macmillan.

Mischel, W. (1974). Processes in delay of gratification. In L. Berkowitz (Ed.), *Advances in experimental social psychology* (Vol. 7, pp. 249–292). San Diego, CA: Academic.

Mischel, W. (1996). From good intentions to willpower. In P. Gollwitzer & J. Bargh (Eds.), *The psychology of action* (pp. 197–218). New York: Guilford.

Mischel, W., Ebbesen, E. B., & Zeiss, A. R. (1973). Selective attention to the self: Situational and dispositional determinants. *Journal of Personality and Social Psychology, 27,* 129–142.

Mischel, W., Ebbesen, E.B., & Zeiss, A. R. (1976). Determinants of selective memory about the self. *Journal of Consulting and Clinical Psychology, 44,* 92–103.

Mischel, W., Shoda, Y., & Peake, P. K. (1988). The nature of adolescent competencies predicted by preschool delay of gratification. *Journal of Personality and Social Psychology, 54,* 687–696.

Model makers: A survey of the Netherlands. (2002, May 4). *Economist.*

Monat, A., Averill, J. R., & Lazarus, R. S. (1972). Anticipatory stress and coping reactions under various conditions of uncertainty. *Journal of Personality and Social Psychology, 24,* 237–253.

Mook, C. G. (1987). *Motivation: The organization of action.* New York: Norton.

Morf, C. C., & Rhodewalt, F. (2001). Unraveling the paradoxes of narcissism: A dynamic self-regulatory processing model. *Psychological Inquiry, 12,* 177–196.

Moscovici, S., & Zavalloni, M. (1969). The group as polarizer of attitudes. *Journal of Personality and Social Psychology, 12,* 125–135.

Muraven, M., Baumeister, R. F., & Tice, D. M. (1999). Longitudinal improvement of self-regulation through practice: Building self-control through repeated exercise. *Journal of Social Psychology, 139,* 446–457.

Muraven, M. R., & Baumeister, R. F. (2000). Self-regulation and depletion of limited resources: Does self-control resemble a muscle? *Psychological Bulletin, 126,* 247–259.

Murphy, S. (1992). *A delicate dance: Sexuality, celibacy, and relationships among Catholic clergy and religious.* New York: Crossroad.

Murray, C. (1998). *Income inequality and IQ.* Washington, DC: AIE.

Myers, D. (1992). *The pursuit of happiness.* New York: Morrow.

Nagin, D., & Tremblay, R. E. (1999). Trajectories of boys' physical aggression, opposition, and hyperactivity on the path to physically violent and nonviolent juvenile delinquency. *Child Development, 70,* 1181–1196.

Nationline. (1998, June 8). Twins killed. *USA Today,* p. 2A.

Neuberg, S. L., & Fiske, S. T. (1987). Motivational influences on impression formation: Outcome dependency, accuracy-driven attention, and individuating processes. *Journal of Personality and Social Psychology, 53,* 431–444.

Niedenthal, P. M., Halberstadt, J. B., & Innes-Ker, A. H. (1999). Emotional response categorization. *Psychological Review, 106,* 337–361.

Nisbett, R. E., Peng, K., Choi, I., & Norenzayan, A. (2001). Culture and systems of thought: Holistic versus analytic cognition. *Psychological Review, 108,* 291–310.

Nisbett, R. E., & Wilson, T. D. (1977). Telling more than we can know: Verbal reports on mental processes. *Psychological Review, 84,* 231–259.

Oaten, M., & Cheng, K. (2002). *Strengthening the regulatory muscle: The longitudinal benefit of exercising self-control.* Unpublished data, Macquarie University, Australia.

Oehman, A., Lundqvist, D., & Esteves, F. (2001). The face in the crowd revisited: A threat advantage with schematic stimuli. *Journal of Personality and Social Psychology, 80,* 381–396.

Oettingen, G., & Gollwitzer, P. M. (2001). Goal setting and goal striving. In A. Tesser & N. Schwarz (Eds.), *Blackwell handbook of social psychology: Intraindividual processes* (pp. 329–348). Oxford: Blackwell.

Ohman, A., & Mineka, S. (2001). Fears, phobias, and preparedness: Toward an evolved module of fear and fear learning. *Psychological Review, 108,* 483–522.

O'Sullivan, C. S., & Durso, F. T. (1984). Effect of schema-incongruent information on memory for stereotypical attributes. *Journal of Personality and Social Psychology, 47,* 55–70.

O'Toole, B. J. (1990). Intelligence and behavior and motor vehicle accident mortality. *Accident Analysis and Prevention, 22,* 211–221.

Overmier, J. B., & Seligman, M. E. P. (1967). Effects of inescapable shock upon subsequent escape and avoidance learning. *Journal of Comparative and Physiological Psychology, 63,* 23–33.

Palmer, S. E. (1975). The effects of contextual scenes on the identification of objects. *Memory and Cognition, 3,* 519–526.

Patterson, G. R., DeBaryshe, B. D., & Ramsey, E. (2000). A developmental perspective on antisocial behavior. In W. Craig (Ed.), *Childhood social development: The essential readings* (pp. 333–348). Oxford: Blackwell.

Peele, S., & Brodsky, A. (1991). *Love and addiction.* New York: Penguin.

Pelham, B. W., Mirenberg, M. C., & Jones, J. T. (2002). Why Susie sells seashells by the seashore: Implicit egoism and major life decisions. *Journal of Personality and Social Psychology, 82,* 469–487.

Petty, R. E., & Cacioppo, J. T. (1986). The elaboration likelihood model of persuasion. In L. Berkowitz (Ed.), *Advances in experimental social psychology* (Vol. 19, pp. 123–205). San Diego, CA: Academic.

Piers, G., & Singer, M. (1971). *Shame and guilt: A psychoanalytic and cultural study.* New York: Norton. (Original work published 1953)

Pines, M., & Aronson, E. (1983). Antecedents, correlates, and consequences of sexual jealousy. *Journal of Personality, 51,* 108–135.

Pinker, S. (1994). *The language instinct.* New York: HarperCollins.

Pinker, S. (1997). *How the mind works.* New York: Norton.

Pinker, S. (2002). *The blank slate: The modern denial of human nature.* New York: Viking.

Platt, J. (1973). Social traps. *American Psychologist, 28,* 641–651.

Polivy, J. (1981). On the induction of mood in the laboratory: Discrete moods or multiple affect states? *Journal of Personality and Social Psychology, 41,* 803–817.

Povinelli, D. J., & Bering, J. M. (2002). The mentality of apes revisited. *Current Directions in Psychological Science, 20,* 115–119.

Powers, W. T. (1973). *Behavior: The control of perception.* Chicago: Aldine.

Prentice, D. A., & Miller, D. T. (1992). When small effects are impressive. *Psychological Bulletin, 112,* 160–164.

Pryor, J. B., & Kriss, M. (1977). The cognitive dynamics of salience in the attribution process. *Journal of Personality and Social Psychology, 35,* 850–856.

Pullum, G. K. (1991). *The great Eskimo vocabulary hoax and other irreverent essays on the study of language.* Chicago: University of Chicago Press.

Pyszczynski, T., & Greenberg, J. (1987). Toward an integration of cognitive and motivational perspectives on social inference: A biased hypothesis-testing model. In L. Berkowitz (Ed.), *Advances in experimental social psychology* (Vol. 20, pp. 297–340). New York: Academic.

Pyszczynski, T., Greenberg, J., & Holt, K. (1985). Maintaining consistency between self-serving beliefs and available data: A bias in information processing. *Personality and Social Psychology Bulletin, 11,* 179–190.

Pyszczynski, T., Greenberg, J., & Solomon, S. (1997). Why do we need what we need? A terror management perspective on the roots of human social motivation. *Psychological Inquiry, 8,* 1–20.

Rahman, Q., & Wilson, G. D. (2001). *The psychobiology of sexual orientation.* Manuscript submitted for publication.

Reis, H. T. (1990). The role of intimacy in interpersonal relations. *Journal of Social and Clinical Psychology, 9,* 15–30.

Reiss, I. L. (1986). A sociological journey into sexuality. *Journal of Marriage and the Family, 48,* 233–242.

Rhodewalt, F., & Eddings, S. (2002). Narcissus reflects: Memory distortion in response to ego relevant feedback in high and low narcissistic men. *Journal of Research in Personality, 36,* 97–116.

Ridley, M. (1993). *The red queen: Sex and evolution in human nature.* New York: Penguin.

Robbins, T. (1988). *Cults, converts, and charisma: The sociology of new religious movements.* London, England: Sage.

Roberts, B .W., & Caspi, A. (2001). Personality development and the person-situation debate: It's déjà vu all over again. *Psychological Inquiry, 12,* 104–109.

Roberts, W. A. (2002). Are animals stuck in time? *Psychological Bulletin, 128,* 473–489.

Rodin, J., & Langer, E. J. (1977). Long term effects of a control-relevant intervention with the institutionalized aged. *Journal of Personality and Social Psychology, 35,* 897–902.

Rogers, T. B., Kuiper, N. A., & Kirker, W. S. (1977). Self-reference and the encoding of personal information. *Journal of Personality and Social Psychology, 35,* 677–688.

Rohner, R. P., & Veneziano, R. A. (2001). The importance of father love: History and contemporary evidence. *Review of General Psychology, 5,* 382–405.

Rosenfeld, D., Folger, R., & Adelman, H. F. (1980). When rewards reflect competence: A qualification of the overjustification effect. *Journal of Personality and Social Psychology, 39,* 368–376.

Ross, M. (1989). The relation of implicit theories to the construction of personal histories. *Psychological Review, 96,* 341–357.

Ross, M., & Sicoly, F. (1979). Egocentric biases in availability and attribution. *Journal of Personality and Social Psychology, 37,* 322–336.

Rothbart, M. K. (1989). Temperament and development. In J. Bates, G. Kohnstamm, & M. Rothbart (Eds.), *Temperament in childhood* (pp. 187–247). New York: Wiley.

Rothbaum, F., Weisz, J. R., & Snyder, S. S. (1982). Changing the world and changing the self: A two-process model of perceived control. *Journal of Personality and Social Psychology, 42,* 5–37.

Rowe, D. C. (1998). Genes, environment, and psychological development. In A. Campbell & S. Muncer (Eds.), *The social child* (pp. 51–83). East Sussex, England: Psychology Press/Taylor & Francis.

Rowe, D. C., Jacobson, K. C., & Van den Oord, E. J. C. G. (1999). Genetic and environmental influences on vocabulary IQ: Parental education level as a moderator. *Child Development, 70,* 1151–1162.

Rozin, P., Millman, L., & Nemeroff, C. (1986). Operation of the laws of sympathetic magic in disgust and other domains. *Journal of Personality and Social Psychology, 50,* 703–712.

Rubin, L. (1990). *Erotic wars: What happened to the sexual revolution?* New York: Farrar, Straus, & Giroux.

Russell, J. A. (1994). Is there a universal recognition of emotion from facial expressions? A review of the cross-cultural studies. *Psychological Bulletin, 115,* 102–141.

Russell, J. A. (1995). Facial expressions of emotion: What lies beyond minimal universality? *Psychological Bulletin, 118,* 379–391.

Russell, J. A., & Feldman Barrett, L. (1999). Core affect, prototypical emotional episodes, and other things called emotion: Dissecting the elephant. *Journal of Personality and Social Psychology, 76,* 805–819.

Rutter, M. (1979). Maternal deprivation, 1972–1978: New findings, new concepts, new approaches. *Child Development, 50,* 283–305.

Sackeim, H. A., & Gur, R. C. (1979). Self-deception, other-deception, and self-reported psychopathology. *Journal of Consulting and Clinical Psychology, 47,* 213–215.

Sahlins, M. (1999). Two or three things that I know about culture. *Journal of the Royal Anthropological Institute, 5,* 399–421.

Sampson, R. J., & Laub, J. H. (1990). Crime and deviance over the life course: The salience of adult social bonds. *American Sociological Review, 55,* 609–627.

Sampson, R. J., & Laub, J. H. (1993). *Crime in the making: Pathways and turning points through life.* Cambridge, MA: Harvard University Press.

Sartre, J.-P. (1953). *Existential psychoanalysis.* New York: Philosophical Library.

Sartre, J.-P. (1974). *Being and nothingness.* Secaucus, NJ: Citadel. (Original work published 1943)

Schachter, S., & Singer, J. E. (1962). Cognitive, social and physiological determinants of emotional state. *Psychological Review, 69,* 379–399.

Schacter, D. L. (2001). *The seven sins of memory.* New York: Houghton Mifflin.

Schaffner, P. E. (1985). Specious learning about reward and punishment. *Journal of Personality and Social Psychology, 48,* 1377–1386.

Schimmel, S. (1992). *The seven deadly sins: Jewish, Christian, and classical reflections on human nature.* New York: Free Press.

Schlenker, B. R. (1980). *Impression management: The self-concept, social identity, and interpersonal relations.* Monterey, CA: Brooks/Cole.

Schlenker, B. R., & Leary, M. R. (1982). Social anxiety and self-presentation. *Psychological Bulletin, 92,* 641–669.

Schmidt, F. L., & Hunter, J. E. (1992). Development of a causal model of processes determining job performance. *Current Directions in Psychological Science, 1,* 89–92.

Schmidt, F. L., & Hunter, J. E. (1998). The validity and utility of selection methods in personnel psychology: Practical and theoretical implications of 85 years of research findings. *Psychological Bulletin, 124,* 262–274.

Schmitt, D. P., & Buss, D. M. (2001). Human mate poaching: Tactics and temptations for infiltrating existing mateships. *Journal of Personality and Social Psychology, 80,* 894–917.

Schneider, W., & Shiffrin, R. M. (1977). Controlled and automatic human information processing: I. Detection, search, and attention. *Psychological Review, 84,* 1–66.

Schwartz, B. (2000). Self-determination: The tyranny of freedom. *American Psychologist, 55,* 79–88.

Searle, J. R. (2001). *Rationality in action.* Cambridge, MA: MIT Press.

Sedikides, C. (1993). Assessment, enhancement, and verification determinants of the self-evaluation process. *Journal of Personality and Social Psychology, 65,* 317–338.

Sedikides, C., Gaertner, L., & Toguchi, Y. (2003). Pancultural self-enhancement. *Journal of Personality and Social Psychology, 84,* 60–70.

Seligman, M. E. P. (1975). *Helplessness: On depression, development, and death.* San Francisco: Freeman.

Sewell, W. H. (1999). The concept(s) of culture. In V. Bonnell & L. Hunt (Eds.), *Beyond the cultural turn* (pp. 35–61). Berkeley: University of California Press.

Shoda, Y., Mischel, W., & Peake, P. K. (1990). Predicting adolescent cognitive and self-regulatory competencies from preschool delay of gratification: Identifying diagnostic conditions. *Developmental Psychology, 26,* 978–986.

Shrauger, J. A., & Schoeneman, T. J. (1979). Symbolic interactionist view of self-concept: Through the looking glass darkly. *Psychological Bulletin, 86,* 549–573.

Shrauger, J. S. (1975). Responses to evaluation as a function of initial self-perceptions. *Psychological Bulletin, 82,* 581–596.

Shrauger, J. S., & Sorman, P. B. (1977). Self-evaluations, initial success and failure, and improvement as determinants of persistence. *Journal of Consulting and Clinical Psychology, 45,* 784–795.

Sipe, A. W. R. (1995). *Sex, priests, and power: Anatomy of a crisis.* New York: Brunner/ Mazel.

Skinner, E. A. (1995). *Perceived control, motivation, and coping.* Thousand Oaks, CA: Sage.

Slobin, D. I. (1996). From "thought and language" to "thinking for speaking." In J. Gumperz & S. Levinson (Eds.), *Rethinking linguistic relativity* (pp. 70–96). Cambridge: Cambridge University Press.

Sloman, S. A. (2002). Two systems of reasoning. In T. Gilovich, D. Griffin, & D. Kahneman (Eds.), *Heuristics and biases* (pp. 379–396). New York: Cambridge University Press.

Slovic, P., Finucane, M., Peters, E., & MacGregor, D. G. (2002). The affect heuristic. In T. Gilovich, D. Griffin, & D. Kahneman (Eds.), *Heuristics and biases: The psychology of intuitive judgment* (pp. 397–420). New York: Cambridge University Press.

Smith, G., & Engel, R. (1968). Influence of a female model on perceived characteristics of an automobile. *Proceedings of the 76th Annual Convention of the American Psychological Association, 168,* 681–682.

Smith, T. (1994). Attitudes toward sexual permissiveness: Trends, correlates, and behavioral connections. In A. S. Rossi (Ed.), *Sexuality across the life course* (pp. 63–97). Chicago: University of Chicago Press.

Smith, T. W., Ingram, R. E., & Brehm, S. S. (1983). Social anxiety, anxious self-preoccupation, and recall of self-relevant information. *Journal of Personality and Social Psychology, 44,* 1276–1283.

Snyder, A. I. (1978). Periodic marital separation and physical illness. *American Journal of Orthopsychiatry, 48,* 637–643.

Spanier, G. B., & Casto, R. F. (1979). Adjustment to separation and divorce: A qualitative analysis. In G. Levinger & O. C. Moles (Eds.), *Divorce and separation: Context, causes, and consequences* (pp. 211–227). New York: Basic.

Spence, J. T., & Segner, L. L. (1967). Verbal vs. nonverbal reinforcement combinations in the discrimination learning of middle and lower class children. *Child Development, 38,* 29–38.

Sprecher, S. (1999). "I love you more today than yesterday": Romantic partners' perceptions of changes in love and related affect over time. *Journal of Personality and Social Psychology, 76,* 46–53.

Stark, R., & Bainbridge, W. S. (1985). *The future of religion: Secularization, revival and cult formation.* Berkeley: University of California Press.

Stasser, G., & Titus, W. (1985). Pooling of unshared information in group decision making: Biased information sampling during discussion. *Journal of Personality and Social Psychology, 48,* 1467–1478.

Stasser, G., & Titus, W. (1987). Effects of information load and percentage of shared information o the dissemination of unshared information during group discussion. *Journal of Personality and Social Psychology, 53,* 81–93.

Steele, C. M., & Southwick, L. (1985). Alcohol and social behavior: I. The mediating role of inhibitory conflict. *Journal of Personality and Social Psychology, 48,* 18–34.

Stephan, W. G., & Stephan, C. W. (1985). Intergroup anxiety. *Journal of Social Issues, 41,* 157–175.

Sternberg, R. J. (1997). *Successful intelligence: How practical and creative intelligence determine success in life.* New York: Plume.

Suicide technologies: Exit this way. (2001, December 8). *Economist,* pp. 69–70.

Sullivan, H.S. (1953). *The interpersonal theory of psychiatry.* New York: Norton.

Suls, J., & Wan, C. K. (1987). In search of the false uniqueness phenomenon: Fear and estimates of social consensus. *Journal of Personality and Social Psychology, 52,* 211–217.

Swann, W. B., Jr. (1987). Identity negotiation: Where two roads meet. *Journal of Personality and Social Psychology, 53,* 1038–1051.

Swann, W. B., Jr., Griffin, J. J., Predmore, S., & Gaines, B. (1987). The cognitive-affective crossfire: When self-consistency confronts self-enhancement. *Journal of Personality and Social Psychology, 52,* 881–889.

Symanski, R. (1980). Prostitution in Nevada. In E. Muga, *Studies in prostitution* (pp. 246–279). Nairobi: Kenya Literature Bureau.

Symons, D. (1979). *The evolution of human sexuality.* New York: Oxford University Press.

Tajfel, H. (1970). Experiments in intergroup discrimination. *Scientific American, 223,* 96–102.

Tajfel, H., & Billig, M. (1974). Familiarity and categorization in intergroup behavior. *Journal of Experimental Social Psychology, 10,* 159–170.

Tajfel, H., Flament, C., Billig, M. G., & Bundy, R. F. (1971). Social categorization and intergroup behaviour. *European Journal of Social Psychology, 1,* 149–177.

Tangney, J. P., Baumeister, R. F., & Boone, A. L. (in press). High self-control predicts good adjustment, less pathology, better grades, and interpersonal success. *Journal of Personality.*

Tannahill, R. (1980). *Sex in history.* New York: Stein and Day/Scarborough.

Tavris, C. (1989). *Anger: The misunderstood emotion.* New York: Simon & Schuster.

Taylor, S. E. (1983). Adjustment to threatening events: A theory of cognitive adaptation. *American Psychologist, 38,* 1161–1173.

Taylor, S. E., & Brown, J. D. (1988). Illusion and well-being: A social psychological perspective on mental health. *Psychological Bulletin, 103,* 193–210.

Tedeschi, J. T., & Felson, R. B. (1994). *Violence, aggression, and coercive actions.* Washington, DC: American Psychological Association.

Teger, A. I. (1980). *Too much invested to quit.* New York: Pergamon.

Tellegen, A., Lykken, D. T., Bouchard, T. J., Wilcox, K. J., Segal, N. L., & Rich, S. (1988). Personality similarity in twins reared apart and together. *Journal of Personality and Social Psychology, 54,* 1031–1039.

Tetlock, P. E. (1981). Pre- to post-election shifts in presidential rhetoric: Impression management or cognitive adjustment? *Journal of Personality and Social Psychology, 41,* 207–212.

Tetlock, P. E. (1983). Accountability and the complexity of thought. *Journal of Personality and Social Psychology, 45,* 74–83.

Tetlock, P. E. (1986). A value pluralism model of ideological reasoning. *Journal of Personality and Social Psychology, 50,* 819–827.

Tetlock, P. E., & Boettger, R. (1989). Accountability: A social magnifier of the dilution effect. *Journal of Personality and Social Psychology, 57,* 388–398.

Tetlock, P. E, & Kim, J. I. (1987). Accountability and judgment processes in a personality prediction task. *Journal of Personality and Social Psychology, 52,* 700–709.

Thorndike, E. L., & Lorge, I. (1944). *The teacher's word book of 30,000 words.* New York: Columbia University Bureau of Publications.

Tice, D. M., & Baumeister, R. F. (1997). Longitudinal study of procrastination, performance, stress, and health: The costs and benefits of dawdling. *Psychological Science, 8,* 454–458.

Tice, D. M., Bratslavsky, E., & Baumeister, R. F. (2001). Emotional distress regulation takes precedence over impulse control: If you feel bad, do it! *Journal of Personality and Social Psychology, 80,* 53–67.

Tindall, R. C., & Ratliff, R. G. (1974). Interaction of reinforcement conditions and developmental level in a two-choice discrimination task with children. *Journal of Experimental Child Psychology, 18,* 183–189.

Tomasello, M. (1999). *The cultural origins of human cognition.* Cambridge, MA: Harvard University Press.

Tremblay, R. E. (2000). The development of aggressive behavior during childhood: What have we learned in the past century? *International Journal of Behavioral Development, 24,* 129–141.

Tremblay, R. E. (2003). Why socialization fails: The case of chronic physical aggression. In B. B. Lahey, T. E. Moffitt, & A. Caspi (Eds.), *The causes of conduct disorder and serious juvenile delinquency* (pp. 182–224). New York: Guilford.

Tremblay, R. E., Nagin, D. S., Sguin, J. R., Zoccolillo, M., Zelazo, P. D., Boivin, M., Prusse, D., & Japel, C. (in press). Physical aggression during early childhood: Trajectories and predictors. *Pediatrics.*

Trope, Y. (1983). Self-assessment in achievement behavior. In J. Suls & A. Greenwald (Eds.), *Psychological perspectives on the self* (Vol. 2, pp. 93–121). Hillsdale, NJ: Erlbaum.

Trope, Y. (1986). Self-enhancement and self-assessment in achievement behavior. In R. Sorrentino & E. T. Higgins (Eds.), *Handbook of motivation and cognition* (Vol. 2, pp. 350–378). New York: Guilford.

Trout, D. L. (1980). The role of social isolation in suicide. *Suicide and Life-Threatening Behavior, 10,* 10–23.

Turner, J. C. (1985). Social categorization and the self-concept: A social cognitive theory of group behavior. In E. J. Lawler (Ed.), *Advances in group processes: Theory and research* (Vol. 2, pp. 77–121). Greenwich, CT: JAI.

Tversky, A., & Kahneman, D. (1973). Availability: A heuristic for judging frequency and probability. *Cognitive Psychology, 5,* 207–232.

Twenge, J. M., Baumeister, R. F., Tice, D. M., & Stucke, T. S. (2001). If you can't join them, beat them: Effects of social exclusion on aggressive behavior. *Journal of Personality and Social Psychology, 81,* 1058–1069.

Twenge, J. M., Catanese, K. R., & Baumeister, R. F. (2002). Social exclusion causes self-defeating behavior. *Journal of Personality and Social Psychology, 83,* 606–615.

Udry, J. R. (1980). Changes in the frequency of marital intercourse from panel data. *Archives of Sexual Behavior, 9,* 319–325.

Vallacher, R. R., & Wegner, D. M. (1985). *A theory of action identification.* Hillsdale, NJ: Erlbaum.

Vallacher, R. R., & Wegner, D. M. (1987). What do people think they're doing? Action identification and human behavior. *Psychological Review, 94,* 3–15.

Vaughan, D. (1986). *Uncoupling.* New York: Oxford University Press.

Viscusi, K., & Magat, W. (1987). *Learning about risk.* Cambridge, MA: Harvard University Press.

Vohs, K. D., Twenge, J. M., Baumeister, R. F., Schmeichel, B. J., & Tice, D. M. (2002). *Decision fatigue: Making multiple personal decisions depletes the self's resources.* Unpublished manuscript.

Von Fersen, L., Wynne, C. D. L., & Delius, J. D. (1991). Transitive inference formation in pigeons. *Journal of Experimental Psychology: Animal Behavior Processes, 17,* 334–341.

Wahba, M. A., & Bridwell, L. G. (1983). Maslow reconsidered: A review of research on the need hierarchy theory. In R. Steers & L. Porter (Eds.), *Motivation and work behavior* (pp. 34–41). New York: McGraw-Hill.

Waldman, S. (1992, January 27). The tyranny of choice: Why the consumer revolution is ruining your life. *New Republic,* pp. 22–25.

Wallace, H.M., & Baumeister, R.F. (2002). The performance of narcissists rises and falls with perceived opportunity for glory. *Journal of Personality and Social Psychology, 82,* 819–834.

Wason, P. (1966). Reasoning. In B. M. Foss (Ed.), *New horizons in psychology* (pp. 106–137). Harmondsworth, England: Penguin.

Wason, P., & Johnson-Laird, P. N. (1972). *The psychology of reasoning.* London: Batsford.

Watson, D., & Clark, L. A. (1992). Affects separable and inseparable: On the hierarchical arrangement of the negative affects. *Journal of Personality and Social Psychology, 62,* 489–505.

Watson, D., & Tellegen, A. (1985). Toward a consensual structure of mood. *Psychological Bulletin, 98,* 219–235.

Wegner, D. M. (2002). *The illusion of conscious will.* Cambridge, MA: MIT Press.

Wegner, D. M. (in press). Who is the controller of controlled processes? In R. Hassin, J. Uleman, & J. Bargh (Eds.), *Unintended thought* (Vol. 2). New York: Guilford.

Weinberger, D. A., Schwartz, G. E., & Davidson, R. J. (1979). Low-anxious, high-anxious, and repressive coping styles: Psychometric patterns and behavioral and physiological responses to stress. *Journal of Abnormal Psychology, 88,* 369–380.

Weiner, B. (1985). "Spontaneous" causal thinking. *Psychological Bulletin, 97,* 74–84.

Weiner, B., Frieze, I., Kukla, A., Reed, L., Rest, S., & Rosenbaum, R. M. (1971). Perceiving the causes of success and failure. In E. E. Jones, D. E. Kanouse, H. H. Kelley, R. E. Nisbett, S. Valins, & B. Weiner (Eds.), *Attribution: Perceiving the causes of behavior* (pp. 95–120). Morristown, NJ: General Learning.

Weintraub, K. J. (1978). *The value of the individual: Self and circumstance in autobiography.* Chicago: University of Chicago Press.

Weiss, J. M. (1971a). Effects of coping behavior in different warning signal conditions on stress pathology in rats. *Journal of Comparative and Physiological Psychology, 77,* 1–13.

Weiss, J. M. (1971b). Effects of coping behavior with and without a feedback signal on stress pathology in rats. *Journal of Comparative and Physiological Psychology, 77,* 22–30.

Weiss, J. M. (1971c). Effects of punishing the coping response (conflict) on stress pathology in rats. *Journal of Comparative and Physiological Psychology, 77,* 14–21.

Wells, L. E., & Rankin, J. H. (1991). Families and delinquency: A meta-analysis of the impact of broken homes. *Social Problems, 38,* 71–93.

Wenzlaff, R. M., Wegner, D. M., & Roper, D. (1988). Depression and mental control: The resurgence of unwanted negative thoughts. *Journal of Personality and Social Psychology, 55,* 882–892.

Wheeler, L., & Nezlek, J. (1977). Sex differences in social participation. *Journal of Personality and Social Psychology, 35,* 742–754.

Wheeler, L., Reis, H. T., & Nezlek, J. (1983). Loneliness, social interaction, and sex roles. *Journal of Personality and Social Psychology, 45,* 943–953.

Wicker, A. M. (1969). Attitudes vs. actions: The relationship of verbal and overt behavioral responses to attitude objects. *Journal of Social Issues, 22,* 41–78.

Will, G. F. (1990, May 21). The budget (yawn) battle. *Newsweek,* p. 100.

Will, G. F. (2002a, September 29). The billions between tort and extort. *Cleveland Plain Dealer,* p. H5.

Will, G. F. (2002b). *With a happy eye but . . . : America and the world.* New York: Free Press.

Wills, T.A. (1981). Downward comparison principles in social psychology. *Psychological Bulletin, 90,* 245–271.

Williams, K. D. (2001). *Ostracism: The power of silence.* New York: Guilford.

Wilson, J. Q. (2002). *The marriage problem: How our culture has weakened families.* New York: HarperCollins.

Wilson, T. D. (2002). *Strangers to ourselves: Discovering the adaptive unconscious.* Cambridge, MA: Harvard University Press.

Wilson, T. D., & Gilbert, D. T. (2003). Affective forecasting. In M. Zanna (Ed.), *Advances in experimental social psychology* (Vol. 35, pp. 345–411). New York: Elsevier.

Wilson, T. D., Meyers, J., & Gilbert, D. T. (2001). Lessons from the past: Do people learn from experience that emotional reactions are short lived? *Personality and Social Psychology Bulletin, 27,* 1648–1661.

Winfield, F. E. (1985). *Commuter marriage.* New York: Columbia University Press.

Winter, D. G. (1973). *The power motive.* New York: Free Press.

Wong, R. (2000). *Motivation: A biobehavioural approach.* Cambridge: Cambridge University Press.

Wood, W., Quinn, J., & Kashy, D. (2002). Habits in everyday life: Thought, emotion, and action. *Journal of Personality and Social Psychology, 83*(6), 1281–1297.

Wright, K. N., & Wright, K. E. (1992). Does getting married reduce the likelihood of criminality? A review of the literature. *Federal Probation, 56,* 50–56.

Wyer, R. S., & Frey, D. (1983). The effects of feedback about self and others on the cognitive processing of feedback-relevant information. *Journal of Experimental Social Psychology, 19,* 540–559.

Yerkes, R. M., & Dodson, J. D. (1908). The relation of strength of stimulus to rapidity of habit-formation. *Journal of Comparative Neurology and Psychology, 18,* 459–482.

Zajonc, R. B. (1985). Emotion and facial efference: A theory reclaimed. *Science, 228,* 15–21.

Zanna, M. P., Higgins, E. T., & Taves, P. A. (1976). Is dissonance phenomenologically aversive? *Journal of Experimental Social Psychology, 12,* 530–538.

Zillman, D. (1993). Mental control of angry aggression. In D. M. Wegner & J. W. Pennebaker (Eds.), *Handbook of mental control* (pp. 370–392). Englewood Cliffs, NJ: Prentice-Hall.

Zuckerman, M. (1979). Attribution of success and failure revisited; or, The motivational bias is alive and well in attribution theory. *Journal of Personality, 47,* 245–287.

Zullow, H. M., & Seligman, M. E. (1990). Pessimistic rumination predicts defeat of presidential candidates, 1900 to 1984. *Psychological Inquiry, 1,* 52–61.

Index